Managerial Accounting for Managers

Managerial Accounting for Managers

Sixth Edition

Eric W. Noreen, Ph.D., CMA

Professor Emeritus
University of Washington

Peter C. Brewer, Ph.D.

Wake Forest University

Ray H. Garrison, D.B.A., CPA

Professor Emeritus
Brigham Young University

MANAGERIAL ACCOUNTING FOR MANAGERS, SIXTH EDITION

Published by McGraw Hill LLC, 1325 Avenue of the Americas, New York, NY 10019. Copyright ©2023 by McGraw Hill LLC. All rights reserved. Printed in the United States of America. Previous editions ©2020, 2017, and 2014. No part of this publication may be reproduced or distributed in any form or by any means, or stored in a database or retrieval system, without the prior written consent of McGraw Hill LLC, including, but not limited to, in any network or other electronic storage or transmission, or broadcast for distance learning.

Some ancillaries, including electronic and print components, may not be available to customers outside the United States.

This book is printed on acid-free paper.

1 2 3 4 5 6 7 8 9 LWI 27 26 25 24 23 22

ISBN 978-1-264-10059-0 (bound edition)
MHID 1-264-10059-0 (bound edition)
ISBN 978-1-264-44539-4 (loose-leaf edition)
MHID 1-264-44539-3 (loose-leaf edition)

Senior Portfolio Manager: *Noelle Bathurst*
Product Developer: *Erin Quinones*
Executive Marketing Manager: *Lauren Schur*
Lead Content Project Managers: *Pat Frederickson and Angela Norris*
Buyer: *Laura Fuller*
Designer: *Matt Diamond*
Content Licensing Specialist: *Lori Hancock*
Cover Image: *Cavan Images/Alamy Stock Photo*
Compositor: *Straive*

All credits appearing on page or at the end of the book are considered to be an extension of the copyright page.

Library of Congress Cataloging-in-Publication Data

Cataloging-in-Publication Data has been requested from the Library of Congress.

The Internet addresses listed in the text were accurate at the time of publication. The inclusion of a website does not indicate an endorsement by the authors or McGraw Hill LLC, and McGraw Hill LLC does not guarantee the accuracy of the information presented at these sites.

mheducation.com/highered

About the Authors

Courtesy of Eric W. Noreen

Eric W. Noreen has taught at INSEAD in France and the Hong Kong Institute of Science and Technology and is emeritus professor of accounting at the University of Washington. Currently, he is the Accounting Circle Professor of Accounting, Fox School of Business, Temple University.

He received his BA degree from the University of Washington and MBA and PhD degrees from Stanford University. A Certified Management Accountant, he was awarded a Certificate of Distinguished Performance by the Institute of Certified Management Accountants.

Professor Noreen has served as associate editor of *The Accounting Review* and the *Journal of Accounting and Economics.* He has numerous articles in academic journals, including the *Journal of Accounting Research; The Accounting Review;* the *Journal of Accounting and Economics; Accounting Horizons; Accounting, Organizations and Society; Contemporary Accounting Research;* the *Journal of Management Accounting Research;* and the *Review of Accounting Studies.*

Professor Noreen has won a number of awards from students for his teaching. ■

Courtesy of Louise St. Romain—
Fast Cat Studios

Peter C. Brewer teaches in the Department of Accountancy at Wake Forest University. Prior to joining the faculty at Wake Forest, he was an accounting professor at Miami University for 19 years. He holds a BS degree in accounting from Penn State University, an MS degree in accounting from the University of Virginia, and a PhD from the University of Tennessee. He has published more than 40 articles in a variety of journals, including *Management Accounting Research;* the *Journal of Information Systems; Cost Management; Strategic*

Finance; the *Journal of Accountancy; Issues in Accounting Education;* and the *Journal of Business Logistics.*

Professor Brewer has served on the editorial boards of the *Journal of Accounting Education* and *Issues in Accounting Education.* His article "Putting Strategy into the Balanced Scorecard" won the 2003 International Federation of Accountants' Articles of Merit competition, and his articles "Using Six Sigma to Improve the Finance Function" and "Lean Accounting: What's It All About?" were awarded the Institute of Management Accountants' Lybrand Gold and Silver Medals in 2005 and 2006. He has received Miami University's Richard T. Farmer School of Business Teaching Excellence Award.

Prior to joining the faculty at Miami University, Professor Brewer was employed as an auditor for Touche Ross in the firm's Philadelphia office. He also worked as an internal audit manager for the Board of Pensions of the Presbyterian Church (U.S.A.). ■

Courtesy of Ray H. Garrison

Ray H. Garrison is emeritus professor of accounting at Brigham Young University, Provo, Utah. He received his BS and MS degrees from Brigham Young University and his DBA degree from Indiana University.

As a certified public accountant, Professor Garrison has been involved in management consulting work with both national and regional accounting firms. He has published articles in *The Accounting Review, Management Accounting,* and other professional journals. Innovation in the classroom has earned Professor Garrison the Karl G. Maeser Distinguished Teaching Award from Brigham Young University. ■

Dedication

To our families and to our many colleagues who use this book.

—*Eric W. Noreen, Peter C. Brewer,
and Ray H. Garrison*

Focus on the Future Manager

with Noreen/Brewer/Garrison

In *Managerial Accounting for Managers,* the authors have crafted a streamlined managerial accounting book that is perfect for non-accounting majors who intend to move into managerial positions. The traditional Process Costing, Statement of Cash Flows, and Financial Statement Analysis chapters have been dropped to enable instructors to **focus their attention on the bedrocks of managerial accounting**—planning, control, and decision making. Noreen/Brewer/Garrison focuses on the fundamentals, allowing students to develop the conceptual framework managers need to succeed.

In its sixth edition, *Managerial Accounting for Managers* continues to adhere to three core standards:

FOCUS. Noreen/Brewer/Garrison pinpoint the key managerial concepts students will need in their future careers. With no journal entries or financial accounting topics to worry about, students can focus on the fundamental principles of managerial accounting. The manager approach in Noreen allows students to develop the conceptual framework needed to succeed, with a focus on decision making and analytical skills.

"This textbook is well written and is very suitable for an introductory managerial accounting course. This textbook provides many resources for instructors and students. The focus companies in the beginning of every chapter are very interesting; they help students appreciate the importance of managerial accounting in real companies. Connect is very useful and is well-integrated with the textbook."

Wan-Ting (Alexandra) Wu, University of Massachusetts Boston

"I was pleased with the content, depth, examples and problems presented in the text. I would definitely recommend using this book to a colleague. One of my favorite aspects of the books is the Real World example that each chapter starts with. Automatically students are able to bridge the gap between the concepts and the real world as they read through the chapter."

Jaclyn Boichat, Johnson & Wales University

RELEVANCE. Building student interest with its insightful Entrepreneur Spotlights opening each chapter, current In Business examples throughout the text, and tried-and-true end-of-chapter material, students will always see the real-world applicability of Noreen/Brewer/Garrison.

BALANCE. There is more than one type of business, and so Noreen/Brewer/Garrison covers a variety of business models, including nonprofit, retail, service, wholesale, and manufacturing organizations. Service company examples are highlighted with icons in the margins of the text.

Cavan Images/Alamy Stock Photo

New in the Sixth Edition

Faculty feedback helps us continue to improve *Managerial Accounting for Managers.* In response to reviewer suggestions, the authors have made the following changes to the text:

- New, auto-graded **Excel Data Analytics Exercises** help prepare students with career-ready skills and an analytical mindset. These exercises teach students how to analyze data using Excel-based tools such as Goal Seek, Solver, and Pivot Tables, while also teaching them how to communicate their resulting insights using a variety of Excel's charting capabilities.

- New, auto-graded **Tableau Data Visualization Exercises** that introduce students to this widely used data visualization software package, which they will likely encounter during their careers.

- A **Data Analytics Implementation Guide** (in Connect) to help instructors integrate **Data Analytics Exercises** into their managerial accounting class, and a **Data Analytics Exercise Tutorial** to help students as they work through Excel exercises.

- Over 1,200 new multiple-choice test bank questions are now included in **Connect.** These questions include a variety of conceptual and computational formats as well as static and algorithmic formats.

- The chapter previously titled "Performance Measurement in Decentralized Organizations" has been split into two chapters. One of those two chapters, titled "Strategic Performance Measurement," greatly expands our coverage of the balanced scorecard—a topic that is pervasive in practice. This chapter also provides more than 70 examples of scorecard measures that will enrich your students' understanding of nonfinancial performance measurement within the learning and growth, internal business process, and customer perspectives of the scorecard. This chapter also extends our coverage of how companies measure their performance with respect to corporate social responsibility.

- The **Integration Exercises,** included in the back of the book, have been expanded from 8 to 12. These exercises help students see how the learning objectives across chapters integrate with one another. They are also suitable for both a flipped classroom model and an in-class active learning environment as they engage students and encourage critical thinking.

- **Audio Hints** have been added to certain problems in **Connect** and offer brief explanations of the key steps students need to solve a specific end-of-chapter problem. With callouts to individual chapter learning objectives, audio hints are both a helpful tool for completing an assignment as well as an additional opportunity for students to link their work back to the chapter content.

- **Entrepreneur Spotlights** are new chapter openers for the sixth edition of *Managerial Accounting for Managers.* With the majority of businesses being small businesses, we felt it important to emphasize a diverse group of entrepreneurs and their roles in the economy.

- **In Business boxes** are updated throughout to provide relevant and current real-world examples for use in classroom discussion and to support student understanding of key concepts as they read through a chapter.

New in the Sixth Edition

Prologue

- The Prologue has a new discussion of Big Data and Data Analytics, added coverage of the CSCA exam, and an updated version of the IMA's Statement of Ethical Professional Practice. It also includes a new In Business box that introduces students to the IMA's Management Accounting Competency Framework.

Chapter 1

- Learning objective 1–5 was restated to focus on relevant and irrelevant costs. The terms *controllable* and *uncontrollable costs* as well as *value-added* and *non-value-added costs* were added to the chapter. Four new In Business boxes were added. The Cost of Quality appendix was deleted, and a subset of the deleted material was moved to Chapter 12 (Strategic Performance Measurement).

Chapter 2

- The operating leverage discussion was adjusted to better highlight its emphasis on analyzing changes in unit sales. Problems 2–19, 2–24, and 2–25 were revised, and three new In Business boxes were added.

Chapter 3

- We added a new learning objective related to calculating ending inventories for the balance sheet and cost of goods sold for the income statement. Also, Foundational 15, Exercise 3–17, and Problem 3–22 were revised, and three new In Business boxes were added.

Chapter 4

- This chapter added three new In Business boxes

Chapter 5

- This chapter added two new In Business boxes

Chapter 6

- We changed the language accompanying learning objective 6–3 from the manufacturing-centric "make or buy decisions" to the broader business language of "sourcing decisions." We created three new end-of-chapter exercises (6–11, 6–18, and 6–20) to illustrate (1) the decision to add a product line, (2) sourcing decisions in a nonmanufacturing context, and (3) the relevance of replacement costs in decision making. Also, three new In Business boxes were added.

Chapter 7

- The formula for the profitability index was revised to become "Present value of cash inflows ÷ Investment required." A new footnote explains how to use Microsoft Excel's IRR functionality to compute the internal rate of return. Also, we added four new In Business boxes.

Chapter 8

- The "Why and How Organizations Create Budgets" discussion was cut in half while retaining all of the key insights. This chapter added two new In Business boxes.

Chapter 9

- We replaced the learning objective related to "common errors" with a learning objective focusing on preparing a flexible budget performance report with more than one cost driver. We added two new In Business boxes.

Chapter 10

- This chapter added two new In Business boxes.

Chapter 11

- We changed the chapter title to Responsibility Accounting Systems. Coverage of operating performance measures and the balanced scorecard was removed. The subject matter previously in Appendices 11A (Transfer Pricing) and 11B (Service Department Charges) was integrated into the main body of the chapter. We added two new In Business boxes.

Chapter 12

- This is a new chapter. It greatly expands our coverage of the balanced scorecard and corporate social responsibility. The chapter includes nine new end-of-chapter exercises and problems.

Noreen's Powerful Pedagogy

Managerial Accounting for Managers includes pedagogical elements that engage and instruct students without cluttering the pages or interrupting student learning. Noreen's key pedagogical tools enhance and support students' understanding of the concepts rather than compete with the narrative for their attention.

Microsoft Excel

Microsoft Excel

NEW* Data Analytics Exercises

NEW Data Analytics Exercises are created to foster creating career-ready students by teaching them how to use software tools to derive managerial insights and communicate them to stakeholders. These new exercises, which appear in Connect, are linked to a diverse range of learning objectives that span numerous chapters, are auto-graded, and offer a scaffolded approach to introducing data analytics to students.

- **NEW Tableau Dashboard Activities** allow students to explore live Tableau dashboards directly integrated into Connect and include auto-graded questions focused on both calculations and analysis. Students can check their understanding and apply what they are learning within the framework of analytics and critical thinking.

- **NEW Applying Tableau Exercises** featuring Tableau at the end of each chapter. These exercises are auto-gradable in Connect and help students develop in-demand skills in analyzing and interpreting data and effectively communicating findings. Students will be provided datasets as well as numerous training and video tutorials and step-by-step instructions to build dashboards that visualize data using Tableau software. Over the course of these exercises, students will gain both managerial insights as well as confidence in telling the story of data through visualization software.

- **NEW Power BI Exercises** will introduce and teach students to drive better business decisions by analyzing data for insights via Microsoft's Power BI software. Power BI aims to provide interactive visualizations, business intelligence capabilities, and supports users' ability to gain deeper data insight. Users create their own reports and dashboards, harnessing data to tell a compelling business story. As with Applying Tableau, students will be provided datasets, numerous training and video tutorials, and step-by-step instructions to learn how to visualize data using Power BI software.

- **NEW Excel Analytics** were created to allow students to work with complex datasets in Excel. Created to support student Career Readiness, students need to use Excel-based tools to analyze datasets and derive solutions using a variety of data management, data analysis, and data visualization techniques. Students are provided datasets via Connect, video training embedded in Connect, and step-by-step tutorials. These go beyond basic data manipulations with Excel skills.

NEW* Integrated Excel Assignments

Integrated Excel assignments pair the power of Microsoft Excel with the power of Connect. A seamless integration of Excel within Connect, Integrated Excel questions allow students to work in live, auto-graded Excel spreadsheets—no additional logins, no need to upload or download files. Instructors can choose to grade by formula or solution value, and students receive instant cell-level feedback via integrated Check My Work functionality.

NEW* Entrepreneur Spotlight

All chapters begin with a new **Entrepreneur Spotlight** that serves four purposes. First, this new feature acknowledges the importance of small business owners and the instrumental role they play in supporting a thriving economy. Second, each spotlight links the principles of managerial accounting to a real-world small business context. Third, each spotlight describes the company's commitments to its corporate social responsibilities, thereby exposing our students to a stakeholder-based philosophy of organizational management. Finally, the collective body of Entrepreneurial Spotlights depicts the diverse backgrounds of our world's entrepreneurs, thereby helping **all** of our students understand that starting a new business is an opportunity available to them.

WARBY PARKER

NICE TO SEE YOU

Interim Archives/Contributor/Getty Images

ENTREPRENEUR SPOTLIGHT

Neil Blumenthal and Dave Gilboa co-founded Warby Parker to solve what they saw as a simple problem—the price of eyeglasses was too high. By designing their own glasses and interacting directly with customers, they were able "to provide high quality, better-looking prescription eyewear at a fraction of the going price." Today the company is

NEW* Connect-Only Test Bank

A new online-only test bank is now available in Connect, containing more than **1,200 new multiple-choice** test bank questions. These new, author-created **Connect-Only Test Bank** questions were written in such a way to prevent students from finding answers on external sites. The questions are presented in a combination of static and algorithmic (both quantitative and qualitative algo) modes and they cover all learning objectives in all of the chapters. The questions are qualitative and quantitative in nature, and they span the entire "degree-of-difficulty" continuum, including easy, medium, and hard.

NEW* Author-Created Learning Objective Videos

Author Pete Brewer created narrated PowerPoint videos for each chapter. There is one video for every learning objective plus chapter overview videos. Each video is three to eight minutes in duration and includes a brief explanation of the learning objective's key concepts accompanied by a numerical example.

Writing Assignment

Available within McGraw Hill Connect and McGraw Hill Connect Master, the **Writing Assignment** tool delivers a learning experience to help students improve their written communication skills and conceptual understanding. As an instructor, you can assign, monitor, grade, and provide feedback on writing more efficiently and effectively.

Additional Integration Exercises

We have added four new Integration Exercises for a total of twelve (located in the back of the book) that integrate learning objectives across chapters. These exercises will increase the students' level of interest in the course because they forge the connections across chapters. Rather than seeing each chapter as an isolated set of learning objectives, students begin to see how "it all fits together" to provide greater managerial insight and more effective planning, controlling, and decision making. The integration exercises also are tailor-made for flipping the classroom because they offer challenging questions that require students to work in teams to derive solutions that synthesize what they have been learning throughout the semester.

The Foundational 15

Each chapter contains one **Foundational 15** exercise that includes 15 "building-block" questions related to one concise set of data. These exercises can be used for in-class discussion or as homework assignments. They are found before the Exercises and are available in Connect.

"This is my favorite part of the text. Its really helps students to go through all the concepts in the chapters with the same data. Shorter exercises that only do one step are okay, but as a wrap up, the Foundational 15 is much better."

Sandra Copa, North Hennepin Community College

Concept Overview Videos

Concept Overview Videos, available within Connect, teach the core concepts of the content in an animated, narrated, and interactive multimedia format, bringing the key learning objectives of the course to life. Checkpoint questions allow instructors to assign points to knowledge checks and grade for accuracy, not just completion. Concept Overview Videos are particularly helpful for online courses and for those audio and visual learners who struggle reading the textbook page by page.

In Business Boxes

These helpful **In Business** boxed features offer a glimpse into how real companies use the managerial accounting concepts discussed within the chapter. Each chapter contains multiple current examples.

Managerial Accounting in Action Vignettes

The **Managerial Accounting in Action** vignettes depict cross-functional teams working together in real-life settings, working with the products and services that students recognize from their own lives. Students are shown step-by-step how accounting concepts are implemented in organizations and how these concepts are applied to solve everyday business problems. First, "The Issue" is introduced through a dialogue; the student then walks through the implementation process; finally, "The Wrap-up" summarizes the big picture.

To help explain the role of CVP analysis in business decisions, we'll turn our attention to the case of Acoustic Concepts, Inc., a company founded by Prem Narayan.

MANAGERIAL ACCOUNTING IN ACTION
THE ISSUE

ACOUSTIC concepts inc

Prem, who was a graduate student in engineering at the time, started Acoustic Concepts, Inc., to market a radical new speaker he had designed for automobile sound systems. The speaker, called the Sonic Blaster, uses an advanced microprocessor and proprietary software to boost amplification to awesome levels. Prem contracted with a Taiwanese electronics manufacturer to produce the speaker. With seed money provided by his family, Prem placed an order with the manufacturer and ran advertisements in auto magazines.

The Sonic Blaster was an immediate success, and sales grew to the point that Prem moved the company's headquarters out of his apartment and into rented quarters in a nearby industrial park. He also hired a receptionist, an accountant, a sales manager, and a small sales staff to sell the speakers to retail stores. The accountant, Bob Luchinni, had worked for several small companies where he had acted as a business advisor, as well as accountant and bookkeeper. The following discussion occurred soon after Bob was hired:

Prem: Bob, I've got a lot of questions about the company's finances I hope you can help answer.

Bob: We're in great shape. The loan from your family will be paid off within a few months.

Prem: I know, but I am worried about the risks I've taken on by expanding operations. What would happen if a competitor entered the market and our sales slipped? How far could sales drop without putting us into the red? Another question I've been trying to resolve is how much our sales would have to increase to justify the

Test Builder in Connect

Available within Connect, **Test Builder** is a cloud-based tool that enables instructors to format tests that can be printed or administered within an LMS. Test Builder offers a modern, streamlined interface for easy content configuration that matches course needs without requiring a download.

Test Builder allows you to

- Access all test bank content from a particular title.
- Easily pinpoint the most relevant content through robust filtering options.
- Manipulate the order of questions or scramble questions and/or answers.
- Pin questions to a specific location within a test.
- Determine your preferred treatment of algorithmic questions.
- Choose the layout and spacing.
- Add instructions and configure default settings.

Test Builder provides a secure interface for better protection of content and allows for just-in-time updates to flow directly into assessments.

Remote Proctoring & Browser-Locking Capabilities

New remote proctoring and browser-locking capabilities, hosted by Proctorio within Connect, provide control of the assessment environment by enabling security options and verifying the identity of the student. Seamlessly integrated within Connect, these services allow instructors to control students' assessment experience by restricting browser activity, recording students' activity, and verifying students are doing their own work. Instant and detailed reporting gives instructors an at-a-glance view of potential academic integrity concerns, thereby avoiding personal bias and supporting evidence-based claims.

Tegrity: Lectures 24/7

Tegrity in Connect is a tool that makes class time available 24/7 by automatically capturing every lecture. With a simple one-click start-and-stop process, you capture all computer screens and corresponding audio in a format that is easy to search, frame by frame. Students can replay any part of any class with easy-to-use, browser-based viewing on a PC, Mac, iPod, or other mobile device.

Educators know that the more students can see, hear, and experience class resources, the better they learn. In fact, studies prove it. Tegrity's unique search feature helps students efficiently find what they need, when they need it, across an entire semester of class recordings. Help turn your students' study time into learning moments immediately supported by your lecture. With Tegrity, you also increase intent listening and class participation by easing students' concerns about notetaking. Using Tegrity in Connect will make it more likely you will see students' faces, not the tops of their heads.

Custom Publishing through Create

McGraw Hill Create is a new, self-service website that allows instructors to create custom course materials by drawing upon McGraw Hill's comprehensive, cross-disciplinary content. Instructors can add their own content quickly and easily and tap into other rights-secured third-party sources as well, then arrange the content in a way that makes the most sense for their course. Instructors can even personalize their book with the course name and information and choose the best format for their students: color print, black-and-white print, or an eBook.

Through Create, instructors can

- Select and arrange the content in a way that makes the most sense for their course.
- Combine material from different sources and even upload their own content.
- Choose the best format for their students: print or eBook.
- Edit and update their course materials as often as they like.

Begin creating now at **www.mcgrawhillcreate.com**.

McGraw Hill Customer Experience
Group Contact Information

At McGraw Hill, we understand that getting the most from new technology can be challenging. That's why our services don't stop after you purchase our products. You can contact our Product Specialists 24 hours a day to get product training online. Or you can search the knowledge bank of Frequently Asked Questions on our support website. For Customer Support, call **800-331-5094,** or visit **www.mhhe.com/support**. One of our Technical Support Analysts will be able to assist you in a timely fashion.

Microsoft Excel

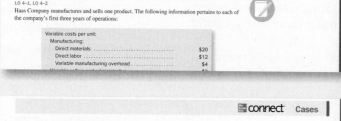

End-of-Chapter Material

Managerial Accounting for Managers has earned a reputation for the best end-of-chapter practice material of any text on the market. Our problem and case material continues to conform to AACSB recommendations and makes a great starting point for class discussions and group projects. When the authors first wrote *Managerial Accounting for Managers,* they started with the end-of-chapter material, then wrote the narrative in support of it. This unique approach to textbook authoring not only ensured consistency between the end-of-chapter material and text content but also underscored the fundamental belief in the importance of applying theory through practice. It is not enough for students to read; they must also understand. To this day, the guiding principle of that first edition remains, and Noreen's superior end-of-chapter material continues to provide accurate, current, and relevant practice for students.

Assurance of Learning Ready

Many educational institutions today are focused on the notion of assurance of learning, an important element of some accreditation standards. *Managerial Accounting for Managers,* 6e, is designed specifically to support your assurance of learning initiatives with a simple, yet powerful, solution.

Each question for *Managerial Accounting for Managers,* 6e, maps to a specific chapter learning outcome/objective listed in the text. The reporting features of Connect can aggregate students to make the collection and presentation of assurance of learning data simple and easy.

Author-Written Supplements

Unlike other managerial accounting texts, the book's authors write the major supplements such as the test bank and solution files, ensuring a perfect fit between text and supplements.

Utilizing the Icons

 To reflect our service-based economy, the text is replete with examples from service-based businesses. A helpful icon distinguishes service-related examples in the text.

 Ethics assignments and examples serve as a reminder that good conduct is vital in business. Icons call out content that relates to ethical behavior for students.

 The writing icon denotes problems that require students to use critical thinking as well as writing skills to explain their decisions.

 This icon indicates Data Analytic Exercises in Connect tied to chapter learning objectives.

AACSB Statement

McGraw Hill Education is a proud corporate member of AACSB International. Recognizing the importance and value of AACSB accreditation, we have sought to recognize the curricula guidelines detailed in AACSB standards for business accreditation by connecting selected questions in *Managerial Accounting for Managers,* 6e, to the general knowledge and skill guidelines found in the AACSB standards. The statements contained in *Managerial Accounting for Managers,* 6e, are provided only as a guide for the users of this text. The AACSB leaves content coverage and assessment clearly within the realm and control of individual schools, the mission of the school, and the faculty. The AACSB does also charge schools with the obligation of doing assessment against their own content and learning goals. While *Managerial Accounting for Managers,* 6e, and its teaching package makes no claim of any specific AACSB qualification or evaluation, we have, within *Managerial Accounting for Managers,* 6e, tagged questions according to the six general knowledge and skills areas. The labels or tags within *Managerial Accounting for Managers,* 6e, are as indicated. There are, of course, many more within the test bank, the text, and the teaching package, which might be used as a "standard" for your course. However, the labeled questions are suggested for your consideration.

Instructors: Student Success Starts with You

Tools to enhance your unique voice

Want to build your own course? No problem. Prefer to use an OLC-aligned, prebuilt course? Easy. Want to make changes throughout the semester? Sure. And you'll save time with Connect's auto-grading too.

65%
Less Time
Grading

Laptop: McGraw Hill; Woman/dog: George Doyle/Getty Images

Study made personal

Incorporate adaptive study resources like SmartBook® 2.0 into your course and help your students be better prepared in less time. Learn more about the powerful personalized learning experience available in SmartBook 2.0 at **www.mheducation.com/highered/connect/smartbook**

Affordable solutions, added value

Make technology work for you with LMS integration for single sign-on access, mobile access to the digital textbook, and reports to quickly show you how each of your students is doing. And with our Inclusive Access program you can provide all these tools at a discount to your students. Ask your McGraw Hill representative for more information.

Padlock: Jobalou/Getty Images

Solutions for your challenges

A product isn't a solution. Real solutions are affordable, reliable, and come with training and ongoing support when you need it and how you want it. Visit **www.supportateverystep.com** for videos and resources both you and your students can use throughout the semester.

Checkmark: Jobalou/Getty Images

Students: Get Learning that Fits You

Effective tools for efficient studying

Connect is designed to help you be more productive with simple, flexible, intuitive tools that maximize your study time and meet your individual learning needs. Get learning that works for you with Connect.

Study anytime, anywhere

Download the free ReadAnywhere app and access your online eBook, SmartBook 2.0, or Adaptive Learning Assignments when it's convenient, even if you're offline. And since the app automatically syncs with your Connect account, all of your work is available every time you open it. Find out more at **www.mheducation.com/readanywhere**

> *"I really liked this app—it made it easy to study when you don't have your text-book in front of you."*
>
> - Jordan Cunningham, Eastern Washington University

Calendar: owattaphotos/Getty Images

Everything you need in one place

Your Connect course has everything you need—whether reading on your digital eBook or completing assignments for class, Connect makes it easy to get your work done.

Learning for everyone

McGraw Hill works directly with Accessibility Services Departments and faculty to meet the learning needs of all students. Please contact your Accessibility Services Office and ask them to email accessibility@mheducation.com, or visit **www.mheducation.com/about/accessibility** for more information.

Acknowledgments

Suggestions have been received from many of our colleagues throughout the world. Each of those who have offered comments and suggestions has our thanks.

The efforts of many people are needed to develop and improve a text. Among these people are the reviewers and consultants who point out areas of concern, cite areas of strength, and make recommendations for change. In this regard, the following professors provided feedback that was enormously helpful in preparing the sixth edition of *Managerial Accounting for Managers:*

Wagdy Abdallah, *Seton Hall University*
Linda Abernathy, *Kirkwood Community College*
James Andrews, *Central New Mexico Community College*
Rick Andrews, *Sinclair Community College*
Frank Aquilino, *Montclair State University*
Jane Austin, *Oklahoma City University*
Kashi R. Balachandran, *New York University*
Linda Benz, *Jefferson Technical College*
Sheila Betz, *J. Sargeant Reynolds Community College*
Surasakdi Bhamornsiri, *University of North Carolina–Charlotte*
Larry N. Bitner, *Shippensburg University*
Jaclyn Boichat, *Johnson & Wales University*
Jorja Bradford, *Alabama State University*
Janet Butler, *Texas State University–San Marcos*
Jennifer Cainas, *University of South Florida*
Rusty Calk, *New Mexico State University*
Dana Carpenter, *MATC Truax*
Chiaho Chang, *Montlcair State University*
Cathy Claiborne, *University of Colorado–Colorado Springs*
Robert Clarke, *Brigham Young University–Idaho*
Curtis Clements, *Abilene Christian University*
Darlene Coarts, *University of Northern Iowa*
Elizabeth Connors, *University of Massachusetts–Boston*
Sandy Copa, *North Hennepin Community College*
Deb Cosgrove, *University of Nebraska–Lincoln*
Nancy Coulmas, *Bloomsburg University of Pennsylvania*
Jean Crawford, *Alabama State University*
Janet Dausey, *Northeast Wisconsin Technical College*
Patricia Doherty, *Boston University*
David L. Doyon, *Southern New Hampshire University*
Andrea Drake, *Louisiana Tech University*
Jan Duffy, *Iowa State University*
Cindy Easterwood, *Virginia Tech*
Gene Elrod, *University of North Texas*

Rebecca Evans, *Florida State College–Jacksonville*
Amanda Farmer, *University of Georgia*
Janice Fergusson, *University of South Carolina*
Annette Fisher, *Glendale Community College*
Ananda Ganguly, *Claremont College*
J. Marie Gibson, *University of Nevada, Reno*
Olen Greer, *Missouri State University*
Cynthia Greeson, *Ivy Tech Community College*
Andrew S. Griffith, *Iona College*
Robert Hammond, *Camden County College*
Richard O. Hanson, *Southern New Hampshire University*
Ken Harmon, *Kennesaw State University*
Christine Haynes, *University of West Georgia*
David Henderson, *College of Charleston*
Kathy Ho, *Niagara University*
Mark Holtzman, *Seton Hall University*
Maggie Houston, *Wright State University*
Tom Hrubec, *Franklin University*
Ronald Huefner, *SUNY Buffalo*
Yousef Jahmani, *Savannah State University*
Robyn Jarnagin, *Montana State University*
Iris Jenkel, *St. Norbert College*
Randy Johnston, *Michigan State University*
Nancy Jones, *San Diego State University*
Jai Kang, *San Francisco State University*
Catherine Katagiri, *College of Saint Rose*
Carl Keller, *Indiana Purdue University/Fort Wayne*
Cynthia Khanlarian, *University of North Carolina–Greensboro*
James Kinard, *Ohio State University–Columbus*
Gary Kleinman, *Montclair State University*
Leon Korte, *The University of South Dakota*
Wikil Kwak, *University of Nebraska at Omaha*
Marco Lam, *Western Carolina University*
Christy Land, *Catawba Valley Community College*
Ron Lazer, *University of Houston*
Chuo-Hsuan Lee, *SUNY–Plattsburgh*
Candace Leuck, *Clemson University*
Natasha Librizzi, *Milwaukee Area Technical College*

William R. Link, *University of Missouri–St. Louis*
Kathy Long, *University of Tennessee–Chattanooga*
Patti Lopez, *Valencia Community College East*
Jim Lukawitz, *University of Memphis*
Anna Lusher, *Slippery Rock University*
Linda Malgeri, *Kennesaw State University*
Mary Loretta Manktelow, *James Madison University*
Steve Markoff, *Montclair State University*
Melissa Martin, *Arizona State University–Tempe*
Christian Mastilak, *Xavier University*
Karen Bardshaw McCarron, *Georgia Gwinnett College*
Gary McCombs, *College of Charleston*
Noel McKeon, *Florida State College–Jacksonville*
Jim McKittrick, *University of Portland*
Laurie McWhorter, *Mississippi State University*
James Meddaugh, *Ohio University*
Tammy Metzke, *Milwaukee Area Technical College–West Allis*
Tony Mifsud, *Catawba Valley Community College*
Tim Mills, *Eastern Illinois University*
Mark E. Motluck, *Anderson University*
Dennis Mullen, *City College of San Francisco*
Gerald M. Myers, *Pacific Lutheran University*
Albert Nagy, *John Carroll University*
Michael Newman, *University of Houston–Houston*
Joseph M. Nicassio, *Westmoreland County Community College*
Alfonso R. Oddo, *Niagara University*
Tamara Phelan, *Northern Illinois University*
JoAnn Pinto, *Montclair State University*
Terence Pitre, *University of St. Thomas*
Shirley Polejewski, *University of St. Thomas*
Kay Poston, *Francis Marion University*
Les Price, *Pierce College*
Kamala Raghavan, *Robert Morris University*
Rama Ramamurthy, *Georgetown University*
Raul Ramos, *Lorain County Community College*

John Reisch, *East Carolina University*
Michelle Reisch, *East Carolina University*
Therese Rice, *North Hennepin Community College*
Rhonda Richards, *Southeastern Oklahoma State University*
Luther L. Ross Sr., *Central Piedmont Community College*
Pamela Rouse, *Butler University*
Amy Santos, *Manatee Community College*
Rex Schildhouse, *Miramar College*
Ann E. Selk, *University of Wisconsin–Green Bay*
Daniel Sevall, *Lincoln University*
Ken Snow, *Florida State College–Jacksonville*
Debra Snyder, *Calvin College*
Vic Stanton, *University of California–Berkeley*
Dennis Stovall, *Grand Valley State University*
Ellen Sweatt, *Georgia Perimeter College*
Rick Tabor, *Auburn University*
Diane Tanner, *University of North Florida*
Samantha Ternes, *Kirkwood Community College*
Chuck Thompson, *University of Massachusetts*
Dorothy Thompson, *North Central Texas College*
Kiran Verma, *University of Massachusetts–Boston*
Terri Walsh, *Seminole State College of Florida*
James White, *Boston University*
Lori White, *West Liberty University*
James Wilhelm, *Chapman University*
Michael Wilson, *University of Indianapolis*
Jeffrey Wong, *University of Nevada–Reno*
Peter Woodlock, *Youngstown State University*
Janet Woods, *Macon State College*
Christine Wright, *Seminole State College of Florida*
Wan-Ting (Alexandra) Wu, *University of Massachusetts–Boston*
James Yang, *Montclair State University*
Marjorie Yuschak, *Rutgers University*
Ronald Zhao, *Monmouth University*

We are grateful for the outstanding support from McGraw Hill. In particular, we would like to thank Tim Vertovec, Portfolio VP; Becky Olson, Senior Director; Noelle Bathurst, Senior Portfolio Manager; Erin Quinones, Product Developer; Kevin Moran, Director of Digital Content; Pat Frederickson and Angela Norris, Lead Content Project Managers; Lauren Schur, Executive Marketing Manager; Matt Diamond, Designer; Laura Fuller, Buyer; and Lori Hancock, Content Licensing Specialist.

Thank you to Julie Hankins for acting as lead subject matter expert on Connect content, along with Julie Hampton, Emily Bello, and Beth Kobylarz for their efforts as subject matter experts on Connect EOC and Test Bank content. Patti Lopez (Valencia College) for her efforts as lead subject matter expert on LearnSmart. Thank you to Beth Kobylarz for her feedback to the text revisions and a special thank you to Jacob Shortt for his contributions to the Data Analalytics offerings for this edition.

We are grateful to the Institute of Certified Management Accountants for permission to use questions and/or unofficial answers from past Certificate in Management Accounting (CMA) examinations.

Eric W. Noreen · Peter C. Brewer · Ray H. Garrison

Brief Contents

Table of Contents

Chapter 2

Cost-Volume-Profit Relationships 62

Chapter 3

Job-Order Costing: Calculating Unit Product Costs 122

Chapter

Variable Costing and Segment Reporting: Tools for Management   171

Chapter

Activity-Based Costing: A Tool to Aid Decision Making   225

Chapter 6

Differential Analysis: The Key to Decision Making 277

Chapter 7

Capital Budgeting Decisions 349

Chapter 10

Chapter 11

Chapter 12

Strategic Performance Measurement 572

Managerial Accounting: An Overview

Cavan Images/Alamy Stock Photo

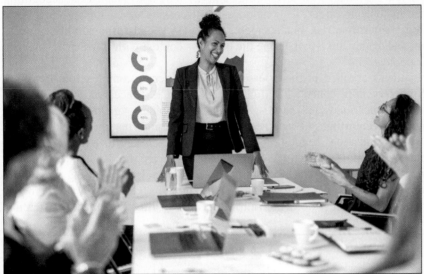

AzmanJaka/E+/Getty Images

ENTREPRENEUR SPOTLIGHT

Maria Contreras-Sweet "sees entrepreneurship as a force that can change lives and lift whole communities around the world." In 2006, she started ProAmérica Bank—the first commercial bank started in California by a person of Latino origin in more than 35 years. The bank focuses on serving small and medium-sized businesses in Latino neighborhoods, based on her belief "that the lack of access to capital means a lack of opportunity."

Managerial Accounting: The Practical Application

ProAmérica Bank maintains internal controls (as summarized in Exhibit P–8) to minimize various risks, such as incurring financial reporting errors. For example, the bank uses physical safeguards to limit access to its cash and other tangible assets. It also requires proper authorizations for transactions over pre-established dollar amounts. In addition, the bank prepares periodic reconciliations that compare its cash on hand with its underlying accounting records to identify and resolve any discrepancies.

Corporate Social Responsibility: Serving all Stakeholders

In addition to her entrepreneurial ventures, Contreras-Sweet has also served her community in various other capacities. For example, she served in President Barack Obama's cabinet as the 24th Administrator of the United States Small Business Administration. She also was a founding member of a nonprofit organization called Hispanas Organized for Political Equality (HOPE). The organization seeks to empower its communities "through advocacy, Latina leadership training, and increasing knowledge on the contributions Latinas have made to advance the status of women." ■

Sources: www.contrerassweet.com, https://smallbiztrends.com/2019/10/successful-hispanic-entrepreneurs.html, http://www.hispaniclifestyle.com/articles/latina-of-influence-maria-contreras-sweet/, https://www.latinas.org/hope-leadership.

What Is Managerial Accounting?

The prologue explains why managerial accounting is important to the future careers of all business students. It begins by answering two questions: (1) What is managerial accounting? and (2) Why does managerial accounting matter to your career? It concludes by discussing seven topics—Big Data, ethics, strategy, enterprise risk management, corporate social responsibility, process management, and leadership—that define the business context within which managerial accounting operates.

Many students enrolled in this course will have recently completed an introductory *financial accounting* course. **Financial accounting** is concerned with reporting financial information to external parties, such as stockholders, creditors, and regulators. **Managerial accounting** is concerned with providing information to managers for use within the organization. Exhibit P–1 summarizes seven key differences between financial and managerial accounting. It recognizes that the fundamental difference between financial and managerial accounting is that financial accounting serves the needs of those *outside* the organization, whereas managerial accounting serves the needs of managers employed *inside* the organization. Because of this fundamental difference

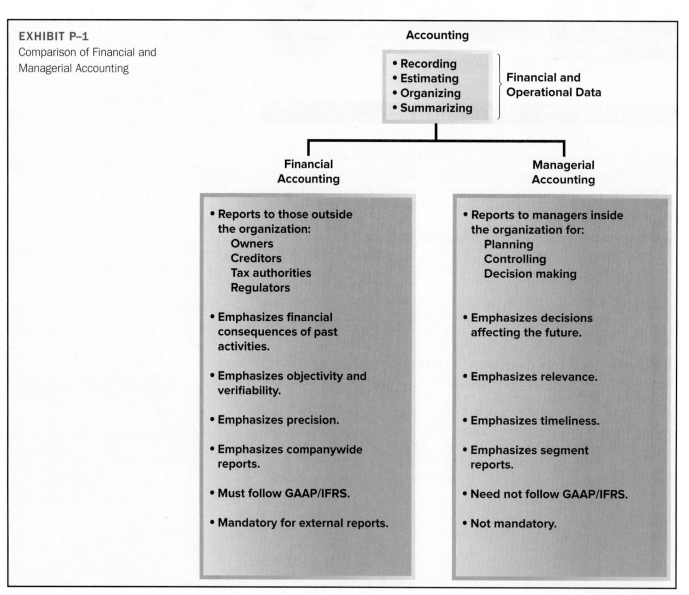

EXHIBIT P–1
Comparison of Financial and Managerial Accounting

Accounting

- Recording
- Estimating
- Organizing
- Summarizing

Financial and Operational Data

Financial Accounting

- Reports to those outside the organization:
    Owners
    Creditors
    Tax authorities
    Regulators

- Emphasizes financial consequences of past activities.

- Emphasizes objectivity and verifiability.

- Emphasizes precision.

- Emphasizes companywide reports.

- Must follow GAAP/IFRS.

- Mandatory for external reports.

Managerial Accounting

- Reports to managers inside the organization for:
    Planning
    Controlling
    Decision making

- Emphasizes decisions affecting the future.

- Emphasizes relevance.

- Emphasizes timeliness.

- Emphasizes segment reports.

- Need not follow GAAP/IFRS.

- Not mandatory.

in users, financial accounting emphasizes the financial consequences of past activities, objectivity and verifiability, precision, and companywide performance, whereas managerial accounting emphasizes decisions affecting the future, relevance, timeliness, and *segment* performance. A **segment** is a part or activity of an organization about which managers would like cost, revenue, or profit data. Examples of business segments include product lines, customer groups (segmented by age, ethnicity, gender, volume of purchases, etc.), geographic territories, divisions, plants, and departments. Finally, financial accounting is mandatory for external reports, and it needs to comply with rules, such as generally accepted accounting principles (GAAP) and international financial reporting standards (IFRS), whereas managerial accounting is not mandatory and does not need to comply with externally imposed rules.

As mentioned in Exhibit P–1, managerial accounting helps managers perform three vital activities—*planning, controlling,* and *decision making.* **Planning** involves establishing goals and specifying how to achieve them. **Controlling** involves gathering feedback to ensure that the plan is being properly executed or modified as circumstances change. **Decision making** involves selecting a course of action from competing alternatives. Now let's take a closer look at these three pillars of managerial accounting.

Planning

Assume you work for Procter & Gamble (P&G) and are in charge of the company's campus recruiting for all undergraduate business majors. In this example, your planning process would begin by establishing a goal such as: our goal is to recruit the "best and brightest" college graduates. The next stage of the planning process would require specifying how to achieve this goal by answering numerous questions such as:

- How many students do we need to hire in total and from each major?
- What schools do we plan to include in our recruiting efforts?
- Which of our employees will be involved in each school's recruiting activities?
- When will we conduct our interviews?
- How will we compare students to one another to decide who will be extended job offers?
- What salary will we offer our new hires? Will the salaries differ by major?
- How much money can we spend on our recruiting efforts?

As you can see, there are many questions that need to be answered as part of the planning process. Plans are often accompanied by a *budget.* A **budget** is a detailed plan for the future that is usually expressed in formal quantitative terms. As the head of recruiting at P&G, your budget would include two key components. First, you would have to work with other senior managers inside the company to establish a budgeted amount of total salaries that can be offered to all new hires. Second, you would have to create a budget that quantifies how much you intend to spend on your campus recruiting activities.

IN BUSINESS

LABOR VS. EQUIPMENT: AN IMPORTANT PLANNING DECISION

As e-commerce companies such as Amazon.com continue to thrive, brick-and-mortar retailers are looking for ways to improve customer satisfaction by eliminating the hassle of long checkout lines. For example, Tesco PLC, one of the world's largest supermarket operators, is experimenting with cashierless stores. Its automated process relies on 150 ceiling-mounted cameras to detect what customers buy and then automatically charges them for their groceries as they exit the store. Numerous other companies, such as Carrefour SA, Walmart, and Kroger, are also exploring ways to deliver what Tesco describes as "frictionless shopping" for their customers. While each company's approach to streamlining the shopping process may be unique, they all have important planning and budgeting implications with respect to investing in labor versus equipment.

Source: Parmy Olson, "Grocers Swap Cashiers for Cameras," *The Wall Street Journal,* July 8, 2019, pp. B1–B2.

Controlling

Once you established and started implementing P&G's recruiting plan, you would transition to the control process. This process would involve gathering, evaluating, and responding to feedback to ensure that this year's recruiting process meets expectations. It would also include evaluating the feedback in search of ways to run a more effective recruiting campaign next year. The control process would involve answering questions such as:

- Did we succeed in hiring the planned number of students within each major and at each school?
- Did we lose too many exceptional candidates to competitors?
- Did each of our employees involved in the recruiting process perform satisfactorily?
- Is our method of comparing students to one another working?
- Did the on-campus and office interviews run smoothly?
- Did we stay within our budget in terms of total salary commitments to new hires?
- Did we stay within our budget regarding spending on recruiting activities?

As you can see, there are many questions that need to be answered as part of the control process. When answering these questions, your goal would be to go beyond simple yes or no answers in search of the underlying reasons why performance exceeded or failed to meet expectations. Part of the control process includes preparing *performance reports*. A **performance report** compares budgeted data to actual data in an effort to identify and learn from excellent performance and to identify and eliminate sources of unsatisfactory performance. Performance reports can also be used as one of many inputs to help evaluate and reward employees.

Although this example focused on P&G's campus recruiting efforts, we could have described how planning enables FedEx to deliver packages across the globe overnight or how it helps Apple develop and market successive generations of the iPhone. We could have discussed how the control process helps Pfizer, Eli Lilly, and Abbott Laboratories ensure that their pharmaceutical drugs are produced in conformance with rigorous quality standards, or how Publix relies on the control process to keep its grocery shelves stocked. We also could have looked at planning and control failures such as Takata's recall of more than 30 million defective driver-side airbags installed by a variety of automakers such as Honda, Ford, Toyota, and Subaru. In short, all managers (and that probably includes you someday) perform planning and controlling activities.

Decision Making

Perhaps the most basic managerial skill is the ability to make intelligent, data-driven decisions. Broadly speaking, many of those decisions revolve around the following three questions: *What* should we be selling? *Who* should we be serving? *How* should we execute? Exhibit P–2 provides examples of decisions pertaining to each of these three categories.

EXHIBIT P–2
Examples of Decisions

What should we be selling?	Who should we be serving?	How should we execute?
What products and services should be the focus of our marketing efforts?	Who should be the focus of our marketing efforts?	How should we supply our parts and services?
What new products and services should we offer?	Who should we start serving?	How should we expand our capacity?
What prices should we charge for our products and services?	Who should pay price premiums or receive price discounts?	How should we reduce our capacity?
What products and services should we discontinue?	Who should we stop serving?	How should we improve our efficiency and effectiveness?

The left-hand column of Exhibit P–2 suggests that every company must make decisions related to the products and services it sells. For example, each year Procter & Gamble must decide how to allocate its marketing budget across numerous brands that each generate over $1 billion in sales as well as other brands that have promising growth potential. Mattel must decide what new toys to introduce to the market. Southwest Airlines must decide what ticket prices to establish for each of its thousands of flights per day. Hyundai must decide whether to discontinue certain models of automobiles.

The middle column of Exhibit P–2 indicates that all companies must make decisions related to the customers they serve. For example, Duluth Trading Company must decide how to allocate its marketing budget between products that tend to appeal to male versus female customers. FedEx must decide whether to expand its services into new markets across the globe. HP must decide what price discounts to offer corporate clients who purchase large volumes of its products. A bank must decide whether to discontinue customers who may be unprofitable.

The right-hand column of Exhibit P–2 shows that companies also make decisions related to how they execute. For example, Boeing must decide whether to rely on outside vendors such as Goodrich, Saab, and Rolls-Royce to manufacture many of the parts used to make its airplanes. Cintas must decide whether to expand its laundering and cleaning capacity in a given geographic region by adding square footage to an existing facility or constructing an entirely new facility. In an economic downturn, a manufacturer might have to decide whether to eliminate one 8-hour shift at three plants or to close one plant. Finally, all companies have to decide among competing improvement opportunities. For example, a company may have to decide whether to implement a new software system, to upgrade a piece of equipment, or to provide extra training to its employees.

This portion of the prologue has explained that the three pillars of managerial accounting are planning, controlling, and decision making. This book helps prepare you to become an effective manager by explaining how to make intelligent data-driven decisions, how to create financial plans for the future, and how to continually make progress toward achieving goals by obtaining, evaluating, and responding to feedback.

Why Does Managerial Accounting Matter to Your Career?

Many students feel anxious about choosing a major because they are unsure if it will provide a fulfilling career. To reduce these anxieties, we recommend deemphasizing what you cannot control about the future; instead, focusing on what you can control right now. More specifically, concentrate on answering the following question: What can you do now to prepare for success in an unknown future career? The best answer is to learn skills that will make it easier for you to adapt to an uncertain future. You need to become adaptable!

Whether you end up working in the United States or abroad, for a large corporation, a small entrepreneurial company, a nonprofit organization, or a governmental entity, you'll need to know how to plan for the future, how to make progress toward achieving goals, and how to make intelligent decisions. In other words, managerial accounting skills are useful in just about any career, organization, and industry. If you commit energy to this course, you'll be making a smart investment in your future—even though you cannot clearly envision it. Next, we will elaborate on this point by explaining how managerial accounting relates to the future careers of business majors and accounting majors.

Business Majors

Exhibit P–3 provides examples of how planning, controlling, and decision making affect three majors other than accounting—marketing, supply chain management, and human resource management.

The left-hand column of Exhibit P–3 describes some planning, controlling, and decision-making applications in the marketing profession. For example, marketing managers make planning decisions related to allocating advertising dollars across various communication mediums and to staffing new sales territories. From a control standpoint,

EXHIBIT P–3

Relating Managerial Accounting to Three Business Majors

	Marketing	Supply Chain Management	Human Resource Management
Planning	How much should we budget for TV, print, and Internet advertising?	How many units should we plan to produce next period?	How much should we plan to spend for occupational safety training?
	How many salespeople should we plan to hire to serve a new territory?	How much should we budget for next period's utility expense?	How much should we plan to spend on employee recruitment advertising?
Controlling	Is the budgeted price cut increasing unit sales as expected?	Did we spend more or less than expected for the units we actually produced?	Is our employee retention rate exceeding our goals?
	Are we accumulating too much inventory during the holiday shopping season?	Are we achieving our goal of reducing the number of defective units produced?	Are we meeting our goal of completing timely performance appraisals?
Decision Making	Should we sell our services as one bundle or sell them separately?	Should we transfer production of a component part to an overseas supplier?	Should we hire an on-site medical staff to lower our health care costs?
	Should we sell directly to customers or use a distributor?	Should we redesign our manufacturing process to lower inventory levels?	Should we hire temporary workers or full-time employees?

they may closely track sales data to see if a budgeted price cut is generating an anticipated increase in unit sales, or they may study inventory levels during the holiday shopping season so that they can adjust prices as needed to optimize sales. Marketing managers also make many important decisions, such as whether to bundle services together and sell them for one price or to sell each service separately. They may also decide whether to sell products directly to the customer or to sell to a distributor, who then sells to the end consumer.

The middle column of Exhibit P–3 states that supply chain managers have to plan how many units to produce to satisfy anticipated customer demand. They also need to budget for operating expenses such as utilities, supplies, and labor costs. In terms of control, they monitor actual spending relative to the budget and closely watch operational measures such as the number of defects produced relative to the plan. Supply chain managers make numerous decisions, such as deciding whether to transfer production of a component part to an overseas supplier. They also decide whether to invest in redesigning a manufacturing process to reduce inventory levels.

The right-hand column of Exhibit P–3 explains how human resource managers make a variety of planning decisions, such as budgeting how much to spend on occupational safety training and employee recruitment advertising. They monitor feedback related to numerous management concerns, such as employee retention rates and the timely completion of employee performance appraisals. They also help make many important decisions, such as whether to hire on-site medical staff in an effort to lower health-care costs and whether to hire temporary workers or full-time employees in an uncertain economy.

For brevity, Exhibit P–3 does not include all business majors, such as finance, information technology, and economics. Can you explain how planning, controlling, and decision-making activities would relate to these majors?

Accounting Majors

Many accounting graduates begin their careers working for public accounting firms that provide a variety of valuable services for their clients. Some of these graduates will build successful and fulfilling careers in the public accounting industry; however, most will leave public accounting at some point to work in other organizations. In fact, the Institute of Management Accountants (IMA) estimates that more than 80 percent of professional accountants in the United States work in nonpublic accounting environments.[1]

The public accounting profession has a strong financial accounting orientation. Its most important function is to protect investors and other external parties by assuring them that companies are reporting historical financial results that comply with applicable accounting rules. Managerial accountants also have strong financial accounting skills. For example, they play an important role in helping their organizations design and maintain financial reporting systems that generate reliable financial disclosures. However, the primary role of managerial accountants is to partner with their co-workers within the organization to improve performance.

Given the 80 percent figure mentioned above, if you are an accounting major, there is a very high likelihood that your future will involve working for a nonpublic accounting employer. Your employer will expect you to have strong financial accounting skills, but more importantly, it will expect you to help improve organizational performance by applying the planning, controlling, and decision-making skills that are the foundation of managerial accounting.

IN BUSINESS

A NETWORKING OPPORTUNITY

The Institute of Management Accountants (IMA) is a network of more than 100,000 accounting and finance professionals from over 140 countries. Every year the IMA hosts a student leadership conference that attracts 300 students from over 50 colleges and universities. Guest speakers at past conferences have discussed topics such as leadership, advice for a successful career, how to market yourself in a difficult economy, and excelling in today's multigenerational workforce. One student who attended the conference said, "I liked that I was able to interact with professionals who are in fields that could be potential career paths for me." For more information on this worthwhile networking opportunity, contact the IMA at the phone number shown below or visit https://www.imastudentconference.org.

Source: Conversation with Jodi Ryan, Institute of Management Accountants' Director, Student & Academic Relations. She can be contacted at (201) 474-1556.

The Institute of Management Accountants

Professional Certification—A Smart Investment If you plan to become an accounting major, the Certified Management Accountant (CMA), Certified in Strategy and Competitive Analysis (CSCA), and Chartered Global Management Accountant (CGMA) designations are globally respected credentials that will increase your credibility, upward mobility, and compensation.

The CMA exam is sponsored by the Institute of Management Accountants (IMA) in Montvale, New Jersey. To become a CMA requires membership in the IMA, a bachelor's degree from an accredited college or university, two continuous years of relevant professional experience, and passage of the CMA exam. Exhibit P–4 summarizes the topics covered in the IMA's two-part CMA exam. For brevity, we are not going to define all the terms included in this exhibit. Its purpose is simply to emphasize that the CMA exam focuses on the planning, controlling, and decision-making skills that are critically important to all managers. Information about becoming a CMA is available on the IMA's website (www.imanet.org) or by calling 1-800-638-4427.

The IMA also sponsors the CSCA exam, which is a three-hour exam that includes 60 multiple-choice questions and one case study. The exam covers three content areas: strategic analysis, creating competitive advantage, and strategy implementation and performance evaluation. It is intended for people who have earned the CMA designation and hold positions ranging from staff accountant to chief financial officer (CFO).

---

[1] This statistic was provided by Raef Lawson, the Institute of Management Accountants Vice-President of Research & Policy and Professor in Residence.

EXHIBIT P–4
CMA Exam Content
Specifications

Part 1	*Financial Planning, Performance, and Analytics*
	External financial reporting decisions
	Planning, budgeting, and forecasting
	Performance management
	Cost management
	Internal controls
	Technology and Analytics
Part 2	*Strategic Financial Management*
	Financial statement analysis
	Corporate finance
	Decision analysis
	Risk management
	Investment decisions
	Professional ethics

The CGMA designation is co-sponsored by the American Institute of Certified Public Accountants (AICPA) and the Chartered Institute of Management Accountants (CIMA), each of whom provides a distinct pathway to becoming a CGMA. The AICPA pathway requires a bachelor's degree in accounting (accompanied by a total of 150 college credit-hours), passage of the Certified Public Accountant (CPA) exam, membership in the AICPA, three years of relevant management accounting work experience, and passage of the CGMA exam—which is a case-based exam that focuses on technical skills, business skills, leadership skills, people skills, and ethics, integrity, and professionalism. Notice that the AICPA's pathway to becoming a CGMA requires passage of the multipart CPA exam, which emphasizes rule-based compliance—assurance standards, financial accounting standards, business law, and the tax code. Information on becoming a CGMA is available at www.cgma.org.

IN BUSINESS

HOW'S THE PAY?

The Institute of Management Accountants has created the following table that allows individuals to estimate what their salary would be as a management accountant.

			Your Calculation
Start with this base amount.		$63,835	$63,835
If you are top-level management	ADD	$64,786	
OR, if you are senior-level management . .	ADD	$56,064	
OR, if you are middle-level management .	ADD	$22,587	
If you have an advanced degree	ADD	$15,490	
If you hold the CMA.	ADD	$13,151	
If you hold the CPA	ADD	$16,990	_____
Your estimated salary level.			_____

For example, if you make it to top-level management, have an advanced degree, and a CMA, your estimated salary would be $157,262 ($63,835 + $64,786 + $15,490 + $13,151)

Source: Shannon Charles and Kip Krumwiede, "IMA's 2021 Global Salary Survey," *Strategic Finance*, March 2021, pp. 28–37.

Managerial Accounting: Understanding the Broader Context

Exhibit P–5 summarizes how each chapter of the book teaches measurement skills that managers use on the job every day. For example, Chapter 8 teaches you the measurement skills that managers use to answer the question—how should I create a financial plan for next year? Chapters 9 and 10 teach you the measurement skills that managers use to answer the question—how well am I performing relative to my plan? Chapter 5 teaches you measurement skills related to product, service, and customer profitability. However, it is vitally important that you also understand that managers need to apply these measurement skills in a broader business context to enable intelligent planning, control, and decision making. This context includes topics such as Big Data, ethics, strategy, enterprise risk management, and corporate social responsibility, as well as process management and leadership.

Big Data

Experts estimate that every second of every day, we are creating 1.7 megabytes of new information per person. Given our global population of more than 7.5 billion people, this is a truly astonishing rate of data generation. However, less than 0.5% of this data is currently being analyzed and used to support decision making,[2] thereby suggesting that business managers have an extraordinary opportunity to harness what is known as the *Big Data* phenomenon. **Big Data** refers to large collections of data that are gathered from inside or outside a company to provide opportunities for ongoing reporting and analysis.[3] Big Data can be both "structured," such as memos and reports, and "unstructured," such as videos, pictures, audio, and other digital forms.

Big Data is often discussed in terms of five Vs. The first three of those Vs—variety, volume, velocity—refine the definition of Big Data. *Variety* refers to the data formats in which information is stored. This includes traditional forms and digital formats, including social media, as well as click-streams on a webpage, sensor-enabled feedback, and internet-based audio/video files. *Volume* refers to the continuously expanding quantity of data that companies must gather, cleanse, organize, and analyze. For larger companies,

---

EXHIBIT P–5
Measurement Skills: A Manager's Perspective

Chapter Number	The Key Question from a Manager's Perspective
Chapter 1	What cost classifications do I use for different management purposes?
Chapter 2	How will my profits change if I change my selling price, sales volume, or costs?
Chapter 3	How much does it cost us to manufacture customized jobs for each of our customers?
Chapter 4	How should the income statement be presented?
Chapter 5	How profitable is each of our products, services, and customers?
Chapter 6	How do I quantify the financial impact of pursuing one course of action versus another?
Chapter 7	How do I make long-term capital investment decisions?
Chapter 8	How should I create a financial plan for next year?
Chapters 9 & 10	How well am I performing relative to my plan?
Chapters 11 & 12	How should I implement a performance measurement system to help ensure we achieve our strategic goals?

---

[2] Source: Bernard Marr, "Big Data: 20 Mind-Boggling Facts Everyone Must Read," *Forbes,* September 30, 2015.
[3] Source: Lisa Arthur, "What Is Big Data," *Forbes,* August 15, 2013.

this can be hundreds of petabytes of data (where one petabyte equals one million gigabytes). *Velocity* speaks to the rate at which data is received and acted on by organizations. This is particularly important where the data has a limited shelf-life. For example, retailers can better match supply with demand if they are receiving and responding to sales data in seconds or minutes rather than days or weeks.

The remaining Vs—value and veracity—define users' expectations with respect to Big Data. The concept of *Value* implies that the time and money organizations expend to analyze Big Data need to result in insights that are valued by stakeholders. For example, shareholders expect Big Data analysis to translate into financial benefits, such as rising sales, increased return on investment, and a higher stock price. *Veracity* refers to the fact that users expect their data to be accurate and trustworthy. For accounting professionals, veracity may be the most important of the "five Vs" because their analysis and opinions, which are relied on by numerous stakeholders (such as managers, investors, and regulators), must be supported by verifiable data.

From a managerial accounting standpoint, the goal for managers is to use *data analytics* to derive value from big data. **Data analytics** refers to the process of analyzing data with the aid of specialized systems and software to draw conclusions about the information they contain.[4] Managers often communicate the findings from their data analysis to others through the use of *data visualization* techniques, such as graphs, charts, maps, and diagrams.

Data analytics can be used for descriptive, diagnostic, predictive, and prescriptive purposes. *Descriptive analytics* are used to answer the question: What happened? For example, managers may use them to better understand historical trends in revenues and expenses. *Diagnostic analytics* are used to answer the question: Why did it happen? For example, managers may analyze economic indicators, such as changes in the unemployment rate, to help explain why sales increased or decreased. *Predictive analytics* are used to answer the question: What will happen? For example, managers can use predictive techniques, such as regression analysis, to estimate sales or expenses for the next month, quarter, or year. Finally, *prescriptive analytics* can be used to answer the question: What should I do? For example, managers may use prescriptive analytics to decide which products should be promoted, deemphasized, or discontinued.[5]

Ethics

Ethical behavior is the lubricant that keeps the economy running. Without that lubricant, the economy would operate much less efficiently—less would be available to consumers, quality would be lower, and prices would be higher. In other words, without fundamental

---

[4] Source: https://searchdatamanagement.techtarget.com/definition/data-analytics.
[5] Source: Jake Frankenfield, "Data Analytics," published by Investopedia and available at the following link: https://www.investopedia.com/terms/d/data-analytics.asp.

trust in the integrity of business, the economy would operate much less efficiently. Thus, for the good of everyone—including profit-making companies—it is vitally important that business be conducted within an ethical framework that builds and sustains trust.

Code of Conduct for Management Accountants The Institute of Management Accountants (IMA) has adopted an ethical code called the *Statement of Ethical Professional Practice* that describes in some detail the ethical responsibilities of management accountants. Even though the standards were developed specifically for management accountants, they have much broader applications. The standards consist of two parts that are presented in full in Exhibit P–6. The first part provides general guidelines for ethical behavior. In a nutshell, a management accountant has ethical responsibilities in four broad areas: first, to maintain a high level of professional competence; second, to treat sensitive matters with confidentiality; third, to maintain personal integrity; and fourth, to disclose information in a credible fashion. The second part of the standards specifies what should be done if an individual finds evidence of ethical misconduct.

The ethical standards provide sound, practical advice for management accountants and managers. Most of the rules in the ethical standards are motivated by a very practical consideration—if these rules were not generally followed in business, then the economy and all of us would suffer. Consider the following specific examples of the consequences of not abiding by the standards:

- Suppose employees could not be trusted with confidential information. Then top managers would be reluctant to distribute such information within the company and, as a result, decisions would be based on incomplete information and operations would deteriorate.
- Suppose employees accepted bribes from suppliers. Then contracts would tend to go to the suppliers who pay the highest bribes rather than to the most competent suppliers. Would you like to fly in aircraft whose wings were made by the subcontractor who paid the highest bribe? Would you fly as often? What would happen to the airline industry if its safety record deteriorated due to shoddy workmanship on contracted parts and subassemblies?
- Suppose the presidents of companies routinely lied in their annual reports and financial statements. If investors could not rely on the basic integrity of a company's financial statements, they would have little basis for making informed decisions. Suspecting the worst, rational investors would pay less for stocks issued by companies and may not be willing to invest at all. As a consequence, companies would have less money for productive investments—leading to slower economic growth, fewer goods and services, and higher prices.

Not only is ethical behavior the lubricant for our economy, it is the foundation of managerial accounting. The numbers that managers rely on for planning, controlling, and decision making are meaningless unless they have been competently, objectively, and honestly gathered, analyzed, and reported. As your career unfolds, you will inevitably face decisions with ethical implications. Before making such decisions, consider performing the following steps. First, define your alternative courses of action. Second, identify all of the parties that will be affected by your decision. Third, define how each course of action will favorably or unfavorably impact each affected party. Once you have a complete understanding of the decision context, seek guidance from external sources such as the IMA Statement of Ethical Professional Practice (see Exhibit P–6), the IMA Ethics Helpline at (800) 245-1383, or a trusted confidant. Before executing your decision ask yourself one final question—would I be comfortable disclosing my chosen course of action on the front page of *The Wall Street Journal?*

Strategy

Companies do not succeed by sheer luck; instead, they need to develop a *strategy* that defines how they intend to succeed in the marketplace. A **strategy** is a "game plan" that

EXHIBIT P–6

Institute of Management Accountants (IMA) Statement of Ethical Professional Practice

Members of IMA shall behave ethically. A commitment to ethical professional practice includes: overarching principles that express our values, and standards that guide our conduct.

PRINCIPLES

IMA's overarching ethical principles include: Honesty, Fairness, Objectivity, and Responsibility. Members shall act in accordance with these principles and shall encourage others within their organizations to adhere to them.

STANDARDS

IMA members have a responsibility to comply with and uphold the standards of Competence, Confidentiality, Integrity, and Credibility. Failure to comply may result in disciplinary action.

I. COMPETENCE

1. Maintain an appropriate level of professional leadership and expertise by enhancing knowledge and skills.
2. Perform professional duties in accordance with relevant laws, regulations, and technical standards.
3. Provide decision support information and recommendations that are accurate, clear, concise, and timely. Recognize and help manage risk.

II. CONFIDENTIALITY

1. Keep information confidential except when disclosure is authorized or legally required.
2. Inform all relevant parties regarding appropriate use of confidential information. Monitor to ensure compliance.
3. Refrain from using confidential information for unethical or illegal advantage.

III. INTEGRITY

1. Mitigate actual conflicts of interest. Regularly communicate with business associates to avoid apparent conflicts of interest. Advise all parties of any potential conflicts of interest.
2. Refrain from engaging in any conduct that would prejudice carrying out duties ethically.
3. Abstain from engaging in or supporting any activity that might discredit the profession.
4. Contribute to a positive ethical culture and place integrity of the profession above personal interests.

IV. CREDIBILITY

1. Communicate information fairly and objectively.
2. Provide all relevant information that could reasonably be expected to influence an intended user's understanding of the reports, analyses, or recommendations.
3. Report any delays or deficiencies in information, timeliness, processing, or internal controls in conformance with organization policy and/or applicable law.
4. Communicate professional limitations or other constraints that would preclude responsible judgment or successful performance of an activity.

RESOLVING ETHICAL ISSUES

In applying the Standards of Ethical Professional Practice, the member may encounter unethical issues or behavior. In these situations, the member should not ignore them, but rather should actively seek resolution of the issue. In determining which steps to follow, the member should consider all risks involved and whether protections exist against retaliation.

When faced with unethical issues, the member should follow the established policies of his or her organization, including use of an anonymous reporting system if available.

If the organization does not have established policies, the member should consider the following courses of action:

- The resolution process could include a discussion with the member's immediate supervisor. If the supervisor appears to be involved, the issue could be presented to the next level of management.
- IMA offers an anonymous helpline that the member may call to request how key elements of the *IMA Statement of Ethical Professional Practice* could be applied to the ethical issue.
- The member should consider consulting his or her own attorney to learn of any legal obligations, rights, and risks concerning the issue.

If resolution efforts are not successful, the member may wish to consider disassociating from the organization.

enables a company to attract customers by distinguishing itself from competitors. The focal point of a company's strategy should be its target customers. A company can only succeed if it creates a reason for its target customers to choose it over a competitor. These reasons, or what are more formally called *customer value propositions,* are the essence of strategy.

Customer value propositions tend to fall into three broad categories—*customer intimacy, operational excellence,* and *product leadership.* Companies that adopt a *customer intimacy* strategy are, in essence, saying to their customers, "You should choose us because we can customize our products and services to meet your individual needs better than our competitors." Ritz-Carlton, Nordstrom, and Virtuoso (a premium service travel agency) rely primarily on a customer intimacy value proposition for their success. Companies that pursue the second customer value proposition, called *operational excellence,* are saying to their target customers, "You should choose us because we deliver products and services faster, more conveniently, and at a lower price than our competitors." Southwest Airlines, Walmart, and Google are examples of companies that succeed first and foremost because of their operational excellence. Companies pursuing the third customer value proposition, called *product leadership,* are saying to their target customers, "You should choose us because we offer higher quality products than our competitors." Apple, Cisco Systems, and W.L. Gore (the creator of GORE-TEX® fabrics) are examples of companies that succeed because of their product leadership.[6]

The plans managers set forth, the variables they seek to control, and the decisions they make are all influenced by their company's strategy. For example, Walmart would not make plans to build ultra-expensive clothing boutiques because these plans would conflict with the company's strategy of operational excellence and "everyday low prices." Apple would not seek to control its operations by selecting performance measures that focus solely on cost-cutting because those measures would conflict with its product leadership customer value proposition. Finally, it is unlikely that Rolex would decide to implement drastic price reductions for its watches even if a financial analysis indicated that establishing a lower price might boost short-run profits. Rolex would oppose this course of action because it would diminish the luxury brand that forms the foundation of the company's product leadership customer value proposition.

Enterprise Risk Management

Every strategy, plan, and decision involves risks. **Enterprise risk management** is a process used by a company to identify those risks and develop responses to them that enable it to be reasonably assured of meeting its goals. The left-hand column of Exhibit P–7 provides 10 examples of the types of business risks that companies face. They range from risks that relate to the weather to risks associated with computer hackers, complying with the law, supplier strikes, and products harming customers. The right-hand column of Exhibit P–7 provides an example of a control that could be implemented to help reduce each of the risks mentioned in the left-hand column of the exhibit.[7] Although these types of controls cannot completely eliminate risks, they enable companies to proactively manage their risks rather than passively reacting to unfortunate events that have already occurred.

In managerial accounting, companies use controls to reduce the risk that their plans will not be achieved. For example, if a company plans to build a new manufacturing facility within a predefined budget and time frame, it will establish and monitor control measures to ensure that the project is concluded on time and within the budget. Risk management is also a critically important aspect of decision making. For example, when

---

[6] These three customer value propositions were defined by Michael Treacy and Fred Wiersema in "Customer Intimacy and Other Value Disciplines," *Harvard Business Review,* Volume 71 Issue 1, pp. 84–93.

[7] Besides using controls to reduce risks, companies can also choose other risk responses, such as accepting or avoiding a risk.

EXHIBIT P–7
Identifying and Controlling Business Risks

Examples of Business Risks	Examples of Controls to Reduce Business Risks
• Intellectual assets being stolen from computer files	• Create firewalls that prohibit computer hackers from corrupting or stealing intellectual property
• Products harming customers	• Develop a formal and rigorous new product testing program
• Losing market share due to the unforeseen actions of competitors	• Develop an approach for legally gathering information about competitors' plans and practices
• Poor weather conditions shutting down operations	• Develop contingency plans for overcoming weather-related disruptions
• A website malfunctioning	• Thoroughly test the website before going "live" on the Internet
• A supplier strike halting the flow of raw materials	• Establish a relationship with two companies capable of providing needed raw materials
• A poorly designed incentive compensation system causing employees to make bad decisions	• Create a balanced set of performance measures that motivates the desired behavior
• Poor environmental stewardship causing reputational and financial damage	• Create a reporting system that tracks key environmental performance indicators
• Inaccurate budget estimates causing excessive or insufficient production	• Implement a rigorous budget review process
• Failing to comply with equal employment opportunity laws	• Create a report that tracks key metrics related to compliance with the laws

a company quantifies the labor cost savings that it can realize by sending jobs overseas, it should complement its financial analysis with a prudent assessment of the accompanying risks. Will the overseas manufacturer use child labor? Will the product's quality decline, thereby leading to more warranty repairs, customer complaints, and lawsuits? Will the elapsed time from customer order to delivery dramatically increase? Will terminating domestic employees diminish morale within the company and harm perceptions within the community? These are the types of risks that managers should incorporate into their decision-making processes.

Companies also use controls in financial accounting to safeguard assets and minimize the risk of financial reporting errors. Exhibit P–8 describes seven types of controls that companies use to safeguard their assets and to reduce their financial reporting risks. Each item in the exhibit is labeled as a *preventive control* and/or a *detective control*. A **preventive control** deters undesirable events from occurring. A **detective control** detects undesirable events that have already occurred.

As shown in Exhibit P–8, requiring *authorizations* for certain types of transactions is a preventive control. For example, companies frequently require that a specific senior manager sign all checks above a particular dollar amount to reduce the risk of an inappropriate cash disbursement. *Reconciliations* are a detective control. If you have ever compared a bank statement to your checkbook to resolve any discrepancies, then you have performed a type of reconciliation known as a bank reconciliation. This is a detective control because you are seeking to identify any mistakes already made by the bank or existing mistakes in your own records. Another type of reconciliation occurs when a company performs a physical count of its inventory. The value of the physical inventory on hand is compared to the accounting records so that any discrepancies can be identified and resolved.

Exhibit P–8 also mentions *segregation of duties,* which is a preventive control that separates responsibilities for authorizing transactions, recording transactions, and

EXHIBIT P–8
Types of Internal Controls for Financial Reporting

Type of Control	Classification	Description
Authorizations	Preventive	Requiring management to formally approve certain types of transactions.
Reconciliations	Detective	Relating data sets to one another to identify and resolve discrepancies.
Segregation of duties	Preventive	Separating responsibilities related to authorizing transactions, recording transactions, and maintaining custody of the related assets.
Physical safeguards	Preventive	Using cameras, locks, and physical barriers to protect assets.
Performance reviews	Detective	Comparing actual performance to various benchmarks to identify unexpected results.
Maintaining records	Detective	Maintaining written and/or electronic evidence to support transactions.
Information systems security	Preventive/Detective	Using controls such as passwords and access logs to ensure appropriate data restrictions.

maintaining custody of the related assets. For example, the same employee should not have the ability to authorize inventory purchases, account for those purchases, and manage the inventory storeroom. *Physical safeguards* prevent unauthorized employees from having access to assets such as inventories and computer equipment. *Performance reviews* are a detective control performed by employees in supervisory positions to ensure that actual results are reasonable when compared to relevant benchmarks. If actual results unexpectedly deviate from expectations, then it triggers further analysis to determine the root cause of the deviation. Companies *maintain records* to provide evidence that supports each transaction. For example, companies use serially numbered checks (a detective control) so they can readily track all of their cash disbursements. Finally, companies maintain *information systems security* by using passwords (a preventive control) and access logs (a detective control) to restrict electronic data access as appropriate.

It bears reemphasizing that these types of controls may help a company reduce its risks, but they cannot guarantee a company will achieve its objectives. For example, two or more employees may collude to circumvent the control system, or a company's senior leaders may manipulate financial results by intentionally overriding prescribed policies and procedures. This reality highlights the importance of having senior leaders (including the chief executive officer and the chief financial officer) who are committed to creating an ethical "tone at the top" of the organization.

IN BUSINESS

TARGET'S CHECK-OUT LANES GRIND TO A HALT
When a glitch during routine computer maintenance shut down all of Target's check-out lanes for a two-hour span, many disgruntled customers took to Twitter to complain using the hashtag #TargetDown. Notice that this computer outage not only inconvenienced numerous customers within Target's stores, but it also created additional reputational damage through social media–enabled "word-of-mouth." This experience highlights why companies invest heavily in enterprise risk management to prevent adverse events such as this from occurring.

Source: Khadeeja Safdar, "Outage Paralyzes Shopping at Target," *The Wall Street Journal*, June 17, 2019, p. B3.

QualityHD/Shutterstock

Corporate Social Responsibility

Companies are responsible for creating strategies that produce financial results that satisfy stockholders. However, they also have a *corporate social responsibility* to serve other stakeholders—such as customers, employees, suppliers, communities, and environmental and human rights advocates—whose interests are tied to the company's performance. **Corporate social responsibility** (CSR) is a concept whereby organizations consider the needs of all stakeholders when making decisions. CSR extends beyond legal compliance to include voluntary actions that satisfy stakeholder expectations. Numerous companies, such as Pirelli, 3M, Eli Lilly and Company, Starbucks, Microsoft, Genentech, Johnson & Johnson, Baxter International, Abbott Laboratories, REI, PNC Bank, Deloitte, Timberland, and Caterpillar, prominently describe their corporate social performance on their websites.

Exhibit P–9 presents examples of corporate social responsibilities that are of interest to six stakeholder groups.[8] If a company fails to meet the needs of these six stakeholder groups, it can adversely affect its financial performance. For example, if a company pollutes the environment or fails to provide safe and humane working conditions for its employees, the negative publicity from environmental and human rights activists could cause the company's customers to defect and its "best and brightest" job candidates to apply elsewhere—both of which are likely to eventually harm financial performance. This explains why in managerial accounting, a manager must establish plans, implement controls, and make decisions that consider impacts on all stakeholders.

EXHIBIT P–9
Examples of Corporate Social Responsibilities

Companies should provide *customers* with:
- Safe, high-quality products that are fairly priced.
- Competent, courteous, and rapid delivery of products and services.
- Full disclosure of product-related risks.
- Easy-to-use information systems for shopping and tracking orders.

Companies should provide *suppliers* with:
- Fair contract terms and prompt payments.
- Reasonable time to prepare orders.
- Hassle-free acceptance of timely and complete deliveries.
- Cooperative rather than unilateral actions.

Companies should provide *stockholders* with:
- Competent management.
- Easy access to complete and accurate financial information.
- Full disclosure of enterprise risks.
- Honest answers to knowledgeable questions.

Companies and their suppliers should provide *employees* with:
- Safe and humane working conditions.
- Nondiscriminatory treatment and the right to organize and file grievances.
- Fair compensation.
- Opportunities for training, promotion, and personal development.

Companies should provide *communities* with:
- Payment of fair taxes.
- Honest information about plans such as plant closings.
- Resources that support charities, schools, and civic activities.
- Reasonable access to media sources.

Companies should provide *environmental and human rights advocates* with:
- Greenhouse gas emissions data.
- Recycling and resource conservation data.
- Child labor transparency.
- Full disclosure of suppliers located in developing countries.

---

[8] Many of the examples in Exhibit P–9 were drawn from Terry Leap and Misty L. Loughry, "The Stakeholder-Friendly Firm," *Business Horizons,* March/April 2004, pp. 27–32.

THE ENVIRONMENTAL IMPACTS OF FAST FASHION

McKinsey & Co. estimates that, over a 14-year span, the number of times people wore a clothing item before discarding it declined by 36 percent. Given that 53 million metric tons of fiber—less than 13 percent of which is recycled—is annually used in clothing, this trend presents a worrisome environmental problem. More specifically, McKinsey estimates that by 2030 our annual global clothing consumption will use 118 billion cubic meters of water. It will also produce 2.79 billion tons of carbon dioxide and 148 million tons of waste, most of which is landfilled or incinerated. In an effort to tackle this problem, some companies such as Inditex SA and Lenzing AG are investing in recycling technologies, while others such as JCPenney and Macy's are starting to sell secondhand clothing.

Source: Saabira Chaudhuri, "Fast Fashion Leads to New Recycling Effort," *The Wall Street Journal*, October 13, 2019, pp. B1–B2.

Process Management Perspective

Most companies organize themselves by functional departments, such as the Marketing Department, the Research and Development Department, and the Accounting Department. These departments tend to have a clearly defined "chain of command" that specifies superior and subordinate relationships. However, effective managers understand that *business processes,* more so than functional departments, serve the needs of a company's most important stakeholders—its customers. A **business process** is a series of steps that are followed in order to carry out some task in a business. These steps often span departmental boundaries, thereby requiring managers to cooperate across functional departments. The term *value chain* is often used to describe how an organization's functional departments interact with one another to form business processes. A **value chain,** as shown in Exhibit P–10, consists of the major business functions that add value to a company's products and services.

Managers need to understand the value chain to be effective in terms of planning, control, and decision making. For example, if a company's engineers plan to design a new product, they must communicate with the Manufacturing Department to ensure the product can actually be produced, the Marketing Department to ensure customers will buy the product, the Distribution Department to ensure large volumes of the product can be cost-effectively transported to customers, and the Accounting Department to ensure the product will increase profits. From a control and decision-making standpoint, managers also need to focus on process excellence instead of functional performance. For example, if the Purchasing Department focuses solely on minimizing the cost of purchased materials, this narrowly focused attempt at cost reduction may lead to greater scrap and rework in the Manufacturing Department, more complaints in the Customer Service Department, and greater challenges in the Marketing Department because dissatisfied customers are turning their attention to competitors.

Managers frequently use a process management method known as *lean resource management,* or what is called *Lean Production* in the manufacturing sector. **Lean Production** is a management approach that organizes resources such as people and machines

---

EXHIBIT P–10
Business Functions Making Up the Value Chain

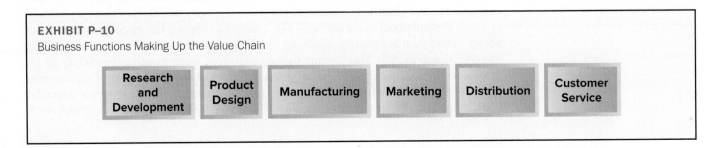

around the flow of business processes and only produces units in response to customer orders. It is often called *just-in-time* production (or *JIT*) because products are only manufactured in response to customer orders, and they are completed just-in-time to be shipped to customers. Lean Production differs from traditional manufacturing methods that organize work departmentally and encourage departments to maximize their output even if it exceeds customer demand and bloats inventories. Because Lean Production only allows production in response to customer orders, the number of units produced tends to equal the number of units sold, thereby resulting in minimal inventory. The lean approach also results in fewer defects, less wasted effort, and quicker customer response times than traditional production methods.

Leadership

An organization's employees bring diverse needs, beliefs, and goals to the workplace. Therefore, an important role for organizational leaders is to unite the behaviors of their fellow employees around two common themes—pursuing strategic goals and making optimal decisions. To fulfill this responsibility, leaders need to understand how *intrinsic motivation, extrinsic incentives,* and *cognitive bias* influence human behavior.

Intrinsic Motivation

Intrinsic motivation refers to motivation that comes from within us. Stop for a moment and identify the greatest accomplishment of your life. Then ask yourself what motivated you to achieve this goal? In all likelihood, you achieved it because you wanted to, not because someone forced you to do it. In other words, you were intrinsically motivated. Similarly, an organization is more likely to prosper when its employees are intrinsically motivated to pursue its interests. A leader, who employees perceive as *credible* and *respectful* of their value to the organization, can increase the extent to which those employees are intrinsically motivated to pursue strategic goals. As your career evolves, to be perceived as a credible leader, you'll need to possess three attributes—technical competence (that spans the value chain), personal integrity (in terms of work ethic and honesty), and strong communication skills (including oral presentation skills and writing skills). To be perceived as a leader who is respectful of your co-workers' value to the organization, you'll need to possess three more attributes—strong mentoring skills (to help others realize their potential), strong listening skills (to learn from your co-workers and be responsive to their needs), and personal humility (in terms of deferring recognition to all employees who contribute to the organization's success). If you possess these six traits, then you'll have the potential to become a leader who inspires others to readily and energetically channel their efforts toward achieving organizational goals.

Extrinsic Incentives

Many organizations use *extrinsic incentives* to highlight important goals and to motivate employees to achieve them. For example, assume a company establishes the goal of reducing the time needed to perform a task by 20 percent. In addition, assume the company agrees to pay bonus compensation to its employees if they achieve the goal within three months. In this example, the company is using a type of extrinsic incentive known as a bonus to highlight a particular goal and to presumably motivate employees to achieve it.

While proponents of extrinsic incentives rightly assert that these types of rewards can have a powerful influence on employee behavior, many critics warn that they can also produce dysfunctional consequences. For example, suppose the employees mentioned above earned their bonuses by achieving the 20 percent time reduction goal within three months. However, let's also assume that during those three months, the quality of the employees' output plummeted, thereby causing a spike in the company's repair costs, product returns, and customer defections. In this instance, did the extrinsic incentive work properly? The answer is yes and no. The bonus system did motivate employees to attain the time reduction goal; however, it also had the unintended consequences of causing employees to neglect product quality, thereby increasing repair costs, product returns, and customer defections. In other words, what may have seemed like a well-intended extrinsic incentive actually produced dysfunctional results for the company. This example highlights an important leadership challenge that you are likely to face someday—designing financial compensation systems that fairly reward employees for their efforts without inadvertently creating extrinsic incentives that motivate them to take actions that harm the company.

Cognitive Bias Leaders need to be aware that all people (including themselves) possess *cognitive biases,* or distorted thought processes, that can adversely affect planning, controlling, and decision making. To illustrate how cognitive bias works, let's consider the scenario of a television "infomercial" where someone is selling a product with a proclaimed value of $200 for $19.99 if viewers call within the next 30 minutes. Why do you think the seller claims that the product has a $200 value? The seller is relying on a cognitive bias called *anchoring bias* in an effort to convince viewers that a $180 discount is simply too good to pass up. The "anchor" is the false assertion that the product is actually worth $200. If viewers erroneously attach credibility to this contrived piece of information, their distorted analysis of the situation may cause them to spend $19.99 on an item whose true economic value is much less than that amount.

While cognitive biases cannot be eliminated, effective leaders should take two steps to reduce their negative impacts. First, they should acknowledge their own susceptibility to cognitive bias. For example, a leader's judgment might be clouded by optimism bias (being overly optimistic in assessing the likelihood of future outcomes) or self-enhancement bias (overestimating one's strengths and underestimating one's weaknesses relative to others). Second, they should acknowledge the presence of cognitive bias in others and introduce techniques to minimize their adverse consequences. For example, to reduce the risks of confirmation bias (a bias where people pay greater attention to information that confirms their preconceived notions, while devaluing information that contradicts them) or groupthink bias (a bias where some group members support a course of action solely because other group members do), a leader may routinely appoint independent teams of employees to assess the credibility of recommendations set forth by other individuals and groups.

IN BUSINESS

A BROADER VIEW OF THE MANAGEMENT ACCOUNTING PROFESSION

The Institute of Management Accountants (IMA) has established a competency framework to describe the breadth of skills it believes management accountants need to be successful in the marketplace. The centerpiece of the framework is *Leadership,* which refers to the competencies required to collaborate with others and inspire teams to achieve organizational goals. The framework's foundation is *Professional Ethics & Values,* and its four remaining competencies include *Strategy, Planning & Performance, Reporting & Control, Technology & Analytics,* and *Business Acumen & Operations.*

This framework expands upon the pillars of planning, controlling, and decision making described earlier in the Prologue. The IMA has defined this expanded set of competencies to guide accounting professionals in developing their own skills and to help them mentor co-workers who are also interested in career advancement.

Source: The 44-page document that provides a detailed description of this framework is available at https://www.imanet.org/career-resources/management-accounting-competencies.

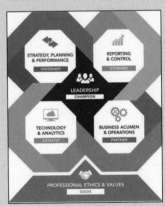

Source: Institute of Management Accountants

Summary

The prologue defined managerial accounting and explained why it is relevant to business and accounting majors. It also discussed seven topics—Big Data, ethics, strategic management, enterprise risk management, corporate social responsibility, process management, and leadership—that define the context for applying the quantitative aspects of managerial accounting. The most important goal of the prologue was to help you understand that managerial accounting matters to your future career regardless of your major. Accounting is the language of business, and you'll need to speak it to communicate effectively with and influence fellow managers.

Glossary

Big Data Large collections of data that are gathered from inside or outside a company to provide opportunities for ongoing reporting and analysis. (p. 9)

Budget A detailed plan for the future that is usually expressed in formal quantitative terms. (p. 3)

Business process A series of steps that are followed in order to carry out some task in a business. (p. 17)

Controlling The process of gathering feedback to ensure a plan is being properly executed or modified as circumstances change. (p. 3)

Corporate social responsibility A concept whereby organizations consider the needs of all stakeholders when making decisions. (p. 16)

Data analytics The process of analyzing data with the aid of specialized systems and software to draw conclusions about the information they contain. (p. 10)

Decision making Selecting a course of action from competing alternatives. (p. 3)

Detective control A control that detects undesirable events that have already occurred. (p. 14)

Enterprise risk management A process used by a company to identify its risks and develop responses to them that enable it to be reasonably assured of meeting its goals. (p. 13)

Financial accounting The phase of accounting concerned with reporting historical financial information to external parties, such as stockholders, creditors, and regulators. (p. 2)

Lean Production A management approach that organizes resources such as people and machines around the flow of business processes and that only produces units in response to customer orders. (p. 17)

Managerial accounting The phase of accounting concerned with providing information to managers for use within the organization. (p. 2)

Performance report A report that compares budgeted data to actual data to highlight instances of excellent and unsatisfactory performance. (p. 4)

Planning The process of establishing goals and specifying how to achieve them. (p. 3)

Preventive control A control that deters undesirable events from occurring. (p. 14)

Segment Any part or activity of an organization about which managers seek cost, revenue, or profit data. (p. 3)

Strategy A company's "game plan" for attracting customers by distinguishing itself from competitors. (p. 11)

Value chain The major business functions that add value to a company's products and services, such as research and development, product design, manufacturing, marketing, distribution, and customer service. (p. 17)

Questions

P–1 How does managerial accounting differ from financial accounting?

P–2 Pick any major television network and describe some planning and control activities that its managers would engage in.

P–3   If you had to decide whether to continue making a component part or to begin buying the part from an overseas supplier, what quantitative and qualitative factors would influence your decision?

P–4   Why do companies prepare budgets?

P–5   Why is managerial accounting relevant to business majors and their future careers?

P–6   Why is managerial accounting relevant to accounting majors and their future careers?

P–7   Pick any large company and describe its strategy using one of the three customer value propositions defined in the prologue.

P–8   Why do management accountants need to understand their company's strategy?

P–9   Pick any large company and describe three risks that it faces and how it responds to those risks.

P–10 Pick three industries and describe how the risks faced by companies within those industries can influence their planning, controlling, and decision-making activities.

P–11 Pick any large company and explain three ways that it could segment its companywide performance.

P–12 Locate the website of any company that publishes a corporate social responsibility report (also referred to as a sustainability report). Describe three nonfinancial performance measures included in the report. Why do you think the company publishes this report?

P–13 Why do companies that implement Lean Production tend to have minimal inventories?

P–14 Why are leadership skills important to managers?

P–15 Why is ethical behavior important to business?

P–16 If you were a restaurant owner, what internal controls would you implement to help maintain control of your cash?

P–17 As a form of internal control, what documents would you review prior to paying an invoice received from a supplier?

P–18 What internal controls would you implement to help maintain control of your credit sales and accounts receivable?

P–19 Why do companies take a physical count of their inventory on hand at least once per year?

P–20 Why do companies use sequential prenumbering for documents such as checks, sales invoices, and purchase orders?

 Exercises

EXERCISE P–1 Planning and Control

Assume you are a sales manager working with your boss to create a sales budget for next year. Once the sales budget is established, it will influence how other departments within your company plan to deploy their resources. For example, the manufacturing manager will plan to produce enough units to meet the budgeted unit sales. If the sales budget is too high, it will result in excess inventories, and if it is too low, it will result in lost sales.

You have studied all of the pertinent data and concluded that the "most likely" outcome is estimated sales of $1,000,000. You also believe that if the sales team works extra hard and has a terrific year, it has a modest chance of achieving an "optimistic" sales forecast of $1,200,000. Conversely, if the economy sours, you believe that your sales team can still achieve a "pessimistic" sales forecast of $900,000.

Required:

1. Assume your company uses its sales budget for only one purpose—to match the supply of manufactured products with customer demand, thereby minimizing inventories and lost sales. What sales forecast would you provide to your boss?

2. Assume your company also uses its sales budget as a motivational tool to help employees strive for "stretch goals" and exceptional results. What sales forecast would you provide to your boss?

3. Assume your company's sales budget is also used for a third purpose—to determine your pay raise, bonus, and potential for promotion. If actual sales exceed the sales budget, it bodes

well for your career. If actual sales are less than budgeted sales, it will diminish your financial compensation and potential for promotion. What sales forecast would you provide to your boss?

4. Are your answers to the first three questions the same or different? Why? If you know from past experience that your boss usually adds 5–10% to your forecast, how would this affect your answers to the first three questions?
5. Do you think it would be appropriate for your boss to establish the sales budget without any input from you? Why?
6. Do you think the company would allow you to establish the sales budget without any input from your boss? Why?

EXERCISE P–2 Controlling

Assume that you work for an airline unloading luggage from airplanes. Your boss has said that, on average, each airplane contains 100 pieces of luggage. Furthermore, your boss has stated that you should be able to unload 100 pieces of luggage from an airplane in 10 minutes. Today an airplane arrived with 150 pieces of luggage, and you unloaded all of it in 13 minutes. After finishing with the 150 pieces of luggage, your boss yelled at you for exceeding the 10-minute allowance for unloading luggage from an airplane.

Required:

How would you feel about being yelled at for taking 13 minutes to unload 150 pieces of luggage? How does this scenario relate to the larger issue of how companies design control systems?

EXERCISE P–3 Decision Making

Exhibit P–2 from within the prologue includes 12 questions related to 12 types of decisions that companies often face. In the prologue, these 12 decisions were discussed within the context of for-profit companies; however, they are also readily applicable to nonprofit organizations. To illustrate this point, assume that you are a senior leader, such as a president, provost, or dean, in a university setting.

Required:

For each of the 12 decisions in Exhibit P–2, provide an example of how that type of decision might be applicable to a university setting.

EXERCISE P–4 Ethics and the Manager

Richmond, Inc., operates a chain of 44 department stores. Two years ago, the board of directors of Richmond approved a large-scale remodeling of its stores to attract a more upscale clientele.

Before finalizing these plans, two stores were remodeled as a test. Linda Perlman, assistant controller, was asked to oversee the financial reporting for these test stores, and she and other management personnel were offered bonuses based on the sales growth and profitability of these stores. While completing the financial reports, Perlman discovered a sizable inventory of outdated goods that should have been discounted for sale or returned to the manufacturer. She discussed the situation with her management colleagues; the consensus was to ignore reporting this inventory as obsolete because reporting it would diminish the financial results and their bonuses.

Required:

1. According to the IMA's Statement of Ethical Professional Practice, would it be ethical for Perlman *not* to report the inventory as obsolete?
2. Would it be easy for Perlman to take the ethical action in this situation?

(CMA, adapted)

EXERCISE P–5 Strategy

The table below contains the names of six companies.

Required:

For each company, categorize its strategy as being focused on customer intimacy, operational excellence, or product leadership. If you wish to improve your understanding of each company's customer value proposition before completing the exercise, review its most recent annual report. To obtain electronic access to this information, perform an Internet search on each company's name followed by the words "annual report."

Company	Strategy
1. Deere	?
2. FedEx	?
3. State Farm Insurance	?
4. BMW	?
5. Amazon.com	?
6. Charles Schwab	?

EXERCISE P–6 Enterprise Risk Management

The table below refers to seven industries.

Required:

For each industry, provide an example of a business risk faced by companies that compete within that industry. Then, describe an example of a control that could be used to reduce the business risk that you have identified.

Industry	Example of Business Risk	Example of Control to Reduce the Business Risk
1. Airlines (e.g., Delta Airlines)		
2. Pharmaceutical drugs (e.g., Merck)		
3. Package delivery (e.g., United Parcel Service)		
4. Banking (e.g., Bank of America)		
5. Oil & gas (e.g., ExxonMobil)		
6. E-commerce (e.g., eBay)		
7. Automotive (e.g., Toyota)		

EXERCISE P–7 Ethics in Business

Consumers and attorney generals in more than 40 states accused a prominent nationwide chain of auto repair shops of misleading customers and selling them unnecessary parts and services, from brake jobs to front-end alignments. Lynn Sharpe Paine reported the situation as follows in "Managing for Organizational Integrity," *Harvard Business Review,* Volume 72 Issue 3:

> In the face of declining revenues, shrinking market share, and an increasingly competitive market . . . management attempted to spur performance of its auto centers. . . . The auto-motive service advisers were given product-specific sales quotas—sell so many springs, shock absorbers, alignments, or brake jobs per shift—and paid a commission based on sales. . . . [F]ailure to meet quotas could lead to a transfer or a reduction in work hours. Some employees spoke of the "pressure, pressure, pressure" to bring in sales.
>
> This pressure-cooker atmosphere created conditions under which employees felt that the only way to satisfy top management was by selling products and services to customers that they didn't really need.

Suppose all automotive repair businesses routinely followed the practice of attempting to sell customers unnecessary parts and services.

Required:

1. How would this behavior affect customers? How might customers attempt to protect themselves against this behavior?

2. How would this behavior probably affect profits and employment in the automotive service industry?

EXERCISE P–8 Cognitive Bias

In the 1970s, one million college-bound students were surveyed and asked to compare themselves to their peers. Some of the key findings of the survey were as follows:

a. 70% of the students rated themselves as above average in leadership ability, while only 2% rated themselves as below average in this regard.

b. With respect to athletic skills, 60% of the students rated their skills as above the median and only 6% of students rated themselves as below the median.

c. 60% of the students rated themselves in the top 10% in terms of their ability to get along with others, while 25% of the students felt that they were in the top 1% in terms of this interpersonal skill.

Required:

1. What type of cognitive bias reveals itself in the data mentioned above?
2. How might this cognitive bias adversely influence a manager's planning, controlling, and decision-making activities?
3. What steps could managers take to reduce the possibility that this cognitive bias would adversely influence their actions?

Source: Dan Lovallo and Daniel Kahneman, "Delusions of Success: How Optimism Undermines Executives' Decisions," *Harvard Business Review,* July 2003, pp. 56–63.

EXERCISE P–9 Ethics and Decision Making

Assume you are the chair of the Department of Accountancy at Mountain State University. One of the accounting professors in your department, Dr. Candler, has been consistently and uniformly regarded by students as an awful teacher for more than 10 years. Other accounting professors within your department have observed Dr. Candler's classroom teaching, and they concur that his teaching skills are very poor. However, Dr. Candler was granted tenure 12 years ago, thereby ensuring him lifelong job security at Mountain State University.

Much to your surprise, today you received a phone call from an accounting professor at Oregon Coastal University. During this phone call, you are informed that Oregon Coastal University is on the verge of making a job offer to Dr. Candler. However, before extending the job offer, the faculty at Oregon Coastal wants your input regarding Dr. Candler's teaching effectiveness while at Mountain State University.

Required:

How would you respond to the professor from Oregon Coastal University? What would you say about Dr. Candler's teaching ability? Would you describe your answer to this inquiry as being ethical? Why?

EXERCISE P–10 Corporate Social Responsibility

In his book *Capitalism and Freedom,* economist Milton Friedman wrote on page 133: "There is one and only one social responsibility of business—to use its resources and engage in activities designed to increase its profits so long as it . . . engages in open and free competition, without deception or fraud."

Required:

Explain why you agree or disagree with this quote.

EXERCISE P–11 Intrinsic Motivation and Extrinsic Incentives

In a *Harvard Business Review* article titled "Why Incentive Plans Cannot Work" (Volume 71, Issue 5), author Alfie Kohn wrote: "Research suggests that, by and large, rewards succeed at securing one thing only: temporary compliance. When it comes to producing lasting change in attitudes and behavior, however, rewards, like punishment, are strikingly ineffective. Once the rewards run out, people revert to their old behaviors. . . . Incentives, a version of what psychologists call extrinsic motivators, do not alter the attitudes that underlie our behaviors. They do not create an enduring *commitment* to any value or action. Rather, incentives merely—and temporarily— change what we do."

Required:
1. Do you agree with this quote? Why?
2. As a manager, how would you seek to motivate your employees?
3. As a manager, would you use financial incentives to compensate your employees? If so, what would be the keys to using them effectively? If not, then how would you compensate your employees?

EXERCISE P–12 Cognitive Bias and Decision Making

During World War II, the U.S. military was studying its combat-tested fighter planes to determine the parts of the plane most vulnerable to enemy fire. The purpose of the study was to identify the most vulnerable sections of each plane and then take steps to reinforce those sections to improve pilot safety and airplane durability. The data gathered by the U.S. military showed that certain sections of its combat-tested fighter planes were consistently hit more often with enemy fire than other sections of the plane.

Required:
1. Would you recommend reinforcing the sections of the plane that were hit most often by enemy fire, or would you reinforce the sections that were hit less frequently by enemy fire? Why?
2. Do you think cognitive bias had the potential to influence the U.S. military's decision-making process with respect to reinforcing its fighter planes?

Source: Jerker Denrell, "Selection Bias and the Perils of Benchmarking," *Harvard Business Review,* Volume 83, Issue 4, pp. 114–119.

EXERCISE P–13 Ethics and Decision Making

Assume you just completed a December weekend vacation to a casino within the United States. During your trip, you won $10,000 gambling. When the casino exchanged your chips for cash, it did not record any personal information, such as your driver's license number or social security number. Four months later while preparing your tax returns for the prior year, you stop to contemplate the fact that the Internal Revenue Service requires taxpayers to report all gambling winnings on Form 1040.

Required:
Would you report your gambling winnings to the Internal Revenue Service so you could pay federal income taxes on those winnings? Do you believe your actions are ethical? Why?

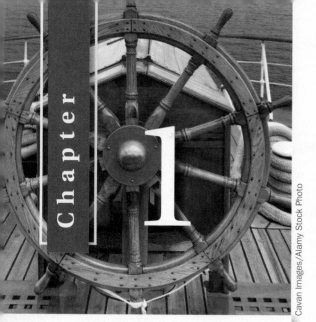

Cavan Images/Alamy Stock Photo

Managerial Accounting and Cost Concepts

Mary Altaffer/AP Photo

LEARNING OBJECTIVES

After studying Chapter 1, you should be able to:

LO 1–1 Understand cost classifications used for assigning costs to cost objects: direct costs and indirect costs.

LO 1–2 Identify and give examples of each of the three basic manufacturing cost categories.

LO 1–3 Understand cost classifications used to prepare financial statements: product costs and period costs.

LO 1–4 Understand cost classifications used to predict cost behavior: variable costs, fixed costs, and mixed costs.

LO 1–5 Understand cost classifications used in making decisions: relevant costs and irrelevant costs.

LO 1–6 Prepare income statements for a merchandising company using the traditional and contribution formats.

Data Analytics Exercise available in Connect to complement this chapter

ENTREPRENEUR SPOTLIGHT

Coss Marte is a former prison inmate who lost 70 pounds during six months of incarceration. He accomplished this remarkable transformation without any gym equipment or a personal trainer—just the walls and floor in his 9' by 6' prison cell. After his release, Marte started a company called CONBODY that provides military-style bodyweight training for its customers. The company offers more than 50 online, on-demand exercise classes as well as live virtual workout opportunities.

Managerial Accounting: The Practical Application

In managing his company, Marte has numerous opportunities to apply managerial accounting cost concepts. For example, when preparing a budget, he'd need to distinguish between variable costs (such as instructor labor costs that vary with respect to the number of classes taught) and fixed costs (such as his monthly website maintenance costs). He'd also need to separate relevant costs from irrelevant costs when deciding whether to add a new class or discontinue an existing class.

Corporate Social Responsibility: Serving all Stakeholders

CONBODY's mission "is to bridge a gap between two communities: young professionals and formerly incarcerated individuals." The company also partners with nonprofit organizations to provide former inmates educational resources, mentorship, housing, and employment opportunities. To date, Marte has hired over 40 former inmates as fitness instructors with an astonishing 0% recidivism rate. ■

Source: www.conbody.com

In accounting, costs can be classified differently depending on the needs of management. For example, the Prologue mentioned that **financial accounting** is concerned with reporting financial information to external parties, such as stockholders, creditors, and regulators. In this context, costs are classified in accordance with externally imposed rules to enable the preparation of financial statements. Conversely, **managerial accounting** is concerned with providing information to managers within an organization so that they can formulate plans, control operations, and make decisions. In these contexts, costs are classified in diverse ways that enable managers to predict future costs, to compare actual costs to budgeted costs, to assign costs to segments of the business (such as product lines, geographic regions, and distribution channels), and to properly contrast the costs associated with competing alternatives.

The notion of *different cost classifications for different purposes* is the most important unifying theme of this chapter and one of the key foundational concepts of the entire textbook. Exhibit 1–1 summarizes five types of cost classifications that will be used throughout the textbook, namely cost classifications (1) for assigning costs to cost objects, (2) for manufacturing companies, (3) for preparing financial statements, (4) for predicting cost behavior, and (5) for making decisions. As we begin defining the cost terminology related to each of these cost classifications, please refer back to this exhibit to help improve your understanding of the overall organization of the chapter.

Cost Classifications for Assigning Costs to Cost Objects

Costs are assigned to cost objects for a variety of purposes, including pricing, preparing profitability studies, and controlling spending. A **cost object** is anything for which cost data are desired—including products, customers, plants, office locations, and departments. For purposes of assigning costs to cost objects, costs are classified as either *direct* or *indirect*.

LEARNING OBJECTIVE 1–1
Understand cost classifications used for assigning costs to cost objects: direct costs and indirect costs.

EXHIBIT 1–1
Summary of Cost Classifications

Purpose of Cost Classification	Cost Classifications
Assigning costs to cost objects	• Direct costs (can be easily traced) • Indirect costs (cannot be easily traced)
Accounting for costs in manufacturing companies	• Manufacturing costs • Direct materials • Direct labor • Manufacturing overhead • Nonmanufacturing costs • Selling costs • Administrative costs
Preparing financial statements	• Product costs (inventoriable) • Period costs (expensed)
Predicting cost behavior in response to changes in activity	• Variable costs (proportional to activity) • Fixed costs (constant in total) • Mixed costs (have variable and fixed elements)
Making decisions	• Relevant costs (differ between alternatives) • Irrelevant costs (should be ignored)

Direct Cost

A **direct cost** is a cost that can be easily and conveniently traced to a specified cost object. For example, if Adidas is assigning costs to its various regional and national sales offices, then the salary of the sales manager in its Tokyo office would be a direct cost of that office. If a printing company made 10,000 brochures for a specific customer, then the cost of the paper used to make the brochures would be a direct cost of that customer.

Indirect Cost

An **indirect cost** is a cost that cannot be easily and conveniently traced to a specified cost object. For example, a Campbell Soup factory may produce dozens of varieties of canned soups. The factory manager's salary would be an indirect cost of a particular variety, such as chicken noodle soup. The reason is that the factory manager's salary is incurred as a consequence of running the entire factory—it is not incurred to produce any one soup variety. *To be traced to a cost object such as a particular product, the cost must be caused by the cost object.* The factory manager's salary is called a *common cost* of producing the various products of the factory. A **common cost** is a cost that is incurred to support a number of cost objects but cannot be traced to them individually. A common cost is a type of indirect cost.

A particular cost may be direct or indirect, depending on the cost object. While the Campbell Soup factory manager's salary is an *indirect* cost of manufacturing chicken noodle soup, it is a *direct* cost of the manufacturing department. In the first case, the cost object is chicken noodle soup. In the second case, the cost object is the entire manufacturing department.

Cost Classifications for Manufacturing Companies

LEARNING OBJECTIVE 1–2
Identify and give examples of each of the three basic manufacturing cost categories.

Manufacturing companies such as Samtec, Mack Trucks, and 3M separate their costs into two broad categories—manufacturing and nonmanufacturing costs.

Manufacturing Costs

Most manufacturing companies further separate their manufacturing costs into two direct cost categories, direct materials and direct labor, and one indirect cost category, manufacturing overhead. A discussion of these three categories follows.

Direct Materials The materials that go into the final product are called **raw materials.** This term is somewhat misleading because it seems to imply unprocessed natural resources like wood pulp or iron ore. Actually, raw materials refer to any materials used in the final product; and the finished product of one company can become the raw materials of another company. For example, the plastics produced by DuPont are a raw material used by HP in its personal computers.

Direct materials refers to raw materials that become an integral part of the finished product and whose costs can be conveniently traced to the finished product. This would include, for example, the seats Airbus purchases from subcontractors to install in its commercial aircraft, the electronic components Samsung uses in its cell phones, and the doors Whirlpool installs on its refrigerators.

SAY GOODBYE TO SINGLE-USE DRINKING STRAWS

For decades food and beverage retailers' direct materials cost included single-use plastic drinking straws. However, when a YouTube video showed a sea turtle with a plastic straw stuck in its nose, it prompted a social-media outcry to end single-use straws. Starbucks responded to this concern by introducing a new lid that eliminates the need for drinking straws. The company says that phasing out plastic drinking straws from its 30,000 stores across the globe will eliminate the use of more than one billion straws per year.

Source: Micah Maidenberg, "Starbucks Unveils New Lids to Cut Out Straws," *The Wall Street Journal,* March 21, 2019, p. B3.

MichellePatrickPhotographyLLC/Getty Images

Direct Labor **Direct labor** consists of labor costs that can be easily traced to individual units of product. Direct labor is sometimes called *touch labor* because direct labor workers typically touch the product while it is being made. Examples of direct labor include assembly-line workers at Mazda, carpenters at the home builder KB Home, and electricians who install equipment on aircraft at Bombardier Learjet.

Managers occasionally refer to their two direct manufacturing cost categories as *prime costs.* **Prime cost** is the sum of direct materials cost and direct labor cost.

Manufacturing Overhead **Manufacturing overhead,** the third manufacturing cost category, includes all manufacturing costs except direct materials and direct labor. From a product costing standpoint, manufacturing overhead costs are indirect costs because they cannot be readily traced to specific products. For example, manufacturing overhead includes a portion of raw materials known as *indirect materials* as well as *indirect labor.* **Indirect materials** are raw materials, such as the solder used to make electrical connections in a Toshiba HDTV and the glue used to assemble an Ethan Allen chair, whose costs cannot be easily or conveniently traced to finished products. **Indirect labor** refers to employees, such as janitors, supervisors, materials handlers, maintenance workers, and night security guards, that play an essential role in running a manufacturing facility; however, the cost of compensating these people cannot be easily or conveniently traced to specific units of product. Because indirect materials and indirect labor are difficult to trace to specific products, their costs are included in manufacturing overhead.

Manufacturing overhead also includes other indirect costs that cannot be readily traced to finished products, such as depreciation of manufacturing equipment and the utility costs, property taxes, and insurance premiums incurred to operate a manufacturing facility. Although companies also incur depreciation, utility costs, property taxes, and insurance premiums to sustain their nonmanufacturing operations, these costs are not included as part of manufacturing overhead. Only those indirect costs associated with *operating the factory* are included in manufacturing overhead.

In practice, managers use various names for manufacturing overhead, such as *indirect manufacturing cost, factory overhead,* and *factory burden.* All of these terms are synonyms for manufacturing overhead. Another term that managers frequently use in practice is *conversion cost.* **Conversion cost** refers to the sum of direct labor and manufacturing overhead. The term conversion cost is used to describe direct labor and manufacturing overhead because these costs are incurred to *convert* direct materials into finished products.

Nonmanufacturing Costs

Nonmanufacturing costs are often divided into two categories: (1) *selling costs* and (2) *administrative costs.* **Selling costs** include all costs incurred to secure customer orders and get the finished product to the customer. These costs are sometimes called *order-getting* and *order-filling costs.* Examples of selling costs include advertising, shipping, sales travel, sales commissions, sales salaries, and costs of finished goods warehouses. Selling costs can be either direct or indirect costs. For example, the cost of an advertising campaign dedicated to one specific product is a direct cost of that product, whereas the salary of a marketing manager who oversees numerous products is an indirect cost with respect to individual products.

Administrative costs include all costs associated with the *general management* of an organization rather than with manufacturing or selling. Examples of administrative costs include executive compensation, general accounting, legal counsel, secretarial, public relations, and similar costs involved in the overall general administration of the organization *as a whole.* Administrative costs can be either direct or indirect costs. For example, the salary of an accounting manager in charge of accounts receivable collections in the East region is a direct cost of that region, whereas the salary of a chief financial officer who oversees all of a company's regions is an indirect cost with respect to individual regions.

Nonmanufacturing costs are also often called selling, general, and administrative (SG&A) costs or just selling and administrative costs.

Cost Classifications for Preparing Financial Statements

LEARNING OBJECTIVE 1–3
Understand cost classifications used to prepare financial statements: product costs and period costs.

When preparing a balance sheet and an income statement, companies need to classify their costs as *product costs* or *period costs.* To understand the difference between product costs and period costs, we must first discuss the matching principle from financial accounting.

Generally, costs are recognized as expenses on the income statement in the period that benefits from the cost. For example, if a company pays for liability insurance in advance for two years, the entire amount is not considered an expense of the year in which the payment is made. Instead, one-half of the cost would be recognized as an expense each year. The reason is that both years—not just the first year—benefit from the insurance payment. The unexpensed portion of the insurance payment is carried on the balance sheet as an asset called prepaid insurance.

The *matching principle* is based on the *accrual* concept that *costs incurred to generate a particular revenue should be recognized as expenses in the same period that the revenue is recognized.* This means that if a cost is incurred to acquire or make something that will eventually be sold, then the cost should be recognized as an expense only when the sale takes place—that is, when the benefit occurs. Such costs are called *product costs.*

Product Costs

For financial accounting purposes, **product costs** include all costs involved in acquiring or making a product. Product costs "attach" to a unit of product as it is purchased or manufactured, and they stay attached to each unit of product as long as it remains in inventory awaiting sale. When units of product are sold, their costs are released from inventory as expenses (typically called cost of goods sold) and matched against sales on the income statement. Because product costs are initially assigned to inventories, they are also known as **inventoriable costs.**

For manufacturing companies, product costs include direct materials, direct labor, and manufacturing overhead.[1] A manufacturer's product costs flow through three inventory accounts on the balance sheet—*Raw Materials, Work in Process,* and *Finished Goods*—prior to being recorded in cost of goods sold on the income statement. Raw materials include any materials that go into the final product. **Work in process** consists of units of product that are only partially complete and will require further work before

---

[1] For internal management purposes, product costs may exclude some manufacturing costs. For example, see Appendix 3B and the discussion in Chapter 4.

they are ready for sale to the customer. **Finished goods** consist of completed units of product that have not yet been sold to customers.

When direct materials are used in production, their costs are transferred from Raw Materials to Work in Process. Direct labor and manufacturing overhead costs are added to Work in Process to convert direct materials into finished goods. Once units of product are completed, their costs are transferred from Work in Process to Finished Goods. When a manufacturer sells its finished goods to customers, the costs are transferred from Finished Goods to Cost of Goods Sold.

We want to emphasize that product costs are not necessarily recorded as expenses on the income statement in the period in which they are incurred. Rather, as explained above, they are recorded as expenses in the period in which the related products *are sold.*

Period Costs

Period costs are all the costs that are not product costs. *All selling and administrative expenses are treated as period costs.* For example, sales commissions, advertising, executive salaries, public relations, and the rental costs of administrative offices are all period costs. Period costs are not included as part of the cost of either purchased or manufactured goods; instead, period costs are expensed on the income statement in the period in which they are incurred using the usual rules of accrual accounting. Keep in mind that the period in which a cost is incurred is not necessarily the period in which cash changes hands. For example, as discussed earlier, the cost of liability insurance is spread across the periods that benefit from the insurance—regardless of the period in which the insurance premium is paid.

Exhibit 1–2 summarizes the product and period cost flows for manufacturers that were just discussed. Notice that product costs flow through three inventory accounts on the balance sheet prior to being recognized as part of cost of goods sold in the income statement. Conversely, period costs do not flow through the inventory accounts on the

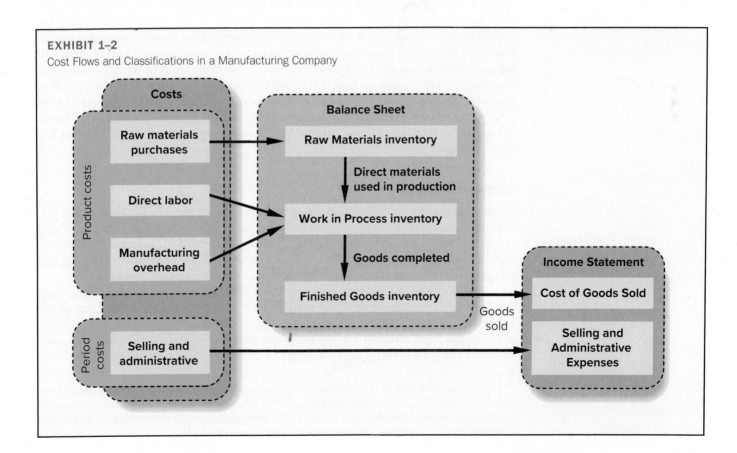

EXHIBIT 1–2
Cost Flows and Classifications in a Manufacturing Company

balance sheet, and they are not included in cost of goods sold in the income statement. Instead, they are recorded as selling and administrative expenses in the income statement during the period incurred.

THE ADMINISTRATIVE COSTS OF REDESIGNING THE OFFICE

Deliris/Shutterstock

For decades American companies sought to "cram workers into tighter spaces with few separations between colleagues . . . [spending] millions of dollars . . . to create rows of open desks, intimate conference rooms, and elaborate communal gathering areas." However, in the post-COVID-19 era companies are incurring additional administrative costs as they reexamine and redesign their office spaces. For example, HP welcomed back each employee to one of its offices with a kit containing three new office essentials—hand sanitizer, a mask, and gloves. McCann Worldgroup's New York office has closed its cafeteria and ordered dozens of refrigerators and microwaves so employees can bring their lunches to work. Discover Financial Services is considering seating its employees at every other workstation, whereas WeWork is removing 30,000 conference-room chairs from its global offices to enable proper social distancing.

Source: Chip Cutter and Suzanne Vranica, "Offices Revamp to Keep Germs at Bay," *The Wall Street Journal,* May 12, 2020, pp. B1 and B5.

Cost Classifications for Predicting Cost Behavior

LEARNING OBJECTIVE 1–4
Understand cost classifications used to predict cost behavior: variable costs, fixed costs, and mixed costs.

It is often necessary to predict how a certain cost will behave in response to a change in activity. For example, a manager at Under Armour may want to estimate the impact a 5% increase in sales would have on the company's total direct materials cost. **Cost behavior** refers to how a cost reacts to changes in the level of activity. As the activity level rises and falls, a particular cost may rise and fall as well—or it may remain constant. For planning purposes, a manager must be able to anticipate which of these will happen; and if a cost can be expected to change, the manager must be able to estimate how much it will change. To help make such distinctions, costs are often categorized as *variable, fixed,* or *mixed.* The relative proportion of each type of cost in an organization is known as its **cost structure.** For example, an organization might have many fixed costs but few variable or mixed costs. Alternatively, it might have many variable costs but few fixed or mixed costs.

Variable Cost

A **variable cost** varies, in total, in direct proportion to changes in the level of activity. Common examples of variable costs include cost of goods sold for a merchandising company, direct materials, direct labor, variable elements of manufacturing overhead, such as indirect materials, supplies, and power, and variable elements of selling and administrative expenses, such as commissions and shipping costs.[2]

For a cost to be variable, it must be variable *with respect to something.* That "something" is its *activity base.* An **activity base** is a measure of whatever causes the incurrence of a variable cost. An activity base is sometimes referred to as a *cost driver.* Some of the most common activity bases are direct labor-hours, machine-hours, units produced, and units sold. Other examples of activity bases (cost drivers) include the

---

[2] Direct labor costs often can be fixed instead of variable for a variety of reasons. For example, in some countries, such as France, Germany, and Japan, labor regulations and cultural norms may limit management's ability to adjust the labor force in response to changes in activity. In this textbook, always assume that direct labor is a variable cost unless you are explicitly told otherwise.

number of miles driven by salespersons, the number of pounds of laundry cleaned by a hotel, the number of calls handled by technical support staff at a software company, and the number of beds occupied in a hospital. *While there are many activity bases within organizations, throughout this textbook, unless stated otherwise, you should assume that the activity base under consideration is the total volume of goods and services provided by the organization. We will specify the activity base only when it is something other than total output.*

To provide an example of a variable cost, consider Nooksack Expeditions, a small company that provides daylong whitewater rafting excursions on rivers in the North Cascade Mountains. The company provides all of the necessary equipment and experienced guides, and it serves gourmet meals to its guests. The meals are purchased from a caterer for $30 a person for a daylong excursion. The behavior of this variable cost, on both a per-unit and a total basis, is shown below:

Number of Guests	Cost of Meals per Guest	Total Cost of Meals
250	$30	$7,500
500	$30	$15,000
750	$30	$22,500
1,000	$30	$30,000

While total variable costs change as the activity level changes, it is important to note that a variable cost is constant if expressed on a *per-unit* basis. For example, the per-unit cost of the meals remains constant at $30 even though the total cost of the meals increases and decreases with activity. The graph on the left-hand side of Exhibit 1–3 illustrates that the total variable cost rises and falls as the activity level rises and falls. At an activity level of 250 guests, the total meal cost is $7,500. At an activity level of 1,000 guests, the total meal cost rises to $30,000.

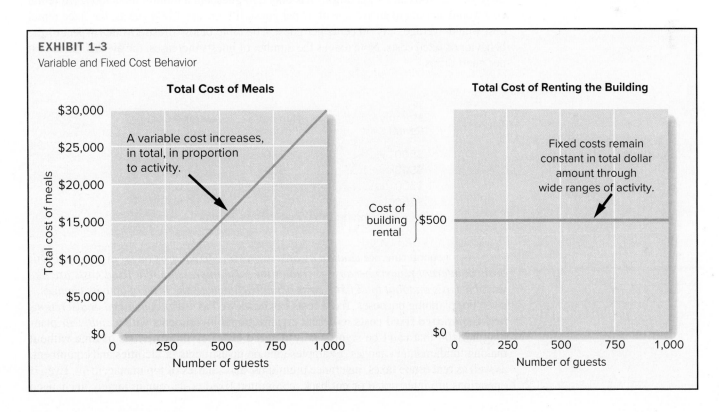

EXHIBIT 1–3
Variable and Fixed Cost Behavior

Fixed Cost

A **fixed cost** is a cost that remains constant, in total, regardless of changes in the level of activity. Manufacturing overhead usually includes various fixed costs such as depreciation, insurance, property taxes, rent, and supervisory salaries. Similarly, selling and administrative costs often include fixed costs such as administrative salaries, advertising, and depreciation of nonmanufacturing assets. Unlike variable costs, fixed costs are not affected by changes in activity. Consequently, as the activity level rises and falls, total fixed costs remain constant unless influenced by some outside force, such as a landlord increasing your monthly rent. To continue the Nooksack Expeditions example, assume the company rents a building for $500 per month to store its equipment. The total amount of rent paid is the same regardless of the number of guests the company takes on its expeditions during any given month. The concept of a fixed cost is shown graphically on the right-hand side of Exhibit 1–3.

Because total fixed costs remain constant for large variations in the level of activity, the average fixed cost *per unit* becomes progressively smaller as the level of activity increases. If Nooksack Expeditions has only 250 guests in a month, the $500 fixed rental cost would amount to an average of $2 per guest. If there are 1,000 guests, the fixed rental cost would average only 50 cents per guest. The table below illustrates this aspect of the behavior of fixed costs. Note that as the number of guests increases, the average fixed cost per guest drops.

Monthly Rental Cost	Number of Guests	Average Cost per Guest
$500	250	$2.00
$500	500	$1.00
$500	750	$0.67
$500	1,000	$0.50

As a general rule, *we caution against expressing fixed costs on an average per-unit basis in internal reports because it creates the false impression that fixed costs are like variable costs and that total fixed costs actually change as the level of activity changes.*

For planning purposes, fixed costs can be viewed as either *committed* or *discretionary*. **Committed fixed costs** represent organizational investments with a *multiyear* planning horizon that can't be significantly reduced even for short periods of time without making fundamental changes. Examples include investments in facilities and equipment, as well as real estate taxes, insurance premiums, and salaries of top management. Even if operations are interrupted or cut back, committed fixed costs remain largely unchanged in the short term because the costs of restoring them later are likely to be far greater than any short-run savings that might be realized. **Discretionary fixed costs** (often referred to as *managed fixed costs*) usually arise from *annual* decisions by management to spend on certain fixed cost items. Examples of discretionary fixed costs include advertising, research, public relations, management development programs, and internships for students. Discretionary fixed costs can be cut for short periods of time with minimal damage to the long-run goals of the organization.

The Linearity Assumption and the Relevant Range

Management accountants ordinarily assume that costs are strictly linear; that is, the relation between cost on the one hand and activity on the other can be represented by a straight line within a narrow band of activity known as the *relevant range*. The **relevant range** is the range of activity within which the assumption that cost behavior is strictly linear is reasonably valid.[3]

The concept of the relevant range is important in understanding fixed costs. For example, suppose the Mayo Clinic rents a machine for $20,000 per month that tests blood samples for the presence of leukemia cells. Furthermore, suppose that the capacity of the leukemia diagnostic machine is 3,000 tests per month. The assumption that the rent for the diagnostic machine is $20,000 per month is only valid within the relevant range of 0 to 3,000 tests per month. If the Mayo Clinic needed to test 5,000 blood samples per month, then it would need to rent another machine for an additional $20,000 per month. It would be difficult to rent half of a diagnostic machine; therefore, the step pattern depicted in Exhibit 1–4 is typical for such costs. This exhibit shows that the fixed rental cost is $20,000 for a relevant range of 0 to 3,000 tests. The fixed rental cost increases to $40,000 within the relevant range of 3,001 to 6,000 tests. The rental cost increases in discrete steps or increments of 3,000 tests, rather than increasing in a linear fashion per test.

This step-oriented cost behavior pattern can also be used to describe other costs, such as some labor costs. For example, the cost of compensating salaried employees can

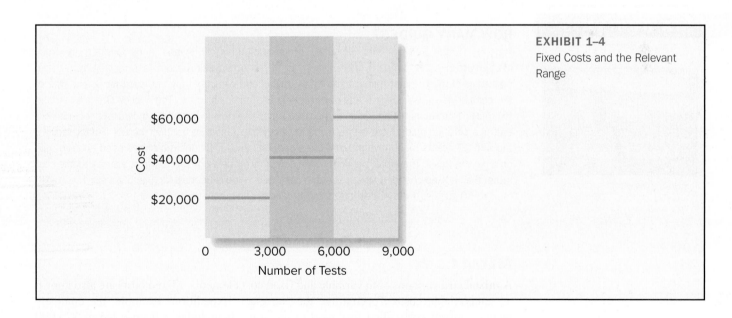

EXHIBIT 1–4
Fixed Costs and the Relevant Range

---

[3] Recent research has focused on how costs respond to changes in activity. That research is broadly consistent with the accountant's linear model, with anticipated activity outside of the relevant range often leading to adjustments in fixed costs. See Rajiv Banker and Dmitri Byzalov, "Asymmetric Cost Behavior," *Journal of Management Accounting Research*, 2014, Vol. 26, No. 2, pages 43–79, and Eric Noreen, "Capacity Constraints and Asymmetric Cost Behavior," working paper, 2017.

EXHIBIT 1–5
Summary of Variable and Fixed
Cost Behavior

	Behavior of the Cost (within the relevant range)	
Cost	In Total	Per Unit
Variable cost	Total variable cost increases and decreases in proportion to changes in the activity level.	Variable cost per unit remains constant.
Fixed cost	Total fixed cost is not affected by changes in the activity level within the relevant range.	Average fixed cost per unit decreases as the activity level rises and increases as the activity level falls.

be characterized using a step pattern. Salaried employees are paid a fixed amount, such as $40,000 per year, for providing the capacity to work a prespecified amount of time, such as 40 hours per week for 50 weeks a year (= 2,000 hours per year). In this example, the total salary cost is $40,000 within a relevant range of 0 to 2,000 hours of work. The total salary cost increases to $80,000 (or two employees) if the organization's work requirements expand to a relevant range of 2,001 to 4,000 hours of work. Cost behavior patterns, such as salaried employees, are often called *step-variable costs.* Step-variable costs can often be adjusted quickly as conditions change. Furthermore, the width of the steps for step-variable costs is generally so narrow that these costs can be treated essentially as variable costs for most purposes. The width of the steps for fixed costs, on the other hand, is so wide that these costs should be treated as entirely fixed within the relevant range.

Exhibit 1–5 summarizes four key concepts related to variable and fixed costs. Study it carefully before reading further.

Kuznetcov_Konstantin/Shutterstock

HOW MANY GUIDES?

Majestic Ocean Kayaking, of Ucluelet, British Columbia, is owned and operated by Tracy Morben-Eeftink. The company offers a number of guided kayaking excursions ranging from three-hour tours of the Ucluelet harbor to six-day kayaking and camping trips in Clayoquot Sound. One of the company's excursions is a four-day kayaking and camping trip to The Broken Group Islands in the Pacific Rim National Park. Special regulations apply to trips in the park—including a requirement that one certified guide must be assigned for every five guests or fraction thereof. For example, a trip with 12 guests must have at least three certified guides. Guides are not salaried and are paid on a per-day basis. Therefore, the cost to the company of the guides for a trip is a step-variable cost rather than a fixed cost or a strictly variable cost. One guide is needed for 1 to 5 guests, two guides for 6 to 10 guests, three guides for 11 to 15 guests, and so on.

Mixed Costs

A **mixed cost** contains both variable and fixed cost elements. Mixed costs are also known as semivariable costs. To continue the Nooksack Expeditions example, the company incurs a mixed cost called *fees paid to the state.* It includes a license fee of $25,000 per year plus $3 per rafting party paid to the state's Department of Natural Resources. If the company runs 1,000 rafting parties this year, then the total fees paid to the state would be $28,000, made up of $25,000 in fixed cost plus $3,000 in variable cost. Exhibit 1–6 depicts the behavior of this mixed cost.

Even if Nooksack fails to attract any customers, the company will still have to pay the license fee of $25,000. This is why the cost line in Exhibit 1–6 intersects the vertical

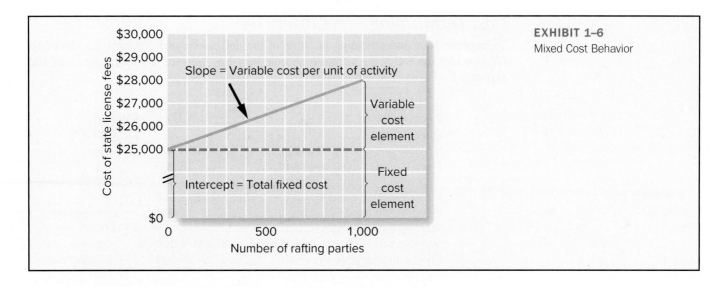

EXHIBIT 1–6
Mixed Cost Behavior

cost axis at the $25,000 point. For each rafting party the company organizes, the total cost of the state fees will increase by $3. Therefore, the total cost line slopes upward as the variable cost of $3 per party is added to the fixed cost of $25,000 per year.

Because the mixed cost in Exhibit 1–6 is represented by a straight line, the following equation for a straight line can be used to express the relationship between a mixed cost and the level of activity:

$$Y = a + bX$$

In this equation,

Y = The total mixed cost

a = The total fixed cost (the vertical intercept of the line)

b = The variable cost per unit of activity (the slope of the line)

X = The level of activity

Because the variable cost per unit equals the slope of the straight line, the steeper the slope, the higher the variable cost per unit.

In the case of the state fees paid by Nooksack Expeditions, the equation is written as follows:

$$Y = \$25,000 + \$3.00X$$

| Total mixed cost | Total fixed cost | Variable cost per unit of activity | Activity level |

This equation makes it easy to calculate the total mixed cost for any activity level within the relevant range. For example, suppose the company expects to organize 800 rafting parties in the next year. The total state fees would be calculated as follows:

$$Y = \$25,000 + (\$3.00 \text{ per rafting party} \times 800 \text{ rafting parties})$$
$$= \$27,400$$

Cost Terminology—A Closer Look

To improve your understanding of some of the definitions and concepts introduced so far, consider the following scenario. A company has reported the following costs and expenses for the most recent month:

Direct materials		$69,000
Direct labor.		$35,000
Variable manufacturing overhead	$15,000	
Fixed manufacturing overhead.	28,000	
Total manufacturing overhead		$43,000
Variable selling expense	$12,000	
Fixed selling expense.	18,000	
Total selling expense		$30,000
Variable administrative expense.	$ 4,000	
Fixed administrative expense	25,000	
Total administrative expense.		$29,000

These costs and expenses can be categorized in a number of ways, some of which are shown below:

$$
\begin{aligned}
\text{Product cost} &= \text{Direct materials} + \text{Direct labor} + \text{Manufacturing overhead} \\
&= \$69,000 + \$35,000 + \$43,000 \\
&= \$147,000 \\
\text{Period cost} &= \text{Selling expense} + \text{Administrative expense} \\
&= \$30,000 + \$29,000 \\
&= \$59,000 \\
\text{Conversion cost} &= \text{Direct labor} + \text{Manufacturing overhead} \\
&= \$35,000 + \$43,000 \\
&= \$78,000 \\
\text{Prime cost} &= \text{Direct materials} + \text{Direct labor} \\
&= \$69,000 + \$35,000 \\
&= \$104,000 \\
\text{Variable manufacturing cost} &= \text{Direct materials} + \text{Direct labor} + \text{Variable manufacturing overhead} \\
&= \$69,000 + \$35,000 + \$15,000 \\
&= \$119,000 \\
\text{Total fixed cost} &= \frac{\text{Fixed manufacturing}}{\text{overhead}} + \frac{\text{Fixed selling}}{\text{expense}} + \frac{\text{Fixed administrative}}{\text{expense}} \\
&= \$28,000 + \$18,000 + \$25,000 \\
&= \$71,000
\end{aligned}
$$

Cost Classifications for Decision Making

LEARNING OBJECTIVE 1–5
Understand cost classifications used in making decisions: relevant costs and irrelevant costs.

Every decision involves choosing from among at least two alternatives. The key to choosing among alternatives is distinguishing between *relevant* and *irrelevant* costs and benefits. **Relevant costs** and **relevant benefits** should be considered when making decisions. Irrelevant costs and irrelevant benefits should be ignored when making decisions. The remainder of this section expands on these concepts by defining the terms *differential cost* and *revenue, incremental cost, opportunity cost,* and *sunk cost.*

Differential Cost and Revenue

In business decisions, each alternative will have costs and benefits that must be compared to the costs and benefits of other available alternatives. A future cost that differs between any two alternatives is known as a **differential cost.** Differential costs are always relevant costs. Future revenue that differs between any two alternatives is known as **differential revenue.** Differential revenue is an example of a relevant benefit. Any future cost or benefit that does not differ between the alternatives is irrelevant and should be ignored.

A differential cost is also known as an **incremental cost.** Although technically an incremental cost should refer only to an increase in cost from one alternative to another, whereas decreases in cost should be referred to as *decremental costs.* Differential cost is a broader term, encompassing both cost increases (incremental costs) and cost decreases (decremental costs) between alternatives.

The accountant's differential cost concept can be compared to the economist's marginal cost concept. In speaking of changes in cost and revenue, the economist uses the terms *marginal cost* and *marginal revenue.* The revenue obtained from selling one more unit of product is called marginal revenue, and the cost involved in producing one more unit of product is called marginal cost. The economist's marginal concept is basically the same as the accountant's differential concept applied to a single unit of output.

Differential costs can be either fixed or variable. To illustrate, assume that Natural Cosmetics, Inc., is thinking about changing its marketing method from distribution through retailers to distribution by a network of neighborhood sales representatives. Present costs and revenues are compared to projected costs and revenues in the following table:

	Retailer Distribution (present)	Sales Representatives (proposed)	Differential Costs and Revenues
Sales (*variable*)	$700,000	$800,000	$100,000
Cost of goods sold (*variable*)	350,000	400,000	50,000
Advertising (*fixed*)	80,000	45,000	(35,000)
Commissions (*variable*)	0	40,000	40,000
Warehouse depreciation (*fixed*)	50,000	80,000	30,000
Other expenses (*fixed*)	60,000	60,000	0
Total expenses.	540,000	625,000	85,000
Net operating income.	$160,000	$175,000	$ 15,000

According to the above analysis, the differential revenue is $100,000 and the differential costs total $85,000, leaving a positive differential net operating income of $15,000 in favor of using sales representatives.

In general, only the differences between alternatives are relevant in decisions. Those items that are the same under all alternatives and that are not affected by the decision can be ignored. For example, in the Natural Cosmetics, Inc., example above, the "Other expenses" category, which is $60,000 under both alternatives, can be ignored because it has no effect on the decision. If it were removed from the calculations, the sales representatives would still be preferred by $15,000. This is an extremely important principle in management accounting that we will revisit in later chapters.

Opportunity Cost and Sunk Cost

Opportunity cost is the potential benefit that is given up when one alternative is selected over another. For example, assume that you have a part-time job while attending college that pays $200 per week. If you spend one week at the beach during spring break without pay, then the $200 in lost wages would be an opportunity cost of taking the week off to be at the beach. Opportunity costs are not usually found in accounting records, but they are relevant costs that must be explicitly considered in every decision a manager makes. Virtually every alternative involves an opportunity cost.

A **sunk cost** is a cost *that has already been incurred* and cannot be changed by any decision made now or in the future. Because sunk costs cannot be changed by any decision, they are not differential costs. And because only differential costs are relevant in a decision, sunk costs are irrelevant costs that should always be ignored.

To illustrate a sunk cost, assume that a company paid $50,000 several years ago for a special-purpose machine. The machine was used to make a product that is now obsolete and is no longer being sold. Even though in hindsight purchasing the machine may have been unwise, the $50,000 cost has already been incurred and cannot be undone. It would be folly to continue making the obsolete product in a misguided attempt to "recover" the original cost of the machine. In short, the $50,000 originally paid for the machine is a sunk cost that should be ignored in current decisions.

Before moving to the next section, we want to emphasize that managers can use cost classifications for other purposes besides those described thus far in this chapter. For example, managers may wish to classify costs as controllable or uncontrollable for employee performance evaluation purposes. A *controllable cost* can be influenced by the manager being evaluated. An *uncontrollable cost* cannot be influenced by the manager being evaluated. A company's managers may also wish to classify costs as value-added or non-value-added for process improvement purposes. A *value-added cost* increases the value of products and services provided to the company's stakeholders, whereas a *non-value-added cost* does not provide any benefit to the company's stakeholders. The overarching theme of the chapter is to first identify the needs of management and then classify costs accordingly.

IS EATING LUNCH AT A RESTAURANT BECOMING OBSOLETE?

NPD Group estimates that Americans are eating lunch at a restaurant 433 million fewer times than in prior years. Faced with three options—eating lunch at a restaurant, having food delivered to their office, and bringing food from home—business professionals are increasingly choosing the latter two options because it saves them time and money.

Scott Colosi, president of Texas Roadhouse, says his employees are eating lunch at the office so often that they know the local delivery drivers by name. They are choosing to work through lunch in an effort to save time and be more efficient. Meanwhile, the average price of a restaurant lunch has risen 19.5% to $7.59, whereas grocery stores are experiencing the longest stretch of falling prices in more than 50 years. These divergent trends explain why many employees are choosing to bring their lunch from home rather than eating at a restaurant.

Source: Julie Jargon, "Lunch Business Serves Up Less for Restaurants," *The Wall Street Journal,* May 31, 2017, pp. B1–B2.

Using Different Cost Classifications for Different Purposes

LEARNING OBJECTIVE 1–6
Prepare income statements for a merchandising company using the traditional and contribution formats.

This section of the chapter discusses how to prepare traditional and contribution format income statements for a merchandising company.[4] Merchandising companies do not manufacture the products they sell to customers. For example, Lowe's and Home Depot are merchandising companies because they buy finished products from manufacturers and then resell them to end consumers.

Contrasting these two types of income statements enables us to illustrate the chapter's unifying theme of *different cost classifications for different purposes*. Traditional income statements are prepared primarily for *external reporting purposes*. They rely on cost classifications for preparing financial statements (product and period costs) to depict the financial consequences of *past* transactions. Contribution format income statements are prepared for *internal management purposes*. They use cost classifications for predicting cost behavior (variable and fixed costs) to better inform decisions affecting the *future*.

---

[4] Subsequent chapters compare the income statement formats for manufacturing companies.

The two different purposes served by these income statements highlight what is arguably the most important difference between financial accounting and managerial accounting—an emphasis on recording past performance versus an emphasis on making predictions and decisions that affect future performance.

The Traditional Format Income Statement

The left-hand side of Exhibit 1–7 shows a traditional income statement format for merchandising companies. This type of income statement organizes costs into two categories—cost of goods sold and selling and administrative expenses. Sales minus cost of goods sold equals the *gross margin*. The gross margin minus selling and administrative expenses equals net operating income.

The cost of goods sold reports the *product costs* attached to the merchandise sold during the period. The selling and administrative expenses report all *period costs* that have been expensed as incurred. The cost of goods sold for a merchandising company can be computed directly by multiplying the number of units sold by their unit cost or indirectly using the equation below:

$$\text{Cost of goods sold} = \text{Beginning merchandise inventory} + \text{Purchases} - \text{Ending merchandise inventory}$$

For example, let's assume the company depicted in Exhibit 1–7 purchased $3,000 of merchandise inventory during the period and had beginning and ending merchandise inventory balances of $7,000 and $4,000, respectively. The equation above could be used to compute the cost of goods sold as follows:

$$\text{Cost of goods sold} = \text{Beginning merchandise inventory} + \text{Purchases} - \text{Ending merchandise inventory}$$
$$= \$7,000 + \$3,000 - \$4,000$$
$$= \$6,000$$

EXHIBIT 1–7

Comparing Traditional and Contribution Format Income Statements for Merchandising Companies (all numbers are given)

Traditional Format			Contribution Format		
Sales		$12,000	Sales		$12,000
Cost of goods sold*		6,000	Variable expenses:		
Gross margin		6,000	Cost of goods sold	$6,000	
Selling and administrative expenses:			Variable selling	600	
Selling	$3,100		Variable administrative	400	7,000
Administrative	1,900	5,000	Contribution margin		5,000
Net operating income		$ 1,000	Fixed expenses:		
			Fixed selling	2,500	
			Fixed administrative	1,500	4,000
			Net operating income		$ 1,000

* For a manufacturing company, the cost of goods sold would include some variable costs, such as direct materials, direct labor, and variable overhead, and some fixed costs, such as fixed manufacturing overhead. Income statement formats for manufacturing companies will be explored in greater detail in a subsequent chapter.

Although the traditional income statement is useful for external reporting pur-poses, it has serious limitations when used for internal purposes. It does not distinguish between fixed and variable costs. For example, under the heading "Selling and adminis-trative expenses," both variable administrative costs ($400) and fixed administrative costs ($1,500) are lumped together ($1,900). Internally, managers need cost data organized by cost behavior to aid in planning, controlling, and decision making. The contribution format income statement has been developed in response to these needs.

The Contribution Format Income Statement

The crucial distinction between fixed and variable costs is at the heart of the **contri-bution approach** to constructing income statements. The unique thing about the con-tribution approach is that it provides managers with an income statement that clearly distinguishes between fixed and variable costs and therefore aids planning, controlling, and decision making. The right-hand side of Exhibit 1–7 shows a contribution format income statement for merchandising companies.

The contribution approach separates costs into fixed and variable categories, first deducting all variable expenses from sales to obtain the *contribution margin*. For a merchandising company, cost of goods sold is a variable cost that gets included in the "Variable expenses" portion of the contribution format income statement. The **contribution margin** is the amount remaining from sales revenues after all variable expenses have been deducted. This amount *contributes* toward covering fixed expenses and then toward profits for the period. The contribution margin can also be stated on a per-unit basis. For example, if the company depicted in Exhibit 1–7 sold 500 units, then its contribution margin per unit would be $10 per unit (= $5,000 ÷ 500 units).

The contribution format income statement is used as an internal planning and decision-making tool. Its emphasis on cost behavior aids cost-volume-profit analysis, management performance appraisals, and budgeting. Moreover, the contribution approach helps managers organize data pertinent to numerous decisions such as product-line analysis, pricing, use of scarce resources, and make or buy analysis. All of these topics are covered in later chapters.

Summary

In this chapter, we have discussed ways in which managers classify costs. How the costs will be used—for assigning costs to cost objects, preparing external reports, predicting cost behavior, or decision making—will dictate how the costs are classified.

For purposes of assigning costs to cost objects such as products or departments, costs are classified as direct or indirect. Direct costs can be conveniently traced to cost objects. Indirect costs cannot be conveniently traced to cost objects.

For external reporting purposes, costs are classified as either product costs or period costs. Product costs are assigned to inventories and are considered assets until the products are sold. At the point of sale, product costs become cost of goods sold on the income statement. In contrast, period costs are taken directly to the income statement as expenses in the period in which they are incurred.

For purposes of predicting how costs will react to changes in activity, costs are classified into three categories—variable, fixed, and mixed. Variable costs, in total, are strictly proportional to activity. The variable cost per unit is constant. Fixed costs, in total, remain the same as the activity level changes within the relevant range. The average fixed cost per unit decreases as the activity level increases. Mixed costs consist of variable and fixed elements and can be expressed in equation form as $Y = a + bX$, where Y is the total mixed cost, a is the total fixed cost, b is the variable cost per unit of activity, and X is the activity level.

For purposes of making decisions, managers must distinguish between relevant and irrelevant costs and benefits. To do this, they must understand the concepts of differential cost and revenue, opportunity cost, and sunk cost. Differential costs and revenues are the costs and revenues that differ between alternatives. Opportunity cost is the benefit that is forgone when one alternative is selected over another. Sunk cost is a cost that occurred in the past and cannot be altered. Differential costs and opportunity costs are relevant costs that should be carefully considered in decisions. Sunk costs are irrelevant costs and should be ignored when making decisions.

Different cost classifications for different purposes is the unifying theme of this chapter, and it can be highlighted by contrasting traditional and contribution format income statements. The traditional income statement format is used primarily for external reporting purposes. It organizes costs using product and period cost classifications. The contribution format income statement aids decision making because it organizes costs using variable and fixed cost classifications.

 Data Analytics Exercise available in Connect to complement this chapter

Review Problem 1: Cost Terms

Many new cost terms have been introduced in this chapter. It will take you some time to learn what each term means and how to properly classify costs in an organization. Consider the following example: Porter Company manufactures furniture, including tables. Selected costs are given below:

1. The tables are made of wood that costs $100 per table.
2. The tables are assembled by workers at a wage cost of $40 per table.
3. Workers assembling the tables are supervised by a factory supervisor who is paid $45,000 per year.
4. Electrical costs are $2 per machine-hour. Four machine-hours are required to produce a table.
5. The depreciation on the machines used to make the tables totals $10,000 per year. The machines have no resale value and do not wear out through use.
6. The salary of the president of the company is $200,000 per year.
7. The company spends $250,000 per year to advertise its products.
8. Salespersons are paid a commission of $30 for each table sold.
9. Instead of producing the tables, the company could rent its factory space for $50,000 per year.

Required:
Classify these costs according to the various cost terms used in the chapter. *Carefully study the classification of each cost.* If you don't understand why a particular cost is classified the way it is, reread the section of the chapter discussing the particular cost term. The terms *variable cost* and *fixed cost* refer to how costs behave with respect to the number of tables produced in a year.

Solution to Review Problem 1

	Variable Cost	Fixed Cost	Period (Selling and Administrative) Cost	Product Cost Direct Materials	Direct Labor	Manufacturing Overhead	Sunk Cost	Opportunity Cost
1. Wood used in a table ($100 per table)	X			X				
2. Labor cost to assemble a table ($40 per table)	X				X			
3. Salary of the factory supervisor ($45,000 per year)		X				X		
4. Cost of electricity to produce tables ($2 per machine-hour)	X					X		
5. Depreciation of machines used to produce tables ($10,000 per year).		X				X	X*	
6. Salary of the company president ($200,000 per year)		X	X					
7. Advertising expense ($250,000 per year)		X	X					
8. Commissions paid to salespersons ($30 per table sold)	X		X					
9. Rental income forgone on factory space ($50,000 per year)								X†

* This is a sunk cost because the outlay for the equipment was made in a previous period.

† This is an opportunity cost because it represents the potential benefit that is lost or sacrificed as a result of using the factory space to produce tables. Opportunity cost is a special category of cost that is not ordinarily recorded in an organization's accounting records. To avoid possible confusion with other costs, we will not attempt to classify this cost in any other way except as an opportunity cost.

Review Problem 2: Income Statement Formats

McFarland, Inc., is a merchandiser that provided the following information:

	Amount
Number of units sold	35,000
Selling price per unit.	$40
Variable selling expense per unit.	$3
Variable administrative expense per unit	$1
Total fixed selling expense	$45,000
Total fixed administrative expense.	$28,000
Beginning merchandise inventory	$21,000
Ending merchandise inventory.	$35,000
Merchandise purchases.	$805,000

Required:

1. Prepare a traditional income statement.
2. Prepare a contribution format income statement.

Solution to Review Problem 2

1. Traditional income statement

McFarland, Inc. Traditional Income Statement		
Sales ($40 per unit × 35,000 units)......................		$1,400,000
Cost of goods sold ($21,000 + $805,000 − $35,000)....		791,000
Gross margin		609,000
Selling and administrative expenses:		
Selling expense (($3 per unit × 35,000 units) + $45,000)..	$150,000	
Administrative expense (($1 per unit × 35,000 units) + $28,000)..	63,000	213,000
Net operating income..................................		$ 396,000

2. Contribution format income statement

McFarland, Inc. Contribution Format Income Statement		
Sales..		$1,400,000
Variable expenses:		
Cost of goods sold ($21,000 + $805,000 − $35,000)	$791,000	
Selling expense ($3 per unit × 35,000 units)	105,000	
Administrative expense ($1 per unit × 35,000 units)	35,000	931,000
Contribution margin.....................................		469,000
Fixed expenses:		
Selling expense	45,000	
Administrative expense................................	28,000	73,000
Net operating income		$ 396,000

Glossary

Activity base A measure of whatever causes the incurrence of a variable cost. For example, the total cost of surgical gloves in a hospital will increase as the number of surgeries increases. Therefore, the number of surgeries is the activity base that explains the total cost of surgical gloves. (p. 32)

Administrative costs All executive, organizational, and clerical costs associated with the general management of an organization rather than with manufacturing or selling. (p. 30)

Committed fixed costs Investments in facilities, equipment, and basic organizational structure that can't be significantly reduced even for short periods of time without making fundamental changes. (p. 34)

Common cost A cost that is incurred to support a number of cost objects but that cannot be traced to them individually. For example, the wage cost of the pilot of a 747 airliner is a common cost of all of the passengers on the aircraft. Without the pilot, there would be no flight and no passengers. But no part of the pilot's wage is caused by any one passenger taking the flight. (p. 28)

Contribution approach An income statement format that organizes costs by their behavior. Costs are separated into variable and fixed categories rather than being separated into product and period costs for external reporting purposes. (p. 42)

Contribution margin The amount remaining from sales revenues after all variable expenses have been deducted. (p. 42)

Conversion cost Direct labor cost plus manufacturing overhead cost. (p. 29)

Cost behavior The way in which a cost reacts to changes in the level of activity. (p. 32)

Cost object Anything for which cost data are desired. Examples of cost objects are products, customers, geographic regions, and parts of the organization such as departments or divisions. (p. 27)

Cost structure The relative proportion of fixed, variable, and mixed costs in an organization. (p. 32)

Differential cost A future cost that differs between any two alternatives. (p. 39)

Differential revenue Future revenue that differs between any two alternatives. (p. 39)

Direct cost A cost that can be easily and conveniently traced to a specified cost object. (p. 28)

Direct labor Factory labor costs that can be easily traced to individual units of product. Also called *touch labor*. (p. 29)

Direct materials Materials that become an integral part of a finished product and whose costs can be conveniently traced to it. (p. 28)

Discretionary fixed costs Those fixed costs that arise from annual decisions by management to spend on certain fixed cost items, such as advertising and research. (p. 35)

Financial accounting The phase of accounting that is concerned with reporting historical financial information to external parties, such as stockholders, creditors, and regulators. (p. 27)

Finished goods Units of product that have been completed but not yet sold to customers. (p. 31)

Fixed cost A cost that remains constant, in total, regardless of changes in the level of activity within the relevant range. If a fixed cost is expressed on a per-unit basis, it varies inversely with the level of activity. (p. 34)

Incremental cost An increase in cost between two alternatives. (p. 39)

Indirect cost A cost that cannot be easily and conveniently traced to a specified cost object. (p. 28)

Indirect labor The labor costs of janitors, supervisors, materials handlers, and other factory workers that cannot be conveniently traced to particular products. (p. 29)

Indirect materials Small items of material such as glue and nails that may be an integral part of a finished product, but whose costs cannot be easily or conveniently traced to it. (p. 29)

Inventoriable costs Synonym for product costs. (p. 30)

Managerial accounting The phase of accounting that is concerned with providing information to managers for use within the organization. (p. 27)

Manufacturing overhead All manufacturing costs except direct materials and direct labor. (p. 29)

Mixed cost A cost that contains both variable and fixed cost elements. (p. 36)

Opportunity cost The potential benefit that is given up when one alternative is selected over another. (p. 39)

Period costs Costs that are taken directly to the income statement as expenses in the period in which they are incurred or accrued. (p. 31)

Prime cost Direct materials cost plus direct labor cost. (p. 29)

Product costs All costs that are involved in acquiring or making a product. In the case of manufactured goods, these costs consist of direct materials, direct labor, and manufacturing overhead. Also see *Inventoriable costs*. (p. 30)

Raw materials Any materials that go into the final product. (p. 28)

Relevant benefit A benefit that should be considered when making decisions. (p. 38)

Relevant cost A cost that should be considered when making decisions. (p. 38)

Relevant range The range of activity within which assumptions about variable and fixed cost behavior are valid. (p. 35)

Selling costs All costs that are incurred to secure customer orders and get the finished product or service into the hands of the customer. (p. 29)

Sunk cost A cost that has already been incurred and that cannot be changed by any decision made now or in the future. (p. 40)

Variable cost A cost that varies, in total, in direct proportion to changes in the level of activity. A variable cost is constant per unit. (p. 32)

Work in process Units of product that are only partially complete and will require further work before they are ready for sale to the customer. (p. 30)

Questions

1–1   What are the three major types of product costs in a manufacturing company?

1–2   Define the following: (*a*) direct materials, (*b*) indirect materials, (*c*) direct labor, (*d*) indirect labor, and (*e*) manufacturing overhead.

1–3 Explain the difference between a product cost and a period cost.

1–4 Distinguish between (*a*) a variable cost, (*b*) a fixed cost, and (*c*) a mixed cost.

1–5 What effect does an increase in the activity level have on:

   a. Average fixed costs per unit?

   b. Variable costs per unit?

   c. Total fixed costs?

   d. Total variable costs?

1–6 Define the following terms: (*a*) cost behavior and (*b*) relevant range.

1–7 What is meant by an *activity base* when dealing with variable costs? Give several examples of activity bases.

1–8 Managers often assume a strictly linear relationship between cost and the level of activity. Under what conditions would this be a valid or invalid assumption?

1–9 Distinguish between discretionary fixed costs and committed fixed costs.

1–10 Does the concept of the relevant range apply to fixed costs? Explain.

1–11 What is the difference between a traditional format income statement and a contribution format income statement?

1–12 What is the contribution margin?

1–13 Define the following terms: (*a*) differential cost, (*b*) sunk cost, and (*c*) opportunity cost.

1–14 Only variable costs can be differential costs. Do you agree? Explain.

Mc Graw Hill connect Applying Excel

This Excel worksheet form is to be used to recreate Exhibit 1–7. The workbook, and instructions on how to complete the file, can be found in Connect.

LEARNING OBJECTIVE 1–6

	A	B	C	D
1	Chapter 1: Applying Excel			
2				
3	**Data**			
4	Sales	$12,000		
5	Variable costs:			
6	Cost of goods sold	$6,000		
7	Variable selling	$600		
8	Variable administrative	$400		
9	Fixed costs:			
10	Fixed selling	$2,500		
11	Fixed administrative	$1,500		
12				
13	*Enter a formula into each of the cells marked with a ? below*			
14	**Exhibit 1-7**			
15				
16	**Traditional Format Income Statement**			
17	Sales		?	
18	Cost of goods sold		?	
19	Gross margin		?	
20	Selling and administrative expenses:			
21	Selling	?		
22	Administrative	?	?	
23	Net operating income		?	
24				
25	**Contribution Format Income Statement**			
26	Sales		?	
27	Variable expenses:			
28	Cost of goods sold	?		
29	Variable selling	?		
30	Variable administrative	?	?	
31	Contribution margin		?	
32	Fixed expenses:			
33	Fixed selling	?		
34	Fixed administrative	?	?	
35	Net operating income		?	
36				

H ◀ ▶ H | **Chapter 1 Form** / Filled in Chapter 1 Form

Microsoft Excel

Required:

1. Check your worksheet by changing the variable selling cost in the Data area to $900, keeping all of the other data the same as in Exhibit 1–7. If your worksheet is operating properly, the net operating income under the traditional format income statement and under the contribution format income statement should now be $700 and the contribution margin should now be $4,700. If you do not get these answers, find the errors in your worksheet and correct them.
    How much is the gross margin? Did it change? Why or why not?

2. Suppose that sales are 10% higher, as shown below:

Sales	$13,200
Variable costs:	
Cost of goods sold	$6,600
Variable selling	$660
Variable administrative	$440
Fixed costs:	
Fixed selling	$2,500
Fixed administrative	$1,500

Enter these new data into your worksheet. Make sure you change all of the data that are different—not just the sales. Print or copy the income statements from your worksheet.
    What happened to the variable costs and to the fixed costs when sales increased by 10%? Why? Did the contribution margin increase by 10%? Why or why not? Did the net operating income increase by 10%? Why or why not?

The Foundational 15   Mc Graw Hill connect

LEARNING OBJECTIVES 1–1, 1–2, 1–3, 1–4, 1–5, 1–6

Martinez Company's relevant range of production is 7,500 units to 12,500 units. When it produces and sells 10,000 units, its average costs per unit are as follows:

	Average Cost per Unit
Direct materials	$6.00
Direct labor	$3.50
Variable manufacturing overhead	$1.50
Fixed manufacturing overhead	$4.00
Fixed selling expense	$3.00
Fixed administrative expense	$2.00
Sales commissions	$1.00
Variable administrative expense	$0.50

Required:

1. For financial accounting purposes, what is the total amount of product costs incurred to make 10,000 units?
2. For financial accounting purposes, what is the total amount of period costs incurred to sell 10,000 units?
3. If 8,000 units are produced and sold, what is the variable cost per unit produced and sold?
4. If 12,500 units are produced and sold, what is the variable cost per unit produced and sold?
5. If 8,000 units are produced and sold, what is the total amount of variable costs related to the units produced and sold?
6. If 12,500 units are produced and sold, what is the total amount of variable costs related to the units produced and sold?
7. If 8,000 units are produced, what is the average fixed manufacturing cost per unit produced?
8. If 12,500 units are produced, what is the average fixed manufacturing cost per unit produced?
9. If 8,000 units are produced, what is the total amount of fixed manufacturing cost incurred to support this level of production?

10. If 12,500 units are produced, what is the total amount of fixed manufacturing cost incurred to support this level of production?

11. If 8,000 units are produced, what is the total amount of manufacturing overhead cost incurred to support this level of production? What is this total amount expressed on a per-unit basis?

12. If 12,500 units are produced, what is the total amount of manufacturing overhead cost incurred to support this level of production? What is this total amount expressed on a per-unit basis?

13. If the selling price is $22 per unit, what is the contribution margin per unit?

14. If 11,000 units are produced, what are the total amounts of direct and indirect manufacturing costs incurred to support this level of production?

15. What incremental manufacturing cost will Martinez incur if it increases production from 10,000 to 10,001 units?

 Exercises

EXERCISE 1–1 Identifying Direct and Indirect Costs LO1–1

Northwest Hospital is a full-service hospital that provides everything from major surgery and emergency room care to outpatient clinics.

Required:

For each cost incurred at Northwest Hospital, indicate whether it would most likely be a direct cost or an indirect cost of the specified cost object by placing an X in the appropriate column.

	Cost	Cost Object	Direct Cost	Indirect Cost
Ex.	Catered food served to patients	A particular patient	X	
1.	The wages of pediatric nurses	The pediatric department		
2.	Prescription drugs	A particular patient		
3.	Heating the hospital	The pediatric department		
4.	The salary of the head of pediatrics	The pediatric department		
5.	The salary of the head of pediatrics	A particular pediatric patient		
6.	Hospital chaplain's salary	A particular patient		
7.	Lab tests by outside contractor	A particular patient		
8.	Lab tests by outside contractor	A particular department		

EXERCISE 1–2 Classifying Manufacturing Costs LO1–2

The PC Works assembles custom computers from components supplied by various manufacturers. The company is very small, and its assembly shop and retail sales store are housed in a single facility in a Redmond, Washington, industrial park. Listed below are some of the costs that the company incurs.

Required:

For each cost, indicate whether it would most likely be classified as direct materials, direct labor, manufacturing overhead, selling, or an administrative cost.

1. The cost of a hard drive installed in a computer.
2. The cost of advertising in the *Puget Sound Computer User* newspaper.
3. The wages of employees who assemble computers from components.
4. Sales commissions paid to the company's salespeople.
5. The salary of the assembly shop's supervisor.
6. The salary of the company's accountant.
7. Depreciation on equipment used to test assembled computers before release to customers.
8. Rent on the facility in the industrial park.

EXERCISE 1–3 Classifying Costs as Product or Period Costs LO1–3

Suppose you have a summer job as an intern at Issac Aircams, a company that manufactures sophisticated spy cameras for remote-controlled military reconnaissance aircraft. The company, which is privately owned, has approached a bank for a loan to help finance its growth. The bank requires financial statements before approving the loan.

Required:

Classify each cost listed below as either a product cost or a period cost for the purpose of preparing financial statements for the bank.

1. Depreciation on salespersons' cars.
2. Rent on equipment used in the factory.
3. Lubricants used for machine maintenance.
4. Salaries of personnel who work in the finished goods warehouse.
5. Soap and paper towels used by factory workers at the end of a shift.
6. Factory supervisors' salaries.
7. Heat, water, and power consumed in the factory.
8. Materials used for boxing products for shipment overseas. (Units are not normally boxed.)
9. Advertising costs.
10. Workers' compensation insurance for factory employees.
11. Depreciation on chairs and tables in the factory lunchroom.
12. The wages of the receptionist in the administrative offices.
13. Cost of leasing the corporate jet used by the company's executives.
14. The cost of renting rooms at a Florida resort for the annual sales conference.
15. The cost of packaging the company's product.

EXERCISE 1–4 Fixed and Variable Cost Behavior LO1–4

Espresso Express operates a number of espresso coffee stands in busy suburban malls. The fixed weekly expense of a coffee stand is $1,200 and the variable cost per cup of coffee served is $0.22.

Required:

1. Fill in the following table with your estimates of the company's total cost and average cost per cup of coffee at the indicated levels of activity. Round off the average cost per cup of coffee to the nearest tenth of a cent.

	Cups of Coffee Served in a Week		
	2,000	2,100	2,200
Fixed cost	?	?	?
Variable cost	?	?	?
Total cost.	?	?	?
Average cost per cup of coffee served.	?	?	?

2. Does the average cost per cup of coffee served increase, decrease, or remain the same as the number of cups of coffee served in a week increases? Explain.

EXERCISE 1–5 Differential, Sunk, and Opportunity Costs LO1–5

Northeast Hospital's Radiology Department is considering replacing an old inefficient X-ray machine with a state-of-the-art digital X-ray machine. The new machine would provide higher quality X-rays in less time and at a lower cost per X-ray. It would also require less power and would use a color laser printer to produce easily readable X-ray images. Instead of investing the funds in the new X-ray machine, the Laboratory Department is lobbying the hospital's management to buy a new DNA analyzer.

Required:

For each of the items below, indicate by placing an *X* in the appropriate column whether it should be considered a differential cost, a sunk cost, or an opportunity cost in the decision to replace the old X-ray machine with a new machine. If none of the categories apply for a particular item, leave all columns blank.

Item	Differential Cost	Sunk Cost	Opportunity Cost
Ex. Cost of X-ray film used in the old machine	X		
1. Cost of the old X-ray machine.........................			
2. The salary of the head of the Radiology Department.....			
3. The salary of the head of the Laboratory Department			
4. Cost of the new color laser printer			
5. Rent on the space occupied by Radiology			
6. The cost of maintaining the old machine			
7. Benefits from a new DNA analyzer.....................			
8. Cost of electricity to run the X-ray machines			

EXERCISE 1–6 Traditional and Contribution Format Income Statements LO1–6

Cherokee Inc. is a merchandiser that provided the following information:

	Amount
Number of units sold.....................	20,000
Selling price per unit	$30
Variable selling expense per unit	$4
Variable administrative expense per unit......	$2
Total fixed selling expense.................	$40,000
Total fixed administrative expense	$30,000
Beginning merchandise inventory	$24,000
Ending merchandise inventory	$44,000
Merchandise purchases	$180,000

Required:

1. Prepare a traditional income statement.
2. Prepare a contribution format income statement.

EXERCISE 1–7 Direct and Indirect Costs LO1–1

Kubin Company's relevant range of production is 18,000 to 22,000 units. When it produces and sells 20,000 units, its average costs per unit are as follows:

	Average Cost per Unit
Direct materials..........................	$7.00
Direct labor	$4.00
Variable manufacturing overhead..........	$1.50
Fixed manufacturing overhead	$5.00
Fixed selling expense	$3.50
Fixed administrative expense	$2.50
Sales commissions.......................	$1.00
Variable administrative expense...........	$0.50

Required:

1. Assume the cost object is units of production:
   a. What is the total direct manufacturing cost incurred to make 20,000 units?
   b. What is the total indirect manufacturing cost incurred to make 20,000 units?
2. Assume the cost object is the Manufacturing Department and its total output is 20,000 units.
   a. How much total manufacturing cost is directly traceable to the Manufacturing Department?
   b. How much total manufacturing cost is an indirect cost that cannot be easily traced to the Manufacturing Department?

3. Assume the cost object is the company's various sales representatives. Furthermore, assume the company spent $50,000 of its total fixed selling expense on advertising, and the remainder of the total fixed selling expense comprised the fixed portion of the company's sales representatives' compensation.
   a. When the company sells 20,000 units, what is the total direct selling expense that can be readily traced to individual sales representatives?
   b. When the company sells 20,000 units, what is the total indirect selling expense that cannot be readily traced to individual sales representatives?
4. Are Kubin's administrative expenses always going to be treated as indirect costs in its internal management reports?

EXERCISE 1–8 Product Costs and Period Costs; Variable and Fixed Costs LO1–3, LO1–4
Refer to the data given in Exercise 1–7. Answer all questions independently.

Required:
1. For financial accounting purposes, what is the total amount of product costs incurred to make 20,000 units?
2. For financial accounting purposes, what is the total amount of period costs incurred to sell 20,000 units?
3. For financial accounting purposes, what is the total amount of product costs incurred to make 22,000 units?
4. For financial accounting purposes, what is the total amount of period costs incurred to sell 18,000 units?

EXERCISE 1–9 Fixed, Variable, and Mixed Costs LO1–4
Refer to the data given in Exercise 1–7. Answer all questions independently.

Required:
1. If 18,000 units are produced and sold, what is the variable cost per unit produced and sold?
2. If 22,000 units are produced and sold, what is the variable cost per unit produced and sold?
3. If 18,000 units are produced and sold, what is the total amount of variable cost related to the units produced and sold?
4. If 22,000 units are produced and sold, what is the total amount of variable cost related to the units produced and sold?
5. If 18,000 units are produced, what is the average fixed manufacturing cost per unit produced?
6. If 22,000 units are produced, what is the average fixed manufacturing cost per unit produced?
7. If 18,000 units are produced, what is the total amount of fixed manufacturing overhead incurred to support this level of production?
8. If 22,000 units are produced, what is the total amount of fixed manufacturing overhead incurred to support this level of production?

EXERCISE 1–10 Differential Costs and Sunk Costs LO1–5
Refer to the data given in Exercise 1–7. Answer all questions independently.

Required:
1. What is the incremental manufacturing cost incurred if the company increases production from 20,000 to 20,001 units?
2. What is the incremental cost incurred if the company increases production *and* sales from 20,000 to 20,001 units?
3. Assume Kubin Company produced 20,000 units and expects to sell 19,800 of them. If a new customer unexpectedly emerges and expresses interest in buying the 200 extra units that have been produced by the company and would otherwise remain unsold, what is the incremental manufacturing cost per unit incurred to sell these units to the customer?
4. Assume Kubin Company produced 20,000 units and expects to sell 19,800 of them. If a new customer unexpectedly emerges and expresses interest in buying the 200 extra units that have

been produced by the company and would otherwise remain unsold, what incremental selling and administrative cost per unit is incurred to sell these units to the customer?

EXERCISE 1–11 Cost Behavior; Contribution Format Income Statement LO1–4, LO1–6

Harris Company manufactures and sells a single product. A partially completed schedule of the company's total costs and costs per unit over the relevant range of 30,000 to 50,000 units is given below:

	Units Produced and Sold		
	30,000	40,000	50,000
Total costs:			
Variable cost...............	$180,000	?	?
Fixed cost	300,000	?	?
Total cost	$480,000	?	?
Costs per unit:			
Variable cost...............	?	?	?
Fixed cost	?	?	?
Total cost per unit...........	?	?	?

Required:

1. Complete the above schedule of the company's total costs and costs per unit.
2. Assume the company produces and sells 45,000 units during the year at a selling price of $16 per unit. Prepare a contribution format income statement for the year.

EXERCISE 1–12 Product and Period Cost Flows LO1–3

The Devon Motor Company produces automobiles. On April 1st, the company had no beginning inventories, and it purchased 8,000 batteries at a cost of $80 per battery. It withdrew 7,600 batteries from the storeroom during the month. Of these, 100 were used to replace batteries in cars being used by the company's traveling sales staff. The remaining 7,500 batteries withdrawn from the storeroom were placed in cars being produced by the company. Of the cars in production during April, 90% were completed and transferred from work in process to finished goods. Of the cars completed during the month, 30% were unsold at April 30th.

Required:

1. Determine the cost of batteries that would appear in each of the following accounts on April 30th.
   - a. Raw Materials
   - b. Work in Process
   - c. Finished Goods
   - d. Cost of Goods Sold
   - e. Selling Expense
2. Specify whether each of the above accounts would appear on the balance sheet or on the income statement at the end of the month.

EXERCISE 1–13 Variable and Fixed Cost Behavior LO1–4

Munchak Company's relevant range of production is between 9,000 and 11,000 units. Last month the company produced 10,000 units. Its total manufacturing cost per unit produced was $70. At this level of activity, the company's variable manufacturing costs are 40% of its total manufacturing costs.

Required:

Assume next month Munchak produces 10,050 units and its cost behavior patterns remain unchanged. Label each of the following statements as true or false with respect to next month.

Do not use a calculator to answer items 1 through 6. You can use a calculator to answer items 7 through 12. Record your answers by placing an X under the appropriate heading.

	True	False
1. The variable manufacturing cost per unit will remain the same as last month.		
2. The total fixed manufacturing cost will be greater than last month.		
3. The total manufacturing cost will be greater than last month.		
4. The average fixed manufacturing cost per unit will be less than last month.		
5. The total variable manufacturing cost will be less than last month.		
6. The total manufacturing cost per unit will be greater than last month.		
7. The variable manufacturing cost per unit will equal $28.		
8. The total fixed manufacturing cost will equal $422,100.		
9. The total manufacturing cost will equal $701,400.		
10. The average fixed manufacturing cost per unit (rounded to the nearest cent) will equal $41.79.		
11. The total variable manufacturing cost will equal $280,000.		
12. The total manufacturing cost per unit (rounded to the nearest cent) will equal $69.79.		

EXERCISE 1–14 Cost Classification LO1–2, LO1–3, LO1–4, LO1–5

Wollogong Group Ltd. of New South Wales, Australia, acquired its factory building 10 years ago. For several years, the company has rented out a small annex attached to the rear of the building for $30,000 per year. The renter's lease will expire soon, and rather than renewing the lease, the company has decided to use the annex to manufacture a new product.

Direct materials cost for the new product will total $80 per unit. To have a place to store its finished goods, the company will rent a small warehouse for $500 per month. In addition, the company must rent equipment for $4,000 per month to produce the new product. Direct laborers will be hired and paid $60 per unit to manufacture the new product. As in prior years, the space in the annex will continue to be depreciated at $8,000 per year.

The annual advertising cost for the new product will be $50,000. A supervisor will be hired and paid $3,500 per month to oversee production. Electricity for operating machines will be $1.20 per unit. The cost of shipping the new product to customers will be $9 per unit.

To provide funds to purchase materials, meet payrolls, and so forth, the company will have to liquidate some temporary investments. These investments are presently yielding a return of $3,000 per year.

Required:

Using the table shown below, describe each of the costs associated with the new product decision in four ways. In terms of cost classifications for predicting cost behavior (column 1), indicate whether the cost is fixed or variable. With respect to cost classifications for manufacturers (column 2), if the item is a manufacturing cost, indicate whether it is direct materials, direct labor, or manufacturing overhead. If it is a nonmanufacturing cost, then select "none" as your answer. With respect to cost classifications for preparing financial statements (column 3), indicate whether the item is a product cost or period cost. Finally, in terms of cost classifications for decision making (column 4), identify any items that are sunk costs or opportunity costs. If you identify an item as an opportunity cost, then select "none" as your answer in columns 1–3.

	Cost Classifications for:			
Cost Item	(1) Predicting Cost Behavior	(2) Manufacturers	(3) Preparing Financial Statements	(4) Decision Making

EXERCISE 1–15 Traditional and Contribution Format Income Statements LO1–6

The Alpine House, Inc., is a large retailer of snow skis. The company assembled the information shown below for the quarter ended March 31:

	Amount
Sales...	$150,000
Selling price per pair of skis........................	$750
Variable selling expense per pair of skis............	$50
Variable administrative expense per pair of skis	$10
Total fixed selling expense.........................	$20,000
Total fixed administrative expense	$20,000
Beginning merchandise inventory	$30,000
Ending merchandise inventory	$40,000
Merchandise purchases	$100,000

Required:
1. Prepare a traditional income statement for the quarter ended March 31.
2. Prepare a contribution format income statement for the quarter ended March 31.
3. What was the contribution margin per unit?

EXERCISE 1–16 Cost Classifications for Decision Making LO1–5

Warner Corporation purchased a machine seven years ago for $319,000 when it launched product P50. Unfortunately, this machine has broken down and cannot be repaired. The machine could be replaced by a new model 300 machine costing $313,000 or by a new model 200 machine costing $275,000. Management has decided to buy the model 200 machine. It has less capacity than the model 300 machine, but its capacity is sufficient to continue making product P50. Management also considered, but rejected, the alternative of dropping product P50 and not replacing the old machine. If that were done, the $275,000 invested in the new machine could instead have been invested in a project that would have returned a total of $374,000.

Required:
1. What is the total differential cost regarding the decision to buy the model 200 machine rather than the model 300 machine?
2. What is the total sunk cost regarding the decision to buy the model 200 machine rather than the model 300 machine?
3. What is the total opportunity cost regarding the decision to invest in the model 200 machine?

EXERCISE 1–17 Classifying Variable and Fixed Costs and Product and Period Costs

LO1–3, LO1–4

Below are listed various costs that are found in organizations.
1. Hamburger buns in a Wendy's restaurant.
2. Advertising by a dental office.
3. Apples processed and canned by Del Monte.
4. Shipping canned apples from a Del Monte plant to customers.
5. Insurance on a Bausch & Lomb factory producing contact lenses.
6. Insurance on Nucor's corporate headquarters.
7. Salary of a supervisor overseeing production of printers at Ricoh.
8. Commissions paid to automobile salespersons.
9. Depreciation of factory lunchroom facilities at a General Electric plant.
10. Steering wheels installed in Tesla electric vehicles.

Required:
Using the table shown below, describe each of the costs mentioned above in two ways. In terms of cost classifications for predicting cost behavior (column 1), indicate whether the cost is fixed or

variable with respect to the number of units produced and sold. With respect to cost classifications for preparing financial statements (column 2), indicate whether the item is a product cost or period cost (selling and administrative cost).

	Cost Classifications for:	
Cost Item	(1) Predicting Cost Behavior	(2) Preparing Financial Statements

Problems   Mc Graw Hill connect

PROBLEM 1–18 Direct and Indirect Costs; Variable Costs LO1–1, LO1–4

The following cost data pertain to the operations of Montgomery Department Stores, Inc., for the month of July.

Corporate legal office salaries	$56,000
Apparel Department cost of sales—Evendale Store	$90,000
Corporate headquarters building lease	$48,000
Store manager's salary—Evendale Store	$12,000
Apparel Department sales commission—Evendale Store	$7,000
Store utilities—Evendale Store................................	$11,000
Apparel Department manager's salary—Evendale Store	$8,000
Central warehouse lease cost.................................	$15,000
Janitorial costs—Evendale Store.............................	$9,000

The Evendale Store is one of many stores owned and operated by the company. The Apparel Department is one of many departments at the Evendale Store. The central warehouse serves all of the company's stores.

Required:
1. What is the total amount of the costs listed above that are direct costs of the Apparel Department?
2. What is the total amount of the costs listed above that are direct costs of the Evendale Store?
3. What is the total amount of the Apparel Department's direct costs that are also variable costs with respect to total departmental sales?

PROBLEM 1–19 Traditional and Contribution Format Income Statements LO1–6

Todrick Company is a merchandiser that reported the following information based on 1,000 units sold:

Sales	$300,000
Beginning merchandise inventory...........	$20,000
Purchases.................................	$200,000
Ending merchandise inventory..............	$7,000
Fixed selling expense......................	?
Fixed administrative expense	$12,000
Variable selling expense	$15,000
Variable administrative expense	?
Contribution margin	$60,000
Net operating income	$18,000

Required:

1. Prepare a contribution format income statement.
2. Prepare a traditional format income statement.
3. Calculate the selling price per unit.
4. Calculate the variable cost per unit.
5. Calculate the contribution margin per unit.
6. Which income statement format (traditional format or contribution format) would be more useful to managers in estimating how net operating income will change in response to changes in unit sales? Why?

PROBLEM 1–20 Variable and Fixed Costs; Subtleties of Direct and Indirect Costs LO1–1, LO1–4

Madison Seniors Care Center is a nonprofit organization that provides a variety of health services to the elderly. The center is organized into a number of departments, one of which is the Meals-On-Wheels program that delivers hot meals to seniors in their homes on a daily basis. Below are listed a number of costs of the center and the Meals-On-Wheels program.

example The cost of groceries used in meal preparation.
    a. The cost of leasing the Meals-On-Wheels van.
    b. The cost of incidental supplies such as salt, pepper, napkins, and so on.
    c. The cost of gasoline consumed by the Meals-On-Wheels van.
    d. The rent on the facility that houses Madison Seniors Care Center, including the Meals-On-Wheels program.
    e. The salary of the part-time manager of the Meals-On-Wheels program.
    f. Depreciation on the kitchen equipment used in the Meals-On-Wheels program.
    g. The hourly wages of the caregiver who drives the van and delivers the meals.
    h. The costs of complying with health safety regulations in the kitchen.
    i. The costs of mailing letters soliciting donations to the Meals-On-Wheels program.

Required:

For each cost listed above, indicate whether it is a direct or indirect cost of the Meals-On-Wheels program, whether it is a direct or indirect cost of particular seniors served by the program, and whether it is variable or fixed with respect to the number of seniors served. Use the form below for your answer.

Item	Description	Direct or Indirect Cost of the Meals-on-Wheels Program		Direct or Indirect Cost of Particular Seniors Served by the Meals-on-Wheels Program		Variable or Fixed with Respect to the Number of Seniors Served by the Meals-on-Wheels Program	
		Direct	Indirect	Direct	Indirect	Variable	Fixed
Example	The cost of groceries used in meal preparation..............	X		X		X	

PROBLEM 1–21 Traditional and Contribution Format Income Statements LO1–6

Marwick's Pianos, Inc., purchases pianos from a large manufacturer for an average cost of $2,450 per unit and then sells them to retail customers for an average price of $3,125 each. The company's selling and administrative costs for a typical month are presented below:

Costs	Cost Formula
Selling:	
Advertising	$700 per month
Sales salaries and commissions	$950 per month, plus 8% of sales
Delivery of pianos to customers	$30 per piano sold
Utilities.....................................	$350 per month
Depreciation of sales facilities..............	$800 per month
Administrative:	
Executive salaries.........................	$2,500 per month
Insurance..................................	$400 per month
Clerical....................................	$1,000 per month, plus $20 per piano sold
Depreciation of office equipment	$300 per month

During August, Marwick's Pianos, Inc., sold and delivered 40 pianos.

Required:

1. Prepare a traditional format income statement for August.
2. Prepare a contribution format income statement for August. Show costs and revenues on both a total and a per-unit basis down through contribution margin.
3. Refer to the income statement you prepared in (2) above. Why might it be misleading to show the fixed costs on a per-unit basis?

PROBLEM 1–22 Cost Terminology; Contribution Format Income Statement LO1–2, LO1–4, LO1–6

Miller Company's total sales are $120,000. The company's direct labor cost is $15,000, which represents 30% of its total conversion cost and 40% of its total prime cost. Its total selling and administrative expense is $18,000, and its only variable selling and administrative expense is a sales commission of 5% of sales. The company maintains no beginning or ending inventories, and its manufacturing overhead costs are entirely fixed costs.

Required:

1. What is the total manufacturing overhead cost?
2. What is the total direct materials cost?
3. What is the total manufacturing cost?
4. What is the total variable selling and administrative cost?
5. What is the total variable cost?
6. What is the total fixed cost?
7. What is the total contribution margin?

PROBLEM 1–23 Cost Classification LO1–1, LO1–3, LO1–4

Listed below are costs found in various organizations.

1. Property taxes, factory.
2. Boxes used for packaging detergent produced by the company.
3. Salespersons' commissions.
4. Supervisor's salary, factory.
5. Depreciation, executive autos.
6. Wages of workers assembling computers.
7. Insurance, finished goods warehouses.
8. Lubricants for production equipment.
9. Advertising costs.
10. Microchips used in producing calculators.
11. Shipping costs on merchandise sold.
12. Magazine subscriptions, factory lunchroom.
13. Thread in a garment factory.
14. Executive life insurance.
15. Ink used in textbook production.

16. Fringe benefits, materials handling workers.
17. Yarn used in sweater production.
18. Wages of receptionist, executive offices.

Required:
Prepare an answer sheet with column headings as shown below. For each cost item, indicate whether it would be variable or fixed with respect to the number of units produced and sold; and then whether it would be a selling cost, an administrative cost, or a manufacturing cost. If it is a manufacturing cost, indicate whether it is a direct cost or an indirect cost with respect to units of product. Three sample answers are provided for illustration.

Cost Item	Variable or Fixed	Selling Cost	Administrative Cost	Manufacturing (Product) Cost Direct	Manufacturing (Product) Cost Indirect
Direct labor	V			X	
Executive salaries	F		X		
Factory rent	F				X

PROBLEM 1–24 Different Cost Classifications for Different Purposes LO1–1, LO1–2, LO1–3, LO1–4, LO1–5

Dozier Company produced and sold 1,000 units during its first month of operations. It reported the following costs and expenses for the month:

Direct materials.		$69,000
Direct labor		$35,000
Variable manufacturing overhead.	$15,000	
Fixed manufacturing overhead	28,000	
Total manufacturing overhead.		$43,000
Variable selling expense.	$12,000	
Fixed selling expense	18,000	
Total selling expense.		$30,000
Variable administrative expense	$ 4,000	
Fixed administrative expense	25,000	
Total administrative expense		$29,000

Required:
1. With respect to cost classifications for preparing financial statements:
   a. What is the total product cost?
   b. What is the total period cost?
2. With respect to cost classifications for assigning costs to cost objects:
   a. What is total direct manufacturing cost?
   b. What is the total indirect manufacturing cost?
3. With respect to cost classifications for manufacturers:
   a. What is the total manufacturing cost?
   b. What is the total nonmanufacturing cost?
   c. What is the total conversion cost and prime cost?
4. With respect to cost classifications for predicting cost behavior:
   a. What is the total variable manufacturing cost?
   b. What is the total fixed cost for the company as a whole?
   c. What is the variable cost per unit produced and sold?
5. With respect to cost classifications for decision making:
   a. If Dozier had produced 1,001 units instead of 1,000 units, how much incremental manufacturing cost would it have incurred to make the additional unit?

PROBLEM 1–25 Traditional and Contribution Format Income Statements LO1–6

Milden Company is a merchandiser that plans to sell 12,000 units during the next quarter at a selling price of $100 per unit. The company also gathered the following cost estimates for the next quarter:

Cost	Cost Formula
Cost of good sold....................	$35 per unit sold
Advertising expense................	$210,000 per quarter
Sales commissions.................	6% of sales
Shipping expense..................	$28,000 per quarter + $9.10 per unit sold
Administrative salaries..............	$145,000 per quarter
Insurance expense.................	$9,000 per quarter
Depreciation expense..............	$76,000 per quarter

Required:

1. Prepare a contribution format income statement for the next quarter.
2. Prepare a traditional format income statement for the next quarter.

Cases

Select cases are available in Connect.

CASE 1–26 Cost Classification and Cost Behavior LO1–1, LO1–2, LO1–3, LO1–4

The Dorilane Company produces a set of wood patio furniture consisting of a table and four chairs. The company has enough customer demand to justify producing its full capacity of 2,000 sets per year. Annual cost data at full capacity follow:

Direct labor......................................	$118,000
Advertising......................................	$50,000
Factory supervision.............................	$40,000
Property taxes, factory building....................	$3,500
Sales commissions.............................	$80,000
Insurance, factory................................	$2,500
Depreciation, administrative office equipment......	$4,000
Lease cost, factory equipment....................	$12,000
Indirect materials, factory........................	$6,000
Depreciation, factory building....................	$10,000
Administrative office supplies (billing).............	$3,000
Administrative office salaries.....................	$60,000
Direct materials used (wood, bolts, etc.)...........	$94,000
Utilities, factory.................................	$20,000

Required:

1. Prepare an answer sheet with the column headings shown below. Enter each cost item on your answer sheet, placing the dollar amount under the appropriate headings. As examples, this has been done already for the first two items in the list above. Note that each cost item is classified in two ways: first, as variable or fixed with respect to the number of units produced and sold;

and second, as a selling and administrative cost or a product cost. (If the item is a product cost, it should also be classified as either direct or indirect, as shown.)

Cost Item	Cost Behavior		Period (Selling or Administrative) Cost	Product Cost	
	Variable	Fixed		Direct	Indirect*
Direct labor	$118,000			$118,000	
Advertising		$50,000	$50,000		

* To units of product.

2. Total the dollar amounts in each of the columns in (1) above. Compute the average product cost of one patio set.
3. Assume production drops to only 1,000 sets annually. Would you expect the average product cost per set to increase, decrease, or remain unchanged? Explain. No computations are necessary.
4. Refer to the original data. The president's brother-in-law considered making himself a patio set and priced the necessary materials at a building supply store. The brother-in-law asked the president if he could purchase a patio set from the Dorilane Company "at cost," and the president agreed to let him do so.
   a. Would you expect any disagreement between the two men over the price the brother-in-law should pay? Explain. What price does the president probably have in mind? The brother-in-law?
   b. Because the company is operating at full capacity, what cost term used in the chapter might be justification for the president to charge the full, regular price to the brother-in-law and still be selling "at cost"?

CASE 1–27 Ethics and the Manager LO1–3

M. K. Gallant is president of Kranbrack Corporation, a company whose stock is traded on a national exchange. In a meeting with investment analysts at the beginning of the year, Gallant had predicted that the company's earnings would grow by 20% this year. Unfortunately, sales have been less than expected for the year, and Gallant concluded within two weeks of the end of the fiscal year that it would be impossible to report an increase in earnings as large as predicted unless some drastic action was taken. Accordingly, Gallant has ordered that wherever possible, expenditures should be postponed to the new year—including canceling or postponing orders with suppliers, delaying planned maintenance and training, and cutting back on end-of-year advertising and travel. Additionally, Gallant ordered the company's controller to carefully scrutinize all costs currently classified as period costs and reclassify as many as possible as product costs. The company is expected to have substantial inventories at the end of the year.

Required:

1. Why would reclassifying period costs as product costs increase this period's reported earnings?
2. Do you believe Gallant's actions are ethical? Why or why not?

Cost-Volume-Profit Relationships

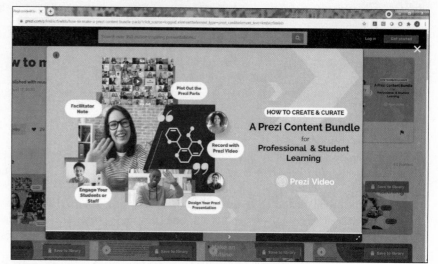

Prezi Inc.

LEARNING OBJECTIVES

After studying Chapter 2, you should be able to:

LO 2–1 Explain how changes in sales volume affect contribution margin and net operating income.

LO 2–2 Prepare and interpret a cost-volume-profit (CVP) graph and a profit graph.

LO 2–3 Use the contribution margin ratio (CM ratio) to compute changes in contribution margin and net operating income resulting from changes in sales volume.

LO 2–4 Show the effects on net operating income of changes in variable costs, fixed costs, selling price, and sales volume.

LO 2–5 Determine the break-even point.

LO 2–6 Determine the level of sales needed to achieve a desired target profit.

LO 2–7 Compute the margin of safety and explain its significance.

LO 2–8 Compute the degree of operating leverage at a particular level of sales and explain how it can be used to predict changes in net operating income.

LO 2–9 Compute the break-even point for a multiproduct company and explain the effects of shifts in the sales mix on contribution margin and the break-even point.

LO 2–10 *(Appendix 2A) Analyze a mixed cost using a scattergraph plot and the high-low method.*

LO 2–11 *(Appendix 2A) Analyze a mixed cost using a scattergraph plot and the least-squares regression method.*

Data Analytics Exercise available in Connect to complement this chapter

ENTREPRENEUR SPOTLIGHT

Peter Arvai is the cofounder of Prezi, a company that sells state-of-the-art presentation software. His company's products help oral presenters to better organize and deliver their thoughts, thereby enabling the audience to reach "that 'ah-hah' moment faster." Today Prezi supports over 100 million users who have made more than 360 million presentations. The company's website cites user-based research that claims Prezi is 12.5% more organized, 16.4% more engaging, 21.9% more persuasive, and 25.3% more effective than PowerPoint.

Managerial Accounting: The Practical Application
Prezi sells three main product lines (Prezi Present, Prezi Video, and Prezi Design) on one software platform in standard, plus, and premium packages to three customer segments—individual, students & educators, and business. As the company considers what prices to charge for its various software packages across its three customer segments, it would use cost-volume-profit (CVP) analysis to answer the question: What will be the impact on profits of implementing one pricing plan versus another? If the company raises its prices, it will likely cause unit sales to decline, and vice versa—lowering its prices will likely cause unit sales to increase. CVP analysis can help the company find the price points it believes will maximize profits.

Corporate Social Responsibility: Serving all Stakeholders
Peter Arvai played an instrumental role in founding WeAreOpen—a nonprofit entity that promotes diversity and inclusion in the workplace. The organization's core belief is that a company's employees and its business partners should be "judged solely on the basis of their actions and their work performance, and without regard for their sex, age, sexual orientation, national or ethnic background, political convictions, physical abilities, or other characteristics." To date, more than 1,000 companies have publicly joined and supported the WeAreOpen mission. Arvai has also founded another non-profit called BridgeBudapest "to encourage young Hungarians to believe that global success can happen from Hungary." ■

Sources: www.prezi.com, https://nyitottakvagyunk.hu/en/about-us/, https://bridgebudapest.org/.

Cavan Images/Alamy Stock Photo

Cost-volume-profit (CVP) analysis helps managers make many important decisions, such as what products and services to offer, what prices to charge, what marketing strategy to use, and what cost structure to maintain. Its primary purpose is to estimate how profits are affected by the following five factors:

1. Selling prices.
2. Sales volume.
3. Unit variable costs.
4. Total fixed costs.
5. Mix of products sold.

To simplify CVP calculations, managers typically adopt the following assumptions with respect to these factors[1]:

1. Selling price is constant. The price of a product or service will not change as volume changes.
2. Costs are linear and can be accurately divided into variable and fixed components. The variable costs are constant per unit, and the fixed costs are constant in total over the entire relevant range.
3. In multiproduct companies, the mix of products sold remains constant.

While these assumptions may be violated in practice, the results of CVP analysis are often "good enough" to be quite useful. Perhaps the greatest danger lies in relying on simple CVP analysis when a manager is contemplating a large change in sales volume that lies outside the relevant range. However, even in these situations, the CVP model can be adjusted to take into account anticipated changes in selling prices, variable costs per unit, total fixed costs, and the sales mix that arise when the estimated sales volume falls outside the relevant range.

To help explain the role of CVP analysis in business decisions, we'll turn our attention to the case of Acoustic Concepts, Inc., a company founded by Prem Narayan.

MANAGERIAL ACCOUNTING IN ACTION

THE ISSUE

ACOUSTIC concepts inc

Prem, who was a graduate student in engineering at the time, started Acoustic Concepts, Inc., to market a radical new speaker he had designed for automobile sound systems. The speaker, called the Sonic Blaster, uses an advanced microprocessor and proprietary software to boost amplification to awesome levels. Prem contracted with a Taiwanese electronics manufacturer to produce the speaker. With seed money provided by his family, Prem placed an order with the manufacturer and ran advertisements in auto magazines.

The Sonic Blaster was an immediate success, and sales grew to the point that Prem moved the company's headquarters out of his apartment and into rented quarters in a nearby industrial park. He also hired a receptionist, an accountant, a sales manager, and a small sales staff to sell the speakers to retail stores. The accountant, Bob Luchinni, had worked for several small companies where he had acted as a business advisor, as well as accountant and bookkeeper. The following discussion occurred soon after Bob was hired:

Prem: Bob, I've got a lot of questions about the company's finances I hope you can help answer.

Bob: We're in great shape. The loan from your family will be paid off within a few months.

Prem: I know, but I am worried about the risks I've taken on by expanding operations. What would happen if a competitor entered the market and our sales slipped? How far could sales drop without putting us into the red? Another question I've been trying to resolve is how much our sales would have to increase to justify the big marketing campaign the sales staff is pushing for.

Bob: Marketing always wants more money for advertising.

---

[1] One additional assumption often used in manufacturing companies is that inventories do not change. The number of units produced equals the number of units sold.

Prem: And they are always pushing me to drop the selling price on the speaker. I agree with them that a lower price will boost our sales volume, but I'm not sure the increased volume will offset the loss in revenue from the lower price.

Bob: It sounds like these questions are all related in some way to the relationships among our selling prices, our costs, and our volume. I shouldn't have a problem coming up with some answers.

Prem: Can we meet again in a couple of days to see what you have come up with?

Bob: Sounds good. By then I'll have some preliminary answers for you as well as a model you can use for answering similar questions in the future.

The Basics of Cost-Volume-Profit (CVP) Analysis

Bob Luchinni's preparation for his forthcoming meeting with Prem Narayan begins with the contribution format income statement introduced in the previous chapter. The contribution income statement emphasizes the behavior of costs and, therefore, is extremely helpful to managers in judging how changes in selling price, cost, or volume impact profits. Bob will base his analysis on the following contribution income statement he prepared last month:

Acoustic Concepts, Inc. Contribution Format Income Statement For the Month of June		
	Total	Per Unit
Sales (400 speakers)..........	$100,000	$250
Variable expenses	60,000	150
Contribution margin............	40,000	$100
Fixed expenses................	35,000	
Net operating income..........	$ 5,000	

Notice that sales, variable expenses, and contribution margin are expressed on a per-unit basis, as well as in total on this contribution income statement. The per-unit figures will be very helpful to Bob in some of his calculations. Note that this contribution income statement has been prepared for management's use inside the company and would not ordinarily be made available to those outside the company.

Contribution Margin

LEARNING OBJECTIVE 2-1

Explain how changes in sales volume affect contribution margin and net operating income.

Contribution margin is the amount remaining from sales revenue after variable expenses have been deducted. Thus, it is the amount available to cover fixed expenses and then to provide profits for the period. Notice the sequence here—contribution margin is used *first* to cover the fixed expenses, and then whatever remains goes toward profits. If the contribution margin is not sufficient to cover the fixed expenses, then a loss occurs for the period. To illustrate with an extreme example, assume that Acoustic Concepts sells only one speaker during a particular month. The company's income statement would appear as follows:

Contribution Format Income Statement Sale of 1 Speaker		
	Total	Per Unit
Sales (1 speaker)............	$ 250	$250
Variable expenses	150	150
Contribution margin..........	100	$100
Fixed expenses..............	35,000	
Net operating loss...........	$(34,900)	

For each additional speaker the company sells during the month, $100 more in contribution margin becomes available to help cover the fixed expenses. If a second speaker is sold, for example, then the total contribution margin will increase by $100 (to a total of $200) and the company's loss will decrease by $100, to $34,800:

Contribution Format Income Statement
Sales of 2 Speakers

	Total	Per Unit
Sales (2 speakers).............	$ 500	$250
Variable expenses.............	300	150
Contribution margin	200	$100
Fixed expenses	35,000	
Net operating loss	$(34,800)	

If enough speakers can be sold to generate $35,000 in contribution margin, then all of the fixed expenses will be covered and the company will *break even* for the month—that is, it will show neither profit nor loss but just cover all of its costs. To reach the break-even point, the company will have to sell 350 speakers in a month because each speaker sold yields $100 in contribution margin:

Contribution Format Income Statement
Sales of 350 Speakers

	Total	Per Unit
Sales (350 speakers)	$87,500	$250
Variable expenses.............	52,500	150
Contribution margin	35,000	$100
Fixed expenses	35,000	
Net operating income..........	$ 0	

Computation of the break-even point is discussed in detail later in the chapter; for the moment, note that the **break-even point** is the level of sales at which profit is zero.

Once the break-even point has been reached, net operating income will increase by the amount of the unit contribution margin for each additional unit sold. For example, if 351 speakers are sold in a month, then the net operating income for the month will be $100 because the company will have sold 1 speaker more than the number needed to break even:

Contribution Format Income Statement
Sales of 351 Speakers

	Total	Per Unit
Sales (351 speakers)	$87,750	$250
Variable expenses.............	52,650	150
Contribution margin	35,100	$100
Fixed expenses	35,000	
Net operating income..........	$ 100	

If 352 speakers are sold (2 speakers above the break-even point), the net operating income for the month will be $200. If 353 speakers are sold (3 speakers above the break-even point), the net operating income for the month will be $300, and so forth. To estimate the profit at any sales volume above the break-even point, multiply the number of units sold in excess of the break-even point by the unit contribution margin. The result represents the anticipated profits for the period. Or, to estimate the effect of a planned increase in sales volume on profits, simply multiply the increase in units sold by the unit contribution margin. The result will be the expected increase in profits. To illustrate, if Acoustic Concepts is currently selling 400 speakers per month and plans to increase sales to 425 speakers per month, the anticipated impact on profits can be computed as follows:

Additional speakers to be sold...............	25
Contribution margin per speaker.............	× $100
Increase in net operating income	$2,500

These calculations can be verified as follows:

	Sales Volume			
	400 Speakers	**425 Speakers**	**Difference (25 Speakers)**	**Per Unit**
Sales (@ $250 per speaker)......	$100,000	$106,250	$6,250	$250
Variable expenses				
(@ $150 per speaker)	60,000	63,750	3,750	150
Contribution margin.............	40,000	42,500	2,500	$100
Fixed expenses.................	35,000	35,000	0	
Net operating income...........	$ 5,000	$ 7,500	$2,500	

To summarize, if sales are zero, the company's loss would equal its fixed expenses. Each unit sold reduces the loss by the amount of the unit contribution margin. Once the break-even point has been reached, each additional unit sold increases the company's profit by the amount of the unit contribution margin.

CVP Relationships in Equation Form

The contribution format income statement can be expressed in equation form as follows:

$$\text{Profit} = (\text{Sales} - \text{Variable expenses}) - \text{Fixed expenses}$$

For brevity, we use the term *profit* to stand for net operating income in equations.

When a company has only a *single* product, as at Acoustic Concepts, we can further refine the equation as follows:

$$\text{Sales} = \text{Selling price per unit} \times \text{Quantity sold} = P \times Q$$

$$\text{Variable expenses} = \text{Variable expenses per unit} \times \text{Quantity sold} = V \times Q$$

$$\text{Profit} = (P \times Q - V \times Q) - \text{Fixed expenses}$$

We can do all of the calculations of the previous section using this simple equation. For example, earlier we computed the net operating income (profit) from sales of 351 speakers would be $100. We arrive at the same conclusion using the above equation as follows:

$$\text{Profit} = (P \times Q - V \times Q) - \text{Fixed expenses}$$
$$\text{Profit} = (\$250 \times 351 - \$150 \times 351) - \$35,000$$
$$= (\$250 - \$150) \times 351 - \$35,000$$
$$= (\$100) \times 351 - \$35,000$$
$$= \$35,100 - \$35,000$$
$$= \$100$$

It is often useful to express the simple profit equation in terms of the unit contribution margin (Unit CM) as follows:

Unit CM = Selling price per unit − Variable expenses per unit = $P − V$

Profit = $(P \times Q − V \times Q)$ − Fixed expenses

Profit = $(P − V) \times Q$ − Fixed expenses

Profit = Unit CM $\times Q$ − Fixed expenses

We could also have used this equation to determine the profit from sales of 351 speakers as follows:

$$\text{Profit} = \text{Unit CM} \times Q − \text{Fixed expenses}$$

$$= \$100 \times 351 − \$35,000$$

$$= \$35,100 − \$35,000$$

$$= \$100$$

For those who are comfortable with algebra, the quickest and easiest approach to solving the problems in this chapter may be to use the simple profit equation in one of its forms.

CVP Relationships in Graphic Form

The relationships among revenue, cost, profit, and volume are illustrated on a **cost-volume-profit (CVP) graph.** A CVP graph highlights CVP relationships over wide ranges of activity. To help explain his analysis to Prem Narayan, Bob Luchinni prepared a CVP graph for Acoustic Concepts.

LEARNING OBJECTIVE 2–2
Prepare and interpret a cost-volume-profit (CVP) graph and a profit graph.

Preparing the CVP Graph In a CVP graph (sometimes called a *break-even chart*), unit volume is represented on the horizontal (*X*) axis and dollars on the vertical (*Y*) axis. Preparing a CVP graph involves the three steps depicted in Exhibit 2–1:

1. Draw a line parallel to the volume axis to represent total fixed expense. For Acoustic Concepts, total fixed expenses are $35,000.
2. Choose some volume of unit sales and plot the point representing total expense (fixed and variable) at the sales volume you have selected. In Exhibit 2–1, Bob Luchinni chose a volume of 600 speakers. Total expense at that sales volume is:

Fixed expense	$ 35,000
Variable expense (600 speakers × $150 per speaker)	90,000
Total expense	$125,000

After the point has been plotted, draw a line through it back to the point where the fixed expense line intersects the dollars axis.
3. Again choose some sales volume and plot the point representing total sales dollars at the activity level you have selected. In Exhibit 2–1, Bob Luchinni again chose a volume of 600 speakers. Sales at that volume total $150,000 (600 speakers × $250 per speaker). Draw a line through this point back to the origin.

The interpretation of the completed CVP graph is given in Exhibit 2–2. The anticipated profit or loss at any given level of sales is measured by the vertical distance between the total revenue line (sales) and the total expense line (variable expense plus fixed expense).

EXHIBIT 2–1
Preparing the CVP Graph

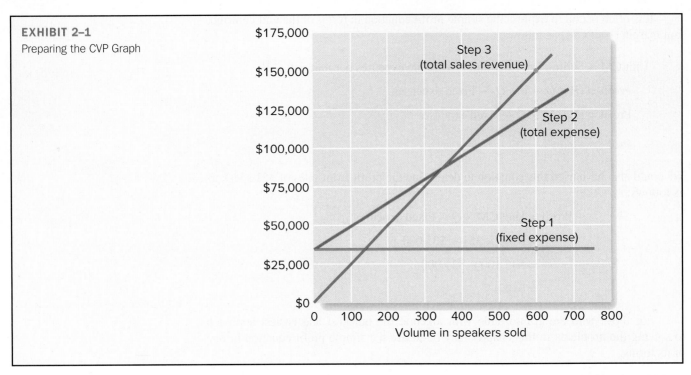

EXHIBIT 2–2
The Completed CVP Graph

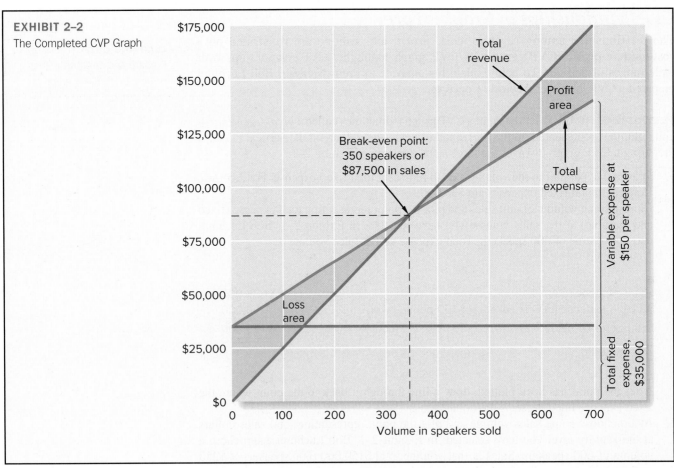

The break-even point is where the total revenue and total expense lines cross. The break-even point of 350 speakers in Exhibit 2–2 agrees with the break-even point computed earlier.

When sales are below the break-even point—in this case, 350 units—the company suffers a loss. Note that the loss (represented by the vertical distance between the total expense

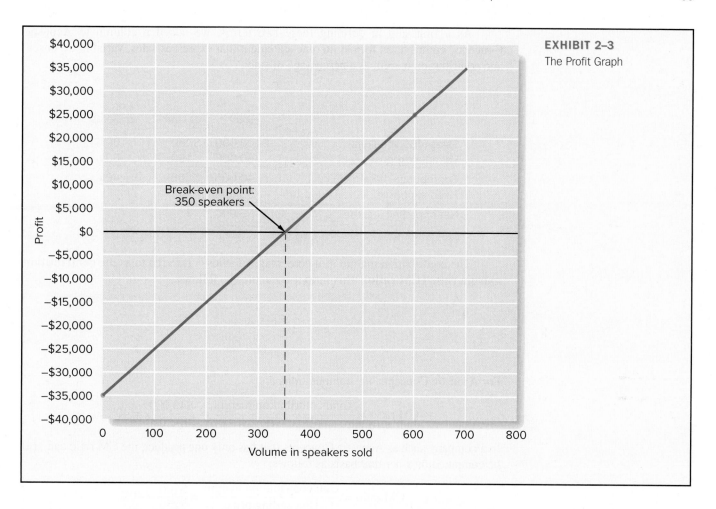

EXHIBIT 2–3
The Profit Graph

and total revenue lines) gets bigger as sales decline. When sales are above the break-even point, the company earns a profit and the size of the profit (represented by the vertical distance between the total revenue and total expense lines) increases as sales increase.

An even simpler form of the CVP graph, which we call a profit graph, is presented in Exhibit 2–3. That graph is based on the following equation:

$$\text{Profit} = \text{Unit CM} \times Q - \text{Fixed expenses}$$

In the case of Acoustic Concepts, the equation can be expressed as:

$$\text{Profit} = \$100 \times Q - \$35,000$$

Because this is a linear equation, it plots as a single straight line. To plot the line, compute the profit at two different sales volumes, plot the points, and then connect them with a straight line. For example, when the sales volume is zero (i.e., $Q = 0$), the profit is −$35,000 (= $100 × 0 − $35,000). When Q is 600, the profit is $25,000 (= $100 × 600 − $35,000). These two points are plotted in Exhibit 2–3 and a straight line has been drawn through them.

The break-even point on the profit graph is the volume of sales at which profit is zero and is indicated by the dashed line on the graph. Note that the profit steadily increases to the right of the break-even point as the sales volume increases and the loss becomes steadily worse to the left of the break-even point as the sales volume decreases.

Contribution Margin Ratio (CM Ratio) and the Variable Expense Ratio

In the previous section, we explored how CVP relationships can be visualized. This section begins by defining the *contribution margin ratio* and the *variable expense ratio*. Then it demonstrates how to use the contribution margin ratio in CVP calculations.

As a first step in defining these two terms, we added a column to Acoustic Concepts' contribution format income statement that expresses sales, variable expenses, and contribution margin as a percentage of sales:

	Total	Per Unit	Percent of Sales
Sales (400 speakers)............	$100,000	$250	100%
Variable expenses...............	60,000	150	60%
Contribution margin.............	40,000	$100	40%
Fixed expenses.................	35,000		
Net operating income...........	$ 5,000		

The contribution margin as a percentage of sales is referred to as the **contribution margin ratio (CM ratio).** This ratio is computed as follows:

$$\text{CM ratio} = \frac{\text{Contribution margin}}{\text{Sales}}$$

For Acoustic Concepts, the computations are:

$$\text{CM ratio} = \frac{\text{Total contribution margin}}{\text{Total sales}} = \frac{\$40,000}{\$100,000} = 40\%$$

In a company such as Acoustic Concepts that has only one product, the CM ratio can also be computed on a per-unit basis as follows:

$$\text{CM ratio} = \frac{\text{Unit contribution margin}}{\text{Unit selling price}} = \frac{\$100}{\$250} = 40\%$$

Similarly, the variable expenses as a percentage of sales is referred to as the **variable expense ratio.** This ratio is computed as follows:

$$\text{Variable expense ratio} = \frac{\text{Variable expenses}}{\text{Sales}}$$

For Acoustic Concepts, the computations are:

$$\text{Variable expense ratio} = \frac{\text{Total variable expenses}}{\text{Total sales}} = \frac{\$60,000}{\$100,000} = 60\%$$

Because Acoustic Concepts has only one product, the variable expense ratio can also be computed on a per-unit basis as follows:

$$\text{Variable expense ratio} = \frac{\text{Variable expense per unit}}{\text{Unit selling price}} = \frac{\$150}{\$250} = 60\%$$

Having defined the two terms, it bears emphasizing that the contribution margin ratio and the variable expense ratio can be mathematically related to one another:

$$\text{CM ratio} = \frac{\text{Contribution margin}}{\text{Sales}}$$

$$\text{CM ratio} = \frac{\text{Sales} - \text{Variable expenses}}{\text{Sales}}$$

$$\text{CM ratio} = 1 - \text{Variable expense ratio}$$

So, in the case of Acoustic Concepts, this relationship would be as follows:

$$\text{CM ratio} = 1 - \text{Variable expense ratio}$$
$$= 1 - 60\%$$
$$= 40\%$$

Applications of the Contribution Margin Ratio The CM ratio shows how the contribution margin will be affected by a change in sales volume. Acoustic Concepts' CM ratio of 40% means that for each dollar increase in sales, total contribution margin will increase by 40 cents ($1 sales × CM ratio of 40%). Net operating income will also increase by 40 cents, assuming that fixed costs are not affected by the increase in unit sales. Generally, the effect of a change in sales volume on the contribution margin is expressed in equation form as:

LEARNING OBJECTIVE 2–3
Use the contribution margin ratio (CM ratio) to compute changes in contribution margin and net operating income resulting from changes in sales volume.

$$\text{Change in contribution margin} = \text{CM ratio} \times \text{Change in sales}$$

As this equation shows, *the impact on net operating income of a change in the sales volume can be computed by multiplying the CM ratio by the corresponding change in dollar sales.* For example, if Acoustic Concepts plans to increase unit sales by 120 speakers next month, it will increase total sales by $30,000 (= 120 speakers × $250 per speaker). Using the equation shown above, we can quickly determine that this increase in sales will also increase contribution margin by $12,000 ($30,000 increase in sales × CM ratio of 40%). If fixed costs do not change, net operating income will also increase by $12,000. This is verified by the following table:

	Sales Volume			Percent of Sales
	Present	Expected	Increase	
Sales......................	$100,000	$130,000	$30,000	100%
Variable expenses	60,000	78,000*	18,000	60%
Contribution margin...........	40,000	52,000	12,000	40%
Fixed expenses...............	35,000	35,000	0	
Net operating income	$ 5,000	$ 17,000	$12,000	

*$130,000 expected sales ÷ $250 per unit = 520 units. 520 units × $150 per unit = $78,000.

The relation between profit and the CM ratio can also be expressed using the following equation:

$$\text{Profit} = \text{CM ratio} \times \text{Sales} - \text{Fixed expenses}^2$$

or, in terms of changes,

$$\text{Change in profit} = \text{CM ratio} \times \text{Change in sales} - \text{Change in fixed expenses}$$

---

[2]   This equation can be derived using the basic profit equation and the definition of the CM ratio as follows:

Profit = (Sales − Variable expenses) − Fixed expenses

Profit = Contribution margin − Fixed expenses

$$\text{Profit} = \frac{\text{Contribution margin}}{\text{Sales}} \times \text{Sales} - \text{Fixed expenses}$$

Profit = CM ratio × Sales − Fixed expenses

For example, at sales of $130,000, the profit is expected to be $17,000 as shown below:

$$\text{Profit} = \text{CM ratio} \times \text{Sales} - \text{Fixed expenses}$$
$$= 0.40 \times \$130,000 - \$35,000$$
$$= \$52,000 - \$35,000$$
$$= \$17,000$$

Again, if you are comfortable with algebra, this approach is usually quicker than constructing contribution format income statements.

The CM ratio is particularly valuable in situations where the dollar sales of one product must be traded off against the dollar sales of another product. In this situation, products that yield the greatest amount of contribution margin per dollar of sales should be emphasized.

Additional Applications of CVP Concepts

LEARNING OBJECTIVE 2–4

Show the effects on net operating income of changes in variable costs, fixed costs, selling price, and sales volume.

Having demonstrated how to use the contribution margin ratio in CVP calculations, Bob Luchinni, the accountant at Acoustic Concepts, wanted to offer the company's president, Prem Narayan, five additional examples of how CVP analysis can be used to answer the types of questions their company is facing. So, he began by reminding Prem that the company's fixed expenses are $35,000 per month, and he restated the following key pieces of data:

	Per Unit	Percent of Sales
Selling price................	$250	100%
Variable expenses	150	60%
Contribution margin	$100	40%

Example 1: Change in Fixed Cost and Sales Volume Acoustic Concepts is currently selling 400 speakers per month at $250 per speaker for total monthly sales of $100,000. The sales manager feels that a $10,000 increase in the monthly advertising budget would increase monthly sales by $30,000 to a total of 520 units. Should the advertising budget be increased? The table below shows the financial impact of the proposed change in the monthly advertising budget.

	Current Sales	Sales with Additional Advertising Budget	Difference	Percent of Sales
Sales.............................	$100,000	$130,000	$30,000	100%
Variable expenses	60,000	78,000*	18,000	60%
Contribution margin.................	40,000	52,000	12,000	40%
Fixed expenses....................	35,000	45,000'	10,000	
Net operating income	$ 5,000	$ 7,000	$ 2,000	

*520 units × $150 per unit = $78,000.
'$35,000 + additional $10,000 monthly advertising budget = $45,000.

Assuming no other factors need to be considered, the increase in the advertising budget should be approved because it would increase net operating income by $2,000. There are two shorter ways to arrive at this solution. The first alternative solution follows:

Alternative Solution 1

Expected total contribution margin:	
$130,000 × 40% CM ratio	$52,000
Present total contribution margin:	
$100,000 × 40% CM ratio	40,000
Increase in total contribution margin	12,000
Change in fixed expenses:	
Less incremental advertising expense	10,000
Increased net operating income	$ 2,000

Because in this case only the fixed costs and the sales volume change, the solution can also be quickly derived as follows:

Alternative Solution 2

Incremental contribution margin:	
$30,000 × 40% CM ratio	$12,000
Less incremental advertising expense	10,000
Increased net operating income	$ 2,000

Notice that this approach does not depend on knowledge of previous sales. Also note that it is unnecessary under either shorter approach to prepare an income statement. Both of the alternative solutions involve **incremental analysis**—that is, they consider only the costs and revenues that will change if the new program is implemented. Although in each case a new income statement could have been prepared, the incremental approach is simpler and more direct and focuses attention on the specific changes that would occur as a result of the decision.

Example 2: Change in Variable Costs and Sales Volume Refer to the original data. Recall that Acoustic Concepts is currently selling 400 speakers per month. Prem is considering the use of higher-quality components, which would increase variable costs (and thereby reduce the contribution margin) by $10 per speaker. However, the sales manager predicts using higher-quality components will increase sales to 480 speakers per month. Should the higher-quality components be used?

The $10 increase in variable costs would decrease the unit contribution margin by $10—from $100 down to $90.

Solution

Expected total contribution margin with higher-quality components:	
480 speakers × $90 per speaker	$43,200
Present total contribution margin:	
400 speakers × $100 per speaker	40,000
Increase in total contribution margin	$ 3,200

According to this analysis, the higher-quality components should be used. Because fixed costs would not change, the $3,200 increase in contribution margin shown above should result in a $3,200 increase in net operating income.

Example 3: Change in Fixed Cost, Selling Price, and Sales Volume

Refer to the original data and recall again that Acoustic Concepts is currently selling 400 speakers per month. To increase sales, the sales manager would like to cut the selling price by $20 per speaker and increase the advertising budget by $15,000 per month.

The sales manager believes if these two steps are taken, unit sales will increase by 50 percent to 600 speakers per month. Should the changes be made?

A decrease in the selling price of $20 per speaker would decrease the unit contribution margin by $20 down to $80.

Solution

Expected total contribution margin with lower selling price:	
600 speakers × $80 per speaker...............	$48,000
Present total contribution margin:	
400 speakers × $100 per speaker	40,000
Incremental contribution margin	8,000
Change in fixed expenses:	
Less incremental advertising expense...........	15,000
Reduction in net operating income	$ (7,000)

According to this analysis, the changes should not be made. The $7,000 reduction in net operating income shown above can be verified by preparing comparative contribution format income statements as shown here:

	Present 400 Speakers per Month		Expected 600 Speakers per Month		
	Total	Per Unit	Total	Per Unit	Difference
Sales.......................	$100,000	$250	$138,000	$230	$38,000
Variable expenses	60,000	150	90,000	150	30,000
Contribution margin..........	40,000	$100	48,000	$ 80	8,000
Fixed expenses..............	35,000		50,000*		15,000
Net operating income (loss)...	$ 5,000		$ (2,000)		$ (7,000)

*$35,000 + Additional monthly advertising budget of $15,000 = $50,000.

Example 4: Change in Variable Cost, Fixed Cost, and Sales Volume

Refer to Acoustic Concepts' original data. As before, the company is currently selling 400 speakers per month. The sales manager would like to pay salespersons a sales commission of $15 per speaker sold, rather than the flat salaries that now total $6,000 per month. The sales manager is confident the change would increase the monthly sales volume by 15 percent to 460 speakers per month. Should the change be made?

Solution Changing the sales staff's compensation from salaries to commissions would affect both variable and fixed expenses. Variable expenses per unit would increase by $15, from $150 to $165, and the unit contribution margin would decrease from $100 to $85. Fixed expenses would decrease by $6,000, from $35,000 to $29,000.

Expected total contribution margin with sales staff on commissions:	
460 speakers × $85 per speaker...............	$39,100
Present total contribution margin:	
400 speakers × $100 per speaker	40,000
Decrease in total contribution margin	(900)
Change in fixed expenses:	
Add salaries avoided if a commission is paid.....	6,000
Increase in net operating income	$ 5,100

According to this analysis, the changes should be made. Again, the same answer can be obtained by preparing comparative contribution income statements:

	Present 400 Speakers per Month		Expected 460 Speakers per Month		
	Total	Per Unit	Total	Per Unit	Difference
Sales	$100,000	$250	$115,000	$250	$ 15,000
Variable expenses	60,000	150	75,900	165	15,900
Contribution margin...........	40,000	$100	39,100	$ 85	900
Fixed expenses	35,000		29,000		(6,000)*
Net operating income	$ 5,000		$ 10,100		$ 5,100

*Note: A reduction in fixed expenses has the effect of increasing net operating income.

Example 5: Change in Selling Price Refer to the original data where Acoustic Concepts is currently selling 400 speakers per month. The company has an opportunity to make a bulk sale of 150 speakers to a wholesaler if an acceptable price can be negotiated. This sale would not alter the company's regular sales and would not affect the company's total fixed expenses. What price per speaker should be quoted to the wholesaler if Acoustic Concepts is seeking a profit of $3,000 on the bulk sale?

Solution

Variable cost per speaker.......................	$150
Desired profit per speaker:	
$3,000 ÷ 150 speakers	20
Quoted price per speaker	$170

Notice that fixed expenses are not included in the computation. This is because fixed expenses are not affected by the bulk sale, so all of the additional contribution margin increases the company's profits.

Break-Even and Target Profit Analysis

Managers use break-even and target profit analysis to answer questions, such as how much would we have to sell to avoid incurring a loss or how much would we have to sell to make a profit of $10,000 per month? We'll discuss break-even analysis first, followed by target profit analysis.

Break-Even Analysis

LEARNING OBJECTIVE 2-5
Determine the break-even point.

Earlier in the chapter we defined the break-even point as *the level of sales at which the company's profit is zero.* To calculate the break-even point (in unit sales and dollar sales), managers can use either of two approaches, the equation method or the formula method. We'll demonstrate both approaches using the data from Acoustic Concepts.

The Equation Method The equation method relies on the basic profit equation introduced earlier in the chapter. Because Acoustic Concepts has only one product, we'll use the contribution margin form of this equation to perform the break-even calculations. Remembering that Acoustic Concepts' unit contribution margin is $100, and its fixed expenses are $35,000, the company's break-even point is computed as follows:

$$\text{Profit} = \text{Unit CM} \times Q - \text{Fixed expense}$$
$$\$0 = \$100 \times Q - \$35,000$$
$$\$100 \times Q = \$0 + \$35,000$$
$$Q = \$35,000 \div \$100$$
$$Q = 350$$

Thus, as we determined earlier in the chapter, Acoustic Concepts will break even (or earn zero profit) at a sales volume of 350 speakers per month.

The Formula Method The formula method is a shortcut version of the equation method. It centers on the idea discussed earlier in the chapter that each unit sold provides a certain amount of contribution margin that goes toward covering fixed expenses. In a single-product situation, the formula for computing the unit sales to break even is:

$$\text{Unit sales to break even} = \frac{\text{Fixed expenses}^3}{\text{Unit CM}}$$

In the case of Acoustic Concepts, the unit sales needed to break even is computed as follows:

$$\text{Unit sales to break even} = \frac{\text{Fixed expenses}}{\text{Unit CM}}$$
$$= \frac{\$35,000}{\$100}$$
$$= 350$$

---

[3] This formula can be derived as follows:
$$\text{Profit} = \text{Unit CM} \times Q - \text{Fixed expenses}$$
$$\$0 = \text{Unit CM} \times Q - \text{Fixed expenses}$$
$$\text{Unit CM} \times Q = \$0 + \text{Fixed expenses}$$
$$Q = \text{Fixed expenses} \div \text{Unit CM}$$

Notice that 350 units is the same answer we got when using the equation method. This will always be the case because the formula method and equation method are mathematically equivalent. The formula method simply skips a few steps in the equation method.

Break-Even in Dollar Sales In addition to finding the break-even point in unit sales, we can also find the break-even point in dollar sales using three methods. First, we could solve for the break-even point in *unit* sales using the equation method or formula method and then simply multiply the result by the selling price. In the case of Acoustic Concepts, the break-even point in dollar sales using this approach would be computed as 350 speakers × $250 per speaker, or $87,500 in total sales.

Second, we can use the equation method to compute the break-even point in dollar sales. Remembering that Acoustic Concepts' contribution margin ratio is 40 percent and its fixed expenses are $35,000, the equation method calculates the break-even point in dollar sales as follows:

$$\text{Profit} = \text{CM ratio} \times \text{Sales} - \text{Fixed expenses}$$
$$\$0 = 0.40 \times \text{Sales} - \$35,000$$
$$0.40 \times \text{Sales} = \$0 + \$35,000$$
$$\text{Sales} = \$35,000 \div 0.40$$
$$\text{Sales} = \$87,500$$

Third, we can use the formula method to compute the dollar sales needed to break even as shown below:

$$\text{Dollar sales to break even} = \frac{\text{Fixed expenses}^4}{\text{CM ratio}}$$

In the case of Acoustic Concepts, the computations are performed as follows:

$$\text{Dollar sales to break even} = \frac{\text{Fixed expenses}}{\text{CM ratio}}$$
$$= \frac{\$35,000}{0.40}$$
$$= \$87,500$$

Again, you'll notice that the break-even point in dollar sales ($87,500) is the same under all three methods. This will always be the case because these methods are mathematically equivalent.

Target Profit Analysis

Target profit analysis is one of the key uses of CVP analysis. In **target profit analysis,** we estimate the level of sales needed to achieve a desired target profit. For example, suppose Prem Narayan of Acoustic Concepts, Inc., would like to estimate the sales needed to attain a target profit of $40,000 per month. To determine the unit sales and dollar sales needed to achieve a target profit, we can rely on the same two approaches we have been discussing thus far, the equation method or the formula method.

LEARNING OBJECTIVE 2–6
Determine the level of sales needed to achieve a desired target profit.

---

4 This formula can be derived as follows:
$$\text{Profit} = \text{CM ratio} \times \text{Sales} - \text{Fixed expenses}$$
$$\$0 = \text{CM ratio} \times \text{Sales} - \text{Fixed expenses}$$
$$\text{CM ratio} \times \text{Sales} = \$0 + \text{Fixed expenses}$$
$$\text{Sales} = \text{Fixed expenses} \div \text{CM ratio}$$

The Equation Method To compute the unit sales required to achieve a target profit of $40,000 per month, Acoustic Concepts can use the same profit equation that was used for its break-even analysis. Remembering that the company's contribution margin per unit is $100 and its total fixed expenses are $35,000, the equation method could be applied as follows:

$$\text{Profit} = \text{Unit CM} \times Q - \text{Fixed expense}$$
$$\$40,000 = \$100 \times Q - \$35,000$$
$$\$100 \times Q = \$40,000 + \$35,000$$
$$Q = \$75,000 \div \$100$$
$$Q = 750$$

Thus, the target profit can be achieved by selling 750 speakers per month. Notice the only difference between this equation and the equation used for Acoustic Concepts' break-even calculation is the profit figure. In the break-even scenario, the profit is $0, whereas in the target profit scenario, the profit is $40,000.

The Formula Method In general, in a single-product situation, we can compute the unit sales required to attain a specific target profit using the following formula:

$$\text{Unit sales to attain the target profit} = \frac{\text{Target profit} + \text{Fixed expenses}}{\text{Unit CM}}$$

In the case of Acoustic Concepts, the unit sales needed to attain a target profit of 40,000 is computed as follows:

$$\text{Unit sales to attain the target profit} = \frac{\text{Target profit} + \text{Fixed expenses}}{\text{Unit CM}}$$
$$= \frac{\$40,000 + \$35,000}{\$100}$$
$$= 750$$

Target Profit Analysis in Terms of Dollar Sales When quantifying the dollar sales needed to attain a target profit, we can apply the same three methods we used for calculating the dollar sales needed to break even. First, we can solve for the *unit* sales needed to attain the target profit using the equation method or formula method and then simply multiply the result by the selling price. In the case of Acoustic Concepts, the dollar sales to attain its target profit would be computed as 750 speakers × $250 per speaker, or $187,500 in total sales.

Second, we can use the equation method to compute the dollar sales needed to attain the target profit. Remembering that Acoustic Concepts' target profit is $40,000, its contribution margin ratio is 40 percent, and its fixed expenses are $35,000, the equation method calculates the answer as follows:

$$\text{Profit} = \text{CM ratio} \times \text{Sales} - \text{Fixed expenses}$$
$$\$40,000 = 0.40 \times \text{Sales} - \$35,000$$
$$0.40 \times \text{Sales} = \$40,000 + \$35,000$$
$$\text{Sales} = \$75,000 \div 0.40$$
$$\text{Sales} = \$187,500$$

Third, we can use the formula method to compute the dollar sales needed to attain the target profit as shown below:

$$\text{Dollar sales to attain the target profit} = \frac{\text{Target profit} + \text{Fixed expenses}}{\text{CM ratio}}$$

In the case of Acoustic Concepts, the computations would be:

$$\text{Dollar sales to attain the target profit} = \frac{\text{Target profit} + \text{Fixed expenses}}{\text{CM ratio}}$$

$$= \frac{\$40,000 + \$35,000}{\$0.40}$$

$$= \$187,500$$

Again, you'll notice the answers are the same regardless of which method we use. This is because all of the methods discussed are simply different roads to the same destination.

The Margin of Safety

The **margin of safety** is the excess of budgeted or actual sales dollars over the break-even sales dollars. It is the amount by which sales can drop before losses are incurred. The higher the margin of safety, the lower the risk of not breaking even and incurring a loss. The formula for the margin of safety is:

LEARNING OBJECTIVE 2–7
Compute the margin of safety and explain its significance.

Margin of safety in dollars = Total budgeted (or actual) sales − Break-even sales

The margin of safety also can be expressed in percentage form by dividing the margin of safety in dollars by total dollar sales:

$$\text{Margin of safety percentage} = \frac{\text{Margin of safety in dollars}}{\text{Total budgeted (or actual) sales in dollars}}$$

The calculation of the margin of safety for Acoustic Concepts is:

Sales (at the current volume of 400 speakers) (a)	$100,000
Break-even sales (at 350 speakers)	87,500
Margin of safety in dollars (b)	$ 12,500
Margin of safety percentage, (b) ÷ (a)	12.5%

This margin of safety means that at the current level of sales and with the company's current prices and cost structure, a reduction in sales of $12,500, or 12.5%, would result in just breaking even.

In a single-product company like Acoustic Concepts, the margin of safety also can be expressed in terms of the number of units sold by dividing the margin of safety in dollars by the selling price per unit. In this case, the margin of safety is 50 speakers ($12,500 ÷ $250 per speaker = 50 speakers).

ACOUSTIC
concepts

Prem Narayan and Bob Luchinni met to discuss the results of Bob's analysis.

Prem: Bob, everything you have shown me is pretty clear. I can see what impact the sales manager's suggestions would have on our profits. Some of those suggestions are quite good, and others are not so good. I am concerned that our margin of safety is only 50 speakers. What can we do to increase this number?

Bob: Well, we have to increase total sales or decrease the break-even point, or both.

Prem: And to decrease the break-even point, we have to either decrease our fixed expenses or increase our unit contribution margin?

Bob: Exactly.

Prem: And to increase our unit contribution margin, we must either increase our selling price or decrease the variable cost per unit?

Bob: Correct.

Prem: So what do you suggest?

Bob: Well, the analysis doesn't tell us which of these to do, but it does indicate we have a potential problem here.

Prem: If you don't have any immediate suggestions, I would like to call a general meeting next week to discuss ways we can work on increasing the margin of safety. I think everyone will be concerned about how vulnerable we are to even small downturns in sales.

CVP Considerations in Choosing a Cost Structure

Cost structure refers to the relative proportion of fixed and variable costs in an organization. Managers often have some latitude in trading off between these two types of costs. For example, fixed investments in automated equipment can reduce variable labor costs. In this section, we discuss the choice of a cost structure. We also introduce the concept of *operating leverage.*

Cost Structure and Profit Stability

Which cost structure is better—high variable costs and low fixed costs, or the opposite? No single answer to this question is possible; each approach has its advantages. To show what we mean, refer to the following contribution format income statements for two blueberry farms. Bogside Farm pays employees an hourly wage to pick its berries by hand, whereas Sterling Farm has invested in expensive berry-picking machines. Consequently, Bogside Farm has higher variable costs, but Sterling Farm has higher fixed costs:

	Bogside Farm		Sterling Farm	
	Amount	Percent	Amount	Percent
Sales....................	$100,000	100%	$100,000	100%
Variable expenses.........	60,000	60%	30,000	30%
Contribution margin........	40,000	40%	70,000	70%
Fixed expenses...........	30,000		60,000	
Net operating income......	$ 10,000		$ 10,000	

Which farm has the better cost structure? The answer depends on many factors, including the long-run trend in sales, year-to-year fluctuations in the level of sales, and the attitude of the owners toward risk. If sales are expected to exceed $100,000 in the future, then Sterling Farm probably has the better cost structure. The reason is that its CM ratio is higher, and its profits will therefore increase more rapidly as unit sales increase. To illustrate, assume each farm experiences a 10 percent increase in unit sales without any increase in fixed costs. The new contribution income statements would be as follows:

	Bogside Farm		Sterling Farm	
	Amount	Percent	Amount	Percent
Sales....................	$110,000	100%	$110,000	100%
Variable expenses	66,000	60%	33,000	30%
Contribution margin........	44,000	40%	77,000	70%
Fixed expenses............	30,000		60,000	
Net operating income	$ 14,000		$ 17,000	

Sterling Farm has experienced a greater increase in net operating income due to its higher CM ratio even though the increase in unit sales was the same for both farms.

What if sales drop below $100,000? What are the farms' break-even points? What are their margins of safety? The computations needed to answer these questions are shown below using the formula method:

	Bogside Farm	Sterling Farm
Fixed expenses.............................	$ 30,000	$ 60,000
Contribution margin ratio	÷ 0.40	÷ 0.70
Dollar sales to break even	$ 75,000	$ 85,714
Total current sales (a)......................	$100,000	$100,000
Break-even sales	75,000	85,714
Margin of safety in sales dollars (b)...........	$ 25,000	$ 14,286
Margin of safety percentage (b) ÷ (a)	25.0%	14.3%

Bogside Farm's margin of safety is greater and its contribution margin ratio is lower than Sterling Farm's. Therefore, Bogside Farm is less vulnerable to downturns than Sterling Farm. Due to its lower contribution margin ratio, Bogside Farm will not lose contribution margin as rapidly as Sterling Farm when unit sales decline. Thus, Bogside Farm's profit will be less volatile. We saw earlier that this is a drawback when the sales volume increases, but it provides more protection when unit sales drop. And because its break-even point is lower, Bogside Farm can suffer a larger decline in unit sales before losses emerge.

To summarize, without knowing the future, it is not obvious which cost structure is better. Both have advantages and disadvantages. Sterling Farm, with its higher fixed costs and lower variable costs, will experience wider swings in net operating income as unit sales fluctuate, with greater profits in good years and greater losses in bad years. Bogside Farm, with its lower fixed costs and higher variable costs, will enjoy greater profit stability and will be more protected from losses during bad years, but at the cost of lower net operating income in good years. Moreover, if the higher fixed costs in Sterling Farm reflect greater capacity, Sterling Farm will be better able than Bogside Farm to profit from unexpected surges in demand.

Operating Leverage

LEARNING OBJECTIVE 2–8
Compute the degree of operating leverage at a particular level of sales and explain how it can be used to predict changes in net operating income.

A lever is a tool for multiplying force. Using a lever, a massive object can be moved with only a modest amount of force. In business, *operating leverage* serves a similar purpose. **Operating leverage** is a measure of how sensitive net operating income is to a given percentage change in unit sales. Operating leverage acts as a multiplier. If operating leverage is high, a small percentage increase in unit sales can produce a much larger percentage increase in net operating income.

Operating leverage can be illustrated by returning to the data for the two blueberry farms. We previously showed that a 10 percent increase in sales (from $100,000 to $110,000 in each farm) results in a 70 percent increase in the net operating income of Sterling Farm (from $10,000 to $17,000) and only a 40 percent increase in the net operating income of Bogside Farm (from $10,000 to $14,000). Thus, for a 10 percent increase in unit sales, Sterling Farm experiences a much greater percentage increase in profits than does Bogside Farm. Therefore, Sterling Farm has greater operating leverage than Bogside Farm.

The **degree of operating leverage** at a given level of sales is computed by the following formula:

$$\text{Degree of operating leverage} = \frac{\text{Contribution margin}}{\text{Net operating income}}$$

The degree of operating leverage is a measure, at a given level of sales, of how a percentage change in sales volume will affect profits. To illustrate, the degree of operating leverage for the two farms at $100,000 sales would be computed as follows:

$$\text{Bogside Farm:} \frac{\$40,000}{\$10,000} = 4$$

$$\text{Sterling Farm:} \frac{\$70,000}{\$10,000} = 7$$

Because the degree of operating leverage for Bogside Farm is 4, the farm's net operating income grows four times as fast as its sales. In contrast, Sterling Farm's net operating income grows seven times as fast as its sales. Thus, if the sales volume increases by 10 percent, then we can expect the net operating income of Bogside Farm to increase by four times this amount, or by 40 percent, and the net operating income of Sterling Farm to increase by seven times this amount, or by 70 percent. In general, this relation between the percentage change in unit sales and the percentage change in net operating income is given by the following formula:

$$\frac{\text{Percentage change in}}{\text{net operating income}} = \frac{\text{Degree of}}{\text{operating leverage}} \times \frac{\text{Percentage}}{\text{change in sales}}$$

Bogside Farm: Percentage change in net operating income = 4 × 10% = 40%

Sterling Farm: Percentage change in net operating income = 7 × 10% = 70%

What is responsible for the higher operating leverage at Sterling Farm? The only difference between the two farms is their cost structure. If two companies have the same total revenue and same total expense but different cost structures, then the company with the higher proportion of fixed costs in its cost structure will have higher operating leverage. Referring back to the original data, when both farms have sales of $100,000 and total expenses of $90,000, one-third of Bogside Farm's costs are fixed but two-thirds of Sterling Farm's costs are fixed. As a consequence, Sterling's degree of operating leverage is higher than Bogside's.

The degree of operating leverage is not a constant; it is greatest at sales levels near the break-even point and decreases as sales and profits rise. The following table shows the degree of operating leverage for Bogside Farm at various sales levels. (Data used earlier for Bogside Farm are shown in color.)

Sales	$75,000	$80,000	$100,000	$150,000	$225,000
Variable expenses	45,000	48,000	60,000	90,000	135,000
Contribution margin (a)	30,000	32,000	40,000	60,000	90,000
Fixed expenses	30,000	30,000	30,000	30,000	30,000
Net operating income (b)	$ 0	$ 2,000	$ 10,000	$ 30,000	$ 60,000
Degree of operating leverage, (a) ÷ (b)	∞	16	4	2	1.5

Thus, a 10 percent increase in unit sales would increase profits by only 15 percent (10% × 1.5) if sales were previously $225,000, as compared to the 40 percent increase we computed earlier at the $100,000 sales level. The degree of operating leverage will continue to decrease the farther the company moves from its break-even point. At the break-even point, the degree of operating leverage is infinitely large ($30,000 contribution margin ÷ $0 net operating income = ∞).

The degree of operating leverage can be used to quickly estimate what impact various percentage changes in unit sales will have on profits, without the necessity of preparing detailed contribution format income statements. As shown by our examples, the effects of operating leverage can be dramatic. If a company is near its break-even point, then even a small percentage increase in sales volume can cause a huge percentage increase in profits. *This explains why management will often work very hard for only a small increase in sales volume.* If the degree of operating leverage is 5, then a 6 percent increase in unit sales would translate into a 30 percent increase in profits.

Sales Mix

LEARNING OBJECTIVE 2–9
Compute the break-even point for a multiproduct company and explain the effects of shifts in the sales mix on contribution margin and the break-even point.

Before concluding our discussion of CVP concepts, we need to consider the impact of changes in *sales mix* on a company's profit.

The Definition of Sales Mix

The term **sales mix** refers to the relative proportions in which a company's products are sold. The idea is to achieve the combination, or mix, that will yield the greatest profits. Most companies have many products, and often these products are not equally profitable. Hence, profits will depend to some extent on the company's sales mix. Profits will be greater if high-margin rather than low-margin items make up a relatively large proportion of total sales.

Changes in the sales mix can cause perplexing variations in a company's profits. A shift in the sales mix from high-margin items to low-margin items can cause total profits to decrease even though total sales may increase. Conversely, a shift in the sales mix from low-margin items to high-margin items can cause the reverse effect—total profits may increase even though total sales decrease. It is one thing to achieve a particular sales volume; it is quite another to sell the most profitable mix of products.

Sales Mix and Break-Even Analysis

If a company sells more than one product, break-even analysis is more complex than discussed to this point. The reason is that different products will have different selling prices, different costs, and different contribution margins. Consequently, the break-even point depends on the mix in which the various products are sold. To illustrate, consider Virtual Journeys Unlimited, a small company that sells two DVDs: the Monuments DVD, a tour of the United States' most popular National Monuments; and the Parks DVD, which tours the United States' National Parks. The company's September sales, expenses, and break-even point are shown in Exhibit 2–4.

As shown in the exhibit, the break-even point is $60,000 in sales, which was computed by dividing the company's fixed expenses of $27,000 by its overall CM ratio of 45 percent. However, this is the break-even point only if the company's sales mix does not change. Currently, the Monuments DVD is responsible for 20 percent and the Parks DVD for 80 percent of the company's dollar sales. Assuming this sales mix does not change, if total sales are $60,000, the sales of the Monuments DVD would be $12,000 (20% of $60,000) and the sales of the Parks DVD would be $48,000 (80% of $60,000). As shown in Exhibit 2–4, at these levels of sales, the company would indeed break even. But $60,000 in sales represents the break-even point for the company only if the sales mix does not change. *If the sales mix changes, then the break-even point will also usually change.* This is illustrated by the results for October in which the sales mix shifted away from the more profitable Parks DVD (which has a 50% CM ratio) toward the less profitable Monuments DVD (which has a 25% CM ratio). These results appear in Exhibit 2–5.

Although sales have remained unchanged at $100,000, the sales mix is exactly the reverse of what it was in Exhibit 2–4, with the bulk of the sales now coming from the less profitable Monuments DVD. Notice that this shift in the sales mix has caused both the overall CM ratio and total profits to drop sharply from the prior month even though total sales are the same. The overall CM ratio has dropped from 45 percent in September to only 30 percent in October, and net operating income has dropped from $18,000 to only $3,000. In addition, with the drop in the overall CM ratio, the company's break-even point is no longer $60,000 in sales. Because the company is now realizing less average contribution margin per dollar of sales, it takes more sales to cover the same amount of fixed costs. Thus, the break-even point has increased from $60,000 to $90,000 in sales per year.

In preparing a break-even analysis, an assumption must be made concerning the sales mix. Usually the assumption is that it will not change. However, if the sales mix is expected to change, then this must be explicitly considered in any CVP computations.

EXHIBIT 2–4
Multiproduct Break-Even Analysis

Virtual Journeys Unlimited
Contribution Format Income Statement
For the Month of September

	Monuments DVD		Parks DVD		Total	
	Amount	Percent	Amount	Percent	Amount	Percent
Sales	$20,000	100%	$80,000	100%	$100,000	100%
Variable expenses................	15,000	75%	40,000	50%	55,000	55%
Contribution margin	$ 5,000	25%	$40,000	50%	45,000	45%
Fixed expenses					27,000	
Net operating income.............					$ 18,000	

Computation of the break-even point:

$$\frac{\text{Fixed expenses}}{\text{Overall CM ratio}} = \frac{\$27,000}{0.45} = \$60,000$$

Verification of the break-even point:

	Monuments DVD	Parks DVD	Total
Current dollar sales.................	$20,000	$80,000	$100,000
Percentage of total dollar sales......	20%	80%	100%
Sales at the break-even point	$12,000	$48,000	$60,000

	Monuments DVD		Parks DVD		Total	
	Amount	Percent	Amount	Percent	Amount	Percent
Sales	$12,000	100%	$48,000	100%	$60,000	100%
Variable expenses................	9,000	75%	24,000	50%	33,000	55%
Contribution margin	$ 3,000	25%	$24,000	50%	27,000	45%
Fixed expenses					27,000	
Net operating income.............					$ 0	

EXHIBIT 2–5
Multiproduct Break-Even Analysis: A Shift in Sales Mix (see Exhibit 2–4)

Virtual Journeys Unlimited
Contribution Format Income Statement
For the Month of October

	Monuments DVD		Parks DVD		Total	
	Amount	Percent	Amount	Percent	Amount	Percent
Sales	$80,000	100%	$20,000	100%	$100,000	100%
Variable expenses................	60,000	75%	10,000	50%	70,000	70%
Contribution margin	$20,000	25%	$10,000	50%	30,000	30%
Fixed expenses					27,000	
Net operating income					$ 3,000	

Computation of the break-even point:

$$\frac{\text{Fixed expenses}}{\text{Overall CM ratio}} = \frac{\$27,000}{0.30} = \$90,000$$

Summary

CVP analysis is based on a simple model of how profits respond to prices, costs, and volume. This model can be used to answer a variety of critical questions, such as what is the company's break-even volume, what is its margin of safety, and what is likely to happen if specific changes are made in prices, costs, and volume.

A CVP graph depicts the relationships between unit sales on the one hand and fixed expenses, variable expenses, total expenses, total sales, and profits on the other hand. The profit graph is simpler than the CVP graph and shows how profits depend on sales. The CVP and profit graphs are useful for developing intuition about how costs and profits respond to changes in sales.

The contribution margin ratio is the ratio of contribution margin to sales. This ratio can be used to quickly estimate what impact a change in sales volume would have on net operating income. The ratio is also useful in break-even analysis.

Break-even analysis is used to estimate the sales needed to break even. The unit sales required to break even can be estimated by dividing the fixed expense by the unit contribution margin. Target profit analysis is used to estimate the sales needed to attain a specified target profit. The unit sales required to attain the target profit can be estimated by dividing the sum of the target profit and fixed expense by the unit contribution margin.

The margin of safety is the amount by which the company's budgeted (or actual) sales exceeds break-even sales.

The degree of operating leverage allows quick estimation of what impact a given percentage change in unit sales would have on the company's net operating income. The higher the degree of operating leverage, the greater is the impact on the company's profits. The degree of operating leverage is not constant—it depends on the company's current level of sales.

The profits of a multiproduct company are affected by its sales mix. Changes in the sales mix can affect the break-even point, margin of safety, and other critical factors.

 Data Analytics Exercise available in Connect to complement this chapter

Review Problem: CVP Relationships

Voltar Company manufactures and sells a specialized cordless telephone for high electromagnetic radiation environments. The company's contribution format income statement for the most recent year is given below:

	Total	Per Unit	Percent of Sales
Sales (20,000 units)	$1,200,000	$60	100%
Variable expenses.........................	900,000	45	?%
Contribution margin	300,000	$15	?%
Fixed expenses	240,000		
Net operating income	$ 60,000		

Management is anxious to increase the company's profit and has asked for an analysis of a number of items.

Required:

1. Compute the company's CM ratio and variable expense ratio.
2. Compute the company's break-even point in both unit sales and dollar sales. Use the equation method.
3. Assume an increase in unit sales causes total sales to increase by $400,000 next year. If cost behavior patterns remain unchanged, by how much will the company's net operating income increase? Use the CM ratio to compute your answer.
4. Refer to the original data. Assume next year management wants the company to earn a profit of at least $90,000. How many units will have to be sold to earn this target profit?
5. Refer to the original data. Compute the company's margin of safety in both dollar and percentage form.
6. a. Compute the company's degree of operating leverage at the present level of sales.
   b. Assume that through a more intense effort by the sales staff, the company's unit sales increase by 8% next year. By what percentage would you expect net operating income to increase? Use the degree of operating leverage to obtain your answer.
   c. Verify your answer to (b) by preparing a new contribution format income statement showing an 8% increase in unit sales.
7. Refer to the original data. In an effort to increase sales and profits, management is considering the use of a higher-quality speaker. The higher-quality speaker would increase variable costs by $3 per unit, but management could eliminate one quality inspector who is paid a salary of $30,000 per year. The sales manager estimates that the higher-quality speaker would increase annual unit sales by at least 20%.
   a. Assuming changes are made as described above, prepare a projected contribution format income statement for next year. Show data on a total, per unit, and percentage basis.
   b. Compute the company's new break-even point in both unit sales and dollar sales. Use the formula method.
   c. Would you recommend the changes be made?

Solution to Review Problem

1.

$$\text{CM ratio} = \frac{\text{Unit contribution margin}}{\text{Unit selling price}} = \frac{\$15}{\$60} = 25\%$$

$$\text{Variable expense ratio} = \frac{\text{Variable expense}}{\text{Selling price}} = \frac{\$45}{\$60} = 75\%$$

2.
$$\text{Profit} = \text{Unit CM} \times Q - \text{Fixed expenses}$$
$$\$0 = \$15 \times Q - \$240,000$$
$$\$15Q = \$240,000$$
$$Q = \$240,000 \div \$15$$
$$Q = 16,000 \text{ units; or, at } \$60 \text{ per unit, } \$960,000$$

3.

Increase in sales	$ 400,000
Contribution margin ratio	× 25%
Expected increase in contribution margin......................	$ 100,000

Because the fixed expenses are not expected to change, net operating income will increase by the entire $100,000 increase in contribution margin computed above.

4.   Equation method:

$$\text{Profit} = \text{Unit CM} \times Q - \text{Fixed expenses}$$
$$\$90,000 = \$15 \times Q - \$240,000$$
$$\$15Q = \$90,000 + \$240,000$$
$$Q = \$330,000 \div \$15$$
$$Q = 22,000 \text{ units}$$

Formula method:

$$\frac{\text{Unit sales to attain}}{\text{the target profit}} = \frac{\text{Target profit} + \text{Fixed expenses}}{\text{Contribution margin per unit}} = \frac{\$90,000 + \$240,000}{\$15 \text{ per unit}} = 22,000 \text{ units}$$

5.   Margin of safety in dollars   = Total sales − Break-even sales
$$= \$1,200,000 - \$960,000 = \$240,000$$

$$\text{Margin of safety percentage} = \frac{\text{Margin of safety in dollars}}{\text{Total sales}} = \frac{\$240,000}{\$1,200,000} = 20\%$$

6.   *a.* $\text{Degree of operating leverage} = \dfrac{\text{Contribution margin}}{\text{Net operating income}} = \dfrac{\$300,000}{\$60,000} = 5$

b.

Expected increase in sales	8%
Degree of operating leverage	× 5
Expected increase in net operating income	40%

c.   If unit sales increase by 8%, then 21,600 units (20,000 × 1.08 = 21,600) will be sold next year. The new contribution format income statement would be as follows:

	Total	Per Unit	Percent of Sales
Sales (21,600 units)	$1,296,000	$60	100%
Variable expenses	972,000	45	75%
Contribution margin	324,000	$15	25%
Fixed expenses	240,000		
Net operating income	$ 84,000		

Thus, the $84,000 expected net operating income for next year represents a 40% increase over the $60,000 net operating income earned during the current year:

$$\frac{\$84,000 - \$60,000}{\$60,000} = \frac{\$24,000}{\$60,000} = 40\% \text{ increase}$$

Note the increase in sales from 20,000 to 21,600 units has increased *both* total sales and total variable expenses.

7. *a.* A 20% increase in unit sales would result in 24,000 units being sold next year: 20,000 units × 1.20 = 24,000 units.

	Total	Per Unit	Percent of Sales
Sales (24,000 units)	$1,440,000	$60	100%
Variable expenses.	1,152,000	48*	80%
Contribution margin	288,000	$12	20%
Fixed expenses	210,000†		
Net operating income.	$ 78,000		

* $45 + $3 = $48; $48 ÷ $60 = 80%.
† $240,000 − $30,000 = $210,000.

Note the change in per-unit variable expenses results in a change in both the per-unit contribution margin and the CM ratio.

b. $$\text{Unit sales to break even} = \frac{\text{Fixed expenses}}{\text{Unit contribution margin}}$$

$$= \frac{\$210,000}{\$12 \text{ per unit}} = 17,500 \text{ units}$$

$$\text{Dollar sales to break even} = \frac{\text{Fixed expenses}}{\text{CM ratio}}$$

$$= \frac{\$210,000}{0.20} = \$1,050,000$$

c. Yes, based on these data, the changes should be made. The changes increase the company's net operating income from the present $60,000 to $78,000 per year. Although the changes also result in a higher break-even point (17,500 units as compared to the present 16,000 units), the company's margin of safety actually becomes greater than before:

$$\text{Margin of safety in dollars} = \text{Total sales} - \text{Break-even sales}$$
$$= \$1,440,000 - \$1,050,000 = \$390,000$$

As shown in (5), the company's present margin of safety is only $240,000. Thus, several benefits will result from the proposed changes.

Glossary

Break-even point The level of sales at which profit is zero. (p. 65)

Contribution margin ratio (CM ratio) A ratio computed by dividing contribution margin by sales. (p. 70)

Cost-volume-profit (CVP) graph A graphical representation of the relationships between an organization's revenues, costs, and profits on the one hand and its sales volume on the other hand. (p. 67)

Degree of operating leverage A measure, at a given level of sales, of how a percentage change in sales volume will affect profits. The degree of operating leverage is computed by dividing contribution margin by net operating income. (p. 82)

Incremental analysis An analytical approach that focuses only on those costs and revenues that change as a result of a decision. (p. 73)

Margin of safety The excess of budgeted or actual dollar sales over the break-even dollar sales. (p. 79)

Operating leverage A measure of how sensitive net operating income is to a given percentage change in unit sales. (p. 82)

Sales mix The relative proportions in which a company's products are sold. Sales mix is computed by expressing the sales of each product as a percentage of total sales. (p. 84)

Target profit analysis Estimating the level of sales needed to achieve a desired target profit. (p. 77)

Variable expense ratio A ratio computed by dividing variable expenses by sales. (p. 70)

Questions

2–1 What is the meaning of *contribution margin ratio?* How is this ratio useful in planning business operations?

2–2 Often the most direct route to a business decision is an incremental analysis. What is meant by an *incremental analysis?*

2–3 In all respects, Company A and Company B are identical except that Company A's costs are mostly variable, whereas Company B's costs are mostly fixed. When sales increase, which company will tend to realize the greatest increase in profits? Explain.

2–4 What is the meaning of *operating leverage?*

2–5 What is the meaning of *break-even point?*

2–6 In response to a request from your immediate supervisor, you prepared a CVP graph portraying the cost and revenue characteristics of your company's product and operations. Explain how the lines on the graph and the break-even point would change if (*a*) the selling price per unit decreased, (*b*) fixed cost increased throughout the entire range of activity portrayed on the graph, and (*c*) variable cost per unit increased.

2–7 What is the meaning of *margin of safety?*

2–8 What is meant by the term *sales mix?* What assumption is usually made concerning sales mix in CVP analysis?

2–9 Explain how a shift in the sales mix could result in both a higher break-even point and a lower net operating income.

Applying Excel Mc Graw Hill connect

LEARNING OBJECTIVES 2–4, 2–5, 2–7, 2–8

The Excel worksheet form that appears below is to be used to recreate portions of the Review Problem relating to Voltar Company. The workbook, and instructions on how to complete the file, can be found in Connect.

	A	B	C	D
1	Chapter 2: Applying Excel			
2				
3	**Data**			
4	Unit sales	20,000	units	
5	Selling price per unit	$60	per unit	
6	Variable expenses per unit	$45	per unit	
7	Fixed expenses	$240,000		
8				
9	*Enter a formula into each of the cells marked with a ? below*			
10	**Review Problem: CVP Relationships**			
11				
12	*Compute the CM ratio and variable expense ratio*			
13	Selling price per unit	?	per unit	
14	Variable expenses per unit	?	per unit	
15	Contribution margin per unit	?	per unit	
16				
17	CM ratio	?		
18	Variable expense ratio	?		
19				
20	*Compute the break-even*			
21	Break-even in unit sales	?	units	
22	Break-even in dollar sales	?		
23				
24	*Compute the margin of safety*			
25	Margin of safety in dollars	?		
26	Margin of safety percentage	?		
27				
28	*Compute the degree of operating leverage*			
29	Sales	?		
30	Variable expenses	?		
31	Contribution margin	?		
32	Fixed expenses	?		
33	Net operating income	?		
34				
35	Degree of operating leverage	?		
36				

◄ ◄ ► ►◄   **Chapter 2 Form**   Filled in Chapter 2 Form

Microsoft Excel

You should proceed to the requirements below only after completing your worksheet.

Required:

1. Check your worksheet by changing the fixed expenses to $270,000. If your worksheet is operating properly, the degree of operating leverage should be 10. If you do not get this answer, find the errors in your worksheet and correct them. How much is the margin of safety percentage? Did it change? Why or why not?

2. Enter the following data from a different company into your worksheet:

Unit sales	10,000
Selling price per unit	$120
Variable expenses per unit	$72
Fixed expenses	$420,000

What is the margin of safety percentage? What is the degree of operating leverage?

3. Using the degree of operating leverage and without changing anything in your worksheet, calculate the percentage change in net operating income if unit sales increase by 15%.

4. Confirm the calculations you made in part (3) above by increasing the unit sales in your work-sheet by 15%. What is the new net operating income and by what percentage did it increase?

5. Thad Morgan, a motorcycle enthusiast, has been exploring the possibility of relaunching the Western Hombre brand of cycle that was popular in the 1930s. The retro-look cycle would be sold for $10,000 and at that price, Thad estimates he could sell 600 units each year. The variable cost to produce and sell the cycles would be $7,500 per unit. The annual fixed cost would be $1,200,000.

    a. Using your worksheet, what would be the unit sales to break even, the margin of safety in dollars, and the degree of operating leverage?

    b. Thad is worried about the selling price. Rumors are circulating that other retro brands of cycles may be revived. If so, the selling price for the Western Hombre would have to be reduced to $9,000 to compete effectively. In that event, Thad also would reduce fixed expenses by $300,000 by reducing advertising expenses, but he still hopes to sell 600 units per year. Do you think this is a good plan? Explain. Also, explain the degree of operating leverage that appears on your worksheet.

The Foundational 15 ⓂⒼⒽ connect

LEARNING OBJECTIVES 2–1, 2–3,
2–4, 2–5, 2–6, 2–7, 2–8

Oslo Company prepared the following contribution format income statement based on a sales volume of 1,000 units (the relevant range of production is 500 units to 1,500 units):

Sales	$20,000
Variable expenses	12,000
Contribution margin	8,000
Fixed expenses	6,000
Net operating income	$ 2,000

Required:

(Answer each question independently and always refer to the original data unless instructed otherwise.)

1. What is the contribution margin per unit?
2. What is the contribution margin ratio?
3. What is the variable expense ratio?
4. If sales increase to 1,001 units, what would be the increase in net operating income?
5. If sales decline to 900 units, what would be the net operating income?
6. If the selling price increases by $2 per unit and the sales volume decreases by 100 units, what would be the net operating income?
7. If the variable cost per unit increases by $1, spending on advertising increases by $1,500, and unit sales increase by 250 units, what would be the net operating income?
8. What is the break-even point in unit sales?
9. What is the break-even point in dollar sales?
10. How many units must be sold to achieve a target profit of $5,000?
11. What is the margin of safety in dollars? What is the margin of safety percentage?
12. What is the degree of operating leverage?
13. Using the degree of operating leverage, what is the estimated percent increase in net operating income that would result from a 5% increase in unit sales?
14. Assume that the amounts of the company's total variable expenses and total fixed expenses were reversed. In other words, assume that the total variable expenses are $6,000 and the total fixed expenses are $12,000. Under this scenario and assuming that total sales remain the same, what is the degree of operating leverage?
15. Using the degree of operating leverage that you computed in the previous question, what is the estimated percent increase in net operating income that would result from a 5% increase in unit sales?

EXERCISE 2–1 The Effect of Changes in Sales Volume on Net Operating Income LO2–1

Whirly Corporation's contribution format income statement for the most recent month is shown below:

	Total	Per Unit
Sales (10,000 units)	$350,000	$35.00
Variable expenses	200,000	20.00
Contribution margin	150,000	$15.00
Fixed expenses	135,000	
Net operating income.	$ 15,000	

Required:

(Consider each case independently):

1. What would be the revised net operating income per month if the sales volume increases by 100 units?
2. What would be the revised net operating income per month if the sales volume decreases by 100 units?
3. What would be the revised net operating income per month if the sales volume is 9,000 units?

EXERCISE 2–2 Prepare a Cost-Volume-Profit (CVP) Graph LO2–2

Karlik Enterprises distributes a single product whose selling price is $24 per unit and whose variable expense is $18 per unit. The company's monthly fixed expense is $24,000.

Required:

1. Prepare a cost-volume-profit graph for the company up to a sales volume of 8,000 units.
2. Estimate the company's break-even point in unit sales using your cost-volume-profit graph.

EXERCISE 2–3 Prepare a Profit Graph LO2–2

Jaffre Enterprises distributes a single product whose selling price is $16 per unit and whose variable expense is $11 per unit. The company's fixed expense is $16,000 per month.

Required:

1. Prepare a profit graph for the company up to a sales volume of 4,000 units.
2. Estimate the company's break-even point in unit sales using your profit graph.

EXERCISE 2–4 Computing and Using the CM Ratio LO2–3

Last month when Holiday Creations, Inc., sold 50,000 units, total sales were $200,000, total variable expenses were $120,000, and fixed expenses were $65,000.

Required:

1. What is the company's contribution margin (CM) ratio?
2. What is the estimated change in the company's net operating income if it can increase sales volume by 250 units and total sales by $1,000?

EXERCISE 2–5 Changes in Variable Costs, Fixed Costs, Selling Price, and Volume LO2–4

Data for Hermann Corporation are shown below:

	Per Unit	Percent of Sales
Selling price	$90	100%
Variable expenses	63	70
Contribution margin	$27	30%

Fixed expenses are $30,000 per month and the company is selling 2,000 units per month.

Required:

1. How much will net operating income increase (decrease) per month if the monthly advertising budget increases by $5,000, the monthly sales volume increases by 100 units, and the total monthly sales increase by $9,000?
2. Refer to the original data. How much will net operating income increase (decrease) per month if the company uses higher-quality components that increase the variable expense by $2 per unit and increase unit sales by 10%.

EXERCISE 2–6 Break-Even Analysis LO2–5

Mauro Products distributes a single product, a woven basket whose selling price is $15 per unit and whose variable expense is $12 per unit. The company's monthly fixed expense is $4,200.

Required:

1. Calculate the company's break-even point in unit sales.
2. Calculate the company's break-even point in dollar sales.
3. If the company's fixed expenses increase by $600, what would become the new break-even point in unit sales? In dollar sales?

EXERCISE 2–7 Target Profit Analysis LO2–6

Lin Corporation has a single product whose selling price is $120 per unit and whose variable expense is $80 per unit. The company's monthly fixed expense is $50,000.

Required:

1. Calculate the unit sales needed to attain a target profit of $10,000.
2. Calculate the dollar sales needed to attain a target profit of $15,000.

EXERCISE 2–8 Compute the Margin of Safety LO2–7

Molander Corporation is a distributor of a sun umbrella used at resort hotels. Data concerning the next month's budget appear below:

Selling price per unit	$30
Variable expense per unit	$20
Fixed expense per month	$7,500
Unit sales per month	1,000

Required:

1. What is the company's margin of safety?
2. What is the company's margin of safety as a percentage of its sales?

EXERCISE 2–9 Compute and Use the Degree of Operating Leverage LO2–8

Engberg Company installs lawn sod in home yards. The company's most recent monthly contribution format income statement follows:

	Amount	Percent of Sales
Sales	$80,000	100%
Variable expenses	32,000	40%
Contribution margin	48,000	60%
Fixed expenses	38,000	
Net operating income	$10,000	

Required:

1. What is the company's degree of operating leverage?
2. Using the degree of operating leverage, estimate the impact on net operating income of a 5% increase in unit sales.
3. Verify your estimate from part (2) above by constructing a new contribution format income statement for the company assuming a 5% increase in unit sales.

EXERCISE 2–10 Multiproduct Break-Even Analysis LO2–9

Lucido Products markets two computer games: Claimjumper and Makeover. A contribution format income statement for a recent month for the two games appears below:

	Claimjumper	Makeover	Total
Sales	$30,000	$70,000	$100,000
Variable expenses.................	20,000	50,000	70,000
Contribution margin	$10,000	$20,000	30,000
Fixed expenses			24,000
Net operating income			$ 6,000

Required:
1. What is the overall contribution margin (CM) ratio for the company?
2. What is the company's overall break-even point in dollar sales?
3. Verify the overall break-even point for the company by constructing a contribution format income statement showing the appropriate levels of sales for the two products.

EXERCISE 2–11 Missing Data; Basic CVP Concepts LO2–1, LO2–9

Fill in the missing amounts in each of the eight case situations below. Each case is independent of the others. (*Hint:* One way to find the missing amounts would be to prepare a contribution format income statement for each case, enter the known data, and then compute the missing items.)

a. Assume only one product is being sold in each of the four following case situations:

Case	Units Sold	Sales	Variable Expenses	Contribution Margin per Unit	Fixed Expenses	Net Operating Income (Loss)
1.........	15,000	$180,000	$120,000	?	$50,000	?
2.........	?	$100,000	?	$10	$32,000	$8,000
3.........	10,000	?	$70,000	$13	?	$12,000
4.........	6,000	$300,000	?	?	$100,000	$(10,000)

b. Assume more than one product is being sold in each of the four following case situations:

Case	Sales	Variable Expenses	Average Contribution Margin Ratio	Fixed Expenses	Net Operating Income (Loss)
1.........	$500,000	?	20%	?	$7,000
2.........	$400,000	$260,000	?	$100,000	?
3.......	?	?	60%	$130,000	$20,000
4........	$600,000	$420,000	?	?	$(5,000)

EXERCISE 2–12 Multiproduct Break-Even Analysis LO2–9

Olongapo Sports Corporation distributes two premium golf balls—Flight Dynamic and Sure Shot. Monthly sales and the contribution margin ratios for the two products follow:

	Product		
	Flight Dynamic	Sure Shot	Total
Sales	$150,000	$250,000	$400,000
CM ratio	80%	36%	?

Fixed expenses total $183,750 per month.

Required:

1. Prepare a contribution format income statement for the company as a whole. Carry computations to one decimal place.
2. What is the company's break-even point in dollar sales based on the current sales mix?
3. If sales increase by $100,000 a month, by how much would you expect the monthly net operating income to increase? What are your assumptions?

EXERCISE 2–13 Changes in Selling Price, Sales Volume, Variable Cost per Unit, and Total Fixed Costs LO2–1, LO2–4

Miller Company's contribution format income statement for the most recent month is shown below:

	Total	Per Unit
Sales (20,000 units)	$300,000	$15.00
Variable expenses	180,000	9.00
Contribution margin	120,000	$ 6.00
Fixed expenses	70,000	
Net operating income	$ 50,000	

Required:

(Consider each case independently):

1. What is the revised net operating income if unit sales increase by 15%?
2. What is the revised net operating income if the selling price decreases by $1.50 per unit and the number of units sold increases by 25%?
3. What is the revised net operating income if the selling price increases by $1.50 per unit, fixed expenses increase by $20,000, and the number of units sold decreases by 5%?
4. What is the revised net operating income if the selling price per unit increases by 12%, variable expenses increase by 60 cents per unit, and the number of units sold decreases by 10%?

EXERCISE 2–14 Break-Even and Target Profit Analysis LO2–3, LO2–4, LO2–5, LO2–6

Lindon Company is the exclusive distributor for an automotive product that sells for $40 per unit and has a CM ratio of 30%. The company's fixed expenses are $180,000 per year. The company plans to sell 16,000 units this year.

Required:

1. What are the variable expenses per unit?
2. What is the break-even point in unit sales and in dollar sales?
3. What amount of unit sales and dollar sales is required to attain a target profit of $60,000 per year?
4. Assume that by using a more efficient shipper, the company is able to reduce its variable expenses by $4 per unit. What is the company's new break-even point in unit sales and in dollar sales? What dollar sales are required to attain a target profit of $60,000?

EXERCISE 2–15 Operating Leverage LO2–1, LO2–8

Magic Realm, Inc., developed a new fantasy board game and sold 15,000 units last year at a selling price of $20 per game. Fixed expenses associated with the game are $182,000 per year, and variable expenses are $6 per game. Production of the game was outsourced to a printing contractor, so variable expenses consist mostly of payments to this contractor.

Required:

1. Prepare a contribution format income statement for the game last year and compute the degree of operating leverage.
2. Management is confident the company can sell 18,000 games next year (an increase of 3,000 games, or 20%, over last year). Given this assumption:
   a. What is the expected percentage increase in net operating income for next year?
   b. What is the expected amount of net operating income for next year? (Do not prepare an income statement; use the degree of operating leverage to compute your answer.)

EXERCISE 2–16 Break-Even Analysis and CVP Graphing LO2–2, LO2–4, LO2–5

The Hartford Symphony Guild is planning its annual dinner-dance. The dinner-dance committee assembled the following expected costs for the event:

Dinner (per person).............................	$18
Favors and program (per person)...................	$2
Band	$2,800
Rental of ballroom.............................	$900
Professional entertainment during intermission	$1,000
Tickets and advertising	$1,300

The committee members would like to charge $35 per person for the evening's activities.

Required:
1. What is the break-even point for the dinner-dance (in terms of the number of persons who must attend)?
2. Assume only 300 persons attended the dinner-dance last year. If the same number attend this year, what price per ticket must be charged in order to break even?
3. Refer to the original data ($35 ticket price per person). Prepare a CVP graph for the dinner-dance from zero tickets up to 600 tickets sold.

EXERCISE 2–17 Break-Even and Target Profit Analysis LO2–4, LO2–5, LO2–6

Outback Outfitters sells recreational equipment. One of the company's products, a small camp stove, sells for $50 per unit. Variable expenses are $32 per stove, and fixed expenses associated with the stove total $108,000 per month.

Required:
1. What is the break-even point in unit sales and in dollar sales?
2. If the variable expenses per stove increase as a percentage of the selling price, will it result in a higher or a lower break-even point? Why? (Assume the fixed expenses remain unchanged.)
3. At present, the company is selling 8,000 stoves per month. The sales manager is convinced a 10% reduction in the selling price would result in a 25% increase in monthly sales of stoves. Prepare two contribution format income statements, one under present operating conditions, and one as operations would appear after the proposed changes. Show both total and per-unit data on your statements.
4. Refer to the data in (3) above. How many stoves would have to be sold at the new selling price to attain a target profit of $35,000 per month?

EXERCISE 2–18 Break-Even and Target Profit Analysis; Margin of Safety; CM Ratio LO2–1, LO2–3, LO2–5, LO2–6, LO2–7

Menlo Company distributes a single product. The company's sales and expenses for last month follow:

	Total	Per Unit
Sales	$450,000	$30
Variable expenses................	180,000	12
Contribution margin	270,000	$18
Fixed expenses	216,000	
Net operating income.............	$ 54,000	

Required:
1. What is the monthly break-even point in unit sales and in dollar sales?
2. Without resorting to computations, what is the total contribution margin at the break-even point?
3. How many units would have to be sold each month to attain a target profit of $90,000? Verify your answer by preparing a contribution format income statement at the target sales level.
4. Refer to the original data. Compute the company's margin of safety in both dollar and percentage terms.
5. What is the company's CM ratio? If the company can sell more units, thereby increasing sales by $50,000 per month, and there is no change in fixed expenses, by how much would you expect monthly net operating income to increase?

Problems   Mc Graw Hill connect

PROBLEM 2–19 Break-Even Analysis; Pricing LO2–1, LO2–4, LO2–5

Last year Minden Company introduced a new product and sold 15,000 units of it at a price of $70 per unit. The product's variable expenses are $40 per unit and its fixed expenses are $540,000 per year.

Required:

1. What was this product's net operating income (loss) last year?
2. What is the product's break-even point in unit sales and dollar sales?
3. Assume the company conducted a marketing study that estimates it can increase annual sales of this product by 5,000 units for each $2 reduction in its selling price. If the company will only consider price reductions in increments of $2 (e.g., $68, $66, etc.), what is the maximum annual profit it can earn on this product? What sales volume and selling price per unit generate the maximum profit?
4. What would be the break-even point in unit sales and in dollar sales using the selling price that you determined in requirement 3? Why is this break-even point different from the break-even point you computed in requirement 2?

PROBLEM 2–20 CVP Applications: Break-Even Analysis; Cost Structure; Target Sales
LO2–1, LO2–3, LO2–4, LO2–5, LO2–6, LO2–8

Northwood Company manufactures basketballs. The company has a ball that sells for $25. At present, the ball is manufactured in a small plant that relies heavily on direct labor workers. Thus, variable expenses are high, totaling $15 per ball, of which 60% is direct labor cost.

Last year, the company sold 30,000 of these balls, with the following results:

Sales (30,000 balls)	$750,000
Variable expenses	450,000
Contribution margin	300,000
Fixed expenses	210,000
Net operating income	$ 90,000

Required:

1. Compute (*a*) last year's CM ratio and the break-even point in balls and (*b*) the degree of operating leverage at last year's sales level.
2. Due to an increase in labor rates, the company estimates that next year's variable expenses will increase by $3 per ball. If this change takes place and the selling price per ball remains constant at $25, what will be next year's CM ratio and the break-even point in balls?
3. Refer to the data in (2) above. If the expected change in variable expenses takes place, how many balls will have to be sold next year to earn the same net operating income, $90,000, as last year?
4. Refer again to the data in (2) above. The president feels the company must raise the selling price of its basketballs. If Northwood Company wants to maintain the same CM ratio as last year (as computed in requirement 1a), what selling price per ball must it charge next year to cover the increased labor costs?
5. Refer to the original data. The company is discussing the construction of a new, automated manufacturing plant. The new plant would slash variable expenses per ball by 40%, but it would cause fixed expenses per year to double. If the new plant is built, what would be the company's new CM ratio and new break-even point in balls?
6. Refer to the data in (5) above.
   a. If the new plant is built, how many balls will have to be sold next year to earn the same net operating income, $90,000, as last year?
   b. Assume the new plant is built and next year the company manufactures and sells 30,000 balls (the same number as sold last year). Prepare a contribution format income statement and compute the degree of operating leverage.
   c. If you were a member of top management, would you have been in favor of constructing the new plant? Explain.

PROBLEM 2–21 Sales Mix; Multiproduct Break-Even Analysis LO2–9

Gold Star Rice, Ltd., of Thailand exports Thai rice throughout Asia. The company grows three varieties of rice—White, Fragrant, and Loonzain. Budgeted sales by product and in total for the coming month are shown below:

| | Product | | | | | | | |
	White		Fragrant		Loonzain		Total	
Percentage of total sales	20%		52%		28%		100%	
Sales.....................	$150,000	100%	$390,000	100%	$210,000	100%	$750,000	100%
Variable expenses	108,000	72%	78,000	20%	84,000	40%	270,000	36%
Contribution margin..................	$ 42,000	28%	$312,000	80%	$126,000	60%	480,000	64%
Fixed expenses.......................							449,280	
Net operating income							$ 30,720	

$$\frac{\text{Dollar sales to}}{\text{break even}} = \frac{\text{Fixed expenses}}{\text{CM ratio}} = \frac{\$449,280}{0.64} = \$702,000$$

As shown by these data, net operating income is budgeted at $30,720 for the month, and the estimated break-even sales is $702,000.

Assume that actual sales for the month total $750,000 as planned; however, actual sales by product are White, $300,000; Fragrant, $180,000; and Loonzain, $270,000.

Required:
1. Prepare a contribution format income statement for the month based on the actual sales data. Present the income statement in the format shown above.
2. Compute the break-even point in dollar sales for the month based on your actual data.
3. Considering the fact that the company met its $750,000 sales budget for the month, the president is shocked at the results shown on your income statement in (1) above. Prepare a brief memo for the president explaining why the net operating income (loss) and the break-even point in dollar sales are different from what was budgeted.

PROBLEM 2–22 CVP Applications; Contribution Margin Ratio; Break-Even Analysis; Cost Structure LO2–1, LO2–3, LO2–4, LO2–5, LO2–6

PEM, Inc., is experiencing financial difficulty due to erratic sales of its only product, a high-capacity battery for laptop computers. The company's contribution format income statement for the most recent month is given below:

Sales (19,500 units × $30 per unit)...............	$585,000
Variable expenses.............................	409,500
Contribution margin	175,500
Fixed expenses...............................	180,000
Net operating loss.............................	$ (4,500)

Required:
1. Compute the company's CM ratio and its break-even point in unit sales and dollar sales.
2. The president believes a $16,000 increase in the monthly advertising budget, combined with an intensified effort by the sales staff, will increase unit sales and the total sales by $80,000 per month. If the president is right, what will be the increase (decrease) in the company's monthly net operating income?
3. Refer to the original data. The sales manager is convinced a 10% reduction in the selling price, combined with an increase of $60,000 in the monthly advertising budget, will double unit sales. If the sales manager is right, what will be the revised net operating income (loss)?
4. Refer to the original data. The Marketing Department thinks a fancy new package for the laptop computer battery would grow sales. The new package would increase packaging costs by 75 cents per unit. Assuming no other changes, how many units would have to be sold each month to attain a target profit of $9,750?

5. Refer to the original data. By automating, the company could reduce variable expenses by $3 per unit. However, fixed expenses would increase by $72,000 each month.

   a. Compute the new CM ratio and the new break-even point in unit sales and dollar sales.

   b. Assume the company expects to sell 26,000 units next month. Prepare two contribution format income statements, one assuming that operations are not automated and one assuming they are. (Show data on a per-unit and percentage basis, as well as in total, for each alternative.)

   c. Would you recommend that the company automate its operations? Explain.

PROBLEM 2–23 CVP Applications; Contribution Margin Ratio: Degree of Operating Leverage LO2–1, LO2–3, LO2–4, LO2–5, LO2–8

Feather Friends, Inc., distributes a high-quality wooden birdhouse that sells for $20 per unit. Variable expenses are $8 per unit, and fixed expenses total $180,000 per year. Its operating results for last year were as follows:

Sales	$400,000
Variable expenses	160,000
Contribution margin	240,000
Fixed expenses	180,000
Net operating income	$ 60,000

Required:

Answer each question independently based on the original data:

1. What is the product's CM ratio?
2. Use the CM ratio to determine the break-even point in dollar sales.
3. Assume this year's unit sales and total sales increase by 3,750 units and $75,000, respectively. If the fixed expenses do not change, how much will net operating income increase?
4. *a.* What is the degree of operating leverage based on last year's sales?
    b. Assume the president expects this year's unit sales to increase by 20%. Using the degree of operating leverage from last year, what percentage increase in net operating income will the company realize this year?
5. The sales manager is convinced a 10% reduction in the selling price, combined with a $30,000 increase in advertising, would increase this year's unit sales by 25%. If the sales manager is right, what would be this year's net operating income if his ideas are implemented? Do you recommend implementing the sales manager's suggestions? Why?
6. The president does not want to change the selling price. Instead, he wants to increase the sales commission by $1 per unit. He thinks this move, combined with some increase in advertising, would increase this year's unit sales by 25%. How much could the president increase this year's advertising expense and still earn the same $60,000 net operating income as last year?

PROBLEM 2–24 Break-Even and Target Profit Analysis LO2–5, LO2–6

The Shirt Works sells a large variety of tee shirts and sweatshirts. Steve Hooper, the owner, is thinking of expanding his sales by hiring high school students, on a commission basis, to sell sweatshirts bearing the name and mascot of the local high school.

These sweatshirts would have to be ordered from the manufacturer six weeks in advance and could not be returned because of the unique printing required. The sweatshirts would cost Hooper $8 each with a minimum order of 75 sweatshirts. Any additional sweatshirts would have to be ordered in increments of 75.

Because Hooper's plan would not require any additional facilities, the only costs associated with the project would be the costs of the sweatshirts and the costs of the sales commissions. The selling price of the sweatshirts would be $13.50 each. Hooper would pay the students a commission of $1.50 for each shirt sold.

Required:

1. What level of unit sales and dollar sales is needed to attain a target profit of $1,200?
2. Assume Hooper places an initial order for 75 sweatshirts. What is his break-even point in unit sales and dollar sales?
3. How many sweatshirts would Hooper need to sell to earn a target profit of $1,320?

PROBLEM 2–25 Changes in Fixed and Variable Costs; Break-Even and Target Profit Analysis LO2–4, LO2–5, LO2–6

Neptune Company has developed a small inflatable toy it is anxious to introduce to its customers. The company's Marketing Department estimates that demand for the new toy will range between 15,000 units and 35,000 units per month. The new toy will sell for $3 per unit. Enough capacity exists in the company's plant to produce 18,000 units of the toy each month. Variable expenses to manufacture and sell one unit would be $1.00, and incremental fixed expenses associated with the toy would total $22,000 per month.

Neptune has also identified an outside supplier who could produce the toy for a price of $1.75 per unit, plus a fixed fee of $15,000 per month for any production volume up to 20,000 units. For a production volume between 20,001 and 40,000 units, the fixed fee would increase to a total of $30,000 per month.

Required:

1. Calculate the break-even point in unit sales assuming Neptune does not hire the outside supplier.
2. How much profit will Neptune earn assuming:
   a. It produces and sells 18,000 units?
   b. It does not produce any units and instead outsources the production of 18,000 units to the outside supplier and then sells those units to its customers?
3. Calculate the break-even point in unit sales assuming Neptune plans to use all of its production capacity to produce the first 18,000 units that it sells and also commits to hiring the outside supplier to produce up to 17,000 additional units.
4. Assume Neptune plans to use all of its production capacity to produce the first 18,000 units it sells and also commits to hiring the outside supplier to produce up to 17,000 additional units.
   a. What total unit sales would Neptune need to achieve in order to equal the profit earned in requirement 2a?
   b. What total unit sales would Neptune need to achieve in order to attain a target profit of $16,500 per month?
   c. How much profit will Neptune earn if it sells 35,000 units per month?
   d. How much profit will Neptune earn if it sells 35,000 units per month and agrees to pay its marketing manager a bonus of 10 cents for each unit sold above the break-even point from requirement 3?
5. If Neptune outsources all production to the outside supplier, how much profit will the company earn if it sells 35,000 units?

PROBLEM 2–26 CVP Applications; Break-Even Analysis; Graphing LO2–1, LO2–2, LO2–4, LO2–5

The Fashion Shoe Company operates a chain of women's shoe shops that carry many styles of shoes that are all sold at the same price. Sales personnel in the shops are paid a sales commission on each pair of shoes sold plus a small base salary.

The following data pertain to Shop 48 and are typical of the company's many outlets:

	Per Pair of Shoes
Selling price	$30.00
Variable expenses:	
Invoice cost	$13.50
Sales commission	4.50
Total variable expenses	$18.00

	Annual
Fixed expenses:	
Advertising	$ 30,000
Rent	20,000
Salaries	100,000
Total fixed expenses	$150,000

Required:

1. What is Shop 48's annual break-even point in unit sales and dollar sales?
2. Prepare a CVP graph showing cost and revenue data for Shop 48 from zero shoes up to 17,000 pairs of shoes sold each year. Clearly indicate the break-even point on the graph.
3. If 12,000 pairs of shoes are sold in a year, what would be Shop 48's net operating income (loss)?
4. The company is considering paying the Shop 48 store manager an incentive commission of 75 cents per pair of shoes (in addition to the salesperson's commission). If this change is made, what will be the new break-even point in unit sales and dollar sales?
5. Refer to the original data. As an alternative to (4) above, the company is considering paying the Shop 48 store manager 50 cents commission on each pair of shoes sold in excess of the break-even point. If this change is made, what will be Shop 48's net operating income (loss) if 15,000 pairs of shoes are sold?
6. Refer to the original data. The company is considering eliminating sales commissions entirely in its shops and increasing fixed salaries by $31,500 annually. If this change is made, what will be Shop 48's new break-even point in unit sales and dollar sales? Would you recommend that the change be made? Explain.

PROBLEM 2–27 Sales Mix; Break-Even Analysis; Margin of Safety LO2–7, LO2–9

Island Novelties, Inc., of Palau makes two products—Hawaiian Fantasy and Tahitian Joy. Each product's selling price, variable expense per unit, and annual sales volume are as follows:

	Hawaiian Fantasy	Tahitian Joy
Selling price per unit....................	$15	$100
Variable expense per unit..............	$9	$20
Number of units sold annually	20,000	5,000

Fixed expenses total $475,800 per year.

Required:

1. Assuming the sales mix given above, do the following:
    a. Prepare a contribution format income statement showing both dollar and percent columns for each product and for the company as a whole.
    b. Compute the company's break-even point in dollar sales. Also, compute its margin of safety in dollars and its margin of safety percentage.
2. The company has developed a new product called Samoan Delight that sells for $45 each and has variable expenses of $36 per unit. If the company can sell 10,000 units of Samoan Delight without incurring any additional fixed expenses:
    a. Prepare a revised contribution format income statement that includes Samoan Delight. Assume that sales of the other two products do not change.
    b. Compute the company's revised break-even point in dollar sales. Also, compute its revised margin of safety in dollars and margin of safety percentage.
3. The president of the company examines your figures and says, "There's something strange here. Our fixed expenses haven't changed and you show greater total contribution margin if we add the new product, but you also show our break-even point going up. With greater contribution margin, the break-even point should go down, not up. You've made a mistake somewhere." Explain to the president what happened.

PROBLEM 2–28 Sales Mix; Multiproduct Break-Even Analysis LO2-9

Topper Sports, Inc., produces high-quality sports equipment. The company's Racket Division manufactures three tennis rackets—the Standard, the Deluxe, and the Pro—that are widely used in amateur play. Selected information on the rackets is given below:

	Standard	Deluxe	Pro
Selling price per racket...............	$40.00	$60.00	$90.00
Variable expenses per racket:			
Production........................	$22.00	$27.00	$31.50
Selling (5% of selling price).........	$2.00	$3.00	$4.50

All sales are made through the company's own retail outlets. The Racket Division has the following fixed costs:

	Per Month
Fixed production costs	$120,000
Advertising expense	100,000
Administrative salaries	50,000
Total	$270,000

Sales, in units, over the past two months have been as follows:

	Standard	Deluxe	Pro	Total
April	2,000	1,000	5,000	8,000
May............	8,000	1,000	3,000	12,000

Required:
1. Prepare contribution format income statements for April and May. Use the following headings:

	Standard		Deluxe		Pro		Total	
	Amount	Percent	Amount	Percent	Amount	Percent	Amount	Percent
Sales.................								
Etc.								

Place the fixed expenses only in the Total column. Do not show percentages for the fixed expenses.

2. Upon seeing the income statements in (1) above, the president stated, "I can't believe this! We sold 50% more rackets in May than in April, yet profits went down. It's obvious that costs are out of control in that division." What other explanation can you give for the drop in net operating income?

3. Compute the Racket Division's break-even point in dollar sales for April.

4. Without doing any calculations, explain whether the break-even point would be higher or lower with May's sales mix than with April's sales mix.

5. Assume sales of the Standard racket increase by $20,000. What would be the effect on net operating income? What would be the effect if Pro racket sales increased by $20,000? Do not prepare income statements; use the incremental analysis approach in determining your answer.

PROBLEM 2–29 Changes in Cost Structure; Break-Even Analysis; Operating Leverage; Margin of Safety LO2–4, LO2–5, LO2–7, LO2–8

Morton Company's contribution format income statement for last month is given below:

Sales (15,000 units × $30 per unit)........	$450,000
Variable expenses	315,000
Contribution margin	135,000
Fixed expenses	90,000
Net operating income	$ 45,000

The industry in which Morton Company operates is quite sensitive to cyclical movements in the economy. Thus, profits vary considerably from year to year according to general economic conditions. The company has a large amount of unused capacity and is studying ways of improving profits.

Required:
1. New equipment has come onto the market that would allow Morton Company to automate a portion of its operations. Variable expenses would be reduced by $9 per unit. However, fixed expenses would increase to a total of $225,000 each month. Prepare two contribution format income statements, one showing present operations and one showing how operations would

appear if the new equipment is purchased. Show an Amount column, a Per Unit column, and a Percent column on each statement. Do not show percentages for the fixed expenses.

2. Refer to the income statements in (1). For the present operations and the proposed new operations, compute (*a*) the degree of operating leverage, (*b*) the break-even point in dollar sales, and (*c*) the margin of safety in dollars and the margin of safety percentage.

3. Refer again to the data in (1). As a manager, what factor would be paramount in your mind in deciding whether to purchase the new equipment? (Assume enough funds are available to make the purchase.)

4. Refer to the original data. Rather than purchase new equipment, the marketing manager argues that the company's marketing strategy should be changed. Rather than pay sales commissions, which are currently included in variable expenses, the company would pay salespersons fixed salaries and would invest heavily in advertising. The marketing manager claims this new approach would increase unit sales by 30% without any change in selling price; the company's new monthly fixed expenses would be $180,000; and its net operating income would increase by 20%. Compute the company's break-even point in dollar sales under the new marketing strategy. Do you agree with the marketing manager's proposal?

PROBLEM 2–30 Graphing; Incremental Analysis; Operating Leverage LO2–2, LO2–4, LO2–5, LO2–6, LO2–8

Angie Silva recently opened The Sandal Shop in Brisbane, Australia, a store that specializes in fashionable sandals. In time, she hopes to open a chain of sandal shops. As a first step, she gathered the following data for her new store:

Sales price per pair of sandals	$40
Variable expenses per pair of sandals	16
Contribution margin per pair of sandals	$24
Fixed expenses per year:	
Building rental	$15,000
Equipment depreciation	7,000
Selling	20,000
Administrative	18,000
Total fixed expenses	$60,000

Required:

1. What is the break-even point in unit sales and dollar sales?

2. Prepare a CVP graph or a profit graph for the store from zero pairs up to 4,000 pairs of sandals sold each year. Indicate the break-even point on your graph.

3. Angie decided she must earn a profit of $18,000 the first year to justify her time and effort. How many pairs of sandals must be sold to attain this target profit?

4. Angie now has two salespersons working in the store—one full time and one part time. It will cost her an additional $8,000 per year to convert the part-time position to a full-time position. Angie believes that the change would increase annual sales by $25,000. Should she convert the position? Use the incremental approach. (Do not prepare an income statement.)

5. Refer to the original data. During the first year, the store sold only 3,000 pairs of sandals and reported the following operating results:

Sales (3,000 pairs)	$120,000
Variable expenses	48,000
Contribution margin	72,000
Fixed expenses	60,000
Net operating income	$ 12,000

a. What is the store's degree of operating leverage?

b. Angie is confident that with a more intense sales effort and a more creative advertising program she can increase unit sales by 50% next year. Using the degree of operating leverage, what would be the expected percentage increase in net operating income if Angie is able to increase unit sales by 50%?

PROBLEM 2–31 Interpretive Questions on the CVP Graph LO2–2, LO2–5

A CVP graph, such as the one shown below, is a useful technique for showing relationships among an organization's costs, volume, and profits.

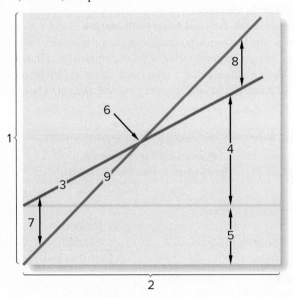

Required:

1. Identify the numbered components in the CVP graph.
2. State the effect of each of the following actions on line 3, line 9, and the break-even point. For line 3 and line 9, state whether the action will cause the line to:

   Remain unchanged.
   Shift upward.
   Shift downward.
   Have a steeper slope (i.e., rotate upward).
   Have a flatter slope (i.e., rotate downward).
   Shift upward *and* have a steeper slope.
   Shift upward *and* have a flatter slope.
   Shift downward *and* have a steeper slope.
   Shift downward *and* have a flatter slope.

   In the case of the break-even point, state whether the action will cause the break-even point to:

   Remain unchanged.
   Increase.
   Decrease.
   Probably change, but the direction is uncertain.

   Treat each case independently.

   x.   *Example.*   Fixed expenses are reduced by $5,000 per period.
        Answer (see choices above):   Line 3: Shift downward.
                                                Line 9: Remain unchanged.
                                                Break-even point: Decrease.

   a.   The unit selling price is increased from $18 to $20.
   b.   Unit variable expenses are decreased from $12 to $10.
   c.   Fixed expenses are increased by $3,000 per period.
   d.   Two thousand more units are sold during the period than were budgeted.
   e.   Due to paying salespersons a commission rather than a flat salary, fixed expenses are reduced by $8,000 per period and unit variable expenses are increased by $3.
   f.   Due to an increase in the cost of materials, both unit variable expenses and the selling price are increased by $2.
   g.   Advertising costs are increased by $10,000 per period, resulting in a 10% increase in the number of units sold.
   h.   Due to automating an operation previously done by workers, fixed expenses are increased by $12,000 per period and unit variable expenses are reduced by $4.

Case connect

Select cases are available in Connect.

CASE 2–32 Cost Structure; Break-Even and Target Profit Analysis LO2–4, LO2–5, LO2–6

Pittman Company is a small but growing manufacturer of telecommunications equipment. The company has no sales force of its own; rather, it relies completely on independent sales agents to market its products. These agents are paid a sales commission of 15% for all items sold.

Barbara Cheney, Pittman's controller, just prepared the company's budgeted income statement for next year as follows:

Pittman Company Budgeted Income Statement For the Year Ended December 31		
Sales		$16,000,000
Manufacturing expenses:		
Variable	$7,200,000	
Fixed overhead	2,340,000	9,540,000
Gross margin		6,460,000
Selling and administrative expenses:		
Commissions to agents	$2,400,000	
Fixed marketing expenses	120,000*	
Fixed administrative expenses	1,800,000	4,320,000
Net operating income		2,140,000
Fixed interest expenses		540,000
Income before income taxes		1,600,000
Income taxes (30%)		480,000
Net income		$ 1,120,000

* Primarily depreciation on storage facilities.

As Barbara handed the statement to Karl Vecci, Pittman's president, she commented, "I went ahead and used the agents' 15% commission rate in completing these statements, but we've just learned that they refuse to handle our products next year unless we increase the commission rate to 20%."

"That's the last straw," Karl replied angrily. "Those agents have been demanding more and more, and this time they've gone too far. How can they possibly defend a 20% commission rate?"

"They claim that after paying for advertising, travel, and the other costs of promotion, there's nothing left over for profit," replied Barbara.

"I say it's just plain robbery," retorted Karl. "And I also say it's time we dumped those guys and got our own sales force. Can you get your people to work up some cost figures for us to look at?"

"We've already worked them up," said Barbara. "Several companies we know about pay a 7.5% commission to their own salespeople, along with a small salary. Of course, we would have to handle all promotion costs, too. We figure our fixed expenses would increase by $2,400,000 per year, but that would be more than offset by the $3,200,000 (20% × $16,000,000) that we would avoid on agents' commissions."

The breakdown of the $2,400,000 cost follows:

Salaries:	
Sales manager	$ 100,000
Salespersons	600,000
Travel and entertainment	400,000
Advertising	1,300,000
Total	$2,400,000

"Super," replied Karl. "And I noticed that the $2,400,000 equals what we're paying the agents under the old 15% commission rate."

"It's even better than that," explained Barbara. "We can actually save $75,000 a year because that's what we're paying our auditors to check out the agents' reports. So our overall administrative expenses would be less."

"Pull all of these numbers together and we'll show them to the executive committee tomorrow," said Karl. "With the approval of the committee, we can move on the matter immediately."

Required:

1. Compute Pittman Company's break-even point in dollar sales for next year assuming:
    a. The agents' commission rate remains unchanged at 15%.
    b. The agents' commission rate is increased to 20%.
    c. The company employs its own sales force.

2. Assume Pittman Company decides to continue selling through agents and pays the 20% commission rate. Determine the dollar sales required to generate the same net income as contained in the budgeted income statement for next year.

3. Determine the dollar sales at which net income would be equal regardless of whether Pittman Company sells through agents (at a 20% commission rate) or employs its own sales force.

4. Compute the degree of operating leverage the company would expect to have at the end of next year assuming:
    a. The agents' commission rate remains unchanged at 15%.
    b. The agents' commission rate is increased to 20%.
    c. The company employs its own sales force.
    Use income *before* income taxes in your operating leverage computation.

5. Based on the data in (1) through (4) above, make a recommendation as to whether the company should continue to use sales agents (at a 20% commission rate) or employ its own sales force. Give reasons for your answer.

(CMA, adapted)

Appendix 2A: Analyzing Mixed Costs

The main body of Chapter 2 assumed all costs could be readily classified as variable or fixed. In reality, many costs contain both variable *and* fixed components—they are *mixed costs*. The purpose of this appendix is to describe various methods companies can use to separate mixed costs into their variable and fixed components, thereby enabling cost-volume-profit (CVP) analysis.

Mixed costs are very common in most organizations. For example, the overall cost of performing surgeries for patients at the Harvard Medical School Hospital is a mixed cost. The costs of equipment depreciation and surgeons' and nurses' salaries are fixed, but the costs of surgical gloves, power, and other supplies are variable. At Southwest Airlines, maintenance costs are a mixed cost. The company incurs fixed costs for renting maintenance facilities and for keeping skilled mechanics on the payroll, but the costs of replacement parts, lubricating oils, tires, and so forth, are variable with respect to how often and how far the company's aircraft are flown.

The fixed portion of a mixed cost represents the minimum cost of having a service *ready and available* for use. The variable portion represents the cost incurred for *actual consumption* of the service; thus, it varies in proportion to the amount of service actually consumed.

Managers can use a variety of methods to estimate the fixed and variable components of a mixed cost such as *account analysis,* the *engineering approach,* the *high-low method,* and *least-squares regression analysis.* In **account analysis,** an account is classified as either variable or fixed based on the analyst's prior knowledge of how the cost in the account behaves. For example, direct materials would be classified as variable and a building lease cost would be classified as fixed because of the nature of those costs. The **engineering approach** to cost analysis involves a detailed analysis of what cost behavior should be, based on an industrial engineer's evaluation of the production methods to be used, the materials specifications, labor requirements, equipment usage, production efficiency, power consumption, and so on.

The high-low method and least-squares regression method estimate the fixed and variable elements of a mixed cost by analyzing past records of cost and activity data. Throughout the remainder of this appendix, we will define these two cost estimation methods and use an example from Brentline Hospital to illustrate how they each derive their respective fixed and variable cost estimates. The least-squares regression computations will be explained using Microsoft Excel because it can perform the underlying mathematics much faster than using a pencil and a calculator.

Diagnosing Cost Behavior with a Scattergraph Plot

LEARNING OBJECTIVE 2–10

Analyze a mixed cost using a scattergraph plot and the high-low method.

Assume Brentline Hospital is interested in predicting future monthly maintenance costs for budgeting purposes. The senior management team believes that maintenance cost is a mixed cost and the variable portion of this cost is driven by the number of patient-days. Each day a patient is in the hospital counts as one patient-day. The hospital's chief financial officer gathered the following data for the most recent seven-month period:

Month	Activity Level: Patient-Days	Maintenance Cost Incurred
January...............	5,600	$7,900
February..............	7,100	$8,500
March	5,000	$7,400
April..................	6,500	$8,200
May	7,300	$9,100
June..................	8,000	$9,800
July	6,200	$7,800

The first step in applying the high-low method or the least-squares regression method is to diagnose cost behavior with a scattergraph plot. The scattergraph plot of maintenance costs versus patient-days at Brentline Hospital is shown in Exhibit 2A–1. Two things should be noted about this scattergraph:

EXHIBIT 2A–1

Scattergraph Method of Cost Analysis

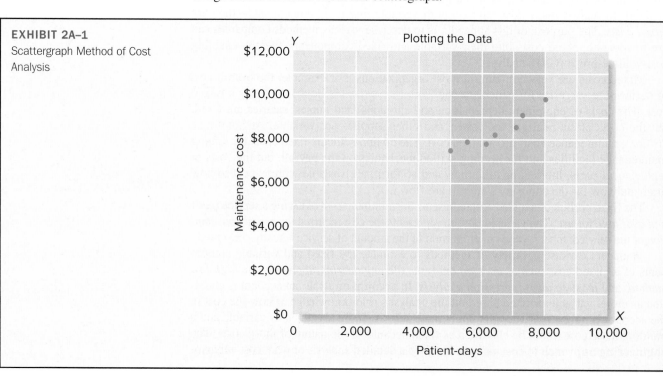

1. The total maintenance cost, Y, is plotted on the vertical axis. Cost is known as the **dependent variable** because the amount of cost incurred during a period depends on the level of activity for the period. (That is, as the level of activity increases, total cost also will ordinarily increase.)

2. The activity, X (patient-days in this case), is plotted on the horizontal axis. Activity is known as the **independent variable** because it causes variations in the cost.

From the scattergraph plot, it is evident that maintenance costs do increase with the number of patient-days in an approximately *linear* fashion. In other words, the points lie more or less along a straight line that slopes upward and to the right. **Linear cost behavior** exists whenever a straight line is a reasonable approximation for the relation between cost and activity.

Plotting the data on a scattergraph is an essential diagnostic step that should be performed before performing the high-low or least-squares regression calculations. If the scattergraph plot reveals linear cost behavior, then it makes sense to perform the high-low or least-squares regression calculations to separate the mixed cost into its variable and fixed components. If the scattergraph plot does not depict linear cost behavior, then it makes no sense to proceed any further in analyzing the data.

Once we determine that the dependent and independent variables have a linear relationship, the high-low and least-squares regression methods both rely on the following equation for a straight line (as introduced in Chapter 1) to express the relationship between a mixed cost and the level of activity:

$$Y = a + bX$$

In this equation,

Y = The total mixed cost

a = The total fixed cost (the vertical intercept of the line)

b = The variable cost per unit of activity (the slope of the line)

X = The level of activity

The High-Low Method

The high-low method is based on the rise-over-run formula for the slope of a straight line. Assuming the relation between cost and activity can be represented by a straight line, then the slope of the straight line is equal to the variable cost per unit of activity. Consequently, the following formula can be used to estimate the variable cost:

$$\text{Variable cost} = \text{Slope of the line} = \frac{\text{Rise}}{\text{Run}} = \frac{Y_2 - Y_1}{X_2 - X_1}$$

To analyze mixed costs with the **high-low method,** begin by identifying the period with the lowest level of activity and the period with the highest level of activity. The period with the lowest activity is selected as the first point in the above formula and the period with the highest activity is selected as the second point. Consequently, the formula becomes:

$$\text{Variable cost} = \frac{Y_2 - Y_1}{X_2 - X_1} = \frac{\text{Cost at the high activity level} - \text{Cost at the low activity level}}{\text{High activity level} - \text{Low activity level}}$$

or

$$\text{Variable cost} = \frac{\text{Change in cost}}{\text{Change in activity}}$$

Therefore, when the high-low method is used, the variable cost is estimated by dividing the difference in cost between the high and low levels of activity by the change in activity between those two points.

To return to the Brentline Hospital example, using the high-low method, we first identify the periods with the highest and lowest *activity*—in this case, June and March. We then use the activity and cost data from these two periods to estimate the variable cost component as follows:

	Patient-Days	Maintenance Cost Incurred
High activity level (June)	8,000	$9,800
Low activity level (March).	5,000	7,400
Change	3,000	$2,400

$$\text{Variable cost} = \frac{\text{Change in cost}}{\text{Change in activity}} = \frac{\$2,400}{3,000 \text{ patient-days}} = \$0.80 \text{ per patient-day}$$

Having determined the variable maintenance cost is 80 cents per patient-day, we can now calculate the amount of fixed cost. This is done by taking the total cost at *either* the high or the low activity level and deducting the variable cost element. In the computation below, total cost at the high activity level is used in computing the fixed cost element:

$$
\begin{aligned}
\text{Fixed cost element} &= \text{Total cost} - \text{Variable cost element} \\
&= \$9,800 - (\$0.80 \text{ per patient-day} \times 8,000 \text{ patient-days}) \\
&= \$3,400
\end{aligned}
$$

Given that we have estimated the variable and fixed cost elements, the maintenance cost can now be expressed as $3,400 per month plus 80 cents per patient-day, or as:

$$Y = \$3,400 + \$0.80X$$

↑	↑
Total maintenance cost	Total patient-days

The data used in this illustration are shown graphically in Exhibit 2A–2. Notice a straight line has been drawn through the points corresponding to the low and high levels of activity. In essence, that is what the high-low method does—it draws a straight line through those two points.

Sometimes the high and low levels of activity don't coincide with the high and low amounts of cost. For example, the period that has the highest level of activity may not have the highest amount of cost. Nevertheless, the costs at the highest and lowest levels of *activity* are always used to analyze a mixed cost under the high-low method. The reason is that the analyst would like to use data that reflect the greatest possible variation in activity.

The high-low method is very simple to apply, but it suffers from a major (and sometimes critical) defect—it utilizes only two data points. Generally, two data points are not enough to produce accurate estimates. Additionally, the periods with the highest and lowest activity tend to be unusual. A cost formula estimated solely using data from these unusual periods may misrepresent the true cost behavior during normal periods. Such a distortion is evident in Exhibit 2A–2. The straight line should probably be shifted down somewhat so it is closer to more of the data points. For these reasons, least-squares regression will generally be more accurate than the high-low method.

The Least-Squares Regression Method

LEARNING OBJECTIVE 2–11
Analyze a mixed cost using a scattergraph plot and the least-squares regression method.

The **least-squares regression method,** unlike the high-low method, uses all of the data to separate a mixed cost into its fixed and variable components. A *regression line* of the form $Y = a + bX$ is fitted to the data, where a (the intercept) represents the total fixed

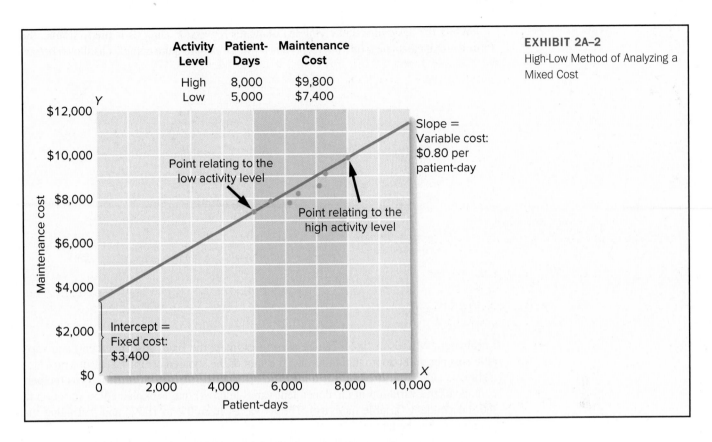

Activity Level	Patient-Days	Maintenance Cost
High	8,000	$9,800
Low	5,000	$7,400

EXHIBIT 2A–2

High-Low Method of Analyzing a Mixed Cost

cost and *b* (the slope) represents the variable cost per unit of activity. The basic idea underlying the least-squares regression method is illustrated in Exhibit 2A–3 using hypothetical data points. Notice from the exhibit that the deviations from the plotted points to the regression line are measured vertically on the graph. These vertical deviations are called the regression errors. There is nothing mysterious about the least-squares regression method. It simply computes the regression line that minimizes the sum of these squared errors.

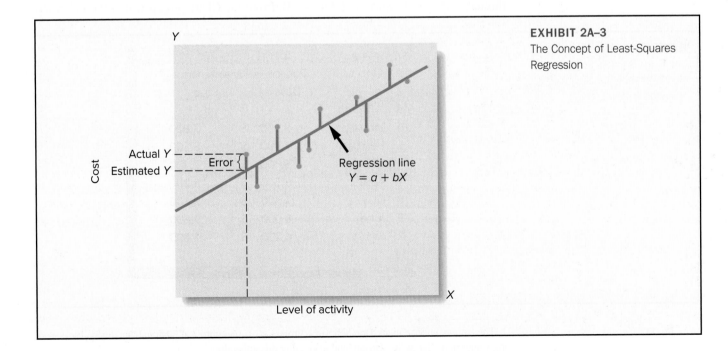

EXHIBIT 2A–3

The Concept of Least-Squares Regression

While the basic idea underlying least-squares regression analysis is pretty simple, the formulas that calculate a (the intercept) and b (the slope) are quite complex as shown below:

$$b = \frac{n(\Sigma XY) - (\Sigma X)(\Sigma Y)}{n(\Sigma X^2) - (\Sigma X)^2}$$

$$a = \frac{(\Sigma Y) - b(\Sigma X)}{n}$$

where:

X = The level of activity (independent variable)

Y = The total mixed cost (dependent variable)

a = The total fixed cost (the vertical intercept of the line)

b = The variable cost per unit of activity (the slope of the line)

n = Number of observations

Σ = Sum across all n observations

Fortunately, Microsoft Excel can be used to estimate the fixed cost (intercept) and variable cost per unit (slope) that minimize the sum of the squared errors. Excel also provides a statistic called the R^2, which is a measure of "goodness of fit." The R^2 tells us the percentage of the variation in the dependent variable (cost) that is explained by variation in the independent variable (activity). The R^2 varies from 0% to 100%, and the higher the percentage, the better.

As mentioned earlier, you should always plot the data in a scattergraph, but it is particularly important to check the data visually when the R^2 is low. A quick look at the scattergraph can reveal that there is little relation between the cost and the activity or that the relation is something other than a simple straight line. In such cases, additional analysis would be required.

Exhibit 2A–4 uses Excel to depict the Brentline Hospital data we used earlier to illustrate the high-low method. We'll be using this same data set to illustrate how Excel can be used to create a scattergraph plot and to calculate the intercept a, the slope b, and the R^2 using least-squares regression.[5]

To prepare a scattergraph plot in Excel, begin by highlighting the data in cells B4 through C10 (as shown in Exhibit 2A–4). From the Charts group within the Insert tab,

EXHIBIT 2A–4

The Least-Squares Regression Worksheet for Brentline Hospital

	A	B	C
1		Patient	Maintenance
2		Days	Cost
3	Month	X	Y
4	January	5,600	$ 7,900
5	February	7,100	$ 8,500
6	March	5,000	$ 7,400
7	April	6,500	$ 8,200
8	May	7,300	$ 9,100
9	June	8,000	$ 9,800
10	July	6,200	$ 7,800
11			

Least-squares regression

Microsoft Excel

[5] The authors wish to thank Don Schwartz, Professor of Accounting at National University, for providing suggestions that were instrumental in creating this appendix.

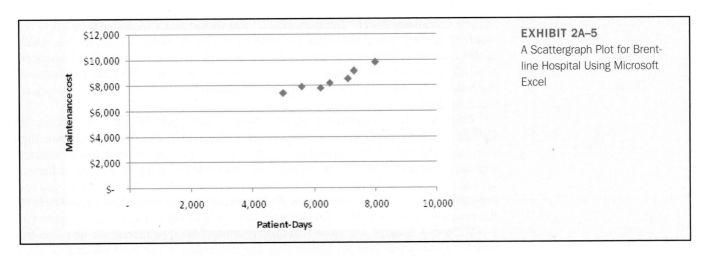

EXHIBIT 2A–5
A Scattergraph Plot for Brent-
line Hospital Using Microsoft
Excel

select the "Scatter" subgroup and then click on the choice that has no lines connecting the data points. This should produce a scattergraph plot similar to the one shown in Exhibit 2A–5. Notice the number of patient-days is plotted on the X-axis and the maintenance cost is plotted on the Y-axis.[6] As we saw verified earlier in Exhibit 2A–1, the data are approximately linear, so it makes sense to proceed with estimating a regression equation that minimizes the sum of the squared errors.

To determine the intercept a, the slope b, and the R^2, begin by right-clicking on any data point in the scattergraph plot and selecting "Add Trendline." This should produce the screen shown in Exhibit 2A–6. Notice under "Trendline Options" you should select

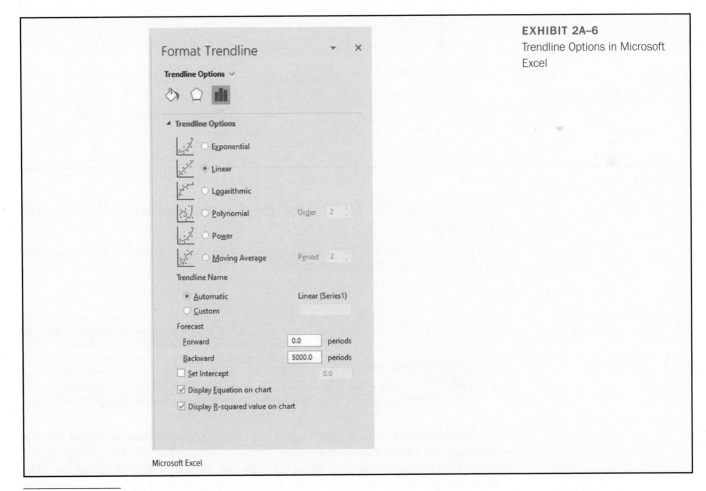

EXHIBIT 2A–6
Trendline Options in Microsoft
Excel

---

[6] To insert labels for the X-axis and Y-axis, go to the Layout tab in Excel. Then, within the Labels group, select Axis Titles.

"Linear." Similarly, under "Trendline Name" you should select "Automatic." Next to the word "Backward" you should input the lowest value for the independent variable, which in this example is 5000 patient-days. Taking this particular step instructs Excel to extend your fitted line until it intersects the Y-axis. Finally, you should check the two boxes at the bottom of Exhibit 2A–6 that say "Display Equation on chart" and "Display R-squared value on chart."

Once you have established these settings, then click "Close." As shown in Exhibit 2A–7, this will automatically insert a line within the scattergraph plot that minimizes the sum of the squared errors. It will also cause the estimated least-squares regression equation and R^2 to be inserted into your scattergraph plot. Instead of depicting the results using the form $Y = a + bX$, Excel uses an equivalent form of the equation depicted as $Y = bX + a$. In other words, Excel reverses the two terms shown to the right of the equals sign. So, in Exhibit 2A–7, Excel shows a least-squares regression equation of $y = 0.7589x + 3,430.9$. The slope b in this equation of $0.7589 represents the estimated variable maintenance cost per patient-day. The intercept a in this equation of $3,430.90 (or approximately $3,431) represents the estimated fixed monthly maintenance cost. Note that the R^2 is approximately 0.90, which is quite good and indicates that 90% of the variation in maintenance cost is explained by the variation in patient-days.

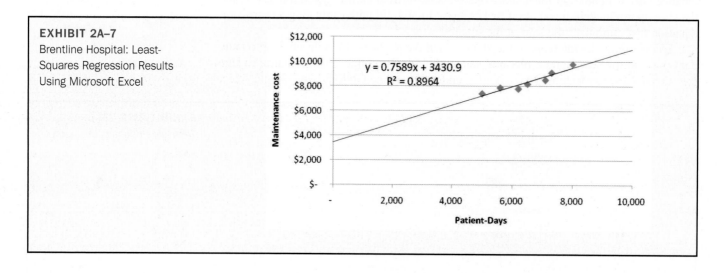

EXHIBIT 2A–7
Brentline Hospital: Least-Squares Regression Results Using Microsoft Excel

y = 0.7589x + 3430.9
R² = 0.8964

Comparing the High-Low and Least-Squares Regression Methods

The table below compares Brentline Hospital's cost estimates using the high-low method and the least-squares regression method:

	High-Low Method	Least-Squares Regression Method
Variable cost estimate per patient-day	$0.800	$0.759
Fixed cost estimate per month	$3,400	$3,431

When Brentline uses the least-squares regression method to create a straight line that minimizes the sum of the squared errors, it results in estimated fixed costs that are $31 higher than the amount derived using the high-low method. It also decreases the slope of the straight line, resulting in a lower variable cost estimate of $0.759 per patient-day rather than $0.80 per patient-day as derived using the high-low method.

Glossary (Appendix 2A)

Account analysis A method for analyzing cost behavior in which an account is classified as either variable or fixed based on the analyst's prior knowledge of how the cost in the account behaves. (p. 107)

Dependent variable A variable that responds to some causal factor; total cost is the dependent variable, as represented by the letter Y, in the equation $Y = a + bX$. (p. 109)

Engineering approach A detailed analysis of cost behavior based on an industrial engineer's evaluation of the inputs that are required to carry out a particular activity and of the prices of those inputs. (p. 107)

High-low method A method of separating a mixed cost into its fixed and variable elements by analyzing the change in cost between the high and low activity levels. (p. 109)

Independent variable A variable that acts as a causal factor; activity is the independent variable, as represented by the letter X, in the equation $Y = a + bX$. (p. 109)

Least-squares regression method A method of separating a mixed cost into its fixed and variable elements by fitting a regression line that minimizes the sum of the squared errors. (p. 110)

Linear cost behavior Cost behavior is said to be linear whenever a straight line is a reasonable approximation for the relation between cost and activity. (p. 109)

R^2 A measure of goodness of fit in least-squares regression analysis. It is the percentage of the variation in the dependent variable that is explained by variation in the independent variable. (p. 112)

connect Appendix 2A: Exercises and Problems

EXERCISE 2A–1 High-Low Method LO2–10

The Cheyenne Hotel in Big Sky, Montana, has accumulated records of the total electrical costs of the hotel and the number of occupancy-days over the last year. An occupancy-day represents a room rented for one day. The hotel's business is highly seasonal, with peaks occurring during the ski season and in the summer.

Month	Occupancy-Days	Electrical Costs
January	1,736	$4,127
February	1,904	$4,207
March	2,356	$5,083
April	960	$2,857
May	360	$1,871
June	744	$2,696
July	2,108	$4,670
August	2,406	$5,148
September	840	$2,691
October	124	$1,588
November	720	$2,454
December	1,364	$3,529

Required:

1. Using the high-low method, estimate the fixed cost of electricity per month and the variable cost of electricity per occupancy-day. Round off the fixed cost to the nearest whole dollar and the variable cost to the nearest whole cent.

2. What other factors in addition to occupancy-days are likely to affect the variation in electrical costs from month to month?

EXERCISE 2A–2 Least-Squares Regression LO2–11

Bargain Rental Car offers rental cars in an off-airport location near a major tourist destination in California. Management would like to better understand the variable and fixed portions of its car washing costs. The company operates its own car wash facility in which each returned rental car is thoroughly cleaned before being released for rental to another customer. Management believes that the variable portion of its car washing costs relates to the number of rental returns. Accordingly, the following data have been compiled:

Month	Rental Returns	Car Wash Costs
January...............	2,380	$10,825
February..............	2,421	$11,865
March	2,586	$11,332
April.................	2,725	$12,422
May	2,968	$13,850
June..................	3,281	$14,419
July	3,353	$14,935
August................	3,489	$15,738
September	3,057	$13,563
October...............	2,876	$11,889
November.............	2,735	$12,683
December.............	2,983	$13,796

Required:
1. Prepare a scattergraph plot. (Place car wash costs on the vertical axis and rental returns on the horizontal axis.)
2. Using least-squares regression, estimate the variable cost per rental return and the monthly fixed cost incurred to wash cars. The total fixed cost should be estimated to the nearest dollar and the variable cost per rental return to the nearest cent.

EXERCISE 2A–3 Cost Behavior; High-Low Method LO2–10
Hoi Chong Transport, Ltd., operates a fleet of delivery trucks in Singapore. The company determined if a truck is driven 105,000 kilometers during a year, the average operating cost is 11.4 cents per kilometer. If a truck is driven only 70,000 kilometers during a year, the average operating cost increases to 13.4 cents per kilometer.

Required:
1. Using the high-low method, estimate the variable operating cost per kilometer and the annual fixed operating cost associated with the fleet of trucks.
2. Express the variable and fixed costs in the form $Y = a + bX$.
3. If a truck were driven 80,000 kilometers during a year, what total operating cost would you expect to be incurred?

EXERCISE 2A–4 High-Low Method; Scattergraph Analysis LO2–10
Archer Company is a wholesaler of custom-built air-conditioning units for commercial buildings. It gathered the following monthly data relating to units shipped and total shipping expense:

Month	Units Shipped	Total Shipping Expense
January...............	3	$1,800
February..............	6	$2,300
March	4	$1,700
April.................	5	$2,000
May	7	$2,300
June..................	8	$2,700
July	2	$1,200

Required:
1. Prepare a scattergraph using the data given above. Plot cost on the vertical axis and activity on the horizontal axis. Is there an approximately linear relationship between shipping expense and the number of units shipped?
2. Using the high-low method, estimate the cost formula for shipping expense. Draw a straight line through the high and low data points shown in the scattergraph that you prepared in requirement 1. Make sure your line intersects the Y-axis.

3. Comment on the accuracy of your high-low estimates assuming a least-squares regression analysis estimated the total fixed costs to be $910.71 per month and the variable cost to be $217.86 per unit. How would the straight line you drew in requirement 2 differ from a straight line that minimizes the sum of the squared errors?

4. What factors, other than the number of units shipped, are likely to affect the company's shipping expense? Explain.

EXERCISE 2A–5 Least-Squares Regression LO2–11

George Caloz & Frères, located in Grenchen, Switzerland, makes luxury custom watches in small lots. One of the company's products, a platinum diving watch, goes through an etching process. The company recorded etching costs as follows over the last six weeks:

Week	Units	Total Etching Cost
1..........................	4	$ 18
2..........................	3	17
3..........................	8	25
4..........................	6	20
5..........................	7	24
6..........................	2	16
	30	$120

For planning purposes, management would like to know the variable etching cost per unit and the total fixed etching cost per week.

Required:

1. Prepare a scattergraph plot. (Plot etching costs on the vertical axis and units on the horizontal axis.)

2. Using the least-squares regression method, estimate the variable etching cost per unit and the total fixed etching cost per week. Express these estimates in the form $Y = a + bX$.

3. If the company processes five units next week, what would be the expected total etching cost? (Round your answer to the nearest cent.)

PROBLEM 2A–6 Least-Squares Regression; Scattergraph; Comparison of Activity Bases LO2–11

The Hard Rock Mining Company is developing cost formulas for management planning and decision-making purposes. The company's cost analyst concluded that utilities cost is a mixed cost, and he is attempting to find a base that correlates with the cost. The controller suggested that tons mined might be a good base to use in developing a cost formula. The production superintendent disagrees; she thinks that direct labor-hours would be a better base. The cost analyst decided to try both bases and assembled the following information:

Quarter	Tons Mined	Direct Labor-Hours	Utilities Cost
Year 1:			
First	15,000	5,000	$50,000
Second	11,000	3,000	$45,000
Third	21,000	4,000	$60,000
Fourth	12,000	6,000	$75,000
Year 2:			
First	18,000	10,000	$100,000
Second	25,000	9,000	$105,000
Third	30,000	8,000	$85,000
Fourth	28,000	11,000	$120,000

Required:

1. Using tons mined as the independent variable, prepare a scattergraph that plots tons mined on the horizontal axis and utilities cost on the vertical axis. Using the least-squares regression method, estimate the variable utilities cost per ton mined and the total fixed utilities cost per quarter. Express these estimates in the form $Y = a + bX$.

2. Using direct labor-hours as the independent variable, prepare a scattergraph that plots direct labor-hours on the horizontal axis and utilities cost on the vertical axis. Using the least-squares regression method, estimate the variable utilities cost per direct labor-hour and the total fixed utilities cost per quarter. Express these estimates in the form $Y = a + bX$.

3. Would you recommend the company use tons mined or direct labor-hours as a base for planning utilities cost?

PROBLEM 2A–7 Cost Behavior; High-Low Method; Contribution Format Income Statement LO2–10

Morrisey & Brown, Ltd., of Sydney is a merchandising company that is the sole distributor of a product that is increasing in popularity among Australian consumers. The company's income statements for the three most recent months follow:

Morrisey & Brown, Ltd. Income Statements For the Three Months Ended September 30			
	July	August	September
Sales in units	4,000	4,500	5,000
Sales	$400,000	$450,000	$500,000
Cost of goods sold	240,000	270,000	300,000
Gross margin	160,000	180,000	200,000
Selling and administrative expenses:			
Advertising expense	21,000	21,000	21,000
Shipping expense	34,000	36,000	38,000
Salaries and commissions	78,000	84,000	90,000
Insurance expense	6,000	6,000	6,000
Depreciation expense	15,000	15,000	15,000
Total selling and administrative expenses	154,000	162,000	170,000
Net operating income	$ 6,000	$ 18,000	$ 30,000

Required:

1. By analyzing the data from the company's income statements, classify each of its expenses (including cost of goods sold) as either variable, fixed, or mixed.
2. Using the high-low method, separate each mixed expense into variable and fixed elements. Express the variable and fixed portions of each mixed expense in the form $Y = a + bX$.
3. Redo the company's income statement at the 5,000-unit level of activity using the contribution format.

PROBLEM 2A–8 High-Low Method; Predicting Cost LO2–10

Nova Company's total overhead cost at various levels of activity are presented below:

Month	Machine-Hours	Total Overhead Cost
April	70,000	$198,000
May	60,000	$174,000
June	80,000	$222,000
July	90,000	$246,000

Assume the total overhead cost above consists of utilities, supervisory salaries, and maintenance. The breakdown of these costs at the 60,000 machine-hour level of activity is:

Utilities (variable)	$ 48,000
Supervisory salaries (fixed)	21,000
Maintenance (mixed)	105,000
Total overhead cost	$174,000

Nova Company's management wants to break down the maintenance cost into its variable and fixed cost elements.

Required:

1. Estimate how much of the $246,000 of overhead cost in July was maintenance cost. (*Hint:* To do this, it may be helpful to first determine how much of the $246,000 consisted of utilities and supervisory salaries. Think about the behavior of variable and fixed costs.)
2. Using the high-low method, estimate a cost formula for maintenance in the form $Y = a + bX$.
3. Express the company's *total* overhead cost in the form $Y = a + bX$.
4. What *total* overhead cost would you expect to be incurred at an activity level of 75,000 machine-hours?

PROBLEM 2A–9 High-Low Method; Contribution Format Income Statement LO2–10

Milden Company is a distributor who wants to start using a contribution format income statement for planning purposes. The company analyzed its expenses and developed the following cost formulas:

Cost	Cost Formula
Cost of good sold	$35 per unit sold
Advertising expense.	$210,000 per quarter
Sales commissions	6% of sales
Shipping expense	?
Administrative salaries	$145,000 per quarter
Insurance expense	$9,000 per quarter
Depreciation expense	$76,000 per quarter

Because shipping expense is a mixed cost, the company needs to estimate the variable shipping expense per unit sold and the fixed shipping expense per quarter using the following data:

Quarter	Units Sold	Shipping Expense
Year 1:		
First	10,000	$119,000
Second	16,000	$175,000
Third	18,000	$190,000
Fourth	15,000	$164,000
Year 2:		
First	11,000	$130,000
Second	17,000	$185,000
Third	20,000	$210,000
Fourth	13,000	$147,000

Required:

1. Using the high-low method, estimate a cost formula for shipping expense in the form $Y = a + bX$.
2. In the first quarter of Year 3, the company plans to sell 12,000 units at a selling price of $100 per unit. Prepare a contribution format income statement for the quarter.

PROBLEM 2A–10 Least-Squares Regression Method; Scattergraph; Cost Behavior LO2–11

Professor John Morton has just been appointed chairperson of the Finance Department at Westland University. In reviewing the department's cost records, Professor Morton found the following total cost associated with Finance 101 over the last five terms:

Term	Number of Sections Offered	Total Cost
Fall, last year	4	$10,000
Winter, last year	6	$14,000
Summer, last year	2	$7,000
Fall, this year	5	$13,000
Winter, this year	3	$9,500

Professor Morton knows there are some variable costs, such as amounts paid to graduate assistants, associated with the course. He would like to have the variable and fixed costs separated for planning purposes.

Required:

1. Prepare a scattergraph plot. (Plot total cost on the vertical axis and number of sections offered on the horizontal axis.)

2. Using the least-squares regression method, estimate the variable cost per section and the total fixed cost per term for Finance 101. Express these estimates in the form $Y = a + bX$.

3. Assume that because of the small number of sections offered during the Winter Term this year, Professor Morton will have to offer eight sections of Finance 101 during the Fall Term. Compute the expected total cost for Finance 101. Can you see any problem with using the cost formula from (2) above to derive this total cost figure? Explain.

CASE 2A–11 Mixed Cost Analysis and the Relevant Range LO2–10

The Ramon Company is a manufacturer interested in developing a cost formula to estimate the variable and fixed components of its monthly manufacturing overhead costs. The company wishes to use machine-hours as its measure of activity and has gathered the data below for this year and last year:

| | Last Year | | This Year | |
| | Machine-Hours | Overhead Costs | Machine-Hours | Overhead Costs |
Month				
January............	21,000	$84,000	21,000	$86,000
February...........	25,000	$99,000	24,000	$93,000
March	22,000	$89,500	23,000	$93,000
April..............	23,000	$90,000	22,000	$87,000
May	20,500	$81,500	20,000	$80,000
June..............	19,000	$75,500	18,000	$76,500
July	14,000	$70,500	12,000	$67,500
August............	10,000	$64,500	13,000	$71,000
September.........	12,000	$69,000	15,000	$73,500
October...........	17,000	$75,000	17,000	$72,500
November..........	16,000	$71,500	15,000	$71,000
December..........	19,000	$78,000	18,000	$75,000

The company leases all of its manufacturing equipment. The lease arrangement calls for a flat monthly fee up to 19,500 machine-hours. If the machine-hours used exceed 19,500, then the fee becomes strictly variable with respect to the total number of machine-hours consumed during the month. Lease expense is a major element of overhead cost.

Required:

1. Using the high-low method, estimate a manufacturing overhead cost formula in the form $Y = a + bX$.

2. Prepare a scattergraph using all of the data for the two-year period. Fit a straight line or lines to the plotted points using a ruler. Describe the cost behavior pattern revealed by your scattergraph plot.

3. Assume a least-squares regression analysis using all of the given data points estimated the total fixed cost to be $40,102 and the variable cost to be $2.13 per machine-hour. Do you have any concerns about the accuracy of the high-low estimates you have computed or the least-squares regression estimates provided?

4. Assume the company consumes 22,500 machine-hours during a month. Using the high-low method, estimate the total overhead cost incurred at this level of activity. Be sure to consider only the data points contained in the relevant range of activity when performing your computations.

5. Comment on the accuracy of your high-low estimates assuming a least-squares regression analysis using only the data points in the relevant range of activity estimated the total fixed cost to be $10,090 and the variable cost to be $3.53 per machine-hour.

CASE 2A–12 Analysis of Mixed Costs in a Pricing Decision LO2–11

Maria Chavez owns a catering company that serves food and beverages at parties and business functions. Chavez's business is seasonal, with a heavy schedule during the summer months and holidays and a lighter schedule at other times.

One of the major events Chavez's customers request is a cocktail party. She offers a standard cocktail party and estimates the cost per guest as follows:

Food and beverages	$15.00
Labor (0.5 hr. @ $10.00/hr.)	5.00
Overhead (0.5 hr. @ $13.98/hr.)	6.99
Total cost per guest	$26.99

The standard cocktail party lasts three hours, and Chavez hires one worker for every six guests, so that works out to one-half hour of labor per guest. These workers are hired only as needed and are paid only for the hours they actually work.

When bidding on cocktail parties, Chavez adds a 15% markup to yield a price of about $31 per guest. She is confident about her estimates of the costs of food and beverages and labor but is not as comfortable with the estimate of overhead cost. The $13.98 overhead cost per labor-hour was determined by dividing total overhead expenses for the last 12 months by total labor-hours for the same period. Monthly data concerning overhead costs and labor-hours follow:

Month	Labor-Hours	Overhead Expenses
January	2,500	$ 55,000
February	2,800	59,000
March	3,000	60,000
April	4,200	64,000
May	4,500	67,000
June	5,500	71,000
July	6,500	74,000
August	7,500	77,000
September	7,000	75,000
October	4,500	68,000
November	3,100	62,000
December	6,500	73,000
Total	57,600	$805,000

Chavez received a request to bid on a 180-guest fundraising cocktail party to be given next month by an important local charity. (The party would last the usual three hours.) She would like to win this contract because the guest list for this charity event includes many prominent individuals whom she would like to secure as future clients. Maria is confident these potential customers would be favorably impressed by her company's services at the charity event.

Required:

1. Prepare a scattergraph plot that puts labor-hours on the *X*-axis and overhead expenses on the *Y*-axis. What insights are revealed by your scattergraph?

2. Use the least-squares regression method to estimate the fixed and variable components of overhead expenses. Express these estimates in the form $Y = a + bX$.

3. If Chavez charges her usual price of $31 per guest for the 180-guest cocktail party, how much contribution margin will she earn by serving this event?

4. How low could Chavez bid for the charity event in terms of a price per guest and still break even on the event itself?

5. The individual who is organizing the charity's fundraising event indicated he has already received a bid under $30 from another catering company. Do you think Chavez should bid below her normal $31 per guest price for the charity event? Why or why not?

(CMA, adapted)

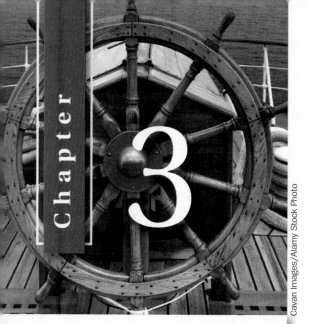

Cavan Images/Alamy Stock Photo

Job-Order Costing: Calculating Unit Product Costs

Dmytro Amanzholov/Shutterstock

Data Analytics Exercise available in Connect to complement this chapter

ENTREPRENEUR SPOTLIGHT

When Spencer Kelly was 14 years old, his bike was stolen—and it ended up changing his life for the better! His father bought him a replacement bike on the condition that he figure out how to repay his dad by the end of the summer. While in the shower early that summer, Spencer had the thought—why can't I make a better soap?—and his company, Expedition Soaps, was born. Today the company produces over 130 products. Every one of the company's soap bars "begins with 5 skin-loving plant oils to delight your skin, including coconut oil, olive oil, corn oil, soybean oil, and sunflower oil."

Managerial Accounting: The Practical Application
Expedition Soaps sells its products at numerous craft shows throughout the state of Michigan. In 2020, most of those shows were canceled due to the coronavirus pandemic. However, when the craft shows eventually resume, Spencer can use the principles of job-order costing to decide which craft shows to attend. He would view each craft show as a job and record its sales and costs (e.g., materials cost, labor cost, registration cost). After calculating the profitability of each show (or job), Spencer could retain profitable shows on his calendar while possibly discontinuing his company's presence at unprofitable shows.

Corporate Social Responsibility: Serving all Stakeholders
Expedition Soaps is an avid supporter of the autism community. For example, each year the company donates to OU CARES, an autism support program at Oakland University. It also makes annual contributions to USAutism.org to support the nonprofit organization's College Autism Project. Through a separate fundraising website, Expedition Soaps also makes its products available to local nonprofit organizations to support their fundraising efforts. In fact, Spencer's company contributes about 40% of its fundraising revenues back to the local partnering organization. ∎

Source: https://expeditionsoaps.com/, https://expeditionsoapsfundraising.com/.

Companies usually assign costs to their products and services for two main reasons. First, it helps them fulfill their planning, controlling, and decision-making responsibilities. For example, a company may use product cost information to better understand each product's profitability or to establish each product's selling price. Second, it helps them determine the value of ending inventories and cost of goods sold for external reporting purposes. The costs attached to products that have not sold are included in ending inventories on the balance sheet, whereas the costs attached to units that have sold are included in cost of goods sold on the income statement.

It is very common for external financial reporting requirements to heavily influence how companies assign costs to their products and services. Because most countries (including the United States) require some form of *absorption costing* for external financial reports, many companies use some form of absorption costing for product costing purposes. In **absorption costing,** all manufacturing costs, both fixed and variable, are assigned to units of product—units are said to *fully absorb manufacturing costs.* Conversely, all nonmanufacturing costs are treated as period costs, and they are not assigned to units of product.

This chapter discusses the role of job-order costing systems in planning, control, and decision making. Our focus will be on assigning manufacturing costs to individual jobs for internal management purposes rather than external reporting purposes.

Job-Order Costing—An Overview

Job-order costing is used in situations where many *different* products, each with individual and unique features, are produced each period. For example, a Diesel clothing factory would typically make many different types of jeans for both men and women during a month. A particular order might consist of 1,000 boot-cut men's blue denim jeans, style number A312. This order of 1,000 jeans is called a *job.* In a job-order costing system, costs are traced and allocated to jobs, and then the costs of the job are divided by the number of units in the job to arrive at an average cost per unit. This average cost per unit is also referred to as the *unit product cost.*

Other examples of situations where job-order costing would be used include large-scale construction projects managed by Bechtel International; commercial aircraft produced by Boeing; business cards designed, printed, and shipped by Vistaprint; and airline meals prepared by LSG SkyChefs. All of these examples are characterized by diverse outputs. Each Bechtel project is unique and different from every other—the company may be simultaneously constructing a dam in Nigeria and a bridge in Indonesia. Likewise, each airline orders a different type of meal from LSG SkyChefs' catering service.

Job-order costing is also used extensively in service industries. For example, hospitals, law firms, movie studios, accounting firms, advertising agencies, and repair shops all use a variation of job-order costing to accumulate costs. Although the detailed example of job-order costing provided in the following section deals with a manufacturing company, the same basic concepts and procedures are used by many service organizations.

Sandee Noreen

Sandee Noreen

IS THIS REALLY A JOB?

VBT Bicycling Vacations of Bristol, Vermont, offers deluxe bicycling vacations in the United States, Canada, Europe, and other locations throughout the world. For example, the company offers a 10-day tour of the Puglia region of Italy—the "heel of the boot." The tour price includes international airfare, 10 nights of lodging, most meals, use of a bicycle, and ground transportation as needed. Each tour is led by at least two local tour leaders, one of whom rides with the guests along the tour route. The other tour leader drives a "sag wagon" that carries extra water, snacks, and bicycle repair equipment and is available for a shuttle back to the hotel or up a hill. The sag wagon also transports guests' luggage from one hotel to another.

Each specific tour can be considered a job. For example, Giuliano Astore and Debora Trippetti, two natives of Puglia, led a VBT tour with 17 guests over 10 days in late April. At the end of the tour, Giuliano submitted a report to VBT headquarters. This report detailed the on-the-ground costs incurred for this specific tour, including fuel and operating costs for the van, lodging costs for the guests, the costs of meals provided to guests, the costs of snacks, the cost of hiring additional ground transportation as needed, and the wages of the tour leaders. In addition to these costs, some costs are paid directly by VBT in Vermont to vendors. The total cost incurred for the tour is then compared to the total revenue collected from guests to determine the gross profit for the tour.

Sources: Giuliano Astore and Gregg Marston, President, VBT Bicycling Vacations. For more information about VBT, see www.vbt.com.

Job-Order Costing—An Example

To introduce job-order costing, we will follow a specific job as it progresses through the manufacturing process. This job consists of two experimental couplings Yost Precision Machining has agreed to produce for Loops Unlimited, a manufacturer of roller coasters. Couplings connect the cars on the roller coaster and are a critical component in the performance and safety of the ride. Before we begin our discussion, it bears reemphasizing that companies generally classify manufacturing costs into three broad categories: (1) direct materials, (2) direct labor, and (3) manufacturing overhead. As we study the operation of a job-order costing system, we will see how each of these three types of product costs is assigned to jobs for purposes of computing unit product costs.

YOST
Precision Machining

Yost Precision Machining is a small company in Michigan specializing in fabricating precision metal parts used in a variety of applications ranging from deep-sea exploration vehicles to the inertial triggers in automobile air bags. The company's top managers gather every morning at 8:00 A.M. in the company's conference room for the daily planning meeting. Attending the meeting this morning are Jean Yost, the company's president; David Cheung, the marketing manager; Debbie Turner, the production manager; and Marc White, the company controller. The president opened the meeting:

Jean: The production schedule indicates we'll be starting Job 2B47 today. Isn't that the special order for experimental couplings, David?

David: That's right. That's the order from Loops Unlimited for two couplings for their new roller coaster ride for Magic Mountain.

Debbie: Why only two couplings? Don't they need a coupling for every car?

David: Yes. But this is a completely new roller coaster. The cars will go faster and will be subjected to more twists, turns, drops, and loops than on any other existing roller coaster. To hold up under these stresses, Loops Unlimited's engineers completely redesigned the cars and couplings. They want us to make just two of these new couplings for testing purposes. If the design works, then we'll have the inside track on the order to supply couplings for the whole ride.

Jean: We agreed to take on this initial order at our cost just to get our foot in the door. Marc, will there be any problem documenting our cost so we can get paid?

Marc: No problem. The contract with Loops stipulates that they will pay us an amount equal to each coupling's unit product cost as determined by our job-order costing system. I can finalize each coupling's direct materials, direct labor, and manufacturing overhead costs on the day the job is completed.

Jean: Good. Is there anything else we should discuss about this job at this time? No? Well then, let's move on to the next item of business.

Measuring Direct Materials Cost

The blueprints submitted by Loops Unlimited indicate that each experimental coupling will require three parts that are classified as *direct materials:* two G7 Connectors and one M46 Housing. Because each coupling requires two connectors and one housing, the production of two couplings requires four connectors and two housings. This is a custom product that is being made for the first time, but if this were one of the company's standard products, it would have an established *bill of materials.* A **bill of materials** is a document that lists the quantity of each type of direct material needed to complete a unit of product.

When an agreement has been reached with the customer concerning the quantities, prices, and shipment date for the order, a *production order* is issued. The Production Department then prepares a *materials requisition form* similar to the form in Exhibit 3–1. The **materials requisition form** is a document that specifies the type and quantity of materials to be drawn from the storeroom and identifies the job that will be charged for the cost of the materials.

The Yost Precision Machining materials requisition form in Exhibit 3–1 shows the company's Milling Department has requisitioned two M46 Housings and four G7 Connectors for the Loops Unlimited job, which has been designated as Job 2B47.

Job Cost Sheet

After a production order has been issued, the Accounting Department's job-order costing software system automatically generates a *job cost sheet* like the one presented in Exhibit 3–2. A **job cost sheet** records the materials, labor, and manufacturing overhead costs charged to that job.

EXHIBIT 3–1
Materials Requisition Form

Materials Requisition Number	14873	Date	March 2
Job Number to Be Charged	2B47		
Department	Milling		

Description	Quantity	Unit Cost	Total Cost
M46 Housing	2	$124	$248
G7 Connector	4	$103	412
			$660

EXHIBIT 3–2
Job Cost Sheet

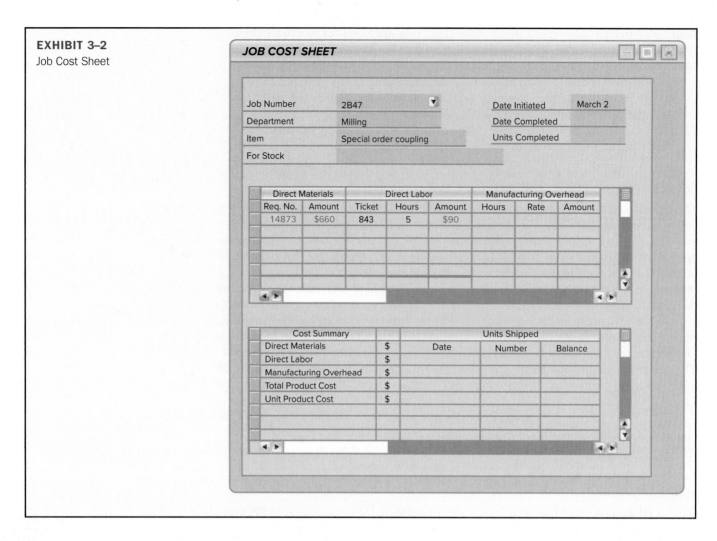

After direct materials are issued, the cost of these materials are automatically recorded on the job cost sheet. Note from Exhibit 3–2, for example, that the $660 cost for direct materials shown earlier on the materials requisition form has been charged to Job 2B47 on its job cost sheet. The requisition number 14873 from the materials requisition form appears on the job cost sheet to make it easier to identify the source document for the direct materials charge.

Measuring Direct Labor Cost

Direct labor consists of labor charges that are easily traced to a particular job. Labor charges that cannot be easily traced to specific jobs are treated as part of manufacturing overhead. As discussed in the previous chapter, this latter category of labor cost is called *indirect labor* and includes tasks such as maintenance, supervision, and cleanup.

Most companies rely on computerized systems to maintain employee *time tickets.* A completed **time ticket** is an hour-by-hour summary of the employee's activities throughout the day. One computerized approach to creating time tickets uses bar codes to capture data. Each employee and each job has a unique bar code. When beginning work on a job, the employee scans three bar codes using a handheld device, much like the bar code readers at grocery store checkout stands. The first bar code indicates that a task is being started; the second is the unique bar code on the employee's identity badge; and the third is the unique bar code of the job itself. This information is fed automatically via an electronic network to a computer that notes the time and records all of the data. When the task is completed, the employee scans a bar code indicating the task is complete, the bar code on his or her

EXHIBIT 3–3
Employee Time Ticket

identity badge, and the bar code attached to the job. This information is relayed to the computer that again notes the time, and a time ticket, such as the one shown in Exhibit 3–3, is automatically prepared. Because all of the source data is already in computer files, the labor costs can be automatically posted to job cost sheets. For example, Exhibit 3–3 shows $90 of direct labor cost related to Job 2B47. This amount is automatically posted to the job cost sheet shown in Exhibit 3–2. The time ticket in Exhibit 3–3 also shows $18 of indirect labor cost related to performing maintenance. This cost is treated as part of manufacturing overhead and does not get directly posted on a job cost sheet.

DIRECT LABOR COST PER HOUR VERSUS DIRECT LABOR COST PER UNIT

Bollman Hat Company recently moved its production facilities from Guangzhou, China, to Adamstown, Pennsylvania. However, the company is encountering challenges managing its direct labor costs. The direct labor cost per hour at the U.S. facility is $15.50 per hour compared to a little more than $2.50 per hour in China. Furthermore, the Adamstown employees are completing 200–250 hats per day, whereas each employee in China was completing 350–400 hats per day. This translates to a direct labor cost per hat of about $0.50 in the U.S. versus $0.05 in China.

Source: Michelle Ma, "For Kangol Hats, a Costly Move to U.S.," *The Wall Street Journal*, September 29, 2017, p. B5.

Computing Predetermined Overhead Rates

Recall that, in absorption costing, product costs include manufacturing overhead as well as direct materials and direct labor. Therefore, manufacturing overhead also needs to be recorded on the job cost sheet. However, assigning manufacturing overhead to a specific job is complicated by three circumstances:

LEARNING OBJECTIVE 3–1
Compute a predetermined overhead rate.

1. Manufacturing overhead is an *indirect cost*. This means it is either impossible or difficult to trace these costs to a particular product or job.
2. Manufacturing overhead consists of many different types of costs ranging from the grease used in machines to the annual salary of the production manager. Some of these costs are *variable overhead costs* because they vary in direct proportion to changes in the level of production (e.g., indirect materials, supplies, and power) and

some are *fixed overhead costs* because they remain constant as the level of production fluctuates (e.g., heat and light, property taxes, and insurance).

3. Many companies have large amounts of fixed manufacturing overhead. Therefore, their total manufacturing overhead costs tend to remain relatively constant from one period to the next even though the number of units they produce can fluctuate widely. Consequently, the average cost per unit will vary from one period to the next.

Given these circumstances, an allocation method is used to assign overhead costs to products. Allocation is accomplished by selecting an *allocation base* common to all of the company's products and services. An **allocation base** is a measure such as direct labor-hours (DLH) or machine-hours (MH) used to assign overhead costs to products and services. The most widely used allocation bases in manufacturing are direct labor-hours, direct labor cost, machine-hours, and (where a company has only a single product) units of product.

Manufacturing overhead is commonly assigned to products using a *predetermined overhead rate*. The **predetermined overhead rate** is computed by dividing the total estimated manufacturing overhead cost for the period by the estimated total amount of the allocation base as follows:

$$\text{Predetermined overhead rate} = \frac{\text{Estimated total manufacturing overhead cost}}{\text{Estimated total amount of the allocation base}}$$

The predetermined overhead rate is computed before the period begins using a four-step process. The first step is to estimate the total amount of the allocation base (the denominator) required for next period's estimated level of production. The second step is to estimate the total fixed manufacturing overhead cost for the coming period and the variable manufacturing overhead cost per unit of the allocation base. The third step is to use the cost formula shown below to estimate the total manufacturing overhead cost (the numerator) for the coming period:

$$Y = a + bX$$

where,

Y = The estimated total manufacturing overhead cost
a = The estimated total fixed manufacturing overhead cost
b = The estimated variable manufacturing overhead cost per unit of the allocation base
X = The estimated total amount of the allocation base

The fourth step is to compute the predetermined overhead rate. Notice, the estimated amount of the allocation base is determined before estimating the total manufacturing overhead cost. This needs to be done because total manufacturing overhead cost includes variable overhead costs that depend on the amount of the allocation base.

Applying Manufacturing Overhead

To repeat, the predetermined overhead rate is computed *before* the period begins. The predetermined overhead rate is then used to apply overhead cost to jobs throughout the period. The process of assigning overhead cost to jobs is called **overhead application.** The formula for determining the amount of overhead cost to apply to a particular job is:

$$\text{Overhead applied to a particular job} = \text{Predetermined overhead rate} \times \text{Amount of the allocation base incurred by the job}$$

For example, if the predetermined overhead rate is $20 per direct labor-hour, then $20 of overhead cost is *applied* to a job for each direct labor-hour incurred on the job. When the allocation base is direct labor-hours, the formula becomes:

$$\begin{matrix} \text{Overhead applied to} \\ \text{a particular job} \end{matrix} = \begin{matrix} \text{Predetermined} \\ \text{overhead rate} \end{matrix} \times \begin{matrix} \text{Actual direct labor-hours} \\ \text{worked on the job} \end{matrix}$$

Note that the amount of overhead applied to a particular job is not the actual amount of overhead caused by the job. Actual overhead costs are not assigned to jobs—if that could be done, the costs would be direct costs, not overhead. The overhead assigned to the job is simply a share of the total overhead estimated at the beginning of the year. This approach to overhead application is known as *normal costing*. A **normal cost system** applies overhead costs to jobs by multiplying a predetermined overhead rate by the actual amount of the allocation base incurred by the jobs.

Manufacturing Overhead—A Closer Look

To illustrate the steps involved in computing and using a predetermined overhead rate, let's return to Yost Precision Machining and make the following assumptions. In step one, the company estimated that 40,000 direct labor-hours would be required to support the production planned for the year. In step two, it estimated $640,000 of total fixed manufacturing overhead cost for the coming year and $4.00 of variable manufacturing overhead cost per direct labor-hour. Given these assumptions, in step three the company used the cost formula shown below to estimate its total manufacturing overhead cost for the year:

$Y = a + bX$

$Y = \$640,000 + (\$4.00 \text{ per direct labor-hour} \times 40,000 \text{ direct labor-hours})$

$Y = \$640,000 + \$160,000$

$Y = \$800,000$

In step four, Yost Precision Machining computed its predetermined overhead rate for the year of $20 per direct labor-hour as shown below:

$$\text{Predetermined overhead rate} = \frac{\text{Estimated total manufacturing overhead cost}}{\text{Estimated total amount of the allocation base}}$$

$$= \frac{\$800,000}{40,000 \text{ direct labor-hours}}$$

$$= \$20 \text{ per direct labor-hour}$$

The job cost sheet in Exhibit 3–4 indicates that 27 direct labor-hours (i.e., DLHs) were charged to Job 2B47. Therefore, a total of $540 of manufacturing overhead cost would be applied to the job:

$$\begin{matrix} \text{Overhead applied to} \\ \text{Job 2B47} \end{matrix} = \begin{matrix} \text{Predetermined} \\ \text{overhead rate} \end{matrix} \times \begin{matrix} \text{Actual direct labor-hours} \\ \text{charged to Job 2B47} \end{matrix}$$

$$= \$20 \text{ per DLH} \times 27 \text{ DLHs}$$

$$= \$540 \text{ of overhead applied to Job 2B47}$$

This amount of overhead has been entered on the job cost sheet in Exhibit 3–4.

EXHIBIT 3–4
A Completed Job Cost Sheet

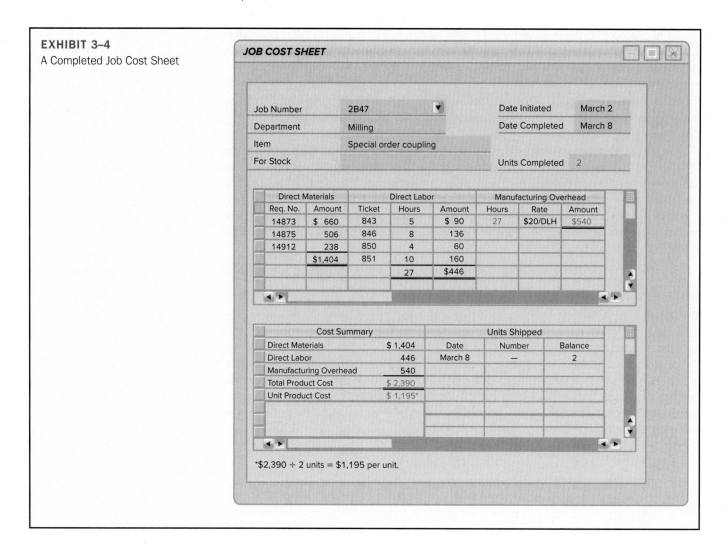

JOB COST SHEET

Job Number	2B47		Date Initiated	March 2
Department	Milling		Date Completed	March 8
Item	Special order coupling			
For Stock			Units Completed	2

Direct Materials		Direct Labor			Manufacturing Overhead		
Req. No.	Amount	Ticket	Hours	Amount	Hours	Rate	Amount
14873	$ 660	843	5	$ 90	27	$20/DLH	$540
14875	506	846	8	136			
14912	238	850	4	60			
	$1,404	851	10	160			
			27	$446			

Cost Summary		Units Shipped		
Direct Materials	$ 1,404	Date	Number	Balance
Direct Labor	446	March 8	—	2
Manufacturing Overhead	540			
Total Product Cost	$ 2,390			
Unit Product Cost	$ 1,195*			

*$2,390 ÷ 2 units = $1,195 per unit.

The Need for a Predetermined Rate

Instead of using a predetermined rate based on estimates, it may be tempting to suggest companies should use the *actual* total manufacturing overhead cost and the *actual* total amount of the allocation base to compute their overhead rates on a monthly, quarterly, or annual basis. However, if an actual rate is computed monthly or quarterly, seasonal factors in overhead costs or in the allocation base can produce fluctuations in the overhead rate. For example, the costs of heating and cooling a factory in Illinois will be highest in the winter and summer months and lowest in the spring and fall. If the overhead rate is recomputed at the end of each month or each quarter based on actual costs and activity, the overhead rate would go up in the winter and summer and down in the spring and fall. As a result, two identical jobs, one completed in the winter and one completed in the spring, would be assigned different manufacturing overhead costs.

To avoid such confusing fluctuations, companies could compute actual overhead rates on an annual basis. However, with this approach, the manufacturing overhead assigned to any particular job would not be known until the end of the year. For example, the cost of Job 2B47 at Yost Precision Machining would not be known until the end of the year, even though the job will be completed and shipped to the customer in March. For these reasons, most companies use predetermined overhead rates rather than actual overhead rates in their cost accounting systems.

CYBER INSURANCE: A NEW NORMAL FOR MANUFACTURERS

Advisen Ltd. estimates manufacturers are now paying more than $36.9 million per year for cyber-specific insurance policies. While these companies have always insured their manufacturing facilities from physical damage, the fact that their factories "are increasingly computerized, automated, and digitally integrated with other parts of the company" necessitates expanding manufacturing overhead costs to include cyber insurance. Daniel Steiner, enterprise risk manager at Kimberly-Clark Corporation, says his company began buying cyber insurance in 2009. More recently, many other manufacturers have followed suit after the German Federal Office for Information Security reported that a cyberattack caused "massive damage" at one of the country's steel manufacturing plants.

Source: Richard Teitelbaum, "More Manufacturers Weigh Insurance for Cyberattacks," *The Wall Street Journal*, April 18, 2017, p B4.

Rawpixel.com/Shutterstock

Computation of Total Job Costs and Unit Product Costs

With the application of Yost Precision Machining's $540 of manufacturing overhead to the job cost sheet in Exhibit 3–4, the job cost sheet is complete except for two final steps. First, the totals for direct materials, direct labor, and manufacturing overhead are transferred to the Cost Summary section of the job cost sheet and added together to obtain the total cost for the job.[1] Then, the total product cost ($2,390) is divided by the number of units (2) to obtain the unit product cost ($1,195). As indicated earlier, *this unit product cost is an average cost and should not be interpreted as the cost that would actually be incurred if another unit were produced.* The incremental cost of an additional unit is something less than the average unit cost of $1,195 because much of the actual overhead costs would not change if another unit were produced.

LEARNING OBJECTIVE 3–3
Compute the total cost and the unit product cost of a job using a plantwide predetermined overhead rate.

In the 8:00 A.M. daily planning meeting on March 9, Jean Yost, the president of Yost Precision Machining, once again drew attention to Job 2B47, the experimental couplings:

Jean: I see Job 2B47 is completed. Let's get those couplings shipped immediately to Loops Unlimited so they can get their testing program under way. Marc, how much are we going to bill Loops for those two units?

Marc: Because we agreed to sell the experimental couplings at cost, we will be charging Loops Unlimited just $1,195 a unit.

Jean: Fine. Let's hope the couplings work out and we make some money on the big order later.

MANAGERIAL ACCOUNTING IN ACTION
The Wrap-Up

YOST
Precision Machining

JOB-ORDER COSTING IN THE SERVICE INDUSTRY

Accenture is one of the world's largest consulting firms with annual revenues greater than $44 billion. Because the firm does not have any inventory on its balance sheet, it might be tempting to conclude that it does not need a job-order costing system. However, that is not true.

Accenture pays its consultants more than $30 billion per year to provide services for clients. Job-order costing enables the firm to compare each client's revenues to the costs of serving those clients. It also enables the firm to determine what portion of its consulting capacity was billable to clients and what portion was not billed to specific clients.

Source: Accenture 2020 Annual Report.

---

[1] Notice, we are assuming Job 2B47 required direct materials and direct labor beyond the charges shown in Exhibits 3–1 and 3–3.

Job-Order Costing—A Managerial Perspective

Managers use job cost information to establish plans and make decisions. For example, managers may use job profitability reports to develop sales and production plans for next year. If certain types of jobs, such as low-volume engineering-intensive jobs, appear to be highly profitable, managers may decide to dedicate future advertising expenditures to growing sales of these types of jobs. Conversely, if other types of jobs, such as high-volume labor-intensive jobs, appear to be unprofitable, managers may take actions to reduce the projected sales and production of these types of jobs.

Managers may also use job cost information to make pricing decisions. For example, if Job A has a total manufacturing cost of $100, managers often use a predefined markup percentage, say 50%, to establish a markup of $50 (= $100 × 50%) and a selling price of $150 (= $100 + $50). Under this approach, known as cost-plus pricing, the managers establish a markup percentage they believe will generate enough revenue to cover all of a job's manufacturing costs and a portion of the company's nonmanufacturing costs, while generating some residual profit.

If a company's job-order costing system does not accurately assign manufacturing costs to jobs, it will adversely influence the types of planning and decision-making scenarios just described. In other words, distorted job cost data may cause managers to use additional advertising dollars to pursue certain types of jobs they believe are profitable but, in actuality, are not. Similarly, inaccurate job costs may cause managers to establish selling prices that are too high or too low relative to the prices established by more savvy competitors.

At this point, you may be wondering, how can this happen? How can a job-order costing system inaccurately assign costs to jobs? The key to answering this question is to focus on *indirect* manufacturing costs, also called manufacturing overhead costs. While job-order costing systems can accurately trace *direct* materials and *direct* labor costs to jobs, they often fail to accurately allocate the manufacturing overhead costs used during the production process to their respective jobs. The root cause of the problem often relates to the choice of an allocation base.

Choosing an Allocation Base—A Key to Job Cost Accuracy

Imagine going to a restaurant with three of your friends. The group orders an extra-large pizza for $20 that is cut into ten slices. One of your friends eats five slices of pizza, your other two friends eat two slices each, and you eat one slice. When the bill arrives, the friend who ate five slices recommends paying the bill using "number of people seated at the table" as the allocation base, thereby requiring you to contribute $5 (= $20 ÷ 4) toward paying the bill. How would you feel about the accuracy of this cost allocation base? In all likelihood, you'd suggest distributing the bill among the four diners using another allocation base called "number of slices eaten." This approach would require each person seated at the table to pay $2 (= $20 ÷ 10) per slice consumed, thereby requiring you to contribute $2 toward paying the bill. While the distortion caused by using "number of people seated at the table" as the allocation base seems obvious, job-order costing systems often make the same error—they use allocation bases that do not reflect how jobs actually use overhead resources.

To improve job cost accuracy, the allocation base in the predetermined overhead rate should *drive* the overhead cost. A **cost driver** is a factor, such as machine-hours, beds occupied, computer time, or flight-hours, that causes overhead costs. If the base in the predetermined overhead rate does not "drive" overhead costs, it will not accurately measure the cost of overhead resources used by each job. Many companies use job-order costing systems that assume direct labor-hours (or direct labor cost) is the only manufacturing overhead cost driver. They use a single predetermined overhead rate, or what is called a **plantwide overhead rate,** to allocate all manufacturing overhead costs to jobs based on their usage of direct-labor hours. However, while direct labor-hours may indeed "drive" some of a company's manufacturing overhead costs, it is often overly simplistic and incorrect to assume that direct-labor hours is a company's *only* manufacturing overhead cost driver. When companies can identify more than one overhead cost driver, they can improve job cost accuracy by using *multiple predetermined overhead rates.*

UNIVERSITY TEES: SERVING OVER 150 CAMPUSES NATIONWIDE

University Tees was founded in 2003 by two Miami University college students to provide screen-printing, embroidery, and promotional products for fraternities, sororities, and student organizations. Today, the company is headquartered in Cleveland, Ohio, and employs as many as four Campus Managers on each of over 150 college campuses across America.

Accurately calculating the cost of each potential customer order is critically important to University Tees because the company needs to be sure the sales price exceeds the cost associated with satisfying the order. The costs include the cost of the blank T-shirts themselves, printing costs (which vary depending on the quantity of shirts produced and the number of colors per shirt), screen costs (which also vary depending on the number of colors included in a design), shipping costs, and the artwork needed to create a design. The company also takes into account its competitors' pricing strategies when developing its own prices.

Given its success on college campuses, University Tees has introduced a sister company called On Point Promos to serve for-profit companies and nonprofit organizations.

Source: Conversation with Joe Haddad, cofounder of University Tees.

Courtesy of University Tees, Inc.

Job-Order Costing Using Multiple Predetermined Overhead Rates

A cost system with **multiple predetermined overhead rates** uses more than one overhead rate to apply overhead costs to jobs. For example, a company may choose to use a predetermined overhead rate for each of its production departments. Such a system, while more complex, is more accurate because it reflects differences across departments in terms of how jobs consume overhead costs. For example, in departments that are relatively labor-intensive, their overhead costs might be applied to jobs based on direct labor-hours, and in departments that are relatively machine-intensive, their overhead costs might be applied to jobs based on machine-hours.

Multiple Predetermined Overhead Rates—A Departmental Approach

Dickson Company has two production departments, Milling and Assembly. The company uses a job-order costing system and computes a predetermined overhead rate in each production department. The predetermined overhead rate in the Milling Department is based on machine-hours, and in the Assembly Department, it is based on direct labor-hours. The company uses *cost-plus pricing* to establish selling prices for its products. **Cost-plus pricing** is a pricing method in which a predetermined markup is applied to a cost base to determine the target selling price. In this instance, Dickson Company uses a markup percentage of 75% of total manufacturing cost to establish selling prices for all of its jobs. At the beginning of the year, the company made the following estimates:

	Department	
	Milling	**Assembly**
Machine-hours	60,000	3,000
Direct labor-hours	8,000	80,000
Total fixed manufacturing overhead cost	$390,000	$500,000
Variable manufacturing overhead per machine-hour	$2.00	—
Variable manufacturing overhead per direct labor-hour ..	—	$3.75

During the current month, the company started and completed Job 407. It wants to use its predetermined departmental overhead rates and the information pertaining to Job 407 shown below to establish a selling price for this job:

	Department	
Job 407	**Milling**	**Assembly**
Machine-hours	90	4
Direct labor-hours...............	5	20
Direct materials.................	$800	$370
Direct labor cost	$70	$280

Exhibit 3–5 explains how Dickson would compute a selling price for Job 407 using a five-step process, the first of which is to calculate the estimated total manufacturing overhead cost in each department using the equation

$$Y = a + bX$$

where:

$Y =$ The estimated total manufacturing overhead cost
$a =$ The estimated total fixed manufacturing overhead cost
$b =$ The estimated variable manufacturing overhead cost per unit of the allocation base
$X =$ The estimated total amount of the allocation base

As shown in Step 1 in Exhibit 3–5, this equation provides the Milling Department's estimated total manufacturing overhead cost of $510,000 and the Assembly Department's estimated total overhead cost of $800,000.

The second step is to calculate the predetermined overhead rate for each department using the following formula:

$$\text{Predetermined overhead rate} = \frac{\text{Estimated total manufacturing overhead cost}}{\text{Estimated total amount of the allocation base}}$$

Per Step 2 in Exhibit 3–5, this formula results in predetermined overhead rates in the Milling and Assembly Departments of $8.50 per machine-hour and $10.00 per direct labor-hour, respectively.

The third step is to use the general equation shown below to calculate the amount of overhead applied from each department to Job 407.

$$\frac{\text{Overhead applied to}}{\text{Job 407}} = \frac{\text{Predetermined}}{\text{overhead rate}} \times \frac{\text{Actual amount of the allocation}}{\text{base used by Job 407}}$$

As depicted in the middle of Exhibit 3–5, $765 of manufacturing overhead would be applied from the Milling Department to Job 407, whereas $200 would be applied from the Assembly Department to this same job.

Finally, Exhibit 3–5 also summarizes Steps 4 and 5, which calculate the total job cost for Job 407 ($2,485) and the selling price of Job 407 ($4,348.75) using the markup percentage of 75%.

It is important to emphasize that using a departmental approach to overhead application results in a different selling price for Job 407 than would have been derived using a plantwide overhead rate based on either direct labor-hours or machine-hours. The appeal of using predetermined departmental overhead rates is they presumably provide a more accurate accounting of the costs caused by jobs, which, in turn, should enhance management planning and decision making.

EXHIBIT 3–5

Dickson Company: An Example Using Multiple Predetermined Overhead Rates

Step 1: Calculate the estimated total manufacturing overhead cost for each department.

Milling Department Overhead Cost (Y):	Assembly Department Overhead Cost (Y):
= $390,000 + ($2.00 per MH × 60,000 MHs)	= $500,000 + ($3.75 per DLH × 80,000 DLHs)
= $390,000 + $120,000	= $500,000 + $300,000
= $510,000	= $800,000

Step 2: Calculate the predetermined overhead rate in each department.

Milling Department Overhead Rate:	Assembly Department Overhead Rate:
$= \dfrac{\$510{,}000}{60{,}000 \text{ machine-hours}}$	$= \dfrac{\$800{,}000}{80{,}000 \text{ direct labor-hours}}$
= $8.50 per machine-hour	= $10.00 per direct labor-hour

Step 3: Calculate the amount of overhead applied from both departments to Job 407.

Milling Department: Overhead Applied to Job 407	Assembly Department: Overhead Applied to Job 407
= $8.50 per MH × 90 MHs	= $10.00 per DLH × 20 DLHs
= $765	= $200

Step 4: Calculate the total job cost for Job 407.

	Milling	Assembly	Total
Direct materials	$800	$370	$1,170
Direct labor	$70	$280	350
Manufacturing overhead applied	$765	$200	965
Total cost of Job 407			$2,485

Step 5: Calculate the selling price for Job 407.

Total cost of Job 407	$2,485.00
Markup ($2,485 × 75%).	1,863.75
Selling price of Job 407	$4,348.75

Multiple Predetermined Overhead Rates—An Activity-Based Approach

Using departmental overhead rates is one approach to creating a job-order costing system that includes multiple predetermined overhead rates. Another approach is to create overhead rates related to the activities performed within departments. This approach usually results in more overhead rates than a departmental approach because each department may perform more than one activity. When a company creates overhead rates based on the activities it performs, it is employing an approach called *activity-based costing*.

For now, our goal is to simply introduce you to the idea of activity-based costing—an alternative approach to developing multiple predetermined overhead rates. Managers use activity-based costing systems to more accurately measure the demands that jobs, products, customers, and other cost objects make on overhead resources. Appendix 3A provides an in-depth discussion of activity-based absorption costing and contrasts it with the plantwide approach described earlier in this chapter. Chapter 5 describes a more refined approach to activity-based costing that better serves the needs of management than the activity-based absorption costing approach discussed in Appendix 3A.

Job-Order Costing—An External Reporting Perspective

LEARNING OBJECTIVE 3–5
Use job cost sheets to calculate ending inventories and cost of goods sold.

This chapter focuses on using job-order costing systems to compute unit product costs for internal management purposes. However, job-order costing systems are also often used to create a balance sheet and income statement for external parties, such as shareholders and lenders. In this section, we explain how a company's job cost sheets provide a subsidiary ledger that summarizes the specific jobs that comprise the amounts reported in *Work-in-Process* and *Finished Goods* on the balance sheet as well as *Cost of Goods Sold* on the income statement.

To illustrate, assume Dixon Company worked on six jobs during May: Jobs A, B, C, D, E, and F. At the end of May, the job cost sheets for these six jobs contained the following data:

	Job A	Job B	Job C	Job D	Job E	Job F
Beginning balance	$64	$50	$110	$100	$116	$132
Charged to the jobs during May:						
Direct materials.................	$100	$88	$142	$106	$180	$160
Direct labor	$80	$60	$90	$70	$120	$100
Manufacturing overhead applied ..	$96	$72	$108	$84	$144	$120
Units completed	0	0	100	60	200	160
Units sold during May	0	0	80	60	200	40

Jobs C, D, E, and F were completed during May. Jobs A and B were incomplete at the end of May. There was no finished goods inventory on May 1, and the company's total manufacturing overhead applied equals its total actual manufacturing overhead.

Given this information, the job cost sheets can be used to calculate *Work in Process* for the May 31 balance sheet by identifying the jobs that have no units completed at the end of the month (Jobs A and B) and summing their total job costs as follows:

	Job A	Job B	Total
Beginning balance	$ 64	$ 50	
Direct materials............................	100	88	
Direct labor	80	60	
Manufacturing overhead applied	96	72	
Cost of ending work in process inventory	$340	$270	$610

The job cost sheets can also be used to calculate *Cost of Goods Sold* for May's income statement using a two-step process. First, calculate the unit product costs for all jobs completed during May (Jobs C, D, E, and F) as follows:

	Job C	Job D	Job E	Job F
Beginning balance	$110	$100	$116	$132
Direct materials...................	142	106	180	160
Direct labor......................	90	70	120	100
Manufacturing overhead applied....	108	84	144	120
Total job cost (a).................	$450	$360	$560	$512
Units completed (b)...............	100	60	200	160
Unit product cost (a) ÷ (b).........	$4.50	$6.00	$2.80	$3.20

Next, calculate the *Cost of Goods Sold* by multiplying each job's unit product cost by the number of units sold:

	Job C	Job D	Job E	Job F	Total
Unit product cost (a)	$4.50	$6.00	$2.80	$3.20	
Units sold (b)	80	60	200	40	
Cost of goods sold (a) × (b) . . .	$360	$360	$560	$128	$1,408

The *Finished Goods* inventory for the May 31 balance sheet can also be calculated using a two-step process. First, calculate the number of units in ending finished goods inventory:

	Job C	Job D	Job E	Job F
Units completed (a).	100	60	200	160
Units sold (b)	80	60	200	40
Units in finished goods inventory (a) − (b) . . .	20	0	0	120

Second, multiply the units in finished goods inventory by each job's respective unit product cost:

	Job C	Job D	Job E	Job F	Total
Units in finished goods inventory (a) . . .	20	0	0	120	
Unit product cost (b).	$4.50	$6.00	$2.80	$3.20	
Cost of ending finished goods inventory (a) × (b)	$90	$0	$0	$384	$474

Overhead Application and the Income Statement

For simplicity, the example we just completed assumes Dixon Company's total manufacturing overhead applied equals its total actual manufacturing overhead. However, in reality, when a company uses predetermined overhead rates to apply overhead cost to jobs, it is almost a certainty that the amount of overhead applied to all jobs will differ from the actual amount of overhead cost. When a company applies less overhead to production than it actually incurs, it creates what is known as *underapplied overhead.* When it applies more overhead to production than it actually incurs, it results in *overapplied overhead.*

The existence of underapplied or overapplied overhead has implications for how a company prepares its financial statements. For example, the cost of goods sold reported on a company's income statement must be adjusted to reflect underapplied or overapplied overhead. The adjustment for underapplied overhead increases cost of goods sold and decreases net operating income, whereas the adjustment for overapplied overhead decreases cost of goods sold and increases net operating income. Nonetheless, all forthcoming exercises and problems pertaining to this learning objective will assume the amounts of applied and actual overhead are the same.

Job-Order Costing in Service Companies

This chapter has focused on manufacturing companies; however, job-order costing is also used in service organizations, such as law firms, movie studios, hospitals, and repair shops. In a law firm, for example, each client is a "job," and the costs of that job are accumulated day by day on a job cost sheet as the client's case is handled by the firm. Legal forms and similar inputs represent the direct materials for the job; the time expended by attorneys is like direct labor; and the costs of secretaries and legal aids, rent, depreciation, and so forth, represent the overhead.

In a movie studio such as Columbia Pictures, each film produced by the studio is a "job," and costs of direct materials (costumes and props) and direct labor (actors, directors, and extras) are charged to each film's job cost sheet. A share of the studio's overhead costs, such as utilities, depreciation of equipment, wages of maintenance workers, and so forth, is also charged to each film.

In summary, job-order costing is a versatile and widely used costing method that may be encountered in virtually any organization that provides diverse products or services.

Summary

Job-order costing is used in situations where the organization offers many different products or services, such as in furniture manufacturing, hospitals, and legal firms. When used in a manufacturing context, job-order costing systems accumulate a job's direct materials, direct labor, and manufacturing overhead costs on a job cost sheet. Selling and administrative costs are not assigned to jobs because they are treated as period costs.

Job-order costing systems use materials requisition forms and labor time tickets to trace direct materials and direct labor costs to jobs. Because manufacturing overhead costs are indirect costs, they must be allocated to jobs. Ideally, the allocation base used to allocate overhead costs to jobs should be a cost driver—it should cause the consumption of overhead costs. The most frequently used allocation bases in job-order costing systems are direct labor-hours and machine-hours.

Normal costing systems allocate overhead costs to jobs using predetermined overhead rates that are estimated before the period begins. A predetermined overhead rate is computed by dividing the estimated total manufacturing overhead cost for the period by the estimated total amount of the allocation base for the period. Job-order costing systems can use only one predetermined overhead rate (also called a plantwide rate) or multiple predetermined overhead rates.

Throughout the period, overhead is applied to jobs by multiplying the predetermined overhead rate by the actual amount of the allocation base recorded for each job. The total manufacturing costs assigned to a job (including direct materials, direct labor, and applied overhead) divided by the number of units within that job equals what is known as the unit product cost.

A company's job cost sheets form a subsidiary ledger that can be used to summarize the amounts of work in process and finished goods on the balance sheet and the cost of goods sold in the income statement.

 Data Analytics Exercise available in Connect to complement this chapter

Review Problem: Calculating Unit Product Costs

Redhawk Company has two manufacturing departments—Assembly and Fabrication. The company considers all of its manufacturing overhead costs to be fixed costs. The first set of data shown below is based on estimates made at the beginning of the year for the expected total output. The second set of data relates to one particular job completed during the year—Job A200.

Estimated Data	Assembly	Fabrication	Total
Manufacturing overhead costs..........	$300,000	$400,000	$700,000
Direct labor-hours.....................	25,000	15,000	40,000
Machine-hours........................	10,000	50,000	60,000

Job A200	Assembly	Fabrication	Total
Direct materials.......................	$110	$50	$160
Direct labor..........................	$70	$45	$115
Direct labor-hours.....................	10 hours	2 hours	12 hours
Machine-hours........................	1 hour	7 hours	8 hours

Required:
1. If Redhawk uses a predetermined plantwide overhead rate with direct labor-hours as the allocation base, how much manufacturing overhead would be applied to Job A200?
2. If Redhawk uses predetermined departmental overhead rates with direct labor-hours as the allocation base in Assembly and machine-hours as the allocation base in Fabrication, how much total manufacturing overhead cost would be applied to Job A200?
3. Assume Redhawk uses the departmental overhead rates mentioned in requirement 2 and Job A200 includes 50 units. What is the unit product cost for Job A200?

Solution to Review Problem

1. The predetermined plantwide overhead rate is computed as follows:

$$\text{Predetermined overhead rate} = \frac{\text{Estimated total manufacturing overhead cost}}{\text{Estimated total amount of the allocation base}}$$

$$= \frac{\$700,000}{40,000 \text{ direct labor-hours}}$$

$$= \$17.50 \text{ per direct labor-hour}$$

The manufacturing overhead applied to Job A200 is computed as follows:

$$\begin{array}{l}\text{Overhead applied to} \\ \text{Job A200}\end{array} = \begin{array}{l}\text{Predetermined} \\ \text{overhead rate}\end{array} \times \begin{array}{l}\text{Actual direct labor-hours} \\ \text{charged to Job A200}\end{array}$$

$$= \$17.50 \text{ per DLH} \times 12 \text{ DLHs}$$

$$= \$210 \text{ of overhead applied to Job A200}$$

2. The predetermined departmental overhead rates are computed as follows:
   Assembly Department:

$$\text{Predetermined overhead rate} = \frac{\text{Estimated total manufacturing overhead cost}}{\text{Estimated total amount of the allocation base}}$$

$$= \frac{\$300,000}{25,000 \text{ direct labor-hours}}$$

$$= \$12 \text{ per direct labor-hour}$$

Fabrication Department:

$$\text{Predetermined overhead rate} = \frac{\text{Estimated total manufacturing overhead cost}}{\text{Estimated total amount of the allocation base}}$$

$$= \frac{\$400,000}{50,000 \text{ machine-hours}}$$

$$= \$8.00 \text{ per machine-hour}$$

The manufacturing overhead applied to Job A200 is computed as follows:

Job A200	(1) Overhead Rate	(2) Actual Hours Used	Applied Overhead (1) × (2)
Assembly Department	$12 per DLH	10 hours	$120
Fabrication Department	$8 per MH	7 hours	56
Total applied overhead.			$176

3. The unit product cost for Job A200 is computed as follows:

Job A200	Assembly	Fabrication	Total
Direct materials	$110	$50	$160
Direct labor.	$70	$45	115
Applied overhead	$120	$56	176
Total job cost (a).			$451
Number of units in Job A200 (b)			50
Unit product cost (a) ÷ (b).			$9.02

Glossary

Absorption costing A costing method that includes all manufacturing costs—direct materials, direct labor, and both variable and fixed manufacturing overhead—in unit product costs. (p. 123)

Allocation base A measure of activity such as direct labor-hours or machine-hours that is used to assign costs to cost objects. (p. 128)

Bill of materials A document that shows the quantity of each type of direct material required to make a product. (p. 125)

Cost driver A factor, such as machine-hours, beds occupied, computer time, or flight-hours, that causes overhead costs. (p. 132)

Cost-plus pricing A pricing method in which a predetermined markup is applied to a cost base to determine the target selling price. (p. 133)

Job cost sheet A form that records the direct materials, direct labor, and manufacturing overhead cost charged to a job. (p. 125)

Job-order costing A costing system used in situations where many different products, jobs, or services are produced each period. (p. 123)

Materials requisition form A document that specifies the type and quantity of materials to be drawn from the storeroom and that identifies the job that will be charged for the cost of those materials. (p. 125)

Multiple predetermined overhead rates A costing system with multiple overhead cost pools and a different predetermined overhead rate for each cost pool, rather than a single predetermined overhead rate for the entire company. Each production department may be treated as a separate overhead cost pool. (p. 133)

Normal cost system A costing system in which overhead costs are applied to a job by multiplying a predetermined overhead rate by the actual amount of the allocation base incurred by the job. (p. 129)

Overhead application The process of assigning overhead cost to specific jobs. (p. 128)

Plantwide overhead rate A single predetermined overhead rate that is used throughout a plant. (p. 132)

Predetermined overhead rate A rate used to charge manufacturing overhead cost to jobs that is established in advance for each period. It is computed by dividing the estimated total manufacturing overhead cost for the period by the estimated total amount of the allocation base for the period. (p. 128)

Time ticket A document that is used to record the amount of time an employee spends on various activities. (p. 126)

Questions

3–1   What is job-order costing?

3–2   What is absorption costing?

3–3   What is normal costing?

3–4   How is the unit product cost of a job calculated?

3–5   Explain the four-step process used to compute a predetermined overhead rate.

3–6   What is the purpose of the job cost sheet in a job-order costing system?

3–7   Explain why some production costs must be assigned to products through an allocation process.

3–8   Why do companies use predetermined overhead rates rather than actual manufacturing overhead costs to apply overhead to jobs?

3–9   What factors should be considered in selecting an allocation base to be used in computing a predetermined overhead rate?

3–10 If a company fully allocates all of its overhead costs to jobs, does this guarantee that a profit will be earned for the period?

3–11 Would you expect the amount of applied overhead for a period to equal the actual overhead costs of the period? Why or why not?

3–12 What is underapplied overhead? Overapplied overhead?

3–13 What is a plantwide overhead rate? Why are multiple overhead rates, rather than a plantwide overhead rate, used in some companies?

 Applying Excel

This Excel worksheet relates to the Dickson Company example summarized in Exhibit 3–5. The workbook, and instructions on how to complete the file, can be found in Connect.

LEARNING OBJECTIVES 3–1, 3–2, 3–3, 3–4

You should proceed to the requirements below only after completing your worksheet.

Required:

1. Check your worksheet by changing the total fixed manufacturing overhead cost for the Milling Department in the Data area to $300,000, keeping all of the other data the same as in the original example. If your worksheet is operating properly, the total cost of Job 407 should now be $2,350. If you do not get this answer, find the errors in your worksheet and correct them.
    How much is the selling price of Job 407? Did it change? Why or why not?

2. Change the total fixed manufacturing overhead cost for the Milling Department in the Data area back to $390,000, keeping all of the other data the same as in the original example.

	A	B	C	D	E
1	Chapter 3: Applying Excel				
2					
3	Data				
4	Markup on job cost	75%			
5					
6		Department			
7		Milling	Assembly		
8	Machine-hours	60,000	3,000		
9	Direct labor-hours	8,000	80,000		
10	Total fixed manufacturing overhead cost	$390,000	$500,000		
11	Variable manufacturing overhead per machine-hour	$2.00			
12	Variable manufacturing overhead per direct labor-hour		$3.75		
13					
14	Cost summary for Job 407	Department			
15		Milling	Assembly		
16	Machine-hours	90	4		
17	Direct labor-hours	5	20		
18	Direct materials	$800	$370		
19	Direct labor cost	$70	$280		
20					
21	Enter a formula into each of the cells marked with a ? below				
22					
23	Step 1: Calculate the estimated total manufacturing overhead cost for each department				
24		Milling	Assembly		
25	Total fixed manufacturing overhead cost	?	?		
26	Variable manufacturing overhead per machine-hour or direct labor-hour	?	?		
27	Total machine-hours or direct labor-hours	?	?		
28	Total variable manufacturing overhead	?	?		
29	Total manufacturing overhead	?	?		
30					
31	Step 2: Calculate the predetermined overhead rate in each department				
32		Milling	Assembly		
33	Total manufacturing overhead	?	?		
34	Total machine-hours or direct labor-hours	?	?		
35	Predetermined overhead rate per machine-hour or direct labor-hour	?	?		
36					
37	Step 3: Calculate the amount of overhead applied from both departments to Job 407				
38		Milling	Assembly		
39	Predetermined overhead rate per machine-hour or direct labor-hour	?	?		
40	Machine-hours or direct labor-hours for the job	?	?		
41	Manufacturing overhead applied	?	?		
42					
43	Step 4: Calculate the total job cost for Job 407				
44		Milling	Assembly	Total	
45	Direct materials	?	?	?	
46	Direct labor cost	?	?	?	
47	Manufacturing overhead applied	?	?	?	
48	Total cost of Job 407			?	
49					
50	Step 5: Calculate the selling price for Job 407				
51	Total cost of Job 407			?	
52	Markup			?	
53	Selling price of Job 407			?	
54					

H ◀ ▶ H   Chapter 3 Form   Filled in Chapter 3 Form

Microsoft Excel

Determine the selling price for a new job, Job 408, with the following characteristics. You need not bother changing the job number from 407 to 408 in the worksheet.

	Department	
Cost summary for Job 408	Milling	Assembly
Machine-hours	40	10
Direct labor-hours	2	6
Direct materials....................	$700	$360
Direct labor cost...................	$50	$150

3. What happens to the selling price for Job 408 if the total number of machine-hours in the Assembly Department increases from 3,000 machine-hours to 6,000 machine-hours? Does it increase, decrease, or stay the same as in part 2 above? Why?

4. Restore the total number of machine-hours in the Assembly Department to 3,000 machine-hours. What happens to the selling price for Job 408 if the total number of direct labor-hours in the Assembly Department decreases from 80,000 direct labor-hours to 50,000 direct labor-hours? Does it increase, decrease, or stay the same as in part 2 above? Why?

Sweeten Company had no jobs in progress at the beginning of the year and no beginning inventories. It started, completed, and sold only two jobs during the year—Job P and Job Q. The company uses a plantwide predetermined overhead rate based on machine-hours. At the beginning of the year, it estimated 4,000 machine-hours would be required for the period's estimated level of production. Sweeten also estimated $25,000 of fixed manufacturing overhead cost for the coming period and variable manufacturing overhead of $1.70 per machine-hour.

LEARNING OBJECTIVES 3–1, 3–2, 3–3, 3–4

Because Sweeten has two manufacturing departments—Molding and Fabrication—it is considering replacing its plantwide overhead rate with departmental rates that would also be based on machine-hours. The company gathered the following additional information to enable calculating departmental overhead rates:

	Molding	Fabrication	Total
Estimated total machine-hours used	2,500	1,500	4,000
Estimated total fixed manufacturing overhead	$10,000	$15,000	$25,000
Estimated variable manufacturing overhead per machine-hour	$1.40	$2.20	

The direct materials cost, direct labor cost, and machine-hours used for Jobs P and Q are as follows:

	Job P	Job Q
Direct materials	$13,000	$8,000
Direct labor cost	$21,000	$7,500
Actual machine-hours used:		
Molding	1,700	800
Fabrication	600	900
Total	2,300	1,700

Sweeten Company had no overapplied or underapplied manufacturing overhead costs during the year.

Required:

For questions 1–8, assume Sweeten Company uses a plantwide predetermined overhead rate with machine-hours as the allocation base. For questions 9–15, assume that the company uses predetermined departmental overhead rates with machine-hours as the allocation base in both departments.

1. What is the company's plantwide predetermined overhead rate?
2. How much manufacturing overhead was applied to Job P, and how much was applied to Job Q?
3. What is the total manufacturing cost assigned to Job P?
4. If Job P includes 20 units, what is its unit product cost?
5. What is the total manufacturing cost assigned to Job Q?
6. If Job Q includes 30 units, what is its unit product cost?
7. Assume Sweeten Company uses cost-plus pricing (and a markup percentage of 80% of total manufacturing cost) to establish selling prices for all of its jobs. What selling price would the company establish for Jobs P and Q? What are the selling prices for both jobs when stated on a per-unit basis?
8. What is Sweeten Company's cost of goods sold for the year?
9. What are the company's predetermined overhead rates in the Molding Department and the Fabrication Department?
10. How much manufacturing overhead was applied from the Molding Department to Job P, and how much was applied to Job Q?
11. How much manufacturing overhead was applied from the Fabrication Department to Job P, and how much was applied to Job Q?
12. If Job P includes 20 units, what is its unit product cost?
13. If Job Q includes 30 units, what is its unit product cost?

14. Assume Sweeten Company uses cost-plus pricing (and a markup percentage of 80% of total manufacturing cost) to establish selling prices for all of its jobs. What selling price would the company establish for Jobs P and Q? What are the selling prices for both jobs when stated on a per-unit basis?
15. What is Sweeten Company's cost of goods sold for the year?

Exercises

EXERCISE 3–1 Compute a Predetermined Overhead Rate LO 3–1
Harris Fabrics computes its plantwide predetermined overhead rate annually on the basis of direct labor-hours. At the beginning of the year, it estimated that 20,000 direct labor-hours would be required for the period's estimated level of production. The company also estimated $94,000 of fixed manufacturing overhead cost for the coming period and variable manufacturing overhead of $2.00 per direct labor-hour. Harris's actual manufacturing overhead cost for the year was $123,900 and its actual total direct labor was 21,000 hours.

Required:
Compute the company's plantwide predetermined overhead rate for the year.

EXERCISE 3–2 Apply Overhead Cost to Jobs LO 3–2
Luthan Company uses a plantwide predetermined overhead rate of $23.40 per direct labor-hour. This predetermined rate was based on a cost formula that estimated $257,400 of total manufacturing overhead cost for an estimated activity level of 11,000 direct labor-hours.

The company incurred actual total manufacturing overhead cost of $249,000 and 10,800 total direct labor-hours during the period.

Required:
Determine the amount of manufacturing overhead cost that would have been applied to all jobs during the period.

EXERCISE 3–3 Computing Total Job Costs and Unit Product Costs Using a Plantwide Predetermined Overhead Rate LO 3–3
Mickley Company's plantwide predetermined overhead rate is $14.00 per direct labor-hour and its direct labor wage rate is $17.00 per hour. The following information pertains to Job A-500:

Direct materials	$231
Direct labor	$153

Required:
1. What is the total manufacturing cost assigned to Job A-500?
2. If Job A-500 consists of 40 units, what is the unit product cost for this job?

EXERCISE 3–4 Computing Total Job Costs and Unit Product Costs Using Multiple Predetermined Overhead Rates LO 3–4
Fickel Company has two manufacturing departments—Assembly and Testing & Packaging. The predetermined overhead rates in Assembly and Testing & Packaging are $16.00 per direct labor-hour and $12.00 per direct labor-hour, respectively. The company's direct labor wage rate is $20.00 per hour. The following information pertains to Job N-60:

	Assembly	Testing & Packaging
Direct materials	$340	$25
Direct labor	$180	$40

Required:
1. What is the total manufacturing cost assigned to Job N-60?
2. If Job N-60 consists of 10 units, what is the unit product cost for this job?

EXERCISE 3–5 Calculating Ending Inventories and Cost of Goods Sold LO 3–5

Morrow Corporation had only one job in process during May—Job X32Z—and had no finished goods inventory on May 1. Job X32Z was started in April and finished during May. Data concerning that job appear below:

	Job X32Z
Beginning balance	$5,000
Charged to the job during May:	
Direct materials	$8,000
Direct labor	$2,000
Manufacturing overhead applied	$4,000
Units completed	100
Units sold during May	40

The company's total manufacturing overhead applied always equals its total actual manufacturing overhead.

Required:

1. What is the cost of goods sold for May?
2. What is the total value of the finished goods inventory at the end of May?
3. What is the total value of the work in process inventory at the end of May?

EXERCISE 3–6 Computing Total Job Costs and Unit Product Costs Using Multiple Predetermined Overhead Rates LO 3–4

Braverman Company has two manufacturing departments—Finishing and Fabrication. The predetermined overhead rates in Finishing and Fabrication are $18.00 per direct labor-hour and 110% of direct materials cost, respectively. The company's direct labor wage rate is $16.00 per hour. The following information pertains to Job 700:

	Finishing	Fabrication
Direct materials	$410	$60
Direct labor	$128	$48

Required:

1. What is the total manufacturing cost assigned to Job 700?
2. If Job 700 consists of 15 units, what is the unit product cost for this job?

EXERCISE 3–7 Job-Order Costing for a Service Company LO 3–1, LO 3–2, LO 3–3

Tech Solutions is a consulting firm that uses a job-order costing system. Its direct materials consist of hardware and software it purchases and installs on behalf of its clients. The firm's direct labor includes salaries of consultants who work at the client's job site, and its overhead consists of costs such as depreciation, utilities, and insurance related to the office headquarters as well as the office supplies that are consumed serving clients.

Tech Solutions computes its predetermined overhead rate annually on the basis of direct labor-hours. At the beginning of the year, it estimated that 80,000 direct labor-hours would be required for the period's estimated level of client service. The company also estimated $680,000 of fixed overhead cost for the coming period and variable overhead of $0.50 per direct labor-hour. The firm's actual overhead cost for the year was $692,000, and its actual total direct labor was 83,000 hours.

Required:

1. Compute the predetermined overhead rate.
2. During the year, Tech Solutions started and completed the Xavier Company engagement. The following information was available with respect to this job:

Direct materials	$38,000
Direct labor cost	$21,000
Direct labor-hours worked	280

Compute the total job cost for the Xavier Company engagement.

EXERCISE 3–8 Job-Order Costing; Working Backwards LO 3–1, LO 3–2, LO 3–3

Hahn Company uses a job-order costing system. Its plantwide predetermined overhead rate uses direct labor-hours as the allocation base. The company pays its direct laborers $15 per hour. During the year, the company started and completed only two jobs—Job Alpha, which used 54,500 direct labor-hours, and Job Omega. The job cost sheets for these two jobs are shown below:

Job Alpha	
Direct materials	?
Direct labor	?
Manufacturing overhead applied	?
Total job cost	$1,533,500

Job Omega	
Direct materials	$235,000
Direct labor	345,000
Manufacturing overhead applied	184,000
Total job cost	$764,000

Required:

1. Calculate the plantwide predetermined overhead rate.
2. Complete the job cost sheet for Job Alpha.

EXERCISE 3–9 Applying Overhead Cost; Computing Unit Product Cost LO 3–2, LO 3–3

Newhard Company assigns overhead cost to jobs on the basis of 125% of direct labor cost. The job cost sheet for Job 313 includes $10,000 in direct materials cost and $12,000 in direct labor cost. A total of 1,000 units were produced in Job 313.

Required:

What is the total manufacturing cost assigned to Job 313? What is the unit product cost for Job 313?

EXERCISE 3–10 Job-Order Costing and Decision Making LO 3–1, LO 3–2, LO 3–3

Taveras Corporation is currently operating at 50% of its available manufacturing capacity. It uses a job-order costing system with a plantwide predetermined overhead rate based on machine-hours. At the beginning of the year, the company made the following estimates:

Machine-hours required to support estimated production	165,000
Fixed manufacturing overhead cost	$1,980,000
Variable manufacturing overhead cost per machine-hour	$2.00

Required:

1. Compute the plantwide predetermined overhead rate.
2. During the year, Job P90 was started, completed, and sold to the customer for $2,500. The following information was available with respect to this job:

Direct materials	$1,150
Direct labor cost	$830
Machine-hours used	72

Compute the total manufacturing cost assigned to Job P90.
3. Upon comparing Job P90's sales revenue to its total manufacturing cost, the company's chief financial officer said, "If this exact same opportunity walked through our front door tomorrow, I'd turn it down rather than making it and selling it for $2,500."
   a. Construct an argument (supported by numerical analysis) that refutes the chief financial officer's assertion.

b.   Construct an argument (accompanied by numerical analysis) that supports the chief financial officer's assertion.

EXERCISE 3–11 Applying Overhead; Calculating Ending Inventories and Cost of Goods Sold LO 3–2, LO 3–5

Heritage Company uses a job-order costing system to assign costs to jobs. It had no work in process or finished goods inventories on hand at the beginning of May. The table below provides data concerning the only three jobs worked on in May.

	Job X	Job Y	Job Z
Direct labor-hours . . .	200	80	120
Direct materials	$4,800	$1,800	$3,600
Direct labor.	$2,400	$1,000	$1,500

Jobs X and Y were completed in May; however, only 150 of the 200 units included in Job X were sold in May, whereas all 100 of Job Y's units were sold in May. Job Z was not completed by the end of the month.

Overhead costs are applied to jobs based on direct labor-hours and the predetermined overhead rate is $45 per direct labor-hour. The company's total applied overhead always equals its total actual overhead.

Required:
1. Compute the amount of overhead cost that would have been applied to each job during May.
2. Compute the work in process inventory that would be reported in the company's May 31 balance sheet.
3. Compute the finished goods inventory that would be reported in the company's May 31 balance sheet.
4. Compute the cost of goods sold that would be reported in the company's income statement for May.

EXERCISE 3–12 Applying Overhead Cost to a Job LO 3–2

Sigma Corporation applies overhead cost to jobs on the basis of direct labor cost. Job V, which was started and completed during the current period, shows charges of $5,000 for direct materials, $8,000 for direct labor, and $6,000 for overhead on its job cost sheet. Job W, which is still in process at year-end, shows charges of $2,500 for direct materials and $4,000 for direct labor.

Required:
1. Should any overhead cost be applied to Job W at year-end? If so, how much? Explain.
2. How will the costs included in Job W's job cost sheet be reported within Sigma Corporation's financial statements at the end of the year?

EXERCISE 3–13 Varying Plantwide Predetermined Overhead Rates LO 3–1, LO 3–2, LO 3–3

Kingsport Containers Company makes a single product that is subject to wide seasonal variations in demand. The company uses a job-order costing system and computes plantwide predetermined overhead rates on a quarterly basis using the number of units to be produced as the allocation base. Its estimated costs, by quarter, for the coming year are given below:

	Quarter			
	First	Second	Third	Fourth
Direct materials	$240,000	$120,000	$ 60,000	$180,000
Direct labor	128,000	64,000	32,000	96,000
Manufacturing overhead	300,000	220,000	180,000	?
Total manufacturing costs (a)	$668,000	$404,000	$272,000	$?
Number of units to be produced (b)	80,000	40,000	20,000	60,000
Estimated unit product cost (a) ÷ (b)	$8.35	$10.10	$13.60	?

Management finds the variation in quarterly unit product costs to be confusing. It has been suggested that the problem lies with manufacturing overhead because it is the largest element of total manufacturing cost. Accordingly, you have been asked to find a more appropriate way of assigning manufacturing overhead cost to units of product.

Required:

1. Assuming the estimated variable manufacturing overhead cost per unit is $2.00, what must be the estimated total fixed manufacturing overhead cost per quarter?
2. Assuming the assumptions about cost behavior from the first three quarters hold constant, what is the estimated unit product cost for the fourth quarter?
3. What is causing the estimated unit product cost to fluctuate from one quarter to the next?
4. How would you recommend stabilizing the company's unit product cost? Support your answer with computations.

EXERCISE 3–14 Computing Predetermined Overhead Rates and Job Costs LO 3–1, LO 3–2, LO 3–3

Moody Corporation uses a job-order costing system with a plantwide predetermined overhead rate based on machine-hours. At the beginning of the year, the company made the following estimates:

Machine-hours required to support estimated production	100,000
Fixed manufacturing overhead cost...........................	$650,000
Variable manufacturing overhead cost per machine-hour........	$3.00

Required:

1. Compute the plantwide predetermined overhead rate.
2. During the year, Job 400 was started and completed. The following information was available with respect to this job:

Direct materials	$450
Direct labor cost	$210
Machine-hours used	40

Compute the total manufacturing cost assigned to Job 400.

3. If Job 400 includes 52 units, what is the unit product cost for this job?
4. If Moody uses a markup percentage of 120% of its total manufacturing cost, then what selling price per unit would it have established for Job 400?
5. If Moody hired you as a consultant to critique its pricing methodology, what would you say?

EXERCISE 3–15 Departmental Predetermined Overhead Rates LO 3–1, LO 3–2, LO 3–4

White Company has two departments, Cutting and Finishing. The company uses a job-order costing system and computes a predetermined overhead rate in each department. The Cutting Department bases its rate on machine-hours, and the Finishing Department bases its rate on direct labor-hours. At the beginning of the year, the company made the following estimates:

	Department	
	Cutting	Finishing
Direct labor-hours	6,000	30,000
Machine-hours	48,000	5,000
Total fixed manufacturing overhead cost	$264,000	$366,000
Variable manufacturing overhead per machine-hour	$2.00	—
Variable manufacturing overhead per direct labor-hour	—	$4.00

Required:

1. Compute the predetermined overhead rate for each department.
2. The job cost sheet for Job 203, which was started and completed during the year, showed the following:

	Department	
	Cutting	Finishing
Direct labor-hours	6	20
Machine-hours	80	4
Direct materials	$500	$310
Direct labor cost	$108	$360

Using the predetermined overhead rates you computed in (1) above, compute the total manufacturing cost assigned to Job 203.

3. Would you expect substantially different amounts of overhead cost to be assigned to some jobs if the company used a plantwide predetermined overhead rate based on direct labor-hours, rather than using departmental rates? Explain. No computations are necessary.

EXERCISE 3–16 Job-Order Costing for a Service Company LO 3–1, LO 3–2, LO 3–3

Yancey Productions is a film studio that uses a job-order costing system. The company's direct materials consist of items such as costumes and props. Its direct labor includes each film's actors, directors, and extras. The company's overhead costs include items such as utilities, depreciation of equipment, senior management salaries, and wages of maintenance workers. Yancey applies its overhead cost to films based on direct labor-dollars.

At the beginning of the year, Yancey made the following estimates:

Direct labor-dollars to support all productions	$8,000,000
Fixed overhead cost	$4,800,000
Variable overhead cost per direct labor-dollar	$0.05

Required:

1. Compute the predetermined overhead rate.
2. During the year, Yancey produced a film titled *You Can Say That Again* that incurred the following costs:

Direct materials	$1,259,000
Direct labor cost	$2,400,000

Compute the total job cost for this particular film.

EXERCISE 3–17 Plantwide and Departmental Predetermined Overhead Rates; Job Costs LO 3–1, LO 3–2, LO 3–3, LO 3–4

Delph Company uses a job-order costing system with a plantwide predetermined overhead rate based on machine-hours. At the beginning of the year, the company estimated that 50,000 machine-hours would be required for the period's estimated level of production. It also estimated $910,000 of fixed manufacturing overhead cost for the coming period and variable manufacturing overhead of $1.80 per machine-hour.

Because Delph has two manufacturing departments—Molding and Fabrication—it is considering replacing its plantwide overhead rate with departmental rates that would also be based on machine-hours. The company gathered the following information to enable calculating departmental overhead rates:

	Molding	Fabrication	Total
Machine-hours	20,000	30,000	50,000
Fixed manufacturing overhead cost	$700,000	$210,000	$910,000
Variable manufacturing overhead cost per machine-hour	$3.00	$1.00	

During the year, the company had no beginning or ending inventories and it started, completed, and sold only two jobs—Job D-70 and Job C-200. It provided the following information related to those two jobs:

Job D-70	Molding	Fabrication	Total
Direct materials cost	$375,000	$325,000	$700,000
Direct labor cost	$200,000	$160,000	$360,000
Machine-hours	14,000	6,000	20,000

Job C-200	Molding	Fabrication	Total
Direct materials cost	$300,000	$250,000	$550,000
Direct labor cost	$175,000	$225,000	$400,000
Machine-hours	6,000	24,000	30,000

Delph had no underapplied or overapplied manufacturing overhead during the year.

Required:

1. Assume Delph uses a plantwide predetermined overhead rate based on machine-hours.
    a. Compute the plantwide predetermined overhead rate.
    b. Compute the total manufacturing cost assigned to Job D-70 and Job C-200.
    c. If Delph establishes bid prices that are 150% of total manufacturing costs, what bid prices would it have established for Job D-70 and Job C-200?
    d. What is Delph's cost of goods sold for the year?
2. Assume Delph uses departmental predetermined overhead rates based on machine-hours.
    a. Compute the departmental predetermined overhead rates.
    b. Compute the total manufacturing cost assigned to Job D-70 and Job C-200.
    c. If Delph establishes bid prices that are 150% of total manufacturing cost, what bid prices would it have established for Job D-70 and Job C-200?
    d. What is Delph's cost of goods sold for the year?
3. What managerial insights are revealed by the computations that you performed in this problem? (*Hint:* Do the cost of goods sold amounts that you computed in requirements 1 and 2 differ from one another? Do the bid prices that you computed in requirements 1 and 2 differ from one another? Why?)

Problems Mc Graw Hill connect

PROBLEM 3–18 Plantwide Predetermined Overhead Rates; Pricing LO 3–1, LO 3–2, LO 3–3

Landen Corporation uses a job-order costing system. At the beginning of the year, the company made the following estimates:

Direct labor-hours required to support estimated production	140,000
Machine-hours required to support estimated production	70,000
Fixed manufacturing overhead cost	$784,000
Variable manufacturing overhead cost per direct labor-hour	$2.00
Variable manufacturing overhead cost per machine-hour	$4.00

During the year, Job 550 was started and completed. The following information is available with respect to this job:

Direct materials	$175
Direct labor cost	$225
Direct labor-hours	15
Machine-hours	5

Required:

1. Assume that Landen has historically used a plantwide predetermined overhead rate with direct labor-hours as the allocation base. Under this approach:
   a. Compute the plantwide predetermined overhead rate.
   b. Compute the total manufacturing cost of Job 550.
   c. If Landen uses a markup percentage of 200% of its total manufacturing cost, what selling price would it establish for Job 550?
2. Assume that Landen's controller believes that machine-hours is a better allocation base than direct labor-hours. Under this approach:
   a. Compute the plantwide predetermined overhead rate.
   b. Compute the total manufacturing cost of Job 550.
   c. If Landen uses a markup percentage of 200% of its total manufacturing cost, what selling price would it establish for Job 550?
3. Assume that Landen's controller is right about machine-hours being a more accurate overhead cost allocation base than direct labor-hours. If the company continues to use direct labor-hours as its only overhead cost allocation base, what implications does this have for pricing jobs such as Job 550?

PROBLEM 3–19 Plantwide and Departmental Predetermined Overhead Rates; Overhead Application LO 3–1, LO 3–2

Wilmington Company has two manufacturing departments—Assembly and Fabrication. It considers all of its manufacturing overhead costs to be fixed costs. The first set of data shown below is based on estimates from the beginning of the year. The second set of data relates to one particular job completed during the year—Job Bravo.

Estimated Data	Assembly	Fabrication	Total
Manufacturing overhead costs	$600,000	$800,000	$1,400,000
Direct labor-hours	50,000	30,000	80,000
Machine-hours	20,000	100,000	120,000

Job Bravo	Assembly	Fabrication	Total
Direct labor-hours	11	3	14
Machine-hours	3	6	9

Required:

1. If Wilmington used a plantwide predetermined overhead rate based on direct labor-hours, how much manufacturing overhead would be applied to Job Bravo?
2. If Wilmington uses departmental predetermined overhead rates with direct labor-hours as the allocation base in Assembly and machine-hours as the allocation base in Fabrication, how much manufacturing overhead would be applied to Job Bravo?

PROBLEM 3–20 Job-Order Costing for a Service Company LO 3–1, LO 3–2, LO 3–3

Speedy Auto Repairs uses a job-order costing system. The company's direct materials consist of replacement parts installed in customer vehicles, and its direct labor consists of the mechanics' hourly wages. Speedy's overhead costs include various items, such as the shop manager's salary, depreciation of equipment, utilities, insurance, and magazine subscriptions and refreshments for the waiting room.

The company applies all of its overhead costs to jobs based on direct labor-hours. At the beginning of the year, it made the following estimates:

Direct labor-hours required to support estimated output	20,000
Fixed overhead cost	$350,000
Variable overhead cost per direct labor-hour	$1.00

Required:

1. Compute the predetermined overhead rate.
2. During the year, Mr. Wilkes brought in his vehicle to replace his brakes, spark plugs, and tires. The following information was available with respect to his job:

Direct materials	$590
Direct labor cost	$109
Direct labor-hours used	6

    Compute Mr. Wilkes' total job cost.

3. If Speedy establishes its selling prices using a markup percentage of 40% of its total job cost, then how much would it have charged Mr. Wilkes?

PROBLEM 3–21 Multiple Predetermined Overhead Rates; Applying Overhead LO 3–1, LO 3–2, LO 3–4

High Desert Potteryworks makes a variety of pottery products that it sells to retailers. The company uses a job-order costing system in which departmental predetermined overhead rates are used to apply manufacturing overhead cost to jobs. The predetermined overhead rate in the Molding Department is based on machine-hours, and the rate in the Painting Department is based on direct labor-hours. At the beginning of the year, the company provided the following estimates:

	Department	
	Molding	Painting
Direct labor-hours	12,000	60,000
Machine-hours	70,000	8,000
Fixed manufacturing overhead cost	$497,000	$615,000
Variable manufacturing overhead per machine-hour	$1.50	–
Variable manufacturing overhead per direct labor-hour	–	$2.00

Job 205 was started on August 1 and completed on August 10. The company's cost records show the following information concerning the job:

	Department	
	Molding	Painting
Direct labor-hours	30	84
Machine-hours	110	20
Direct materials	$770	$1,332
Direct labor cost	$525	$1,470

Required:

1. Compute the predetermined overhead rates used in the Molding Department and the Painting Department.
2. Compute the total overhead cost applied to Job 205.
3. What would be the total manufacturing cost recorded for Job 205? If the job contained 50 units, what would be the unit product cost?

PROBLEM 3–22 Plantwide versus Multiple Predetermined Overhead Rates: Service Industry LO 3–1, LO 3–2, LO 3–3, LO 3–4

McCullough Hospital uses a job-order costing system to assign costs to its patients. Its direct materials include a variety of items such as pharmaceutical drugs, heart valves, artificial hips, and pacemakers. Its direct labor costs (e.g., surgeons, anesthesiologists, radiologists, and nurses) associated with specific surgical procedures and tests are traced to individual patients. All other costs, such as depreciation of medical equipment, insurance, utilities, incidental medical supplies, and the labor costs associated with around-the-clock monitoring of patients are treated as overhead costs.

Historically, McCullough has used one predetermined overhead rate based on the number of patient-days (each night that a patient spends in the hospital counts as one patient-day) to allocate overhead costs to patients. For the most recent period, this predetermined rate was based on three estimates—fixed overhead costs of $17,200,000, variable overhead costs of $110 per patient-day, and a denominator volume of 20,000 patient-days.

Recently a member of the hospital's accounting staff suggested using two predetermined overhead rates (allocated based on the number of patient-days) to improve the accuracy of the costs allocated to patients. The first overhead rate would include all overhead costs within the Intensive Care Unit (ICU) and the second overhead rate would include all Other overhead costs. Information pertaining to these two cost pools and two of the hospital's patients—Patient A and Patient B—is provided below:

	ICU	Other	Total
Estimated number of patient-days	2,000	18,000	20,000
Estimated fixed overhead cost	$3,200,000	$14,000,000	$17,200,000
Estimated variable overhead cost per patient-day	$236	$96	

	Patient A	Patient B
Direct materials	$4,500	$6,200
Direct labor	$25,000	$36,000
Total number of patient-days (including ICU)	14	21
Number of patient-days spent in ICU	0	7

Required:

1. Assuming McCullough continues to use only one predetermined overhead rate, calculate:
   a. The predetermined overhead rate.
   b. The total cost, including direct materials, direct labor, and applied overhead, assigned to Patient A and Patient B.

2. Assuming McCullough calculates two overhead rates as recommended by the staff accountant, calculate:
   a. The ICU and Other overhead rates.
   b. The total cost, including direct materials, direct labor, and applied overhead, assigned to Patient A and Patient B.

3. What insights are revealed by the staff accountant's approach?

PROBLEM 3–23 Calculating Ending Inventories and Cost of Goods Sold LO 3–5

Techuxia Corporation worked on four jobs during October: Job A256, Job A257, Job A258, and Job A260. At the end of October, the job cost sheets for these jobs contained the following data:

	Job A256	Job A257	Job A258	Job A260
Beginning balance	$1,200	$500	$0	$0
Charged to the jobs during October:				
Direct materials	$2,600	$3,500	$1,400	$3,500
Direct labor	$800	$1,000	$600	$400
Manufacturing overhead applied	$1,200	$1,500	$900	$600
Units completed	100	0	200	0
Units sold during October	80	0	40	0

Jobs A256 and A258 were completed during October. The other two jobs were incomplete at the end of October. There was no finished goods inventory on October 1. The company's total manufacturing overhead applied equals its total actual manufacturing overhead.

Required:
1. What is the cost of goods sold for October?
2. What is the total value of the finished goods inventory at the end of October?
3. What is the total value of the work in process inventory at the end of October?

PROBLEM 3–24 Plantwide versus Multiple Predetermined Overhead Rates LO 3–1, LO 3–2

Mason Company has two manufacturing departments—Machining and Assembly. The company considers all of its manufacturing overhead costs to be fixed costs. It provided the following estimates at the beginning of the year as well as the following information with respect to Jobs A and B:

Estimated Data	Machining	Assembly	Total
Manufacturing overhead	$500,000	$100,000	$600,000
Direct labor-hours	10,000	50,000	60,000
Machine-hours	50,000	5,000	55,000

Job A	Machining	Assembly	Total
Direct labor-hours	5	10	15
Machine-hours	11	2	13

Job B	Machining	Assembly	Total
Direct labor-hours	4	5	9
Machine-hours	12	3	15

Required:
1. If Mason Company uses a plantwide predetermined overhead rate with direct labor-hours as the allocation base, how much manufacturing overhead cost would be applied to Job A? Job B?
2. Assume Mason Company uses departmental predetermined overhead rates. The Machining Department is allocated based on machine-hours and the Assembly Department is allocated based on direct labor-hours. How much manufacturing overhead cost would be applied to Job A? Job B?
3. If Mason multiplies its job costs by a markup percentage to establish selling prices, how might plantwide overhead allocation adversely affect the company's pricing decisions?

PROBLEM 3–25 Calculating Ending Inventories and Cost of Goods Sold LO 3–5

Expedition Company worked on five jobs during May: Jobs A10, B20, C30, D40, and E50. At the end of May, the job cost sheets for these five jobs contained the following data:

	Job A10	Job B20	Job C30	Job D40	Job E50
Beginning balance	$73	$90	$166	$114	$185
Charged to the jobs during May:					
Direct materials	$110	$90	$140	$110	$220
Direct labor	$90	$100	$80	$120	$150
Manufacturing overhead applied	$117	$130	$104	$156	$195
Units completed	120	0	50	0	150
Units sold during May	0	0	50	0	100

Jobs A10, C30, and E50 were completed during May. Jobs B20 and D40 were incomplete at the end of May. There was no finished goods inventory on May 1, and the company's total manufacturing overhead applied always equals its total actual manufacturing overhead.

Required:
1. What is the cost of goods sold for May?
2. What is the total value of the finished goods inventory at the end of May?
3. What is the total value of the work in process inventory at the end of May?

McGraw Hill connect Case

Select cases are available in Connect.

CASE 3–26 Plantwide versus Departmental Overhead Rates; Pricing LO 3–1, LO 3–2, LO 3–3, LO 3-4

"Blast it!" said David Wilson, president of Teledex Company. "We've just lost the bid on the Koopers job by $2,000. It seems we're either too high to get the job or too low to make any money on half the jobs we bid."

Teledex Company manufactures products to customers' specifications and uses a job-order costing system. The company uses a plantwide predetermined overhead rate based on direct labor cost to apply its manufacturing overhead (assumed to be all fixed) to jobs. The following estimates were made at the beginning of the year:

	Department			
	Fabricating	Machining	Assembly	Total Plant
Manufacturing overhead	$350,000	$400,000	$90,000	$840,000
Direct labor	$200,000	$100,000	$300,000	$600,000

Jobs require varying amounts of work in the three departments. The Koopers job, for example, would have required manufacturing costs in the three departments as follows:

	Department			
	Fabricating	Machining	Assembly	Total Plant
Direct materials	$3,000	$200	$1,400	$4,600
Direct labor	$2,800	$500	$6,200	$9,500
Manufacturing overhead	?	?	?	?

Required:
1. Using the company's plantwide approach:
   a. Compute the plantwide predetermined rate for the current year.
   b. Determine the amount of manufacturing overhead cost that would have been applied to the Koopers job.
2. Suppose instead of using a plantwide predetermined overhead rate, the company had used departmental predetermined overhead rates based on direct labor cost. Under these conditions:
   a. Compute the predetermined overhead rate for each department for the current year.
   b. Determine the amount of manufacturing overhead cost that would have been applied to the Koopers job.
3. Explain the difference between the manufacturing overhead that would have been applied to the Koopers job using the plantwide approach in question 1(b) and using the departmental approach in question 2(b).
4. Assume it is customary in the industry to bid jobs at 150% of total manufacturing cost (direct materials, direct labor, and applied overhead). What was the company's bid price on the Koopers job using a plantwide predetermined overhead rate? What would have been the bid price if departmental predetermined overhead rates were used to apply overhead cost?

Appendix 3A: Activity-Based Absorption Costing

Chapter 3 described how manufacturing companies use traditional absorption costing systems to calculate unit product costs. In this appendix, we contrast traditional absorption costing with an alternative approach called *activity-based absorption costing.* **Activity-based absorption costing** assigns all manufacturing overhead costs to products based on the *activities* performed to make those products. An **activity** is an event that causes the consumption of manufacturing overhead resources. Rather than relying on plantwide or departmental cost pools, the activity-based approach accumulates each activity's overhead costs in *activity cost pools.* An **activity cost pool** is a "bucket" in which costs are accumulated that relate to a single activity. Each activity cost pool has one *activity measure.* An **activity measure** is an allocation base used as the denominator for an activity cost pool. The costs accumulated in the numerator of an activity cost pool divided by the quantity of the activity measure in its denominator equals what is called an *activity rate.* An activity rate is used to assign costs from an activity cost pool to products.

Activity-based absorption costing differs from traditional absorption costing in two ways. First, the activity-based approach uses more cost pools than a traditional approach. Second, the activity-based approach includes some activities and activity measures that *do not* relate to the volume of units produced, whereas the traditional approach relies exclusively on allocation bases that are driven by the volume of production. For example, the activity-based approach may include *batch-level activities.* A **batch-level activity** is performed each time a batch is handled or processed, regardless of how many units are in the batch. Batch-level activities include tasks such as placing purchase orders, setting up equipment, and transporting batches of component parts. Costs at the batch level depend on the number of batches processed rather than the number of units produced. The activity-based approach may also include *product-level activities.* A **product-level activity** relates to specific products and typically must be carried out regardless of how many batches are run or units of product are produced and sold. Product-level activities include tasks such as designing a product and making engineering design changes to a product. Costs at the product-level depend on the number of products supported rather than the number of batches run or the number of units of product produced and sold.

To illustrate the differences between traditional and activity-based absorption costing, we'll use an example focused on Maxtar Industries, a manufacturer of high-quality smoker/barbecue units. The company has two product lines—Premium and Standard. The company has traditionally applied manufacturing overhead costs to these products using a plantwide predetermined overhead rate based on direct labor-hours. Exhibit 3A–1 details how the unit product costs of the two product lines are computed using the company's traditional costing system. The unit product cost of the Premium product line is $71.60 and the unit product cost of the Standard product line is $53.70 according to this traditional costing system.

Maxtar Industries recently experimented with an activity-based absorption costing system that has three activity cost pools: (1) supporting direct labor; (2) setting up machines; and (3) parts administration. The top of Exhibit 3A–2 displays basic data concerning these activity cost pools. Note the total estimated overhead cost in these three costs pools, $1,520,000, agrees with the total estimated overhead cost in the company's traditional costing system. The company's activity-based approach simply provides an alternative way to allocate the company's manufacturing overhead across the two products.

The activity rates for the three activity cost pools are computed in the second table in Exhibit 3A–2. For example, the total cost in the "setting up machines" activity cost pool, $480,000, is divided by the total activity associated with that cost pool, 800 setups, to determine the activity rate of $600 per setup.

Basic Data		
Total estimated manufacturing overhead cost	$1,520,000	
Total estimated direct labor-hours	400,000 DLHs	

	Premium	Standard
Direct materials per unit	$40.00	$30.00
Direct labor per unit	$24.00	$18.00
Direct labor-hours per unit	2.0 DLHs	1.5 DLHs
Units produced	50,000 units	200,000 units

Computation of the Plantwide Predetermined Overhead Rate

$$\text{Predetermined overhead rate} = \frac{\text{Total estimated manufacturing overhead}}{\text{Total estimated amount of the allocation base}}$$

$$= \frac{\$1,520,000}{400,000 \text{ DLHs}} = \$3.80 \text{ per DLH}$$

Traditional Unit Product Costs

	Premium	Standard
Direct materials	$40.00	$30.00
Direct labor	24.00	18.00
Manufacturing overhead (2.0 DLHs × $3.80 per DLH; 1.5 DLHs × $3.80 per DLH)	7.60	5.70
Unit product cost	$71.60	$53.70

EXHIBIT 3A–1
Maxtar Industries' Traditional Costing System

The activity rates are used to allocate overhead costs to the two products in the third table in Exhibit 3A–2. For example, the activity rate for the "setting up machines" activity cost pool, $600 per setup, is multiplied by the Premium product line's 600 setups to determine the $360,000 machine setup cost allocated to the Premium product line.

The table at the bottom of Exhibit 3A–2 displays the overhead costs per unit and the activity-based unit product costs. The overhead cost per unit is determined by dividing the total overhead cost by the number of units produced. For example, the Premium product line's total overhead cost of $728,000 is divided by 50,000 units to determine the $14.56 overhead cost per unit. Note that the unit product costs differ from those computed using the company's traditional costing system in Exhibit 3A–1. Because the activity-based approach contains both a batch-level (setting up machines) and a product-level (parts administration) activity cost pool, the unit product costs under the activity-based approach follow the usual pattern in which overhead costs are shifted from the high-volume to the low-volume product. The unit product cost of the Standard product line, the high-volume product, has gone down from $53.70 under the traditional costing system to $51.96 under activity-based costing. In contrast, the unit product cost of the Premium product line, the low-volume product, has increased from $71.60 under the traditional costing system to $78.56 under activity-based costing. Instead of using direct labor-hours (which moves in tandem with the volume of the production) to assign all manufacturing overhead costs to products, the activity-based approach uses a batch-level activity measure and a product-level activity measure to assign the batch-level and product-level activity cost pools to the two products.

EXHIBIT 3A–2
Maxtar Industries' Activity-Based Absorption Costing System

Basic Data

Activity Cost Pools and Activity Measures	Estimated Overhead Cost	Expected Activity		
		Premium	Standard	Total
Supporting direct labor (DLHs)	$ 800,000	100,000	300,000	400,000
Setting up machines (setups)	480,000	600	200	800
Parts administration (part types)	240,000	140	60	200
Total manufacturing overhead cost	$1,520,000			

Computation of Activity Rates

Activity Cost Pools	(a) Estimated Overhead Cost	(b) Total Expected Activity	(a) ÷ (b) Activity Rate
Supporting direct labor	$800,000	400,000 DLHs	$2 per DLH
Setting up machines	$480,000	800 setups	$600 per setup
Parts administration	$240,000	200 part types	$1,200 per part type

Assigning Overhead Costs to Products

The Premium Product

Activity Cost Pools	(a) Activity Rate	(b) Activity	(a) × (b) ABC Cost
Supporting direct labor	$2 per DLH	100,000 DLHs	$200,000
Setting up machines	$600 per setup	600 setups	360,000
Parts administration	$1,200 per part type	140 part types	168,000
Total			$728,000

The Standard Product

Activity Cost Pools	(a) Activity Rate	(b) Activity	(a) × (b) ABC Cost
Supporting direct labor	$2 per DLH	300,000 DLHs	$600,000
Setting up machines	$600 per setup	200 setups	120,000
Parts administration	$1,200 per part type	60 part types	72,000
Total			$792,000

Activity-Based Absorption Costing Product Costs

	Premium	Standard
Direct materials	$40.00	$30.00
Direct labor	24.00	18.00
Manufacturing overhead ($728,000 ÷ 50,000 units; $792,000 ÷ 200,000 units)	14.56	3.96
Unit product cost	$78.56	$51.96

Glossary (Appendix 3A)

Activity An event that causes the consumption of overhead resources in an organization. (p. 156)

Activity-based absorption costing A costing method that assigns all manufacturing overhead costs to products based on the *activities* performed to make those products. (p. 156)

Activity cost pool A "bucket" in which costs are accumulated that relate to a single activity measure in an activity-based costing system. (p. 156)

Activity measure An allocation base in an activity-based costing system; ideally, a measure of the amount of activity that drives the costs in an activity cost pool. (p. 156)

Batch-level activity An activity that is performed each time a batch is handled or processed, regardless of how many units are in the batch. The amount of resources consumed depends on the number of batches run rather than on the number of units in the batch. (p. 156)

Product-level activity An activity that relates to specific products and typically must be carried out regardless of how many batches are run or units of product are produced and sold. (p. 156)

Appendix 3A: Exercises, Problems, and Case

EXERCISE 3A–1 Activity-Based Absorption Costing LO 3–6

Fogerty Company makes two products—Hubs and Sprockets. Data regarding the two products follow:

	Direct Labor-Hours per Unit	Annual Production
Hubs	0.80	10,000 units
Sprockets	0.40	40,000 units

Additional information about the company follows:

a. Hubs require $32 in direct materials per unit, and Sprockets require $18.

b. The direct labor wage rate is $15 per hour.

c. Hubs are more complex to manufacture than Sprockets and require special processing.

d. The company's activity-based absorption costing system has the following activity cost pools:

Activity Cost Pool (and Activity Measure)	Estimated Overhead Cost	Expected Activity Hubs	Expected Activity Sprockets	Expected Activity Total
Machine setups (number of setups)	$72,000	100	300	400
Special processing (machine-hours)	$200,000	5,000	0	5,000
General factory (Direct labor-hours)	$816,000	8,000	16,000	24,000

Required:

1. Compute the activity rate for each activity cost pool.

2. Compute the unit product cost for Hubs and Sprockets using activity-based absorption costing.

EXERCISE 3A–2 Activity-Based Absorption Costing as an Alternative to Traditional Product Costing LO 3–6

Harrison Company makes two products and uses a traditional costing system in which a single plantwide predetermined overhead rate is computed based on direct labor-hours. Data for the two products for the upcoming year follow:

	Rascon	Parcel
Direct materials cost per unit	$13.00	$22.00
Direct labor cost per unit	$6.00	$3.00
Direct labor-hours per unit	0.40	0.20
Number of units produced	20,000	80,000

These products are customized to some degree for specific customers.

Required:

1. The company's manufacturing overhead costs for the year are expected to be $576,000. Using the company's traditional costing system, compute the unit product costs for the two products.
2. Management is considering an activity-based absorption costing system in which half of the overhead would continue to be allocated based on direct labor-hours and half would be allocated based on engineering design time. This time is expected to be distributed as follows during the upcoming year:

	Rascon	Parcel	Total
Engineering design time (in hours)	3,000	3,000	6,000

Compute the unit product costs for the two products using the proposed activity-based absorption costing system.

3. Explain why the product costs differ between the two systems.

EXERCISE 3A–3 Activity-Based Absorption Costing as an Alternative to Traditional Product Costing LO 3–6

Stillicum Corporation makes ultralightweight backpacking tents. Data concerning the company's two product lines appear below:

	Deluxe	Standard
Direct materials per unit	$72.00	$53.00
Direct labor per unit	$19.00	$15.20
Direct labor-hours per unit	1.0 DLH	0.8 DLH
Estimated annual production	10,000 units	50,000 units

The company has a traditional costing system in which manufacturing overhead is applied to units based on direct labor-hours. Data concerning manufacturing overhead and direct labor-hours for the upcoming year appear below:

Estimated total manufacturing overhead	$325,000
Estimated total direct labor-hours	50,000 DLHs

Required:

1. Determine the unit product costs of the Deluxe and Standard products under the company's traditional costing system.
2. The company is considering replacing its traditional costing system with an activity-based absorption costing system that would have the following three activity cost pools:

	Estimated	Expected Activity		
Activity Cost Pools (and Activity Measures)	Overhead Cost	Deluxe	Standard	Total
Supporting direct labor (direct labor-hours)	$200,000	10,000	40,000	50,000
Batch setups (setups)	75,000	200	100	300
Safety testing (tests)	50,000	30	70	100
Total manufacturing overhead cost	$325,000			

Determine the unit product costs of the Deluxe and Standard products under the activity-based absorption costing system.

PROBLEM 3A–4 Activity-Based Absorption Costing as an Alternative to Traditional Product Costing

LO 3–6

Ellix Company manufactures two models of ultra-high fidelity speakers—the X200 model and the X99 model. Data regarding the two products follow:

Product	Direct Labor-Hours	Annual Production	Total Direct Labor-Hours
X200.................	1.8 DLHs per unit	5,000 units	9,000 DLHs
X99.................	0.9 DLHs per unit	30,000 units	27,000 DLHs
			36,000 DLHs

Additional information about the company follows:

a. Model X200 requires $72 in direct materials per unit, and model X99 requires $50.
b. The direct labor workers are paid $20 per hour.
c. The company has always used direct labor-hours as the allocation base for applying manufacturing overhead cost to products.
d. Model X200 is more complex to manufacture than model X99 and requires the use of special equipment.
e. Because of the special work required in (d) above, the company is considering the use of activity-based absorption costing to apply manufacturing overhead cost to products. Three activity cost pools have been identified as follows:

Activity Cost Pool	Activity Measure	Estimated Total Cost	Estimated Total Activity X200	X99	Total
Machine setups	Number of setups	$ 360,000	50	100	150
Special processing	Machine-hours	180,000	12,000	0	12,000
General factory	Direct labor-hours	1,260,000	9,000	27,000	36,000
		$1,800,000			

Required:

1. Assume the company continues to use direct labor-hours as the allocation base for applying overhead cost to products.
   a. Compute the plantwide predetermined overhead rate.
   b. Compute the unit product cost of each model.
2. Assume the company decides to use activity-based absorption costing to apply overhead cost to products.
   a. Compute the activity rate for each activity cost pool and determine the amount of overhead cost that would be applied to each model using the activity-based approach.
   b. Compute the unit product cost of each model.
3. Explain why overhead cost shifted from the high-volume model to the low-volume model under the activity-based approach.

PROBLEM 3A–5 Activity-Based Absorption Costing as an Alternative to Traditional Product Costing

LO 3–6

Siegel Company manufactures a product that is available in both a deluxe model and a regular model. The company has manufactured the regular model for years. The deluxe model was introduced several years ago to tap a new segment of the market. Since introduction of the deluxe model, the company's profits have steadily declined and management has become increasingly concerned about the accuracy of its costing system. Sales of the deluxe model have been increasing rapidly.

Manufacturing overhead is assigned to products on the basis of direct labor-hours. For the current year, the company estimated it will incur $900,000 in manufacturing overhead cost and produce 5,000 units of the deluxe model and 40,000 units of the regular model. The deluxe model requires two hours of direct labor time per unit, and the regular model requires one hour. Material and labor costs per unit are as follows:

	Model	
	Deluxe	Regular
Direct materials	$40	$25
Direct labor	$38	$19

Required:

1. Compute the predetermined overhead rate using direct labor-hours as the allocation base. Using this rate and other data from the problem, calculate the unit product cost of each model.
2. Management is considering using activity-based absorption costing to apply manufacturing overhead cost to products. The activity-based system would have the following four activity cost pools:

Activity Cost Pool	Activity Measure	Estimated Overhead Cost
Purchasing	Purchase orders issued	$204,000
Processing	Machine-hours	182,000
Scrap/rework	Scrap/rework orders issued	379,000
Shipping	Number of shipments	135,000
		$900,000

	Expected Activity		
Activity Measure	Deluxe	Regular	Total
Purchase orders issued	200	400	600
Machine-hours	20,000	15,000	35,000
Scrap/rework orders issued	1,000	1,000	2,000
Number of shipments	250	650	900

Determine the predetermined overhead rate for each of the four activity cost pools.

3. Using the predetermined overhead rates you computed in part (2), do the following:
   a. Compute the total amount of manufacturing overhead cost that would be applied to each model using the activity-based absorption costing system. After these totals have been computed, determine the amount of manufacturing overhead cost per unit of each model.
   b. Compute the unit product cost of each model (including direct materials, direct labor, and manufacturing overhead).
4. From the data you developed in parts (1) through (3), identify factors that may account for the company's declining profits.

CASE 3A–6 Activity-Based Absorption Costing and Pricing LO 3–6

Java Source, Inc. (JSI) buys coffee beans from around the world and roasts, blends, and packages them for resale. Some of JSI's coffees are very popular and sell in large volumes, while a few of the newer blends sell in very low volumes. JSI prices its coffees at manufacturing cost plus a markup of 25%.

For the coming year, JSI's budget includes estimated manufacturing overhead cost of $2,200,000. JSI assigns manufacturing overhead to products on the basis of direct labor-hours. The expected direct labor cost totals $600,000, which represents 50,000 hours of direct labor time.

The expected costs for direct materials and direct labor for one-pound bags of two of the company's coffee products appear below.

	Kenya Dark	Viet Select
Direct materials	$4.50	$2.90
Direct labor (0.02 hour per bag)	$0.34	$0.34

JSI's controller believes the company's traditional costing system may be providing misleading cost information. To determine whether or not this is correct, the controller prepared an analysis of the year's expected manufacturing overhead costs, as shown in the following table:

Activity Cost Pool	Activity Measure	Expected Activity for the Year	Expected Cost for the Year
Purchasing	Purchase orders	2,000 orders	$ 560,000
Material handling	Number of setups	1,000 setups	193,000
Quality control	Number of batches	500 batches	90,000
Roasting	Roasting hours	95,000 roasting hours	1,045,000
Blending	Blending hours	32,000 blending hours	192,000
Packaging	Packaging hours	24,000 packaging hours	120,000
Total manufacturing overhead cost			$2,200,000

Data regarding the expected production and sales of Kenya Dark and Viet Select coffee are presented below.

	Kenya Dark	Viet Select
Expected production and sales	80,000 pounds	4,000 pounds
Batch size	5,000 pounds	500 pounds
Setups	2 per batch	2 per batch
Purchase order size	20,000 pounds	500 pounds
Roasting time per 100 pounds	1.5 roasting hours	1.5 roasting hours
Blending time per 100 pounds	0.5 blending hours	0.5 blending hours
Packaging time per 100 pounds	0.3 packaging hours	0.3 packaging hours

Required:

1. Using direct labor-hours as the manufacturing overhead cost allocation base, do the following:
   a. Determine the plantwide predetermined overhead rate that will be used during the year.
   b. Determine the unit product cost of one pound of Kenya Dark coffee and one pound of Viet Select coffee.
2. Using the activity-based absorption costing approach, do the following:
   a. Determine the total amount of manufacturing overhead cost assigned to Kenya Dark coffee and to Viet Select coffee for the year.
   b. Using the data developed in (2a) above, compute the amount of manufacturing overhead cost per pound of Kenya Dark coffee and Viet Select coffee.
   c. Determine the unit product cost of one pound of Kenya Dark coffee and one pound of Viet Select coffee.
3. Write a brief memo to the president of JSI explaining what you found in (1) and (2) above and discuss the implications of using direct labor-hours as the company's only manufacturing overhead cost allocation base.

(CMA, adapted)

Appendix 3B: The Predetermined Overhead Rate and Capacity

LEARNING OBJECTIVE 3-7

Understand the implications of basing the predetermined overhead rate on activity at capacity rather than on estimated activity for the period.

This appendix contrasts two methods of computing predetermined overhead rates. The first method (which was used throughout the chapter) demonstrates the absorption costing approach that company's use for external reporting purposes.[2] It bases the denominator volume for overhead rates on the estimated, or budgeted, amount of the allocation base for the upcoming period. The second method, often used for internal management purposes, bases the denominator volume for overhead rates on the estimated total amount of the allocation base at capacity. To simplify our forthcoming comparison of these two methods, we make two important assumptions that will hold true throughout the entire appendix: (1) all manufacturing overhead costs are fixed and (2) the estimated, or budgeted, fixed manufacturing overhead at the beginning of the period equals the actual fixed manufacturing overhead at the end of the period.

Let's assume Prahad Corporation manufactures DVDs for local production studios. The company's DVD duplicating machine can produce a new DVD every 10 seconds from a master DVD. The company leases the DVD duplicating machine for a fixed cost of $180,000 per year, and this is the company's only estimated (and actual) manufacturing overhead cost. With allowances for setups and maintenance, the machine is theoretically capable of producing up to 900,000 DVDs per year. However, due to a business downturn, Prahad's customers are unlikely to order more than 600,000 DVDs next year. The company uses machine time as the allocation base for applying manufacturing overhead to DVDs. These data are summarized below:

Prahad Corporation Data	
Total estimated and actual manufacturing overhead cost . .	$180,000 per year
Allocation base—machine time per DVD	10 seconds per DVD
Capacity	900,000 DVDs per year
Budgeted output for next year	600,000 DVDs

If Prahad uses the first method mentioned above, which computes predetermined overhead rates using the estimated or budgeted activity for the period, then its predetermined overhead rate for next year would be $0.03 per second of machine time computed as follows:

$$\frac{\text{Predetermined}}{\text{overhad rate}} = \frac{\text{Estimated total manufacturing overhead cost}}{\text{Estimated total amount of the allocation base}}$$

$$= \frac{\$180,000}{600,000 \text{ DVDs} \times 10 \text{ seconds per DVD}}$$

$$= \$0.03 \text{ per second}$$

Because each DVD requires 10 seconds of machine time, each DVD will be charged for $0.30 of overhead cost.

While this absorption approach is commonly used for external reporting purposes, it has two important limitations from a managerial accounting standpoint. First, if predetermined overhead rates are based on budgeted activity and overhead includes significant fixed costs, then the unit product costs will fluctuate depending on the budgeted level of activity for the period. For example, if Prahad's budgeted output for the year was only 300,000 DVDs (instead of 600,000 DVDs), its predetermined overhead rate would be $0.06 per second of machine time or $0.60 per DVD rather than $0.30 per DVD. Notice as the company's budgeted output falls, its overhead cost per unit increases. This, in turn,

---

[2] Statement of Financial Accounting Standards No. 151: *Inventory Costs* and International Accounting Standard 2: *Inventories* require allocating fixed manufacturing overhead costs to products based on normal capacity. Normal capacity reflects the level of output expected to be produced over numerous periods under normal circumstances. This definition mirrors the language used in this book that refers to basing the predetermined overhead rate on the estimated, or budgeted, amount of the allocation base for the upcoming period.

makes it appear as though the cost of producing DVDs has increased, which may tempt managers to raise prices at the worst possible time—just as demand is falling.

The second limitation of the absorption approach is that it charges products for resources they don't use. When the fixed costs of capacity are spread over estimated activity, the units produced must shoulder the costs of any unused capacity. If the level of activity falls, a company's shrinking output of products must absorb a growing share of idle capacity cost that is above and beyond their actual production cost.

Basing the predetermined overhead rate on the estimated total amount of the allocation base at capacity overcomes the two limitations just discussed. It is computed as follows[3]:

$$\text{Predetermined overhead rate based on capacity} = \frac{\text{Estimated total manufacturing overhead cost at capacity}}{\text{Estimated total amount of the allocation base at capacity}}$$

$$= \frac{\$180,000}{900,000 \text{ DVDs} \times 10 \text{ seconds per DVD}}$$

$$= \$0.02 \text{ per second}$$

When Prahad bases its predetermined overhead rate on activity at capacity, its overhead rate is $0.02 per second instead of $0.03 per second as computed under the absorption approach. Consequently, the overhead cost Prahad will apply to each DVD using the capacity-based approach would be $0.20 (= $0.02 × 10 seconds) per unit instead of $0.30 per unit under the absorption method. Notice that the capacity-based amounts per second and per unit are lower than the absorption-based amounts. This occurs because the capacity-based approach uses a higher denominator volume that reflects Prahad's capacity to produce DVDs—9,000,000 seconds.

Prahad's capacity-based rate of $0.02 per second will remain constant even if its budgeted level of activity fluctuates from one period to another. So, if the company's estimated level of activity drops from 600,000 DVDs to 300,000 DVDs, its capacity-based rate would stay at $0.02 per second. The company's unused capacity cost would increase in this situation, but its unit cost to make DVDs would stay constant at $0.20 per unit.

Whenever a company operates at less than full capacity and allocates fixed overhead costs using a capacity-based denominator volume, it will report some amount of unused capacity cost that is computed as follows:

$$\text{Cost of unused capacity} = \left(\text{Amount of the allocation base at capacity} - \text{Actual amount of the allocation base}\right) \times \text{Predetermined overhead rate}$$

For example, let's assume Prahad Company actually used 6,000,000 seconds on the DVD duplicating machine to produce 600,000 DVDs. At this level of output, the company would compute its cost of unused capacity as follows:

$$\text{Cost of unused capacity} = \left(\text{Amount of the allocation base at capacity} - \text{Actual amount of the allocation base}\right) \times \text{Predetermined overhead rate}$$

$$\text{Cost of unused capacity} = (9,000,000 \text{ seconds} - 6,000,000 \text{ seconds}) \times \$0.02 \text{ per second}$$

$$\text{Cost of unused capacity} = 3,000,000 \text{ seconds} \times \$0.02 \text{ per second}$$

$$\text{Cost of unused capacity} = \$60,000$$

[3] Ordinarily, because of variable overhead costs, the estimated total manufacturing overhead cost at capacity will be larger than the estimated total manufacturing overhead cost at the estimated level of activity. However, for simplicity, we assume in this appendix that all overhead costs are fixed. Then the total manufacturing overhead cost will be the same regardless of the level of activity.

EXHIBIT 3B–1

Prahad Corporation: An Income Statement That Recognizes the Cost of Unused Capacity

Prahad Corporation
Income Statement
For the Year Ended December 31

Sales[1]		$1,200,000
Cost of goods sold[2]		1,080,000
Gross margin		120,000
Other expenses:		
Cost of unused capacity	$60,000	
Selling and administrative expenses[3]	90,000	150,000
Net operating loss		$ (30,000)

---

[1] Assume sales of 600,000 CDs at $2 per CD.
[2] Assume the unit product cost of the CDs is $1.80, including $0.20 for manufacturing overhead.
[3] Assume selling and administrative expenses total $90,000.

Exhibit 3B–1 illustrates how Prahad would disclose this cost of unused capacity ($60,000) within an income statement prepared for internal management purposes. Rather than treating it as a product cost (as is done in the absorption approach), Prahad's capacity-based approach would treat this cost as a period expense that is reported below the gross margin. By separately disclosing the *Cost of unused capacity* as a lump sum of $60,000 on the income statement, instead of burying it in Cost of Goods Sold, the need to effectively manage capacity is highlighted for the company's managers. Generally speaking, a company's managers should respond to large unused capacity costs by either seeking new business opportunities that consume the capacity or by cutting costs and shrinking the amount of available capacity.

Appendix 3B: Exercises, Problem, and Case

EXERCISE 3B–1 Overhead Rate Based on Capacity LO 3–7

Wixis Cabinets makes custom wooden cabinets for high-end stereo systems from specialty woods. The company uses a job-order costing system. The capacity of the plant is determined by the capacity of its constraint, which is time on the automated bandsaw that makes finely beveled cuts in wood according to the preprogrammed specifications of each cabinet. The bandsaw can operate up to 180 hours per month. The estimated total manufacturing overhead cost at capacity is $14,760 per month. The company bases its predetermined overhead rate on capacity, so its predetermined overhead rate is $82 per hour of bandsaw use.

The results of a recent month's operations appear below:

Sales	$43,740
Beginning inventories	$0
Ending inventories	$0
Direct materials	$5,350
Direct labor	$8,860
Manufacturing overhead incurred	$14,760
Selling and administrative expense	$8,180
Actual hours of bandsaw use	150

Required:

1. Prepare an income statement following the example in Exhibit 3B–1 that records the cost of unused capacity on the income statement as a period expense.
2. Why do unused capacity costs arise when the predetermined overhead rate is based on capacity?

EXERCISE 3B–2 Overhead Rates and Capacity Issues LO 3–1, LO 3–2, LO 3–7

Security Pension Services helps clients to set up and administer pension plans that are in compliance with tax laws and regulatory requirements. The firm uses a job-order costing system in which overhead is applied to clients' accounts on the basis of professional staff hours charged to the accounts. Data concerning two recent years appear below:

	Last Year	This Year
Estimated professional staff hours to be charged to clients' accounts	4,600	4,500
Estimated overhead cost	$310,500	$310,500
Professional staff hours available	6,000	6,000

"Professional staff hours available" is a measure of the capacity of the firm. Any hours available that are not charged to clients' accounts represent unused capacity. All of the firm's overhead is fixed.

Required:

1. Marta Brinksi is an established client whose pension plan was set up many years ago. In both this year and last year, only 2.5 hours of professional staff time were charged to Ms. Brinksi's account. If the company bases its predetermined overhead rate on the estimated overhead cost and the estimated professional staff hours to be charged to clients, how much overhead cost would have been applied to Ms. Brinksi's account last year? This year?
2. Suppose the company bases its predetermined overhead rate on the estimated overhead cost and the estimated professional staff hours to be charged to clients as in (1) above. Also, suppose the actual professional staff hours charged to clients' accounts and the actual overhead costs turn out to be exactly as estimated in both years. How much unused capacity cost would the company report last year? How about for this year?
3. Refer back to the data concerning Ms. Brinksi in (1) above. If the company bases its predetermined overhead rate on the *professional staff hours available,* how much overhead cost would have been applied to Ms. Brinksi's account last year? This year?
4. Suppose the company bases its predetermined overhead rate on the professional staff hours available as in (3) above. Also, suppose the actual professional staff hours charged to clients' accounts and the actual overhead costs turn out to be exactly as estimated in both years. How much unused capacity cost would the company report last year? How about for this year?

PROBLEM 3B–3 Predetermined Overhead Rate and Capacity LO 3–1, LO 3–2, LO 3–7

Platinum Web Services designs and maintains websites for small business entrepreneurs. Competition has been intensifying in recent years and the company has been losing business to larger web design firms. Summary data concerning the last two years of operations follow:

	Last Year	This Year
Estimated hours of service demanded	1,000	800
Estimated overhead cost	$160,000	$160,000
Actual hours of service provided	750	500
Actual overhead cost incurred	$160,000	$160,000
Hours of service available at capacity	1,600	1,600

The company applies its overhead costs to jobs using the hours of service provided as the allocation base. For example, this year and last year, 40 service-hours were required to maintain the website for a small company called *Verde Consulting*. All of Platinum's overhead costs are fixed, and the actual overhead cost incurred was exactly as estimated at the beginning of the year in last year and this year.

Required:
1. Platinum Web Services computes its predetermined overhead rate at the beginning of each year based on the estimated overhead cost and the estimated hours of service demanded for the year. Using this approach, how much overhead would have been applied to the Verde Consulting job last year? How about this year?
2. The president of Platinum Web Services heard that some companies in the industry changed to a system of computing the predetermined overhead rate based on the hours of service available at capacity. He would like to know what effect this method would have on job costs. How much overhead cost would have been applied to the Verde Consulting job last year using this method? How much would have been applied his year?
3. If Platinum computes its predetermined overhead rate based on the hours of service available at capacity as in (2) above, how much unused capacity cost would the company have incurred last year? This year?
4. What fundamental business problem is Platinum Web Services facing? Which method of computing the predetermined overhead rate is likely to be more helpful in addressing this problem? Explain.

CASE 3B–4 ETHICS; Predetermined Overhead Rate and Capacity LO 3–2, LO 3–7

Pat Miranda, the new controller of Vault Hard Drives, Inc., has just returned from a seminar on the choice of the activity level in the predetermined overhead rate. Even though the subject did not sound exciting at first, she found there were some important ideas presented that should get a hearing at her company. After returning from the seminar, she arranged a meeting with the production manager, J. Stevens, and the assistant production manager, Marvin Washington.

Pat: I ran across an idea I wanted to check out with both of you. It's about the way we compute predetermined overhead rates.
J.: We're all ears.
Pat: We compute the predetermined overhead rate by dividing the estimated total factory overhead for the coming year, which is all a fixed cost, by the estimated total units produced for the coming year.
Marvin: We've been doing that as long as I've been with the company.
J.: And it has been done that way at every other company I've worked at, except at most places they divide by direct labor-hours.
Pat: We use units because it is simpler and we basically make one product with minor variations. But there's another way to do it. Instead of basing the overhead rate on the estimated total units produced for the coming year, we could base it on the total units produced at capacity.
Marvin: Oh, the Marketing Department will love that. It will drop the costs on all of our products. They'll go wild over there cutting prices.
Pat: That is a worry, but I wanted to talk to both of you first before going over to Marketing.
J.: Aren't you always going to have a lot of unused capacity costs?
Pat: That's correct, but let me show you how we would handle it. Here's an example based on our budget for next year.

Budgeted (estimated) production	160,000 units
Budgeted sales	160,000 units
Capacity	200,000 units
Selling price	$60 per unit
Variable manufacturing cost	$15 per unit
Total manufacturing overhead cost (all fixed)	$4,000,000
Selling and administrative expenses (all fixed)	$2,700,000
Beginning inventories	$0

Traditional Approach to Computation of the Predetermined Overhead Rate

$$\frac{\text{Estimated total manufacturing overhead cost, \$4,000,000}}{\text{Estimated total units produced, 160,000}} = \$25 \text{ per unit}$$

Budgeted Income Statement		
Revenue (160,000 units × $60 per unit)		$9,600,000
Cost of goods sold:		
Variable manufacturing (160,000 units × $15 per unit)	$2,400,000	
Manufacturing overhead applied		
(160,000 units × $25 per unit)	4,000,000	6,400,000
Gross margin		3,200,000
Selling and administrative expenses		2,700,000
Net operating income		$ 500,000

New Approach to Computation of the Predetermined Overhead Rate
Using Capacity in the Denominator

$$\frac{\text{Estimated total manufacturing overhead cost at capacity, \$4,000,000}}{\text{Total units at capacity, 200,000}} = \$20 \text{ per unit}$$

Budgeted Income Statement		
Revenue (160,000 units × $60 per unit)		$9,600,000
Cost of goods sold:		
Variable manufacturing (160,000 units × $15 per unit)	$2,400,000	
Manufacturing overhead applied		
(160,000 units × $20 per unit)	3,200,000	5,600,000
Gross margin		4,000,000
Cost of unused capacity [(200,000 units − 160,000 units)		
× $20 per unit]		800,000
Selling and administrative expenses		2,700,000
Net operating income		$ 500,000

J.: Whoa!! I don't think I like the looks of that "Cost of unused capacity." If that thing shows up on the income statement, someone from headquarters is likely to come down here looking for some people to lay off.

Marvin: I'm worried about something else too. What happens when sales are not up to expectations? Can we pull the "hat trick"?

Pat: I'm sorry, I don't understand.

J.: Marvin's talking about something that happens fairly regularly. When sales are down and profits look like they are going to be lower than the president told the owners they were going to be, the president comes down here and asks us to deliver some more profits.

Marvin: And we pull them out of our hat.

J.: Yeah, we just increase production until we get the profits we want.

Pat: I still don't understand. You mean you increase sales?

J.: Nope, we increase production. We're the production managers, not the sales managers.

Pat: I get it. Because you have produced more, the sales force has more units it can sell.

J.: Nope, the marketing people don't do a thing. We just build inventories and that does the trick.

Required:

In all of the questions below, assume the predetermined overhead rate under the traditional method is $25 per unit, and under the new capacity-based method it is $20 per unit.

1. Assume actual sales is 150,000 units and the actual production in units, actual selling price, actual variable manufacturing cost per unit, and actual fixed costs all equal their respective budgeted amounts. Given these assumptions:
   a. Compute net operating income using the traditional income statement format.
   b. Compute net operating income using the new income statement format.

2. What effect does the new capacity-based approach have on the volatility of net operating income?

3. Assume actual sales is 150,000 units and the actual selling price, actual variable manufacturing cost per unit, and actual fixed costs all equal their respective budgeted amounts. Under the traditional approach, how many units would have to be produced to realize net operating income of $500,000?

4. Assume actual sales is 150,000 units and the actual selling price, actual variable manufacturing cost per unit, and actual fixed costs all equal their respective budgeted amounts. Under the new capacity-based approach, how many units would have to be produced to realize net operating income of $500,000?

5. Will the "hat trick" be easier or harder to perform if the new capacity-based method is used?

6. Do you think the "hat trick" is ethical?

Variable Costing and Segment Reporting: Tools for Management

Cavan Images/Alamy Stock Photo

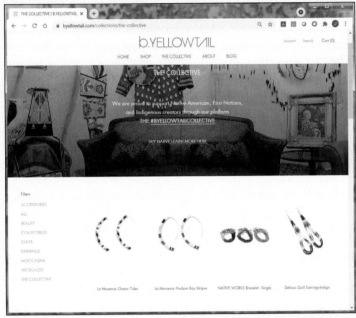

B.YELLOWTAIL

ENTREPRENEUR SPOTLIGHT

Bethany Yellowtail is a graduate of the Fashion Institute of Design and Merchandising. She "started her fashion career at the BCBG Max Ariza Group, moving on to become a lead pattern maker for several private label companies before launching her own brand." She is currently the CEO of B. Yellowtail and the B. Yellowtail Collective, which sell and promote "handmade, heirloom-quality jewelry, textiles and accessories crafted by carefully selected indigenous artists from all corners of North America." The company's product lines include dresses, cuffs, earrings, moccasins, necklaces, scarves, and skirts.

Managerial Accounting: The Practical Application
B. Yellowtail can segment its sales by product line. For example, it could break its total sales into product lines such as those mentioned above—dresses, cuffs, earrings, moccasins, necklaces, scarves, and skirts. Furthermore, it could divide its earring sales into segments, such as horsehair tassel earrings, Mosaic stud earrings, and Cheyanne Symone Pearl Direction earrings. The company also has other product segments such as lotions, soaps, candles, and stationery.

Corporate Social Responsibility: Serving all Stakeholders
At B. Yellowtail, for each face mask the company sells, it donates one face mask to the indigenous communities most affected by COVID-19. To date, the company has donated more than 25,000 face masks to Orenda Tribe to be distributed to indigenous people in the Southwest portion of the United States. Navajo Nation was hit hard by COVID-19 with more than 8,500 confirmed cases and more than 400 deaths. ■

Source: www.byellowtail.com

LEARNING OBJECTIVES

After studying Chapter 4, you should be able to:

LO 4–1 Explain how variable costing differs from absorption costing and compute unit product costs under each method.

LO 4–2 Prepare income statements using both variable and absorption costing.

LO 4–3 Reconcile variable costing and absorption costing net operating incomes and explain why the two amounts differ.

LO 4–4 Prepare a segmented income statement that differentiates traceable fixed costs from common fixed costs and use it to make decisions.

LO 4–5 Compute companywide and segment break-even points for a company with traceable fixed costs.

LO 4–6 *(Appendix 4A) Prepare an income statement using super-variable costing and reconcile this approach with variable costing.*

Data Analytics Exercise available in Connect to complement this chapter

This chapter describes two applications of the contribution format income statement introduced in earlier chapters. First, it explains how manufacturing companies can prepare *variable costing* income statements, which rely on the contribution format, for internal decision-making purposes. The variable costing approach will be contrasted with *absorption costing* income statements, which are generally used for external reports. Ordinarily, variable costing and absorption costing produce different net operating income figures, and the difference can be quite large. In addition to showing how these two methods differ, we will describe the advantages of variable costing for internal reporting purposes, and we will show how management decisions can be affected by the costing method chosen.

Second, the chapter explains how the contribution format can be used to prepare segmented income statements. In addition to companywide income statements, managers need to measure the profitability of individual *segments* of their organizations. A **segment** is a part or activity of an organization about which managers would like cost, revenue, or profit data. This chapter explains how to create contribution format income statements that report profit data for business segments, such as divisions, individual stores, geographic regions, customers, and product lines.

Overview of Variable and Absorption Costing

LEARNING OBJECTIVE 4–1

Explain how variable costing differs from absorption costing and compute unit product costs under each method.

As you read about variable and absorption costing income statements in the coming pages, focus your attention on three key concepts. First, both income statement formats include product costs and period costs, although they define these cost classifications differently. Second, variable costing income statements are grounded in the contribution format. They categorize expenses based on cost behavior—variable expenses are reported separately from fixed expenses. Absorption costing income statements ignore variable and fixed cost distinctions. Third, as mentioned in the paragraph above, variable and absorption costing net operating incomes often differ from one another. The reason for the difference always relates to the fact that variable costing and absorption costing income statements account for fixed manufacturing overhead differently. *Pay very close attention to the two different ways that variable costing and absorption costing account for fixed manufacturing overhead.*

Variable Costing

Under **variable costing,** only those manufacturing costs that vary with output are treated as product costs. This would usually include direct materials, direct labor, and the variable portion of manufacturing overhead. Fixed manufacturing overhead is not treated as a product cost under this method. Rather, fixed manufacturing overhead is treated as a period cost and, like selling and administrative expenses, it is reported as an expense on the income statement in its entirety each period. Consequently, the cost of a unit of product in inventory or in cost of goods sold under the variable costing method does not contain any fixed manufacturing overhead cost. Variable costing is sometimes referred to as *direct costing* or *marginal costing.*

Absorption Costing

Absorption costing treats *all* manufacturing costs as product costs, regardless of whether they are variable or fixed. The cost of a unit of product under the absorption costing method consists of direct materials, direct labor, and *both* variable and fixed manufacturing overhead. Thus, absorption costing allocates a portion of fixed manufacturing overhead cost to each unit of product, along with the variable manufacturing costs. Because absorption costing includes all manufacturing costs in product costs, it is frequently referred to as the *full cost* method.

EXHIBIT 4–1
Variable Costing versus Absorption Costing

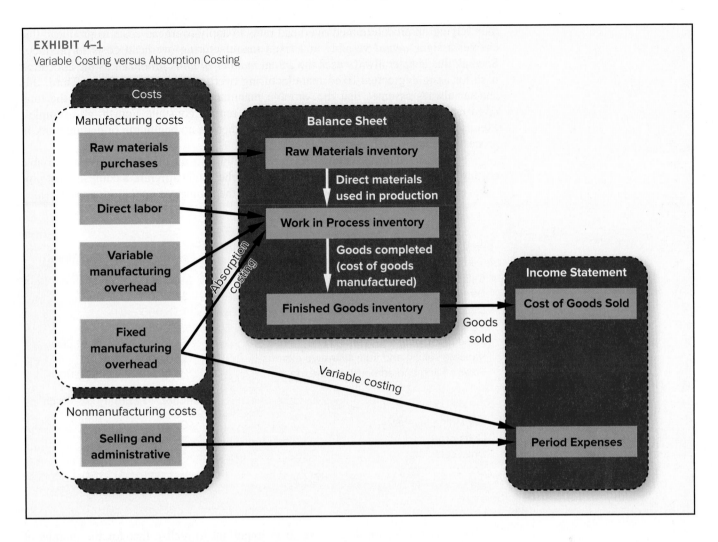

Selling and Administrative Expenses

Selling and administrative expenses are never treated as product costs, regardless of the costing method. Thus, under absorption and variable costing, variable and fixed selling and administrative expenses are always treated as period costs and are reported as expenses on the income statement as incurred.

Summary of Differences The reason variable costing and absorption costing often report different net operating incomes, as illustrated in Exhibit 4–1, is because the two methods account for fixed manufacturing overhead costs differently—all other costs have the same affect on net operating income under the two methods. In absorption costing, fixed manufacturing overhead costs are included in work in process inventory. When units are completed, these costs are transferred to finished goods, and only when the units are sold do these costs flow through to the income statement as part of cost of goods sold. In variable costing, fixed manufacturing overhead costs are considered to be period costs—just like selling and administrative costs—and are taken immediately to the income statement as period expenses.

Variable and Absorption Costing—An Example

We will be making four simplifying assumptions throughout the forthcoming example and the entire chapter. First, this chapter uses *actual costing* rather than the *normal costing* approach that was used in the job-order costing chapters. In other words, rather than relying on predetermined overhead rates to apply overhead costs to products, this chapter assigns *actual* variable and fixed manufacturing overhead costs to products. Second, this chapter always uses the actual *number of units produced* as the allocation base for assigning actual fixed manufacturing overhead costs to products. Third, this chapter always assumes that the variable manufacturing costs per unit and the total fixed manufacturing overhead cost per period remain constant. Fourth, all examples, exercises, and problems in this chapter assume there is no beginning or ending work in process inventory.

Having stated those assumptions, now let's illustrate the difference between variable costing and absorption costing by considering Weber Light Aircraft, a company that produces light recreational aircraft. Data concerning the company's operations appear below:

	Per Aircraft	Per Month
Selling price	$100,000	
Direct materials...............................	$19,000	
Direct labor	$5,000	
Variable manufacturing overhead	$1,000	
Fixed manufacturing overhead		$70,000
Variable selling and administrative expense	$10,000	
Fixed selling and administrative expense		$20,000

	January	February	March
Beginning inventory	0	0	1
Units produced	1	2	4
Units sold	1	1	5
Ending inventory	0	1	0

As you review the data above, it is important to realize that for the months of January, February, and March, the selling price per aircraft, variable costs per aircraft, and total monthly fixed expenses never change. The only data that change in this example are the number of units produced (January = 1 unit produced; February = 2 units produced; March = 4 units produced) and the number of units sold (January = 1 unit sold; February = 1 unit sold; March = 5 units sold).

We will first construct the company's variable costing income statements for January, February, and March. Then we will show how the company's net operating income would be determined for the same months using absorption costing.

Variable Costing Contribution Format Income Statement

LEARNING OBJECTIVE 4–2
Prepare income statements using both variable and absorption costing.

To prepare the company's variable costing income statements for January, February, and March, we begin by computing the unit product cost. Under variable costing, the unit product cost consists solely of variable production costs as shown below:

Variable Costing Unit Product Cost	
Direct materials	$19,000
Direct labor	5,000
Variable manufacturing overhead	1,000
Unit product cost	$25,000

Because each month's unit product cost is $25,000 per aircraft, the variable costing cost of goods sold for all three months can be computed as follows:

Variable Costing Cost of Goods Sold

	January	February	March
Unit product cost (a)	$25,000	$25,000	$25,000
Units sold (b)	1	1	5
Variable cost of goods sold (a) × (b)	$25,000	$25,000	$125,000

And the company's total selling and administrative expense would be derived as follows:

Selling and Administrative Expenses

	January	February	March
Variable selling and administrative expense (@ $10,000 per unit sold)	$10,000	$ 10,000	$50,000
Fixed selling and administrative expense	20,000	20,000	20,000
Total selling and administrative expense	$30,000	$ 30,000	$70,000

Putting it all together, the variable costing income statements would appear as shown in Exhibit 4–2. Notice, the contribution format has been used in these income statements. Also, the monthly fixed manufacturing overhead cost ($70,000) has been recorded as a period expense in the month incurred.

Variable Costing Contribution Format Income Statements

	January	February	March
Sales	$100,000	$100,000	$500,000
Variable expenses:			
Variable cost of goods sold	25,000	25,000	125,000
Variable selling and administrative expense .	10,000	10,000	50,000
Total variable expenses	35,000	35,000	175,000
Contribution margin	65,000	65,000	325,000
Fixed expenses:			
Fixed manufacturing overhead	70,000	70,000	70,000
Fixed selling and administrative expense. . . .	20,000	20,000	20,000
Total fixed expenses	90,000	90,000	90,000
Net operating income (loss)	$ (25,000)	$ (25,000)	$235,000

EXHIBIT 4–2
Variable Costing Income Statements

A simple method for understanding how Weber Light Aircraft computed its variable costing net operating income for each month is to focus on the contribution margin per aircraft sold, which is computed as follows:

Contribution Margin per Aircraft Sold

Selling price per aircraft		$100,000
Variable cost of goods sold per aircraft	$25,000	
Variable selling and administrative expense per aircraft	10,000	35,000
Contribution margin per aircraft		$ 65,000

The variable costing net operating income for each period can always be computed by multiplying the number of units sold by the contribution margin per unit and then subtracting total fixed expenses. For Weber Light Aircraft these computations would appear as follows:

	January	February	March
Number of aircraft sold	1	1	5
Contribution margin per aircraft	× $ 65,000	× $ 65,000	× $ 65,000
Total contribution margin	$ 65,000	$ 65,000	$325,000
Total fixed expenses	90,000	90,000	90,000
Net operating income (loss)	$(25,000)	$(25,000)	$235,000

Notice, January and February have the same net operating loss. This occurs because one aircraft was sold in each month, and, as previously mentioned, the selling price per aircraft, variable costs per aircraft, and total monthly fixed expenses remain constant.

Absorption Costing Income Statement

As we begin the absorption costing portion of the example, remember that the only reason absorption costing income differs from variable costing is that the two methods account for fixed manufacturing overhead differently. Under absorption costing, fixed manufacturing overhead is included in product costs. In variable costing, fixed manufacturing overhead is not included in product costs and instead is treated as a period expense, just like selling and administrative expenses.

The first step in preparing Weber's absorption costing income statements for January, February, and March is to determine the company's unit product costs for each month as follows:

Absorption Costing Unit Product Cost			
	January	February	March
Direct materials	$19,000	$19,000	$19,000
Direct labor	5,000	5,000	5,000
Variable manufacturing overhead	1,000	1,000	1,000
Fixed manufacturing overhead ($70,000 ÷ 1 unit produced in January; $70,000 ÷ 2 units produced in February; $70,000 ÷ 4 units produced in March) ...	70,000	35,000	17,500
Unit product cost	$95,000	$ 60,000	$42,500

Notice in each month, Weber's fixed manufacturing overhead cost of $70,000 is divided by the number of units produced to determine the fixed manufacturing overhead cost per unit.

Given these unit product costs, the company's absorption costing net operating income in each month would be determined as shown in Exhibit 4–3.

The sales for all three months in Exhibit 4–3 are the same as the sales shown in the variable costing income statements. The January cost of goods sold consists of one unit produced during January at a cost of $95,000 according to the absorption costing system. The February cost of goods sold consists of one unit produced during February at a cost of $60,000 according to the absorption costing system. The March cost of goods sold ($230,000) consists of one unit produced during February at an absorption cost of $60,000 plus four units produced in March with a total absorption

Absorption Costing Income Statements				EXHIBIT 4-3
	January	February	March	Absorption Costing Income Statements
Sales	$100,000	$100,000	$500,000	
Cost of goods sold ($95,000 × 1 unit;				
$60,000 × 1 unit;				
$60,000 × 1 unit + $42,500 × 4 units)	95,000	60,000	230,000	
Gross margin	5,000	40,000	270,000	
Selling and administrative expenses	30,000	30,000	70,000	
Net operating income (loss)	$ (25,000)	$ 10,000	$200,000	

cost of $170,000 (= 4 units produced × $42,500 per unit). The selling and administrative expenses equal the amounts reported in the variable costing income statements; however, they are reported as one amount rather than being separated into variable and fixed components.

Note that even though sales were exactly the same in January and February and the cost structure did not change, net operating income was $35,000 higher in February than in January under absorption costing. This occurs because one aircraft produced in February is not sold until March. This aircraft has $35,000 of fixed manufacturing overhead attached to it that was incurred in February but will not be recorded as part of cost of goods sold until March.

Contrasting the variable costing and absorption costing income statements in Exhibits 4–2 and 4–3, note that net operating income is the same in January under variable costing and absorption costing but differs in the other two months. We will discuss this in more depth shortly. Also, note that the format of the variable costing income statement differs from the absorption costing income statement. An absorption costing income statement categorizes costs by function—manufacturing versus selling and administrative. All of the manufacturing costs flow through the absorption costing cost of goods sold, and all of the selling and administrative expenses are listed separately as period expenses. In contrast, in the contribution approach, costs are categorized according to how they behave. All of the variable expenses are listed together, and all of the fixed expenses are listed together. The variable expenses category includes manufacturing costs (i.e., variable cost of goods sold) as well as selling and administrative expenses. The fixed expenses category also includes both manufacturing costs and selling and administrative expenses.

Reconciliation of Variable Costing with Absorption Costing Income

As noted earlier, variable costing and absorption costing net operating incomes may not be the same. In the case of Weber Light Aircraft, the net operating incomes are the same in January but differ in the other two months. These differences occur because under absorption costing, some fixed manufacturing overhead is capitalized in inventories (i.e., included in product costs) rather than being immediately expensed on the income statement. If inventories increase during a period, under absorption costing some of the fixed manufacturing overhead of the current period will be *deferred* in ending inventories. For example, in February, two aircraft were produced, and each carried with it $35,000 (= $70,000 ÷ 2 aircraft produced) in fixed manufacturing overhead. Because only one aircraft was sold, $35,000 of this fixed manufacturing overhead was on February's

LEARNING OBJECTIVE 4-3
Reconcile variable costing and absorption costing net operating incomes and explain why the two amounts differ.

absorption costing income statement as part of cost of goods sold, whereas the other $35,000 attached to the unsold aircraft would be included in February's ending finished goods inventory on the balance sheet. In contrast, under variable costing, *all* of the $70,000 of fixed manufacturing overhead appeared on the February income statement as a period expense. Consequently, net operating income was higher under absorption costing than under variable costing by $35,000 in February. This was reversed in March when four units were produced, but five were sold. In March, under absorption costing $105,000 of fixed manufacturing overhead was included in cost of goods sold ($35,000 for the unit produced in February and sold in March plus $17,500 for each of the four units produced and sold in March), but only $70,000 was recognized as a period expense under variable costing. Hence, the net operating income in March was $35,000 lower under absorption costing than under variable costing.

In general, when the units produced exceed the units sold and hence inventories increase, net operating income is higher under absorption costing than under variable costing. This occurs because some of the fixed manufacturing overhead of the period is *deferred* in inventories under absorption costing. In contrast, when the units sold exceed the units produced, and hence inventories decrease, net operating income is lower under absorption costing than under variable costing. This occurs because some of the fixed manufacturing overhead of previous periods is *released* from inventories under absorption costing. When the units produced and the units sold are equal, no change in inventories occurs, and absorption costing and variable costing net operating incomes are the same.[1]

Variable costing and absorption costing net operating incomes can be reconciled by determining how much fixed manufacturing overhead was deferred in, or released from, inventories during the period:

Fixed Manufacturing Overhead Deferred in, or Released from, Inventories under Absorption Costing			
	January	February	March
Fixed manufacturing overhead in ending inventories	$0	$35,000	$ 0
Deduct: Fixed manufacturing overhead in beginning inventories	0	0	35,000
Fixed manufacturing overhead deferred in (released from) inventories	$0	$35,000	$(35,000)

In equation form, the fixed manufacturing overhead that is deferred in or released from inventories can be determined as follows:

$$\begin{array}{ccc} \text{Manufacturing overhead} & \text{Fixed manufacturing} & \text{Fixed manufacturing} \\ \text{deferred in} & = \quad \text{overhead in} \quad - & \text{overhead in} \\ \text{(released from) inventory} & \text{ending inventories} & \text{beginning inventories} \end{array}$$

The reconciliation would then be reported, as shown in Exhibit 4–4.

Again note that the difference between variable costing net operating income and absorption costing net operating income is entirely due to the amount of fixed

---

[1]   These general statements about the relation between variable costing and absorption costing net operating income assume LIFO is used to value inventories. Even when LIFO is not used, the general statements tend to be correct. Although U.S. GAAP allows LIFO and FIFO inventory flow assumptions, International Financial Reporting Standards do not allow a LIFO inventory flow assumption.

Reconciliation of Variable Costing and Absorption Costing Net Operating Incomes				EXHIBIT 4–4
	January	February	March	Reconciliation of Variable Costing and Absorption Costing Net Operating Incomes
Variable costing net operating income (loss)....	$(25,000)	$(25,000)	$235,000	
Add (deduct) fixed manufacturing overhead deferred in (released from) inventory under absorption costing	0	35,000	(35,000)	
Absorption costing net operating income (loss) .	$(25,000)	$ 10,000	$200,000	

manufacturing overhead that is deferred in, or released from, inventories during the period under absorption costing. Changes in inventories affect absorption costing net operating income—they do not affect variable costing net operating income, providing that variable manufacturing costs per unit are stable.

The reasons for differences between variable and absorption costing net operating incomes are summarized in Exhibit 4–5. When the units produced equal the units sold, as in January for Weber Light Aircraft, absorption costing net operating income will equal variable costing net operating income. This occurs because when production equals sales, all of the fixed manufacturing overhead incurred in the current period flows through to the income statement under both methods. For companies that use Lean Production, the number of units produced tends to equal the number of units sold. This occurs because goods are produced in response to customer orders, thereby eliminating finished goods inventories and reducing work in process inventory to almost nothing. So, when a company uses Lean Production, differences in variable costing and absorption costing net operating income will largely disappear.

When the units produced exceed the units sold, absorption costing net operating income will exceed variable costing net operating income. This occurs because inventories have increased; therefore, under absorption costing, some of the fixed manufacturing overhead incurred in the current period is deferred in ending inventories on the balance

Relation between Production and Sales for the Period	Effect on Inventories	Relation between Absorption and Variable Costing Net Operating Incomes	EXHIBIT 4–5
Units produced = Units sold	No change in inventories	Absorption costing net operating income = Variable costing net operating income	Comparative Income Effects—Absorption and Variable Costing
Units produced > Units sold	Inventories increase	Absorption costing net operating income > Variable costing net operating income*	
Units produced < Units sold	Inventories decrease	Absorption costing net operating income < Variable costing net operating income†	

*Net operating income is higher under absorption costing because fixed manufacturing overhead cost is *deferred* in inventory under absorption costing as inventories increase.
†Net operating income is lower under absorption costing because fixed manufacturing overhead cost is *released* from inventory under absorption costing as inventories decrease.

sheet, whereas under variable costing all of the fixed manufacturing overhead incurred in the current period flows through to the income statement. In contrast, when the units produced are less than the units sold, absorption costing net operating income will be less than variable costing net operating income. This occurs because inventories have decreased; therefore, under absorption costing, fixed manufacturing overhead that had been deferred in inventories during a prior period flows through to the current period's income statement together with all of the fixed manufacturing overhead incurred during the current period. Under variable costing, just the fixed manufacturing overhead of the current period flows through to the income statement.

Advantages of Variable Costing and the Contribution Approach

Variable costing, together with the contribution approach, offers appealing advantages for internal reports. This section discusses three of those advantages.

Enabling CVP Analysis

Cost-volume-profit (CVP) analysis requires that we break costs down into their variable and fixed components. Because variable costing income statements categorize costs as variable and fixed, it is much easier to use this income statement format to perform CVP analysis than attempting to use the absorption costing format, which combines variable and fixed costs.

Moreover, absorption costing net operating income may or may not agree with the results of CVP analysis. For example, let's suppose that you are interested in computing the sales that would be necessary to attain a target profit of $235,000 at Weber Light Aircraft. A CVP analysis based on the January variable costing income statement from Exhibit 4–2 would proceed as follows:

Sales (a)	$100,000
Contribution margin (b)	$65,000
Contribution margin ratio (b) ÷ (a)	65%
Total fixed expenses	$90,000

$$\text{Dollar sales to attain target profit} = \frac{\text{Target profit} + \text{Fixed expenses}}{\text{CM ratio}}$$

$$= \frac{\$235,000 + \$90,000}{0.65} = \$500,000$$

Thus, a CVP analysis based on the January variable costing income statement predicts that the net operating income would be $235,000 when sales are $500,000. And indeed, the net operating income under variable costing *is* $235,000 when the sales are $500,000 in March. However, the net operating income under absorption costing is *not* $235,000 in March, even though the sales are $500,000. Why is this? The reason is that under absorption costing, net operating income can be distorted by changes in inventories. In March, inventories decreased, so some of the fixed manufacturing overhead that had been deferred in February's ending inventories was released to the March income statement, resulting in a net operating income that is $35,000 lower than the $235,000 predicted by CVP analysis. If inventories had increased in March, the opposite would have occurred—the absorption costing net operating income would have been higher than the $235,000 predicted by CVP analysis.

Explaining Changes in Net Operating Income

The variable costing income statements in Exhibit 4–2 are clear and easy to understand. All other things the same, when sales go up, net operating income goes up. When sales go down, net operating income goes down. When sales are constant, net operating income is constant. The number of units produced does not affect net operating income.

Absorption costing income statements can be confusing and are easily misinterpreted. Look again at the absorption costing income statements in Exhibit 4–3. A manager might wonder why net operating income went up from January to February even though sales were exactly the same. Was it a result of lower selling costs, more efficient operations, or some other factor? In fact, it was simply because the number of units produced exceeded the number of units sold in February, and so some of the fixed manufacturing overhead costs were deferred in inventories in that month. These costs have not gone away—they will eventually flow through to the income statement in a later period when inventories go down. There is no way to tell this from the absorption costing income statements.

To avoid mistakes when absorption costing is used, readers of financial statements should be alert to changes in inventory levels. Under absorption costing, if inventories increase, fixed manufacturing overhead costs are deferred in inventories, which in turn increases net operating income. If inventories decrease, fixed manufacturing overhead costs are released from inventories, which in turn decreases net operating income. Thus, when absorption costing is used, fluctuations in net operating income can be caused by changes in inventories as well as changes in unit sales.

Supporting Decision Making

The variable costing method correctly identifies the additional variable costs that will be incurred to make one more unit. It also emphasizes the impact of fixed costs on profits. The total amount of fixed manufacturing costs appears explicitly on the income statement, highlighting that the whole amount of fixed manufacturing costs must be covered for the company to be truly profitable. In the Weber Light Aircraft example, the variable costing income statements correctly report that the cost of producing another unit is $25,000, and they explicitly recognize that $70,000 of fixed manufacturing overhead must be covered to earn a profit.

Under absorption costing, fixed manufacturing overhead costs appear to be variable with respect to the number of units sold, but they are not. For example, in January, the absorption unit product cost at Weber Light Aircraft is $95,000, but the variable portion of this cost is only $25,000. The fixed overhead costs of $70,000 are commingled with variable production costs, thereby obscuring the impact of fixed overhead costs on profits. Because absorption unit product costs are stated on a per-unit basis, managers may mistakenly believe that if another unit is produced, it will cost the company $95,000. But of course, it would not. The cost of producing another unit would be only $25,000. Misinterpreting absorption unit product costs as variable can lead to many problems, including inappropriate pricing decisions and decisions to drop products that are, in fact, profitable.

Segmented Income Statements and the Contribution Approach

In the remainder of the chapter, we'll learn how to use the contribution approach to construct income statements for business segments. These segmented income statements are useful for analyzing the profitability of segments, making decisions, and measuring the performance of segment managers.

LEARNING OBJECTIVE 4–4
Prepare a segmented income statement that differentiates traceable fixed costs from common fixed costs and use it to make decisions.

Traceable and Common Fixed Costs and the Segment Margin

You need to understand three new terms to prepare segmented income statements using the contribution approach—*traceable fixed cost, common fixed cost,* and *segment margin.*

A **traceable fixed cost** of a segment is a fixed cost that is incurred because of the existence of the segment—if the segment had never existed, the fixed cost would not have been incurred; and if the segment were eliminated, the fixed cost would disappear. Examples of traceable fixed costs include the following:

- The salary of the Fritos product manager at PepsiCo is a *traceable* fixed cost of the Fritos business segment of PepsiCo.

- The maintenance cost for the building in which Boeing 747s are assembled is a *traceable* fixed cost of the 747 business segment of Boeing.
- The liability insurance at Disney World is a *traceable* fixed cost of the Disney World business segment of The Walt Disney Corporation.

A **common fixed cost** is a fixed cost that supports the operations of more than one segment but is not traceable in whole or in part to any one segment. Even if a segment were entirely eliminated, there would be no change in a true common fixed cost. For example:

- The salary of the CEO of General Motors is a *common* fixed cost of the various divisions of General Motors.
- The cost of heating a Safeway or Kroger grocery store is a *common* fixed cost of the store's various departments—groceries, produce, bakery, meat, and so forth.
- The cost of the receptionist's salary at an office shared by a number of doctors is a *common* fixed cost of the doctors. The cost is traceable to the office but not to individual doctors.

To prepare a segmented income statement, variable expenses are deducted from sales to yield the contribution margin for the segment. The contribution margin tells us what happens to profits as sales volume changes—holding a segment's capacity and fixed costs constant. The contribution margin is especially useful in decisions involving temporary uses of capacity such as special orders. These types of decisions often involve only sales and variable costs—the two components of contribution margin.

The **segment margin** is obtained by deducting the traceable fixed costs of a segment from the segment's contribution margin. It represents the margin available after a segment has covered all of its own costs. *The segment margin is the best gauge of the long-run profitability of a segment* because it includes only those costs that are caused by the segment. If a segment can't cover its own costs, then that segment probably should be dropped (unless it has important side effects on other segments). Notice, common fixed costs are not allocated to segments.

From a decision-making point of view, the segment margin is most useful in major decisions that affect capacity, such as dropping a segment. By contrast, as we noted earlier, the contribution margin is most useful in decisions involving short-run changes in sales volume, such as pricing special orders that involve temporary use of existing capacity.

AIRPORTS PROVIDE RETAILERS WITH RELIABLE CUSTOMER TRAFFIC

Estée Lauder's global airport sales comprise about 18 percent of its total annual sales of $13.7 billion. In fact, the company's "travel retail" segment revenues now exceed its combined "sales from Macy's, Saks Fifth Avenue, and other department stores in North America." Olivier Bottrie, who heads Estée Lauder's global travel retail business, says the biggest appeal of airports is that they provide continuous access to travelers, who spend an average of 72 minutes waiting between their security clearance and flight departure. Bacardi refers to this 72-minute window as the "golden hour" because numerous travelers choose to spend this time shopping. The spirits maker recently introduced a three-part series for its Aultmore Scotch whisky at London's Heathrow Airport. The company is finding that most customers purchase all three bottles within the series for $1,200.

Source: Jaewon Kang, "Forget the Mall, Hottest Place to Buy Luxury Goods Is the Airport," *The Wall Street Journal,* June 18, 2019, p. B3.

NoyanYalcin/Shutterstock

Identifying Traceable Fixed Costs

The distinction between traceable and common fixed costs is crucial in segment reporting because traceable fixed costs are charged to segments, and common fixed costs are not. In an actual situation, it is sometimes hard to determine whether a cost should be classified as traceable or common.

The general guideline is to treat as traceable costs *only those costs that would disappear over time if the segment itself disappeared.* For example, if one division within a company were sold or discontinued, it would no longer be necessary to pay that division manager's salary. Therefore, the division manager's salary would be classified as a traceable fixed cost of the division. On the other hand, the president of the company undoubtedly would continue to be paid even if one of many divisions was dropped. In fact, he or she might even be paid more if dropping the division was a good idea. Therefore, the president's salary is common to the company's divisions and should not be charged to them.

When assigning costs to segments, the key point is to resist the temptation to allocate costs (such as depreciation of corporate facilities) that are clearly common and that will continue regardless of whether the segment exists or not. *Any allocation of common costs to segments reduces the value of the segment margin as a measure of long-run segment profitability and segment performance.*

Traceable Fixed Costs Can Become Common Fixed Costs

Fixed costs that are traceable to one segment may be a common cost of another segment. For example, United Airlines might want a segmented income statement that shows the segment margin for a particular flight from Chicago to Paris, further broken down into first-class, business-class, and economy-class segment margins. The airline must pay a substantial landing fee at Charles de Gaulle Airport in Paris. This fixed landing fee is a traceable cost of the flight, but it is a common cost of the first-class, business-class, and economy-class segments. Even if the first-class cabin is empty, the entire landing fee must be paid. So the landing fee is not a traceable cost of the first-class cabin. But on the other hand, paying the fee is necessary in order to have any first-class, business-class, or economy-class passengers. So the landing fee is a common cost of these three classes.

IN BUSINESS

SEGMENT REPORTING AT THE VILAR PERFORMING ARTS CENTER

The Vilar Performing Arts Center is a 535-seat theater located in Beaver Creek, Colorado, that presents an unusually wide variety of performances categorized into six business segments—Family Series, Broadway Series, Theatre/Comedy Series, Dance Series, Classical Series, and Concert Series. The executive director of the Vilar, Kris Sabel, must decide which shows to book, what financial terms to offer to the artists, what contributions are likely from underwriters (i.e., donors), and what prices to charge for tickets. He evaluates the profitability of the segments using segmented income statements that include traceable costs (such as the costs of transporting, lodging, and feeding the artists) and exclude common costs (such as his salary, the salaries of his staff, depreciation on the theater, and general marketing expenses).

Data concerning the Classical Series segment for one season appears below:

Number of shows		4
Number of seats budgeted		863
Number of seats sold		655
Average seats sold per show		164
Ticket sales	$46,800	
Underwriting (donors)	65,000	
Total revenue		$111,800
Artists fees	$78,870	
Other traceable expenses	11,231	
Total expenses		90,101
Classical Series segment margin		$ 21,699

Although the Classical Series sold an average of only 164 seats per show, its overall segment margin ($21,699) is positive, thanks to $65,000 of underwriting revenues from donors. Had common costs been allocated to the Classical Series, it may have appeared unprofitable and been discontinued—resulting in fewer shows during the season; less diverse programming; disappointment among a small, but dedicated, number of fans; and lower overall income for the Vilar due to the loss of its Classical Series segment margin.

Segmented Income Statements—An Example

ProphetMax, Inc., is a rapidly growing computer software company. Exhibit 4–6 shows its variable costing income statement for the most recent month. As the company has grown, its senior managers have asked for segmented income statements that could be used to make decisions and evaluate managerial performance. ProphetMax's controller responded by creating examples of contribution format income statements segmented by the company's divisions, product lines, and sales channels. She created Exhibit 4–7

EXHIBIT 4–6
ProphetMax, Inc. Variable
Costing Income Statement

ProphetMax, Inc.
Variable Costing Income Statement

Sales	$500,000
Variable expenses:	
Variable cost of goods sold.	180,000
Other variable expenses	50,000
Total variable expenses	230,000
Contribution margin	270,000
Fixed expenses	256,500
Net operating income	$ 13,500

EXHIBIT 4–7
ProphetMax, Inc.: Examples
of Business Segments

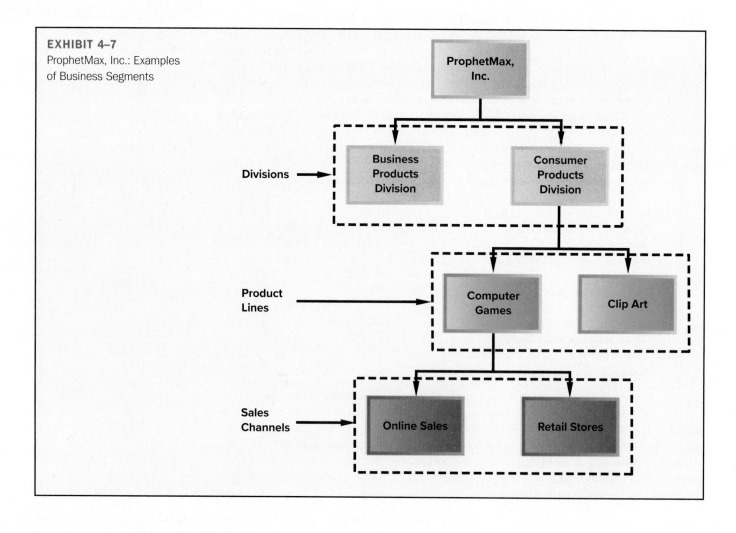

to explain that ProphetMax's profits can be segmented into its two divisions—the Business Products Division and the Consumer Products Division. The Consumer Products Division's profits can be further segmented into the Clip Art and Computer Games product lines. Finally, the Computer Games product line's profits (within the Consumer Products Division) can be segmented into the Online Sales and Retail Stores sales channels.

Levels of Segmented Income Statements

Exhibit 4–8 contains the controller's segmented income statements for the segments depicted in Exhibit 4–7. The contribution format income statement for the entire company appears at the very top of the exhibit under the column labeled Total Company. Notice the net operating income shown in this column ($13,500) is the same as the net operating income shown in Exhibit 4–6. Immediately to the right of the Total Company column are two columns—one for each of the two divisions. We can see that the Business Products Division's traceable fixed expenses are $90,000, and the Consumer Products Division's are $81,000. These $171,000 of traceable fixed expenses (as shown in the Total Company column) plus the $85,500 of common fixed expenses not traceable to individual divisions equals ProphetMax's total fixed expenses ($256,500) as shown in Exhibit 4–6. We can also see that the Business Products Division's segment margin is $60,000 and the Consumer Products Division's is $39,000. These segment margins show the company's divisional managers how much each of their divisions is contributing to the company's profits.

The middle portion of Exhibit 4–8 further segments the Consumer Products Division into its two product lines—Clip Art and Computer Games. The dual nature of some fixed costs can be seen in this portion of the exhibit. Notice, in the top portion of Exhibit 4–8 when segments are defined as divisions, the Consumer Products Division has $81,000 in traceable fixed expenses. However, when we drill down to the product lines (in the middle portion of the exhibit), only $70,000 of the $81,000 expense that was traceable to the Consumer Products Division is traceable to the product lines. The other $11,000 becomes a common fixed expense of the two product lines of the Consumer Products Division.

Why would $11,000 of traceable fixed expense become a common fixed expense when the division is divided into product lines? The $11,000 is the monthly depreciation expense on a machine that is used to encase products in tamper-proof packages for the consumer market. The depreciation expense is a traceable cost of the Consumer Products Division as a whole, but it is a common cost of the division's two product lines. Even if one of the product lines were discontinued entirely, the machine would still be used to wrap the remaining products. Therefore, none of the depreciation expense can really be traced to individual products. Conversely, the $70,000 traceable fixed expense can be traced to the individual product lines because it consists of the costs of product-specific advertising. A total of $30,000 was spent on advertising clip art, and $40,000 was spent on advertising computer programs.

The bottom portion of Exhibit 4–8 further segments the Computer Games product line into two sales channels—Online Sales and Retail Stores. The dual nature of some fixed costs can also be seen in this portion of the exhibit. In the middle portion of Exhibit 4–8 when segments are defined as product lines, the Computer Games product line has $40,000 in traceable fixed expenses. However, when we look at the sales channels in the bottom portion of the exhibit, only $25,000 of the $40,000 that was traceable to Computer Games is traceable to the sales channels. The other $15,000 becomes a common fixed expense of the two sales channels for the Computer Games product line.

EXHIBIT 4–8
ProphetMax, Inc.—Segmented
Income Statements in the
Contribution Format

Segments Defined as Divisions

		Divisions	
	Total Company	Business Products Division	Consumer Products Division
Sales	$500,000	$300,000	$200,000
Variable expenses:			
Variable cost of goods sold	180,000	120,000	60,000
Other variable expenses	50,000	30,000	20,000
Total variable expenses	230,000	150,000	80,000
Contribution margin	270,000	150,000	120,000
Traceable fixed expenses	171,000	90,000	81,000
Divisional segment margin	99,000	$ 60,000	$ 39,000
Common fixed expenses not traceable to individual divisions	85,500		
Net operating income	$ 13,500		

Segments Defined as Product Lines of the Consumer Products Division

		Product Line	
	Consumer Products Division	Clip Art	Computer Games
Sales	$200,000	$ 75,000	$125,000
Variable expenses:			
Variable cost of goods sold	60,000	20,000	40,000
Other variable expenses	20,000	5,000	15,000
Total variable expenses	80,000	25,000	55,000
Contribution margin	120,000	50,000	70,000
Traceable fixed expenses	70,000	30,000	40,000
Product-line segment margin	50,000	$ 20,000	$ 30,000
Common fixed expenses not traceable to individual product lines	11,000		
Divisional segment margin	$ 39,000		

Segments Defined as Sales Channels for One Product Line, Computer Games, of the Consumer Products Division

		Sales Channels	
	Computer Games	Online Sales	Retail Stores
Sales	$125,000	$100,000	$ 25,000
Variable expenses:			
Variable cost of goods sold	40,000	32,000	8,000
Other variable expenses	15,000	5,000	10,000
Total variable expenses	55,000	37,000	18,000
Contribution margin	70,000	63,000	7,000
Traceable fixed expenses	25,000	15,000	10,000
Sales-channel segment margin	45,000	$ 48,000	$ (3,000)
Common fixed expenses not traceable to individual sales channels	15,000		
Product-line segment margin	$ 30,000		

ZARA MAKES POST-PANDEMIC SHIFT TO ONLINE SALES

Inditex SA announced that its post-pandemic future includes closing 1,200 of its more than 7,400 retail store locations worldwide. The closures will "affect as many as 100 of Inditex's Zara, Massimo Dutti, Pull & Bear and other stores in the Americas . . . [that] currently account for between 5 percent and 6 percent in sales." Inditex plans to spend $1.13 billion on digital investments with the goal of boosting online sales from 14 percent to 25 percent of total sales. The company's accelerated shift from brick-and-mortar store locations to online sales punctuates "a yearslong reckoning brought about by a boom in online shopping."

Source: Saabira Chaudhuri, "Zara Owner to Shut 1,200 Stores in Online Push," *The Wall Street Journal*, June 11, 2020, p. B3.

M4OS Photos/Alamy Stock Photo

Segmented Income Statements—Decision Making and Break-Even Analysis

Once a company prepares contribution format segmented income statements, it can use those statements to make decisions and perform break-even analysis.

Decision Making

Let's refer again to the bottom portion of Exhibit 4–8 to illustrate how segmented income statements support decision making. Notice that the Online Sales segment has a segment margin of $48,000, and the Retail Stores segment has a segment margin of $(3,000). Let's assume that ProphetMax wants to know the profit impact of discontinuing the sale of computer games through its Retail Stores sales channel. The company believes that Online Sales of its computer games will increase 10 percent if it discontinues the Retail Stores sales channel. It also believes that the Business Products Division and Clip Art product line will be unaffected by this decision. How would you compute the profit impact of this decision?

The first step is to calculate the profit impact of discontinuing the Retail Stores sales channel. If this sales channel is eliminated, we assume its sales, variable expenses, and traceable fixed expenses would go away. The quickest way to summarize these financial impacts is to focus on the Retail Stores' segment margin. In other words, if the Retail Stores sales channel is discontinued, then its negative segment margin of $3,000 would also be avoided. This would increase ProphetMax's net operating income by $3,000. The second step is to calculate the profit impact of increasing Online Sales of computer games by 10 percent. To perform this calculation, we assume that the Online Sales total traceable fixed expenses ($15,000) remain constant and its contribution margin ratio remains constant at 63% (= $63,000 ÷ $100,000). If Online Sales increase $10,000 (= $100,000 × 10%), then the Online Sales segment's contribution margin will increase by $6,300 (= $10,000 × 63%). The overall profit impact of discontinuing the Retail Stores sales channel can be summarized as follows:

Avoidance of the Retail Stores' segment loss	$3,000
Increase in Online Sales contribution margin	6,300
Increase in ProphetMax's net operating income	$9,300

Break-Even Analysis

In Chapter 2, we learned how to compute a companywide break-even point for a multi-product company with no traceable fixed expenses. Now we are going to use the Prophet-Max, Inc., data in Exhibit 4–8 to explain how to compute companywide and segment break-even points for a company with traceable fixed expenses. Beginning with the

LEARNING OBJECTIVE 4–5
Compute companywide and segment break-even points for a company with traceable fixed costs.

companywide perspective, the formula for computing the break-even point for a multi-product company with traceable fixed expenses is as follows:

$$\frac{\text{Dollar sales for company}}{\text{to break even}} = \frac{\text{Traceable fixed expenses} + \text{Common fixed expenses}}{\text{Overall CM ratop}}$$

In the case of ProphetMax, we should begin by reviewing the information in the Total Company column in the top portion of Exhibit 4–8. This column of data indicates that ProphetMax's total traceable fixed expenses are $171,000, and its total common fixed expenses are $85,500. Furthermore, the company's overall contribution margin of $270,000 divided by its total sales of $500,000 equals its overall CM ratio of 0.54. Given this information, ProphetMax's companywide break-even point is computed as follows:

$$\frac{\text{Dollar sales for company}}{\text{to break even}} = \frac{\text{Traceable fixed expenses} + \text{Common fixed expenses}}{\text{Overall CM ratio}}$$

$$= \frac{\$171,000 + \$85,500}{0.54}$$

$$= \frac{\$256,500}{0.54}$$

$$= \$475,000$$

It is important to emphasize that this computation assumes a constant sales mix. In other words, in the ProphetMax example, it assumes that 60 percent of the total sales ($300,000 ÷ $500,000) will always come from the Business Products Division and 40 percent of the total sales ($200,000 ÷ $500,000) will always come from the Consumer Products Division.

To compute the break-even point for a business segment, the formula is as follows:

$$\frac{\text{Dollar sales for a segment}}{\text{to break even}} = \frac{\text{Segment traceable fixed expenses}}{\text{Segment CM ratio}}$$

In the case of ProphetMax's Business Products Division, we should begin by reviewing the information in the Business Products Division column in the top portion of Exhibit 4–8. This column of data indicates that the Business Products Division's traceable fixed expenses are $90,000 and its CM ratio is 0.50 ($150,000 ÷ $300,000). Given this information, the Business Products Division's break-even point is computed as follows:

$$\frac{\text{Dollar sales for a segment}}{\text{to break even}} = \frac{\text{Segment traceable fixed expenses}}{\text{Segment CM ratio}}$$

$$= \frac{\$90,000}{0.50}$$

$$= \$180,000$$

The same calculation can be performed for the Consumer Products Division using data from the Consumer Products Division column in the top portion of Exhibit 4–8. Given that the Consumer Products Division's traceable fixed expenses are $81,000, and its CM ratio is 0.60 ($120,000 ÷ $200,000), its break-even point is computed as follows:

$$\frac{\text{Dollar sales for a segment}}{\text{to break even}} = \frac{\text{Segment traceable fixed expenses}}{\text{Segment CM ratio}}$$

$$= \frac{\$81,000}{0.60}$$

$$= \$135,000$$

Notice the sum of the segment break-even sales figures of $315,000 ($180,000 + $135,000) is less than the companywide break-even point of $475,000. This occurs because the segment break-even calculations *do not include the company's common fixed expenses.* The exclusion of the company's common fixed expenses can be verified by preparing income statements based on each segment's break-even dollar sales as follows:

	Total Company	Business Products Division	Consumer Products Division
Sales	$315,000	$180,000	$135,000
Variable expenses	144,000	90,000	54,000
Contribution margin	171,000	90,000	81,000
Traceable fixed expenses	171,000	90,000	81,000
Segment margin	0	$ 0	$ 0
Common fixed expenses	85,500		
Net operating loss	$ (85,500)		

When each segment achieves its break-even point, the company's overall net operating loss of $85,500 equals its common fixed expenses of $85,500. This reality can often lead managers astray when making decisions. In an attempt to "cover the company's common fixed expenses," managers will often allocate common fixed expenses to business segments when performing break-even calculations and making decisions. *This is a mistake!* Allocating common fixed expenses to business segments artificially inflates each segment's break-even point. This may cause managers to erroneously discontinue business segments where the inflated break-even point appears unobtainable. The decision to retain or discontinue a business segment should be based on the sales and expenses that would disappear if the segment were dropped. Because common fixed expenses *will persist even if a business segment is dropped,* they should not be allocated to business segments when making decisions.

Segmented Income Statements—Common Mistakes

All of the costs attributable to a segment—and only those costs—should be assigned to the segment. Unfortunately, companies often make mistakes when assigning costs to segments. They omit some costs, inappropriately assign traceable fixed costs, and arbitrarily allocate common fixed costs.

Omission of Costs

The costs assigned to a segment should include all costs attributable to that segment from the company's entire value chain. All of these functions, from research and development, through product design, manufacturing, marketing, distribution, and customer service, are required to bring a product or service to the customer and generate sales.

However, only manufacturing costs are included in product costs under absorption costing, which is widely regarded as required for external financial reporting. To avoid having to maintain two costing systems and to provide consistency between internal and external reports, many companies also use absorption costing for their internal reports, such as segmented income statements. As a result, such companies omit from their profitability analysis part or all of the "upstream" costs in the value chain, which consist of research and development and product design, and the "downstream" costs, which consist of marketing, distribution, and customer service. Yet these nonmanufacturing costs are just as essential in determining product profitability as are the manufacturing costs. These upstream and downstream costs, which are usually included in selling and administrative expenses on absorption costing income statements, can represent half or more of the total costs of an organization. If either the upstream or downstream costs are omitted in profitability analysis, then the product is undercosted, and management may unwittingly develop and maintain products that in the long run result in losses.

Inappropriate Methods for Assigning Traceable Costs among Segments

In addition to omitting costs, many companies do not correctly handle traceable fixed expenses on segmented income statements. First, they do not trace fixed expenses to segments even when it is feasible to do so. Second, they use inappropriate allocation bases to allocate traceable fixed expenses to segments.

Failure to Trace Costs Directly Costs that can be traced directly to a specific segment should be charged directly to that segment and should not be allocated to other segments. For example, the rent for a branch office of an insurance company should be charged directly to the branch office rather than included in a companywide overhead pool and then spread throughout the company.

Inappropriate Allocation Base Some companies use arbitrary allocation bases to allocate costs to segments. For example, some companies allocate selling and administrative expenses on the basis of sales revenues. Thus, if a segment generates 20 percent of total company sales, it would be allocated 20 percent of the company's selling and administrative expenses as its "fair share." This same basic procedure is followed if cost of goods sold or some other measure is used as the allocation base.

Costs should be allocated to segments for internal decision-making purposes only when the allocation base actually drives the cost being allocated (or is very highly correlated with the real cost driver). For example, sales should be used to allocate selling and administrative expenses only if a 10 percent increase in sales will result in a 10 percent increase in selling and administrative expenses. To the extent that selling and administrative expenses are not driven by sales volume, these expenses will be improperly allocated—with a disproportionately high percentage of the selling and administrative expenses assigned to the segments with the largest sales.

Arbitrarily Dividing Common Costs among Segments

The third business practice that leads to distorted segment costs is assigning nontraceable costs to segments. For example, some companies allocate the common costs of the corporate headquarters building to products on segment reports. However, in a multiproduct company, no single product is likely to be responsible for any significant amount of this cost. Even if a product were eliminated entirely, there would usually be no significant effect on any of the costs of the corporate headquarters building. In short, there is no cause-and-effect relationship between the cost of the corporate headquarters building and the existence of any one product. Consequently, any allocation of the cost of the corporate headquarters building to the products must be arbitrary.

Common costs like the costs of the corporate headquarters building are necessary, of course, to have a functioning organization. The practice of arbitrarily allocating common costs to segments is often justified on the grounds that "someone" has to "cover the common costs." While it is undeniably true that a company must cover its common costs to earn a profit, arbitrarily allocating common costs to segments does not ensure that this will happen. In fact, adding a share of common costs to the real costs of a segment may make an otherwise profitable segment appear to be unprofitable. If a manager eliminates the apparently unprofitable segment, the real traceable costs of the segment will be saved, but its sales will be lost. And what happens to the common fixed costs that were allocated to the segment? They don't disappear; they are reallocated to the remaining segments of the company. That makes all of the remaining segments appear to be less profitable—possibly resulting in dropping other segments. The net effect will be to reduce the overall profits of the company and make it even more difficult to "cover the common costs."

Additionally, common fixed costs are not manageable by the manager to whom they are arbitrarily allocated; they are the responsibility of higher-level managers. When common fixed costs are allocated to managers, they are held responsible for those costs even though they cannot control them.

Income Statements—An External Reporting Perspective

Companywide Income Statements

Practically speaking, absorption costing is required for external reports according to U.S. generally accepted accounting principles (GAAP).[2] Furthermore, International Financial Reporting Standards (IFRS) explicitly require companies to use absorption costing. Probably because of the cost and possible confusion of maintaining two separate costing systems—one for external reporting and one for internal reporting—most companies use absorption costing for their external and internal reports.

With all of the advantages of the contribution approach, you may wonder why the absorption approach is used at all. While the answer is partly due to adhering to tradition, absorption costing is also attractive to many accountants and managers because they believe it better matches costs with sales. Advocates of absorption costing argue that *all* manufacturing costs must be assigned to products in order to properly match the costs of producing units of product with their sales. The fixed costs of depreciation, taxes, insurance, supervisory salaries, and so on are just as essential to manufacturing products as are the variable costs.

Advocates of variable costing argue that fixed manufacturing costs are not really the costs of any particular unit of product. These costs are incurred to have the *capacity* to make products during a particular period and will be incurred even if nothing is made during the period. Moreover, whether a unit is made or not, the fixed manufacturing costs

---

[2] The Financial Accounting Standards Board (FASB) has created a single source of authoritative nongovernmental U.S. generally accepted accounting principles (GAAP) called the FASB Accounting Standards Codification (FASB codification). Although the FASB codification does not explicitly disallow variable costing, it does explicitly prohibit companies from excluding all manufacturing overhead costs from product costs. It also provides an in-depth discussion of fixed overhead allocation to products, thereby implying that absorption costing is required for external reports. Although some companies expense significant elements of fixed manufacturing costs on their external reports, practically speaking, U.S. GAAP requires absorption costing for external reports.

will be exactly the same. Therefore, variable costing advocates argue that fixed manufacturing costs are not part of the costs of producing a particular unit of product, and thus, the matching principle dictates that fixed manufacturing costs should be recognized as an expense in the current period.

Segmented Financial Information

U.S. GAAP and IFRS require that publicly traded companies include segmented financial and other data in their annual reports and that the segmented reports prepared for external users *must use the same methods and definitions that the companies use in internal segmented reports that are prepared to aid in making operating decisions.* This is a very unusual stipulation because companies are not ordinarily required to report the same data to external users that are used for internal decision-making purposes. This requirement creates incentives for publicly traded companies to avoid using the contribution format for internal segmented reports. Segmented contribution format income statements contain vital information that companies are often very reluctant to release to the public (and hence competitors). In addition, this requirement creates problems in reconciling internal and external reports.

IN BUSINESS

AIRPORTS DIVERSIFY REVENUES THROUGH LAND DEVELOPMENT

Anne Kitzman/Shutterstock

The Pittsburgh International Airport has historically derived most of its revenue from providing aeronautical services to airline companies. However, the airport plans to change that by using 200 of its 3,000 acres to develop a new business segment—a campus for companies that use 3-D printing in their manufacturing. In fact, airport officials have already signed Arencibia, a "company that supplies and recycles gases for 3-D printing," as their first anchor tenant.

Other American airports are pursuing similar plans to diversify their revenues. For example, the Cincinnati/Northern Kentucky International Airport hopes to develop a 350-acre campus that will lure logistics providers such as Deutsche Post AG's DHL Americas. Airports in Asia, Europe, and the Middle East are also building mini-cities around their core facilities that include exhibition spaces, apartments, and office buildings.

Source: Keiko Morris, "Pittsburgh Airport Ramps Up Side Gig as Land Developer," *The Wall Street Journal*, December 18, 2019, p. B6.

Summary

Variable and absorption costing are alternative methods of determining unit product costs. Under variable costing, only those manufacturing costs that vary with output are treated as product costs. This includes direct materials, variable overhead, and ordinarily direct labor. Fixed manufacturing overhead is treated as a period cost and is expensed on the income statement as incurred. By contrast, absorption costing treats fixed manufacturing overhead as a product cost, along with direct materials, direct labor, and variable overhead. Under both costing methods, selling and administrative expenses are treated as period costs and are expensed on the income statement as incurred.

Because absorption costing treats fixed manufacturing overhead as a product cost, a portion of fixed manufacturing overhead is assigned to each unit as it is produced. If units of product are unsold at the end of a period, then the fixed manufacturing overhead cost attached to those units is carried in ending inventory on the balance sheet rather than being recognized as an expense within cost of goods sold on the income statement. When these units are sold in a subsequent period, the fixed manufacturing overhead cost attached to them is released from the inventory account and recorded as part of cost of goods sold. Thus, under absorption costing, it is possible to defer a portion of the fixed manufacturing overhead cost from one period to a future period through the inventory account.

Unfortunately, this shifting of fixed manufacturing overhead cost between periods can cause erratic fluctuations in net operating income and can result in confusion and unwise decisions. To guard against mistakes when they interpret income statement data, managers should be alert to changes in inventory levels or unit product costs during the period.

Segmented income statements provide information for evaluating the profitability and performance of divisions, product lines, sales territories, and other segments of a company. Under the contribution approach, variable costs and fixed costs are clearly distinguished from each other and only those costs that are traceable to a segment are assigned to the segment. A cost is considered traceable to a segment only if the cost is caused by the segment and could be avoided by eliminating the segment. Fixed common costs are not allocated to segments. The segment margin consists of sales, less variable expenses, and less traceable fixed expenses of the segment.

The dollar sales required for a segment to break even is computed by dividing the segment's traceable fixed expenses by its contribution margin ratio. A company's common fixed expenses should not be allocated to segments when performing break-even calculations because they will not change in response to segment-level decisions.

Data Analytics Exercise available in Connect to complement this chapter

Review Problem 1: Contrasting Variable and Absorption Costing

Dexter Corporation produces and sells a single product, a wooden hand loom for weaving small items such as scarves. Selected cost and operating data relating to the product for two years are given below:

Selling price per unit	$50
Manufacturing costs:	
Variable manufacturing cost per unit produced:	
Direct materials....................................	$11
Direct labor	$6
Variable manufacturing overhead	$3
Fixed manufacturing overhead per year	$120,000
Selling and administrative expenses:	
Variable selling and administrative per unit sold	$4
Fixed selling and administrative per year.............	$70,000

	Year 1	Year 2
Units in beginning inventory.......................	0	2,000
Units produced during the year....................	10,000	6,000
Units sold during the year........................	8,000	8,000
Units in ending inventory	2,000	0

Required:

1. Assume the company uses absorption costing.
   a. Compute the unit product cost in each year.
   b. Prepare an income statement for each year.

2. Assume the company uses variable costing.
   a. Compute the unit product cost in each year.
   b. Prepare an income statement for each year.
3. Reconcile the variable costing and absorption costing net operating incomes.

Solution to Review Problem 1

1. a. Under absorption costing, all manufacturing costs, variable and fixed, are included in unit product costs:

	Year 1	Year 2
Direct materials	$11	$11
Direct labor	6	6
Variable manufacturing overhead	3	3
Fixed manufacturing overhead		
($120,000 ÷ 10,000 units)	12	
($120,000 ÷ 6,000 units)		20
Unit product cost	$32	$40

b. The absorption costing income statements follow:

	Year 1	Year 2
Sales (8,000 units × $50 per unit)	$400,000	$400,000
Cost of goods sold (8,000 units × $32 per unit); [(2,000 units × $32 per unit) + (6,000 units × $40 per unit)]	256,000	304,000
Gross margin	144,000	96,000
Selling and administrative expenses (8,000 units × $4 per unit + $70,000)	102,000	102,000
Net operating income (loss)	$ 42,000	$ (6,000)

2. a. Under variable costing, only the variable manufacturing costs are included in unit product costs:

	Year 1	Year 2
Direct materials	$11	$11
Direct labor	6	6
Variable manufacturing overhead	3	3
Unit product cost	$20	$20

b. The variable costing income statements follow:

	Year 1		Year 2	
Sales (8,000 units × $50 per unit)		$400,000		$400,000
Variable expenses:				
Variable cost of goods sold (8,000 units × $20 per unit)	$160,000		$160,000	
Variable selling and administrative expenses (8,000 units × $4 per unit)	32,000	192,000	32,000	192,000
Contribution margin		208,000		208,000
Fixed expenses:				
Fixed manufacturing overhead	$120,000		$120,000	
Fixed selling and administrative expenses	70,000	190,000	70,000	190,000
Net operating income		$ 18,000		$ 18,000

3. The reconciliation of the variable and absorption costing net operating incomes follows:

	Year 1	Year 2
Fixed manufacturing overhead in ending inventories (2,000 units × $12 per unit; 0 units × $20 per unit)	$24,000	$ 0
Deduct: Fixed manufacturing overhead in beginning inventories (0; 2,000 units × $12 per unit)................	0	24,000
Fixed manufacturing overhead deferred in (released from) inventories	$24,000	$(24,000)

	Year 1	Year 2
Variable costing net operating income	$18,000	$ 18,000
Add: Fixed manufacturing overhead costs deferred in inventory under absorption costing (2,000 units × $12 per unit)	24,000	
Deduct: Fixed manufacturing overhead costs released from inventory under absorption costing (2,000 units × $12 per unit)		(24,000)
Absorption costing net operating income (loss)	$42,000	$ (6,000)

Review Problem 2: Segmented Income Statements

The business staff of the law firm Frampton, Davis & Smythe has constructed the following report that breaks down the firm's overall results for last month into two business segments—family law and commercial law:

	Company Total	Family Law	Commercial Law
Revenues from clients	$1,000,000	$400,000	$600,000
Variable expenses	220,000	100,000	120,000
Contribution margin	780,000	300,000	480,000
Traceable fixed expenses	670,000	280,000	390,000
Segment margin	110,000	20,000	90,000
Common fixed expenses.............	60,000	24,000	36,000
Net operating income (loss)	$ 50,000	$ (4,000)	$ 54,000

However, this report is not quite correct. The common fixed expenses, such as the managing partner's salary, general administrative expenses, and general firm advertising, have been allocated to the two segments based on revenues from clients.

Required:
1. Redo the segment report, eliminating the allocation of common fixed expenses. Would the firm be better off financially if the family law segment were dropped? (Note: Many of the firm's commercial law clients also use the firm for their family law requirements, such as drawing up wills.)
2. The firm's advertising agency has proposed an ad campaign targeted at boosting the revenues of the family law segment. The ad campaign would cost $20,000, and the advertising agency claims it would increase family law revenues by $100,000. The managing partner of Frampton, Davis & Smythe believes this increase in business could be accommodated without any increase in fixed expenses. Estimate the effect this ad campaign would have on the family law segment margin and on the firm's overall net operating income.
3. Compute the companywide break-even point in dollar sales and the dollar sales required for each business segment to break even.

Solution to Review Problem 2

1. The corrected segmented income statement appears below:

	Company Total	Family Law	Commercial Law
Revenues from clients	$1,000,000	$400,000	$600,000
Variable expenses	220,000	100,000	120,000
Contribution margin	780,000	300,000	480,000
Traceable fixed expenses	670,000	280,000	390,000
Segment margin	110,000	$ 20,000	$ 90,000
Common fixed expenses...............	60,000		
Net operating income	$ 50,000		

No, the firm would not be better off financially if the family law practice were dropped. The family law segment is covering all of its own costs and is contributing $20,000 per month to covering the common fixed expenses of the firm. While the segment margin for family law is much lower than for commercial law, it is still profitable. Moreover, family law may be a service that the firm must provide to its commercial clients in order to remain competitive.

2. The ad campaign would increase the family law segment margin by $55,000 as follows:

Increased revenues from clients	$100,000
Family law contribution margin ratio ($300,000 ÷ $400,000)	× 75%
Increased contribution margin	$ 75,000
Less cost of the ad campaign..............................	20,000
Increased segment margin	$ 55,000

Because there would be no increase in fixed expenses (including common fixed expenses), the increase in overall net operating income is also $55,000.

3. The companywide break-even point is computed as follows:

$$\frac{\text{Dollar sales for company}}{\text{to break even}} = \frac{\text{Traceable fixed expenses} + \text{Common fixed expenses}}{\text{Overall CM ratio}}$$

$$= \frac{\$670,000 + \$60,000}{0.78}$$

$$= \frac{\$730,000}{0.78}$$

$$= \$935,897 \text{ (rounded)}$$

The break-even point for the family law segment is computed as follows:

$$\frac{\text{Dollar sales for a segment}}{\text{to break even}} = \frac{\text{Segment traceable fixed expenses}}{\text{Segment CM ratio}}$$

$$= \frac{\$280,000}{0.75}$$

$$= \$373,333 \text{ (rounded)}$$

The break-even point for the commercial law segment is computed as follows:

$$\frac{\text{Dollar sales for a segment}}{\text{to break even}} = \frac{\text{Segment traceable fixed expenses}}{\text{Segment CM ratio}}$$

$$= \frac{\$390,000}{0.80}$$

$$= \$487,500$$

Glossary

Absorption costing A costing method that includes all manufacturing costs—direct materials, direct labor, and both variable and fixed manufacturing overhead—in unit product costs. (p. 172)

Common fixed cost A fixed cost that supports more than one business segment, but is not traceable in whole or in part to any one of the business segments. (p. 182)

Segment Any part or activity of an organization about which managers seek cost, revenue, or profit data. (p. 172)

Segment margin A segment's contribution margin less its traceable fixed costs. It represents the margin available after a segment has covered all of its own traceable costs. (p. 182)

Traceable fixed cost A fixed cost incurred because of the existence of a particular business segment and that would be eliminated if the segment were eliminated. (p. 181)

Variable costing A costing method that includes only variable manufacturing costs—direct materials, direct labor, and variable manufacturing overhead—in unit product costs. (p. 172)

Questions

4–1   What is the difference between absorption costing and variable costing?

4–2   Are selling and administrative expenses treated as product costs or as period costs under variable costing?

4–3   Explain how fixed manufacturing overhead costs are shifted from one period to another under absorption costing.

4–4   What are the arguments in favor of treating fixed manufacturing overhead costs as product costs?

4–5   What are the arguments in favor of treating fixed manufacturing overhead costs as period costs?

4–6   If the units produced equals the units sold, which method would you expect to show the higher net operating income, variable costing or absorption costing? Why?

4–7   If the units produced exceed the units sold, which method would you expect to show the higher net operating income, variable costing or absorption costing? Why?

4–8   If fixed manufacturing overhead costs are released from inventory under absorption costing, what does this tell you about the level of production in relation to the level of unit sales?

4–9   Under absorption costing, how is it possible to increase net operating income without increasing sales?

4–10   How does Lean Production reduce or eliminate the difference in reported net operating income between absorption and variable costing?

4–11   What is a segment of an organization? Give several examples of segments.

4–12   What costs are assigned to a segment under the contribution approach?

4–13   Distinguish between a traceable fixed cost and a common fixed cost. Give several examples of each.

4–14   Explain how the contribution margin differs from the segment margin.

4–15   Why aren't common fixed costs allocated to segments under the contribution approach?

4–16   How is it possible for a fixed cost that is traceable to a segment to become a common fixed cost if the segment is divided into further segments?

4–17   Should a company allocate its common fixed costs to business segments when computing the break-even point for those segments? Why?

 Applying Excel

The Excel worksheet form that appears next is to be used to recreate portions of Review Problem 1 relating to Dexter Corporation. The workbook, and instructions on how to complete the file, can be found in Connect.

LEARNING OBJECTIVE 4–2

	A	B	C	D	E	F
1	Chapter 4: Applying Excel					
2						
3	Data					
4	Selling price per unit	$50				
5	Manufacturing costs:					
6	Variable per unit produced:					
7	Direct materials	$11				
8	Direct labor	$6				
9	Variable manufacturing overhead	$3				
10	Fixed manufacturing overhead per year	$120,000				
11	Selling and administrative expenses:					
12	Variable per unit sold	$4				
13	Fixed per year	$70,000				
14						
15		Year 1	Year 2			
16	Units in beginning inventory	0				
17	Units produced during the year	10,000	6,000			
18	Units sold during the year	8,000	8,000			
19						
20	Enter a formula into each of the cells marked with a ? below					
21	Review Problem 1: Contrasting Variable and Absorption Costing					
22						
23	Compute the Ending Inventory					
24		Year 1	Year 2			
25	Units in beginning inventory	0	?			
26	Units produced during the year	?	?			
27	Units sold during the year	?	?			
28	Units in ending inventory	?	?			
29						
30	Compute the Absorption Costing Unit Product Cost					
31		Year 1	Year 2			
32	Direct materials	?	?			
33	Direct labor	?	?			
34	Variable manufacturing overhead	?	?			
35	Fixed manufacturing overhead	?	?			
36	Absorption costing unit product cost	?	?			
37						
38	Construct the Absorption Costing Income Statement					
39		Year 1	Year 2			
40	Sales	?	?			
41	Cost of goods sold	?	?			
42	Gross margin	?	?			
43	Selling and administrative expenses	?	?			
44	Net operating income	?	?			
45						
46	Compute the Variable Costing Unit Product Cost					
47		Year 1	Year 2			
48	Direct materials	?	?			
49	Direct labor	?	?			
50	Variable manufacturing overhead	?	?			
51	Variable costing unit product cost	?	?			
52						
53	Construct the Variable Costing Income Statement					
54		Year 1		Year 2		
55	Sales	?			?	
56	Variable expenses:					
57	Variable cost of goods sold	?		?		
58	Variable selling and administrative expenses	?	?	?	?	
59	Contribution margin	?			?	
60	Fixed expenses:					
61	Fixed manufacturing overhead	?		?		
62	Fixed selling and administrative expenses	?	?	?	?	
63	Net operating income	?			?	
64						

| ◄ ◄ ► ► | **Chapter 4 Form** | Filled in Chapter 4 Form | Chapter 4 | ◄ |

You should proceed to the requirements below only after completing your worksheet. The LIFO inventory flow assumption is used throughout this problem.

Required:

1. Check your worksheet by changing the units sold in the Data to 6,000 for Year 2. The cost of goods sold under absorption costing for Year 2 should now be $240,000. If it isn't, check cell C41. The formula in this cell should be =IF(C26<C27,C26*C36+(C27− C26)*B36,C27*C36). If your worksheet is operating properly, the net operating income under both absorption costing and variable costing should be $(34,000) for Year 2. That is, the loss in Year 2 is $34,000 under both methods. If you do not get these answers, find the errors in your worksheet and correct them.

   Why is the absorption costing net operating income now equal to the variable costing net operating income in Year 2?

2. Enter the following data from a different company into your worksheet:

Data		
Selling price per unit		$75
Manufacturing costs:		
Variable per unit produced:		
Direct materials		$12
Direct labor		$5
Variable manufacturing overhead		$7
Fixed manufacturing overhead per year		$150,000
Selling and administrative expenses:		
Variable per unit sold		$1
Fixed per year		$60,000
	Year 1	Year 2
Units in beginning inventory	0	
Units produced during the year	15,000	10,000
Units sold during the year	12,000	12,000

   Is the net operating income under variable costing different in Year 1 and Year 2? Why or why not? Explain the relation between the net operating income under absorption costing and variable costing in Year 1. Explain the relation between the net operating income under absorption costing and variable costing in Year 2.

3. At the end of Year 1, the company's board of directors set a target for Year 2 net operating income of $500,000 under absorption costing. If this target is met, a hefty bonus would be paid to the CEO of the company. Keeping everything else the same from part (2) above, change the units produced in Year 2 to 50,000 units. Would this change result in a bonus being paid to the CEO? Do you think this change would be in the best interests of the company? What is likely to happen in Year 3 to the absorption costing net operating income if sales remain constant at 12,000 units per year?

Mc Graw Hill connect | **The Foundational 15**

Diego Company manufactures one product that is sold for $80 per unit in two geographic regions— East and West. The following information pertains to the company's first year of operations, in which it produced 40,000 units and sold 35,000 units.

LEARNING OBJECTIVES 4–1, 4–2, 4–3, 4–4, 4–5

Variable costs per unit:	
Manufacturing:	
Direct materials	$24
Direct labor	$14
Variable manufacturing overhead	$2
Variable selling and administrative	$4
Fixed costs per year:	
Fixed manufacturing overhead	$800,000
Fixed selling and administrative expense	$496,000

The company sold 25,000 units in the East region and 10,000 units in the West region. It determined that $250,000 of its fixed selling and administrative expense is traceable to the West region, $150,000 is traceable to the East region, and the remaining $96,000 is a common fixed expense. The company will continue to incur the total amount of its fixed manufacturing overhead costs as long as it continues to produce any amount of its only product.

Required:

Answer each question independently based on the original data unless instructed otherwise. You do not need to prepare a segmented income statement until question 13.

1. What is the unit product cost under variable costing?
2. What is the unit product cost under absorption costing?
3. What is the company's total contribution margin under variable costing?
4. What is the company's net operating income under variable costing?
5. What is the company's total gross margin under absorption costing?
6. What is the company's net operating income under absorption costing?
7. What is the difference between the variable costing and absorption costing net operating incomes? What is the cause of this difference?
8. What is the company's break-even point in unit sales? Is it above or below the actual unit sales? Compare the break-even point in unit sales to your answer for question 6 and comment.
9. If the sales volumes in the East and West regions had been reversed, what would be the company's overall break-even point in unit sales?
10. What would have been the company's variable costing net operating income if it had produced and sold 35,000 units? You do not need to perform any calculations to answer this question.
11. What would have been the company's absorption costing net operating income if it had produced and sold 35,000 units? You do not need to perform any calculations to answer this question.
12. If the company produces 5,000 fewer units than it sells in its second year of operations, will absorption costing net operating income be higher or lower than variable costing net operating income in Year 2? Why? No calculations are necessary.
13. Prepare a contribution format segmented income statement that includes a Total column and columns for the East and West regions.
14. Diego is considering eliminating the West region because an internally generated report suggests the region's total *gross margin* in the first year of operations was $50,000 less than its traceable fixed selling and administrative expenses. Diego believes that if it drops the West region, the East region's sales will grow by 5% in Year 2. Using the contribution approach for analyzing segment profitability and assuming all else remains constant in Year 2, what would be the profit impact of dropping the West region in Year 2?
15. Assume the West region invests $30,000 in a new advertising campaign in Year 2 that increases its unit sales by 20%. If all else remains constant, what would be the profit impact of pursuing the advertising campaign?

Examples

EXERCISE 4–1 Variable and Absorption Costing Unit Product Costs LO 4–1

Ida Company produces a handcrafted musical instrument called a gamelan that is similar to a xylophone. The gamelans are sold for $850. Selected data for the company's operations last year follow:

Units in beginning inventory	0
Units produced	250
Units sold	225
Units in ending inventory	25
Variable costs per unit:	
Direct materials	$100
Direct labor	$320
Variable manufacturing overhead	$40
Variable selling and administrative	$20
Fixed costs:	
Fixed manufacturing overhead	$60,000
Fixed selling and administrative	$20,000

Required:
1. Assume that the company uses absorption costing. Compute the unit product cost for one gamelan.
2. Assume that the company uses variable costing. Compute the unit product cost for one gamelan.

EXERCISE 4–2 Variable Costing Income Statement; Explanation of Difference in Net Operating Income LO 4–2

Refer to the data in Exercise 4–1 for Ida Company. The absorption costing income statement prepared by the company's accountant for last year appears as shown:

Sales	$191,250
Cost of goods sold	157,500
Gross margin	33,750
Selling and administrative expense	24,500
Net operating income	$ 9,250

Required:
1. Under absorption costing, how much fixed manufacturing overhead cost is included in the company's inventory at the end of last year?
2. Prepare an income statement for last year using variable costing. Explain the difference in net operating income between the two costing methods.

EXERCISE 4–3 Reconciliation of Absorption and Variable Costing Net Operating Incomes LO 4–3

Jorgansen Lighting, Inc., manufactures heavy-duty street lighting systems for municipalities. The company uses variable costing for internal management reports and absorption costing for external reports to shareholders, creditors, and the government. The company has provided the following data:

	Year 1	Year 2	Year 3
Inventories:			
Beginning (units)	200	170	180
Ending (units)	170	180	220
Variable costing net operating income	$1,080,400	$1,032,400	$996,400

The company's fixed manufacturing overhead per unit was constant at $560 for all three years.

Required:
1. Calculate each year's absorption costing net operating income. Present your answer in the form of a reconciliation report.
2. Assume in Year 4 that the company's variable costing net operating income was $984,400 and its absorption costing net operating income was $1,012,400.
   a. Did inventories increase or decrease during Year 4?
   b. How much fixed manufacturing overhead cost was deferred or released from inventory during Year 4?

EXERCISE 4–4 Basic Segmented Income Statement LO 4–4

Royal Lawncare Company produces and sells two packaged products—Weedban and Greengrow. Revenue and cost information relating to the products follow:

	Product	
	Weedban	Greengrow
Selling price per unit	$6.00	$7.50
Variable expenses per unit	$2.40	$5.25
Traceable fixed expenses per year	$45,000	$21,000

Last year the company produced and sold 15,000 units of Weedban and 28,000 units of Green-grow. Its annual common fixed expenses are $33,000.

Required:

Prepare a contribution format income statement segmented by product lines.

EXERCISE 4–5 Companywide and Segment Break-Even Analysis LO 4–5

Piedmont Company segments its business into two regions—North and South. The company prepared the contribution format segmented income statement as shown below:

	Total Company	North	South
Sales	$600,000	$400,000	$200,000
Variable expenses	360,000	280,000	80,000
Contribution margin	240,000	120,000	120,000
Traceable fixed expenses	120,000	60,000	60,000
Segment margin	120,000	$ 60,000	$ 60,000
Common fixed expenses	50,000		
Net operating income	$ 70,000		

Required:

1. Compute the companywide break-even point in dollar sales.
2. Compute the break-even point in dollar sales for the North region.
3. Compute the break-even point in dollar sales for the South region.

EXERCISE 4–6 Variable and Absorption Costing Unit Product Costs and Income Statements LO 4–1, LO 4–2

Lynch Company manufactures and sells a single product. The following costs were incurred during the company's first year of operations:

Variable costs per unit:	
Manufacturing:	
Direct materials	$6
Direct labor	$9
Variable manufacturing overhead	$3
Variable selling and administrative	$4
Fixed costs per year:	
Fixed manufacturing overhead	$300,000
Fixed selling and administrative	$190,000

During the year, the company produced 25,000 units and sold 20,000 units. The selling price of the company's product is $50 per unit.

Required:

1. Assume the company uses absorption costing:
   a. Compute the unit product cost.
   b. Prepare an income statement for the year.
2. Assume the company uses variable costing:
   a. Compute the unit product cost.
   b. Prepare an income statement for the year.

EXERCISE 4–7 Segmented Income Statement LO 4–4

Shannon Company segments its income statement into its North and South Divisions. The company's overall sales, contribution margin ratio, and net operating income are $500,000, 46%, and $10,000, respectively. The North Division's contribution margin and contribution margin ratio are $150,000 and 50%, respectively. The South Division's segment margin is $30,000. The company has $90,000 of common fixed expenses that cannot be traced to either division.

Required:

Prepare an income statement for Shannon Company that uses the contribution format and is segmented by divisions. In addition, for the company as a whole and for each segment, show each item on the segmented income statements as a percent of sales.

EXERCISE 4–8 Deducing Changes in Inventories LO 4–3

Parker Products, Inc., is a manufacturer whose absorption costing income statement reported sales of $123 million and a net operating loss of $18 million. According to a CVP analysis prepared for management, the company's break-even point is $115 million in sales.

Required:

Assuming that the CVP analysis is correct, is it likely that the company's inventory level increased, decreased, or remained unchanged during the year? Explain.

EXERCISE 4–9 Variable and Absorption Costing Unit Product Costs and Income Statements LO 4–1, LO 4–2, LO 4–3

Walsh Company manufactures and sells one product. The following information pertains to each of the company's first two years of operations:

Variable costs per unit:	
Manufacturing:	
Direct materials	$25
Direct labor	$15
Variable manufacturing overhead	$5
Variable selling and administrative	$2
Fixed costs per year:	
Fixed manufacturing overhead	$250,000
Fixed selling and administrative expenses	$80,000

During its first year of operations, Walsh produced 50,000 units and sold 40,000 units. During its second year of operations, it produced 40,000 units and sold 50,000 units. The selling price of the company's product is $60 per unit.

Required:

1. Assume the company uses variable costing:
   a. Compute the unit product cost for Year 1 and Year 2.
   b. Prepare an income statement for Year 1 and Year 2.
2. Assume the company uses absorption costing:
   a. Compute the unit product cost for Year 1 and Year 2.
   b. Prepare an income statement for Year 1 and Year 2.
3. Explain the difference between variable costing and absorption costing net operating income in Year 1. Also, explain why the two net operating incomes differ in Year 2.

EXERCISE 4–10 Companywide and Segment Break-Even Analysis LO 4–5

Crossfire Company segments its business into two regions—East and West. The company prepared a contribution format segmented income statement as shown below:

	Total Company	East	West
Sales	$900,000	$600,000	$300,000
Variable expenses	675,000	480,000	195,000
Contribution margin	225,000	120,000	105,000
Traceable fixed expenses	141,000	50,000	91,000
Segment margin	84,000	$ 70,000	$ 14,000
Common fixed expenses	59,000		
Net operating income	$ 25,000		

Required:

1. Compute the companywide break-even point in dollar sales.
2. Compute the break-even point in dollar sales for the East region.
3. Compute the break-even point in dollar sales for the West region.
4. Prepare a new segmented income statement based on the break-even dollar sales you computed in requirements 2 and 3. Use the same format as shown above. What is Crossfire's net operating income (loss) in your new segmented income statement?
5. Do you think that Crossfire should allocate its common fixed expenses to the East and West regions when computing the break-even points for each region? Why?

EXERCISE 4–11 Segmented Income Statement LO 4–4

Wingate Company, a wholesale distributor of electronic equipment, has been experiencing losses for some time, as shown by its most recent monthly contribution format income statement:

Sales	$1,000,000
Variable expenses	390,000
Contribution margin	610,000
Fixed expenses	625,000
Net operating income (loss)	$ (15,000)

In an effort to resolve the problem, the company would like to prepare an income statement segmented by division. Accordingly, the Accounting Department has developed the following information:

	Division		
	East	Central	West
Sales	$250,000	$400,000	$350,000
Variable expenses as a percentage of sales	52%	30%	40%
Traceable fixed expenses	$160,000	$200,000	$175,000

Required:

1. Prepare a contribution format income statement segmented by divisions.
2. The Marketing Department has proposed increasing the West Division's monthly advertising by $15,000 based on the belief that it would increase that division's sales by 20%. Assuming these estimates are accurate, how much would the company's net operating income increase (decrease) if the proposal is implemented?

EXERCISE 4–12 Variable Costing Income Statement; Reconciliation LO 4–2, LO 4–3

Whitman Company has just completed its first year of operations. The company's absorption costing income statement for the year follows:

Whitman Company Income Statement	
Sales (35,000 units × $25 per unit)	$875,000
Cost of goods sold (35,000 units × $16 per unit)	560,000
Gross margin	315,000
Selling and administrative expenses	280,000
Net operating income	$ 35,000

The company's selling and administrative expenses consist of $210,000 per year in fixed expenses and $2 per unit sold in variable expenses. The $16 unit product cost given above is computed as follows:

Direct materials	$ 5
Direct labor	6
Variable manufacturing overhead	1
Fixed manufacturing overhead ($160,000 ÷ 40,000 units)	4
Absorption costing unit product cost	$16

Required:

1. Redo the company's income statement in the contribution format using variable costing.
2. Reconcile any difference between the net operating income on your variable costing income statement and the net operating income on the absorption costing income statement above.

EXERCISE 4–13 Inferring Costing Method; Unit Product Cost LO 4–1

Sierra Company incurs the following costs to produce and sell its only product.

Variable costs per unit:	
Direct materials	$9
Direct labor	$10
Variable manufacturing overhead	$5
Variable selling and administrative expenses	$3
Fixed costs per year:	
Fixed manufacturing overhead	$150,000
Fixed selling and administrative expenses	$400,000

During this year, 25,000 units were produced, and 22,000 units were sold. The Finished Goods inventory account at the end of this year shows a balance of $72,000 for the 3,000 unsold units.

Required:

1. Calculate this year's ending balance in Finished Goods inventory two ways—using variable costing and using absorption costing. Does it appear that the company is using variable costing or absorption costing to assign costs to the 3,000 units in its Finished Goods inventory?
2. Assume that the company wishes to prepare this year's financial statements for its stockholders.
   a. Is Finished Goods inventory of $72,000 the correct amount to include on the balance sheet for external reporting purposes? Explain.
   b. What balance should be reported in the Finished Goods inventory account for external reporting purposes?

EXERCISE 4–14 Variable Costing Unit Product Cost and Income Statement; Break-Even Analysis
LO 4–1, LO 4–2

Chuck Wagon Grills, Inc., makes a single product—a handmade specialty barbecue grill that it sells for $210. Data for last year's operations follow:

Units in beginning inventory	0
Units produced	20,000
Units sold	19,000
Units in ending inventory	1,000
Variable costs per unit:	
Direct materials	$ 50
Direct labor	80
Variable manufacturing overhead	20
Variable selling and administrative	10
Total variable cost per unit	$160
Fixed costs:	
Fixed manufacturing overhead	$700,000
Fixed selling and administrative	285,000
Total fixed costs	$985,000

Required:

1. Assume the company uses variable costing. Compute the unit product cost for one barbecue grill.
2. Assume the company uses variable costing. Prepare a contribution format income statement for last year.
3. What is the company's break-even point in terms of the number of barbecue grills sold?

EXERCISE 4–15 Absorption Costing Unit Product Cost and Income Statement LO 4–1, LO 4–2

Refer to the data in Exercise 4–14 for Chuck Wagon Grills. Assume in this exercise the company uses absorption costing.

Required:
1.   Compute the unit product cost for one barbecue grill.
2.   Prepare an income statement for last year.

EXERCISE 4–16 Working with a Segmented Income Statement; Break-Even Analysis LO 4–4, LO 4–5
Raner, Harris & Chan is a consulting firm that specializes in information systems for medical and dental clinics. The firm has two offices—one in Chicago and one in Minneapolis. The firm classifies the direct costs of consulting jobs as variable costs. A contribution format segmented income statement for the company's most recent year is given:

| | Total Company | | Office | | | |
			Chicago		Minneapolis	
Sales	$450,000	100%	$150,000	100%	$300,000	100%
Variable expenses	225,000	50%	45,000	30%	180,000	60%
Contribution margin	225,000	50%	105,000	70%	120,000	40%
Traceable fixed expenses	126,000	28%	78,000	52%	48,000	16%
Office segment margin	99,000	22%	$ 27,000	18%	$ 72,000	24%
Common fixed expenses not traceable to offices	63,000	14%				
Net operating income	$ 36,000	8%				

Required:
1.   Compute the companywide break-even point in dollar sales. Also, compute the break-even point for the Chicago office and for the Minneapolis office. Is the companywide break-even point greater than, less than, or equal to the sum of the Chicago and Minneapolis break-even points? Why?
2.   How much would the company's net operating income increase if Minneapolis increased its sales by $75,000 per year? Assume no change in cost behavior patterns.
3.   Refer to the original data. Assume that sales in Chicago increase by $50,000 next year and that sales in Minneapolis remain unchanged. Assume no change in fixed costs.
   a.   Prepare a new segmented income statement for the company using the above format. Show both amounts and percentages.
   b.   Observe from the income statement you have prepared that the contribution margin ratio for Chicago has remained unchanged at 70% (the same as in the above data) but that the segment margin ratio has changed. How do you explain the change in the segment margin ratio?

EXERCISE 4–17 Working with a Segmented Income Statement LO 4–4
Refer to the data in Exercise 4–16. Assume that Minneapolis's sales by major market are:

| | Minneapolis | | Market | | | |
			Medical		Dental	
Sales	$300,000	100%	$200,000	100%	$100,000	100%
Variable expenses	180,000	60%	128,000	64%	52,000	52%
Contribution margin	120,000	40%	72,000	36%	48,000	48%
Traceable fixed expenses	33,000	11%	12,000	6%	21,000	21%
Market segment margin	87,000	29%	$ 60,000	30%	$ 27,000	27%
Common fixed expenses not traceable to markets	15,000	5%				
Office segment margin	$ 72,000	24%				

The company would like to initiate an intensive advertising campaign in one of the two market segments during the next month. The campaign would cost $5,000. Marketing studies indicate that such a campaign would increase Medical market sales by $40,000 or Dental market sales by $35,000.

Required:

1. How much would the company's profits increase (decrease) if it implemented the advertising campaign in the Medical market?
2. How much would the company's profits increase (decrease) if it implemented the advertising campaign in the Dental market?
3. In which of the markets would you recommend that the company focus its advertising campaign?
4. In Exercise 4–16, Minneapolis shows $48,000 in traceable fixed expenses. What happened to the $48,000 in this exercise?

Mc Graw Hill connect   Problems

PROBLEM 4–18 Variable and Absorption Costing Unit Product Costs and Income Statements

LO 4–1, LO 4–2

Haas Company manufactures and sells one product. The following information pertains to each of the company's first three years of operations:

Variable costs per unit:	
Manufacturing:	
Direct materials	$20
Direct labor	$12
Variable manufacturing overhead	$4
Variable selling and administrative	$2
Fixed costs per year:	
Fixed manufacturing overhead	$960,000
Fixed selling and administrative expenses	$240,000

During its first year of operations, Haas produced 60,000 units and sold 60,000 units. During its second year of operations, it produced 75,000 units and sold 50,000 units. In its third year, Haas produced 40,000 units and sold 65,000 units. The selling price of the company's product is $58 per unit.

Required:

1. Compute the company's break-even point in unit sales.
2. Assume the company uses variable costing:
   a. Compute the unit product cost for Year 1, Year 2, and Year 3.
   b. Prepare an income statement for Year 1, Year 2, and Year 3.
3. Assume the company uses absorption costing:
   a. Compute the unit product cost for Year 1, Year 2, and Year 3.
   b. Prepare an income statement for Year 1, Year 2, and Year 3.
4. Compare the net operating incomes that you computed in requirements 2 and 3 to the break-even point in unit sales that you computed in requirement 1. Which net operating income figures (variable costing or absorption costing) seem counterintuitive? Why?

PROBLEM 4–19 Variable Costing Income Statement; Reconciliation LO 4–1, LO 4–2, LO 4–3

During Heaton Company's first two years of operations, it reported absorption costing net operating income as follows:

	Year 1	Year 2
Sales (@ $25 per unit)	$1,000,000	$1,250,000
Cost of goods sold (@ $18 per unit)	720,000	900,000
Gross margin	280,000	350,000
Selling and administrative expenses*	210,000	230,000
Net operating income	$ 70,000	$ 120,000

* $2 per unit variable; $130,000 fixed each year.

The company's $18 unit product cost is computed as follows:

Direct materials	$ 4
Direct labor	7
Variable manufacturing overhead	1
Fixed manufacturing overhead ($270,000 ÷ 45,000 units)	6
Absorption costing unit product cost	$18

Production and cost data for the first two years of operations are:

	Year 1	Year 2
Units produced	45,000	45,000
Units sold	40,000	50,000

Required:
1. Using variable costing, what is the unit product cost for both years?
2. What is the variable costing net operating income in Year 1 and in Year 2?
3. Reconcile the absorption costing and the variable costing net operating income figures for each year.

PROBLEM 4–20 Variable and Absorption Costing Unit Product Costs and Income Statements;
Explanation of Difference in Net Operating Income LO 4–1, LO 4–2, LO 4–3
High Country, Inc., produces and sells many recreational products. The company has just opened a new plant to produce a folding camp cot that will be marketed throughout the United States. The following cost and revenue data relate to May, the first month of the plant's operation:

Beginning inventory	0
Units produced	10,000
Units sold	8,000
Selling price per unit	$75
Selling and administrative expenses:	
Variable per unit	$6
Fixed (per month)	$200,000
Manufacturing costs:	
Direct materials cost per unit	$20
Direct labor cost per unit	$8
Variable manufacturing overhead cost per unit	$2
Fixed manufacturing overhead cost (per month)	$100,000

Management is anxious to assess the profitability of the new camp cot during the month of May.

Required:
1. Assume the company uses absorption costing.
   a. Calculate the unit product cost.
   b. Prepare an income statement for May.
2. Assume the company uses variable costing.
   a. Calculate the unit product cost.
   b. Prepare a contribution format income statement for May.
3. Explain the reason for any difference in the ending inventory balances under the two costing methods and the impact of this difference on reported net operating income.

PROBLEM 4–21 Segment Reporting and Decision Making LO 4–4

Vulcan Company's contribution format income statement for June is as follows:

Vulcan Company Income Statement For the Month Ended June 30	
Sales	$750,000
Variable expenses	336,000
Contribution margin	414,000
Fixed expenses	378,000
Net operating income	$ 36,000

Management is disappointed with the company's performance and is wondering what can be done to improve profits. By examining sales and cost records, you have determined the following:

a. The company is divided into two sales territories—Northern and Southern. The Northern territory recorded $300,000 in sales and $156,000 in variable expenses during June; the remaining sales and variable expenses were recorded in the Southern territory. Fixed expenses of $120,000 and $108,000 are traceable to the Northern and Southern territories, respectively. The rest of the fixed expenses are common to the two territories.

b. The company is the exclusive distributor for two products—Paks and Tibs. Sales of Paks and Tibs totaled $50,000 and $250,000, respectively, in the Northern territory during June. Variable expenses are 22% of the selling price for Paks and 58% for Tibs. Cost records show that $30,000 of the Northern territory's fixed expenses are traceable to Paks and $40,000 to Tibs, with the remainder common to the two products.

Required:

1. Prepare contribution format segmented income statements first showing the total company broken down between sales territories and then showing the Northern territory broken down by product line. In addition, for the company as a whole and for each segment, show each item on the segmented income statements as a percent of sales.

2. Look at the statement you have prepared showing the total company segmented by sales territory. What insights revealed by this statement should be mentioned to management?

3. Look at the statement you have prepared showing the Northern territory segmented by product lines. What insights revealed by this statement should be mentioned to management?

PROBLEM 4–22 Variable Costing Income Statements; Income Reconciliation LO 4–1, LO 4–2, LO 4–3

Denton Company manufactures and sells a single product. Cost data for the product are given:

Variable costs per unit:	
Direct materials	$ 7
Direct labor	10
Variable manufacturing overhead	5
Variable selling and administrative	3
Total variable cost per unit	$25
Fixed costs per month:	
Fixed manufacturing overhead...................	$315,000
Fixed selling and administrative.................	245,000
Total fixed cost per month.....................	$560,000

The product sells for $60 per unit. Production and sales data for July and August, the first two months of operations, follow:

	Units Produced	Units Sold
July	17,500	15,000
August	17,500	20,000

The company's Accounting Department has prepared the following absorption costing income statements for July and August:

	July	August
Sales	$900,000	$1,200,000
Cost of goods sold	600,000	800,000
Gross margin	300,000	400,000
Selling and administrative expenses	290,000	305,000
Net operating income	$ 10,000	$ 95,000

Required:

1. Determine the unit product cost under:
   a. Absorption costing.
   b. Variable costing.
2. Prepare variable costing income statements for July and August.
3. Reconcile the variable costing and absorption costing net operating incomes.
4. The company's Accounting Department determined the company's break-even point to be 16,000 units per month, computed as follows:

$$\frac{\text{Fixed cost per month}}{\text{Unit contribution margin}} = \frac{\$560,000}{\$35 \text{ per unit}} = 16,000 \text{ units}$$

"I'm confused," said the president. "The accounting people say our break-even point is 16,000 units per month, but we sold only 15,000 units in July, and the income statement they prepared shows a $10,000 profit for that month. Either the income statement is wrong or the break-even point is wrong." Prepare a brief memo for the president, explaining what happened on the July absorption costing income statement.

PROBLEM 4–23 Absorption and Variable Costing; Production Constant, Sales Fluctuate LO 4–1, LO 4–2, LO 4–3

Tami Tyler opened Tami's Creations, Inc., a small manufacturing company, at the beginning of the year. Getting the company through its first quarter of operations placed a considerable strain on Ms. Tyler's personal finances. The following income statement for the first quarter was prepared by a friend who just completed a course in managerial accounting at State University.

Tami's Creations, Inc. Income Statement For the Quarter Ended March 31		
Sales (28,000 units)		$1,120,000
Variable expenses:		
Variable cost of goods sold......................	$462,000	
Variable selling and administrative	168,000	630,000
Contribution margin		490,000
Fixed expenses:		
Fixed manufacturing overhead....................	$300,000	
Fixed selling and administrative..................	200,000	500,000
Net operating loss		$ (10,000)

Ms. Tyler is discouraged over the loss shown for the quarter, particularly because she had planned to use the statement as support for a bank loan. Another friend, a CPA, insists that the company should be using absorption costing rather than variable costing and argues that if absorption costing had been used, the company probably would have reported at least some profit for the quarter.

At this point, Ms. Tyler is manufacturing only one product—a swimsuit. Production and cost data relating to the swimsuit for the first quarter follow:

Units produced	30,000
Units sold	28,000
Variable costs per unit:	
Direct materials	$3.50
Direct labor	$12.00
Variable manufacturing overhead	$1.00
Variable selling and administrative	$6.00

Required:

1. Complete the following:
    a. Compute the unit product cost under absorption costing.
    b. What is the company's absorption costing net operating income (loss) for the quarter?
    c. Reconcile the variable and absorption costing net operating income (loss) figures.
2. Was the CPA correct in suggesting that the company really earned a "profit" for the quarter? Explain.
3. During the second quarter of operations, the company again produced 30,000 units but sold 32,000 units. (Assume no change in total fixed costs.)
    a. What is the company's variable costing net operating income (loss) for the second quarter?
    b. What is the company's absorption costing net operating income (loss) for the second quarter?
    c. Reconcile the variable costing and absorption costing net operating incomes for the second quarter.

PROBLEM 4–24 Companywide and Segment Break-Even Analysis; Decision Making LO 4–4, LO 4–5

Toxaway Company is a merchandiser that segments its business into two divisions—Commercial and Residential. The company's accounting intern was asked to prepare segmented income statements that the company's divisional managers could use to calculate their break-even points and make decisions. She took the prior month's companywide income statement and prepared the absorption format segmented income statement shown below:

	Total Company	Commercial	Residential
Sales	$750,000	$250,000	$500,000
Cost of goods sold	500,000	140,000	360,000
Gross margin	250,000	110,000	140,000
Selling and administrative expenses............	240,000	104,000	136,000
Net operating income	$ 10,000	$ 6,000	$ 4,000

In preparing these statements, the intern determined that Toxaway's only variable selling and administrative expense is a 10% sales commission on all sales. The company's total fixed expenses include $72,000 of common fixed expenses that would continue to be incurred even if the Commercial or Residential segment is discontinued, $55,000 of fixed expenses that would disappear if the Commericial segment is dropped, and $38,000 of fixed expenses that would disappear if the Residential segment is dropped.

Required:

1. Do you agree with the intern's decision to use an absorption format for her segmented income statement? Why?
2. Based on a review of the intern's segmented income statement:
    a. How much of the company's common fixed expenses did she allocate to the Commercial and Residential segments?
    b. Which of the following three allocation bases did she most likely use to allocate common fixed expenses to the Commercial and Residential segments: (a) sales, (b) cost of goods sold, or (c) gross margin?
3. Do you agree with the intern's decision to allocate the common fixed expenses to the Commercial and Residential segments? Why?
4. Redo the intern's segmented income statement using the contribution format.
5. Compute the companywide break-even point in dollar sales.
6. Compute the break-even point in dollar sales for the Commercial Division and for the Residential Division.
7. Assume the company decided to pay its sales representatives in the Commercial and Residential Divisions a total monthly salary of $15,000 and $30,000, respectively, and to lower its companywide sales commission percentage from 10% to 5%. Calculate the new break-even point in dollar sales for the Commercial Division and the Residential Division.

PROBLEM 4–25 Prepare and Interpret Income Statements; Changes in Both Sales and Production; Lean Production LO 4–1, LO 4–2, LO 4–3

Starfax, Inc., manufactures a small part that is widely used in various electronic products such as home computers. Results for the first three years of operations were as follows (absorption costing basis):

	Year 1	Year 2	Year 3
Sales	$800,000	$640,000	$800,000
Cost of goods sold	580,000	400,000	620,000
Gross margin	220,000	240,000	180,000
Selling and administrative expenses	190,000	180,000	190,000
Net operating income (loss)	$ 30,000	$ 60,000	$ (10,000)

In the latter part of Year 2, a competitor went out of business, and in the process, dumped a large number of units on the market. As a result, Starfax's sales dropped by 20% during Year 2 even though production increased during the year. Management had expected sales to remain constant at 50,000 units; the increased production was designed to provide the company with a buffer of protection against unexpected spurts in demand. By the start of Year 3, management could see that it had excess inventory and that spurts in demand were unlikely. To reduce the excessive inventories, Starfax cut back production during Year 3, as shown below:

	Year 1	Year 2	Year 3
Production in units	50,000	60,000	40,000
Sales in units	50,000	40,000	50,000

Additional information about the company follows:

a. The company's plant is highly automated. Variable manufacturing expenses (direct materials, direct labor, and variable manufacturing overhead) total only $2 per unit, and fixed manufacturing overhead expenses total $480,000 per year.
b. A new fixed manufacturing overhead rate is computed each year based on that year's actual fixed manufacturing overhead costs divided by the actual number of units produced.

c.   Variable selling and administrative expenses were $1 per unit sold in each year. Fixed selling and administrative expenses totaled $140,000 per year.

d.   The company uses a FIFO inventory flow assumption. (FIFO means first-in first-out. In other words, it assumes the oldest units in inventory are sold first.)

Starfax's management can't understand why profits doubled during Year 2 when sales dropped by 20% and why a loss was incurred during Year 3 when sales recovered to previous levels.

Required:

1.   Prepare a variable costing income statement for each year.

2.   Refer to the absorption costing income statements above.

   a.   Compute the unit product cost in each year under absorption costing. Show how much of this cost is variable and how much is fixed.

   b.   Reconcile the variable costing and absorption costing net operating income figures for each year.

3.   Refer again to the absorption costing income statements. Explain why net operating income was higher in Year 2 than it was in Year 1 under the absorption approach, in light of the fact that fewer units were sold in Year 2 than in Year 1.

4.   Refer again to the absorption costing income statements. Explain why the company suffered a loss in Year 3 but reported a profit in Year 1 although the same number of units was sold each year.

5.   a.   Explain how operations would have differed in Year 2 and Year 3 if the company had been using Lean Production, with the result that ending inventory was zero.

   b.   If Lean Production had been used during Year 2 and Year 3, what would the company's net operating income (or loss) have been in each year under absorption costing? No computations are necessary.

PROBLEM 4–26 Restructuring a Segmented Income Statement LO 4–4

Millard Corporation is a wholesale distributor of office products. It purchases office products from manufacturers and distributes them in the West, Central, and East regions. Each of these regions is about the same size, and each has its own manager and sales staff.

The company has been experiencing losses for many months. In an effort to improve performance, management has requested that the monthly income statement be segmented by sales region. The company's first effort at preparing a segmented income statement for May is given below.

	Sales Region		
	West	Central	East
Sales	$450,000	$800,000	$ 750,000
Regional expenses (traceable):			
Cost of goods sold	162,900	280,000	376,500
Advertising.	108,000	200,000	210,000
Salaries.	90,000	88,000	135,000
Utilities	13,500	12,000	15,000
Depreciation	27,000	28,000	30,000
Shipping expense	17,100	32,000	28,500
Total regional expenses	418,500	640,000	795,000
Regional income (loss) before corporate expenses	31,500	160,000	(45,000)
Corporate expenses:			
Advertising (general)	18,000	32,000	30,000
General administrative expense	50,000	50,000	50,000
Total corporate expenses	68,000	82,000	80,000
Net operating income (loss)	$ (36,500)	$ 78,000	$(125,000)

The cost of goods sold and shipping expense are both variable. All other costs are fixed.

Required:

1. List any weaknesses you see in the company's segmented income statement given above.
2. Explain the basis that is apparently being used to allocate the corporate expenses to the regions. Do you agree with these allocations? Explain.
3. Prepare a new contribution format segmented income statement for May. Show a Total column as well as data for each region. In addition, for the company as a whole and for each sales region, show each item on the segmented income statement as a percent of sales.
4. Analyze the statement you prepared in part (3) above. What insights do those statements reveal that you would bring to management's attention?

PROBLEM 4–27 Incentives Created by Absorption Costing; Ethics and the Manager LO 4–2

Carlos Cavalas, the manager of Echo Products' Brazilian Division, is trying to set the production schedule for the last quarter of the year. The Brazilian Division planned to sell 3,600 units during the year, but by September 30 only the following activity had been reported:

	Units
Inventory, January 1.	0
Production.	2,400
Sales.	2,000
Inventory, September 30	400

The division can rent warehouse space to store up to 1,000 units. The minimum inventory level the division should carry is 50 units. Mr. Cavalas is aware that production must be at least 200 units per quarter in order to retain a nucleus of key employees. Maximum production capacity is 1,500 units per quarter.

Demand has been soft, and the sales forecast for the last quarter is only 600 units. Due to the nature of the division's operations, fixed manufacturing overhead is a major element of product cost.

Required:

1. Assume the division is using variable costing. How many units should be scheduled for production during the last quarter of the year? (The basic formula for computing the required production for the quarter is: Required production = Expected sales + Desired ending inventory − Beginning inventory.) Show computations and explain your answer. Will the number of units scheduled for production affect the division's reported income or loss for the year? Explain.
2. Assume the division is using absorption costing and that the divisional manager is given an annual bonus based on divisional operating income. If Mr. Cavalas wants to maximize his division's operating income for the year, how many units should be scheduled for production during the last quarter? [See the formula in (1) above.] Explain.
3. Identify the ethical issues involved in the decision Mr. Cavalas must make about the level of production for the last quarter of the year.

PROBLEM 4–28 Companywide and Segment Break-Even Analysis LO 4–5

Piedmont Fasteners Corporation makes three different clothing fasteners in its manufacturing facility in North Carolina. All three products are sold in highly competitive markets, so the company is unable to raise prices without losing an unacceptable numbers of customers. Data from the most recent period concerning these products appear below:

	Velcro	Metal	Nylon
Annual sales volume.	100,000	200,000	400,000
Unit selling price	$1.65	$1.50	$0.85
Variable expense per unit	$1.25	$0.70	$0.25
Contribution margin per unit	$0.40	$0.80	$0.60

Total fixed expenses are $400,000 per period. Of the total fixed expenses, $20,000 could be avoided if the Velcro product is dropped, $80,000 if the Metal product is dropped, and $60,000 if the Nylon product is dropped. The remaining fixed expenses of $240,000 consist of common fixed expenses such as administrative salaries and rent on the factory building that could be avoided only by going out of business entirely.

The company's managers would like to compute the break-even point in dollar sales for the company as a whole and the break-even point in unit sales for each product. They are considering two methods for computing each product's break-even point unit sales:

Method #1: Include each product's traceable fixed costs and an allocated share of the common fixed costs in the numerator of each break-even calculation. The common fixed costs would be allocated to the three products using sales dollars as the allocation base.

Method #2: Only include each product's traceable fixed costs in the numerator of each break-even calculation.

Required:
1. Using data from the most recent period, prepare a contribution format segmented income statement. What is the net operating income?
2. What is the company's overall break-even point in dollar sales?
3. Using method 1:
   a. Calculate the break-even point in unit sales for each product.
   b. If the company sells exactly the break-even quantity of each product, what will be the overall profit for the company?
4. Using method 2:
   a. Calculate the break-even point in unit sales for each product.
   b. If the company sells exactly the break-even quantity of each product, what will be the overall profit for the company?
5. Which method should the company use to calculate each product's break-even point in unit sales? Why?

 Cases

Select cases are available in Connect.

CASE 4–29 Variable and Absorption Costing Unit Product Costs and Income Statements LO 4–1, LO 4–2

O'Brien Company manufactures and sells one product. The following information pertains to each of the company's first three years of operations:

Variable costs per unit:	
Manufacturing:	
Direct materials	$32
Direct labor	$20
Variable manufacturing overhead	$4
Variable selling and administrative	$3
Fixed costs per year:	
Fixed manufacturing overhead	$660,000
Fixed selling and administrative expenses	$120,000

During its first year of operations, O'Brien produced 100,000 units and sold 80,000 units. During its second year of operations, it produced 75,000 units and sold 90,000 units. In its third year, O'Brien produced 80,000 units and sold 75,000 units. The selling price of the company's product is $75 per unit.

Required:
1. Assume the company uses variable costing and a FIFO inventory flow assumption (FIFO means first-in first-out; in other words, it assumes the oldest units in inventory are sold first):
   a. Compute the unit product cost for Year 1, Year 2, and Year 3.
   b. Prepare an income statement for Year 1, Year 2, and Year 3.

2. Assume the company uses variable costing and a LIFO inventory flow assumption (LIFO means last-in first-out; in other words, it assumes the newest units in inventory are sold first):
   a. Compute the unit product cost for Year 1, Year 2, and Year 3.
   b. Prepare an income statement for Year 1, Year 2, and Year 3.
3. Assume the company uses absorption costing and a FIFO inventory flow assumption (FIFO means first-in first-out; in other words, it assumes the oldest units in inventory are sold first):
   a. Compute the unit product cost for Year 1, Year 2, and Year 3.
   b. Prepare an income statement for Year 1, Year 2, and Year 3.
4. Assume the company uses absorption costing and a LIFO inventory flow assumption (LIFO means last-in first-out; in other words, it assumes the newest units in inventory are sold first):
   a. Compute the unit product cost for Year 1, Year 2, and Year 3.
   b. Prepare an income statement for Year 1, Year 2, and Year 3.

CASE 4–30 Service Organization; Segment Reporting LO 4–4

Music Teachers, Inc., is an educational association for music teachers that has 20,000 members. The association operates from a central headquarters but has local membership chapters throughout the United States. Monthly meetings are held by the local chapters to discuss recent developments on topics of interest to music teachers. The association's magazine, *Teachers' Forum*, is issued monthly with features about recent developments in the field. The association publishes books and reports and also sponsors professional courses that qualify for continuing professional education credit. The association's statement of revenues and expenses for the current year is presented below.

Music Teachers, Inc. Statement of Revenues and Expenses For the Year Ended November 30	
Revenues	$3,275,000
Expenses:	
Salaries	920,000
Personnel costs	230,000
Occupancy costs	280,000
Reimbursement of member costs to local chapters	600,000
Other membership services	500,000
Printing and paper	320,000
Postage and shipping	176,000
Instructors' fees	80,000
General and administrative	38,000
Total expenses	3,144,000
Excess of revenues over expenses	$ 131,000

The board of directors of Music Teachers, Inc., has requested that a segmented income statement be prepared showing the contribution of each segment to the association. The association has four segments: Membership Division, Magazine Subscriptions Division, Books and Reports Division, and Continuing Education Division. Mike Doyle has been assigned responsibility for preparing the segmented income statement, and he has gathered the following data:

a. The 20,000 members of the association pay dues of $100 per year, of which $20 covers a one-year subscription to the *Teachers' Forum*. Other benefits include membership in the association and chapter affiliation. The portion of the dues covering the magazine subscription ($20) should be assigned to the Magazine Subscriptions Division.

b. A total of 2,500 one-year subscriptions to *Teachers' Forum* were also sold last year to non-members and libraries at $30 per subscription. In addition to subscriptions, the journal generated $100,000 in advertising revenues.

c. The costs to produce the *Teachers' Forum* magazine included $7 per subscription for printing and paper and $4 per subscription for postage and shipping.

d. A total of 28,000 technical reports and professional texts were sold by the Books and Reports Division at an average selling price per unit of $25. Average costs per publication were $4 for printing and paper and $2 for postage and shipping.

e. The association offers a variety of continuing education courses to both members and non-members. The one-day courses had a tuition cost of $75 each and were attended by 2,400 students. A total of 1,760 students took two-day courses at a tuition cost of $125 for each student. Outside instructors were paid to teach some courses.

f. Salary costs and space occupied by division follow:

	Salaries	Space Occupied (square feet)
Membership	$210,000	2,000
Magazine Subscriptions	150,000	2,000
Books and Reports	300,000	3,000
Continuing Education	180,000	2,000
Corporate staff	80,000	1,000
Total	$920,000	10,000

Personnel costs are 25% of salaries in the separate divisions as well as for the corporate staff. The $280,000 in occupancy costs (which can be allocated to segments based on their square feet occupied) includes $50,000 in rental cost for a warehouse used by the Books and Reports Division for storage purposes.

g. Printing and paper costs other than for magazine subscriptions and for books and reports relate to the Continuing Education Division.

h. General and administrative expenses include costs relating to the overall administration of the association as a whole. The company's corporate staff does some mailing of materials for general administrative purposes.

The expenses that can be traced or assigned to the corporate staff, as well as any other expenses that are not traceable to the segments, will be treated as common costs. It is not necessary to distinguish between variable and fixed costs.

Required:
1. Prepare a segmented income statement for Music Teachers, Inc. This statement should show the segment margin for each division as well as results for the association as a whole.
2. Give arguments for and against allocating all costs of the association to the four divisions.

(CMA, adapted)

Appendix 4A: Super-Variable Costing

In the discussion of variable costing in this chapter, we have assumed that direct labor and a portion of manufacturing overhead are variable costs that should be attached to products. However, these assumptions about cost behavior may not be true. For example, it may be easier and more accurate to assume that *all* manufacturing overhead costs are fixed costs because the variable portion of these costs is insignificant or too difficult to estimate. Furthermore, many companies' labor costs (including direct and indirect

LEARNING OBJECTIVE 4–6
Prepare an income statement using super-variable costing and reconcile this approach with variable costing.

labor) are more fixed than variable due to labor regulations, labor contracts, or management policy. In countries such as France, Germany, Spain, and Japan, management often has little flexibility in adjusting the labor force to changes in business activity. Even in countries such as the United States and the United Kingdom, where management usually has greater latitude to adjust the size of its labor force, many managers choose to view labor as a fixed cost. They make this choice because the cost savings from terminating or laying off employees during a short-term business downturn may be swamped by the negative effects on employee morale and by the costs of later finding and training suitable replacements. Moreover, treating employees as variable costs subtly fosters the attitude that employees are expendable and replaceable like materials rather than unique, difficult-to-replace assets.

Super-variable costing is a variation on variable costing in which direct labor and manufacturing overhead costs are considered to be fixed. **Super-variable costing** classifies all direct labor and manufacturing overhead costs as fixed period costs and *only direct materials as a variable product cost.* To simplify, in this appendix we also assume that selling and administrative expenses are entirely fixed.

Super-Variable Costing and Variable Costing—An Example

To illustrate the difference between treating direct labor as a fixed cost (as in super-variable costing) and treating direct labor as a variable cost (as in variable costing), we will use a modified version of the Weber Light Aircraft example from the main body of the chapter. Data concerning the company's operations appear below:

	Per Aircraft	Per Month
Selling price	$100,000	
Direct materials	$19,000	
Direct labor		$20,000
Fixed manufacturing overhead		$74,000
Fixed selling and administrative expense		$40,000

	January	February	March
Beginning inventory	0	0	1
Units produced	2	2	2
Units sold	2	1	3
Ending inventory	0	1	0

The key thing to notice here is that direct labor is a fixed cost—$20,000 per month. Also, notice that Weber Light Aircraft has no variable manufacturing overhead costs and no variable selling and administrative expenses. For the months of January, February, and March, the company's selling price per aircraft, variable cost per aircraft, monthly production in units, and total monthly fixed expenses never change. The only thing that changes in this example is the number of units sold (January = 2 units sold; February = 1 unit sold; March = 3 units sold).

We first will construct the company's super-variable costing income statements for January, February, and March. Then we will show how the company's net operating income would be determined for the same months using variable costing if it were incorrectly assumed that direct labor is a variable cost. As you'll see, both income statements rely on the contribution format.

Super-Variable Costing Income Statements

To prepare the company's super-variable costing income statements for each month, we follow four steps. First, we compute sales by multiplying the number of units sold by the selling price per unit, which in this example is $100,000 per unit. Second, we compute the variable cost of goods sold by multiplying the number of units sold by the unit product cost, which in this example is the direct materials cost of $19,000 per unit. Third, we compute the contribution margin by subtracting variable cost of goods sold from sales. Fourth, we compute net operating income by subtracting total fixed expenses, which in this example is $134,000 per month (= $20,000 + $74,000 + $40,000), from the contribution margin.

Using these four steps, Weber's super-variable costing income statements for each month would appear as shown in Exhibit 4A–1. Notice that the only variable expense is variable cost of goods sold, which is the $19,000 of direct materials per unit sold. For example, in March, the unit product cost of $19,000 is multiplied by three units sold to obtain the variable cost of goods sold of $57,000. The total monthly fixed manufacturing expenses of $94,000 include $20,000 of direct labor and $74,000 of fixed manufacturing overhead.

	January	February	March
Sales (@ $100,000 per unit)	$200,000	$100,000	$300,000
Variable cost of goods sold (@ $19,000 per unit)	38,000	19,000	57,000
Contribution margin	162,000	81,000	243,000
Fixed expenses:			
Fixed manufacturing expenses	94,000	94,000	94,000
Fixed selling and administrative expenses	40,000	40,000	40,000
Total fixed expenses	134,000	134,000	134,000
Net operating income (loss)	$ 28,000	$ (53,000)	$109,000

EXHIBIT 4A–1
Super-Variable Costing Income Statements

Variable Costing Income Statements

The variable costing income statements in this example differ from the super-variable costing income statements in one important respect—we will assume that direct labor is incorrectly classified as a variable cost and is included in unit product costs. Because the monthly direct labor cost is $20,000, and two aircraft are produced each month, if direct labor costs are included in unit product costs, then Weber Light Aircraft will assign $10,000 of direct labor cost to each aircraft that it produces. Thus, the company's unit product costs under variable costing would be computed as follows:

	January	February	March
Direct materials	$19,000	$19,000	$19,000
Direct labor	10,000	10,000	10,000
Unit product cost	$29,000	$29,000	$29,000

Given these unit product cost figures, the company's variable costing income statements would be computed as shown in Exhibit 4A–2. For example, in March, the unit product cost of $29,000 is multiplied by three units sold to obtain the variable cost of goods sold of $87,000. The total fixed manufacturing overhead of $74,000 and total fixed selling and administrative expenses of $40,000 are both recorded as period expenses.

EXHIBIT 4A–2

Variable Costing Income Statements

	January	February	March
Sales (@ $100,000 per unit)	$200,000	$100,000	$300,000
Variable cost of goods sold			
(@ $29,000 per unit)	58,000	29,000	87,000
Contribution margin	142,000	71,000	213,000
Fixed expenses:			
Fixed manufacturing expenses	74,000	74,000	74,000
Fixed selling and administrative expenses ...	40,000	40,000	40,000
Total fixed expenses	114,000	114,000	114,000
Net operating income (loss)	$ 28,000	$ (43,000)	$ 99,000

Reconciliation of Super-Variable Costing and Variable Costing Income

The super-variable costing and variable costing net operating incomes are both $28,000 in January. However, in February, the super-variable costing income is $10,000 lower than the variable costing income, and the opposite holds true in March. In other words, the super-variable costing income in March is $10,000 higher than the variable costing income.

Why do these two costing methods produce different net operating incomes? The answer can be found in the accounting for direct labor costs. Super-variable costing treats direct labor as a fixed period expense, whereas variable costing treats direct labor as a variable product cost. In other words, super-variable costing records the entire direct labor cost of $20,000 as an expense on each month's income statement. Conversely, variable costing assigns $10,000 of direct labor cost to each unit produced. The $10,000 assigned to each unit produced remains in inventory on the balance sheet until the unit is sold—at which point the $10,000 assigned to it is transferred to variable cost of goods sold on the income statement. Given this background, the super-variable costing and variable costing incomes for each month can be reconciled as follows:

	January	February	March
Direct labor cost in ending inventory			
(@ $10,000 per unit).......................	$0	$10,000	$ 0
Deduct: Direct labor cost in beginning inventory			
(@ $10,000 per unit).......................	0	0	10,000
Direct labor cost deferred in			
(released from) inventory	$0	$10,000	$(10,000)

	January	February	March
Super-variable costing net operating			
income (loss)	$28,000	$(53,000)	$109,000
Direct labor deferred in (released from)			
inventory.................................	0	10,000	(10,000)
Variable costing net operating income (loss)	$28,000	$(43,000)	$ 99,000

In January, both costing methods report the same net operating income ($28,000). This occurs because the unit produced in January was also sold in January and, as a result, both methods expense $20,000 of direct labor in the income statement. In February, two units are produced, but only one unit is sold; therefore, super-variable costing income is $10,000 less than variable costing income. This difference arises because super-variable costing expenses $20,000 of direct labor in the income statement, whereas variable costing expenses only $10,000 of direct labor in the income statement ($10,000 per unit × 1 unit sold) while deferring the other $10,000 of direct labor in inventory ($10,000 per unit × 1 unit produced but not sold). In March, two units are produced and three units are sold; hence, super-variable costing income is $10,000 greater than variable costing income. This difference arises because super-variable costing expenses $20,000 of direct labor on the income statement, whereas variable costing expenses $30,000 of direct labor on the income statement ($10,000 per unit × 3 units sold). Notice that one of the units sold in March was actually produced in February. Under variable costing, the $10,000 of direct labor attached to the unit produced in February is released from inventory and included in variable cost of goods sold for March.

In summary, the key issue considered in this appendix is how a company treats direct labor costs. If a company treats direct labor as a variable cost, the cost system may encourage managers to treat labor costs as an expense to be minimized when sales decline, and this may result in reduced morale and eventual problems when business picks up. Second, in practice, management may have little ability to adjust the direct labor force even if they wanted to, resulting in a situation in which direct labor costs are, in fact, fixed. In either case, treating direct labor costs as variable can lead to bad decisions. The super-variable costing approach overcomes this problem by treating labor costs as fixed costs.

Glossary (Appendix 4A)

Super-variable costing A costing method that classifies all direct labor and manufacturing overhead costs as fixed period costs and *only direct materials as a variable product cost.* (p. 218)

connect Appendix 4A: Exercises and Problems

EXERCISE 4A–1 Super-Variable Costing Income Statement LO 4–6
Zola Company manufactures and sells one product. The following information pertains to the company's first year of operations:

Variable cost per unit:	
Direct materials	$18
Fixed costs per year:	
Direct labor	$200,000
Fixed manufacturing overhead	$250,000
Fixed selling and administrative expenses	$80,000

The company does not incur any variable manufacturing overhead costs or variable selling and administrative expenses. During its first year of operations, Zola produced 25,000 units and sold 20,000 units. The selling price of the company's product is $50 per unit.

Required:

Assume the company uses super-variable costing.

- a. Compute the unit product cost for the year.
- b. Prepare an income statement for the year.

EXERCISE 4A–2 Super-Variable Costing and Variable Costing Unit Product Costs and Income Statements LO 4–2, LO 4–6

Lyons Company manufactures and sells one product. The following information pertains to the company's first year of operations:

Variable cost per unit:	
Direct materials	$13
Fixed costs per year:	
Direct labor	$750,000
Fixed manufacturing overhead	$420,000
Fixed selling and administrative expenses	$110,000

The company does not incur any variable manufacturing overhead costs or variable selling and administrative expenses. During its first year of operations, Lyons produced 60,000 units and sold 52,000 units. The selling price of the company's product is $40 per unit.

Required:

1. Assume the company uses super-variable costing:
    - a. Compute the unit product cost for the year.
    - b. Prepare an income statement for the year.
2. Assume the company uses a variable costing system that assigns $12.50 of direct labor cost to each unit produced:
    - a. Compute the unit product cost for the year.
    - b. Prepare an income statement for the year.
3. Prepare a reconciliation explaining the difference between the super-variable costing and variable costing net operating incomes.

EXERCISE 4A–3 Super-Variable Costing and Variable Costing Unit Product Costs and Income Statements LO 4–2, LO 4–6

Kelly Company manufactures and sells one product. The following information pertains to each of the company's first two years of operations:

Variable cost per unit:	
Direct materials	$12
Fixed costs per year:	
Direct labor	$500,000
Fixed manufacturing overhead	$450,000
Fixed selling and administrative expenses	$180,000

The company does not incur any variable manufacturing overhead costs or variable selling and administrative expenses. During its first year of operations, Kelly produced 50,000 units and sold 40,000 units. During its second year of operations, it produced 50,000 units and sold 60,000 units. The selling price of the company's product is $50 per unit.

Required:

1. Assume the company uses super-variable costing:
    - a. Compute the unit product cost for Year 1 and Year 2.
    - b. Prepare an income statement for Year 1 and Year 2.

2. Assume the company uses a variable costing system that assigns $10 of direct labor cost to each unit produced:
    a. Compute the unit product cost for Year 1 and Year 2.
    b. Prepare an income statement for Year 1 and Year 2.
3. Prepare a reconciliation explaining the difference between the super-variable costing and variable costing net operating incomes in Years 1 and 2.

PROBLEM 4A–4 Super-Variable Costing and Variable Costing Unit Product Costs and Income Statements LO 4–2, LO 4–6

Ogilvy Company manufactures and sells one product. The following information pertains to each of the company's first three years of operations:

Variable cost per unit:	
Direct materials	$16
Fixed costs per year:	
Direct labor	$540,000
Fixed manufacturing overhead	$822,000
Fixed selling and administrative expenses.	$370,000

The company does not incur any variable manufacturing overhead costs or variable selling and administrative expenses. During its first year of operations, Ogilvy produced 60,000 units and sold 60,000 units. During its second year of operations, it produced 60,000 units and sold 55,000 units. In its third year, Ogilvy produced 60,000 units and sold 65,000 units. The selling price of the company's product is $45 per unit.

Required:

1. Assume the company uses super-variable costing:
    a. Compute the unit product cost for Year 1, Year 2, and Year 3.
    b. Prepare an income statement for Year 1, Year 2, and Year 3.
2. Assume the company uses a variable costing system that assigns $9 of direct labor cost to each unit produced:
    a. Compute the unit product cost for Year 1, Year 2, and Year 3.
    b. Prepare an income statement for Year 1, Year 2, and Year 3.
3. Prepare a reconciliation explaining the difference between the super-variable costing and variable costing net operating incomes in Years 1, 2, and 3.

PROBLEM 4A–5 Super-Variable Costing, Variable Costing, and Absorption Costing Income Statements LO 4–2, LO 4–6

Bracey Company manufactures and sells one product. The following information pertains to the company's first year of operations:

Variable cost per unit:	
Direct materials	$19
Fixed costs per year:	
Direct labor	$250,000
Fixed manufacturing overhead	$300,000
Fixed selling and administrative expenses.	$90,000

The company does not incur any variable manufacturing overhead costs or variable selling and administrative expenses. During its first year of operations, Bracey produced 20,000 units and sold 18,000 units. The selling price of the company's product is $55 per unit.

Required:

1. Assume the company uses super-variable costing:
   a. Compute the unit product cost for the year.
   b. Prepare an income statement for the year.
2. Assume the company uses a variable costing system that assigns $12.50 of direct labor cost to each unit produced:
   a. Compute the unit product cost for the year.
   b. Prepare an income statement for the year.
3. Assume the company uses an absorption costing system that assigns $12.50 of direct labor cost and $15.00 of fixed manufacturing overhead cost to each unit produced:
   a. Compute the unit product cost for the year.
   b. Prepare an income statement for the year.
4. Prepare a reconciliation explaining the difference between the super-variable costing and variable costing net operating incomes. Prepare another reconciliation explaining the difference between the super-variable costing and absorption costing net operating incomes.

Activity-Based Costing: A Tool to Aid Decision Making

Cavan Images/Alamy Stock Photo

Paul Morigi/Invision for Intuit/AP Images

ENTREPRENEUR SPOTLIGHT

Kavita Shukla is the founder of Fresh Paper—a company that sells patented paper sheets that extend the life of perishable foods. Her paper sheets are stocked by large retailers, such as Whole Foods and Walmart, and are purchased by farmers and families throughout the world. Not only does Kavita hold four patents, but she also "is the youngest woman ever to receive the biennial INDEX Design to Improve Life Award." In fact, her accomplishments caught the attention of Hollywood director Bryce Dallas Howard, who created a short film to tell her story of "simple beginnings, belief, and empowerment."

Managerial Accounting: The Practical Application

In addition to selling its products to wholesale customers, Fresh Paper also welcomes online orders from its retail customers. Its website offers a variety of purchase options, including starter packs, value packs, and monthly subscriptions. The company could use activity-based costing to quantify the cost of its order-processing activities and the profitability of its various wholesale and retail customers. It could implement pricing and marketing strategies that motivate these customers to place orders that maximize revenues earned relative to the batch-level costs associated with fulfilling them.

Corporate Social Responsibility: Serving all Stakeholders

Kavita Shukla founded her company to help tackle the global challenge of reducing food waste. Her company's website offers three statistics that define the magnitude of the problem and the immense benefits that can be realized by solving it. First, one-third of all food produced across the globe is wasted, costing the global economy about $940 billion per year. Second, in spite of this immense waste, 793 million people throughout the world do not have enough food to eat. Third, if 25 percent of our wasted food could be salvaged, it would feed 870 million undernourished people. ■

Sources: https://freshpaper.com.au, https://freshpaper.com.au/food-wastage, https://www.kavitashukla.com

LEARNING OBJECTIVES

After studying Chapter 5, you should be able to:

LO 5–1 Understand activity-based costing and how it differs from a traditional costing system.

LO 5–2 Assign costs to cost pools using a first-stage allocation.

LO 5–3 Compute activity rates for cost pools.

LO 5–4 Assign costs to a cost object using a second-stage allocation.

LO 5–5 Use activity-based costing to compute product and customer margins.

LO 5–6 (Appendix 5A) Use time-driven activity-based costing to assign costs to cost objects.

LO 5–7 (Appendix 5A) Use time-driven activity-based costing to analyze capacity.

Data Analytics Exercise available in Connect to complement this chapter

This chapter introduces the concept of *activity-based costing,* which has been embraced by a wide variety of organizations, including Charles Schwab, Citigroup, Lowe's, Coca-Cola, J&B Wholesale, Fairchild Semiconductor, Assan Aluminum, Sysco Foods, Fisher Scientific International, and Peregrine Outfitters. **Activity-based costing (ABC)** is a costing method that is designed to provide managers with cost information for strategic and other decisions that potentially affect capacity and therefore "fixed" as well as variable costs. Activity-based costing is ordinarily used as a supplement to, rather than as a replacement for, a company's usual costing system. Most organizations that use activity-based costing have two costing systems—the official costing system that is used for preparing external financial reports and the activity-based costing system that is used for internal decision making and for managing activities.

In this chapter we'll explain how organizations use activity-based costing rather than traditional absorption costing to calculate unit product costs for managing overhead and making decisions. Chapter 4 had a similar purpose. That chapter focused on using variable costing to aid decisions that do not affect fixed costs. This chapter extends that idea to show how activity-based costing is used to aid decisions that potentially affect fixed costs as well as variable costs.

Activity-Based Costing: An Overview

LEARNING OBJECTIVE 5–1
Understand activity-based costing and how it differs from a traditional costing system.

Traditional absorption costing is designed to provide data for external financial reports. In contrast, activity-based costing is designed for internal decision making. As a consequence, activity-based costing differs from traditional absorption costing in three ways. In activity-based costing:

1. Nonmanufacturing as well as manufacturing costs may be assigned to products, but only on a cause-and-effect basis.
2. Some manufacturing costs may be excluded from product costs.
3. Numerous overhead cost pools are used, each of which is allocated to products and other cost objects using its own unique measure of activity.

Each of these departures from traditional absorption costing will be discussed in turn.

Nonmanufacturing Costs and Activity-Based Costing

In traditional absorption costing, manufacturing costs are assigned to products, and nonmanufacturing costs are not assigned to products. Conversely, in activity-based costing, we recognize that many nonmanufacturing costs relate to selling, distributing, and servicing specific products. Thus, ABC includes manufacturing *and* nonmanufacturing costs when calculating the entire cost of a product rather than just its manufacturing cost.

There are two types of nonmanufacturing costs that ABC systems assign to products. First, ABC systems trace all direct nonmanufacturing costs to products. Commissions paid to salespersons, shipping costs, and warranty repair costs are examples of nonmanufacturing costs that can be directly traced to individual products. Second, ABC systems allocate indirect nonmanufacturing costs to products whenever the products have presumably caused the costs to be incurred. In fact, in this chapter, we emphasize this point by expanding the definition of *overhead* to include all indirect costs—manufacturing and nonmanufacturing.

In summary, ABC product cost calculations include all direct costs that can be traced to products and all indirect costs that are caused by products. The need to distinguish between manufacturing and nonmanufacturing costs disappears—which is very different from earlier chapters that focused solely on determining the manufacturing cost of a product.

Manufacturing Costs and Activity-Based Costing

In traditional absorption costing systems, *all* manufacturing costs are assigned to products—even manufacturing costs that are not caused by the products. For example, in Chapter 3, we learned that a predetermined plantwide overhead rate is computed by dividing *all* budgeted manufacturing overhead costs by the budgeted amount of the allocation base. So, in the case of a company that uses budgeted direct labor-hours as its allocation base, this approach will assign *all* of the company's manufacturing overhead costs to its products based on each product's direct labor-hour usage. In contrast, activity-based costing systems purposely do not assign two types of manufacturing overhead costs to products—*organization-sustaining costs* and *unused capacity costs* (also called idle capacity costs).

Organization-sustaining costs include costs such as the factory security guard's wages, the plant controller's salary, and the cost of supplies used by the plant manager's secretary. These types of manufacturing overhead costs are assigned to products in a traditional absorption costing system even though they are totally unaffected by which products are made during a period. In contrast, activity-based costing systems treat these types of organization-sustaining costs as period expenses rather than arbitrarily assigning them to products.

Additionally, in a traditional absorption costing system, the cost of unused capacity is assigned to products. If the budgeted level of activity declines, the overhead rate and unit product costs rise, thereby ensuring that the shrinking volume of output absorbs the increasing cost of idle capacity. In contrast, in activity-based costing, products are charged only for the cost of the capacity they use—not for the cost of the capacity they don't use. This provides more stable unit product costs and is consistent with the goal of assigning to products only the costs of the resources that they use.[1]

Exhibit 5–1 summarizes the two departures from traditional absorption costing that we have discussed thus far. The top portion of the exhibit shows that traditional absorption costing treats all manufacturing costs as product costs and all nonmanufacturing costs as period costs. The bottom portion of the exhibit shows that activity-based costing expands the definition of *overhead* to include all indirect costs—manufacturing and nonmanufacturing. The overhead costs caused by products are allocated to them, whereas any overhead costs not caused by products are treated as period costs. It also shows that ABC treats direct nonmanufacturing costs as product costs rather than period costs.

Now we turn our attention to the third and final difference between traditional absorption costing and activity-based costing.

Cost Pools, Allocation Bases, and Activity-Based Costing

Throughout the 19th century and most of the 20th century, cost system designs were simple and satisfactory. Typically, either one plantwide overhead cost pool or a number of departmental overhead cost pools were used to assign overhead costs to products. The plantwide and departmental approaches always had one thing in common—they relied on allocation bases such as direct labor-hours and machine-hours for allocating overhead costs to products. In the labor-intensive production processes of many years ago, direct labor was the most common choice for an overhead allocation base because it represented a large component of product costs, direct labor-hours were closely tracked, and many managers believed that direct labor-hours, the total volume of units produced, and overhead costs were highly correlated. (Three variables, such as direct labor-hours, the total volume of units produced, and overhead costs, are highly correlated if they tend to move together.) Given that most companies at the time were producing a very limited variety of

---

[1] Appendix 3B discusses how the cost of unused capacity can be accounted for as a period cost in an income statement. This treatment highlights the cost of unused capacity rather than burying it in inventory and cost of goods sold. The procedures laid out in this chapter for activity-based costing have the same end effect.

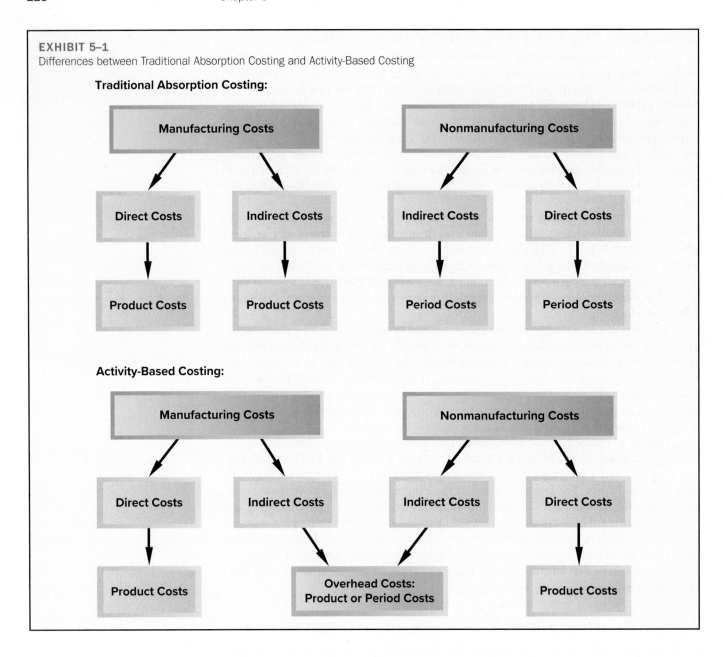

EXHIBIT 5–1
Differences between Traditional Absorption Costing and Activity-Based Costing

products that required similar resources to produce, allocation bases such as direct labor-hours, or even machine-hours, worked fine because, in fact, there was probably little difference in the overhead costs attributable to different products.

Then conditions began to change. As a percentage of total cost, direct labor began declining, and overhead began increasing. Many tasks previously done by direct laborers were being performed by automated equipment—a component of overhead. Companies began creating new products and services at an ever-accelerating rate that differed in volume, batch size, and complexity. Managing and sustaining this product diversity required investing in many more overhead resources, such as production schedulers and product design engineers, that had no obvious connection to direct labor-hours or machine-hours. In this new environment, continuing to rely exclusively on a limited number of overhead cost pools and traditional allocation bases posed the risk that reported unit product costs would be distorted and, therefore, misleading when used for decision-making purposes.

Activity-based costing, thanks to advances in technology that make more complex cost systems feasible, provides an alternative to the traditional plantwide and departmental approaches to defining cost pools and selecting allocation bases. The activity-based approach has appeal in today's business environment because it uses more cost pools and unique measures of activity to better understand the costs of managing and sustaining product diversity.

In activity-based costing, an **activity** is any event that causes the consumption of overhead resources. An **activity cost pool** is a "bucket" in which costs are accumulated that relate to a single activity measure in the ABC system. An **activity measure** is an allocation base in an activity-based costing system. The term *cost driver* is also used to refer to an activity measure because the activity measure should "drive" the cost being allocated. The two most common types of activity measures are *transaction drivers* and *duration drivers*. **Transaction drivers** are simple counts of the number of times an activity occurs, such as the number of bills sent out to customers. **Duration drivers** measure the amount of time required to perform an activity, such as the time spent preparing individual bills for customers. In general, duration drivers are more accurate measures of resource consumption than transaction drivers, but they take more effort to record. For that reason, transaction drivers are often used in practice.

Traditional cost systems rely exclusively on allocation bases that are driven by the volume of production. On the other hand, activity-based costing defines five levels of activity—unit-level, batch-level, product-level, customer-level, and organization-sustaining—that largely do *not* relate to the volume of units produced. The costs and corresponding activity measures for unit-level activities do relate to the volume of units produced; however, the remaining categories do not. These levels are described as follows:[2]

1. **Unit-level activities** are performed each time a unit is produced. The costs of unit-level activities should be proportional to the number of units produced. For example, providing power to run processing equipment would be a unit-level activity because power tends to be consumed in proportion to the number of units produced.

2. **Batch-level activities** are performed each time a batch is handled or processed, regardless of how many units are in the batch. For example, tasks such as placing purchase orders, setting up equipment, and arranging for shipments to customers are batch-level activities. They are incurred once for each batch (or customer order). Costs at the batch level depend on the number of batches processed rather than on the number of units produced, the number of units sold, or other measures of volume. For example, the cost of setting up a machine for batch processing is the same regardless of whether the batch contains one item or thousands of items.

3. **Product-level activities** relate to specific products and typically must be carried out regardless of how many batches are run or units of product are produced or sold. For example, designing a product, advertising a product, and maintaining a product manager and staff are all product-level activities.

4. **Customer-level activities** relate to specific customers and include activities such as sales calls, catalog mailings, and general technical support that are not tied to any specific product.

5. **Organization-sustaining activities** are carried out regardless of which customers are served, which products are produced, how many batches are run, or how many units are made. This category includes activities such as heating the factory, cleaning executive offices, providing a computer network, arranging for loans, preparing annual reports to shareholders, and so on.

Many companies throughout the world continue to base overhead allocations on direct labor-hours or machine-hours. In situations where overhead costs and direct labor-hours are highly correlated or in situations where the goal of the overhead allocation process is to prepare external financial reports, this practice makes sense. However, if plantwide overhead costs do not move in tandem with plantwide direct labor-hours or machine-hours, product costs will be distorted—with the potential of distorting decisions made within the company.

---

[2] Robin Cooper, "Cost Classification in Unit-Based and Activity-Based Manufacturing Cost Systems," *Journal of Cost Management,* Fall 1990, pp. 4–14.

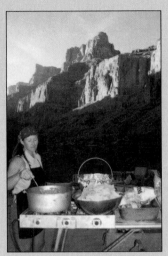

Sandee Noreen

DINING IN THE CANYON

Western River Expeditions (www.westernriver.com) runs river rafting trips on the Colorado, Green, and Salmon rivers. One of its most popular trips is a six-day trip down the Grand Canyon, which features famous rapids such as Crystal and Lava Falls, as well as the awesome scenery accessible only from the bottom of the Grand Canyon. The company runs trips of one or two rafts, each of which carries two guides and up to 18 guests. The company provides all meals on the trip, which are prepared by the guides.

In terms of the hierarchy of activities, a guest can be considered as a unit and a raft as a batch. In that context, the wages paid to the guides are a batch-level cost because each raft requires two guides regardless of the number of guests in the raft. Each guest is given a mug to use during the trip and to take home at the end of the trip as a souvenir. The cost of the mug is a unit-level cost because the number of mugs given away is strictly proportional to the number of guests on a trip.

What about the costs of food served to guests and guides—is this a unit-level cost, a batch-level cost, a product-level cost, or an organization-sustaining cost? At first glance, it might be thought that food costs are a unit-level cost—the greater the number of guests, the higher the food costs. However, that is not quite correct. Standard menus have been created for each day of the trip. For example, the first night's menu might consist of shrimp cocktail, steak, cornbread, salad, and cheesecake. The day before a trip begins, all of the food needed for the trip is taken from the central warehouse and packed in modular containers. It isn't practical to finely adjust the amount of food for the actual number of guests planned to be on a trip—most of the food comes prepackaged in large lots. For example, the shrimp cocktail menu may call for two large bags of frozen shrimp per raft, and that many bags will be packed regardless of how many guests are expected on the raft. Consequently, the costs of food are not a unit-level cost that varies with the number of guests actually on a trip. Instead, the costs of food are a batch-level cost.

Designing an Activity-Based Costing (ABC) System

There are three essential characteristics of a successful activity-based costing implementation. First, top managers must strongly support the ABC implementation because their leadership is instrumental in properly motivating all employees to embrace the need to change. Second, top managers should ensure ABC data are linked to how people are evaluated and rewarded. If employees continue to be evaluated and rewarded using traditional (non-ABC) cost data, they will quickly get the message that ABC is not important, and they will abandon it. Third, a cross-functional team should be created to design and implement the ABC system. The team should include representatives from each area that will use ABC data, such as the marketing, production, engineering, and accounting departments. These cross-functional employees possess intimate knowledge of many parts of an organization's operations that is necessary for designing an effective ABC system. Furthermore, tapping the knowledge of cross-functional managers lessens their resistance to ABC because they feel included in the implementation process. Time after time, when accountants have attempted to implement an ABC system on their own without top-management support and cross-functional involvement, the results have been ignored.

Classic Brass, Inc., makes two main product lines for luxury yachts—standard stanchions and custom compass housings. The president of the company, John Towers, recently attended a management conference at which activity-based costing was discussed. Following the conference, he called a meeting of the company's top managers to discuss what he learned. Attending the meeting were production manager Susan Richter, the marketing manager Tom Olafson, and the accounting manager Mary Goodman. He began the conference by distributing the company's income statement that Mary Goodman had prepared a few hours earlier (see Exhibit 5–2):

EXHIBIT 5–2
Classic Brass Income Statement

Classic Brass
Income Statement
For the Year Ended December 31

Sales		$3,200,000
Cost of goods sold:		
Direct materials	$ 975,000	
Direct labor.	351,250	
Manufacturing overhead*	1,000,000	2,326,250
Gross margin		873,750
Selling and administrative expenses:		
Shipping expense	$ 65,000	
General administrative expense.	510,000	
Marketing expense	300,000	875,000
Net operating loss.		$ (1,250)

*The company's traditional cost system allocates manufacturing overhead to products using a plantwide overhead rate and machine-hours as the allocation base. Inventory levels did not change during the year.

John: Well, it's official. Our company has sunk into the red for the first time in its history—a loss of $1,250.

Tom: I don't know what else we can do! Given our successful efforts to grow sales of the custom compass housings, I was expecting to see a boost to our bottom line, not a net loss. Granted, we have been losing even more bids than usual for standard stanchions because of our recent price increase, but . . .

John: Do you think our prices for standard stanchions are too high?

Tom: No, I don't think our prices are too high. I think our competitors' prices are too low. In fact, I'll bet they are pricing below their cost.

Susan: Why would our competitors price below their cost?

Tom: They are out to grab market share.

Susan: What good is more market share if they are losing money on every unit sold?

John: I think Susan has a point. Mary, what is your take on this?

Mary: If our competitors are pricing standard stanchions below cost, shouldn't they be losing money rather than us? If our company is the one using accurate information to make informed decisions while our competitors are supposedly clueless, then why is our "bottom line" taking a beating? Unfortunately, I think we may be the ones relying on distorted cost data, not our competitors.

John: Based on what I heard at the conference that I just attended, I am inclined to agree. One of the presentations at the conference dealt with activity-based costing. As the speaker began describing the usual insights revealed by activity-based costing systems, I was sitting in the audience getting an ill feeling in my stomach.

Mary: Honestly, John, I have been claiming for years that our existing cost system is okay for external reporting, but it is dangerous to use it for internal decision making. It sounds like you are on board now, right?

John: Yes.

Mary: Well then, how about if all of you commit the time and energy to help me build a fairly simple activity-based costing system that may shed some light on the problems we are facing?

John: Let's do it. I want each of you to appoint one of your top people to a special "ABC team" to investigate how we cost products.

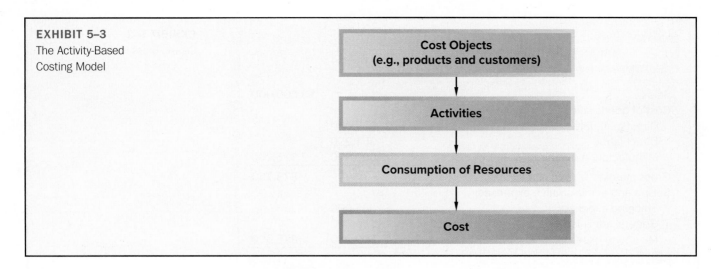

EXHIBIT 5–3
The Activity-Based
Costing Model

Like most other ABC implementations, the ABC team decided that its new ABC system would supplement, rather than replace, the existing cost accounting system, which would continue to be used to prepare financial statements for external parties. The new ABC system would be used to prepare special reports for management decisions such as bidding on new business.

The accounting manager drew the chart appearing in Exhibit 5–3 to explain the general structure of the ABC model to her team members. Cost objects such as products generate activities. For example, a customer order for a custom compass housing requires the activity of preparing a production order. Such an activity consumes resources. A production order uses a sheet of paper and takes time to fill out. And consumption of resources causes costs. The greater the number of sheets used to fill out production orders and the greater the amount of time devoted to filling out such orders, the greater the cost. Activity-based costing attempts to trace through these relationships to identify how products and customers affect costs.

As in most other companies, the ABC team at Classic Brass felt that the company's traditional cost accounting system adequately measured the direct materials and direct labor costs of products because these costs are directly traced to products. Therefore, the ABC study would be concerned solely with the other costs of the company—manufacturing overhead and selling and administrative costs.

Steps for Implementing Activity-Based Costing

The team felt it was important to carefully plan how it would go about implementing the new ABC system at Classic Brass. Accordingly, it broke down the implementation process into five steps:

1. Define activities, activity cost pools, and activity measures.
2. Assign overhead costs to activity cost pools.
3. Calculate activity rates.
4. Assign overhead costs to cost objects.
5. Prepare management reports.

Step 1: Define Activities, Activity Cost Pools, and Activity Measures

The first major step in implementing an ABC system is to identify the activities that will form the foundation for the system. This can be difficult and time-consuming and involves a great deal of judgment. A common procedure is for the individuals on the

ABC implementation team to interview people who work in overhead departments and ask them to describe their major activities. Ordinarily, this results in a very long list of activities.

The length of such lists of activities poses a problem. On the one hand, the greater the number of activities tracked in the ABC system, the more accurate the costs are likely to be. On the other hand, a complex system involving large numbers of activities is costly to design, implement, maintain, and use. Consequently, the original lengthy list of activities is usually reduced to a handful by combining similar activities. For example, several actions may be involved in handling and moving raw materials—from receiving raw materials on the loading dock to sorting them into the appropriate bins in the storeroom. All of these activities might be combined into a single activity called material handling.

When combining activities in an ABC system, activities should be grouped together at the appropriate level. Batch-level activities should not be combined with unit-level activities, or product-level activities with batch-level activities, and so on. In general, it is best to combine only those activities that are highly correlated with each other within a level. For example, the number of customer orders received is likely to be highly correlated with the number of completed customer orders shipped, so these two batch-level activities (receiving and shipping orders) can usually be combined with little loss of accuracy.

At Classic Brass, the ABC team, in consultation with top managers, selected the following *activity cost pools* and *activity measures:*

Activity Cost Pools at Classic Brass

Activity Cost Pool	Activity Measure
Customer orders	Number of customer orders
Product design	Number of product designs
Order size.	Machine-hours
Customer relations	Number of active customers
Other.	Not applicable

The *Customer Orders* cost pool will be assigned all costs of resources consumed by taking and processing customer orders, including costs of processing paperwork and any costs involved in setting up machines for specific orders. The activity measure for this cost pool is the number of customer orders received. This is a batch-level activity because each order generates work that occurs regardless of whether the order is for one unit or 1,000 units.

The *Product Design* cost pool will be assigned all costs of resources consumed by designing products. The activity measure for this cost pool is the number of product designs. This is a product-level activity because the amount of design work on a new product does not depend on the number of units ultimately ordered or batches ultimately run.

The *Order Size* cost pool will be assigned all costs of resources consumed as a consequence of the number of units produced, including the costs of miscellaneous factory supplies, power to run machines, and some equipment depreciation. This is a unit-level activity because each unit requires some of these resources. The activity measure for this cost pool is machine-hours.

The *Customer Relations* cost pool will be assigned all costs associated with maintaining relations with customers, including the costs of sales calls and the costs of entertaining customers. The activity measure for this cost pool is the number of customers the company has on its active customer list. The Customer Relations cost pool represents a customer-level activity.

The *Other* cost pool will be assigned all overhead costs that are not associated with customer orders, product design, the size of the orders, or customer relations. These costs mainly consist of organization-sustaining costs and the costs of unused, idle capacity. These costs *will not* be assigned to products because they represent resources that are *not* consumed by products.

It is unlikely any other company would use exactly the same activity cost pools and activity measures selected by Classic Brass. Because of the amount of judgment involved, the number and definitions of the activity cost pools and activity measures used by companies vary considerably.

The Mechanics of Activity-Based Costing

LEARNING OBJECTIVE 5–2
Assign costs to cost pools using a first-stage allocation.

Step 2: Assign Overhead Costs to Activity Cost Pools

Exhibit 5–4 shows the annual overhead costs (both manufacturing and nonmanufacturing) that Classic Brass intends to assign to its activity cost pools. Notice the data in the exhibit are organized by department (e.g., Production, General Administrative, and Marketing). This is because the data have been extracted from the company's general ledger. General ledgers usually classify costs within the departments where the costs are incurred. For example, salaries, supplies, rent, and so forth incurred in the marketing department are charged to that department. The functional orientation of the general ledger mirrors the presentation of costs in the absorption income statement in Exhibit 5–2. In fact, you'll notice the total costs for the Production Department in Exhibit 5–4 ($1,000,000) equal the total manufacturing overhead costs from the income statement in Exhibit 5–2. Similarly, the total costs for the General Administrative and Marketing Departments in Exhibit 5–4 ($510,000 and $300,000) equal the marketing and general and administrative expenses shown in Exhibit 5–2.

Three costs included in the income statement in Exhibit 5–2—direct materials, direct labor, and shipping expenses—are excluded from the costs shown in Exhibit 5–4. The ABC team purposely excluded these costs from Exhibit 5–4 because the existing cost system can accurately trace direct materials, direct labor, and shipping costs to products. There is no need to incorporate these direct costs in the activity-based allocations of indirect costs.

Classic Brass's activity-based costing system will divide the nine types of overhead costs in Exhibit 5–4 among its five aforementioned activity cost pools via an allocation process called *first-stage allocation.* The **first-stage allocation** in an ABC system is the

Production Department:		
Indirect factory wages	$500,000	
Factory equipment depreciation	300,000	
Factory utilities................................	120,000	
Factory building lease	80,000	$1,000,000
General Administrative Department:		
Administrative wages and salaries.............	400,000	
Office equipment depreciation................	50,000	
Administrative building lease	60,000	510,000
Marketing Department:		
Marketing wages and salaries	250,000	
Selling expenses............................	50,000	300,000
Total overhead cost		$1,810,000

EXHIBIT 5–4
Annual Overhead Costs (Both Manufacturing and Nonmanufacturing) at Classic Brass

process of assigning functionally organized overhead costs derived from a company's general ledger to the activity cost pools.

First-stage allocations are usually based on the results of interviews with employees who have first-hand knowledge of the activities. For example, Classic Brass needs to allocate $500,000 of indirect factory wages to its five activity cost pools. These allocations will be more accurate if the employees who are classified as indirect factory workers (e.g., supervisors, engineers, and quality inspectors) are asked to estimate what percentage of their time is spent dealing with customer orders, product design, processing units of product (i.e., order size), and customer relations. These interviews are conducted with considerable care. Those interviewed must thoroughly understand what the activities encompass and what is expected of them in the interview. In addition, departmental managers are typically interviewed to determine how the nonpersonnel costs should be distributed across the activity cost pools. For example, the Classic Brass production manager would be interviewed to determine how the $300,000 of factory equipment depreciation (shown in Exhibit 5–4) should be allocated to the activity cost pools. The key question that the production manager would need to answer is, "What percentage of the available machine capacity is consumed by each activity, such as the number of customer orders or the number of units processed (i.e., size of orders)?"

The results of the interviews at Classic Brass are displayed in Exhibit 5–5. For example, factory equipment depreciation is distributed 20 percent to Customer Orders, 60 percent to Order Size, and 20 percent to the Other cost pool. The resource in this instance is machine time. According to the estimates made by the production manager, 60 percent of the total available machine time was used to actually process units to fill orders. This percentage is entered in the Order Size column. Each customer order requires setting up, which also requires machine time. This activity consumes 20 percent of the total available machine time and is entered under the Customer Orders column. The remaining 20 percent of available machine time represents idle time and is entered under the Other column.

Exhibit 5–5 and many of the other exhibits in this chapter are presented in the form of Excel spreadsheets. All of the calculations required in activity-based costing can be done by hand. Nevertheless, setting up an activity-based costing system on a spreadsheet or using special ABC software can save a lot of work—particularly in situations involving many activity cost pools and in organizations that periodically update their ABC systems.

We will not go into the details of how all of the percentages in Exhibit 5–5 were determined. However, note that 100 percent of the factory building lease has been assigned to the Other cost pool. Classic Brass has a single production facility. It has

EXHIBIT 5–5

Results of Interviews: Distribution of Resource Consumption across Activity Cost Pools

	A	B	C	D	E	F	G	H
1				Activity Cost Pools				
2		Customer Orders	Product Design	Order Size	Customer Relations	Other	Totals	
4	Production Department:							
5	Indirect factory wages	25%	40%	20%	10%	5%	100%	
6	Factory equipment depreciation	20%	0%	60%	0%	20%	100%	
7	Factory utilities	0%	10%	50%	0%	40%	100%	
8	Factory building lease	0%	0%	0%	0%	100%	100%	
10	General Administrative Department:							
11	Administrative wages and salaries	15%	5%	10%	30%	40%	100%	
12	Office equipment depreciation	30%	0%	0%	25%	45%	100%	
13	Administrative building lease	0%	0%	0%	0%	100%	100%	
15	Marketing Department:							
16	Marketing wages and salaries	22%	8%	0%	60%	10%	100%	
17	Selling expenses	10%	0%	0%	70%	20%	100%	
18								

Exhibit 5-5 / Exhibit 5-6 / Exhibit 5-7 / Exhibit 5-9 / Exhibit 5-10 / Exhibit 5-11 / Exhibit 5-11 (2)

Microsoft Excel

EXHIBIT 5–6

First-Stage Allocations to Activity Cost Pools

	A	B	C	D	E	F	G	H
1				Activity Cost Pools				
2		Customer Orders	Product Design	Order Size	Customer Relations	Other	Totals	
4	Production Department:							
5	Indirect factory wages	$ 125,000	$ 200,000	$ 100,000	$ 50,000	$ 25,000	$ 500,000	
6	Factory equipment depreciation	60,000	0	180,000	0	60,000	300,000	
7	Factory utilities	0	12,000	60,000	0	48,000	120,000	
8	Factory building lease	0	0	0	0	80,000	80,000	
10	General Administrative Department:							
11	Administrative wages and salaries	60,000	20,000	40,000	120,000	160,000	400,000	
12	Office equipment depreciation	15,000	0	0	12,500	22,500	50,000	
13	Administrative building lease	0	0	0	0	60,000	60,000	
15	Marketing Department:							
16	Marketing wages and salaries	55,000	20,000	0	150,000	25,000	250,000	
17	Selling expenses	5,000	0	0	35,000	10,000	50,000	
19	Total	$ 320,000	$ 252,000	$ 380,000	$ 367,500	$ 490,500	$ 1,810,000	

Exhibit 5-5 / Exhibit 5-6 / Exhibit 5-7 / Exhibit 5-9 / Exhibit 5-10 / Exhibit 5-11 / Exhibit 5-11 (2)

Exhibit 5–5 shows that Customer Orders consume 25% of the resources represented by the $500,000 of indirect factory wages.

25% × $500,000 = $125,000

Other entries in the table are computed in a similar fashion.

Microsoft Excel

no plans to expand or to sublease any excess space. The cost of this production facility is treated as an organization-sustaining cost because there is no way to avoid even a portion of this cost if a particular product or customer were to be dropped. (Remember that organization-sustaining costs are assigned to the Other cost pool and are not allocated to products.) In contrast, some companies have separate facilities for manufacturing specific products. The costs of these separate facilities could be directly traced to the specific products.

Once the percentage distributions in Exhibit 5–5 have been established, it is easy to allocate costs to the activity cost pools. The results of this first-stage allocation are displayed in Exhibit 5–6. Each cost is allocated across the activity cost pools by multiplying it by the percentages in Exhibit 5–5. For example, the indirect factory wages of $500,000 are multiplied by the 25 percent entry under Customer Orders in Exhibit 5–5 to arrive at the $125,000 entry under Customer Orders in Exhibit 5–6. Similarly, the indirect factory wages of $500,000 are multiplied by the 40 percent entry under Product Design in Exhibit 5–5 to arrive at the $200,000 entry under Product Design in Exhibit 5–6. All of the entries in Exhibit 5–6 are computed in this way.

Now that the first-stage allocations to the activity cost pools have been completed, the next step is to compute the activity rates.

Step 3: Calculate Activity Rates

The activity rates used for assigning overhead costs to products and customers are computed in Exhibit 5–7. The ABC team determined the total activity for each cost pool that would be required to produce the company's present product mix and to serve its present customers. These numbers are listed in column C of Exhibit 5–7. For example, the ABC team found that 400 new product designs are required each year to serve the company's present customers. The activity rates are computed by dividing the *total* cost for each activity by its *total* activity. For example, the $320,000 total annual cost for the Customer Orders cost pool (which was computed in Exhibit 5–6) is divided by the total of 1,000 customer orders per year to arrive at the activity rate of $320 per customer order. Similarly, the $252,000 *total* cost for the Product Design cost pool is divided by the *total* number of designs (i.e., 400 product designs) to determine the activity rate of $630 per design. Note that an activity rate is not computed for the Other category of costs. This is because the *Other* cost pool consists of organization-sustaining costs and unused capacity costs not allocated to products and customers.

The rates in Exhibit 5–7 indicate that *on average,* a customer order consumes resources that cost $320; a product design consumes resources that cost $630; a unit

LEARNING OBJECTIVE 5–3
Compute activity rates for cost pools.

EXHIBIT 5–7
Computation of Activity Rates

	A	B	C	D	E	F	G
		(a)	(b)		(a) ÷ (b)		
1	Activity Cost Pools	Total Cost*	Total Activity		Activity Rate		
2	Customer orders	$320,000	1,000	orders	$320	per order	
3	Product design	$252,000	400	designs	$630	per design	
4	Order size	$380,000	20,000	MHs	$19	per MH	
5	Customer relations	$367,500	250	customers	$1,470	per customer	
6	Other	$490,500	Not applicable		Not applicable		
7							
8	*From Exhibit 5-6.						
9							

Exhibit 5-5 / Exhibit 5-6 / **Exhibit 5-7** / Exhibit 5-9 / Exhibit 5-10 / Exhibit 5-11 / Exhibit

Microsoft Excel

EXHIBIT 5–8
The Activity-Based Costing Model at Classic Brass

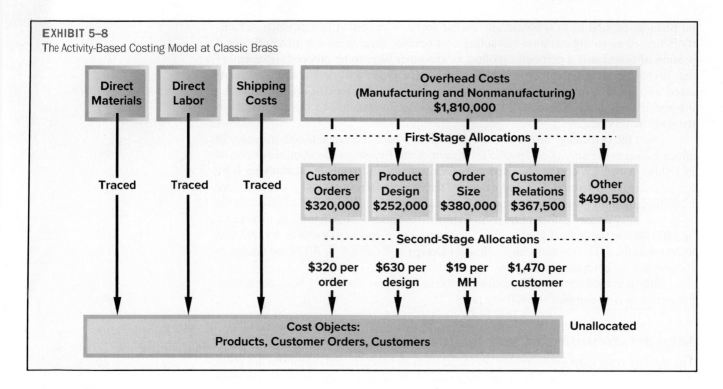

of product consumes resources that cost $19 per machine-hour; and maintaining relations with a customer consumes resources that cost $1,470. Note these are *average* figures. Some members of the ABC design team at Classic Brass argued it would be unfair to charge all new products the same $630 product design cost regardless of how much design time they actually require. After discussing the pros and cons, the team concluded it would not be worth the effort at the present time to keep track of actual design time spent on each new product. They felt the benefits of increased accuracy would not be great enough to justify the higher cost of implementing and maintaining the more detailed costing system. Similarly, some team members were uncomfortable assigning the same $1,470 cost to each customer. Some customers are undemanding—ordering standard products well in advance of their needs. Others are very demanding and consume large amounts of marketing and administrative staff time. These are generally customers who order customized products, tend to order at the last minute, and change their minds. While everyone agreed with this observation, the data required to measure individual customers' demands on resources were not currently available. Rather than delay implementation of the ABC system, the team decided to defer such refinements to a later date.

Before proceeding further, it would be helpful to get a better idea of the overall process of assigning costs to products and other cost objects in an ABC system. Exhibit 5–8 provides a visual perspective of the ABC system at Classic Brass. We recommend that you carefully go over this exhibit. In particular, note that the Other category, which contains organization-sustaining costs and unused capacity costs, is not allocated to products or customers.

Step 4: Assign Overhead Costs to Cost Objects

LEARNING OBJECTIVE 5–4
Assign costs to a cost object using a second-stage allocation.

The fourth step in the implementation of activity-based costing is called *second-stage allocation.* In the **second-stage allocation,** activity rates are used to apply overhead costs to products and customers. First, we illustrate how to assign costs to products, followed by an example of how to assign costs to customers.

The data needed by the ABC team to assign overhead costs to Classic Brass's two products—standard stanchions and custom compass housings—are as follows:

Standard Stanchions

1. This product line does not require any new product design resources.
2. 30,000 units were ordered during the year, comprising 600 separate orders.
3. Each stanchion requires 35 minutes of machine time for a total of 17,500 machine-hours.

Custom Compass Housings

1. This is a custom product that requires new product design resources.
2. There were 400 orders for custom compass housings. Orders for this product are placed separately from orders for standard stanchions.
3. There were 400 custom designs prepared. One custom design was prepared for each order.
4. Because some orders were for more than one unit, a total of 1,250 custom compass housings were produced during the year. A custom compass housing requires an average of 2 machine-hours for a total of 2,500 machine-hours.

Notice, 600 customer orders were placed for standard stanchions and 400 customer orders were placed for custom compass housings, for a total of 1,000 customer orders. All 400 product designs related to custom compass housings; none related to standard stanchions. Producing 30,000 standard stanchions required 17,500 machine-hours and producing 1,250 custom compass housings required 2,500 machine-hours, for a total of 20,000 machine-hours.

Exhibit 5–9 illustrates how overhead costs are assigned to the standard stanchions and custom compass housings. For example, the exhibit shows that $192,000 of overhead costs are assigned from the Customer Orders activity cost pool to the standard stanchions ($320 per order × 600 orders). Similarly, $128,000 of overhead costs are assigned from the Customer Orders activity cost pool to the custom compass housings ($320 per order × 400 orders). The Customer Orders cost pool contained a total of $320,000 (see Exhibit 5–6 or 5–7), and this total amount has been assigned to the two products ($192,000 + $128,000 = $320,000).

EXHIBIT 5–9
Assigning Overhead Costs to Customers

	A	B	C	D	E	F	G
1	**Overhead Cost for the Standard Stanchions**						
2	*Activity Cost Pools*	*(a)* *Activity Rate**		*(b)* *Activity*		*(a) × (b)* *ABC Cost*	
3	Customer orders	$320	per order	600	orders	$ 192,000	
4	Product design	$630	per design	0	designs	0	
5	Order size	$19	per MH	17,500	MHs	332,500	
6	Total					$ 524,500	
7							
8	**Overhead Cost for the Custom Compass Housing**						
9	*Activity Cost Pools*	*(a)* *Activity Rate**		*(b)* *Activity*		*(a) × (b)* *ABC Cost*	
10	Customer orders	$320	per order	400	orders	$ 128,000	
11	Product design	$630	per design	400	designs	252,000	
12	Order size	$19	per MH	2,500	MHs	47,500	
13	Total					$ 427,500	
14							
15	*From Exhibit 5-7.						
16							

Exhibit 5-5 Exhibit 5-6 Exhibit 5-7 Exhibit 5-9 Exhibit 5-10 Exhibit

Microsoft Excel

Exhibit 5–9 shows a total of $952,000 of overhead costs is assigned to Classic Brass's two product lines—$524,500 to standard stanchions and $427,500 to custom compass housings. This amount is less than the $1,810,000 of overhead costs included in the ABC system. Why? The total amount of overhead assigned to products does not match the total amount of overhead cost in the ABC system because the ABC team purposely did not assign the $367,500 of Customer Relations and $490,500 of Other costs to products. The Customer Relations activity is a customer-level activity, and the Other activity is an organization-sustaining activity—neither activity is caused by products. As shown below, when the Customer Relations and Other activity costs are added to the $952,000 of overhead costs assigned to products, the total is $1,810,000.

	Standard Stanchions	Custom Compass Housings	Total
Overhead Costs Assigned to Products			
Customer orders.........................	$192,000	$128,000	$ 320,000
Product design	0	252,000	252,000
Order size..............................	332,500	47,500	380,000
Subtotal (a).............................	$524,500	$427,500	952,000
Overhead Costs Not Assigned to Products			
Customer relations			367,500
Other....................................			490,500
Subtotal (b).............................			858,000
Total overhead cost (a) + (b)			$1,810,000

Next, we describe another example of second-stage allocation—assigning activity costs to customers. The data needed by Classic Brass to assign overhead costs to one of its customers—Windward Yachts—are as follows:

Windward Yachts

1. The company placed a total of three orders.
   a. Two orders were for 150 standard stanchions per order.
   b. One order was for a single custom compass housing unit.
2. A total of 177 machine-hours were used to fulfill the three customer orders.
   a. The 300 standard stanchions required 175 machine-hours.
   b. The custom compass housing required 2 machine-hours.
3. Windward Yachts is one of 250 customers served by Classic Brass.

Exhibit 5–10 illustrates how the ABC system assigns overhead costs to this customer. As shown in Exhibit 5–10, the ABC team calculated that $6,423 of overhead costs should be assigned to Windward Yachts. The exhibit shows that Windward Yachts is assigned $960 ($320 per order × 3 orders) of overhead costs from the Customer Orders activity cost pool; $630 ($630 per design × 1 design) from the Product Design cost pool; $3,363 ($19 per machine-hour × 177 machine-hours) from the Order Size cost pool; and $1,470 ($1,470 per customer × 1 customer) from the Customer Relations cost pool.

With second-stage allocations complete, the ABC design team was ready to turn its attention to creating reports that would help explain the company's first ever net operating loss.

EXHIBIT 5–10
Assigning Overhead Costs to Customers

	A	B	C	D	E	F
1	**Overhead Cost for Windward Yachts**					
2						
3	*Activity Cost Pools*	*(a)* *Activity Rate**		*(b)* *Activity*		*(a) × (b)* *ABC Cost*
4	Customer orders	$320	per order	3	orders	$ 960
5	Product design	$630	per design	1	designs	630
6	Order size	$19	per MH	177	MHs	3,363
7	Customer relations	$1,470	per customer	1	customer	1,470
8	Total overhead cost assigned to customer					$ 6,423
9						
10	*From Exhibit 5-7.					
11						

Exhibit 5-5 / Exhibit 5-6 / Exhibit 5-7 / Exhibit 5-9 / Exhibit 5-10 / Exhibit 5-11 / Exhibit 5-

Microsoft Excel

Step 5: *Prepare Management Reports*

The most common management reports prepared with ABC data are product and customer profitability reports. These reports help companies channel their resources to their most profitable growth opportunities while at the same time highlighting products and customers that drain profits. We begin by illustrating a product profitability report followed by a customer profitability report.

The Classic Brass ABC team realized that the profit from a product, also called the *product margin,* is a function of the product's sales and the direct and indirect costs that the product causes. The ABC cost allocations shown in Exhibit 5–9 only summarize each product's indirect (i.e., overhead) costs. Therefore, to compute a product's profit (i.e., product margin), the design team needed to gather each product's sales and direct costs in addition to the overhead costs previously computed. The pertinent sales and direct cost data for each product are shown below. Notice the numbers in the total column agree with the income statement in Exhibit 5–2.

LEARNING OBJECTIVE 5–5
Use activity-based costing to compute product and customer margins.

	Standard Stanchions	Custom Compass Housings	Total
Sales	$2,660,000	$540,000	$3,200,000
Direct costs:			
Direct materials	$905,500	$69,500	$975,000
Direct labor	$263,750	$87,500	$351,250
Shipping	$60,000	$5,000	$65,000

Having gathered the above data, the design team created the product profitability report shown in Exhibit 5–11. The report revealed that standard stanchions are profitable, with a positive product margin of $906,250, whereas the custom compass housings are unprofitable, with a negative product margin of $49,500. Keep in mind that the product profitability report purposely does not include the costs in the Customer Relations and Other activity cost pools. These costs, which total $858,000, were excluded from the report because they are not caused by the products. Customer Relations costs are caused by customers, not products. The Other costs are organization-sustaining costs and unused capacity costs that are not caused by any particular product.

EXHIBIT 5–11
Product Margins—Activity-Based Costing

	A	B	C	D	E	F	
1	**Product Margins—Activity-Based Costing**						
2		*Standard Stanchions*			*Custom Compass Housings*		
3	Sales		$ 2,660,000			$ 540,000	
4	Costs:						
5	Direct materials	$ 905,500			$ 69,500		
6	Direct labor	263,750			87,500		
7	Shipping	60,000			5,000		
8	Customer orders (from Exhibit 5-9)	192,000			128,000		
9	Product design (from Exhibit 5-9)	-			252,000		
10	Order size (from Exhibit 5-9)	332,500			47,500		
11	Total cost		1,753,750			589,500	
12	Product margin		$ 906,250			$ (49,500)	
13							

Exhibit 5-5 / Exhibit 5-6 / Exhibit 5-7 / Exhibit 5-9 / Exhibit 5-10 / Exhibit 5-11 / Exhib

Microsoft Excel

The product margins can be reconciled with the company's net operating loss as follows:

	Standard Stanchions	Custom Compass Housings	Total
Sales (See Exhibit 5–11)	$2,660,000	$540,000	$3,200,000
Total costs (See Exhibit 5–11).	1,753,750	589,500	2,343,250
Product margins (See Exhibit 5–11)	$ 906,250	$ (49,500)	856,750
Overhead costs not assigned to products:			
Customer relations			367,500
Other......................................			490,500
Total......................................			858,000
Net operating loss.......................			$ (1,250)

Next, the design team created a customer profitability report for Windward Yachts. Similar to the product profitability report, the design team needed to gather data concerning sales to Windward Yachts and the direct materials, direct labor, and shipping costs associated with those sales. Those data are presented below:

	Windward Yachts
Sales	$11,350
Direct costs:	
Direct materials...............	$2,123
Direct labor...................	$1,900
Shipping	$205

Using these data and the data from Exhibit 5–10, the design team created the customer profitability report shown in Exhibit 5–12. The report revealed the customer margin for Windward Yachts is $699. A similar report could be prepared for each of Classic Brass's 250 customers, thereby enabling the company to cultivate relationships with its most profitable customers, while taking steps to reduce the negative impact of unprofitable customers.

	A	B	C
1	**Customer Margin—Activity-Based Costing**		
2			*Windward Yachts*
3	Sales		$11,350
4	Costs:		
5	Direct materials	$ 2,123	
6	Direct labor	1,900	
7	Shipping	205	
8	Customer orders (from Exhibit 5-10)	960	
9	Product design (from Exhibit 5-10)	630	
10	Order size (from Exhibit 5-10)	3,363	
11	Customer relations (from Exhibit 5-10)	1,470	10,651
12	Customer margin		$ 699
13			

Exhibit 5-12 / Exhibit 5-13 / Exhibit 5-14 / Exhibit 5A-1 / Ex

Microsoft Excel

EXHIBIT 5–12
Customer Margin—Activity-Based Costing

USING ACTIVITY-BASED COSTING TO LOWER HEALTH-CARE COSTS

Researchers at Duke University, Harvard University, and Massachusetts General Hospital used activity-based costing to explore an interesting question: If hospital nurses call patients after they are discharged from the hospital, will it lower the hospital's overall operating cost? To answer this question, the researchers needed to compare the cost of performing the post-discharge phone calls to the savings realized from reducing the number of patients that return to the Emergency Department (ED).

The researchers took the process of conducting post-discharge phone calls and broke it into five activities: (1) reviewing the chart, (2) providing discharge instructions to the patient, (3) asking for and receiving patient feedback about their encounter, (4) helping patients with follow-up problems, and (5) documenting the encounter. They concluded that this five-step process costs $243.14 per avoided trip to the ED. However, given that the average cost per ED visit is $378.03, the phone calls produced a savings of $134.89 per avoided ED visit.

Source: Yingna Liu, Ines Luciani-McGillivray, Mary Fran Hughes, Ali S. Raja, Robert S. Kaplan, and Brian J. Yun, "Time-Driven Activity-Based Costing of Emergency Department Postdischarge Nurse Calls," *Journal of Healthcare Management*, November–December 2020, pp. 419–428.

Comparison of Traditional and ABC Product Costs

The ABC team used a two-step process to compare its traditional and ABC product costs. First, the team reviewed the product margins reported by the traditional cost system. Then, it contrasted the differences between the traditional and ABC product margins.

Product Margins Computed Using the Traditional Cost System

Classic Brass's traditional cost system assigns only manufacturing costs to products— this includes direct materials, direct labor, and manufacturing overhead. Selling and administrative costs are not assigned to products. Exhibit 5–13 shows the product margins reported by Classic Brass's traditional cost system. We will explain how these margins were calculated in three steps. First, the sales, direct materials, and direct labor cost data are the same numbers used by the ABC team to prepare Exhibit 5–11. In other

EXHIBIT 5-13

Product Margins—Traditional Cost System

	A	B	C	D	E	F	G	H	I
1	**Product Margins—Traditional Cost System**								
2		*Standard Stanchions*			*Custom Compass Housings*			*Total*	
3	Sales		$2,660,000			$ 540,000			$3,200,000
4	Cost of goods sold:								
5	Direct materials	$ 905,500			$ 69,500			$ 975,000	
6	Direct labor	263,750			87,500			351,250	
7	Manufacturing overhead	875,000	2,044,250		125,000	282,000		1,000,000	2,326,250
8	Product margin		$ 615,750			$ 258,000			873,750
9	Selling and administrative								875,000
10	Net operating loss								$ (1,250)
11									

⊞ ◄ ► ⊞ \ Exhibit 5-12 \ **Exhibit 5-13** \ Exhibit 5-14 \ Exhibit 5A-1 \ Exhibit 5A-2 \ Exhibit 5A-3A \ Exhibit 5A-3B \

Microsoft Excel

words, the traditional cost system and the ABC system treat these three pieces of revenue and cost data identically.

Second, the traditional cost system uses a plantwide overhead rate to assign manufacturing overhead costs to products. The numerator for the plantwide overhead rate is $1,000,000, which is the total amount of manufacturing overhead shown on the income statement in Exhibit 5–2. The footnote in Exhibit 5–2 mentions that the traditional cost system uses machine-hours to assign manufacturing overhead costs to products. The Order Size activity in Exhibit 5–7 used 20,000 machine-hours as its level of activity. These same 20,000 machine-hours would be used in the denominator of the plantwide overhead rate, which is computed as follows:

$$\text{Plantwide overhead rate} = \frac{\text{Total estimated manufacturing overhead}}{\text{Total estimated machine-hours}}$$

$$= \frac{\$1,000,000}{20,000\,\text{machine-hours}}$$

$$= \$50 \text{ per machine-hour}$$

Because 17,500 machine-hours were worked on standard stanchions, this product line is assigned $875,000 (17,500 machine-hours × $50 per machine-hour) of manufacturing overhead cost. Similarly, the custom compass housings required 2,500 machine-hours, so this product line is assigned $125,000 (2,500 machine-hours × $50 per machine-hour) of manufacturing overhead cost. The sales of each product minus its cost of goods sold equals the product margin of $615,750 for standard stanchions and $258,000 for custom compass housings.

Notice, the net operating loss of $1,250 shown in Exhibit 5–13 agrees with the loss reported in the income statement in Exhibit 5–2 and with the loss shown in the table beneath Exhibit 5–11. The company's *total* sales, *total* costs, and resulting net operating loss are the same regardless of whether you are looking at the absorption income statement in Exhibit 5–2, the ABC product profitability analysis, or the traditional product profitability analysis in Exhibit 5–13. Although the "total pie" remains constant across the traditional and ABC systems, what differs is how the pie is divided between the two product lines. The traditional product margin calculations suggest that standard stanchions are generating a product margin of $615,750 and the custom compass housings a product margin of $258,000. However, these product margins differ from the ABC product margins reported in Exhibit 5–11. Indeed, the traditional cost system is sending misleading signals to Classic Brass's managers about each product's profitability. Let's explain why.

The Differences between ABC and Traditional Product Costs

The changes in product margins caused by switching from the traditional cost system to the activity-based costing system are shown below:

	Standard Stanchions	Custom Compass Housings
Product margins—traditional..............	$ 615,750	$ 258,000
Product margins—ABC...................	906,250	(49,500)
Change in reported product margins	$ 290,500	$(307,500)

The traditional cost system overcosts the standard stanchions and consequently reports an artificially low product margin for this product. The switch to an activity-based view of product profitability increases the product margin on standard stanchions by $290,500. In contrast, the traditional cost system undercosts the custom compass housings and reports an artificially high product margin for this product. The switch to activity-based costing decreases the product margin on custom compass housings by $307,500.

The reasons for the change in reported product margins between the two costing methods are revealed in Exhibit 5–14. The top portion of the exhibit shows each product's direct and indirect cost assignments as reported by the traditional cost system in Exhibit 5–13. For example, Exhibit 5–14 includes the following costs for standard

EXHIBIT 5–14

A Comparison of Traditional and Activity-Based Cost Assignments

	A	B	C	D	E	F	G	H	I
1			Standard Stanchions			Custom Compass Housings			
2	**Traditional Cost System**		(a) Amount	(a) ÷ (c) %		(b) Amount	(b) ÷ (c) %		(c) Total
3	Direct materials		$ 905,500	92.9%		$ 69,500	7.1%		$ 975,000
4	Direct labor		263,750	75.1%		87,500	24.9%		351,250
5	Manufacturing overhead		875,000	87.5%		125,000	12.5%		1,000,000
6	Total cost assigned to products		$ 2,044,250			$ 282,000			2,326,250
7	Selling and administrative								875,000
8	Total cost								$ 3,201,250
9									
10	**Activity-Based Costing System**								
11	Direct costs:								
12	Direct materials		$ 905,500	92.9%		$ 69,500	7.1%		$ 975,000
13	Direct labor		263,750	75.1%		87,500	24.9%		351,250
14	Shipping		60,000	92.3%		5,000	7.7%		65,000
15	Indirect costs:								
16	Customer orders		192,000	60.0%		128,000	40.0%		320,000
17	Product design		-	0.0%		252,000	100.0%		252,000
18	Order size		332,500	87.5%		47,500	12.5%		380,000
19	Total cost assigned to products		$ 1,753,750			$ 589,500			2,343,250
20	Costs not assigned to products:								
21	Customer relations								367,500
22	Other								490,500
23	Total cost								$ 3,201,250
24									

Exhibit 5-12 / Exhibit 5-13 / Exhibit 5-14 / Exhibit 5A-1 / Exhibit 5A-2

Microsoft Excel

stanchions: direct materials, $905,500; direct labor, $263,750; and manufacturing overhead, $875,000. Each of these costs corresponds with those reported in Exhibit 5–13. Notice, the selling and administrative costs of $875,000 are purposely not allocated to products because these costs are considered period costs when using traditional costing. Similarly, the bottom portion of Exhibit 5–14 summarizes the direct and indirect cost assignments as reported by the activity-based costing system in Exhibit 5–11. The only new information in Exhibit 5–14 is shown in the two columns of percentages. The first column of percentages shows the percentage of each cost assigned to standard stanchions. For example, the $905,500 of direct materials cost traced to standard stanchions is 92.9 percent of the company's total direct materials cost of $975,000. The second column of percentages does the same thing for custom compass housings.

There are three reasons why the traditional and activity-based costing systems report different product margins. First, Classic Brass's traditional cost system allocates all manufacturing overhead costs to products. This forces both products to absorb all manufacturing overhead costs regardless of whether they actually consumed the costs allocated to them. The ABC system does not assign the manufacturing overhead costs consumed by the Customer Relations activity to products because these costs are caused by customers, not specific products. It also does not assign the manufacturing overhead costs included in the Other activity to products because these organization-sustaining and unused capacity costs are not caused by any particular product. From an ABC point of view, assigning these costs to products is inherently arbitrary and counterproductive.

Second, Classic Brass's traditional cost system allocates all of the manufacturing overhead costs using a volume-related allocation base—machine-hours—that may or may not reflect what actually causes the costs. In other words, in the traditional system, 87.5 percent of each manufacturing overhead cost is implicitly assigned to standard stanchions and 12.5 percent is assigned to custom compass housings. For example, the traditional cost system inappropriately assigns 87.5 percent of the costs of the Customer Orders activity (a batch-level activity) to standard stanchions even though the ABC system revealed that standard stanchions caused only 60 percent of these costs. Conversely, the traditional cost system assigns only 12.5 percent of these costs to custom compass housings even though this product caused 40 percent of these costs. Similarly, the traditional cost system assigns 87.5 percent of the costs of the Product Design activity (a product-level activity) to standard stanchions even though the standard stanchions caused none (0 percent) of these costs. All (100 percent) of the costs of the Product Design activity, rather than just 12.5 percent, should be assigned to custom compass housings. The result is that traditional cost systems overcost high-volume products (such as the standard stanchions) and undercost low-volume products (such as the custom compass housings) because they assign batch-level and product-level costs using volume-related allocation bases.

The third reason the product margins differ between the two cost systems is that the ABC system assigns the nonmanufacturing overhead costs caused by products to those products on a cause-and-effect basis. The traditional cost system disregards these costs because they are classified as period costs. The ABC system directly traces shipping costs to products and includes the nonmanufacturing overhead costs caused by products in the activity cost pools that are assigned to products.

MANAGERIAL ACCOUNTING IN ACTION

THE WRAP-UP

The ABC design team presented the results of its work in a meeting attended by all of the top managers of Classic Brass, including the president John Towers, the production manager Susan Richter, the marketing manager Tom Olafson, and the accounting manager Mary Goodman. The ABC team brought copies of the chart showing the ABC design (Exhibit 5–8) and the table comparing the traditional and ABC cost assignments (Exhibit 5–14). After the formal presentation by the ABC team, the following discussion took place:

John: I would like to personally thank the ABC team for all of the work they have done and for an extremely interesting presentation. I am now beginning to wonder about a lot of the decisions we have made in the past using our old cost accounting system. According to the ABC analysis, we had it all backwards. We are losing money on the custom products and making a fistful on the standard products.

Mary: I have to admit that I had no idea that the Product Design work for custom compass housings was so expensive! I knew burying these costs in our plantwide overhead rate was penalizing standard stanchions, but I didn't understand the magnitude of the problem.

Susan: I never did believe we were making a lot of money on the custom jobs. You ought to see all of the problems they create for us in production.

Tom: I hate to admit it, but the custom jobs always seem to give us headaches in marketing, too.

John: If we are losing money on custom compass housings, why not suggest to our customers that they go elsewhere for that kind of work?

Tom: Wait a minute, we would lose a lot of sales.

Susan: So what, we would save a lot more costs.

Mary: Maybe yes, maybe no. Some of the costs would not disappear if we were to drop the custom business.

Tom: Like what?

Mary: Well, Tom, I believe you said that about 10 percent of your time is spent dealing with new products. As a consequence, 10 percent of your salary was allocated to the Product Design cost pool. If we were to drop all of the products requiring design work, would you be willing to take a 10 percent pay cut?

Tom: I trust you're joking.

Mary: Do you see the problem? Just because 10 percent of your time is spent on custom products doesn't mean that the company would save 10 percent of your salary if the custom products were dropped. Before we take a drastic action like dropping the custom products, we should identify which costs are really relevant.

John: I think I see what you are driving at. We wouldn't want to drop a lot of products only to find that our costs really haven't changed much. It is true that dropping the products would free up resources like Tom's time, but we had better be sure we have some good use for those resources *before* we take such an action.

As this discussion among the managers of Classic Brass illustrates, caution should be exercised before taking action based on an ABC analysis such as the one shown in Exhibit 5–11 and Exhibit 5–12. The product and customer margins computed in these exhibits are a useful starting point for further analysis, but managers need to know what costs are really affected before taking any action, such as dropping a product or customer or changing the prices of products or services. For example, if an ABC system assigns some unavoidable fixed costs to products or customers, those costs should be ignored when making decisions with respect to those cost objects.

IN BUSINESS

MONKEY 47: AN ENTREPRENEUR'S DREAM COMES TRUE

Alexander Stein had been working for Nokia for 10 years when, at age 35, he decided to leave the company to start his own gin distillery. After more than 18 months and 120 test cycles, Stein finally settled on a recipe for his dry gin called Monkey 47. He chose to highlight the number 47 to emphasize the fact that his recipe contains 47 different botanicals, such as juniper and coriander, whereas most gins use only about 12 botanicals.

Rather than using standard stills that process 1,000 liters per batch, Stein uses stills with a capacity of only 100 liters per batch to make his gin, His preference for smaller batch sizes is consistent with his belief that "if you cook for 1,000 people, it won't be as good as cooking for four." This appreciation for handcrafted production may also explain why Monkey 47's employees process all ingredients, such as peeling fruit and prepping lavender, on-site.

Source: John Kell, "Next Gin," *Fortune,* February 1, 2017, p. 28.

Targeting Process Improvements

Activity-based costing can also be used to identify activities that would benefit from process improvements. When used in this way, activity-based costing is often called *activity-based management.* Basically, **activity-based management** involves focusing on activities to eliminate waste, decrease processing time, and reduce defects. Activity-based management is used in organizations as diverse as manufacturing companies, hospitals, and the U.S. Marine Corps.

The first step in any improvement program is to decide what to improve. The activity rates computed in activity-based costing can provide valuable clues concerning where there is waste and opportunity for improvement. For example, looking at the activity rates in Exhibit 5–7, managers at Classic Brass may conclude that $320 to process a customer order is far too expensive for an activity that adds no value to the product. As a consequence, they may target their process improvement efforts toward the Customer Orders activity.[3]

Benchmarking is another way to leverage the information in activity rates. **Benchmarking** is a systematic approach to identifying the activities with the greatest room for improvement. It is based on comparing the performance in an organization with the performance of other, similar organizations known for their outstanding performance. If a particular part of the organization performs far below the world-class standard, managers will be likely to target that area for improvement.

Activity-Based Costing and External Reports

Although activity-based costing generally provides more accurate product costs than traditional costing methods, it is infrequently used for external reports for a number of reasons. First, external reports are less detailed than internal reports prepared for decision making. On the external reports, individual product costs are not reported. Cost of goods sold and inventory valuations are disclosed, but they are not broken down by product. If some products are undercosted and some are overcosted, the errors tend to offset each other when the product costs are added together.

Second, it is often very difficult to make changes in a company's accounting system. The official cost accounting systems in most large companies are usually embedded in complex computer programs that have been modified in-house over the course of many years. It is extremely difficult to make changes in such computer programs without causing numerous bugs.

Third, an ABC system such as the one described in this chapter does not conform to generally accepted accounting principles (GAAP). As discussed in prior chapters, product costs computed for external reports must include all of the manufacturing costs and only manufacturing costs; but in an ABC system as described in this chapter, product costs exclude some manufacturing costs and include some nonmanufacturing costs. It is possible to adjust the ABC data at the end of the period to conform to GAAP, but that requires more work.

Fourth, auditors are likely to be uncomfortable with allocations based on interviews with the company's personnel. Such subjective data can be easily manipulated by management to make earnings and other key variables look more favorable.

For all of these reasons, most companies confine their ABC efforts to special studies for management, and they do not attempt to integrate activity-based costing into their formal cost accounting systems.

---

[3] Chapter 6 discusses another approach to improving processes and growing sales that focuses on effectively managing organizational constraints.

The Limitations of Activity-Based Costing

Implementing an activity-based costing system is a major project that requires substantial resources. And once implemented, an activity-based costing system is more costly to maintain than a traditional costing system—data concerning numerous activity measures must be periodically collected, checked, and entered into the system. The benefits of increased accuracy may not outweigh these costs.

Activity-based costing produces numbers, such as product margins, that are at odds with the numbers produced by traditional costing systems. But managers are accustomed to using traditional costing systems to run their operations, and traditional costing systems are often used in performance evaluations. Essentially, activity-based costing changes the rules of the game. It is a fact of human nature that changes in organizations, particularly those that alter the rules of the game, inevitably face resistance. This underscores the importance of top management support and the full participation of line managers, as well as the accounting staff, in any activity-based costing initiative. If activity-based costing is viewed as an accounting initiative that does not have the full support of top management, it is doomed to failure.

In practice, most managers insist on fully allocating all costs to products, customers, and other costing objects in an activity-based costing system—including the organization-sustaining costs and unused capacity costs. This results in overstated costs and understated margins and mistakes in pricing and other critical decisions.

Activity-based costing data can easily be misinterpreted and must be used with care when used in making decisions. Costs assigned to products, customers, and other cost objects are only *potentially* relevant. Before making any significant decisions using activity-based costing data, managers must identify which costs are really relevant for the decision at hand. For example, if an ABC system assigns some unavoidable fixed costs to cost objects, those costs should be ignored when making decisions.

As discussed in the previous section, reports generated by the best activity-based costing systems do not conform to external reporting requirements. Consequently, an organization involved in activity-based costing should have two cost systems—one for internal use and one for preparing external reports. This is costlier than maintaining just one system and may cause confusion about which system is to be believed and relied on.

Summary

Traditional cost accounting methods suffer from several limitations that can result in distorted costs for decision-making purposes. All manufacturing costs—even those not caused by any specific product—are allocated to products. Nonmanufacturing costs that are caused by products are not assigned to products. And finally, traditional methods tend to place too much reliance on unit-level allocation bases such as direct labor and machine-hours. This results in overcosting high-volume products and undercosting low-volume products and can lead to mistakes when making decisions.

Activity-based costing estimates the costs of the resources consumed by cost objects such as products and customers. The activity-based costing approach assumes that cost objects generate activities that in turn consume costly resources. Activities form the link between costs and cost objects. Activity-based costing is concerned with overhead—both manufacturing overhead and selling and administrative overhead. The accounting for direct labor and direct materials is usually the same under traditional and ABC costing methods.

To build an ABC system, companies typically choose a small set of activities that summarize much of the work performed in overhead departments. Associated with each activity is an activity cost pool. To the extent possible, overhead costs are directly traced to these activity cost pools. The remaining overhead costs are allocated to the activity cost pools in the first-stage allocation. Interviews with managers often form the basis for these allocations.

An activity rate is computed for each cost pool by dividing the costs assigned to the cost pool by the measure of activity for the cost pool. Activity rates provide useful information to managers concerning the costs of performing overhead activities. A particularly high cost for an activity may trigger efforts to improve the way the activity is carried out in the organization.

In the second-stage allocation, activity rates are used to apply costs to cost objects such as products and customers. The costs computed under activity-based costing are often quite different from the costs generated by a company's traditional cost accounting system. While the ABC system is almost certainly more accurate, managers should nevertheless exercise caution before making decisions based on the ABC data. Some of the costs may not be avoidable and hence would not be relevant.

 Data Analytics Exercise available in Connect to complement this chapter

Review Problem: Activity-Based Costing

Ferris Corporation makes a single product—a fire-resistant commercial filing cabinet—that it sells to office furniture distributors. The company has a simple ABC system that it uses for internal decision making. The company has two overhead departments whose costs are as follows:

Manufacturing overhead..........................	$500,000
Selling and administrative overhead...............	300,000
Total overhead costs	$800,000

The company's ABC system has the following activity cost pools and activity measures:

Activity Cost Pool	Activity Measure
Assembling units	Number of units
Processing orders..................	Number of orders
Supporting customers	Number of customers
Other.............................	Not applicable

Costs assigned to the "Other" activity cost pool have no activity measure; they consist of organization-sustaining costs and unused capacity costs—neither of which are assigned to orders, customers, or the product.

Ferris Corporation distributes the costs of manufacturing overhead and selling and administrative overhead to the activity cost pools based on employee interviews, the results of which are reported below:

	Assembling Units	Processing Orders	Supporting Customers	Other	Total
Manufacturing overhead	50%	35%	5%	10%	100%
Selling and administrative overhead....	10%	45%	25%	20%	100%
Total activity.......................	1,000 units	250 orders	100 customers		

Required:

1. Perform the first-stage allocation of overhead costs to the activity cost pools as in Exhibit 5–6.
2. Compute activity rates for the activity cost pools as in Exhibit 5–7.
3. OfficeMart is one of Ferris Corporation's customers. Last year, OfficeMart ordered filing cabinets four different times. OfficeMart ordered a total of 80 filing cabinets during the year. Construct a table as in Exhibit 5–10 showing the overhead costs attributable to OfficeMart.

4. The selling price of a filing cabinet is $595. The cost of direct materials is $180 per filing cabinet, and direct labor is $50 per filing cabinet. What is the customer margin of OfficeMart? See Exhibit 5–12 for an example of how to complete this report.

Solution to Review Problem

1. The first-stage allocation of costs to the activity cost pools appears below:

	Activity Cost Pools				
	Assembling Units	Processing Orders	Supporting Customers	Other	Total
Manufacturing overhead	$250,000	$175,000	$ 25,000	$ 50,000	$500,000
Selling and administrative overhead	30,000	135,000	75,000	60,000	300,000
Total cost.................	$280,000	$310,000	$100,000	$110,000	$800,000

2. The activity rates for the activity cost pools are:

Activity Cost Pools	(a) Total Cost	(b) Total Activity	(a) ÷ (b) Activity Rate
Assembling units...................	$280,000	1,000 units	$280 per unit
Processing orders.................	$310,000	250 orders	$1,240 per order
Supporting customers	$100,000	100 customers	$1,000 per customer

3. The overhead cost attributable to OfficeMart would be computed as follows:

Activity Cost Pools	(a) Activity Rate	(b) Activity	(a) × (b) ABC Cost
Assembling units......................	$280 per unit	80 units	$22,400
Processing orders.....................	$1,240 per order	4 orders	$4,960
Supporting customers	$1,000 per customer	1 customer	$1,000

4. The customer margin can be computed as follows:

Sales ($595 per unit × 80 units).....................		$47,600
Costs:		
Direct materials ($180 per unit × 80 units).........	$14,400	
Direct labor ($50 per unit × 80 units)	4,000	
Assembling units (above)........................	22,400	
Processing orders (above).......................	4,960	
Supporting customers (above)	1,000	46,760
Customer margin..............................		$ 840

Glossary

Activity An event that causes the consumption of overhead resources in an organization. (p. 229)

Activity-based costing (ABC) A costing method based on activities that is designed to provide managers with cost information for strategic and other decisions that potentially affect capacity and therefore fixed as well as variable costs. (p. 226)

Activity-based management (ABM) A management approach that focuses on managing activities as a way of eliminating waste and reducing delays and defects. (p. 248)

Activity cost pool A "bucket" in which costs are accumulated that relate to a single activity measure in an activity-based costing system. (p. 229)

Activity measure An allocation base in an activity-based costing system; ideally, a measure of the amount of activity that drives the costs in an activity cost pool. (p. 229)

Batch-level activities Activities that are performed each time a batch of goods is handled or processed, regardless of how many units are in the batch. The amount of resource consumed depends on the number of batches run rather than on the number of units in the batch. (p. 229)

Benchmarking A systematic approach to identifying the activities with the greatest potential for improvement. (p. 248)

Customer-level activities Activities that are carried out to support customers, but that are not related to any specific product. (p. 229)

Duration driver A measure of the amount of time required to perform an activity. (p. 229)

First-stage allocation The process by which overhead costs are assigned to activity cost pools in an activity-based costing system. (p. 234)

Organization-sustaining activities Activities that are carried out regardless of which customers are served, which products are produced, how many batches are run, or how many units are made. (p. 229)

Product-level activities Activities that relate to specific products that must be carried out regardless of how many units are produced and sold or batches run. (p. 229)

Second-stage allocation The process by which activity rates are used to apply costs to products and customers in activity-based costing. (p. 238)

Transaction driver A simple count of the number of times an activity occurs. (p. 229)

Unit-level activities Activities that are performed each time a unit is produced. (p. 229)

Questions

5–1   In what fundamental ways does activity-based costing differ from traditional costing methods such as job-order costing as described in Chapter 3?

5–2   Why is direct labor a poor base for allocating overhead in many companies?

5–3   Why are top management support and cross-functional involvement crucial when attempting to implement an activity-based costing system?

5–4   What are unit-level, batch-level, product-level, customer-level, and organization-sustaining activities?

5–5   What types of costs should not be assigned to products in an activity-based costing system?

5–6   What are the two stages of allocation in activity-based costing?

5–7   Why is the first stage of the allocation process in activity-based costing often based on interviews?

5–8   When activity-based costing is used, why do manufacturing overhead costs often shift from high-volume products to low-volume products?

5–9   How can the activity rates (i.e., cost per activity) for the various activities be used to target process improvements?

5–10   Why is the form of activity-based costing described in this chapter unacceptable for external financial reports?

Applying Excel   ☒ connect

LEARNING OBJECTIVES 5–1, 5–2, 5–3, 5–4, 5–5

The Excel worksheet form below is to be used to recreate the Review Problem pertaining to Ferris Corporation. The workbook, and instructions on how to complete the file, can be found in Connect. You should proceed to the requirements below only after completing your worksheet.

Required:

1.   Check your worksheet by doubling the units ordered in cell B16 to 160. The customer margin under activity-based costing should now be $7,640 and the traditional costing product margin should be $(21,600). If you do not get these results, find the errors in your worksheet and correct them.

   a.   Why has the customer margin under activity-based costing more than doubled when the number of units ordered is doubled?

   b.   Why has the traditional costing product margin exactly doubled from a loss of $10,800 to a loss of $21,600?

   c.   Which costing system, activity-based costing or traditional costing, provides a more accurate picture of what happens to profits as the number of units ordered increases? Explain.

	A	B	C	D	E	F	G
1	Chapter 5: Applying Excel						
2							
3	**Data**						
4	Manufacturing overhead	$500,000					
5	Selling and administrative overhead	$300,000					
6							
7		Assembling Units	Processing Orders	Supporting Customers	Other		
8	Manufacturing overhead	50%	35%	5%	10%		
9	Selling and administrative overhead	10%	45%	25%	20%		
10	Total activity	1,000	250	100			
11		units	orders	customers			
12							
13	OfficeMart orders:						
14	Customers	1	customer				
15	Orders	4	orders				
16	Number of filing cabinets ordered in total	80	units				
17	Selling price	$595					
18	Direct materials	$180					
19	Direct labor	$50					
20							
21	Enter a formula into each of the cells marked with a ? below						
22	**Review Problem: Activity-Based Costing**						
23							
24	**Perform the first stage allocations**						
25		Assembling Units	Processing Orders	Supporting Customers	Other	Total	
26	Manufacturing overhead	?	?	?	?	?	
27	Selling and administrative overhead	?	?	?	?	?	
28	Total cost	?	?	?	?	?	
29							
30	**Compute the activity rates**						
31	*Activity Cost Pools*	*Total Cost*	*Total Activity*		*Activity Rate*		
32	Assembling units	?	? units		? per unit		
33	Processing orders	?	? orders		? per order		
34	Supporting customers	?	? customers		? per customer		
35							
36	**Compute the overhead cost attributable to the OfficeMart orders**						
37	*Activity Cost Pools*		*Activity Rate*		*Activity*	*ABC Cost*	
38	Assembling units		? per unit		? units	?	
39	Processing orders		? per order		? orders	?	
40	Supporting customers		? per customer		? customer	?	
41							
42	**Determine the customer margin for the OfficeMart orders under Activity-Based Costing**						
43	Sales		?				
44	Costs:						
45	Direct materials	?					
46	Direct labor	?					
47	Unit-related overhead	?					
48	Order-related overhead	?					
49	Customer-related overhead	?	?				
50	Customer margin		?				
51							
52	**Determine the product margin for the OfficeMart orders under a traditional cost system**						
53	Manufacturing overhead	?					
54	Total activity	? units					
55	Manufacturing overhead per unit	? per unit					
56							
57	Sales		?				
58	Costs:						
59	Direct materials	?					
60	Direct labor	?					
61	Manufacturing overhead	?	?				
62	Traditional costing product margin		?				
63							

◄ ◄ ► ►►   **Chapter 5 Form** / Filled in Chapter 5 Form / Chapter 5 Formulas

Microsoft Excel

2. Let's assume OfficeMart places different orders next year, purchasing higher-end filing cabinets more frequently, but in smaller quantities per order. Enter the following data into your worksheet:

Data				
Manufacturing overhead	$500,000			
Selling and administrative overhead	$300,000			

	Assembling Units	Processing Orders	Supporting Customers	Other
Manufacturing overhead	50%	35%	5%	10%
Selling and administrative overhead	10%	45%	25%	20%
Total activity	1,000 units	250 orders	100 customers	

OfficeMart orders:	
Customers	1 customer
Orders	20 orders
Total number of filing cabinets ordered ...	80 units
Selling price	$795
Direct materials	$185
Direct labor	$90

   a. What is the customer margin under activity-based costing?
   b. What is the product margin under the traditional cost system?
   c. Explain why the profitability picture looks much different now than it did when OfficeMart was ordering less expensive filing cabinets less frequently, but in larger quantities per order.

3. Using the data you entered in part (2), change the percentage of selling and administrative overhead attributable to processing orders from 45% to 30% and the percentage attributable to supporting customers from 25% to 40%. That portion of the worksheet should look like this:

	Assembling Units	Processing Orders	Supporting Customers	Other
Manufacturing overhead	50%	35%	5%	10%
Selling and administrative overhead	10%	30%	40%	20%
Total activity	1,000 units	250 orders	100 customers	

   a. Relative to the results from part (2), what has happened to the customer margin under activity-based costing? Why?
   b. Relative to the results from part (2), what has happened to the product margin under the traditional cost system? Why?

The Foundational 15

LEARNING OBJECTIVES 5–1,
5–3, 5–4

Hickory Company manufactures two products—14,000 units of Product Y and 6,000 units of Product Z. The company uses a plantwide overhead rate based on direct labor-hours. It is considering implementing an activity-based costing (ABC) system that allocates all $684,000 of its manufacturing overhead to four cost pools. The following additional information is available for the company as a whole and for Products Y and Z:

Activity Cost Pool	Activity Measure	Estimated Overhead Cost	Expected Activity
Machining.....................	Machine-hours	$200,000	10,000 MHs
Machine setups................	Number of setups	$100,000	200 setups
Product design	Number of products	$84,000	2 products
General factory	Direct labor-hours	$300,000	12,000 DLHs

Activity Measure	Product Y	Product Z
Machine-hours....................	7,000	3,000
Number of setups.................	50	150
Number of products...............	1	1
Direct labor-hours.................	8,000	4,000

Required:

1. What is the company's plantwide overhead rate?
2. Using the plantwide overhead rate, how much manufacturing overhead cost is allocated to Product Y? How much is allocated to Product Z?
3. What is the activity rate for the Machining activity cost pool?
4. What is the activity rate for the Machine Setups activity cost pool?
5. What is the activity rate for the Product Design activity cost pool?
6. What is the activity rate for the General Factory activity cost pool?
7. Which of the four activities is a batch-level activity? Why?
8. Which of the four activities is a product-level activity? Why?
9. Using the ABC system, how much total manufacturing overhead cost would be assigned to Product Y?
10. Using the ABC system, how much total manufacturing overhead cost would be assigned to Product Z?
11. Using the plantwide overhead rate, what percentage of the total overhead cost is allocated to Product Y? What percentage is allocated to Product Z?
12. Using the ABC system, what percentage of the Machining costs is assigned to Product Y? What percentage is assigned to Product Z? Are these percentages similar to those obtained in requirement 11? Why?
13. Using the ABC system, what percentage of Machine Setups cost is assigned to Product Y? What percentage is assigned to Product Z? Are these percentages similar to those obtained in requirement 11? Why?
14. Using the ABC system, what percentage of the Product Design cost is assigned to Product Y? What percentage is assigned to Product Z? Are these percentages similar to those obtained in requirement 11? Why?
15. Using the ABC system, what percentage of the General Factory cost is assigned to Product Y? What percentage is assigned to Product Z? Are these percentages similar to those obtained in requirement 11? Why?

 connect Exercises

EXERCISE 5-1 ABC Cost Hierarchy LO 5-1

The following activities occur at Greenwich Corporation, a company that manufactures a variety of products.

a. Receive raw materials from suppliers.
b. Manage parts inventories.
c. Do rough milling work on products.
d. Interview and process new employees in the personnel department.
e. Design new products.
f. Perform periodic preventive maintenance on general-use equipment.
g. Use the general factory building.
h. Issue purchase orders for a job.

Required:

Classify each of the activities above as either a unit-level, batch-level, product-level, or organization-sustaining activity.

EXERCISE 5-2 First Stage Allocation LO 5-2

SecuriCorp operates a fleet of armored cars that make scheduled pickups and deliveries in the Los Angeles area. The company is implementing an activity-based costing system that has four activity cost pools: Travel, Pickup and Delivery, Customer Service, and Other. The activity measures are miles for the Travel cost pool, number of pickups and deliveries for the Pickup and Delivery cost pool, and number of customers for the Customer Service cost pool. The Other cost pool has no activity measure because it is an organization-sustaining activity. The following costs will be assigned using the activity-based costing system:

Driver and guard wages	$ 720,000
Vehicle operating expense	280,000
Vehicle depreciation	120,000
Customer representative salaries and expenses	160,000
Office expenses	30,000
Administrative expenses	320,000
Total cost	$1,630,000

The distribution of resource consumption across the activity cost pools is as follows:

	Travel	Pickup and Delivery	Customer Service	Other	Totals
Driver and guard wages	50%	35%	10%	5%	100%
Vehicle operating expense	70%	5%	0%	25%	100%
Vehicle depreciation	60%	15%	0%	25%	100%
Customer representative salaries and expenses	0%	0%	90%	10%	100%
Office expenses	0%	20%	30%	50%	100%
Administrative expenses	0%	5%	60%	35%	100%

Required:
Complete the first-stage allocations of costs to activity cost pools as illustrated in Exhibit 5–6.

EXERCISE 5–3 Compute Activity Rates LO 5–3

Green Thumb Gardening is a small gardening service that uses activity-based costing to estimate costs for pricing and other purposes. The proprietor of the company believes costs are driven primarily by the size of customer lawns, the size of customer garden beds, the distance to travel to customers, and the number of customers. In addition, the costs of maintaining garden beds depend on whether the beds are low-maintenance beds (mainly ordinary trees and shrubs) or high-maintenance beds (mainly flowers and exotic plants). Accordingly, the company uses the five activity cost pools listed below:

Activity Cost Pool	Activity Measure
Caring for lawn	Square feet of lawn
Caring for garden beds–low maintenance	Square feet of low-maintenance beds
Caring for garden beds–high maintenance	Square feet of high-maintenance beds
Travel to jobs	Miles
Customer billing and service	Number of customers

The company already has completed its first-stage allocations of costs and has summarized its annual costs and activity as follows:

Activity Cost Pool	Estimated Overhead Cost	Expected Activity
Caring for lawn	$72,000	150,000 square feet of lawn
Caring for garden beds–low maintenance	$26,400	20,000 square feet of low-maintenance beds
Caring for garden beds–high maintenance	$41,400	15,000 square feet of high-maintenance beds
Travel to jobs	$3,250	12,500 miles
Customer billing and service	$8,750	25 customers

Required:

Compute the activity rate for each of the activity cost pools.

EXERCISE 5–4 Second-Stage Allocation LO 5–4

Klumper Corporation is a diversified manufacturer of industrial goods. The company's activity-based costing system contains the following six activity cost pools and activity rates:

Activity Cost Pool	Activity Rates
Supporting direct labor	$6 per direct labor-hour
Machine processing	$4 per machine-hour
Machine setups.........................	$50 per setup
Production orders	$90 per order
Shipments..............................	$14 per shipment
Product sustaining	$840 per product

Activity data have been supplied for the following two products:

	Total Expected Activity	
	K425	M67
Number of units produced per year.............	200	2,000
Direct labor-hours	80	500
Machine-hours..............................	100	1,500
Machine setups.............................	1	4
Production orders	1	4
Shipments.................................	1	10
Product sustaining	1	1

Required:

How much total overhead cost would be assigned to K425 and M67 using the activity-based costing system?

EXERCISE 5–5 Product and Customer Profitability Analysis LO 5–4, LO 5–5

Thermal Rising, Inc., makes paragliders for sale through specialty sporting goods stores. The company has a standard paraglider model, but also makes custom-designed paragliders. Management designed an activity-based costing system with the following activity cost pools and activity rates:

Activity Cost Pool	Activity Rates
Supporting direct labor	$26 per direct labor-hour
Order processing	$284 per order
Custom design processing	$186 per custom design
Customer service	$379 per customer

Management would like an analysis of the profitability of a particular customer, Big Sky Outfitters, which ordered the following products over the last 12 months:

	Standard Model	Custom Design
Number of gliders..........................	20	3
Number of orders	1	3
Number of custom designs..................	0	3
Direct labor-hours per glider.................	26.35	28.00
Selling price per glider......................	$1,850	$2,400
Direct materials cost per glider..............	$564	$634

The company's direct labor rate is $19.50 per hour.

Required:

Using the company's activity-based costing system, compute the customer margin of Big Sky Outfitters.

EXERCISE 5–6 Cost Hierarchy LO 5–1

Flash Express purchases USB flash drives from suppliers and then applies corporate logos to the exterior of those flash drives for its customers. The company maintains a dedicated piece of equipment for each type of product that it processes, such as "top hat" flash drives, credit card flash drives, swing flash drives, and wristband flash drives. The company defines its batches based on customer orders. For example, if one customer places an order for 1,000 credit card flash drives, then that order would be processed as one batch, and it would be shipped as one batch. If another customer places an order for 100 "top hat" flash drives, 100 swing flash drives, and 100 wrist band flash drives, then that order would be processed as three batches and shipped as one batch.

A number of activities carried out at Flash Express are listed below.

a. Sales representatives' periodic visits to customers to keep them informed about the company's existing products and its new product introductions.
b. Engaging in price negotiations with the company's supplier of credit card flash drives.
c. Programming and calibrating the "top hat" logo application machine so it properly applies the logo for a specific customer's production run.
d. Visually inspecting each flash drive that has been produced to ensure the logo has been applied in a defect-free manner.
e. Preparing shipping documents and packaging for a customer order.
f. Periodic maintenance of the equipment used to process wristband flash drives.
g. Lighting and heating the company's production facility.
h. Preparation of the company's quarterly financial reports.

Required:

Classify each of the activities above as either a unit-level, batch-level, product-level, customer-level, or organization-sustaining activity.

EXERCISE 5–7 First-Stage Allocations LO 5–2

The operations vice president of Security Home Bank has been interested in investigating the efficiency of the bank's operations. She has been particularly concerned about the costs of handling routine transactions at the bank and would like to compare these costs at the bank's various branches. If the branches with the most efficient operations can be identified, their methods can be studied and then replicated elsewhere. While the bank maintains meticulous records of wages and other costs, there has been no attempt thus far to show how those costs are related to the various services provided by the bank. The operations vice president has asked for your help in conducting an activity-based costing study of bank operations. In particular, she would like to know the cost of opening an account, the cost of processing deposits and withdrawals, and the cost of processing other customer transactions.

The Westfield branch of Security Home Bank submitted the following cost data for last year:

Teller wages.....................................	$160,000
Assistant branch manager salary.................	75,000
Branch manager salary	80,000
Total..	$315,000

Virtually all other costs of the branch—rent, depreciation, utilities, and so on—are organization-sustaining costs that cannot be meaningfully assigned to individual customer transactions such as depositing checks.

In addition to the cost data above, the employees of the Westfield branch have been interviewed concerning how their time was distributed last year across the activities included in the activity-based costing study. The results of those interviews appear below:

	Opening Accounts	Processing Deposits and Withdrawals	Processing Other Customer Transactions	Other Activities	Total
Teller wages....................	5%	65%	20%	10%	100%
Assistant branch manager salary...	15%	5%	30%	50%	100%
Branch manager salary	5%	0%	10%	85%	100%

Required:

Prepare the first-stage allocation for the activity-based costing study. (See Exhibit 5–6 for an example of a first-stage allocation.)

EXERCISE 5–8 Computing and Interpreting Activity Rates LO 5–3

(This exercise is a continuation of Exercise 5–7; it should be assigned *only* if Exercise 5–7 also is assigned.) The manager of the Westfield branch of Security Home Bank provided the following data concerning the transactions of the branch during the past year:

Activity	Total Activity at the Westfield Branch
Opening accounts.........................	500 new accounts opened
Processing deposits and withdrawals........	100,000 deposits and withdrawals processed
Processing other customer transactions......	5,000 other customer transactions processed

The lowest costs reported by other branches for these activities are displayed below:

Activity	Lowest Cost among All Security Home Bank Branches
Opening accounts................................	$26.75 per new account
Processing deposits and withdrawals...............	$1.24 per deposit or withdrawal
Processing other customer transactions.............	$11.86 per other customer transaction

Required:

1. Using the first-stage allocation from Exercise 5–7 and the above data, compute the activity rates for the activity-based costing system. (Use Exhibit 5–7 as a guide.) Round all computations to the nearest whole cent.
2. What do these results suggest to you concerning operations at the Westfield branch?

EXERCISE 5–9 Second-Stage Allocation to an Order LO 5–4

Durban Metal Products, Ltd., of the Republic of South Africa makes specialty metal parts used in applications ranging from the cutting edges of bulldozer blades to replacement parts for Land Rovers. The company uses an activity-based costing system for internal decision-making purposes. The company has four activity cost pools as listed below:

Activity Cost Pool	Activity Measure	Activity Rate
Order size....................	Number of direct labor-hours	$16.85 per direct labor-hour
Customer orders..............	Number of customer orders	$320.00 per customer order
Product testing	Number of testing hours	$89.00 per testing hour
Selling......................	Number of sales calls	$1,090.00 per sales call

The managing director of the company would like information concerning the cost of a recently completed order for heavy-duty trailer axles. The order required 200 direct labor-hours, 4 hours of product testing, and 2 sales calls.

Required:

What is the total overhead cost assigned to the order for heavy-duty trailer axles?

EXERCISE 5–10 Customer Profitability Analysis LO 5–3, LO 5–4, LO 5–5

Worley Company buys surgical supplies from a variety of manufacturers and then resells and delivers these supplies to hundreds of hospitals. Worley sets its prices for all hospitals by marking up its cost of goods sold to those hospitals by 5%. For example, if a hospital buys supplies from Worley that cost Worley $100 to buy from manufacturers, Worley would charge the hospital $105 to purchase these supplies.

For years, Worley believed that the 5% markup covered its selling and administrative expenses and provided a reasonable profit. However, in the face of declining profits, Worley decided to implement an activity-based costing system to help improve its understanding of customer profitability. The company broke its selling and administrative expenses into five activities as shown:

Activity Cost Pool (Activity Measure)	Total Cost	Total Activity
Customer deliveries (Number of deliveries)...............	$ 500,000	5,000 deliveries
Manual order processing (Number of manual orders)	248,000	4,000 orders
Electronic order processing (Number of electronic orders)................................	200,000	12,500 orders
Line item picking (Number of line items picked)	450,000	450,000 line items
Other organization-sustaining costs (None)..............	602,000	
Total selling and administrative expenses	$2,000,000	

Worley gathered the data below for two of the many hospitals that it serves—University and Memorial (each hospital purchased medical supplies that had cost Worley $30,000 to buy from manufacturers):

	Activity	
Activity Measure	University	Memorial
Number of deliveries	10	25
Number of manual orders	0	30
Number of electronic orders................	15	0
Number of line items picked................	120	250

Required:
1. Compute the total revenue that Worley would receive from University and Memorial.
2. Compute the activity rate for each activity cost pool.
3. Compute the total activity costs that would be assigned to University and Memorial.
4. Compute Worley's customer margin for University and Memorial. (*Hint:* Do not overlook the $30,000 cost of goods sold that Worley incurred serving each hospital.)
5. Describe the purchasing behaviors that are likely to characterize Worley's least profitable customers.

EXERCISE 5–11 Second-Stage Allocation and Margin Calculations LO 5–4, LO 5–5
Foam Products, Inc., makes foam seat cushions for the automotive and aerospace industries. The company's activity-based costing system has four activity cost pools, which are listed below along with their activity measures and activity rates:

Activity Cost Pool	Activity Measure	Activity Rate
Supporting direct labor	Number of direct labor-hours	$5.55 per direct labor-hour
Batch processing.............	Number of batches	$107.00 per batch
Order processing	Number of orders	$275.00 per order
Customer service	Number of customers	$2,463.00 per customer

The company just completed a single order from Interstate Trucking for 1,000 custom seat cushions. The order was produced in two batches. Each seat cushion required 0.25 direct labor-hours. The selling price was $20 per unit, the direct materials cost was $8.50 per unit, and the direct labor cost was $6.00 per unit. This was Interstate Trucking's only order during the year.

Required:
Using Exhibit 5–12 as a guide, calculate the customer margin on sales to Interstate Trucking for the year.

EXERCISE 5–12 Activity Measures LO 5–1

Various activities at Ming Corporation, a manufacturing company, are listed below. Each activity has been classified as a unit-level, batch-level, product-level, or customer-level activity.

Activity	Level of Activity	Examples of Activity Measures
a. Direct labor workers assemble a product.............	Unit	
b. Products are designed by engineers.................	Product	
c. Equipment is set up................................	Batch	
d. Machines are used to shape and cut materials	Unit	
e. Monthly bills are sent out to regular customers........	Customer	
f. Materials are moved from the receiving dock to production lines....................................	Batch	
g. All completed units are inspected for defects	Unit	

Required:

Complete the table by providing an example of an activity measure for each activity.

EXERCISE 5–13 Computing ABC Product Costs LO 5–3, LO 5–4

Fogerty Company makes two products—titanium Hubs and Sprockets. Data regarding the two products follow:

	Direct Labor-Hours per Unit	Annual Production
Hubs	0.80	10,000 units
Sprockets	0.40	40,000 units

Additional information about the company follows:

a.   Hubs require $32 in direct materials per unit, and Sprockets require $18.

b.   The direct labor wage rate is $15 per hour.

c.   Hubs require special equipment and are more complex to manufacture than Sprockets.

d.   The ABC system has the following activity cost pools:

Activity Cost Pool (Activity Measure)	Estimated Overhead Cost	Activity Hubs	Sprockets	Total
Machine setups (number of setups).................	$72,000	100	300	400
Special processing (machine-hours)	$200,000	5,000	0	5,000
General factory (organization-sustaining)............	$816,000	NA	NA	NA

Required:

1.   Compute the activity rate for each activity cost pool. Did you compute an activity rate for all of the activity cost pools? Why?

2.   Determine the unit product cost of each product according to the ABC system.

EXERCISE 5–14 Calculating and Interpreting Activity-Based Costing Data LO 5–3, LO 5–4

Hiram's Lakeside is a popular restaurant located on Lake Washington in Seattle. The restaurant owner has been trying to better understand costs at the restaurant and hired a student intern to conduct an activity-based costing study. The intern, in consultation with the owner, identified three major activities and then completed the first-stage allocations of costs to the activity cost pools. The results appear below.

Activity Cost Pool	Activity Measure	Total Cost	Total Activity
Serving a party of diners	Number of parties served	$33,000	6,000 parties
Serving a diner....................	Number of diners served	$138,000	15,000 diners
Serving drinks	Number of drinks ordered	$24,000	10,000 drinks

The above costs include all of the costs of the restaurant except for organization-sustaining costs such as rent, property taxes, and top-management salaries.

Some costs, such as the cost of cleaning the linens that cover the restaurant's tables, vary with the number of parties served. Other costs, such as washing plates and glasses, depend on the number of diners served or the number of drinks served.

Prior to the activity-based costing study, the owner knew very little about the costs of the restaurant. She knew the total cost for the month (including organization-sustaining costs) was $240,000, and that 15,000 diners had been served. Therefore, the average cost per diner was $16.

Required:

1. According to the activity-based costing system, what is the total cost of serving each of the following parties of diners?
    a. A party of four diners who order three drinks in total.
    b. A party of two diners who do not order any drinks.
    c. A party of one diner who orders two drinks.
2. Convert the total costs you computed in (1) above to costs per diner. In other words, what is the average cost per diner for serving each of the following parties?
    a. A party of four diners who order three drinks in total.
    b. A party of two diners who do not order any drinks.
    c. A party of one diner who orders two drinks.
3. Why do the costs per diner for the three different parties differ from each other and from the overall average cost of $16 per diner?

EXERCISE 5–15 Comprehensive Activity-Based Costing Exercise LO 5–2, LO 5–3, LO 5–4, LO 5–5

Advanced Products Corporation has supplied the following data from its activity-based costing system:

Overhead Costs	
Wages and salaries......................	$300,000
Other overhead costs....................	100,000
Total overhead costs....................	$400,000

Activity Cost Pool	Activity Measure	Total Activity for the Year
Supporting direct labor	Number of direct labor-hours	20,000 DLHs
Order processing	Number of customer orders	400 orders
Customer support...................	Number of customers	200 customers
Other............................	This is an organization-sustaining activity	Not applicable

Distribution of Resource Consumption Across Activities					
	Supporting Direct Labor	Order Processing	Customer Support	Other	Total
Wages and salaries..............	40%	30%	20%	10%	100%
Other overhead costs............	30%	10%	20%	40%	100%

During the year, Advanced Products completed one order for a new customer, Shenzhen Enterprises. This customer did not order any other products during the year. Data concerning that order follow:

Data concerning the Shenzhen Enterprises Order	
Units ordered................................	10 units
Direct labor-hours............................	2 DLHs per unit
Selling price	$300 per unit
Direct materials	$180 per unit
Direct labor.................................	$50 per unit

Required:

1. Using Exhibit 5–6 as a guide, prepare a report showing the first-stage allocations of overhead costs to the activity cost pools.
2. Using Exhibit 5–7 as a guide, compute the activity rates for the activity cost pools.
3. Calculate the total overhead costs for the order from Shenzhen Enterprises including customer support costs.
4. Using Exhibit 5–12 as a guide, calculate the customer margin for Shenzhen Enterprises.

 connect Problems

PROBLEM 5–16 Comparing Traditional and Activity-Based Product Margins LO 5–1, LO 5–3, LO 5–4, LO 5–5

Hi-Tek Manufacturing, Inc., makes two types of industrial component parts—the B300 and the T500. An absorption costing income statement for the most recent period is shown:

Hi-Tek Manufacturing, Inc. Income Statement	
Sales	$2,100,000
Cost of goods sold	1,600,000
Gross margin	500,000
Selling and administrative expenses	550,000
Net operating loss	$ (50,000)

Hi-Tek produced and sold 70,000 units of B300 at a price of $20 per unit and 17,500 units of T500 at a price of $40 per unit. The company's traditional cost system allocates manufacturing overhead to products using a plantwide overhead rate and direct labor dollars as the allocation base. Additional information relating to the company's two product lines is shown below:

	B300	T500	Total
Direct materials	$436,300	$251,700	$ 688,000
Direct labor	$200,000	$104,000	304,000
Manufacturing overhead			608,000
Cost of goods sold			$1,600,000

The company created an activity-based costing system to evaluate the profitability of its products. Hi-Tek's ABC implementation team concluded that $50,000 and $100,000 of the company's advertising expenses could be directly traced to B300 and T500, respectively. The remainder of the selling and administrative expenses was organization-sustaining in nature. The ABC team also distributed the company's manufacturing overhead to four activities as shown:

Activity Cost Pool (and Activity Measure)	Manufacturing Overhead	Activity		
		B300	T500	Total
Machining (machine-hours)	$213,500	90,000	62,500	152,500
Setups (setup hours)	157,500	75	300	375
Product-sustaining (number of products)	120,000	1	1	2
Other (organization-sustaining costs)	117,000	NA	NA	NA
Total manufacturing overhead cost	$608,000			

Required:

1. Using Exhibit 5–13 as a guide, compute the product margins for B300 and T500 under the company's traditional costing system.
2. Using Exhibit 5–11 as a guide, compute the product margins for B300 and T500 under the activity-based costing system.
3. Using Exhibit 5–14 as a guide, prepare a quantitative comparison of the traditional and activity-based cost assignments. Explain why the traditional and activity-based cost assignments differ.

PROBLEM 5–17 Comparing Traditional and Activity-Based Product Margins LO 5–1, LO 5–3, LO 5–4, LO 5–5

Smoky Mountain Corporation makes two types of hiking boots—the Xtreme and the Pathfinder. Data concerning these two product lines appear below:

	Xtreme	Pathfinder
Selling price per unit.	$140.00	$99.00
Direct materials per unit.	$72.00	$53.00
Direct labor per unit	$24.00	$12.00
Direct labor-hours per unit.	2.0 DLHs	1.0 DLHs
Estimated annual production and sales	20,000 units	80,000 units

The company has a traditional costing system in which manufacturing overhead is applied to units based on direct labor-hours. Data concerning manufacturing overhead and direct labor-hours for the upcoming year appear below:

Estimated total manufacturing overhead	$1,980,000
Estimated total direct labor-hours	120,000 DLHs

Required:

1. Using Exhibit 5–13 as a guide, compute the product margins for the Xtreme and the Pathfinder products under the company's traditional costing system.
2. The company is considering replacing its traditional costing system with an activity-based costing system that would assign its manufacturing overhead to the following four activity cost pools (the Other cost pool includes organization-sustaining costs and idle capacity costs):

Activities (and Activity Measures)	Estimated Overhead Cost	Expected Activity		
		Xtreme	Pathfinder	Total
Supporting direct labor (direct labor-hours)	$ 783,600	40,000	80,000	120,000
Batch setups (setups).	495,000	200	100	300
Product sustaining (number of products)	602,400	1	1	2
Other.	99,000	NA	NA	NA
Total manufacturing overhead cost	$1,980,000			

Using Exhibit 5–11 as a guide, compute the product margins for the Xtreme and the Pathfinder products under the activity-based costing system.

3. Using Exhibit 5–14 as a guide, prepare a quantitative comparison of the traditional and activity-based cost assignments. Explain why the traditional and activity-based cost assignments differ.

PROBLEM 5–18 Activity-Based Costing and Bidding on Jobs LO 5–2, LO 5–3, LO 5–4

Mercer Asbestos Removal Company removes potentially toxic asbestos insulation and related products from buildings. There has been a long-simmering dispute between the company's estimator and the work supervisors. The on-site supervisors claim that the estimators do not adequately distinguish between routine work, such as removing asbestos insulation around heating pipes in older homes, and nonroutine work, such as removing asbestos-contaminated ceiling plaster in industrial buildings. The on-site supervisors believe that nonroutine work is far more expensive than routine work and should bear higher customer charges. The estimator sums up his position in this way: "My job is to measure the area to be cleared of asbestos. As directed by top management, I simply multiply the square footage by $2.50 to determine the bid price. Because our average cost is only $2.175 per square foot, that leaves enough cushion to take care of the additional costs of nonroutine work that shows up. Besides, it is difficult to know what is routine or not routine until you actually start tearing things apart."

To shed light on this controversy, the company initiated an activity-based costing study of all of its costs. Data from the activity-based costing system follow:

Activity Cost Pool	Activity Measure	Total Activity
Removing asbestos.................	Thousands of square feet	800 thousand square feet
Estimating and job setup............	Number of jobs	500 jobs
Working on nonroutine jobs	Number of nonroutine jobs	100 nonroutine jobs
Other (organization-sustaining costs and idle capacity costs)......	None	

Note: The 100 nonroutine jobs are included in the total of 500 jobs. Both nonroutine jobs and routine jobs require estimating and setup.

Costs for the Year	
Wages and salaries.........................	$ 300,000
Disposal fees..............................	700,000
Equipment depreciation....................	90,000
On-site supplies...........................	50,000
Office expenses...........................	200,000
Licensing and insurance	400,000
Total cost.................................	$1,740,000

Distribution of Resource Consumption Across Activities

	Removing Asbestos	Estimating and Job Setup	Working on Nonroutine Jobs	Other	Total
Wages and salaries................	50%	10%	30%	10%	100%
Disposal fees.....................	60%	0%	40%	0%	100%
Equipment depreciation............	40%	5%	20%	35%	100%
On-site supplies..................	60%	30%	10%	0%	100%
Office expenses...................	10%	35%	25%	30%	100%
Licensing and insurance	30%	0%	50%	20%	100%

Required:
1. Using Exhibit 5–6 as a guide, perform the first-stage allocation of costs to the activity cost pools.
2. Using Exhibit 5–7 as a guide, compute the activity rates for the activity cost pools.
3. Using the activity rates you have computed, determine the total cost and the average cost per thousand square feet of each of the following jobs according to the activity-based costing system.
   a. A routine 1,000-square-foot asbestos removal job.
   b. A routine 2,000-square-foot asbestos removal job.
   c. A nonroutine 2,000-square-foot asbestos removal job.
4. Given the results you obtained in (3) above, do you agree with the estimator that the company's present policy for bidding on jobs is adequate?

PROBLEM 5–19 Second-Stage Allocations and Product Margins LO 5–4, LO 5–5

Pixel Studio, Inc., is a small company that creates computer-generated animations for films and television. Much of the company's work consists of short commercials for television, but the company also does realistic computer animations for special effects in movies.

The young founders of the company have become increasingly concerned with the economics of the business—particularly because many competitors have sprung up recently in the local area. To help understand the company's cost structure, an activity-based costing system has been designed. Three major activities are carried out in the company: animation concept, animation production, and contract administration. The animation concept activity is carried out at the contract proposal stage when the company bids on projects. This is an intensive activity that involves individuals from all parts of the company in creating storyboards and prototype stills to be shown to the prospective client. Once a project is accepted by the client, the animation goes into production and contract administration begins. Almost all of the work involved in animation production is done by the technical staff, whereas the administrative staff is largely responsible for contract administration. The activity cost pools and their activity measures are listed below:

Activity Cost Pool	Activity Measure	Activity Rate
Animation concept	Number of proposals	$6,040 per proposal
Animation production	Minutes of completed animation	$7,725 per minute
Contract administration	Number of contracts	$6,800 per contract

These activity rates include all of the company's costs, except for its organization-sustaining costs and idle capacity costs. There are no direct labor or direct materials costs.

Preliminary analysis using these activity rates has indicated that the local commercial segment of the market may be unprofitable. This segment is highly competitive. Producers of local commercials may ask three or four companies like Pixel Studio to bid, which results in an unusually low ratio of accepted contracts to bids. Furthermore, the animation sequences tend to be much shorter for local commercials than for other work. Because animation work is billed at fairly standard rates according to the running time of the completed animation, this means that the revenues from these short projects tend to be below average. Data concerning activity in the local commercial market appear below:

Activity Measure	Local Commercials
Number of proposals	25
Minutes of completed animation	5
Number of contracts.	10

The total sales from the 10 contracts for local commercials was $180,000.

Required:

1. Calculate the cost of serving the local commercial market.
2. Calculate the margin earned serving the local commercial market. (Remember, this company has no direct materials or direct labor costs.)
3. What would you recommend to management concerning the local commercial market?

PROBLEM 5–20 Evaluating the Profitability of Services LO 5–2, LO 5–3, LO 5–4, LO 5–5

Gallatin Carpet Cleaning is a small, family-owned business operating out of Bozeman, Montana. For its services, the company has always charged a flat fee per hundred square feet of carpet cleaned. The current fee is $28 per hundred square feet. However, there is some question about whether the company is actually making any money on jobs for some customers—particularly those located on remote ranches that require considerable travel time. The owner's daughter, home for the summer from college, has suggested investigating this question using activity-based costing. After some discussion, she designed a simple system consisting of four activity cost pools. The activity cost pools and their activity measures appear below:

Activity Cost Pool	Activity Measure	Activity for the Year
Cleaning carpets.................	Square feet cleaned (00s)	20,000 hundred square feet
Travel to jobs	Miles driven	60,000 miles
Job support	Number of jobs	2,000 jobs
Other (organization-sustaining costs and idle capacity costs).....	None	Not applicable

The total cost of operating the company for the year is $430,000, which includes the following costs:

Wages.......................................	$150,000
Cleaning supplies	40,000
Cleaning equipment depreciation	20,000
Vehicle expenses	80,000
Office expenses.............................	60,000
President's compensation	80,000
Total cost......................................	$430,000

Resource consumption is distributed across the activities as follows:

	Cleaning Carpets	Travel to Jobs	Job Support	Other	Total
Wages................................	70%	20%	0%	10%	100%
Cleaning supplies	100%	0%	0%	0%	100%
Cleaning equipment depreciation	80%	0%	0%	20%	100%
Vehicle expenses	0%	60%	0%	40%	100%
Office expenses.......................	0%	0%	45%	55%	100%
President's compensation	0%	0%	40%	60%	100%

Job support consists of receiving calls from potential customers at the home office, scheduling jobs, billing, resolving issues, and so on.

Required:

1. Using Exhibit 5–6 as a guide, prepare the first-stage allocation of costs to the activity cost pools.
2. Using Exhibit 5–7 as a guide, compute the activity rates for the activity cost pools.
3. The company recently completed a 500-square-foot carpet-cleaning job at the Flying N Ranch—a 75-mile round-trip journey from the company's offices in Bozeman. Compute the cost of this job using the activity-based costing system.
4. The revenue from the Flying N Ranch was $140 (500 square feet @ $28 per hundred square feet). Using Exhibit 5–12 as a guide, calculate the customer margin earned on this job.
5. What do you conclude concerning the profitability of the Flying N Ranch job? Explain.
6. What advice would you give the president concerning pricing jobs in the future?

Appendix 5A: Time-Driven Activity-Based Costing: A Microsoft Excel–Based Approach

The purpose of this appendix is to introduce you to *time-driven activity-based costing* (TDABC). The approach demonstrated in this appendix overcomes two important limitations that accompany the activity-based costing (ABC) model described in the main body of the chapter. First, TDABC does not require extensive interviews with employees (as depicted in Exhibit 5–5) to perform stage-one allocations. For a company that employs thousands of people, these interviews can be very time-consuming—which limits a company's ability to frequently update its cost model. Second, the ABC model depicted in Exhibits 5–5 and 5–6 assumes employees will self-report their own idle time within the "Other" cost pool. In reality, most employees are very averse to reporting their own idle time because it may signal to management that the size of the labor force can be reduced.

This appendix demonstrates how TDABC can be used to assign indirect costs to cost objects such as products and customers. We'll also explain how TDABC can be used for capacity analysis purposes. For simplicity, we limit the scope of this appendix to focus solely on labor costs. While TDABC systems can include other types of indirect costs such as equipment costs and utility costs, we purposely omit these kinds of costs to simplify our capacity analysis discussion.

Ridley Company: An Example

Ridley Company would like to improve its understanding of customer profitability and capacity utilization. As an initial pilot project, the company decided to use TDABC to analyze its Customer Service Department labor costs. The goals of the project are to obtain a better understanding of how customer service labor costs are used by individual customers and to obtain a more informed basis for making employee staffing decisions within the department. In the past, the company relied on "educated guesses" to make staffing decisions, which often resulted in an imbalance between the number of employees on the payroll and the number of employees needed to serve customers. Ridley hopes that TDABC will enable it to estimate the financial implications of better aligning its labor capacity with its customer demand.

The Data Inputs

Exhibit 5A–1 summarizes three types of data inputs for Ridley's TDABC model—resource data, activity data, and cost object data. The resource data includes the number of employees in the Customer Service Department (30), the average salary per employee ($29,952), the number of weeks in a year (52), the minutes available per week (2,400), and the practical capacity percentage (80%). The practical capacity percentage acknowledges that employees are not serving customers 100 percent of their available minutes. They spend some of their available time on vacation, on breaks, in training, attending to personal needs, etc. Thus, Ridley estimates that 80 percent of an employee's available minutes are spent actually serving customers.

The activity data contained in Exhibit 5A–1 specifies three activities within the Customer Service Department, namely order processing (cell B13), query resolution (cell C13), and credit reviews (cell D13). It also states the average number of minutes required to perform each activity one time. For example, on average, it takes 10 minutes to process one order, 30 minutes to resolve one query from a customer, and 40 minutes to review one customer's credit worthiness.[4] The cost object data shown in Exhibit 5A–1 provide

---

[4] For simplicity, we assume all orders, queries, and credit reviews consume the same amount of minutes per unit of the activity.

activity data for customers A, B, and C, as well as all customers served by the Customer Service Department during the year. For example, customers A, B, and C placed 30, 18, and 7 orders, respectively. A total of 200,000 orders were placed by all of Ridley's customers during the year.

Customer Cost Analysis

Exhibit 5A–2 summarizes the three-step TDABC process that Ridley Company uses to assign Customer Service Department labor costs to customers A, B, and C. The first step is to divide the total cost of the resources supplied in cell B10 ($898,560) by the practical capacity of the resources supplied in cell B14 (2,995,200 minutes) to obtain the cost per minute of the resource supplied in cell B16 ($0.30). Notice that cell B12 shows a practical capacity per employee of 99,840 minutes. This amount is obtained by multiplying together three cells from the data inputs tab shown in Exhibit 5A–1—cell B9 (52 weeks), cell B10 (2,400 minutes per week), and cell B11 (80%).

The second step in Exhibit 5A–2 is to calculate the time-driven activity rate for each of the three activities. For example, the time-driven activity rate for the order processing activity of $3.00 per order (cell B21) is derived by multiplying 10 minutes per unit of the activity (cell B19) by the cost per minute of the resource supplied of $0.30 (cell B20). Similarly, the time-driven activity rate for the query resolution activity of $9.00 per query (cell C21) is derived by multiplying 30 minutes per unit of the activity (cell C19) by the cost per minute of the resource supplied of $0.30 (cell C20).

The third step in Exhibit 5A–2 is to assign customer service labor costs to customers A, B, and C. For example, the total customer service costs assigned to Customer A of $255 (cell B36) is the sum of the order processing costs of $90 (cell B26), the query resolution costs of $153 (cell B30), and the credit review costs of $12 (cell B34). Notice that the number of orders processed in cell B24 (30), the number of customer queries in cell B28 (17), and the number of credit reviews in cell B32 (1) are linked to cells B17 through B19 in the data inputs tab shown in Exhibit 5A–1.

The type of cost assignments summarized in Exhibit 5A–2 could be useful to Ridley Company in larger initiatives, such as measuring customer profitability and managing

EXHIBIT 5A–2

Ridley Company: Customer Cost Analysis

	A	B	C	D
1	Ridley Company			
2	Customer Service Department			
3	Customer Cost Analysis			
4				
5	Step 1: Calculate the cost per minute of the resource supplied			
6				
7	*Customer Service Department:*			
8	Number of employees (a)	30		
9	Average salary per employee (b)	$ 29,952		
10	Total cost of resources supplied (a) × (b)	$ 898,560		
11				
12	Practical capacity per employee (in minutes) (a)	99,840		
13	Number of employees (b)	30		
14	Practical capacity of resources supplied (in minutes) (a) × (b)	2,995,200		
15				
16	Cost per minute of the resource supplied	$ 0.30		
17				
18	Step 2: Calculate the time-driven activity rate	Order processing	Query resolution	Credit reviews
19	Minutes per unit of the activity (a)	10	30	40
20	Cost per minute of the resource supplied (b)	$ 0.30	$ 0.30	$ 0.30
21	Time-driven activity rate (a) × (b)	$ 3.00	$ 9.00	$ 12.00
22				
23	Step 3: Assign costs to cost objects	Customer A	Customer B	Customer C
24	Number of orders processed (a)	30	18	7
25	Time-driven activity rate (b)	$ 3.00	$ 3.00	$ 3.00
26	Order processing costs assigned (a) × (b)	$ 90.00	$ 54.00	$ 21.00
27				
28	Number of customer queries (a)	17	10	8
29	Time-driven activity rate (b)	$ 9.00	$ 9.00	$ 9.00
30	Query resolution costs assigned (a) × (b)	$ 153.00	$ 90.00	$ 72.00
31				
32	Number of credit checks (a)	1	1	1
33	Time-driven activity rate (b)	$ 12.00	$ 12.00	$ 12.00
34	Credit review costs assigned (a) × (b)	$ 12.00	$ 12.00	$ 12.00
35				
36	Total customer service costs assigned	$ 255.00	$ 156.00	$ 105.00
37				

Exhibit 5A-1   Exhibit 5A-2   Exhibit

Microsoft Excel

its customer mix based on those insights. Furthermore, the cost assignments shown in Exhibit 5A–2 were performed without having to interview the 30 employees within the Customer Service Department. Instead, Ridley Company only needed to make a reasonable estimate regarding its practical capacity percentage (80%) and to estimate the amount of time required to perform each activity one time in order to compute its time-driven activity rates.

However, the data in Exhibit 5A–2 does not help Ridley quantify and manage its used and unused capacity costs, nor does it enable the company to estimate the number of customer service department employees that it would need to meet future customer demand. To glean these types of insights from Ridley's TDABC system, we turn our attention to the topic of capacity analysis.

LEARNING OBJECTIVE 5–7

Use time-driven activity-based costing to analyze capacity.

Capacity Analysis

Exhibit 5A–3 shows the four-step process that Ridley Company uses for capacity management purposes. It focuses on *all* of Ridley's customers rather than just customers

EXHIBIT 5A–3
Ridley Company: Capacity Analysis

	A	B	C	D	E
1	Ridley Company				
2	Customer Service Department				
3	Capacity Analysis				
4					
5	Step 1: Calculate the used capacity in minutes	Order processing	Query resolution	Credit reviews	Total
6	Customer demand for each activity (a)	200,000	4,500	8,900	
7	Customer service minutes required per unit of each activity (b)	10	30	40	
8	Customer service minutes used to meet demand (a) × (b)	2,000,000	135,000	356,000	2,491,000
9					
10	Step 2: Calculate the unused capacity in minutes				
11	Total customer service minutes available to meet demand (a)	2,995,200			
12	Total customer service minutes used to meet demand (b)	2,491,000			
13	Unused capacity in minutes (a) − (b)	504,200			
14					
15	Step 3: Calculate the unused capacity in number of employees				
16	Unused capacity in minutes (a)	504,200			
17	Practical capacity per employee (in minutes) (b)	99,840			
18	Unused capacity in number of employees (a) ÷ (b)	5.05			
19					
20	Step 4: Calculate the financial impact of matching capacity with demand				
21	Potential adjustment in number of employees (rounded) (a)	(5.00)			
22	Average salary per employee (b)	$ 29,952			
23	Impact on expenses of matching capacity with demand (a) × (b)	$(149,760)			
24					
25	Note: Cell B21 uses the formula =If(B18>0,rounddown(-B18,0),roundup(-B18,0))				
26					

Exhibit 5A-2 / Exhibit 5A-3 / Exhibit 6A-4 / Exhibit

Microsoft Excel

A, B, and C. The first step is to calculate the total used capacity in minutes of 2,491,000 (= 2,000,000 + 135,000 + 356,000). The second step is to take the total minutes available of 2,995,200 from cell B11 (and as previously computed in cell B14 in Exhibit 5A–2) minus the minutes used of 2,491,000 (from cell B12) to derive the 504,200 minutes of unused capacity shown in cell B13.

The third step translates the unused capacity in minutes to unused capacity in terms of employees. We perform this calculation because customer service employees are a step-fixed cost rather than a variable cost. In other words, Ridley does not purchase customer service capacity by the minute. Instead, it hires individual employees who each provides 99,840 minutes of practical capacity per year. Because the unused capacity in minutes is 504,200 and the practical capacity of one employee is 99,840 minutes, the total unused capacity equates with 5.05 employees (= 504,200 ÷ 99,840).

The fourth step calculates the financial impact of matching capacity with demand. The key to this step is the formula in cell B21 of Exhibit 5A–3, which rounds the value reported in cell B18 to a whole number. We perform this rounding function because Ridley alters its step-fixed employee headcount in terms of whole employees, not portions of an employee. So, for example, cell B18 shows an unused capacity of 5.05 employees; however, Ridley cannot eliminate .05 employees. It could possibly eliminate five or six employees, but nothing in between. Because eliminating six employees would leave the Customer Service Department a little short-handed, we round down to five employees. Given the average salary per employee of $29,952, the impact on expenses of matching labor capacity with demand is a savings of $149,760 (= 5.00 × $29,952).

"What-If" Analysis

The data inputs in Exhibit 5A–1 also enable Ridley to answer some interesting "what if" questions. For example, what if the company was able to lower its credit review time from 40 minutes to 30 minutes? How would this affect the costs assigned to customers A, B, and C? To answer this question, we would change cell D14 in Exhibit 5A–1 from 40 minutes to 30 minutes. The revised customer cost analysis that would be instantly generated is shown in Exhibit 5A–4.

EXHIBIT 5A–4
Ridley Company's Customer Cost Analysis: A "What If" Analysis

	A	B	C	D
1	Ridley Company			
2	Customer Service Department			
3	Customer Cost Analysis			
4				
5	Step 1: Calculate the cost per minute of the resource supplied			
6				
7	*Customer Service Department:*			
8	Number of employees (a)	30		
9	Average salary per employee (b)	$ 29,952		
10	Total cost of resources supplied (a) × (b)	$ 898,560		
11				
12	Practical capacity per employee (in minutes) (a)	99,840		
13	Number of employees (b)	30		
14	Practical capacity of resources supplied (in minutes) (a) × (b)	2,995,200		
15				
16	Cost per minute of the resource supplied	$ 0.30		
17				
18	Step 2: Calculate the time-driven activity rate	Order processing	Query resolution	Credit reviews
19	Minutes per unit of the activity (a)	10	30	30
20	Cost per minute of the resource supplied (b)	$ 0.30	$ 0.30	$ 0.30
21	Time-driven activity rate (a) × (b)	$ 3.00	$ 9.00	$ 9.00
22				
23	Step 3: Assign costs to cost objects	Customer A	Customer B	Customer C
24	Number of orders processed (a)	30	18	7
25	Time-driven activity rate (b)	$ 3.00	$ 3.00	$ 3.00
26	Order processing costs assigned (a) × (b)	$ 90.00	$ 54.00	$ 21.00
27				
28	Number of customer queries (a)	17	10	8
29	Time-driven activity rate (b)	$ 9.00	$ 9.00	$ 9.00
30	Query resolution costs assigned (a) × (b)	$ 153.00	$ 90.00	$ 72.00
31				
32	Number of credit checks (a)	1	1	1
33	Time-driven activity rate (b)	$ 9.00	$ 9.00	$ 9.00
34	Credit review costs assigned (a) × (b)	$ 9.00	$ 9.00	$ 9.00
35				
36	Total customer service costs assigned	$ 252.00	$ 153.00	$ 102.00
37				

Exhibit 5A-4 / Exhibit 5A-5 / Exerci

Microsoft Excel

Notice that cell D19 shows 30 minutes per credit review instead of the 40 minutes shown in the same cell in Exhibit 5A–2. This in turn lowers the cost per credit review to $9.00 (as shown in cell D21) rather than the $12.00 shown in the same cell in Exhibit 5A–2. The lower time-driven activity rate of $9.00 carries forward to cells B33 through D33 and in turn lowers each customer's total customer service costs by $3. For example, customer A's total customer service cost is $252 in cell B36 of Exhibit 5A–4, whereas the corresponding total in cell B36 of Exhibit 5A–2 is $255.

Let's further assume that Ridley Company wants to answer the question: What if we also increase the number of orders processed from 200,000 (as shown in cell E17 in Exhibit 5A–1) to 265,000? How would the projected increase in the number of orders processed affect our staffing needs in the Customer Service Department? After making the appropriate change in cell E17 of Exhibit 5A–1, Exhibit 5A–5 provides the answer to

EXHIBIT 5A–5
Ridley Company's Capacity Analysis: A "What If" Analysis

	A	B	C	D	E
1	Ridley Company				
2	Customer Service Department				
3	Capacity Analysis				
4					
5	**Step 1: Calculate the used capacity in minutes**	Order processing	Query resolution	Credit reviews	Total
6	Customer demand for each activity (a)	265,000	4,500	8,900	
7	Customer service minutes required per unit of each activity (b)	10	30	30	
8	Customer service minutes used to meet demand (a) × (b)	2,650,000	135,000	267,000	3,052,000
9					
10	**Step 2: Calculate the unused capacity in minutes**				
11	Total customer service minutes available to meet demand (a)	2,995,200			
12	Total customer service minutes used to meet demand (b)	3,052,000			
13	Unused capacity in minutes (a) − (b)	(56,800)			
14					
15	**Step 3: Calculate the unused capacity in number of employees**				
16	Unused capacity in minutes (a)	(56,800)			
17	Practical capacity per employee (in minutes) (b)	99,840			
18	Unused capacity in number of employees (a) ÷ (b)	(0.57)			
19					
20	**Step 4: Calculate the financial impact of matching capacity with demand**				
21	Potential adjustment in number of employees (rounded) (a)	1.00			
22	Average salary per employee (b)	$ 29,952			
23	Impact on expenses of matching capacity with demand (a) × (b)	$ 29,952			
24					
25	Note: Cell B21 uses the formula =If(B18>0,rounddown(-B18,0),roundup(-B18,0))				
26					

Exhibit 5A-5 / Exhibit 5A-4 / Exercise 5A-1 Inputs

Microsoft Excel

this question—Ridley Company would need to hire one more employee at an estimated cost of $29,952.

To understand how this answer is derived, let's start with Step 1 within Exhibit 5A–5, which shows 265,000 orders processed in cell B6. This increase in the number of orders processed increases the number of customer service minutes needed to meet customer demand to 3,052,000 (cell E8). Step 2 shows that the total customer service minutes available of 2,995,200 (cell B11) is now less than the number of minutes used to meet demand of 3,052,000 (cell B12), which results in unused capacity of (56,800) minutes as shown in cell B13. Because the unused capacity is a negative number, it implies Ridley does not have enough capacity available to satisfy the estimated customer demand. Step 3 in Exhibit 5A–5 translates the shortage in minutes to a shortfall stated in terms of number of employees—or (0.57) employees as shown in cell B18. Given that Ridley cannot hire slightly more than one-half of an employee, cell B21 rounds this number to 1.00 and then cell B23 translates the estimated cost of hiring one additional employee to $29,952.

This concludes our introduction to TDABC. The strengths of this methodology include (1) it is easy to update because it does not require employee interviews, (2) it quantifies unused capacity costs in an objective fashion that does not require employees to self-report their own idle time, and (3) it helps companies estimate the financial impact of aligning capacity with demand, particularly with respect to step-fixed resources such as the customer service employees in the Ridley Company example.

Appendix 5A: Exercises and Problems

EXERCISE 5A–1 Time-Driven Activity-Based Costing LO 5–6

Saratoga Company manufactures jobs to customer specifications. The company is conducting a time-driven activity-based costing study in its Purchasing Department to better understand how Purchasing Department labor costs are consumed by individual jobs. To aid the study, the company provided the following data regarding its Purchasing Department and three of its many jobs:

Number of employees	12
Average salary per employee	$28,000
Weeks of employment per year	52
Hours worked per week	40
Practical capacity percentage	85%

	Requisition Processing	Bid Evaluation	Inspection
Minutes per unit of the activity	15	45	30

	Job X	Job Y	Job Z
Number of requisitions processed	8	5	4
Number of bid evaluations	3	2	4
Number of inspections	6	2	6

Required:

1. Calculate the cost per minute of the resource supplied in the Purchasing Department.
2. Calculate the time-driven activity rate for each of Saratoga's three activities.
3. Calculate the total purchasing labor costs assigned to Job X, Job Y, and Job Z.

EXERCISE 5A–2 Time-Driven Activity-Based Costing LO 5–7

Refer to the data in Exercise 5A–1. In addition, assume that Saratoga Company provided the following activity data for *all* jobs produced during the year:

	Requisition Processing	Bid Evaluation	Inspection
Activity demands for all jobs	7,000	9,400	10,000

Required:

1. Calculate Saratoga's used capacity in minutes.
2. Calculate Saratoga's unused capacity in minutes.
3. Calculate Saratoga's unused capacity in number of employees. (Do not round your answer to a whole number.)
4. Calculate the impact on expenses of matching capacity with demand. (Be sure to round your potential adjustment in the number of employees to a whole number.)

EXERCISE 5A–3 Time-Driven Activity-Based Costing LO 5–6, LO 5–7

Refer to the data in Exercises 5A–1 and 5A–2. Now assume that Saratoga Company would like to answer the following "what if" question using its time-driven activity-based costing system: Assuming our estimated activity demands for all jobs in the next period will be as shown below, how will this affect our job costs and our staffing levels within the Purchasing Department?

	Requisition Processing	Bid Evaluation	Inspection
Activity demands for all jobs........................	7,600	9,900	11,000

Required:

1. How will these revised activity demands affect the total Purchasing Department labor costs assigned to Job X, Job Y, and Job Z? No calculations are necessary.
2. Using the revised activity demands, calculate Saratoga's used capacity in minutes.
3. Using the revised activity demands, calculate Saratoga's unused capacity in minutes.
4. Using the revised activity demands, calculate Saratoga's unused capacity in number of employees. (Do not round your answer to a whole number.)
5. Based on the revised activity demands, calculate the impact on expenses of matching capacity with demand. (Be sure to round your potential adjustment in the number of employees to a whole number.)

PROBLEM 5A–4 Time-Driven Activity-Based Costing LO 5–6, LO 5–7

Stahl Company is conducting a time-driven activity-based costing study in its Shipping Department. To aid the study, the company provided the following data regarding its Shipping Department and the customers served by the department:

Number of employees	34
Average salary per employee	$34,000
Weeks of employment per year	52
Hours worked per week	40
Practical capacity percentage	80%

	Line-Item Picking	Packaging	Loading Deliveries
Minutes per unit of the activity	5	15	30

	Customer L	Customer M	Customer N	All Customers
Number of line items picked	280	160	90	335,000
Number of boxes packaged	50	20	15	46,800
Number of deliveries loaded	6	2	10	12,100

Required:

1. Using the customer cost analysis shown in Exhibit 5A–2 as your guide, compute the following:
   a. The cost per minute of the resource supplied in the Shipping Department.
   b. The time-driven activity rate for each of Stahl's three activities.
   c. The total labor costs consumed by Customer L, Customer M, and Customer N.
2. Using the capacity analysis shown in Exhibit 5A–3 as your guide, compute the following:
   a. The used capacity in minutes.
   b. The unused capacity in minutes.
   c. The unused capacity in number of employees. (Do not round your answer to a whole number.)
   d. The impact on expenses of matching capacity with demand. (Be sure to round your potential adjustment in the number of employees to a whole number.)

PROBLEM 5A–5 Time-Driven Activity-Based Costing LO 5–6, LO 5–7

Athens Company is conducting a time-driven activity-based costing study in its Engineering Department. To aid the study, the company provided the following data regarding its Engineering Department and the customers served by the department:

Number of employees.	10
Average salary per employee	$90,000
Weeks of employment per year	52
Hours worked per week	40
Practical capacity percentage	85%

	New Product Design	Engineering Change Orders	Product Testing
Hours per unit of the activity	40	20	8

	Customer A	Customer B	Customer C	All Customers
Number of new products designed	3	2	4	180
Number of engineering change orders	5	2	2	250
Number of products tested	8	4	6	160

Required:

1. Using the customer cost analysis shown in Exhibit 5A–2 as your guide, compute the following:
    a. The cost per hour of the resource supplied in the Engineering Department.
    b. The time-driven activity rate per hour for each of Athens' three activities.
    c. The total engineering costs consumed by Customer A, Customer B, and Customer C.

2. Using the capacity analysis shown in Exhibit 5A–3 as your guide, compute the following:
    a. The used capacity in hours.
    b. The unused capacity in hours.
    c. The unused capacity in number of employees. (Do not round your answer to a whole number.)
    d. The impact on expenses of matching capacity with demand. (Be sure to round your potential adjustment in the number of employees to a whole number.)

3. Assume Athens is considering expanding its business such that the estimated number of new products designed would increase to 250, the number of engineering change orders would jump to 320, and the number of products tested would rise to 240. Using these revised figures, calculate the following:
    a. The used capacity in hours.
    b. The unused capacity in hours.
    c. The unused capacity in number of employees. (Do not round your answer to a whole number.)
    d. The impact on expenses of matching capacity with demand. (Be sure to round your potential adjustment in the number of employees to a whole number.)

Differential Analysis: The Key to Decision Making

Cavan Images/Alamy Stock Photo

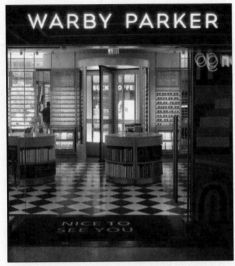

Interim Archives/Contributor/Getty Images

ENTREPRENEUR SPOTLIGHT

Neil Blumenthal and Dave Gilboa co-founded Warby Parker to solve what they saw as a simple problem—the price of eyeglasses was too high. By designing their own glasses and interacting directly with customers, they were able "to provide high quality, better-looking prescription eyewear at a fraction of the going price." Today the company is valued at $3 billion with more than 130 retail locations across the United States accompanied by a market-leading online sales portal. In 2015, *Fast Company* named Warby Parker the most innovative company in the world.

Managerial Accounting: The Practical Application

With more than 130 retail locations throughout the United States, Warby Parker can use differential analysis when deciding to add a new store or to discontinue an existing location. For example, when contemplating closing a store, the company would compare the lost revenue with the avoidable costs. If the avoidable costs exceeded the forgone revenue, it would suggest closing the store. The financial analysis would purposely exclude any costs that would remain unchanged whether the store remains open or closes.

Corporate Social Responsibility: Serving all Stakeholders

Warby Parker says that 1 billion people across the globe lack access to glasses. To help fix this problem, the company "partners with non-profits like VisionSpring to ensure that for every pair of glasses sold, a pair is distributed to someone in need." The company also prepares an annual *Impact Report* that measures its corporate social responsibility performance along four dimensions: (1) customers, (2) employees, (3) community, and (4) sustainability. In addition, Warby Parker has also published a *Racial Equity Strategy* supported by 10 goals, such as increasing "Black representation in the field of optometry and in the technology sector." ▪

Sources: www.warbyparker.com/history, https://www.axios.com/warby-parker-3-billion-valuation-03f53fcc-f18c-4f20-8bf3-1a6fc4f378fb.html, www.warbyparker.com/dave-gilboa, www.warbyparker.com/impact-report-racial-equity-strategy

LEARNING OBJECTIVES

After studying Chapter 6, you should be able to:

LO 6–1 Identify relevant and irrelevant costs and benefits in a decision.

LO 6–2 Prepare an analysis showing whether a product line or other business segment should be added or dropped.

LO 6–3 Identify the relevant costs and benefits associated with sourcing decisions.

LO 6–4 Prepare an analysis showing whether a special order should be accepted.

LO 6–5 Determine the most profitable use of a constrained resource.

LO 6–6 Determine the value of obtaining more of the constrained resource.

LO 6–7 Prepare an analysis showing whether joint products should be sold at the split-off point or processed further.

LO 6–8 *(Appendix 6A) Compute the selling price of a product using the absorption costing approach to cost-plus pricing.*

LO 6–9 *(Appendix 6A) Understand how customers' sensitivity to changes in price should influence pricing decisions.*

LO 6–10 *(Appendix 6A) Analyze pricing decisions using value-based pricing.*

LO 6–11 *(Appendix 6A) Compute the target cost for a new product or service.*

Data Analytics Exercise available in Connect to complement this chapter

This chapter discusses what may be a manager's most important responsibility—making decisions. Examples of decisions include deciding what products to sell, whether to make or buy component parts, what prices to charge, what channels of distribution to use, and whether to accept special orders at special prices. Making such decisions is often a difficult task that is complicated by numerous alternatives and massive amounts of data; however, in this chapter, you will learn how to narrow your focus to the information that matters.

Decision Making: Six Key Concepts

There are six key concepts you need to understand to make intelligent decisions. This section discusses each of those concepts and then concludes by introducing some additional terminology created to help you solve the exercises and problems at the end of the chapter.

Key Concept #1

Every decision involves choosing from among at least two alternatives. Therefore, the first step in decision making is to define the alternatives being considered. For example, if a company is deciding whether to make a component part or buy it from an outside supplier, the alternatives are *make* or *buy* the component part. Similarly, if a company is considering discontinuing a particular product, the alternatives are to *keep* or *drop* the product.

Key Concept #2

Once you have defined the alternatives, you need to identify the criteria for choosing among them. The key to choosing among alternatives is distinguishing between *relevant* and *irrelevant* costs and benefits. **Relevant costs** and **relevant benefits** should be considered when making decisions. *Irrelevant costs* and *irrelevant benefits* should be ignored when making decisions. This is an important concept for two reasons. First, being able to ignore irrelevant data saves decision makers tremendous amounts of time and effort. Second, bad decisions can easily result from erroneously including irrelevant costs and benefits when analyzing alternatives.

Key Concept #3

The key to effective decision making is *differential analysis*—focusing on the future costs and benefits that differ between the alternatives. Everything else is irrelevant and should be ignored. A future cost that differs between any two alternatives is known as a **differential cost.** Differential costs are always relevant costs. Future revenue that differs between any two alternatives is known as **differential revenue.** Differential revenue is an example of a relevant benefit.

The terms *incremental cost* and *avoidable cost* are often used to describe differential costs. An **incremental cost** is an increase in cost between two alternatives. For example, if you are choosing between buying the standard model or the deluxe model of your favorite automobile, the costs of the upgrades contained in the deluxe model are incremental costs. An **avoidable cost** is a cost that can be eliminated by choosing one alternative over another. For example, assume that you have decided to watch a movie tonight; however, you are trying to choose between two alternatives—going to the movie theater or renting a movie. The cost of the ticket to get into the movie theater is an avoidable cost. You would avoid this cost by renting a movie. Similarly, the movie rental fee is an avoidable cost because you could avoid it by going to the movie theater. Avoidable costs (and incremental costs) are always relevant costs.

Differential costs and benefits can be qualitative or quantitative in nature. While qualitative differences between alternatives can have an important impact on decisions, and, therefore, should not be ignored, our goal in this chapter is to hone your quantitative analysis skills. Therefore, our primary focus will be on analyzing quantitative differential costs and benefits—those that have readily measurable impacts on future cash flows.

Key Concept #4

Sunk costs are always irrelevant when choosing among alternatives. A **sunk cost** is a cost that has already been incurred and cannot be changed regardless of what a manager decides to do. Sunk costs have no impact on future cash flows and remain the same no matter what alternatives are being considered; therefore, they are irrelevant and should be ignored when making decisions.

For example, suppose a company purchased a five-year-old truck for $12,000. The amount paid for the truck is a sunk cost because it has already been incurred, and the transaction cannot be undone. The $12,000 paid for the truck is irrelevant in making decisions such as whether to keep, sell, or replace the truck. Furthermore, any accounting depreciation expense related to the truck is irrelevant in making decisions. This is true because accounting depreciation is a noncash expense that has no effect on future cash flows. It simply spreads the sunk cost of the truck over its useful life.[1]

Key Concept #5

Future costs and benefits that *do not differ between alternatives* are irrelevant to the decision-making process. So, continuing with the movie example, assume you plan to buy a Domino's pizza after watching a movie. If you are going to buy the same pizza regardless of your movie-watching venue, the cost of the pizza is irrelevant when choosing between the theater and the rental. The cost of the pizza is *not* a sunk cost because it has not yet been incurred. Nonetheless, the cost of the pizza is irrelevant to the choice of venue because it is a future cost that does not differ between the alternatives.

Key Concept #6

Opportunity costs also need to be considered when making decisions. An **opportunity cost** is the potential benefit given up when one alternative is selected over another. For example, if you were considering giving up a high-paying summer job to travel overseas, the forgone wages would be an opportunity cost of traveling abroad. Opportunity costs are not usually found in accounting records, but they are a type of differential cost that must be explicitly considered in every decision a manager makes.

This chapter covers various decision contexts, such as keep or drop decisions, make or buy decisions, special order decisions, and sell or process further decisions. While tackling these diverse decision contexts may seem a bit overwhelming, keep in mind that they all share a unifying theme—choosing between alternatives based on their differential costs and benefits. To emphasize this common theme, many end-of-chapter exercises and problems that span a variety of learning objectives will often use the same terminology— financial advantage (disadvantage)—when asking you to choose between alternatives. For example, numerous exercises and problems will ask questions such as:

1. What is the financial advantage (disadvantage) of closing the store?
2. What is the financial advantage (disadvantage) of buying the component part from a supplier rather than making it?
3. What is the financial advantage (disadvantage) of accepting the special order?
4. What is the financial advantage (disadvantage) of further processing the intermediate product?

---

[1] See Appendix 7C for a discussion of how depreciation expense impacts decisions when tax implications are considered.

In all of these various contexts, a financial advantage exists if pursuing an alternative, such as closing a store or accepting a special order, passes the cost/benefit test. In other words, it exists if the alternative's differential benefits (i.e., its future cash inflows) exceed its differential costs (i.e., its future cash outflows). Conversely, a financial (disadvantage) exists when an alternative fails the cost/benefit test—its differential benefits are less than its differential costs.[2]

Identifying Relevant Costs and Benefits: An Example

Cynthia is currently a student in an MBA program in Boston and would like to visit a friend in New York City over the weekend. She is trying to decide whether to drive or take the train. Because she is on a tight budget, she wants to carefully consider the costs of the two alternatives. If one alternative is far less expensive than the other, that may be decisive in her choice. By car, the distance between her apartment in Boston and her friend's apartment in New York City is 230 miles. Cynthia has compiled the following list of items to consider:

	Item	Annual Cost of Fixed Items	Cost per Mile (based on 10,000 miles per year)
	Automobile Costs		
(a)	Annual straight-line depreciation on car [($24,000 original cost − $10,000 estimated resale value in 5 years)/5 years]...............	$2,800	$0.280
(b)	Cost of gasoline ($2.40 per gallon ÷ 24 miles per gallon)		0.100
(c)	Annual cost of auto insurance and license.........	$1,380	0.138
(d)	Maintenance and repairs........................		0.065
(e)	Parking fees at school ($45 per month × 8 months)	$360	0.036
(f)	Total average cost per mile......................		$0.619

	Item		
	Additional Data		
(g)	Reduction in the resale value of car due solely to wear and tear........................	$0.080 per mile	
(h)	Cost of round-trip train ticket from Boston to New York City	$114	
(i)	Benefit of relaxing and being able to study during the train ride rather than having to drive..........	?	
(j)	Cost of putting the dog in a kennel while gone......	$80	
(k)	Benefit of having a car available in New York City	?	
(l)	Hassle of parking the car in New York City..........	?	
(m)	Cost of parking the car in New York City	$25 per day	

---

[2] Over the life of a company, cumulative net cash flows equal cumulative net income. Therefore, if a decision maximizes future net cash flows, it will also maximize future cumulative net income. However, because of accruals, in any particular period net income will usually be different from net cash flow. A decision based on maximizing future net cash flows might, in the short run, reduce net income, but in the long run cumulative net income will be higher than it otherwise would have been.

Which costs and benefits are relevant in this decision? Remember, only the differential costs and benefits are relevant—everything else is irrelevant and can be ignored.

Start at the top of the list with item (a): the original cost of the car is a sunk cost. This cost has already been incurred and therefore can never differ between alternatives. Consequently, it is irrelevant and should be ignored. The same is true of the accounting depreciation of $2,800 per year, which simply spreads the sunk cost across five years.

Item (b), the cost of gasoline consumed by driving to New York City, is a relevant cost. If Cynthia takes the train, she would avoid the cost of the gasoline. Hence, the cost differs between alternatives and is therefore relevant.

Item (c), the annual cost of auto insurance and license, is not relevant. Whether Cynthia takes the train or drives on this particular trip, her annual auto insurance premium and her auto license fee will remain the same.[3]

Item (d), the cost of maintenance and repairs, is relevant. While maintenance and repair costs have a large random component, over the long run they should be more or less proportional to the number of miles the car is driven. Thus, the average cost of $0.065 per mile is a reasonable estimate to use.

Item (e), the monthly fee Cynthia pays to park at her school during the academic year, is not relevant. Regardless of which alternative she selects—driving or taking the train—she will still need to pay for parking at school.

Item (f) is the total average cost of $0.619 per mile. As discussed above, some elements of this total are relevant, but some are not relevant. Because it contains some irrelevant costs, it would be incorrect to estimate the cost of driving to New York City and back by simply multiplying the $0.619 by 460 miles (230 miles each way × 2). This erroneous approach would yield a cost of driving of $284.74. Unfortunately, such mistakes are often made in both personal life and business. Because the total cost is stated on a per-mile basis, people are easily misled. Often people think that if the cost is stated as $0.619 per mile, the cost of driving 100 miles is $61.90. But it is not. Many of the costs included in the $0.619 cost per mile are sunk and/or fixed and will not increase if the car is driven another 100 miles. The $0.619 is an average cost, not a differential cost. Beware of such unitized costs (i.e., costs stated in terms of a dollar amount per unit, per mile, per direct labor-hour, per machine-hour, and so on)—they are often misleading.

Item (g), the decline in the resale value of the car that occurs as a consequence of driving more miles, is relevant in the decision. Because she uses the car, its resale value declines, which is a real cost of using the car that should be taken into account. Cynthia estimated this cost by accessing the *Kelley Blue Book* website at www.kbb.com. The reduction in resale value of an asset through use or over time is often called *real* or *economic depreciation*. This is different from accounting depreciation, which attempts to match the sunk cost of an asset with the periods that benefit from that cost.

Item (h), the $114 cost of a round-trip ticket on the train, is relevant in this decision. If she drives, she would avoid the cost of the ticket.

Item (i) is relevant to the decision, even if it is difficult to put a dollar value on relaxing and studying on the train. It is relevant because it is a benefit available under one alternative but not the other.

Item (j), the cost of putting Cynthia's dog in the kennel while she is gone, is irrelevant in this decision. Whether she takes the train or drives to New York City, she will need to put her dog in a kennel.

Like item (i), items (k) and (l) are relevant to the decision even if it is difficult to measure their dollar impacts.

Item (m), the cost of parking in New York City, is relevant to the decision.

---

[3] If Cynthia has an accident while driving to New York City or back, this might affect her insurance premium when the policy is renewed. The increase in the insurance premium would be a relevant cost of this particular trip, but the normal amount of the insurance premium is not relevant in any case.

Bringing together all of the relevant data, Cynthia would estimate the relevant costs of driving and taking the train as follows:

Relevant financial cost of driving to New York City:	
Gasoline (460 miles × $0.100 per mile)	$ 46.00
Maintenance and repairs (460 miles × $0.065 per mile)	29.90
Reduction in the resale value of car due solely to wear and tear (460 miles × $0.080 per mile)	36.80
Cost of parking the car in New York City (2 days × $25 per day)	50.00
Total	$162.70
Relevant financial cost of taking the train to New York City:	
Cost of round-trip train ticket from Boston to New York City	$114.00

What should Cynthia do? From a purely financial standpoint, it would be cheaper by $48.70 ($162.70 − $114.00) to take the train than to drive. Cynthia has to decide if the convenience of having a car in New York City outweighs the additional cost, the disadvantages of being unable to relax and study on the train, and the hassle of finding parking in the city.

EMPLOYERS OFFER TO PAY COLLEGE TUITION

Many employers, such as Walt Disney, Discover Financial Services, and Yum! Brands, are paying their employees to go to college. Instead of only reimbursing tuition costs, these employers are "paying the costs of tuition, fees, books, and other expense upfront and in full." Companies are making this decision because they believe that the benefits of retaining contented and better-trained employees exceed the out-of-pocket costs. Guild Education is a Denver, Colorado–based startup company that brokers deals between companies and colleges. The companies choose the majors they will financially support, such as business, cybersecurity, and computer engineering, and then Guild ensures these employers receive discounted tuition in return for sending large numbers of their employees to pre-selected schools.

Source: Kelsey Gee, "Employers Offer to Pay for College," *The Wall Street Journal*, January 3, 2019, p. B5.

Decision Analysis: The Total Cost and Differential Cost Approaches

The example we just completed focused on identifying the relevant costs and benefits of taking the train versus driving—everything else was ignored. This method of decision analysis is called the *differential approach* because it focuses solely on the relevant costs and benefits. Another method of decision analysis, called the *total cost approach,* includes all of the costs and benefits—relevant or not. When done correctly, the two methods always provide the same correct answer.

To compare and contrast these two methods, let's consider Oak Harbor Woodworks, a company that is contemplating renting a new labor-saving machine for $3,000 per year. The machine will be used on the company's butcher block production line. Data concerning the company's annual sales and costs of butcher blocks with and without the new machine are shown below:

	Without the New Machine	With the New Machine
Units produced and sold	5,000	5,000
Selling price per unit	$40	$40
Direct materials cost per unit	$14	$14
Direct labor cost per unit	$8	$5
Variable overhead cost per unit	$2	$2
Fixed expenses, other	$62,000	$62,000
Fixed expenses, rental of new machine	—	$3,000

	Without New Machine	With New Machine	Differential Costs and Benefits
Sales (5,000 units × $40 per unit)	$200,000	$200,000	$ 0
Variable expenses:			
Direct materials (5,000 units × $14 per unit)	70,000	70,000	0
Direct labor (5,000 units × $8 per unit; 5,000 units × $5 per unit)	40,000	25,000	15,000
Variable overhead (5,000 units × $2 per unit).	10,000	10,000	0
Total variable expenses	120,000	105,000	
Contribution margin	80,000	95,000	
Fixed expenses:			
Other.	62,000	62,000	0
Rental of new machine.	0	3,000	(3,000)
Total fixed expenses.	62,000	65,000	
Net operating income.	$ 18,000	$ 30,000	$12,000

EXHIBIT 6–1

Total and Differential Costs

Given the data above, the net operating income for the product under the two alternatives can be computed, using the *total cost approach,* as shown in the first two columns of Exhibit 6–1. The net operating income in the current situation is $18,000, and the net operating income with the new machine is $30,000. The difference in the net operating incomes in these two columns indicates a $12,000 (= $30,000 − $18,000) financial advantage associated with renting the new machine. The irrelevant items (which includes sales, direct materials, variable overhead, and fixed expenses, other) appear in both columns, so they cancel each other out when isolating the $12,000 difference in favor of renting the machine.

The third column in Exhibit 6–1 uses the *differential cost approach* to derive the same financial advantage of $12,000 (= $15,000 + $(3,000)) associated with renting the new machine. A positive number in the Differential Costs and Benefits column indicates the difference between the alternatives favors the new machine; a negative number indicates the difference favors the current situation. A zero in that column means the total amount for the item is exactly the same for both alternatives. If we properly account for the costs and benefits that do not differ between the alternatives, they will cancel out when we compare the alternatives; hence, they can be ignored.

Rather than setting up comparative income statements, we could have arrived at the same solution much more quickly by completely ignoring the irrelevant costs and benefits.

- The selling price per unit and the number of units sold do not differ between the alternatives. Therefore, the total sales revenues are exactly the same for the two alternatives, as shown in Exhibit 6–1. Because the sales revenues are exactly the same, they have no effect on the difference in net operating income between the two alternatives. That is shown in the last column in Exhibit 6–1, which shows a $0 differential benefit.
- The direct materials cost per unit, the variable overhead cost per unit, and the number of units produced and sold do not differ between the alternatives. Consequently, the total direct materials cost and the total variable overhead cost are the same for the two alternatives and can be ignored.
- The "other" fixed expenses do not differ between the alternatives, so they can be ignored as well.

Indeed, the only costs that do differ between the alternatives are direct labor costs and the fixed rental cost of the new machine. Therefore, the two alternatives can be compared based only on these relevant costs:

Financial Advantage of Renting the New Machine	
Decrease in direct labor costs (5,000 units at a cost savings of $3 per unit)	$15,000
Increase in fixed expenses	(3,000)
Financial advantage of renting the new machine	$12,000

If we focus on just the relevant costs and benefits, we get exactly the same answer ($12,000 in favor of renting the new machine) as when we listed all of the costs and benefits as shown in Exhibit 6–1—including those that do not differ between the alternatives. We get the same answer because the only costs and benefits that matter in the final comparison are those items that differ between the two alternatives and, hence, are not zero in the last column of Exhibit 6–1.

Why Isolate Relevant Costs?

In the preceding example, we used the total cost approach and the differential cost approach to derive the same answer. Thus, it would be natural to ask, "Why bother to isolate relevant costs when total costs will do the job just as well?" Isolating relevant costs is desirable for at least two reasons.

First, only rarely will enough information be available to prepare a detailed income statement for both alternatives. Assume, for example, you are asked to make a decision relating to a portion of a single business process in a multidepartment, multiproduct company. Under these circumstances, it would be virtually impossible to prepare an income statement of any type. You would have to rely on your ability to recognize which costs are relevant and which are not in order to assemble the data necessary to make a decision.

Second, mingling irrelevant costs with relevant costs may cause confusion and distract attention from the information that is really critical. Furthermore, the danger always exists that an irrelevant piece of data may be used improperly, resulting in an incorrect decision. The best approach is to ignore irrelevant data and base the decision entirely on relevant data.

Adding and Dropping Product Lines and Other Segments

LEARNING OBJECTIVE 6–2
Prepare an analysis showing whether a product line or other business segment should be added or dropped.

Decisions relating to whether product lines or other segments of a company should be dropped and new ones added are among the most difficult that a manager has to make. In such decisions, many qualitative and quantitative factors must be considered. Ultimately, however, any final decision to drop a business segment or to add a new one hinges primarily on its financial impact. To assess this impact, costs must be carefully analyzed.

An Illustration of Cost Analysis

Exhibit 6–2 provides sales and cost information for the preceding month for the Discount Drug Company and its three major product lines—drugs, cosmetics, and housewares. A quick review of this exhibit suggests that dropping the housewares segment would increase the company's overall net operating income by $8,000. However, this would be a flawed conclusion because the data in Exhibit 6–2 do not distinguish between fixed expenses that can be avoided if a product line is dropped and common fixed expenses that cannot be avoided by dropping any particular product line.

		Product Line		
	Total	Drugs	Cosmetics	House-wares
Sales	$250,000	$125,000	$75,000	$50,000
Variable expenses	105,000	50,000	25,000	30,000
Contribution margin	145,000	75,000	50,000	20,000
Fixed expenses:				
Salaries	50,000	29,500	12,500	8,000
Advertising	15,000	1,000	7,500	6,500
Utilities	2,000	500	500	1,000
Depreciation—fixtures	5,000	1,000	2,000	2,000
Rent	20,000	10,000	6,000	4,000
Insurance	3,000	2,000	500	500
General administrative	30,000	15,000	9,000	6,000
Total fixed expenses	125,000	59,000	38,000	28,000
Net operating income (loss)	$ 20,000	$ 16,000	$12,000	$ (8,000)

EXHIBIT 6–2
Discount Drug Company Product Lines

In this scenario, the two alternatives under consideration are whether to *keep* the housewares product line or *drop* it. If the housewares line is dropped, then the company will lose $20,000 per month in contribution margin because all of this segment's sales and variable expenses will be eliminated. However, by dropping the housewares line, it may be possible to avoid some fixed costs such as salaries or advertising costs. If dropping the housewares line enables the company to avoid more in fixed costs than it loses in contribution margin, then it would be financially advantageous to eliminate the product line. On the other hand, if the company is not able to avoid as much in fixed costs as it loses in contribution margin, then the housewares line should be kept. Thus, the company's managers need to focus their attention on identifying the costs that differ between the two alternatives (i.e., that can be avoided by dropping the housewares product line). They should be asking themselves—"What costs can we avoid if we drop this product line?"—while purposely ignoring any costs that do not differ between the alternatives.

As we have seen from our earlier discussion, not all costs are avoidable. For example, some of the costs associated with a product line may be sunk costs. Other costs may be allocated fixed costs that will not differ in total regardless of whether the product line is dropped or retained.

To show how to proceed in a product-line analysis, suppose Discount Drug Company analyzed the fixed costs being charged to the three product lines and determined the following:

1. The salaries expense represents salaries paid to employees working directly on the product. All of the employees working in housewares would be discharged if the product line is dropped.
2. The advertising expense represents advertisements specific to each product line and avoidable if the line is dropped.
3. The utilities expense represents utilities costs for the entire company. The amount charged to each product line is an allocation based on space occupied and is not avoidable if the product line is dropped.
4. The depreciation expense represents depreciation on previously purchased fixtures that are used to display the various product lines. Although the fixtures are nearly new, they are custom-built and will have no resale value if the housewares line is dropped.
5. The rent expense represents rent on the entire building housing the company; it is allocated to the product lines on the basis of sales dollars. The monthly rent of $20,000 is fixed under a long-term lease agreement.

6. The insurance expense is for insurance carried on inventories within each of the three product lines. If housewares is dropped, the related inventories will be liquidated and the insurance premiums will decrease proportionately.

7. The general administrative expense represents the costs of accounting, purchasing, and general management, which are allocated to the product lines on the basis of sales dollars. These costs will not change if the housewares line is dropped.

With this information, management can determine that $15,000 of the fixed expenses associated with the housewares product line are avoidable and $13,000 are not:

Fixed Expenses	Total Cost Assigned to Housewares	Not Avoidable*	Avoidable
Salaries	$ 8,000		$ 8,000
Advertising	6,500		6,500
Utilities	1,000	$ 1,000	
Depreciation—fixtures	2,000	2,000	
Rent	4,000	4,000	
Insurance	500		500
General administrative	6,000	6,000	
Total	$28,000	$13,000	$15,000

*These fixed costs represent either sunk costs or future costs that will not change whether the housewares line is retained or discontinued.

As stated earlier, if the housewares product line were dropped, the company would lose the product's contribution margin of $20,000 but would save its associated avoidable fixed expenses. We now know that those avoidable fixed expenses total $15,000. Therefore, the financial disadvantage of dropping the housewares product line is $(5,000), as shown below:

Contribution margin lost if the housewares product line is discontinued (see Exhibit 6–2)	$(20,000)
Fixed expenses that can be avoided if the housewares product line is discontinued (see above)	15,000
Financial (disadvantage) of dropping the housewares product line	$ (5,000)

In this case, the fixed costs that can be avoided by dropping the housewares product line ($15,000) are less than the contribution margin that will be lost ($20,000). Therefore, based on the data given, the housewares line should not be discontinued unless a more profitable use can be found for the floor and counter space it is occupying.

A Comparative Format

This decision can also be approached by preparing comparative income statements showing the effects of either keeping or dropping the product line. Exhibit 6–3 contains such an analysis for the Discount Drug Company. As shown in the last column of the exhibit, if the housewares line is dropped, then overall company net operating income will decrease by $5,000 each period. This is the same answer, of course, as we obtained when we focused just on the lost contribution margin and avoidable fixed costs.

Beware of Allocated Fixed Costs

Go back to Exhibit 6–2. Does this exhibit suggest the housewares product line should be kept—as we have just concluded? No, it does not. Exhibit 6–2 suggests that the housewares product line is losing money. Why keep a product line that is showing a loss?

	Keep Housewares	Drop Housewares	Difference: Net Operating Income Increase (or Decrease)
Sales	$50,000	$ 0	$(50,000)
Variable expenses	30,000	0	30,000
Contribution margin	20,000	0	(20,000)
Fixed expenses:			
Salaries	8,000	0	8,000
Advertising	6,500	0	6,500
Utilities	1,000	1,000	0
Depreciation—fixtures	2,000	2,000	0
Rent	4,000	4,000	0
Insurance	500	0	500
General administrative	6,000	6,000	0
Total fixed expenses	28,000	13,000	15,000
Net operating loss	$ (8,000)	$(13,000)	$ (5,000)

EXHIBIT 6–3
A Comparative Format for Product-Line Analysis

The explanation for this apparent inconsistency lies in part with the common fixed costs being allocated to the product lines. One of the great dangers in allocating common fixed costs is that such allocations can make a product line (or other business segment) look less profitable than it really is. In this instance, allocating the common fixed costs among all product lines makes the housewares product line appear to be unprofitable. However, as we have just shown, there is a $5,000 financial *disadvantage* associated with dropping the product line. This point can be seen clearly if we redo Exhibit 6–2 by eliminating the allocation of the common fixed costs. Exhibit 6–4 uses the segmented approach from Chapter 4 to estimate the profitability of the product lines.

Exhibit 6–4 gives us a much different perspective of the housewares line than does Exhibit 6–2. As shown in Exhibit 6–4, the housewares line is covering all of its own traceable fixed costs and generating a $3,000 segment margin toward covering the common fixed costs of the company. Unless another product line can be found that will generate a segment margin greater than $3,000, the company would be better off keeping the housewares line rather than dropping it.

Additionally, managers may choose to retain an unprofitable product line if it helps sell other products, or if it serves as a "magnet" to attract customers. Bread, for example, may not be an especially profitable line in some food stores, but customers expect it to be available, and many of them would undoubtedly shift their buying elsewhere if a particular store decided to stop carrying it.

24 HOUR FITNESS TO CLOSE 135 OF ITS 445 GYMS

In response to the coronavirus pandemic, 24 Hour Fitness decided to close 135 of its 445 gyms and, along with Gold's Gym International, filed for Chapter 11 bankruptcy protection. 24 Hour Fitness had been struggling before the pandemic "with declining membership and rising costs due to minimum wage increases"; however, its CEO stated, "If it were not for COVID-19 and its devastating effects, we would not be filing for Chapter 11." As 24 Hour Fitness began reopening its remaining locations, it used "an app-based reservation system to enforce social-distancing requirements and a touchless check-in system to limit contact with surfaces."

Source: Alexander Gladstone, "24 Hour Fitness, KO'd by Virus, Files for Bankruptcy," *The Wall Street Journal*, June 16, 2020, p. B3.

Allen J. Schaben/Getty Images

EXHIBIT 6–4

Discount Drug Company Product Lines—Recast in Contribution Format (from Exhibit 6–2)

		Product Line		
	Total	**Drugs**	**Cosmetics**	**House-wares**
Sales	$250,000	$125,000	$75,000	$50,000
Variable expenses	105,000	50,000	25,000	30,000
Contribution margin	145,000	75,000	50,000	20,000
Traceable fixed expenses:				
Salaries	50,000	29,500	12,500	8,000
Advertising	15,000	1,000	7,500	6,500
Depreciation—fixtures	5,000	1,000	2,000	2,000
Insurance	3,000	2,000	500	500
Total traceable fixed expenses	73,000	33,500	22,500	17,000
Product-line segment margin	72,000	$ 41,500	$27,500	$ 3,000*
Common fixed expenses:				
Utilities	2,000			
Rent	20,000			
General administrative	30,000			
Total common fixed expenses	52,000			
Net operating income	$ 20,000			

*If the housewares line is dropped, the company will lose the $3,000 segment margin generated by this product line. In addition, we have seen that the $2,000 depreciation on the fixtures is a sunk cost that cannot be avoided. The sum of these two figures (= $3,000 + $2,000) equals the financial disadvantage of $5,000 associated with discontinuing the housewares product line. Of course, the company may later choose to drop the product if circumstances change—such as a pending decision to replace the fixtures.

Sourcing Decisions

LEARNING OBJECTIVE 6–3

Identify the relevant costs and benefits associated with sourcing decisions.

Providing a product or service to a customer involves many steps. For example, consider all of the steps necessary to develop and sell a product such as a Fitbit fitness watch. First, engineers need to develop the underlying electronics that provide customers with capabilities such as real-time GPS tracking, heart rate monitoring, and activity monitoring. In addition, they need to design a wrist watch that not only houses the electronic circuitry, but that also meets the customers' needs in terms of aesthetics, durability, and functionality. Second, the watches need to be assembled, tested, individually packaged, and then boxed in larger quantities to enable shipping. Third, the finished goods need to be transported to retail sales locations and eventually sold to customers. Finally, the company needs to provide after-sale services such as internet and phone-based help lines, warranty claims, and product returns. All of these activities, from development, to production, to after-sales service, are called a *value chain.*

Separate companies may carry out each of the activities in the value chain, or a single company may carry out several. When a company is involved in more than one activity in the entire value chain, it is **vertically integrated.** Some companies control all of the activities in the value chain from producing basic raw materials right up to the final distribution of finished goods and provision of after-sales service. Other companies are content to integrate on a smaller scale by purchasing many of the parts and materials that go into their finished products. A decision to carry out one of the activities in the value chain internally, rather than to buy externally from a supplier, is called a **sourcing decision.** Quite often these decisions involve whether to make a component part or buy it from a supplier. They also include whether to perform various organizational activities (such as after-sales customer service, payroll, accounting, human resource management, and marketing) or to outsource them to an external provider.

Strategic Aspects of Sourcing Decisions

Vertical integration provides certain advantages. An integrated company is less dependent on its suppliers and may be able to ensure a smoother flow of parts and materials for production than a nonintegrated company. For example, a strike against a major parts supplier can interrupt the operations of a nonintegrated company for many months, whereas an integrated company that is producing its own parts would be able to continue operations. Also, some companies feel that they can control quality better by producing their own parts and materials, rather than by relying on the quality control standards of outside suppliers. In addition, an integrated company realizes profits from the parts and materials that it is "making" rather than "buying," as well as profits from its regular operations.

The advantages of vertical integration are counterbalanced by the advantages of using external suppliers. By pooling demand from a number of companies, a supplier may be able to enjoy economies of scale. These economies of scale can result in higher quality and lower costs than would be possible if the company were to attempt to make the parts or provide the service on its own. A company must be careful, however, to retain control over activities that are essential to maintaining its competitive position. For example, HP controls the software for laser printers that it makes in cooperation with Canon Inc. of Japan. The present trend appears to be toward less vertical integration, with companies like Oracle and HP concentrating on hardware and software design and relying on outside suppliers for almost everything else in the value chain.

An Example of a Sourcing Decision

To provide an illustration of a sourcing decision, consider Mountain Goat Cycles. The company is currently making the heavy-duty gear shifters that it installs on its most popular line of mountain bikes. The company's Accounting Department reports the following costs of making 8,000 shifters each year:

	Per Unit	8,000 Units
Direct materials	$ 6	$ 48,000
Direct labor	4	32,000
Variable overhead	1	8,000
Supervisor's salary	3	24,000
Depreciation of special equipment	2	16,000
Allocated general overhead	5	40,000
Total cost	$21	$168,000

An outside supplier offered to sell 8,000 shifters a year to Mountain Goat Cycles for a price of only $19 each, or a total of $152,000 (= 8,000 shifters × $19 each). Should the company stop making the shifters internally and buy them from the outside supplier? As always, the decision should depend on the relevant costs—those that differ between the alternatives. And the costs that differ between the alternatives consist of the costs that could be avoided by buying the shifters from the outside supplier. If the costs that can be avoided by buying the shifters from the outside supplier total less than $152,000, then the company should continue to make its own shifters and reject the outside supplier's offer. On the other hand, if the costs that can be avoided by buying the shifters from the outside supplier total more than $152,000, the outside supplier's offer should be accepted.

LOWE'S OUTSOURCES MAINTENANCE AND ASSEMBLY WORK

Lowe's, the home improvement chain headquartered in Mooresville, North Carolina, has decided to lay off thousands of its maintenance and assembly workers. Rather than paying its own employees to perform tasks, such as assembling barbecue grills and playsets, the company plans to cut costs by relying on external contractors. The company's outsourcing decision comes at a time when many brick-and-mortar retailers are scrutinizing their labor costs in response to the growing presence of online competitors.

Source: Sarah Nassauer, "Lowe's to Outsource, Lay Off Thousands," *The Wall Street Journal*, August 2, 2019, p. B1.

Exhibit 6–5 contains the relevant cost analysis of the make or buy decision related to the gear shifters. The total amount paid to the supplier of $152,000 is the only relevant cash flow shown in the Buy column. The Make column includes direct materials ($48,000), direct labor ($32,000), and variable overhead ($8,000). All of these costs are relevant to the decision because they could be avoided by purchasing the shifters from the outside supplier. In other words, Mountain Goat Cycles would no longer incur these variable manufacturing costs if it stopped making the shifters. The Make column also includes the supervisor's salary of $24,000. This is a relevant cost because we have assumed that the supervisor of the gear shifter manufacturing process would not be retained if the company stops making the shifters; thus, the supervisory salary of $24,000 would be avoided if the company decides to buy the gear shifters from an outside supplier.[4]

EXHIBIT 6–5

Mountain Goat Cycles' Sourcing Decision

	Total Relevant Costs—8,000 units	
	Make	**Buy**
Outside purchase price		$152,000
Direct materials (8,000 units × $6 per unit)	$ 48,000	
Direct labor (8,000 units × $4 per unit)	32,000	
Variable overhead (8,000 units × $1 per unit)	8,000	
Supervisor's salary	24,000	
Depreciation of special equipment (not relevant)		
Allocated general overhead (not relevant)		
Total cost	$112,000	$152,000
Financial advantage of making the gear shifters	$40,000	

_____

[4] Many companies adhere to a "no layoffs" policy because they believe it improves employee morale, organizational learning, customer satisfaction, and financial results. Furthermore, in some countries, such as France, Germany, and Japan, labor regulations and cultural norms may limit management's ability to reduce the size of the labor force. In these contexts, it would be incorrect to assume that direct labor and supervision are automatically avoidable costs in sourcing decisions. Nonetheless, for the sake of consistency, within this chapter you should assume that direct labor and supervisory salaries are avoidable costs when analyzing sourcing decisions unless you are explicitly told otherwise.

The depreciation of special equipment of $16,000 (as shown in the original data) is an irrelevant cost because the equipment has already been purchased; thus, the cost incurred to buy the equipment is a sunk cost. The depreciation charge of $16,000 simply spreads this sunk cost over the equipment's useful life. If the equipment could be sold, its salvage value would be relevant. Or if the equipment could be used to make other products, this could be relevant as well. However, we will assume that the equipment has no salvage value and that it has no other use except making the heavy-duty gear shifters.

The allocated general overhead of $40,000 (as shown in the original data) is also an irrelevant cost in this decision context. We draw this conclusion because we are assuming that these allocated costs are common to all items produced in the factory and would continue unchanged even if the shifters were bought from an outside supplier. Throughout this chapter, you should assume that these types of allocated common costs are irrelevant to the decision unless you are explicitly told otherwise. If you are explicitly told that a portion of allocated common costs can be avoided by choosing one alternative over another, then by all means, treat the explicitly identified avoidable costs as relevant costs. Otherwise, err on the side of ignoring allocated common costs when choosing between alternatives.

Because the avoidable costs related to making the shifters are $40,000 less than the total amount that would be paid to buy them from the outside supplier, Mountain Goat Cycles should reject the outside supplier's offer. However, the company may wish to consider one additional factor before coming to a final decision—the opportunity cost of the space that it currently uses to produce the shifters.

Opportunity Cost

If the space now being used to produce the shifters *would otherwise be idle,* then Mountain Goat Cycles should continue to make its own shifters and the supplier's offer should be rejected, as stated above. Idle space that has no alternative use has an opportunity cost of zero.

But what if the space now being used to make shifters could be used for some other purpose? In that case, the space would have an opportunity cost equal to the segment margin that could be derived from the best alternative use of the space.

To illustrate, assume the space now being used to make shifters could be used to produce a new cross-country bike that would generate a segment margin of $60,000 per year. Under these conditions, Mountain Goat Cycles would be $20,000 better off by choosing to buy the shifters from the outside supplier (rather than making them) and using the newly available space to produce the cross-country bike:

	Make	Buy
Total annual cost (see Exhibit 6–5)	$112,000	$152,000
Opportunity cost—segment margin forgone on a potential new product line	60,000	
Total cost	$172,000	$152,000
Financial advantage of buying the gear shifters from the outside supplier		$20,000

Opportunity costs are not recorded in the organization's general ledger because they do not represent actual dollar outlays. Rather, they represent economic benefits that are *forgone* as a result of pursuing some course of action. The opportunity cost for Mountain Goat Cycles is sufficiently large in this case to change the decision.

OUTSOURCING COMPANIES CONTINUE TO GROW

Research conducted by S&P Global Market Intelligence indicates that five of the top 20 global employers are outsourcing and "workforce solutions" companies. One of those five companies is Accenture, which now employs 435,000 employees, up from just 200,000 in 2010. The Dublin, Ireland–based company provides consulting and/or outsourcing services to 95 of the Fortune Global 100 companies. Accenture tells companies it "can do their work better and more cheaply, prodding executives to view labor as an on-demand resource they can rent as needed." As the outsourcing sector's annual revenues surpass $37 billion, some economists are expressing concerns because their research suggests "that outsourcing is a significant factor fueling the rise of income inequality in the past decade."

Source: Lauren Weber, "Some of the World's Largest Employers No Longer Sell Things, They Rent Workers," *The Wall Street Journal*, December 28, 2017.

Special Order Decisions

LEARNING OBJECTIVE 6–4
Prepare an analysis showing whether a special order should be accepted.

Managers must often evaluate whether a *special order* should be accepted, and if the order is accepted, the price that should be charged. A **special order** is a one-time order that is not considered part of the company's normal ongoing business. To illustrate, Mountain Goat Cycles has just received a request from the Seattle Police Department to produce 100 specially modified mountain bikes at a price of $558 each. The bikes would be used to patrol some of the more densely populated residential sections of the city. Mountain Goat Cycles can easily modify its City Cruiser model to fit the specifications of the Seattle Police. The normal selling price of the City Cruiser bike is $698, and its unit product cost is $564, as shown below:

Direct materials	$372
Direct labor	90
Manufacturing overhead	102
Unit product cost	$564

The variable portion of the above manufacturing overhead is $12 per unit. The order would have no effect on the company's total fixed manufacturing overhead costs.

The modifications requested by the Seattle Police Department consist of welded brackets to hold radios, nightsticks, and other gear. These modifications would require $34 in incremental variable costs. In addition, the company would have to pay a graphics design studio $2,400 to design and cut stencils that would be used for spray painting the Seattle Police Department's logo and other identifying marks on the bikes. The company's managers believe that this order will have no effect on the company's other sales, and it can be produced without disrupting any of the company's regular scheduled production.

To quantify the financial advantage (disadvantage) of accepting the Seattle Police Department's order, Mountain Goat Cycles should focus its attention on the incremental costs and benefits associated with the order. Because the existing fixed manufacturing overhead costs would not be affected by the order, they are not relevant. The financial advantage (disadvantage) of the special order would be computed as follows:

	Per Unit	Total 100 Bikes
Incremental revenue (a)	$558	$55,800
Less incremental costs:		
Variable costs:		
Direct materials	372	37,200
Direct labor	90	9,000
Variable manufacturing overhead	12	1,200
Special modifications	34	3,400
Total variable cost	$508	50,800
Fixed cost:		
Purchase of stencils		2,400
Total incremental cost (b)		53,200
Financial advantage of accepting the order (a) − (b)		$ 2,600

Therefore, even though the $558 price on the special order is below the normal $564 unit product cost and the order would require additional costs, the company is still better off accepting the order. In general, a special order should be accepted if the incremental revenue from the special order exceeds the incremental costs of the order. However, it is important to make sure that there is indeed idle capacity and that the special order does not cut into normal unit sales or undercut prices on normal sales. For example, if the company was operating at capacity, opportunity costs would have to be taken into account, as well as the incremental costs that have already been detailed above.

Volume Trade-Off Decisions

Companies are forced to make *volume trade-off decisions* when they do not have enough capacity to produce all of the products and sales volumes demanded by their customers. In these situations, companies must trade off or sacrifice production of some products in favor of others in an effort to maximize profits. The key questions become: How should companies manage those trade-offs? Which products should they produce and sell, and which sales opportunities should they intentionally bypass?

To answer these questions, our discussion of volume trade-off decisions will proceed in three steps. First, we'll define the meaning of a constraint. Second, we'll explain how to determine the most profitable use of a constrained resource. Third, we'll discuss how to determine the value of obtaining more of a constrained resource and how to manage constraints to increase profits.

What Is a Constraint?

A **constraint** is anything that prevents you from getting more of what you want. Every individual and every organization face at least one constraint, so it is not difficult to find examples of constraints.[5] You may not have enough time to study thoroughly for every

---

[5] The exercises and problems included at the end of this chapter always assume the company has only one constraint. When companies have more than one constraint, the optimal production mix can be found using a quantitative method known as linear programming, which is available within Microsoft Excel using a feature called Solver. For an introduction to product mix decision making in the presence of more than one constraint, see the Excel Analytics, Applying Tableau, and Applying Power BI exercises that accompany this chapter within Connect.

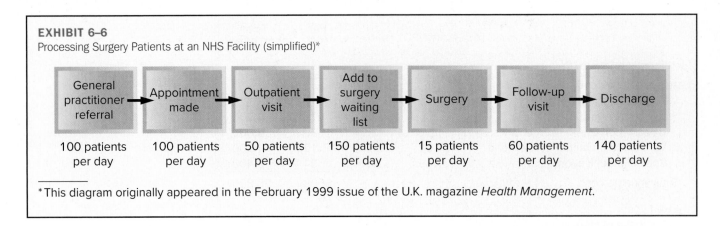

EXHIBIT 6–6
Processing Surgery Patients at an NHS Facility (simplified)*

General practitioner referral	Appointment made	Outpatient visit	Add to surgery waiting list	Surgery	Follow-up visit	Discharge
100 patients per day	100 patients per day	50 patients per day	150 patients per day	15 patients per day	60 patients per day	140 patients per day

*This diagram originally appeared in the February 1999 issue of the U.K. magazine *Health Management.*

subject *and* go out with your friends on the weekend, so time is your constraint. United Airlines has only a limited number of loading gates available at its busy Chicago O'Hare hub, so its constraint is loading gates. Vail Resorts has only a limited amount of land to develop as homesites and commercial lots at its ski areas, so its constraint is land.

As an example, long waiting periods for surgery are a chronic problem in the National Health Service (NHS), the government-funded provider of health care in the United Kingdom. The diagram in Exhibit 6–6 illustrates a simplified version of the steps followed by a surgery patient. The number of patients who can be processed through each step in a day is indicated in the exhibit. For example, appointments for outpatient visits can be made for as many as 100 referrals from general practitioners in a day.

The constraint, or **bottleneck,** in the system is determined by the step that limits total output because it has the smallest capacity—in this case surgery. The total number of patients processed through the entire system cannot exceed 15 per day—the maximum number of patients who can be treated in surgery. No matter how hard managers, doctors, and nurses try to improve the processing rate elsewhere in the system, they will never succeed in driving down wait lists until the capacity of surgery is increased. In fact, improvements elsewhere in the system—particularly before the constraint—are likely to result in even longer waiting times and more frustrated patients and health care providers. Thus, to be effective, improvement efforts must be focused on the constraint. A business process, such as the process for serving surgery patients, is like a chain. If you want to increase the strength of a chain, what is the most effective way to do this? Should you concentrate your efforts on strengthening the strongest link, all the links, or the weakest link? Clearly, focusing your effort on the weakest link will bring the biggest benefit.

The procedure to follow to strengthen the chain is clear. First, identify the weakest link, which is the constraint. In the case of the NHS, the constraint is surgery. Second, do not place a greater strain on the system than the weakest link can handle—if you do, the chain will break. In the case of the NHS, more referrals than surgery can accommodate lead to unacceptably long waiting lists. Third, concentrate improvement efforts on strengthening the weakest link. In the case of the NHS, this means finding ways to increase the number of surgeries that can be performed in a day. Fourth, if the improvement efforts are successful, eventually the weakest link will improve to the point where it is no longer the weakest link. At that point, the new weakest link (i.e., the new constraint) must be identified, and improvement efforts must be shifted over to that link. This simple sequential process provides a powerful strategy for optimizing business processes.

Utilizing a Constrained Resource to Maximize Profits

LEARNING OBJECTIVE 6–5

Determine the most profitable use of a constrained resource.

Managers routinely face the challenge of managing constrained resources in a manner that maximizes profits. A department store, for example, has a limited amount of floor space and therefore cannot stock every product that may be available. A manufacturer has a limited number of machine-hours and a limited number of direct labor-hours at its disposal.

When companies face these types of constraints, their managers must decide which products or services make the most profitable use of those limited resources. Because fixed costs remain the same regardless of how a constrained resource is used, managers should ignore them when making volume trade-off decisions and instead focus their attention on identifying the mix of products that maximizes the total contribution margin.

Given that some products must be cut back when a constraint exists, the key to maximizing the total contribution margin may seem obvious—favor the products with the highest unit contribution margins. Unfortunately, that is not quite correct. Rather, the correct solution is to favor the products that provide the highest *contribution margin per unit of the constrained resource*. To illustrate, in addition to its other products, Mountain Goat Cycles makes saddlebags for bicycles called *panniers*. These panniers come in two models—a touring model and a mountain model. Cost and revenue data for the two models of panniers follow:

	Mountain Pannier	Touring Pannier
Selling price per unit..................................	$25	$30
Variable cost per unit.................................	10	18
Contribution margin per unit.........................	$15	$12
Contribution margin (CM) ratio	60%	40%

The mountain pannier appears to be much more profitable than the touring pannier. It has a $15 per unit contribution margin as compared to only $12 per unit for the touring model, and it has a 60 percent CM ratio as compared to only 40 percent for the touring model.

But now, let us add one more piece of information—the plant that makes the panniers is operating at capacity. This does not mean that every machine and every person in the plant is working at the maximum possible rate. Because machines have different capacities, some machines will be operating at less than 100 percent of capacity. However, if the plant as a whole cannot produce any more units, some machine or process must be operating at capacity. The machine or process that is limiting overall output is called the bottleneck—it is the constraint.

At Mountain Goat Cycles, the bottleneck (i.e., constraint) is a stitching machine. The mountain pannier requires two minutes of stitching time per unit, and the touring pannier requires one minute of stitching time per unit. The stitching machine is available for 12,000 minutes per month, and the company can sell up to 4,000 mountain panniers and 7,000 touring panniers per month. Producing up to this demand for both products would require 15,000 minutes, as shown below:

	Mountain Pannier	Touring Pannier	Total
Monthly demand (a)	4,000 units	7,000 units	
Stitching machine time required to produce one unit (b)........	2 minutes	1 minute	
Total stitching time required (a) × (b)	8,000 minutes	7,000 minutes	15,000 minutes

Producing up to demand would require 15,000 minutes, but only 12,000 minutes are available. This simply confirms that the stitching machine is the bottleneck. By definition, because the stitching machine is a bottleneck, the stitching machine does not have enough capacity to satisfy the existing demand for mountain panniers and touring panniers. Therefore, some orders for the products will have to be turned down. Naturally, managers will want to know which product is less profitable. To answer this question, they should focus on the contribution margin per unit of the constrained resource. This figure is computed by dividing a product's contribution margin per unit by the amount of the constrained resource required to make a unit of that product. These calculations are carried out below for the mountain and touring panniers:

	Mountain Pannier	Touring Pannier
Contribution margin per unit (a)	$15.00	$12.00
Stitching machine time required to produce one unit (b)	2 minutes	1 minute
Contribution margin per unit of the constrained resource (a) ÷ (b)	$7.50 per minute	$12.00 per minute

It is now easy to decide which product is more profitable and should be emphasized. Each minute on the stitching machine devoted to the touring pannier results in an increase of $12.00 in contribution margin and profits. The comparable figure for the mountain pannier is only $7.50 per minute. Therefore, the touring model should be emphasized. Even though the mountain model has the larger contribution margin per unit and the larger CM ratio, the touring model provides the larger contribution margin in relation to the constrained resource.

To verify that the touring model is indeed the more profitable product, suppose an hour of additional stitching time is available and unfilled orders exist for both products. The additional hour on the stitching machine could be used to make either 30 mountain panniers (60 minutes ÷ 2 minutes per mountain pannier) or 60 touring panniers (60 minutes ÷ 1 minute per touring pannier), with the following profit implications:

	Mountain Pannier	Touring Pannier
Contribution margin per unit (a)	$ 15	$ 12
Additional units that can be processed in one hour (b)	30	60
Additional contribution margin (a) × (b)	$450	$720

Because the additional contribution margin would be $720 for the touring panniers and only $450 for the mountain panniers, the touring panniers make the more profitable use of the company's constrained resource—the stitching machine.

The stitching machine is available for 12,000 minutes per month, and producing the touring panniers is the more profitable use of the stitching machine. Therefore, to maximize profits, the company should produce all of the touring panniers the market will demand (7,000 units) and use any remaining capacity to produce mountain panniers. The computations to determine how many mountain panniers can be produced are as follows:

Monthly demand for touring panniers (a)	7,000 units
Stitching machine time required to produce one touring pannier (b)	1 minute
Total stitching time required to produce touring panniers (a) × (b)	7,000 minutes
Remaining stitching time available (12,000 minutes − 7,000 minutes) (c)	5,000 minutes
Stitching machine time required to produce one mountain pannier (d)	2 minutes
Production of mountain panniers (c) ÷ (d)	2,500 units

Therefore, profit would be maximized by producing 7,000 touring panniers and then using the remaining capacity to produce 2,500 mountain panniers. With this product mix, the company can earn a total contribution margin of $121,500 computed as follows:

	Mountain Pannier	Touring Pannier	Total
Contribution margin per unit (a)	$15	$12	
Number of units produced (b).	2,500	7,000	
Contribution margin (a) × (b)	$37,500	$84,000	$121,500

This example clearly shows that looking at each product's unit contribution margin alone is not enough; the contribution margin must be viewed in relation to the amount of the constrained resource each product requires.

AS CHECKOUT LINES GROW, MORE CUSTOMERS BUY ONLINE

Have you ever walked into a large retail store and noticed only three or four of the dozens of check-out lanes are open? To make matters worse, each open check-out lane has numerous customers standing in line waiting to pay for their purchases. In essence, these check-out lanes represent a constraint that does not exist at online retailers, such as Amazon.com.

A survey conducted by Ayden estimates that 86% of shoppers have walked out of a retail store location in the last 12 months due to long check-out lines, thereby costing brick-and-mortar retailers $37.7 billion in lost sales. As retailers such as Macy's, J.C. Penney, Kohl's, Target, and Nordstrom seek to cut costs by reducing headcount, they are losing sales to customers who would rather stay home, save time, avoid the hassles, and shop online.

Source: Suzanne Kapner, "Stores Slash Staffs and Watch Lines Grow," *The Wall Street Journal*, May 1, 2018, pp. B1 and B2.

Worawee Meepian/Shutterstock

Managing Constraints

Effectively managing an organization's constraints is a key to increasing profits. As discussed above, when a constraint exists in the production process, managers can increase profits by producing the products with the highest contribution margin per unit of the constrained resource. However, they can also increase profits by increasing the capacity of the bottleneck operation.

When a manager increases the capacity of the bottleneck, it is called **relaxing (or elevating) the constraint.** In the case of Mountain Goat Cycles, the company is currently working one eight-hour shift. To relax the constraint, the stitching machine operator could be asked to work overtime. No one else would have to work overtime. Because all of the other operations involved in producing panniers have excess capacity, up to a point, the additional panniers processed through the stitching machine during overtime could be finished during normal working hours in the other operations.

The benefits from relaxing the constraint are often enormous and can be easily quantified—the key is the contribution margin per unit of the constrained resource that we have already computed. This number, which was originally stated in terms of minutes in the Mountain Goat Cycles example, is restated below in terms of hours for easier interpretation:

	Mountain Pannier	Touring Pannier
Contribution margin per minute of the constrained resource (a)	$7.50 per minute	$12.00 per minute
Minutes per hour (b)	60 minutes	60 minutes
Contribution margin per hour of the constrained resource (a) × (b)	$450 per hour	$720 per hour

So what is the value of relaxing the constraint—the time on the stitching machine? The manager should first ask, "What would I do with additional capacity at the bottleneck if it were available?" If the time were to be used to make additional mountain panniers, it would be worth $450 per hour. If the time were to be used to make additional touring panniers, it would be worth $720 per hour. In this latter case, the company should be willing to pay an overtime *premium* to the stitching machine operator of up to $720 per hour! Suppose, for example, that the stitching machine operator is paid $20 per hour during normal working hours and time-and-a-half, or $30 per hour, for overtime. In this case, the premium for overtime is only $10 per hour, whereas, in principle, the company should be willing to pay a premium of up to $720 per hour. The difference between what the company should be willing to pay as a premium, $720 per hour, and what it would actually have to pay, $10 per hour, is a pure profit of $710 per hour.

To reinforce this concept, suppose there are only unfilled orders for the mountain pannier. How much would it be worth to the company to run the stitching machine overtime in this situation? Because the additional capacity would be used to make the mountain pannier, the value of that additional capacity would drop to $7.50 per minute or $450 per hour. Nevertheless, the value of relaxing the constraint would still be quite high and the company should be willing to pay an overtime premium of up to $450 per hour.

These calculations indicate managers should pay great attention to the bottleneck operation. If a bottleneck machine breaks down or is ineffectively utilized, the losses to the company can be quite large. In our example, for every minute the stitching machine is down due to breakdowns or setups, the company loses between $7.50 and $12.00.[6] The losses on an hourly basis are between $450 and $720! In contrast, there is no such loss of contribution margin if time is lost on a machine that is not a bottleneck—such machines have excess capacity anyway.

The implications are clear. Managers should focus much of their attention on managing the bottleneck. As we have discussed, managers should emphasize products that make the most profitable use of the constrained resource. They should also make sure that products are processed smoothly through the bottleneck, with minimal lost time due to breakdowns and setups. And they should try to find ways to increase the capacity at the bottleneck.

The capacity of a bottleneck can be effectively increased in a number of ways, including:

- Working overtime on the bottleneck.
- Subcontracting some of the processing that would ordinarily be done at the bottleneck.
- Investing in additional machines at the bottleneck.
- Shifting workers from processes that are not bottlenecks to the process that is the bottleneck.
- Focusing business process improvement efforts on the bottleneck.
- Reducing defective units. Each defective unit that is processed through the bottleneck and subsequently scrapped takes the place of a good unit that could have been sold.

The last three methods of increasing the capacity of the bottleneck are particularly attractive because they are essentially free and may even yield additional cost savings.

---

[6] Setups are required when production switches from one product to another. For example, consider a company that makes automobile side panels. The panels are painted before shipping them to an automobile manufacturer for final assembly. The customer might require 100 blue panels, 50 black panels, and 20 yellow panels. Each time the color is changed, the painting equipment must be purged of the old paint color, cleaned with solvents, and refilled with the new paint color. This takes time. In fact, some equipment may require such lengthy and frequent setups that it is unavailable for actual production more often than not.

Joint Product Costs and Sell or Process Further Decisions

In some industries, two or more products, known as **joint products,** are produced from a single raw material input. For example, in the petroleum refining industry, a large number of joint products are extracted from crude oil, including gasoline, jet fuel, home heating oil, lubricants, asphalt, and various organic chemicals. The point in a manufacturing process where joint products (such as gasoline and jet fuel) can be recognized as separate products is referred to as the **split-off point.**

> **LEARNING OBJECTIVE 6–7**
> Prepare an analysis showing whether joint products should be sold at the split-off point or processed further.

Quite often joint products can be sold at the split-off point, or they can be processed further and sold for a higher price. A decision as to whether a joint product should be sold at the split-off point or processed further is known as a **sell or process further decision.** To make these decisions, managers need to follow a three-step process. First, they should always ignore all **joint costs,** which include all costs incurred up to the split-off point. These costs should be ignored because they are sunk costs that cannot be changed regardless of whether the manager chooses to sell a joint product at the split-off point or process it further.

The second step is to determine the incremental revenue earned by further processing the joint product. This computation is performed by taking the revenue earned after further processing the joint product and subtracting the revenue that could be earned by selling the joint product at the split-off point.

The third step is to take the incremental revenue from step two and subtract the incremental costs associated with processing the joint product beyond the split-off point. If the resulting answer is positive, then the joint product should be processed further and sold for a higher price. If the answer is negative, then the joint product should be sold at the split-off point without any further processing.

Santa Maria Wool Cooperative: An Example

Santa Maria Wool Cooperative buys raw wool from local sheepherders, separates the wool into three grades—coarse, fine, and superfine—and then dyes the wool using traditional methods that rely on pigments from local materials. Exhibit 6–7 contains a diagram of the company's production process.

The company's joint costs include $200,000 for the raw wool and $40,000 for separating the raw wool into three intermediate products. The three types of undyed wool are called intermediate products because they are not finished at this point. Nevertheless, a market does exist for undyed wool—although at a significantly lower price than finished, dyed wool. More specifically and as shown in Exhibit 6–7, the undyed coarse wool, undyed fine wool, and undyed superfine wool each can be sold at the split-off point for $120,000, $150,000, and $60,000, respectively.

Exhibit 6–7 also shows that the cost of further processing the undyed coarse wool, undyed fine wool, and undyed superfine wool is $50,000, $60,000, and $10,000, respectively. Furthermore, the sales values of dyed coarse wool, dyed fine wool, and dyed superfine wool are $160,000, $240,000, and $90,000, respectively.

If Santa Maria Wool Cooperative chooses to further process all three of its intermediate products, it will earn a profit of $130,000, as shown below:

Analysis of the profitability of the overall operation:		
Combined final sales value		
($160,000 + $240,000 + $90,000)		$490,000
Less costs of producing the end products:		
Cost of wool	$200,000	
Cost of separating wool	40,000	
Combined costs of dyeing		
($50,000 + $60,000 + $10,000)	120,000	360,000
Profit		$130,000

EXHIBIT 6–7
Santa Maria Wool Cooperative

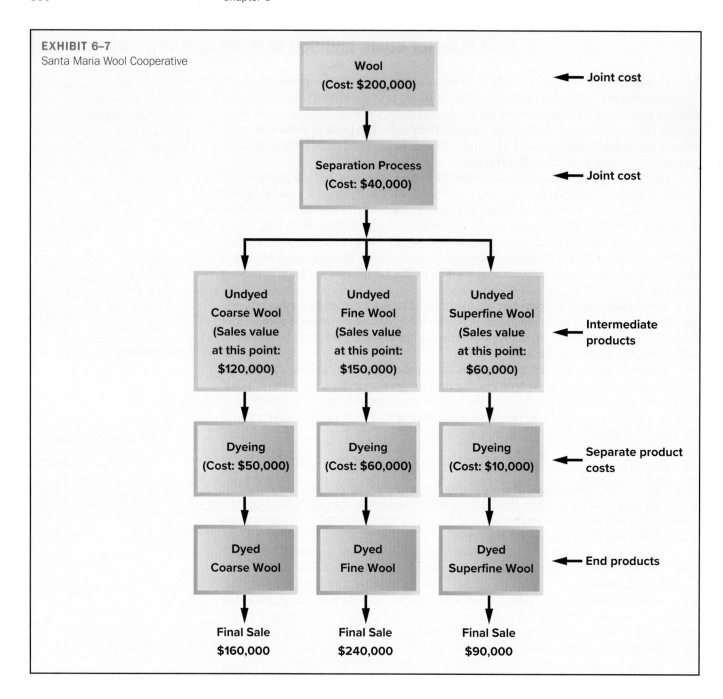

Note that the joint costs of buying the wool ($200,000) and separating the wool ($40,000) are relevant when considering the profitability of the entire operation. This is because these joint costs could be avoided if the entire operation were shut down.

While Santa Maria can make a profit of $130,000 if it further processes all three products, the questions we want to explore further are: Should the company further process all three products? Could the company be financially better off by selling one or more of the three products at the split-off point?

The appropriate way to answer these sell or process further questions is to compare the incremental revenues and incremental costs for each of the joint products as follows:

Analysis of sell or process further:

	Coarse Wool	Fine Wool	Superfine Wool
Final sales value after further processing........	$160,000	$240,000	$90,000
Less sales value at the split-off point............	120,000	150,000	60,000
Incremental revenue from further processing	40,000	90,000	30,000
Less cost of further processing (dyeing).........	50,000	60,000	10,000
Financial advantage (disadvantage) of further processing	$ (10,000)	$ 30,000	$20,000

As this analysis shows, the company would be better off selling the undyed coarse wool at the split-off point rather than processing it further. The other two products should be processed further and dyed before selling them.

Note that the joint costs of the wool ($200,000) and the wool separation process ($40,000) play no role in the decision to sell or further process the intermediate products. These joint costs are relevant in a decision of whether to buy wool and to run the wool separation process, but they are not relevant in decisions about what to do with the intermediate products once they have been separated.

Finally, we can recompute Santa Maria's overall profitability if it chooses to sell the undyed coarse wool at the split-off point and to further process the dyed fine wool and the dyed superfine wool as follows:

Analysis of the profitability of the overall operation:

Combined final sales value ($120,000 + $240,000 + $90,000)		$450,000
Less costs of producing the end products:		
Cost of wool..	$200,000	
Cost of separating wool............................	40,000	
Combined costs of dyeing ($60,000 + $10,000)............................	70,000	310,000
Profit		$140,000

Notice that the revised profit of $140,000 is $10,000 higher than the profit of $130,000 computed earlier when the company further processes all three products. This $10,000 increase in profit equals the $10,000 financial disadvantage of further processing coarse wool that was computed earlier.

Activity-Based Costing and Relevant Costs

As discussed in an earlier chapter, activity-based costing can be used to help identify potentially relevant costs for decision-making purposes. Activity-based costing improves the traceability of costs by focusing on the activities caused by a product or other segment. However, managers should exercise caution against reading more into this "traceability" than really exists. People have a tendency to assume if a cost is traceable to a segment, then the cost is automatically an avoidable cost. That is not true because the costs provided by a well-designed activity-based costing system are only *potentially* relevant. Before making a decision, managers must decide which of the potentially relevant costs are actually avoidable. Only those costs that are avoidable are relevant, and the others should be ignored.

To illustrate, refer again to the data relating to the housewares line in Exhibit 6–4. The $2,000 fixtures depreciation is a traceable cost of the housewares lines because it directly relates to activities in that department. We found, however, that the $2,000 is not avoidable if the housewares line is dropped. The key lesson here is that the method used to assign a cost to a product or other segment does not change the basic nature of the cost. A sunk cost such as depreciation of old equipment is still a sunk cost regardless of whether it is traced directly to a particular segment on an activity basis, allocated to all segments on the basis of labor-hours, or treated in some other way in the costing process. Regardless of the method used to assign costs to products or other segments, the principles discussed in this chapter must be applied to determine the costs that are avoidable in each situation.

Summary

Everything in this chapter consists of applications of one simple but powerful idea—only those costs and benefits that differ between alternatives are relevant in a decision. All other costs and benefits are irrelevant and should be ignored. In particular, sunk costs are irrelevant, as are future costs that do not differ between alternatives.

This simple idea was applied in a variety of situations, including decisions that involve adding or dropping a product line, making or buying a component, accepting or rejecting a special order, using a constrained resource, and further processing joint products. This list includes only a small sample of the possible applications of the differential cost concept. Indeed, any decision involving costs hinges on the proper identification and analysis of the differential costs. We will continue to focus on the concept of differential costs in the following chapter where long-term investment decisions are considered.

 Data Analytics Exercise available in Connect to complement this chapter

Review Problem: Differential Analysis

Charter Sports Equipment manufactures round, rectangular, and octagonal trampolines. Sales and expense data for the past month follow:

| | Total | Trampoline | | |
		Round	Rectangular	Octagonal
Sales	$1,000,000	$140,000	$500,000	$360,000
Variable expenses	410,000	60,000	200,000	150,000
Contribution margin	590,000	80,000	300,000	210,000
Fixed expenses:				
Advertising—traceable	216,000	41,000	110,000	65,000
Depreciation of special equipment	95,000	20,000	40,000	35,000
Line supervisors' salaries	19,000	6,000	7,000	6,000
General factory overhead*	200,000	28,000	100,000	72,000
Total fixed expenses	530,000	95,000	257,000	178,000
Net operating income (loss)	$ 60,000	$ (15,000)	$ 43,000	$ 32,000

*A common fixed cost that is allocated on the basis of sales dollars.

Management is concerned about the continued losses shown by the round trampolines and wants a recommendation as to whether or not the line should be discontinued. The special equipment used to produce the trampolines has no resale value. If the round trampoline model is dropped, the two line supervisors assigned to the model would be discharged.

Required:
1. What is the financial advantage (disadvantage) of discontinuing the round trampolines? The company has no other use for the capacity now being used to produce the round trampolines. Show computations to support your answer.
2. Recast the above data in a format that would be more useful to management in assessing the profitability of the various product lines.

Solution to Review Problem

1. No, production and sale of the round trampolines should not be discontinued. Computations to support this answer follow:

Contribution margin lost if the round trampolines are discontinued		$(80,000)
Less fixed expenses that can be avoided:		
Advertising—traceable.	$41,000	
Line supervisors' salaries.	6,000	47,000
Financial (disadvantage) of discontinuing the round trampolines		$(33,000)

The depreciation of the special equipment is a sunk cost, and therefore, it is not relevant to the decision. The general factory overhead is allocated and will presumably continue regardless of whether or not the round trampolines are discontinued; thus, it is not relevant.

2. If management wants a clearer picture of the profitability of the segments, the general factory overhead should not be allocated. It is a common cost and, therefore, should be deducted from the total product-line segment margin. A more useful income statement format would be as follows:

			Trampoline	
	Total	Round	Rectangular	Octagonal
Sales	$1,000,000	$140,000	$500,000	$360,000
Variable expenses.	410,000	60,000	200,000	150,000
Contribution margin	590,000	80,000	300,000	210,000
Traceable fixed expenses:				
Advertising—traceable.	216,000	41,000	110,000	65,000
Depreciation of special equipment	95,000	20,000	40,000	35,000
Line supervisors' salaries.	19,000	6,000	7,000	6,000
Total traceable fixed expenses.	330,000	67,000	157,000	106,000
Product-line segment margin	260,000	$ 13,000	$143,000	$104,000
Common fixed expenses.	200,000			
Net operating income.	$ 60,000			

Glossary

Avoidable cost A cost that can be eliminated by choosing one alternative over another in a decision. This term is synonymous with *differential cost* and *relevant cost*. (p. 278)

Bottleneck A machine or some other part of a process that limits the total output of the entire system. (p. 294)

Constraint A limitation under which a company must operate, such as limited available machine time or raw materials, that restricts the company's ability to satisfy demand. (p. 293)

Differential cost A future cost that differs between any two alternatives. (p. 278)

Differential revenue Future revenue that differs between any two alternatives. (p. 278)

Incremental cost An increase in cost between two alternatives. (p. 278)

Joint costs Costs that are incurred up to the split-off point in a process that produces joint products. (p. 299)

Joint products Two or more products that are produced from a common input. (p. 299)

Opportunity cost The potential benefit given up when one alternative is selected over another. (p. 279)

Relaxing (or elevating) the constraint An action that increases the amount of a constrained resource. Equivalently, an action that increases the capacity of the bottleneck. (p. 297)

Relevant benefit A benefit that should be considered when making decisions. (p. 278)

Relevant cost A cost that should be considered when making decisions. (p. 278)

Sell or process further decision A decision as to whether a joint product should be sold at the split-off point or sold after further processing. (p. 299)

Sourcing decision A decision concerning whether a product or service should be produced or provided internally or purchased from an outside vendor. (p. 289)

Special order A one-time order that is not considered part of the company's normal ongoing business. (p. 292)

Split-off point That point in the manufacturing process where some or all of the joint products can be recognized as individual products. (p. 299)

Sunk cost A cost has already been incurred and that cannot be changed by any decision made now or in the future. (p. 279)

Vertical integration The involvement by a company in more than one of the activities in the entire value chain from development through production, distribution, sales, and after-sales service. (p. 288)

Questions

6–1 What is a *relevant cost?*

6–2 Define the following terms: *incremental cost, opportunity cost,* and *sunk cost.*

6–3 Are variable costs always relevant costs? Explain.

6–4 "Sunk costs are easy to spot—they're the fixed costs associated with a decision." Do you agree? Explain.

6–5 "Variable costs and differential costs mean the same thing." Do you agree? Explain.

6–6 "All future costs are relevant in decision making." Do you agree? Why?

6–7 Prentice Company is considering dropping one of its product lines. What costs of the product line would be relevant to this decision? What costs would be irrelevant?

6–8 "If a product is generating a loss, then it should be discontinued." Do you agree? Explain.

6–9 What is the danger in allocating common fixed costs among products or other segments of an organization?

6–10 How does opportunity cost enter into a sourcing decision?

6–11 Give at least four examples of possible constraints.

6–12 How will relating product contribution margins to the amount of the constrained resource they consume help a company maximize its profits?

6–13 Define the following terms: *joint products, joint costs,* and *split-off point.*

6–14 From a decision-making point of view, should joint costs be allocated among joint products?

6–15 What guideline should be used in determining whether a joint product should be sold at the split-off point or processed further?

6–16 Airlines sometimes offer reduced rates during certain times of the week to members of a businessperson's family if they accompany him or her on trips. How does the concept of relevant costs enter into the decision by the airline to offer reduced rates of this type?

The Excel worksheet form that appears below is to be used to recreate the example in the text related to Santa Maria Wool Cooperative. The workbook, and instructions on how to complete the file, can be found in Connect.

	A	B	C	D	E
1	Chapter 6: Applying Excel				
2					
3	**Data**				
4	**Exhibit 6-7 Santa Maria Wool Cooperative**				
5	Cost of wool	$200,000			
6	Cost of separation process	$40,000			
7	Sales value of intermediate products at split-off point:				
8	Undyed coarse wool	$120,000			
9	Undyed fine wool	$150,000			
10	Undyed superfine wool	$60,000			
11	Costs of further processing (dyeing) intermediate products:				
12	Undyed coarse wool	$50,000			
13	Undyed fine wool	$60,000			
14	Undyed superfine wool	$10,000			
15	Sales value of end products:				
16	Dyed coarse wool	$160,000			
17	Dyed fine wool	$240,000			
18	Dyed superfine wool	$90,000			
19					
20	*Enter a formula into each of the cells marked with a ? below*				
21	**Example: Joint Product Costs and the Contribution Approach**				
22					
23	**Analysis of the profitability of the overall operation:**				
24	Combined final sales value		?		
25	Less costs of producing the end products:				
26	Cost of wool	?			
27	Cost of separation process	?			
28	Combined costs of dyeing	?	?		
29	Profit		?		
30					
31	**Analysis of sell or process further:**				
32		Coarse	Fine	Superfine	
33		Wool	Wool	Wool	
34	Final sales value after further processing	?	?	?	
35	Less sales value at the split-off point	?	?	?	
36	Incremental revenue from further processing	?	?	?	
37	Less cost of further processung (dyeing)	?	?	?	
38	Financial advantage (disadvantage) of further processing	?	?	?	
39					

H ◀ ▶ H   Chapter 6 Form   Chapter 6 Forf

Microsoft Excel

You should proceed to the requirements below only after completing your worksheet.

Required:

1. Check your worksheet by changing the cost of further processing undyed coarse wool in cell B12 to $30,000. The overall profit from processing all intermediate products into final products should now be $150,000, and the financial advantage of further processing coarse wool should now be $10,000. If you do not get these answers, find the errors in your worksheet and correct them.

   How should operations change in response to this change in cost?

2. In industries that process joint products, the costs of the raw materials inputs and the sales values of intermediate and final products are often volatile. Change the data area of your worksheet to match the following:

Data Exhibit 6–7 Santa Maria Wool Cooperative	
Cost of wool..	$290,000
Cost of separation process	$40,000
Sales value of intermediate products at split-off point:	
Undyed coarse wool.....................................	$100,000
Undyed fine wool	$110,000
Undyed superfine wool	$90,000
Costs of further processing (dyeing) intermediate products:	
Undyed coarse wool	$50,000
Undyed fine wool	$60,000
Undyed superfine wool	$10,000
Sales value of end products:	
Dyed coarse wool......................................	$180,000
Dyed fine wool...	$210,000
Dyed superfine wool	$90,000

a. What is the overall profit if all intermediate products are processed into final products?

b. What is the financial advantage (disadvantage) from further processing each of the intermediate products?

c. With these new costs and selling prices, what recommendations would you make concerning the company's operations? If your recommendation is followed, what should be the overall profit of the company?

The Foundational 15 McGraw Hill connect

LEARNING OBJECTIVE 6–2, 6–3, 6–4, 6–5, 6–6

Cane Company manufactures two products called Alpha and Beta that sell for $120 and $80, respectively. Each product uses only one type of raw material that costs $6 per pound. The company has the capacity to annually produce 100,000 units of each product. Its average cost per unit for each product at this level of activity is given below:

	Alpha	Beta
Direct materials	$ 30	$12
Direct labor......................................	20	15
Variable manufacturing overhead	7	5
Traceable fixed manufacturing overhead............	16	18
Variable selling expenses	12	8
Common fixed expenses..........................	15	10
Total cost per unit	$100	$68

The company considers its traceable fixed manufacturing overhead to be avoidable, whereas its common fixed expenses are unavoidable and have been allocated to products based on sales dollars.

Required:

(Answer each question independently unless instructed otherwise.)

1. What is the total amount of traceable fixed manufacturing overhead for each of the two products?

2. What is the company's total amount of common fixed expenses?

3. Assume that Cane expects to produce and sell 80,000 Alphas during the current year. One of Cane's sales representatives found a new customer who is willing to buy 10,000 additional Alphas for a price of $80 per unit. What is the financial advantage (disadvantage) of accepting the new customer's order?

4. Assume that Cane expects to produce and sell 90,000 Betas during the current year. One of Cane's sales representatives found a new customer who is willing to buy 5,000 additional Betas for a price of $39 per unit. What is the financial advantage (disadvantage) of accepting the new customer's order?

5. Assume that Cane expects to produce and sell 95,000 Alphas during the current year. One of Cane's sales representatives has found a new customer who is willing to buy 10,000 additional Alphas for a price of $80 per unit; however, pursuing this opportunity will decrease Alpha sales to regular customers by 5,000 units. What is the financial advantage (disadvantage) of accepting the new customer's order?

6. Assume Cane normally produces and sells 90,000 Betas per year. What is the financial advantage (disadvantage) of discontinuing the Beta product line?

7. Assume Cane normally produces and sells 40,000 Betas per year. What is the financial advantage (disadvantage) of discontinuing the Beta product line?

8. Assume Cane normally produces and sells 60,000 Betas and 80,000 Alphas per year. If Cane discontinues the Beta product line, its sales representatives could increase sales of Alpha by 15,000 units. What is the financial advantage (disadvantage) of discontinuing the Beta product line?

9. Assume Cane expects to produce and sell 80,000 Alphas during the current year. A supplier has offered to manufacture and deliver 80,000 Alphas to Cane for a price of $80 per unit. What is the financial advantage (disadvantage) of buying 80,000 units from the supplier instead of making those units?

10. Assume Cane expects to produce and sell 50,000 Alphas during the current year. A supplier has offered to manufacture and deliver 50,000 Alphas to Cane for a price of $80 per unit. What is the financial advantage (disadvantage) of buying 50,000 units from the supplier instead of making those units?

11. How many pounds of raw material are needed to make one unit of each of the two products?

12. What contribution margin per pound of raw material is earned by each of the two products?

13. Assume Cane's customers would buy a maximum of 80,000 units of Alpha and 60,000 units of Beta. Also assume that the raw material available for production is limited to 160,000 pounds. How many units of each product should Cane produce to maximize its profits?

14. If Cane follows your recommendation in requirement 13, what total contribution margin will it earn?

15. If Cane uses its 160,000 pounds of raw materials as you recommended in requirement 13, up to how much should it be willing to pay per pound for additional raw materials?

 Exercises

EXERCISE 6–1 Identification of Relevant Costs LO 6–1

Kristen Lu purchased a used automobile for $8,000 at the beginning of last year and incurred the following operating costs:

Depreciation ($8,000 ÷ 5 years).............	$1,600
Insurance	$1,200
Garage rent	$360
Automobile tax and license.................	$40
Variable operating cost	$0.14 per mile

The variable operating cost consists of gasoline, oil, tires, maintenance, and repairs. Kristen estimates that, at her current rate of usage, the car will have zero resale value in five years, so the annual straight-line depreciation is $1,600. The car is kept in a garage for a monthly fee.

Required:

1. Kristen drove the car 10,000 miles last year. Compute the average cost per mile of owning and operating the car.

2. Kristen is unsure about whether she should use her own car or rent a car to go on an extended cross-country trip for two weeks during spring break. What costs above are relevant in this decision? Explain.

3. Kristen is thinking about buying an expensive sports car to replace the car she bought last year. She would drive the same number of miles regardless of which car she owns and would rent the same parking space. The sports car's variable operating costs would be roughly the same as the variable operating costs of her old car. However, her insurance and automobile tax and license costs would go up. What costs are relevant in estimating the incremental cost of owning the more expensive car? Explain.

EXERCISE 6–2 Dropping or Retaining a Segment LO 6–2

The Regal Cycle Company manufactures three types of bicycles—a dirt bike, a mountain bike, and a racing bike. Data on sales and expenses for the past quarter follow:

	Total	Dirt Bikes	Mountain Bikes	Racing Bikes
Sales	$300,000	$90,000	$150,000	$60,000
Variable manufacturing and selling expenses	120,000	27,000	60,000	33,000
Contribution margin	180,000	63,000	90,000	27,000
Fixed expenses:				
Advertising, traceable	30,000	10,000	14,000	6,000
Depreciation of special equipment	23,000	6,000	9,000	8,000
Salaries of product-line managers.........	35,000	12,000	13,000	10,000
Allocated common fixed expenses*	60,000	18,000	30,000	12,000
Total fixed expenses......................	148,000	46,000	66,000	36,000
Net operating income (loss)	$ 32,000	$17,000	$ 24,000	$ (9,000)

*Allocated on the basis of sales dollars.

Management is concerned about the continued losses shown by the racing bikes and wants a recommendation as to whether or not the line should be discontinued. The special equipment used to produce racing bikes has no resale value and does not wear out.

Required:

1. What is the financial advantage (disadvantage) per quarter of discontinuing the Racing Bikes?
2. Should the production and sale of racing bikes be discontinued?
3. Prepare a properly formatted segmented income statement that would be more useful to management in assessing the long-run profitability of the various product lines.

EXERCISE 6–3 Sourcing Decisions LO 6–3

Troy Engines, Ltd., manufactures a variety of engines for use in heavy equipment. The company has always produced all of the necessary parts for its engines, including all of the carburetors. An outside supplier has offered to sell one type of carburetor to Troy Engines, Ltd., for a cost of $35 per unit. To evaluate this offer, Troy Engines, Ltd., has gathered the following information relating to its own cost of producing the carburetor internally:

	Per Unit	15,000 Units per Year
Direct materials	$14	$210,000
Direct labor...	10	150,000
Variable manufacturing overhead	3	45,000
Fixed manufacturing overhead, traceable	6*	90,000
Fixed manufacturing overhead, allocated..............	9	135,000
Total cost...	$42	$630,000

*One-third supervisory salaries; two-thirds depreciation of special equipment (no resale value).

Required:

1. Assuming the company has no alternative use for the facilities now being used to produce the carburetors, what would be the financial advantage (disadvantage) of buying 15,000 carburetors from the outside supplier?
2. Should the outside supplier's offer be accepted?
3. Suppose if the carburetors were purchased, Troy Engines, Ltd., could use the freed capacity to launch a new product. The segment margin of the new product would be $150,000 per year.

Given this new assumption, what would be the financial advantage (disadvantage) of buying 15,000 carburetors from the outside supplier?

4.   Given the new assumption in requirement 3, should the outside supplier's offer be accepted?

EXERCISE 6–4 Special Order Decision LO 6–4

Imperial Jewelers manufactures and sells a gold bracelet for $189.95. The company's accounting system says the unit product cost for this bracelet is $149.00 as shown below:

Direct materials	$ 84.00
Direct labor	45.00
Manufacturing overhead	20.00
Unit product cost	$149.00

The members of a wedding party approached Imperial Jewelers about buying 20 of these gold bracelets for the discounted price of $169.95 each. The members of the wedding party would like special filigree applied to the bracelets that would increase the direct materials cost per bracelet by $2.00. Imperial Jewelers would have to buy a special tool for $250 to apply the filigree to the bracelets. The special tool would have no other use once the special order is completed.

To analyze this special order opportunity, Imperial Jewelers determined that most of its manufacturing overhead is fixed and unaffected by variations in how much jewelry is produced in any given period. However, $4.00 of the overhead is variable with respect to the number of bracelets produced. The company also believes that accepting this order would have no effect on its ability to produce and sell jewelry to other customers. Furthermore, the company could fulfill the wedding party's order using its existing manufacturing capacity.

Required:

1.   What is the financial advantage (disadvantage) of accepting the special order from the wedding party?

2.   Should the company accept the special order?

EXERCISE 6–5 Volume Trade-Off Decisions LO 6–5

Outdoor Luggage, Inc., makes high-end hard-sided luggage for sports equipment. Data concerning three of the company's most popular models appear below.

	Ski Guard	Golf Guard	Fishing Guard
Selling price per unit.	$200	$300	$255
Variable cost per unit	$60	$140	$55
Plastic injection molding machine processing time required to produce one unitt	2 minutes	5 minutes	4 minutes
Pounds of plastic pellets per unit.	7 pounds	4 pounds	8 pounds

Required:

1.   If we assume the total time available on the plastic injection molding machine is the constraint in the production process, how much contribution margin per minute of the constrained resource is earned by each product?

2.   Which product offers the most profitable use of the plastic injection molding machine?

3.   If we assume that a severe shortage of plastic pellets has required the company to cut back its production so much that its new constraint has become the total available pounds of plastic pellets, how much contribution margin per pound of the constrained resource is earned by each product?

4.   Which product offers the most profitable use of the plastic pellets?

5.   Which product has the largest contribution margin per unit? Why wouldn't this product be the most profitable use of the constrained resource in either case?

EXERCISE 6–6 Managing a Constrained Resource LO 6–6

Portsmouth Company makes upholstered furniture. Its only variable cost is direct materials. The demand for the company's products far exceeds its manufacturing capacity. The bottleneck (or constraint) in the production process is upholstery labor-hours. Information concerning three of Portsmouth's products appears below:

	Recliner	Sofa	Love Seat
Selling price per unit.	$1,400	$1,800	$1,500
Variable cost per unit	$800	$1,200	$1,000
Upholstery labor-hours per unit	8 hours	10 hours	5 hours

Required:

1. Portsmouth is considering paying its upholstery laborers hourly compensation, in addition to their usual salaries, to work overtime. Assuming that this extra time would be used to produce sofas, up to how much of an overtime rate per hour should the company be willing to pay to keep the upholstery shop open after normal working hours?

2. A small nearby upholstering company has offered to upholster furniture for Portsmouth at a price of $45 per hour. The management of Portsmouth is confident that this upholstering company's work is high quality, and its craftsmen can work as quickly as Portsmouth's own craftsmen on the simpler upholstering jobs such as the Love Seat. How much additional contribution margin per hour can Portsmouth earn if it hires the nearby upholstering company to make Love Seats?

3. Should Portsmouth hire the nearby upholstering company? Explain.

EXERCISE 6–7 Sell or Process Further Decisions LO 6–7

Dorsey Company manufactures three products from a common input in a joint processing operation. Joint processing costs up to the split-off point total $350,000 per quarter. For financial reporting purposes, the company allocates these costs to the joint products on the basis of their relative sales value at the split-off point. Unit selling prices and total output at the split-off point are as follows:

Product	Selling Price	Quarterly Output
A.	$16 per pound	15,000 pounds
B.	$8 per pound	20,000 pounds
C.	$25 per gallon	4,000 gallons

Each product can be processed further after the split-off point. Additional processing requires no special facilities. The additional processing costs (per quarter) and unit selling prices after further processing are given below:

Product	Additional Processing Costs	Selling Price
A.	$63,000	$20 per pound
B.	$80,000	$13 per pound
C.	$36,000	$32 per gallon

Required:

1. What is the financial advantage (disadvantage) of further processing each of the three products beyond the split-off point?

2. Based on your analysis in requirement 1, which product or products should be sold at the split-off point and which product or products should be processed further?

EXERCISE 6–8 Volume Trade-Off Decisions LO 6–5, LO 6–6

Barlow Company manufactures three products—A, B, and C. The selling price, variable costs, and contribution margin for one unit of each product follow:

	Product		
	A	B	C
Selling price...................................	$180	$270	$240
Variable expenses:			
Direct materials...............................	24	80	32
Other variable expenses......................	102	90	148
Total variable expenses.........................	126	170	180
Contribution margin	$ 54	$100	$ 60
Contribution margin ratio	30%	37%	25%

The same raw material is used in all three products. Barlow Company has only 6,000 pounds of raw material on hand and will not be able to obtain any more of it for several weeks due to a strike in its supplier's plant. Management is trying to decide which product(s) to concentrate on next week in filling its backlog of orders. The material costs $8 per pound.

Required:
1. Calculate the contribution margin per pound of the constraining resource for each product.
2. Assuming that Barlow has unlimited demand for each of its three products, what is the maximum contribution margin the company can earn when using the 6,000 pounds of raw material on hand?
3. Assuming that Barlow's estimated customer demand is 500 units per product line, what is the maximum contribution margin the company can earn when using the 6,000 pounds of raw material on hand?
4. A foreign supplier could furnish Barlow with additional stocks of the raw material at a substantial premium over the usual price. Assuming Barlow's estimated customer demand is 500 units per product line and that the company has used its 6,000 pounds of raw material in an optimal fashion, what is the highest price Barlow Company should be willing to pay for an additional pound of materials? Explain.

EXERCISE 6–9 Special Order Decision LO 6–4

Delta Company produces a single product. The cost of producing and selling a single unit of this product at the company's normal activity level of 60,000 units per year is:

Direct materials......................................	$5.10
Direct labor...	$3.80
Variable manufacturing overhead	$1.00
Fixed manufacturing overhead	$4.20
Variable selling and administrative expense	$1.50
Fixed selling and administrative expense	$2.40

The normal selling price is $21 per unit. The company's capacity is 75,000 units per year. An order has been received from a mail-order house for 15,000 units at a special price of $14.00 per unit. This order would not affect regular sales or the company's total fixed costs.

Required:
1. What is the financial advantage (disadvantage) of accepting the special order?
2. As a separate matter from the special order, assume the company's inventory includes 1,000 units of this product that were produced last year and are inferior to the current model. The units must be sold through regular channels at reduced prices. The company does not expect the selling of these inferior units to have any affect on the sales of its current model. What unit cost is relevant for establishing a minimum selling price for the inferior units? Explain.

EXERCISE 6–10 Sourcing Decisions LO 6–3

Futura Company purchases the 40,000 starters that it installs in its standard line of farm tractors from a supplier for the price of $8.40 per unit. Due to a reduction in output, the company now has idle capacity that could be used to produce the starters rather than buying them from an outside supplier. However, the company's chief engineer is opposed to making the starters because the production cost per unit is $9.20 as shown below:

	Per Unit	Total
Direct materials	$3.10	
Direct labor.	2.70	
Supervision.	1.50	$60,000
Depreciation.	1.00	$40,000
Variable manufacturing overhead	0.60	
Rent	0.30	$12,000
Total production cost	$9.20	

If Futura decides to make the starters, a supervisor would have to be hired (at a salary of $60,000) to oversee production. However, the company has sufficient idle tools and machinery such that no new equipment would have to be purchased. The rent charge above is based on space utilized in the plant. The total rent on the plant is $80,000 per period. Depreciation is due to obsolescence rather than wear and tear.

Required:

What is the financial advantage (disadvantage) of making the 40,000 starters instead of buying them from an outside supplier?

EXERCISE 6–11 Adding a Product Line LO 6–2

Cabin Creek Company is considering adding of a new line of kitchen cabinets. The company's accountant provided the following estimated data for these cabinets:

Annual sales.	800 units
Selling price per unit.	$3,500
Variable manufacturing costs per unit.	$1,500
Variable selling costs per unit.	$350
Incremental fixed costs per year:	
Manufacturing	$475,400
Selling	$55,000
Allocated common costs per year:	
Manufacturing	$80,000
Selling and administrative	$112,000

If the kitchen cabinets are added as a new product line, the company expects that the contribution margin earned from selling its other products will decrease by $200,000 per year.

Required:

1. What is the annual financial advantage (disadvantage) of adding the new line of kitchen cabinets?
2. What is the lowest selling price per unit that could be charged for the cabinets and still make it economically desirable for the company to add the new product line?

EXERCISE 6–12 Sourcing Decisions LO 6–3

Han Products manufactures 30,000 units of part S-6 each year for use on its production line. At this level of activity, the cost per unit for part S-6 is:

Direct materials	$ 3.60
Direct labor.	10.00
Variable manufacturing overhead	2.40
Fixed manufacturing overhead.	9.00
Total cost per part	$25.00

An outside supplier has offered to sell 30,000 units of part S-6 each year to Han Products for $21 per part. If Han Products accepts this offer, the facilities now being used to manufacture part S-6 could be rented to another company at an annual rental of $80,000. However, Han Products has determined that two-thirds of the fixed manufacturing overhead being applied to part S-6 would continue even if part S-6 were purchased from the outside supplier.

Required:

What is the financial advantage (disadvantage) of accepting the outside supplier's offer?

EXERCISE 6–13 Volume Trade-Off Decisions LO 6–5

Benoit Company produces three products—A, B, and C. Data concerning the three products follow (per unit):

	Product		
	A	**B**	**C**
Selling price	$80	$56	$70
Variable expenses:			
Direct materials	24	15	9
Other variable expenses	24	27	40
Total variable expenses	48	42	49
Contribution margin	$32	$14	$21
Contribution margin ratio.	40%	25%	30%

The company estimates it can sell 800 units of each product per month. The same raw material is used in each product. The material costs $3 per pound with a maximum of 5,000 pounds available each month.

Required:

1. Calculate the contribution margin per pound of the constraining resource for each product.
2. Which orders would you advise the company to accept first, those for A, B, or C? Which orders second? Third?
3. What is the maximum contribution margin the company can earn per month if it makes optimal use of its 5,000 pounds of materials?

EXERCISE 6–14 Sell or Process Further Decision LO 6–7

Wexpro, Inc., produces several products from processing 1 ton of clypton, a rare mineral. Material and processing costs total $60,000 per ton, one-fourth of which is allocated to product X15. Seven thousand units of product X15 are produced from each ton of clypton. The units can be either sold at the split-off point for $9 each or processed further at a total cost of $9,500 and then sold for $12 each.

Required:

1. What is the financial advantage (disadvantage) of further processing product X15?
2. Should product X15 be processed further or sold at the split-off point?

EXERCISE 6–15 Dropping or Retaining a Segment LO 6–2

Thalassines Kataskeves, S.A., of Greece makes marine equipment. The company has been experiencing losses on its bilge pump product line for several years. The most recent quarterly contribution format income statement for the bilge pump product line follows:

Thalassines Kataskeves, S.A.
Income Statement—Bilge Pump
For the Quarter Ended March 31

Sales		$850,000
Variable expenses:		
Variable manufacturing expenses	$330,000	
Sales commissions	42,000	
Shipping	18,000	
Total variable expenses		390,000
Contribution margin		460,000
Fixed expenses:		
Advertising (for the bilge pump product line)	270,000	
Depreciation of equipment (no resale value)	80,000	
General factory overhead	105,000*	
Salary of product-line manager	32,000	
Insurance on inventories	8,000	
Purchasing department	45,000†	
Total fixed expenses		540,000
Net operating loss		$ (80,000)

*Common costs allocated on the basis of machine-hours.
†Common costs allocated on the basis of sales dollars.

Discontinuing the bilge pump product line would not affect sales of other product lines and would have no effect on the company's total general factory overhead or total Purchasing Department expenses.

Required:

What is the financial advantage (disadvantage) of discontinuing the bilge pump product line?

EXERCISE 6–16 Identification of Relevant Costs LO 6–1

Bill just returned from a duck hunting trip. He brought home eight ducks. Bill's friend, John, disapproves of duck hunting, and to discourage Bill from further hunting, John presented him with the following cost estimate per duck:

Camper and equipment:	
Cost, $12,000; usable for eight seasons; 10 hunting trips per season	$150
Travel expense (pickup truck):	
100 miles at $0.31 per mile (gas, oil, and tires—$0.21 per mile; depreciation and insurance—$0.10 per mile)	31
Shotgun shells (two boxes per hunting trip)	20
Boat:	
Cost, $2,320, usable for eight seasons; 10 hunting trips per season	29
Hunting license:	
Cost, $30 for the season; 10 hunting trips per season	3
Money lost playing poker:	
Loss, $24 (Bill plays poker every weekend whether he goes hunting or stays at home)	24
Bottle of whiskey:	
Cost, $15 per hunting trip (used to ward off the cold)	15
Total cost	$272
Cost per duck ($272 ÷ 8 ducks)	$ 34

Required:

1. Assuming the duck hunting trip Bill completed is typical, what costs are relevant to a decision as to whether Bill should go duck hunting again this season?
2. Suppose Bill gets lucky on his next hunting trip and shoots 10 ducks using the same amount of shotgun shells he used on his previous hunting trip to bag 8 ducks. How much would it have cost him to shoot the last two ducks? Explain.
3. Which costs are relevant in a decision of whether Bill should give up hunting? Explain.

EXERCISE 6–17 Dropping or Retaining a Segment LO 6–2

Bed & Bath, a retailing company, has two departments—Hardware and Linens. The company's most recent monthly contribution format income statement follows:

	Total	Department	
		Hardware	Linens
Sales	$4,000,000	$3,000,000	$1,000,000
Variable expenses....................	1,300,000	900,000	400,000
Contribution margin	2,700,000	2,100,000	600,000
Fixed expenses	2,200,000	1,400,000	800,000
Net operating income (loss)	$ 500,000	$ 700,000	$ (200,000)

A study indicates that $340,000 of the fixed expenses being charged to Linens are sunk costs or allocated costs that will continue even if the Linens Department is dropped. In addition, the elimination of the Linens Department will result in a 10% decrease in the sales of the Hardware Department.

Required:

What is the financial advantage (disadvantage) of discontinuing the Linens Department?

EXERCISE 6–18 Special Order Decisions LO 6–4

Shortt Company has been approached by a customer who is offering a one-time-only special order to buy 4,000 units of a customer-designed part. Each one of these parts requires 4 units of raw material A10 and 4 units of raw material C70. Data concerning these two raw materials follow:

	Units in Raw Materials Inventory	Cost per Unit in Raw Materials Inventory	Current Market Price per Unit	Disposal Value per Unit
A10	1,800	$5.50	$6.50	$2.00
C70	14,000	$6.00	$7.00	$2.50

The current market price per unit mentioned above reflects the prices currently charged by Shortt Company's raw materials supplier. The disposal value per unit mentioned above reflects the price that a recycling company would pay Shortt to purchase any unused raw materials that it wishes to liquidate. Material A10 is used by many of the company's products and is routinely replaced. Material C70 is no longer used by the company in any of its normal products.

Required:

1. What is the relevant cost of the raw materials that the company should include in its analysis when deciding whether to accept or reject the special order?
2. Assume that A10 and C70 are both no longer used in any of the company's normal products. What is the relevant cost of the raw materials that the company should include in its analysis when deciding whether to accept or reject the special order?

Problems Mc Graw Hill connect

PROBLEM 6–19 Relevant Cost Analysis in a Variety of Situations LO 6–2, LO 6–3, LO 6–4

Andretti Company has a single product called a Dak. The company normally produces and sells 60,000 Daks each year at a selling price of $32 per unit. The company's unit costs at this level of activity are given below:

Direct materials	$10.00	
Direct labor.	4.50	
Variable manufacturing overhead	2.30	
Fixed manufacturing overhead.	5.00	($300,000 total)
Variable selling expenses	1.20	
Fixed selling expenses.	3.50	($210,000 total)
Total cost per unit	$26.50	

A number of questions relating to the production and sale of Daks follow. Each question is independent.

Required:

1. Assume Andretti Company has sufficient capacity to produce 90,000 Daks each year without any increase in fixed manufacturing overhead costs. The company could increase its unit sales by 25% above the present 60,000 units each year if it were willing to increase the fixed selling expenses by $80,000. What is the financial advantage (disadvantage) of investing an additional $80,000 in fixed selling expenses? Would the additional investment be justified?

2. Assume again that Andretti Company has sufficient capacity to produce 90,000 Daks each year. A customer in a foreign market wants to purchase 20,000 Daks. If Andretti accepts this order, it would have to pay import duties on the Daks of $1.70 per unit and an additional $9,000 for permits and licenses. The only selling costs that would be associated with the order would be $3.20 per unit shipping cost. What is the break-even price per unit on this order?

3. The company has 1,000 Daks on hand that have some irregularities and are therefore considered to be "seconds." Due to the irregularities, it will be impossible to sell these units at the normal price through regular distribution channels. What is the unit cost figure that is relevant for setting a minimum selling price? Explain.

4. Due to a strike in its supplier's plant, Andretti Company is unable to purchase more material for the production of Daks. The strike is expected to last for two months. Andretti Company has enough material on hand to operate at 30% of normal levels for the two-month period. As an alternative, Andretti could close its plant down entirely for the two months. If the plant were closed, fixed manufacturing overhead costs would continue at 60% of their normal level during the two-month period, and the fixed selling expenses would be reduced by 20% during the two-month period.

   a. How much total contribution margin will Andretti forgo if it closes the plant for two months?
   b. How much total fixed cost will the company avoid if it closes the plant for two months?
   c. What is the financial advantage (disadvantage) of closing the plant for the two-month period?
   d. Should Andretti close the plant for two months?

5. An outside manufacturer has offered to produce 60,000 Daks and ship them directly to Andretti's customers. If Andretti Company accepts this offer, the facilities that it uses to produce Daks would be idle; however, fixed manufacturing overhead costs would be reduced by 75%. Because the outside manufacturer would pay for all shipping costs, the variable selling expenses would be only two-thirds of their present amount. What is Andretti's avoidable cost per unit that it should compare to the price quoted by the outside manufacturer?

PROBLEM 6–20 Sourcing Decisions LO 6–3

Express Delivery Company (EDC) is considering outsourcing its Payroll Department to a payroll processing company for an annual fee of $220,000. An internally prepared report summarizes the Payroll Department's annual operating costs as follows:

Supplies	$ 30,000
Payroll clerks' salaries	120,000
Payroll supervisor's salary	58,000
Payroll employee training expenses	10,000
Depreciation of equipment	20,000
Allocated share of common building operating costs	15,000
Allocated share of common administrative overhead	28,000
Total annual operating cost	$281,000

EDC currently rents overflow office space for $36,000 per year. If the company closes its Payroll Department, the employees occupying the rented office space could be brought in-house and the lease agreement on the rented space could be terminated with no penalty.

If the Payroll Department is outsourced, the payroll clerks will not be retained; however, the supervisor would be transferred to the company's Human Resource Management Department. As a result of this transfer, the company would discontinue its efforts to hire a new Human Resource Manager that it expected to pay an annual salary of $56,000.

The Payroll Department's equipment would be transferred to other departments within the company to replace outdated equipment that would be recycled for zero salvage value.

Required:

What is the financial advantage (disadvantage) of outsourcing the Payroll Department?

PROBLEM 6–21 Dropping or Retaining a Segment LO 6–2

Jackson County Senior Services is a nonprofit organization devoted to providing essential services to seniors who live in their own homes within the Jackson County area. Three services are provided for seniors—home nursing, Meals On Wheels, and housekeeping. Data on revenue and expenses for the past year follow:

	Total	Home Nursing	Meals On Wheels	House- keeping
Revenues	$900,000	$260,000	$400,000	$240,000
Variable expenses	490,000	120,000	210,000	160,000
Contribution margin	410,000	140,000	190,000	80,000
Fixed expenses:				
Depreciation	68,000	8,000	40,000	20,000
Liability insurance	42,000	20,000	7,000	15,000
Program administrators' salaries	115,000	40,000	38,000	37,000
General administrative overhead*	180,000	52,000	80,000	48,000
Total fixed expenses	405,000	120,000	165,000	120,000
Net operating income (loss)	$ 5,000	$ 20,000	$ 25,000	$ (40,000)

*Allocated on the basis of program revenues.

The head administrator of Jackson County Senior Services, Judith Miyama, considers last year's net operating income of $5,000 to be unsatisfactory; therefore, she is considering the possibility of discontinuing the housekeeping program.

The depreciation in housekeeping is for a small van used to carry the housekeepers and their equipment from job to job. If the program were discontinued, the van would be donated to a charitable organization. None of the general administrative overhead would be avoided if the housekeeping program was dropped, but the liability insurance and the salary of the program administrator would be avoided.

Required:

1. What is the financial advantage (disadvantage) of discontinuing the Housekeeping program? Should the Housekeeping program be discontinued? Explain.

2. Prepare a properly formatted segmented income statement that would be more useful to management in assessing the long-run financial viability of its various services.

PROBLEM 6–22 Sell or Process Further Decision LO 6–7

(Prepared from a situation suggested by Professor John W. Hardy.) Lone Star Meat Packers is a major processor of beef and other meat products. The company has a large amount of T-bone steak on hand, and it is trying to decide whether to sell the T-bone steaks as they are initially cut or to process them further into filet mignon and the New York cut.

If the T-bone steaks are sold as initially cut, the company figures that a 1-pound T-bone steak would yield the following profit:

Selling price ($7.95 per pound)	$7.95
Less joint costs incurred up to the split-off point where T-bone steak can be identified as a separate product	3.80
Profit per pound	$4.15

If the company were to further process the T-bone steaks, then cutting one side of a T-bone steak provides the filet mignon, and cutting the other side provides the New York cut. One 16-ounce T-bone steak cut in this way will yield one 6-ounce filet mignon and one 8-ounce New York cut; the remaining ounces are waste. It costs $0.55 to further process one T-bone steak into the filet mignon and New York cuts. The filet mignon can be sold for $12.00 per pound, and the New York cut can be sold for $8.80 per pound.

Required:

1. What is the financial advantage (disadvantage) of further processing one T-bone steak into filet mignon and New York cut steaks?
2. Would you recommend the T-bone steaks be sold as initially cut or processed further? Why?

PROBLEM 6–23 Dropping or Retaining a Flight LO 6–2

Profits have been decreasing for several years at Pegasus Airlines. In an effort to improve the company's performance, the company is thinking about dropping several flights that appear to be unprofitable.

A typical income statement for one round-trip of one such flight (flight 482) is as follows:

Ticket revenue (175 seats × 40% occupancy × $200 ticket price)	$14,000	100.0%
Variable expenses ($15 per person)	1,050	7.5
Contribution margin	12,950	92.5%
Flight expenses:		
Salaries, flight crew	1,800	
Flight promotion	750	
Depreciation of aircraft	1,550	
Fuel for aircraft	5,800	
Liability insurance	4,200	
Salaries, flight assistants	1,500	
Baggage loading and flight preparation	1,700	
Overnight costs for flight crew and assistants at destination	300	
Total flight expenses	17,600	
Net operating loss	$ (4,650)	

The following additional information is available about flight 482:
- a. Members of the flight crew are paid fixed annual salaries, whereas the flight assistants are paid based on the number of round trips they complete.
- b. One-third of the liability insurance is a special charge assessed against flight 482 because, in the opinion of the insurance company, the destination of the flight is in a "high-risk" area. The remaining two-thirds would be unaffected by a decision to drop flight 482.
- c. The baggage loading and flight preparation expense is an allocation of ground crews' salaries and depreciation of ground equipment. Dropping flight 482 would have no effect on the company's total baggage loading and flight preparation expenses.

  d. If flight 482 is dropped, Pegasus Airlines has no authorization at present to replace it with
      another flight.
  e. Aircraft depreciation is due entirely to obsolescence. Depreciation due to wear and tear is
      negligible.
  f. Dropping flight 482 would not allow Pegasus Airlines to reduce the number of aircraft in
      its fleet or the number of flight crew on its payroll.

Required:
1. What is the financial advantage (disadvantage) of discontinuing flight 482?
2. The airline's scheduling officer has been criticized because only about 50% of the seats on Pega-
    sus's flights are being filled compared to an industry average of 60%. The scheduling officer has
    explained that Pegasus's average seat occupancy could be improved considerably by eliminating
    about 10% of its flights, but that doing so would reduce profits. Explain how this could happen.

PROBLEM 6–24 Special Order Decisions LO 6–4
Polaski Company manufactures and sells a single product called a Ret. Operating at capacity, the
company can produce and sell 30,000 Rets per year. Costs associated with this level of production
and sales are given below:

	Unit	Total
Direct materials	$15	$ 450,000
Direct labor.	8	240,000
Variable manufacturing overhead	3	90,000
Fixed manufacturing overhead.	9	270,000
Variable selling expense	4	120,000
Fixed selling expense.	6	180,000
Total cost.	$45	$1,350,000

     The Rets normally sell for $50 each. Fixed manufacturing overhead is $270,000 per year
within the range of 25,000 through 30,000 Rets per year.

Required:
1. Assume that due to a recession, Polaski Company expects to sell only 25,000 Rets through
    regular channels next year. A large retail chain has offered to purchase 5,000 Rets if Polaski is
    willing to accept a 16% discount off the regular price. There would be no sales commissions
    on this order; thus, variable selling expenses would be slashed by 75%. However, Polaski
    Company would have to purchase a special machine to engrave the retail chain's name on the
    5,000 units. This machine would cost $10,000. Polaski Company has no assurance that the
    retail chain will purchase additional units in the future. What is the financial advantage (dis-
    advantage) of accepting the special order?
2. Refer to the original data. Assume again that Polaski Company expects to sell only 25,000
    Rets through regular channels next year. The U.S. Army would like to make a one-time-only
    purchase of 5,000 Rets. The Army would reimburse Polaski for all of the variable and fixed
    production costs assigned to the units by the company's absorption costing system, plus it
    would pay an additional fee of $1.80 per unit. Because the army would pick up the Rets with
    its own trucks, there would be no variable selling expenses associated with this order. What is
    the financial advantage (disadvantage) of accepting the U.S. Army's special order?
3. Assume the same situation as described in (2) above, except that the company expects to sell
    30,000 Rets through regular channels next year. Thus, accepting the U.S. Army's order would
    require giving up regular sales of 5,000 Rets. Given this new information, what is the finan-
    cial advantage (disadvantage) of accepting the U.S. Army's special order?

PROBLEM 6–25 Sourcing Decisions LO 6–3
Silven Industries, which manufactures and sells a highly successful line of summer lotions and
insect repellents, has decided to diversify in order to stabilize sales throughout the year. A natural
area for the company to consider is the production of winter lotions and creams to prevent dry and
chapped skin.

After considerable research, a winter products line has been developed. However, Silven's president has decided to introduce only one of the new products for this coming winter. If the product is a success, further expansion in future years will be initiated.

The product selected (called Chap-Off) is a lip balm that will be sold in a lipstick-type tube. The product will be sold to wholesalers in boxes of 24 tubes for $8 per box. Because of excess capacity, no additional fixed manufacturing overhead costs will be incurred to produce the product. However, a $90,000 charge for fixed manufacturing overhead will be absorbed by the product under the company's absorption costing system.

Using the estimated sales and production of 100,000 boxes of Chap-Off, the Accounting Department developed the following manufacturing cost per box:

Direct material	$3.60
Direct labor.	2.00
Manufacturing overhead	1.40
Total cost.	$7.00

The costs above relate to making both the lip balm and the tube that contains it. As an alternative to making the tubes for Chap-Off, Silven has approached a supplier to discuss the possibility of buying the tubes. The purchase price of the supplier's empty tubes would be $1.35 per box of 24 tubes. If Silven Industries stops making the tubes and buys them from the outside supplier, its direct labor and variable manufacturing overhead costs per box of Chap-Off would be reduced by 10%, and its direct materials costs would be reduced by 25%.

Required:
1. If Silven buys its tubes from the outside supplier, how much of its own Chap-Off manufacturing costs per box will it be able to avoid? (Hint: You need to separate the manufacturing overhead of $1.40 per box shown above into its variable and fixed components to derive the correct answer.)
2. What is the financial advantage (disadvantage) per box of Chap-Off if Silven buys its tubes from the outside supplier?
3. What is the financial advantage (disadvantage) in total (not per box) if Silven buys 100,000 boxes of tubes from the outside supplier?
4. Should Silven Industries make or buy the tubes?
5. What is the maximum price that Silven should be willing to pay the outside supplier for a box of 24 tubes? Explain.
6. Instead of sales of 100,000 boxes, revised estimates show a sales volume of 120,000 boxes. At this higher sales volume, Silven would need to rent extra equipment at a cost of $40,000 per year to make the additional 20,000 boxes of tubes. Assuming that the outside supplier will not accept an order for less than 120,000 boxes, what is the financial advantage (disadvantage) in total (not per box) if Silven buys 120,000 boxes of tubes from the outside supplier? Given this new information, should Silven Industries make or buy the tubes?
7. Refer to the data in (6) above. Assume that the outside supplier will accept an order of any size for the tubes at a price of $1.35 per box. How many boxes of tubes should Silven make? How many boxes of tubes should it buy from the outside supplier?
8. What qualitative factors should Silven Industries consider in determining whether it should make or buy the tubes?

(CMA, adapted)

PROBLEM 6–26 Shutting Down or Continuing to Operate a Plant LO 6–2
Birch Company normally produces and sells 30,000 units of RG-6 each month. The selling price is $22 per unit, variable costs are $14 per unit, fixed manufacturing overhead costs total $150,000 per month, and fixed selling costs total $30,000 per month.

Employment-contract strikes in the companies that purchase the bulk of the RG-6 units have caused Birch Company's sales to temporarily drop to only 8,000 units per month. Birch Company estimates that the strikes will last for two months, after which time sales of RG-6 should return to normal. Due to the current low level of sales, Birch Company is thinking about closing down its own plant during the strike, which would reduce its fixed manufacturing overhead costs by $45,000 per month and its fixed selling costs by 10%. Start-up costs at the end of the shutdown period would total $8,000. Because Birch Company uses Lean Production methods, no inventories are on hand.

Required:

1. What is the financial advantage (disadvantage) if Birch closes its own plant for two months?
2. Should Birch close the plant for two months? Explain.
3. At what level of unit sales for the two-month period would Birch Company be indifferent between closing the plant or keeping it open? (Hint: This is a type of break-even analysis, except that the fixed cost portion of your break-even computation should include only those fixed costs that are relevant [i.e., avoidable] over the two-month period.)

PROBLEM 6–27 Volume Trade-Off Decisions LO 6–5, LO 6–6

The Walton Toy Company manufactures a line of dolls and a sewing kit. Demand for the company's products is increasing, and management requests assistance from you in determining an economical sales and production mix for the coming year. The company provided the following data:

Product	Demand Next Year (units)	Selling Price per Unit	Direct Materials	Direct Labor
Debbie	50,000	$16.70	$4.30	$6.40
Trish....................	42,000	$7.50	$1.10	$4.00
Sarah..................	35,000	$26.60	$6.44	$11.20
Mike....................	40,000	$14.00	$2.00	$8.00
Sewing kit..............	325,000	$9.60	$3.20	$3.20

The following additional information is available:

 a. The company's plant has a capacity of 130,000 direct labor-hours per year on a single-shift basis. The company's present employees and equipment can produce all five products.
 b. The direct labor rate of $16 per hour is expected to remain unchanged during the coming year.
 c. Fixed costs total $520,000 per year. Variable overhead costs are $2 per direct labor-hour.
 d. All of the company's nonmanufacturing costs are fixed.
 e. The company's finished goods inventory is negligible and can be ignored.

Required:

1. How many direct labor-hours are used to manufacture one unit of each of the company's five products?
2. How much variable overhead cost is incurred to manufacture one unit of each of the company's five products?
3. What is the contribution margin per direct labor-hour for each of the company's five products?
4. Assuming direct labor-hours is the company's constraining resource, what is the highest total contribution margin that the company can earn if it makes optimal use of its constrained resource?
5. Assuming the company has made optimal use of its 130,000 direct labor-hours, what is the highest direct labor rate per hour that Walton Toy Company would be willing to pay for additional capacity (that is, for added direct labor time)?
6. Identify changes the company could make to enable it to satisfy the customers' demand for *all* of its products.

(CMA, adapted)

PROBLEM 6–28 Close or Retain a Store LO 6–2

Superior Markets, Inc., operates three stores in a large metropolitan area. A segmented absorption costing income statement for the company for the last quarter is given below:

Superior Markets, Inc. Income Statement For the Quarter Ended September 30				
	Total	North Store	South Store	East Store
Sales	$3,000,000	$720,000	$1,200,000	$1,080,000
Cost of goods sold	1,657,200	403,200	660,000	594,000
Gross margin	1,342,800	316,800	540,000	486,000
Selling and administrative expenses:				
Selling expenses...................	817,000	231,400	315,000	270,600
Administrative expenses	383,000	106,000	150,900	126,100
Total expenses......................	1,200,000	337,400	465,900	396,700
Net operating income (loss)	$ 142,800	$ (20,600)	$ 74,100	$ 89,300

The North Store has consistently shown losses over the past two years. For this reason, management is giving consideration to closing the store. The company asked you to make a recommendation as to whether the store should be closed or kept open. The following additional information is available for your use:

a. The breakdown of the selling and administrative expenses that are shown above is as follows:

	Total	North Store	South Store	East Store
Selling expenses:				
Sales salaries.....................	$239,000	$ 70,000	$ 89,000	$ 80,000
Direct advertising	187,000	51,000	72,000	64,000
General advertising*..............	45,000	10,800	18,000	16,200
Store rent	300,000	85,000	120,000	95,000
Depreciation of store fixtures	16,000	4,600	6,000	5,400
Delivery salaries	21,000	7,000	7,000	7,000
Depreciation of delivery				
equipment	9,000	3,000	3,000	3,000
Total selling expenses	$817,000	$231,400	$315,000	$270,600

*Allocated on the basis of sales dollars.

	Total	North Store	South Store	East Store
Administrative expenses:				
Store managers' salaries	$ 70,000	$ 21,000	$ 30,000	$ 19,000
General office salaries*	50,000	12,000	20,000	18,000
Insurance on fixtures and inventory.......	25,000	7,500	9,000	8,500
Utilities	106,000	31,000	40,000	35,000
Employment taxes......................	57,000	16,500	21,900	18,600
General office—other*	75,000	18,000	30,000	27,000
Total administrative expenses.............	$383,000	$106,000	$150,900	$126,100

*Allocated on the basis of sales dollars.

b. The lease on the building housing the North Store can be broken with no penalty.
c. The fixtures being used in the North Store would be transferred to the other two stores if the North Store were closed.
d. The general manager of the North Store would be retained and transferred to another position in the company if the North Store were closed. She would be filling a position that would otherwise be filled by hiring a new employee at a salary of $11,000 per quarter. The general manager of the North Store would continue to earn her normal salary of $12,000 per quarter. All other managers and employees in the North Store would be discharged.
e. The company has one delivery crew that serves all three stores. One delivery person could be discharged if the North Store were closed. This person's salary is $4,000 per quarter. The delivery equipment would be distributed to the other stores. The equipment does not wear out through use, but does eventually become obsolete.
f. The company pays employment taxes equal to 15% of their employees' salaries.
g. One-third of the insurance in the North Store is on the store's fixtures.
h. The "General office salaries" and "General office—other" relate to the overall management of Superior Markets, Inc. If the North Store were closed, one person in the general office could be discharged because of the decrease in overall workload. This person's compensation is $6,000 per quarter.

Required:
1. How much employee salaries will the company avoid if it closes the North Store?
2. How much employment taxes will the company avoid if it closes the North Store?
3. What is the financial advantage (disadvantage) of closing the North Store?
4. Assuming that the North Store's floor space can't be subleased, would you recommend closing the North Store?
5. Assume that the North Store's floor space can't be subleased. However, let's introduce three more assumptions. First, assume that if the North Store were closed, one-fourth of its sales would transfer to the East Store due to strong customer loyalty to Superior Markets. Second, assume that the East Store has enough capacity to handle the increased sales that would arise from closing the North Store. Third, assume that the increased sales in the East Store would yield the same gross margin as a percentage of sales as present sales in the East Store. Given these new assumptions, what is the financial advantage (disadvantage) of closing the North Store?

PROBLEM 6–29 Sell or Process Further Decisions LO 6–7
Come-Clean Corporation produces a variety of cleaning compounds and solutions for both industrial and household use. While most of its products are processed independently, a few are related, such as the company's Grit 337 and its Sparkle silver polish.

Grit 337 is a coarse cleaning powder with many industrial uses. It costs $1.60 a pound to make, and it has a selling price of $2.00 a pound. A small portion of the annual production of Grit 337 is retained in the factory for further processing. It is combined with several other ingredients to form a paste that is marketed as Sparkle silver polish. The silver polish sells for $4.00 per jar.

This further processing requires one-fourth pound of Grit 337 per jar of silver polish. The additional direct variable costs involved in the processing of a jar of silver polish are:

Other ingredients	$0.65
Direct labor	1.48
Total direct cost	$2.13

Overhead costs associated with processing the silver polish are:

Variable manufacturing overhead cost	25% of direct labor cost
Fixed manufacturing overhead cost (per month):	
Production supervisor	$3,000
Depreciation of mixing equipment	$1,400

The production supervisor has no duties other than to oversee production of the silver polish. The mixing equipment is special-purpose equipment acquired specifically to produce the silver polish. It can produce up to 15,000 jars of polish per month. Its resale value is negligible, and it does not wear out through use.

Advertising costs for the silver polish total $4,000 per month. Variable selling costs associated with the silver polish are 7.5% of sales.

Due to a recent decline in the demand for silver polish, the company is wondering whether its continued production is advisable. The sales manager feels that it would be more profitable to sell all of the Grit 337 as a cleaning powder.

Required:

1. How much incremental revenue does the company earn per jar of polish by further processing Grit 337 rather than selling it as a cleaning powder?
2. How much incremental contribution margin does the company earn per jar of polish by further processing Grit 337 rather than selling it as a cleaning powder?
3. How many jars of silver polish must be sold each month to exactly offset the avoidable fixed costs incurred to produce and sell the polish? Explain.
4. If the company sells 9,000 jars of polish, what is the financial advantage (disadvantage) of choosing to further process Grit 337 rather than selling it as a cleaning powder?
5. If the company sells 11,500 jars of polish, what is the financial advantage (disadvantage) of choosing to further process Grit 337 rather than selling it as a cleaning powder?

(CMA, adapted)

PROBLEM 6–30 Sourcing Decisions LO 6–3

"In my opinion, we ought to stop making our own drums and accept that outside supplier's offer," said Wim Niewindt, managing director of Antilles Refining, N.V., of Aruba. "At a price of $18 per drum, we would be paying $5.20 less than it costs us to manufacture the drums in our own plant. Because we use 60,000 drums a year, that would be an annual cost savings of $312,000." Antilles Refining's current cost to manufacture one drum is given below (based on 60,000 drums per year):

Direct materials	$10.35
Direct labor.	6.10
Variable overhead.	1.60
Fixed overhead ($2.80 general company overhead, $1.60 depreciation, and $0.75 supervision)	5.15
Total cost per drum.	$23.20

A decision about whether to make or buy the drums is especially important at this time because the equipment being used to make the drums is completely worn out and must be replaced. The choices facing the company are:

Alternative 1: Rent new equipment and continue to make the drums. The equipment would be rented for $135,800 per year.

Alternative 2: Purchase the drums from an outside supplier at $18 per drum.

The new equipment would be more efficient than the equipment that Antilles Refining has been using and, according to the manufacturer, would reduce direct labor and variable overhead costs by 30%. The old equipment has no resale value. Supervision cost ($45,000 per year) and direct materials cost per drum would not be affected by the new equipment. The new equipment's capacity would be 100,000 drums per year.

The company's total general company overhead would be unaffected by this decision.

Required:

1. Assuming 60,000 drums are needed each year, what is the financial advantage (disadvantage) of buying the drums from an outside supplier?
2. Assuming 80,000 drums are needed each year, what is the financial advantage (disadvantage) of buying the drums from an outside supplier?
3. Assuming 100,000 drums are needed each year, what is the financial advantage (disadvantage) of buying the drums from an outside supplier?
4. What other factors would you recommend the company consider before making a decision?

Select cases are available in Connect.

CASE 6–31 Sell or Process Further Decision LO 6–7

The Scottie Sweater Company produces sweaters under the "Scottie" label. The company buys raw wool and processes it into wool yarn from which the sweaters are woven. One spindle of wool yarn is required to produce one sweater. The costs and revenues associated with the sweaters are given below:

		Per Sweater
Selling price		$30.00
Cost to manufacture:		
Raw materials:		
Buttons, thread, lining	$ 2.00	
Wool yarn	16.00	
Total raw materials	18.00	
Direct labor	5.80	
Manufacturing overhead	8.70	32.50
Manufacturing profit (loss)		$ (2.50)

Originally, all of the wool yarn was used to produce sweaters, but in recent years a market has developed for the wool yarn itself. The yarn is purchased by other companies for use in the production of wool blankets and other wool products. Since the development of the market for the wool yarn, a continuing dispute has existed in the Scottie Sweater Company as to whether the yarn should be sold simply as yarn or processed into sweaters. Current cost and revenue data on the yarn are given below:

		Per Spindle of Yarn
Selling price		$20.00
Cost to manufacture:		
Raw materials (raw wool)	$7.00	
Direct labor	3.60	
Manufacturing overhead	5.40	16.00
Manufacturing profit		$ 4.00

The market for sweaters is temporarily depressed due to unusually warm weather in the western states where the sweaters are sold. This has made it necessary for the company to discount the selling price of the sweaters to $30 from the normal $40 price. Because the market for wool yarn has remained strong, the dispute has again surfaced over whether the yarn should be sold outright rather than processed into sweaters. The sales manager thinks that the production of sweaters should be discontinued; she is upset about having to sell sweaters at a $2.50 loss when the yarn could be sold for a $4.00 profit. However, the production superintendent does not want to close down a large portion of the factory. He argues the company is in the sweater business, not the yarn business, and the company should focus on its core strength.

All of the manufacturing overhead costs are fixed and would not be affected even if sweaters were discontinued. Manufacturing overhead is assigned to products on the basis of 150% of direct labor cost. Materials and direct labor costs are variable.

Required:

1. What is the financial advantage (disadvantage) of further processing one spindle of wool yarn into a sweater?
2. Would you recommend the wool yarn be sold outright or processed into sweaters? Explain.
3. What is the lowest price the company should accept for a sweater? Support your answer with appropriate computations and explain your reasoning.

CASE 6–32 Ethics and the Manager; Shut Down or Continue Operations LO 6–2

Haley Romeros had just been appointed vice president of the Rocky Mountain Region of the Bank Services Corporation (BSC). The company provides check processing services for small banks. The banks send checks presented for deposit or payment to BSC, which records the data on each check in a computerized database. BSC then sends the data electronically to the nearest Federal Reserve Bank check-clearing center where the appropriate transfers of funds are made between banks. The Rocky Mountain Region has three check processing centers, which are located in Billings, Montana; Great Falls, Montana; and Clayton, Idaho. Prior to her promotion to vice president, Ms. Romeros had been the manager of a check processing center in New Jersey.

Immediately after assuming her new position, Ms. Romeros requested a complete financial report for the just-ended fiscal year from the region's controller, John Littlebear. Ms. Romeros specified that the financial report should follow the standardized format required by corporate headquarters for all regional performance reports. That report follows:

Bank Services Corporation (BSC) Rocky Mountain Region Financial Performance				
			Check Processing Centers	
	Total	**Billings**	**Great Falls**	**Clayton**
Sales	$50,000,000	$20,000,000	$18,000,000	$12,000,000
Operating expenses:				
Direct labor	32,000,000	12,500,000	11,000,000	8,500,000
Variable overhead	850,000	350,000	310,000	190,000
Equipment depreciation	3,900,000	1,300,000	1,400,000	1,200,000
Facility expense*	2,800,000	900,000	800,000	1,100,000
Local administrative expense†	450,000	140,000	160,000	150,000
Regional administrative expense‡	1,500,000	600,000	540,000	360,000
Corporate administrative expense§	4,750,000	1,900,000	1,710,000	1,140,000
Total operating expense	46,250,000	17,690,000	15,920,000	12,640,000
Net operating income (loss)	$ 3,750,000	$ 2,310,000	$ 2,080,000	$ (640,000)

*Includes building rental expense for the Billings and Great Falls locations and building depreciation for the Clayton location.
†Local administrative expenses are the administrative expenses incurred at the check processing centers.
‡Regional administrative expenses are allocated to the check processing centers based on sales.
§Corporate administrative expenses are charged to segments of the company such as the Rocky Mountain Region and the check processing centers at the rate of 9.5% of their sales.

Upon seeing this report, Ms. Romeros summoned John Littlebear for an explanation.

Romeros: What's the story on Clayton? It didn't have a loss the previous year, did it?
Littlebear: No, the Clayton facility has had a nice profit every year since it opened six years ago, but Clayton lost a big contract this year.
Romeros: Why?
Littlebear: One of our national competitors entered the local market and bid very aggressively on the contract. We couldn't afford to meet the bid. Clayton's costs—particularly their facility expenses—are just too high. When Clayton lost the contract, we had to lay off a lot of employees, but we could not reduce the fixed costs of the Clayton facility.
Romeros: Why is Clayton's facility expense so high? It's a smaller facility than either Billings or Great Falls, and yet its facility expense is higher.
Littlebear: The problem is that we are able to rent suitable facilities very cheaply at Billings and Great Falls. No such facilities were available at Clayton; we had them built. Unfortunately, there were big cost overruns. The contractor we hired was inexperienced at this kind of work and, in fact, went bankrupt before the project was completed. After hiring another contractor to finish the work, we were way over budget. The large depreciation charges on the facility didn't matter at first because we didn't have much competition at the time and could charge premium prices.

Romeros: Well, we can't do that anymore. The Clayton facility will obviously have to be shut down. Its business can be shifted to the other two check processing centers in the region.

Littlebear: I would advise against that. The $1,100,000 in facility depreciation at the Clayton location is misleading. That facility should last indefinitely with proper maintenance. And it has no resale value; there is no other commercial activity around Clayton.

Romeros: What about the other costs at Clayton?

Littlebear: If we shifted Clayton's sales over to the other two processing centers in the region, we wouldn't save anything on direct labor or variable overhead costs. We might save $90,000 or so in local administrative expense, but we would not save any regional administrative expense and corporate headquarters would still charge us 9.5% of our sales as corporate administrative expense.

In addition, we would have to rent more space in Billings and Great Falls in order to handle the work transferred from Clayton; that would probably cost us at least $600,000 a year. And don't forget that it will cost us something to move the equipment from Clayton to Billings and Great Falls. And the move will disrupt service to customers.

Romeros: I understand all of that, but a money-losing processing center on my performance report is completely unacceptable.

Littlebear: And if you shut down Clayton, you are going to throw some loyal employees out of work.

Romeros: That's unfortunate, but we have to face hard business realities.

Littlebear: And you would have to write off the investment in the facilities at Clayton.

Romeros: I can explain a write-off to corporate headquarters; hiring an inexperienced contractor to build the Clayton facility was my predecessor's mistake. But they'll have my head at headquarters if I show operating losses every year at one of my processing centers. Clayton has to go. At the next corporate board meeting, I am going to recommend the Clayton facility be closed.

Required:

1. From the standpoint of the company as a whole, what is the financial advantage (disadvantage) of closing the Clayton processing center and redistributing its work to other processing centers in the region? Explain.

2. Why might it be in Haley Romeros's self-interest to shut down the Clayton facility? Do you think Haley Romeros is conducting herself in an ethical fashion? Explain.

3. What influence should the depreciation on the facilities at Clayton have on prices charged by Clayton for its services?

CASE 6–33 Integrative Case: Relevant Costs; Pricing LO 6–1, LO 6–4

Wesco Incorporated's only product is a combination fertilizer/weedkiller called GrowNWeed. GrowNWeed is sold nationwide to retail nurseries and garden stores.

Zwinger Nursery plans to sell a similar fertilizer/weedkiller compound through its regional nursery chain under its own private label. Zwinger does not have manufacturing facilities of its own, so it has asked Wesco (and several other companies) to submit a bid for manufacturing and delivering a 20,000-pound order of the private brand compound to Zwinger. While the chemical composition of the Zwinger compound differs from that of GrowNWeed, the manufacturing processes are very similar.

The Zwinger compound would be produced in 1,000-pound lots. Each lot would require 25 direct labor-hours and the following chemicals:

Chemicals	Quantity in Pounds
AG-5	300
KL-2	200
CW-7	150
DF-6	175

The first three chemicals (AG-5, KL-2, and CW-7) are all used in the production of GrowNWeed. DF-6 was used in another compound that Wesco discontinued several months ago. The supply of DF-6 that Wesco had on hand when the other compound was discontinued was not discarded. Wesco could sell its supply of DF-6 at the prevailing market price less $0.10 per pound selling and handling expenses.

Wesco also has on hand a chemical called BH-3, which was manufactured for use in another product that is no longer produced. BH-3, which cannot be used in GrowNWeed, can be substituted for AG-5 on a one-for-one basis without affecting the quality of the Zwinger compound. The BH-3 in inventory has a salvage value of $600.

Inventory and cost data for the chemicals that can be used to produce the Zwinger compound are shown below:

Raw Material	Pounds in Inventory	Actual Price per Pound When Purchased	Current Market Price per Pound
AG-5	18,000	$1.15	$1.20
KL-2	6,000	$1.10	$1.05
CW-7	7,000	$1.35	$1.35
DF-6	3,000	$0.80	$0.70
BH-3	3,500	$0.90	(Salvage)

The current direct labor wage rate is $14 per hour. The predetermined overhead rate is based on direct labor-hours (DLH). The predetermined overhead rate for the current year, based on a two-shift capacity with no overtime, is as follows:

Variable manufacturing overhead	$ 3.00	per DLH
Fixed manufacturing overhead	10.50	per DLH
Combined predetermined overhead rate	$13.50	per DLH

Wesco's production manager reports that the present equipment and facilities are adequate to manufacture the Zwinger compound. Therefore, the order would have no effect on total fixed manufacturing overhead costs. However, Wesco is within 400 hours of its two-shift capacity this month. Any additional hours beyond the 400 hours must be done in overtime. If need be, the Zwinger compound could be produced on regular time by shifting a portion of GrowNWeed production to overtime. Wesco's direct labor wage rate for overtime is $21 per hour. There is no allowance for any overtime premium in the predetermined overhead rate.

Required:
1. Wesco has decided to submit a bid for the 20,000-pound order of Zwinger's new compound. The order must be delivered by the end of the current month. Zwinger has indicated that this is a one-time order that will not be repeated. Calculate the lowest price that Wesco could bid for the order and still exactly cover its incremental manufacturing costs.
2. Refer to the original data. Assume that Zwinger Nursery plans to place regular orders for 20,000-pound lots of the new compound. Wesco expects the demand for GrowNWeed to remain strong. Therefore, the recurring orders from Zwinger would put Wesco over its two-shift capacity. However, production could be scheduled so that 90% of each Zwinger order could be completed during regular hours. As another option, some GrowNWeed production could be shifted temporarily to overtime so that the Zwinger orders could be produced on regular time. Current market prices are the best available estimates of future market prices. Wesco's standard markup policy for new products is 40% of the full manufacturing cost, including fixed manufacturing overhead. Calculate the price that Wesco, Inc., would quote Zwinger Nursery for each 20,000-pound lot of the new compound, assuming that it is to be treated as a new product and this pricing policy is followed.

(CMA, adapted)

Some products have an established market price. Consumers will not pay more than this price, and there is no reason for a supplier to charge less—the supplier can sell all that it produces at this price. Under these circumstances, the supplier simply charges the prevailing market price for the product. Markets for basic raw materials such as farm products and minerals follow this pattern.

In this appendix, we are concerned with the more common situation in which a business needs to set its own prices. For example, Delta Airlines has to establish ticket prices for all of its flights. Accenture needs to establish bid prices when it responds to inquiries from prospective consulting clients. Procter & Gamble has to set prices for Bounty, Tide, Pampers, Crest, and its many other product lines. If these companies choose prices that are too high or too low, it can dramatically decrease profits.

Factors That Influence Pricing Decisions

Many factors can influence how companies establish their selling prices. In this section, we'd like to discuss three of those factors—customers, competitors, and costs.

Customers Customers usually possess two things—latitude and private information—that complicate the pricing process. In terms of latitude, the customer can choose to buy your product, or a competitor's product, or nothing at all. Customers also have private information regarding their level of interest in your product or service and how much they might be willing to pay for it.

For example, consider a scenario where a prospective customer invites numerous suppliers to place competitive bids in hopes of winning a contract. The customer has access to private information because it can compare and choose among the bids submitted by each supplier. If a particular supplier sets a bid price that is too high, the customer will award the contract to a competitor. Conversely, if that same supplier is awarded the contract based on a bid price that is much lower than its competitors', it may forgo revenue that the customer would have been willing to pay.

Many companies do not continuously set bid prices for individual contracts; instead, they sell products and services to large volumes of diverse customers who do not have an identical willingness to pay a particular price for a given product. In these situations, companies are keenly interested in quantifying the customers' *price elasticity of demand*. The **price elasticity of demand** measures the degree to which a change in price affects unit sales. Demand for a product or service is said to be *inelastic* if a change in price has little effect on the number of units sold. On the other hand, demand for a product or service is *elastic* if a change in price has a substantial effect on the volume of units sold. Generally speaking, managers should set higher prices when demand is inelastic and lower prices when demand is elastic.

Competitors Competitors have an important effect on a company's pricing decisions because they provide *reference prices* that influence the price elasticity of demand. For example, gasoline buyers usually have readily available reference prices when buying fuel. If a gas station raises its prices higher than the reference price of its competitor across the street, then demand is likely to drop significantly. In this instance, demand is elastic because gasoline is a commodity; therefore, customers are unwilling to pay more than the competitor's reference price. If the same gas station lowered its prices expecting elastic demand to create market share gains, the competitor across the street would probably match the price reduction, thereby holding each gas station's market share constant while lowering both competitors' profits.

If a company wants to charge higher prices than its competitors, then the company must differentiate its products or services from competing choices in a manner that motivates its customers to accept higher prices. For example, brands such as Prada, Rolex, and

Rolls Royce have created product quality and an elite social status that differentiates their products from competitors' and creates inelastic demand among wealthy customers willing to pay extremely high prices.

Costs   Customers and competitors play important roles in determining the *price ceiling* for a company's products and services. The price ceiling represents the highest price customers are willing to pay. A company's *price floor* is determined by its incremental costs. The price floor represents the lowest price a company can charge and still make incremental profit on the sales transaction.

It is important to recognize that if a company prices all of its products above the price floor, it does not guarantee the company will earn a profit. This is because the total sales revenue earned minus incremental costs may not cover the company's fixed costs. A company increases its likelihood of covering all of its costs and maximizing profits if it is capable of choosing optimal prices based on customer demand data rather than computing prices that are arbitrarily chosen without the benefit of customer feedback.

Cost-Plus Pricing

Companies frequently use a pricing approach where they *mark up* cost.[7] A product's **markup** is the difference between its selling price and its cost and is usually expressed as a percentage of cost.

$$\text{Selling price} = (1 + \text{Markup percentage}) \times \text{Cost}$$

For example, a company that uses a markup of 50% adds 50% to the costs of its products to determine selling prices. If a product costs $10, then the company would apply a markup of $5 to derive a selling price of $15 for the product. This approach is called **cost-plus pricing** because a predetermined markup percentage is applied to a cost base to determine the selling price.

Companies define the cost base that they use for cost-plus pricing in a variety of ways. For example, some companies may use absorption costing to define a cost base that includes direct materials, direct labor, variable manufacturing overhead, and fixed manufacturing overhead, whereas other companies may rely on a product's variable cost as the cost base. Furthermore, companies can use various types of cost systems, such as normal costing or standard costing, when quantifying the cost base. If a company uses normal costing for its absorption approach, it would calculate unit product costs based on actual direct materials and direct labor costs plus applied overhead. A company that uses standard costing for its absorption approach would derive unit product costs based on standard direct materials and direct labor costs per unit plus the amount of applied overhead allowed per unit produced.

In the next section, we will discuss the absorption costing approach to cost-plus pricing. As the name implies, the absorption approach uses an absorption-based unit product cost for the cost base when calculating the markup percentage.

The Absorption Costing Approach to Cost-Plus Pricing

LEARNING OBJECTIVE 6–8
Compute the selling price of a product using the absorption costing approach to cost-plus pricing.

Surveys consistently reveal that many managers use the absorption costing approach to cost-plus pricing. This method can be explained in a three-step process.

First, a company needs to calculate its *unit product costs* (including direct materials, direct labor, variable manufacturing overhead, and fixed manufacturing overhead).

---

[7]   There are some legal restrictions on prices. Antitrust laws prohibit "predatory" prices, which are generally interpreted by the courts to mean a price below average variable cost. "Price discrimination"—charging different prices to customers in the same market for the same product or service—is also prohibited by the law.

Second, it needs to determine its markup percentage on absorption cost. Third, it needs to multiply a product's unit product cost by the sum of one plus the markup percentage to determine the product's selling price.

Ritter Company: An Example

Let's assume Ritter Company wants to set the selling price on a product that has just undergone some design modifications. The company invested $100,000 in operating assets to sell an estimated sales volume of 10,000 units. Its required return on investment (ROI) in its operating assets is 20%. The accounting department provided the following cost estimates for the redesigned product:

	Per Unit	Total
Direct materials	$6	
Direct labor.	$4	
Variable manufacturing overhead	$3	
Fixed manufacturing overhead.		$70,000
Variable selling and administrative expenses	$2	
Fixed selling and administrative expenses.		$60,000

In step one of its absorption cost-plus pricing process, Ritter Company would compute the redesigned product's unit product cost as follows (absorption basis):

Direct materials	$ 6
Direct labor.	4
Variable manufacturing overhead	3
Fixed manufacturing overhead ($70,000 ÷ 10,000 units).	7
Unit product cost	$20

Ritter's second step would be to determine the markup percentage that will be multiplied by the unit product cost ($20) to derive the selling price. The formula used to determine the markup percentage is as follows:

$$\frac{\text{Markup percentage}}{\text{on absorption cost}} = \frac{(\text{Required ROI} \times \text{Investment}) + \text{Selling and administrative expenses}}{\text{Unit product cost} \times \text{Unit sales}}$$

Referring to Ritter's background information, the markup percentage on absorption cost would be calculated as follows:

$$\frac{\text{Markup percentage}}{\text{on absorption cost}} = \frac{(20\% \times \$100,000) + (\$2 \text{ per unit} \times 10,000 \text{ units} + \$60,000)}{\$20 \text{ per unit} \times 10,000 \text{ units}}$$

$$= \frac{(\$20,000) + (\$80,000)}{\$200,000}$$

$$= 50\%$$

Notice that the 50% markup on absorption cost is designed to provide the company's required return on investment (20% × $100,000 = $20,000) and to cover the product's selling and administrative expenses ($2 per unit × 10,000 units + $60,000 = $80,000).

The third step is to establish the selling price per unit using the cost-plus pricing equation introduced earlier:

$$\text{Selling price} = (1 + \text{Markup percentage}) \times \text{Cost}$$
$$= (1 + 50\%) \times \$20$$
$$= \$30$$

EXHIBIT 6A–1

Income Statement and ROI Analysis—Ritter Company

Actual Unit Sales = 10,000 Units; Selling Price = $30

Direct materials	$ 6
Direct labor.	4
Variable manufacturing overhead	3
Fixed manufacturing overhead ($70,000 ÷ 10,000 units).	7
Unit product cost.	$20

Absorption Costing Income Statement

Sales ($30 per unit × 10,000 units).	$300,000
Cost of goods sold ($20 per unit × 10,000 units).	200,000
Gross margin	100,000
Selling and administrative expenses ($2 per unit × 10,000 units + $60,000)	80,000
Net operating income.	$ 20,000

ROI

$$\text{ROI} = \frac{\text{Net operating income}}{\text{Average operating assets}}$$

$$= \frac{\$20,000}{\$100,000}$$

$$= 20\%$$

The selling price of $30 covers the unit product cost of $20, plus it provides $10 more to cover selling and administrative expenses and to provide the required ROI.

As shown in Exhibit 6A–1, *if Ritter actually realizes its forecasted sales of 10,000 units,* the product will indeed earn a net operating income of $20,000 and an ROI of 20%. However, if it turns out that more than 10,000 units are sold at this price, the ROI will be greater than 20%. If less than 10,000 units are sold, the ROI will be less than 20%. *The required ROI will be attained only if the forecasted unit sales volume is attained.*

Problems with the Absorption Costing Approach

The absorption costing approach makes pricing look deceptively simple. All a company needs to do is compute its unit product cost, decide how much profit it wants, and then set its price. It appears a company can ignore customer demand and arrive at a price that will safely yield whatever profit it wants. Given that the absorption approach forecasts unit sales *before* establishing a selling price, it appears to operate on the faulty assumption that customers have no latitude—that they are required to buy the product at whatever price the seller deems appropriate. That is not true! Customers have a choice. If the price is too high, they can buy from a competitor or they may choose not to buy at all.

Suppose, for example, that when Ritter Company sets its price at $30, it sells only 7,000 units rather than the forecasted volume of 10,000 units. As shown in Exhibit 6A–2, this lower sales volume would cause the unit product cost to increase from $20 to $23. Furthermore, and as also shown in Exhibit 6A–2, the company would have a loss of $25,000 on the product instead of a profit of $20,000.

If Ritter responds to this situation by raising its price in an effort to restore profitability at a sales volume of 7,000 units, it would recalculate the markup percentage on absorption cost as follows:

Direct materials	$ 6
Direct labor.	4
Variable manufacturing overhead	3
Fixed manufacturing overhead ($70,000 ÷ 7,000 units)	10
Unit product cost.	$23

EXHIBIT 6A–2
Income Statement and ROI Analysis—Ritter Company Actual Unit Sales = 7,000 Units; Selling Price = $30

Absorption Costing Income Statement

Sales ($30 per unit × 7,000 units)	$210,000
Cost of goods sold ($23 per unit × 7,000 units)	161,000
Gross margin	49,000
Selling and administrative expenses ($2 per unit × 7,000 units + $60,000)	74,000
Net operating loss.	$ (25,000)

ROI

$$\text{ROI} = \frac{\text{Net operating income}}{\text{Average operating assets}}$$

$$= \frac{-\$25,000}{\$100,000}$$

$$= -25\%$$

$$\frac{\text{Markup percentage}}{\text{on absorption cost}} = \frac{(20\% \times \$100,000) + (\$2 \text{ per unit} \times 7,000 \text{ units} + \$60,000)}{\$23 \text{ per unit} \times 7,000 \text{ units}}$$

$$= \frac{(\$20,000) + (\$74,000)}{\$161,000}$$

$$= 58.4\%$$

This higher markup percentage would in turn raise the price on the redesigned product from $30.00 to $36.43, which is calculated as follows:

$$\text{Selling price} = (1 + \text{Markup percentage}) \times \text{Cost}$$
$$= (1 + 58.4\%) \times \$23$$
$$= \$36.43$$

While Ritter may hope that a price increase of $6.43 (= $36.43 − $30.00) will restore profitability, in all likelihood, the price hike will cause additional customer defections and lower profits. This is because Ritter's customers are not required to pay whatever price is necessary for Ritter to meet its financial goals. The customers have the latitude to reject Ritter's price and spend their money elsewhere.

Pricing and Customer Latitude

As discussed in the previous section, customers have latitude in their purchasing decisions. They can purchase a competitor's product or allocate their spending budget to some other product altogether. This latitude should be taken into account when setting prices. To illustrate, consider Nature's Garden, a company that sells many products including Apple-Almond Shampoo. The company provided the following data regarding this product:

LEARNING OBJECTIVE 6–9
Understand how the customers' sensitivity to changes in price should influence pricing decisions.

	Apple-Almond Shampoo
Unit sales (a)...............................	200,000
Selling price per unit........................	$5.00
Variable cost per unit	2.00
Contribution margin per unit (b)	$3.00
Total contribution margin (a) × (b).............	$600,000
Traceable fixed expenses	570,000
Net operating income.......................	$ 30,000

Management is considering increasing the price of Apple-Almond Shampoo from $5.00 to $5.50, but is fully aware that this 10% increase in price [= ($5.50 − $5.00) ÷ $5.00] will result in a decline in unit sales because of the latitude customers have in their purchasing decisions. If unit sales drop too much, profit (i.e., net operating income) may actually decline despite the increase in the selling price. The company's marketing managers have estimated that this price hike could decrease unit sales by as much as 15%, from 200,000 units to 170,000 units.

The question the company would like to answer is which price ($5.00 or $5.50) will generate higher profits? To answer this question, the company can use the following equation to calculate Apple-Almond Shampoo's profit at each price:

$$\text{Profit} = (P - V) \times Q - \text{Fixed expenses}$$

where P is the selling price per unit, V is the variable cost per unit, and Q is the unit sales.

At a price of $5.00 and a sales volume of 200,000 units, Apple-Almond Shampoo earns a profit of $30,000 as shown below:

$$\begin{aligned}
\text{Profit} &= (P - V) \times Q - \text{Fixed expenses} \\
&= (\$5.00 - \$2.00) \times 200,000 - \$570,000 \\
&= \$3.00 \times 200,000 - \$570,000 \\
&= \$600,000 - \$570,000 \\
&= \$30,000
\end{aligned}$$

At a price of $5.50 and a sales volume of 170,000 units, assuming fixed expenses are not affected by the decrease in unit sales, Apple-Almond Shampoo earns a profit of $25,000 as shown below:

$$\begin{aligned}
\text{Profit} &= (P - V) \times Q - \text{Fixed expenses} \\
&= (\$5.50 - \$2.00) \times 170,000 - \$570,000 \\
&= \$3.50 \times 170,000 - \$570,000 \\
&= \$595,000 - \$570,000 \\
&= \$25,000
\end{aligned}$$

Given these results, Nature's Garden should not raise the price of this product to $5.50 because its profits would be $5,000 higher (= $30,000 − $25,000) at the lower price of $5.00.

Customer Latitude: A Closer Look

Thus far, our example assumed that management has only two options: either keep the price of Apple-Almond Shampoo at $5.00 or increase it to $5.50 with a resulting drop in unit sales of 15%. However, keep in mind the 15% figure is an estimate, not a certainty. Based on our previous calculations, we know that increasing the price from $5.00 to

$5.50 would reduce profits if unit sales decrease by 15%. If unit sales decrease by more than 15%, profits will decline even more. But what would be the financial implications if unit sales actually decreased by something *less than* 15%?

Management could explore this possibility by calculating the unit sales (Q) needed at the higher price ($5.50) to achieve the same profit ($30,000) that is earned at the lower price ($5.00). Assuming that fixed expenses remain unchanged, that critical value of unit sales (Q) can be solved for as follows:

$$\text{Profit} = (P - V) \times Q - \text{Fixed expenses}$$
$$\$30,000 = (\$5.50 - \$2.00) \times Q - \$570,000$$
$$\$600,000 = \$3.50Q$$
$$Q = 171{,}429 \text{ units (rounded)}$$

This calculation tells us that if the company sells 171,429 units at the selling price of $5.50, the company will earn the same profit that it earned at the lower price of $5.00. But if the company sells *more* than 171,429 units, then increasing the selling price by 10% will *increase* profit. However, if the company sells *fewer* than 171,429 units, then increasing the selling price by 10% will *decrease* profit. The critical value of 171,429 units is sort of a break even in this situation.

The sales volume of 171,429 units reflects a percentage change in sales of −14.3% [= (171,429 − 200,000) ÷ 200,000]. Thus, if management believes unit sales will drop by *less* than 14.3%, it should choose a price of $5.50. If management believes unit sales will drop by *more* than 14.3%, it should choose a price of $5.00. Let's suppose that management believes unit sales will drop by less than 14.3%, and therefore the selling price is increased to $5.50. Further suppose that management is correct and after increasing the price, unit sales drop by only 13%—from 200,000 units to 174,000 units. Then Apple-Almond Shampoo would earn a profit of $39,000 as shown below:

$$\text{Profit} = (P - V) \times Q - \text{Fixed expenses}$$
$$= (\$5.50 - \$2.00) \times 174{,}000 - \$570{,}000$$
$$= \$3.50 \times 174{,}000 - \$570{,}000$$
$$= \$39{,}000$$

In this case, because unit sales drop by only 13%, the higher price of $5.50 causes profits to increase by $9,000 (= $39,000 − $30,000).

Choosing Optimal Prices: The Influence of Customer Latitude

If we assume a 10% increase in the price of Apple-Almond Shampoo causes a 13% decrease in unit sales, then a price of $5.50 will generate $9,000 (= $39,000 − $30,000) of additional profit compared to a price of $5.00. However, it would be incorrect to conclude that $5.50 is the *optimal price* for Apple-Almond Shampoo; in other words, the price that would maximize profit.

A price of $5.50 is not necessarily the optimal price because Nature's Garden is not limited to choosing a price of either $5.00 or $5.50. Perhaps the company would be better off considering an 8% or 12% price increase rather than just a 10% increase. For that matter, the company can establish any price it wants for Apple-Almond Shampoo. It could establish a very low price, such as $2.00 per unit, or a very high price, such as $50 per unit, or anything in between. The low price of $2.00 would be a bad idea because it equals the product's variable cost per unit and would lead to a loss of $570,000, whereas the high price of $50 per unit may be a bad idea because very few customers, if any, would pay $50 for a bottle of shampoo. Thus, the management challenge becomes leveraging knowledge of how customers will respond to changes in price to determine the selling price that will maximize profits—keeping in mind that this optimal price could be higher or lower than the current price of $5.00.

EXHIBIT 6A–3
Nature's Garden Apple-
Almond Shampoo: An Optimal
Pricing Model

	A	B	C	D	E	F
1		Optimal Pricing Model				
2	Apple-Almond Shampoo:					
3	Current unit sales	200,000				
4	Current selling price per unit	$5.00				
5	Variable cost per unit	$2.00				
6	Traceable fixed costs	$570,000				
7						
8	Percentage change in selling price	10%				
9	Percentage change in unit sales	-13%				
10						
11		Per Unit		Unit Sales		Total
12	Sales	$ 6.34	×	141,467	=	$ 896,481
13	Variable expenses	2.00	×	141,467	=	282,934
14	Contribution margin	$ 4.34	×	141,467	=	613,547
15	Traceable fixed expenses					570,000
16	Net operating income					$ 43,547
17						

H ◄ ► H   **Chapter 6 Form**   Chapter 6 Form

Microsoft Excel

Note: The price shown in cell B12 is rounded to the nearest penny, whereas Excel used the unrounded price (which is approximately $6.337) to compute the total sales in cell F12.

Exhibit 6A–3 uses Microsoft Excel to illustrate a pricing model that calculates an optimal price for any product or service once the percentage change in price and percentage change in unit sales have been specified.[8] The specific calculations shown in Exhibit 6A–3 relate to Nature Garden's Apple-Almond Shampoo assuming a 10% increase in price causes a 13% decrease in unit sales.

The first thing to notice with respect to the output from our optimal price calculations shown in Exhibit 6A–3 is that the optimal price is not $5.00 or $5.50. It is $6.34 as shown in cell B12. At this price, the company earns a profit of $43,547 (cell F16), which is $4,547 (= $43,547 − $39,000) higher than the previously computed profit obtained at a price of $5.50. While the mathematics underlying this pricing model are beyond the scope of this course, if you choose to download the model and familiarize yourself with it, we want you to understand how to input data into the model and how to interpret the results.[9]

To input data into the model, you should follow a four-step process. First, input the product's current unit sales (cell B3), current selling price (cell B4), variable cost per unit (cell B5), and traceable fixed costs (cell B6). Second, input the percentage change in selling price (cell B8) and the percentage change in unit sales (cell B9). Third, input the current selling price in cell B12. Fourth, click on the Data tab in Microsoft Excel and select Solver in the upper right-hand portion of your screen.[10] When the Solver window opens, click "Solve," and the optimal price will be calculated and automatically inserted into cell B12. In addition, the optimal profit will be automatically calculated in cell F16.

---

[8] This pricing model assumes a constant elasticity demand curve and fixed expenses that are unaffected by the changes in unit sales. Other demand curves, such as a linear demand curve, could be assumed. While there is some empirical support for using the constant elasticity demand curve, it should be acknowledged that the "optimal" selling price will depend on the demand curve that is assumed. Because of this, as well as the uncertainty that usually surrounds estimates of customer responses to price changes, the "optimal" price produced by this model should be viewed as an estimate and not taken too literally.

[9] To obtain a copy of this Excel-based pricing model, go to www.mhhe.com/noreen_opm.

[10] Solver is an Add-in offered within Microsoft Excel. To activate Solver if you do not see it in your Data tab, click the File tab and select Options. Within the Excel Options menu that appears on your screen, click Add-ins and then select Solver Add-in and click OK.

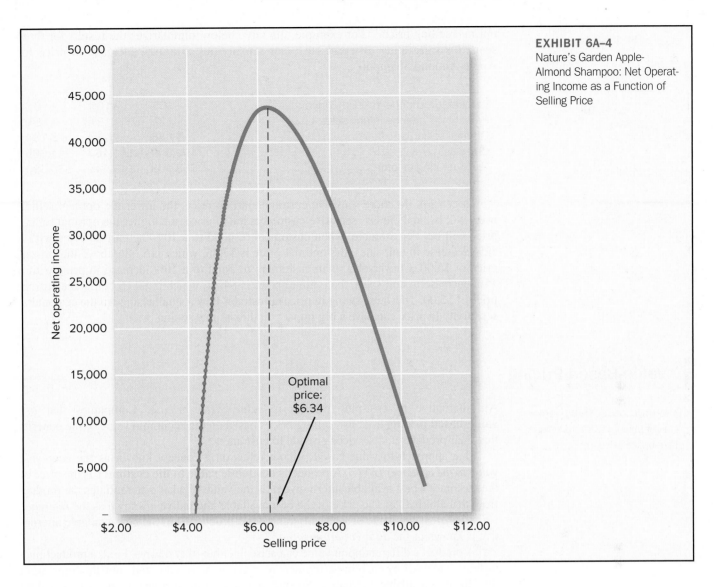

EXHIBIT 6A–4
Nature's Garden Apple-
Almond Shampoo: Net Operat-
ing Income as a Function of
Selling Price

A Visual Perspective of the Optimal Pricing Model

Exhibit 6A–4 plots Apple-Almond Shampoo's net operating income as a function of the selling price when we assume that a 10% increase in price decreases unit sales by 13%.[11]

This plot provides a visual aid in understanding what the optimal pricing model is doing. Essentially, Excel Solver efficiently searches along this graph for the price that maximizes the profit, which in this case is a selling price of $6.34 that results in a total profit of $43,547.

For a variety of reasons, this optimal selling price should not be taken too literally. A prudent manager would make a small change in price in the direction of the optimal price and then observe what happens to unit sales and the net operating income. Nevertheless, the Excel workbook can provide us with important insights into pricing. If we wanted to adjust the percentage change in unit sales or the percentage change in selling price, we could rerun the Solver function to automatically compute the revised

---

[11] As with the Solver solution to the optimal pricing problem, this graph assumes a constant elasticity demand curve and that the fixed expenses are constant throughout the entire range of unit sales that result from the various prices.

optimal selling price.[12] For example, the table below summarizes the results for three scenarios illustrating different customer sensitivities to a 10% increase in price for Apple-Almond Shampoo:

Percentage change in selling price	+10%	+10%	+10%
Percentage change in unit sales	−12%	−13%	−15%
Optimal selling price.	$7.86	$6.34	$4.84
Unit sales	109,009	141,467	211,685
Net operating income.	$68,908	$43,547	$30,390

In general, the more sensitive customers are to price, the lower the optimal selling price will be, and the less sensitive customers are to price, the higher the optimal selling price will be. For example, when customers respond to a 10% increase in price with a 12% decrease in unit sales, the optimal price is $7.86, which is $2.86 above the current price of $5.00. Conversely, when customers respond to a 10% increase in price with a 15% decrease in unit sales, the optimal price is $4.84, which is $0.16 below the current price of $5.00. This large swing in prices illustrates how a small change in the customers' sensitivity to price can have a big impact on the optimal selling price.

Value-Based Pricing

LEARNING OBJECTIVE 6–10
Analyze pricing decisions using value-based pricing.

An alternative to cost-plus pricing is *value-based pricing*. Companies that use **value-based pricing** establish selling prices based on the economic value of the benefits that their products and services provide to customers.

One approach to value-based pricing relies on a concept known as the *economic value to the customer (EVC)*. A product's **economic value to the customer** is the price of the customer's best available alternative plus the value of what differentiates the product from that alternative. The price of the best available alternative is known as the *reference value,* whereas the value of what differentiates a product from the best available alternative is known as the *differentiation value.*[13]

A product's differentiation value can arise in either of two ways. First, a product may differentiate itself by enabling customers to generate more sales and contribution margin than the best available alternative. Second, a product may differentiate itself by enabling customers to realize greater cost savings than the best available alternative.

In equation form, the EVC is computed as follows:

$$\text{Economic value to the customer} = \text{Reference value} + \text{Differentiation value}$$

Once the seller computes the EVC, it seeks to negotiate a value-based selling price with the customer that falls within the following range:

$$\text{Reference value} \leq \text{Value-based price} \leq \text{EVC}$$

---

[12] If Solver is unable to find a solution, the most likely cause is that the combination of the percentage change in price and the percentage change in unit sales that you have inputted has resulted in an infinite optimal price. For example, if a 10% increase in price always leads to only a 5% decrease in units sold and fixed costs are constant, then profits always go up when the price is increased. This obviously cannot happen in practice. At some point customers will stop buying the product altogether.

[13] The terms *reference value* and *differentiation value,* as well as the forthcoming example grounded in the magazine publishing industry, were adapted from *The Strategy and Tactics of Pricing: A Guide to Profitable Decision Making* by Thomas T. Nagle and Reed K. Holden, 2002, Pearson Education, Upper Saddle River, New Jersey.

Economic Value to the Customer: An Example

The managers of *Hike America* magazine want to establish a selling price for a one-month full-page advertisement in their magazine. While their primary competitor, *Hiking Trails* magazine, charges $5,000 per month for a full-page ad, the managers of *Hike America* believe they can justify a higher selling price by quantifying the EVC of a full-page ad in their magazine. To enable their analysis, the managers gathered the following data pertaining to the two magazines:

	Hike America	Hiking Trails
Number of readers	200,000	300,000
Percent of readers who buy advertised products each month	0.2%	0.1%
Monthly spending per reader who buys advertised products	$100	$80
Contribution margin ratio of advertisers	25%	25%

Although *Hike America* has fewer readers than *Hiking Trails* magazine (200,000 vs. 300,000), a higher percentage of *Hike America*'s "hard core" subscribers buy advertised products each month (0.2% vs. 0.1%), and they spend more per person on advertised products ($100 vs. $80). Given the assumption that advertisers in both magazines earn a contribution margin ratio of 25% on all merchandise sales, *Hike America*'s managers computed the differentiation value of an ad placed in their magazine as follows:

	Hike America	Hiking Trails
Number of readers (a).	200,000	300,000
Percent of readers who buy advertised products each month (b).	0.2%	0.1%
Number of readers per month buying advertised products (a) × (b)	400	300
Monthly sales per reader who buys advertised products (a).	$100	$80
Contribution margin ratio (b)	25%	25%
Monthly contribution margin per reader who buys advertised products (a) × (b)	$25	$20
Number of readers per month buying advertised products (a)	400	300
Monthly contribution margin per reader who buys advertised products (b)	$25	$20
Contribution margin per month provided by a full-page ad (a) × (b).	$10,000	$6,000
Differentiation value	**$4,000**	

Given that *Hike America*'s reference value is $5,000—the price charged by *Hiking Trails* for a full-page ad—the EVC would be computed as follows:

Economic value to the customer = Reference value + Differentiation value

= $5,000 + $4,000

= $9,000

Hike America would seek to negotiate a value-based selling price for a full-page adver-tisement within the following range:

$$\text{Reference value} \le \text{Value-based price} \le \text{EVC}$$
$$\$5{,}000 \le \text{Value-based price} \le \$9{,}000$$

It bears emphasizing that the EVC of $9,000 does not necessarily represent the price that *Hike America* should charge customers for a full-page advertisement. Instead, it provides the magazine's managers a starting point for understanding the economic benefit (in terms of additional contribution margin) that a full-page ad in their magazine can offer to prospective customers. In fact, the data shown below suggest that *Hike America* probably needs to establish a price less than $9,000.

| | Hike America | | |
	Price = $9,000	Price = $8,000	Hiking Trails
Contribution margin provided by the ad.....	$10,000	$10,000	$6,000
Investment in the ad (a)	9,000	8,000	5,000
Incremental profit from the ad (b)...........	$ 1,000	$ 2,000	$1,000
Return on investment (b) / (a)	11%	25%	20%

Notice that the right-hand column of numbers shows that *Hiking Trails* magazine provides its customers with a 20% ROI for a full-page advertisement. Conversely, the left-hand column of numbers shows that *Hike America*'s customers would only earn an 11% ROI if they paid $9,000 for a full-page ad. Thus, if *Hike America* established a price of $9,000, it would provide advertisers with a lower ROI than they could earn by placing a full-page ad in *Hiking Trails* magazine. However, *Hike America* might consider touting a lower price, such as $8,000, to its prospective customers. As shown in the middle col-umn of data, this lower price would provide prospective advertisers with an ROI of 25%, which compares favorably with *Hiking Trails'* ROI of 20%.

Target Costing

LEARNING OBJECTIVE 6–11
Compute the target cost for a new product or service.

Our discussion thus far has presumed that a product has already been developed, has been costed, and is ready to be marketed as soon as a price is set. In many cases, the sequence of events is just the reverse. That is, the company already *knows* what price should be charged, and the problem is to *develop* a product that can be marketed profitably at the desired price. Even in this situation, where the normal sequence of events is reversed, cost is still a crucial factor. The company can use an approach called *target costing*. **Target costing** is the process of determining the maximum allowable cost for a new product and then developing a prototype that can be profitably made for that maximum target cost figure. A number of companies have used target costing, including Compaq, Culp, Cum-mins Engine, Daihatsu Motors, Chrysler, Ford, Isuzu Motors, ITT Automotive, Komatsu, Matsushita Electric, Mitsubishi Kasei, NEC, Nippondenso, Nissan, Olympus, Sharp, Texas Instruments, and Toyota.

The target cost for a product is computed by starting with the product's anticipated selling price and then deducting the desired profit, as follows:

$$\text{Target cost} = \text{Anticipated selling price} - \text{Desired profit}$$

The product development team is then given the responsibility of designing the product so that it can be made for no more than the target cost.

Reasons for Using Target Costing

The target costing approach was developed in recognition of two important characteristics of markets and costs. The first is that many companies have less control over price than they would like to think. The market (i.e., supply and demand) really determines price, and a company that attempts to ignore this does so at its peril. Therefore, the anticipated market price is taken as a given in target costing.

The second observation is that most of a product's cost is determined in the design stage. Once a product has been designed and has gone into production, not much can be done to significantly reduce its cost. Most of the opportunities to reduce cost come from designing the product so that it is simple to make, uses fewer parts, and is robust and reliable. If the company has little control over market price and little control over cost once the product has gone into production, then it follows that the major opportunities for affecting profit come during a product's design stage. So that is where the effort is concentrated—in designing and developing cost-effective products that possess features valued by customers.

The difference between target costing and other approaches to product development is profound. Instead of designing the product and then finding out how much it costs, the target cost is set first, and then the product is designed so that the target cost is attained.

An Example of Target Costing

To provide a simple example of target costing, assume the following situation: Handy Company wishes to invest $2,000,000 to design, develop, and produce a new hand mixer. The company's Marketing Department surveyed the features and prices of competing products and determined that a price of $30 would enable Handy to sell an estimated 40,000 hand mixers per year. Because the company desires a 15% ROI, the target cost to manufacture, sell, distribute, and service one mixer is $22.50 as computed below:

Projected sales (40,000 mixers × $30 per mixer)............	$1,200,000
Less desired profit (15% × $2,000,000)...................	300,000
Target cost for 40,000 mixers............................	$ 900,000
Target cost per mixer ($900,000 ÷ 40,000 mixers)	$ 22.50

This $22.50 target cost would be broken down into target costs for the various functions: manufacturing, marketing, distribution, after-sales service, and so on. Each functional area would be responsible for keeping its actual costs within target.

Summary (Appendix 6A)

Pricing involves a delicate balancing act. Higher prices result in more revenue per unit but drive down unit sales. Exactly where to set prices to maximize profit is a difficult problem.

Managers often rely on cost-plus pricing to establish selling prices. The absorption approach to cost-plus pricing applies a markup to the absorption costing unit product cost that is intended to cover nonmanufacturing costs and to provide an adequate return on investment. With the absorption approach, costs will be covered and the return on investment will be adequate *only* if the unit sales forecast used in the cost-plus formula is accurate. If applying the cost-plus formula results in a price that is too high, the unit sales forecast will not be attained.

Customers have latitude in their purchasing decisions. They can choose to buy your product, a competitor's product, or nothing at all. This latitude should be taken into account when setting prices. The customers' sensitivity to price is said to be *inelastic* if a change in price has little effect on the number of units sold. On the other hand, the customers' sensitivity to price is *elastic* if a change in price has a substantial effect on the volume of units sold. In general, the more sensitive customers are to price, the lower the optimal selling price will be, and the less sensitive customers are to price, the higher the optimal selling price will be.

Value-based pricing is an alternative to cost-plus pricing. Companies that use value-based pricing establish selling prices based on the economic value of the benefits that their products and services provide to customers. One approach to value-based pricing relies on quantifying the *economic value to the customer (EVC)*. A product's EVC is the price of the customer's best alternative (the reference value) plus the value of what differentiates the seller's product from that alternative (the differentiation value). Once the seller computes the EVC, it establishes a value-based selling price that falls between the reference value and the EVC.

Companies that use target costing estimate what a new product's market price is likely to be based on its anticipated features and the prices of products already on the market. They subtract desired profit from the estimated market price to arrive at the product's target cost. The design and development team is then given the responsibility of ensuring the actual cost of the new product does not exceed the target cost.

Glossary (Appendix 6A)

Cost-plus pricing A pricing method in which a predetermined markup is applied to a cost base to determine the target selling price. (p. 330)

Economic value to the customer (EVC) The price of a customer's best alternative (called the reference value) plus the value of what differentiates a product from that alternative (called the differentiation value). (p. 338)

Markup The difference between the selling price of a product or service and its cost. The markup is usually expressed as a percentage of cost. (p. 330)

Price elasticity of demand A measure of the degree to which a change in price affects the unit sales of a product or service. (p. 329)

Target costing The process of determining the maximum allowable cost for a new product and then developing a prototype that can be profitably made for that maximum target cost figure. (p. 340)

Value-based pricing A pricing method in which a company establishes selling prices based on the economic value of the benefits that their products and services provide to customers. (p. 338)

Appendix 6A: Exercises and Problems   Mc Graw Hill **connect**

EXERCISE 6A–1 Absorption Costing Approach to Cost-Plus Pricing LO 6–8

Martin Company uses the absorption costing approach to cost-plus pricing. It is considering the introduction of a new product. To determine a selling price, the company gathered the following information:

Number of units to be produced and sold each year............	14,000
Unit product cost..	$25
Estimated annual selling and administrative expenses	$50,000
Estimated investment required by the company................	$750,000
Desired return on investment (ROI)	12%

Required:

1. Compute the markup percentage on absorption cost required to achieve the desired ROI.
2. Compute the selling price per unit.

EXERCISE 6A–2 Customer Latitude and Pricing LO 6–9

Maria Lorenzi owns an ice cream stand that she operates during the summer months in West Yellowstone, Montana. She is unsure how to price her ice cream cones and has experimented with two prices in successive weeks during the busy August season. The number of people who entered the store was roughly the same each week. During the first week, she priced the cones at $3.50, and 1,800 cones were sold. During the second week, she priced the cones at $4.00 and 1,400 cones were sold. The variable cost of a cone is $0.80 and consists solely of the costs of the ice cream and the cone itself. The fixed expenses of the ice cream stand are $2,675 per week.

Required:
1. What profit did Maria earn during the first week when her price was $3.50?
2. At the start of the second week, Maria increased her selling price by what percentage? What percentage did unit sales decrease? (Round your answers to one-tenth of a percent.)
3. What profit did Maria earn during the second week when her price was $4.00?
4. What was Maria's increase (decrease) in profits from the first week to the second week?

EXERCISE 6A–3 Value-Based Pricing LO 6–10

McDermott Company developed a new industrial component called IC-75. The company is excited about IC-75 because it offers superior performance relative to the comparable component sold by McDermott's primary competitor. The competing part sells for $1,200 and needs to be replaced after 2,000 hours of use. It also requires $200 of preventive maintenance during its useful life.

The IC-75's performance capabilities are similar to its competing product with two important exceptions—it needs to be replaced after 4,000 hours of use and it requires $300 of preventive maintenance during its useful life.

Required:
From a value-based pricing standpoint:
1. What is the reference value McDermott should consider when pricing IC-75?
2. What is the differentiation value offered by IC-75 relative the competitor's offering for each 4,000 hours of usage?
3. What is IC-75's economic value to the customer over its 4,000-hour life?
4. What range of possible prices should McDermott consider when setting a price for IC-75?

EXERCISE 6A–4 Target Costing LO 6–11

Shimada Products Corporation of Japan plans to introduce a new electronic component to the market at a target selling price of $15 per unit. The company is investing $5,000,000 to purchase the equipment it needs to produce and sell 300,000 units per year. Its required rate of return on all investments is 12%.

Required:
Compute the component's target cost per unit.

EXERCISE 6A–5 Customer Latitude and Optimal Pricing LO 6–9

Northport Company manufactures numerous products, one of which is called Sea Breeze Skin Cleanser. The company provided the following data regarding this product:

Unit sales (a).	120,000
Selling price per unit.	$20.00
Variable cost per unit	13.00
Contribution margin per unit (b)	$ 7.00
Total contribution margin (a) × (b).	$840,000
Traceable fixed expenses	800,000
Net operating income.	$ 40,000

Management is considering increasing the price of Sea Breeze by 20%, from $20.00 to $24.00. The company's marketing managers estimate that this price hike could decrease unit sales by as much as 30%, from 120,000 units to 84,000 units.

Required:

In all of the below requirements, assume the traceable fixed expenses are not affected by the pricing decision.

1. Assuming the marketing managers' estimate is accurate, what profit will Sea Breeze Skin Cleanser earn at a price of $24.00?
2. How many units would Northport need to sell at a price of $24.00 to earn the exact same profit that it currently earns at a price of $20.00? (Round your answer up to the nearest whole number.)
3. If Northport raises the price of Sea Breeze Skin Cleanser to $24.00, what percentage decrease in unit sales could be absorbed while still providing the same profit currently being earned at a price of $20.00? (Round your answer to the nearest one-tenth of a percent.)
4. Download the optimal pricing model from www.mhhe.com/noreen_opm. Input all of the pertinent data related to Sea Breeze Skin Cleanser into the model (including the assumptions that a 20% increase in selling price will cause a 30% decrease in unit sales). Be sure to input the current price in cell B12. Click on the Data tab in Microsoft Excel and select Solver in the upper right-hand portion of your screen. When the Solver window opens, click "Solve."
    a. What is the optimal selling price?
    b. What profit is earned at the optimal selling price?
    c. How much additional profit is earned at the optimal price compared to a price of $24.00?
5. Assume that a 20% increase in selling price would actually cause a 35% decline in unit sales instead of a 30% drop. Using the optimal pricing model, determine your answers to the following questions:
    a. What are the optimal selling price and optimal profit if unit sales decline by 35% instead of 30%?
    b. Is the optimal price from requirement 5*a* higher or lower than your answer in requirement 4*a*? Why?
    c. If a 20% increase in price causes unit sales to decrease by 35% instead of 30%, would you recommend retaining a price of $20 or implementing your optimal price from requirement 5*a*? Why?

EXERCISE 6A–6 Value-Based Pricing; Absorption Costing Approach to Cost-Plus Pricing LO 6–8, LO 6–10

Valmont Company has developed a new industrial piece of equipment called the XP-200. The company is considering two methods of establishing a selling price for the XP-200—absorption cost-plus pricing and value-based pricing.

Valmont's cost accounting system reports an absorption unit product cost for XP-200 of $8,400. Its markup percentage on absorption cost is 85%. The company's marketing managers have expressed concerns about the use of absorption cost-plus pricing because it seems to overlook the fact that the XP-200 offers superior performance relative to the comparable piece of equipment sold by Valmont's primary competitor. More specifically, the XP-200 can be used for 20,000 hours before replacement. It only requires $1,000 of preventive maintenance during its useful life, and it consumes $120 of electricity per 1,000 hours used.

These figures compare favorably to the competing piece of equipment that sells for $15,000, needs to be replaced after 10,000 hours of use, requires $2,000 of preventive maintenance during its useful life, and consumes $140 of electricity per 1,000 hours used.

Required:

1. If Valmont uses absorption cost-plus pricing, what price will it establish for the XP-200?
2. What is XP-200's economic value to the customer (EVC) over its 20,000-hour life?
3. If Valmont uses value-based pricing, what range of possible prices should it consider when setting a price for the XP-200?
4. What advice would you give Valmont's managers when choosing between absorption cost-plus pricing and value-based pricing?

EXERCISE 6A–7 Customer Latitude and Pricing LO 6–9

The postal service of St. Vincent, an island in the West Indies, obtains a significant portion of its revenues from sales of special souvenir sheets to stamp collectors. The postal service purchases the souvenir sheets from a supplier for $0.80 each. St. Vincent has been selling the souvenir sheets for $8.00 each and ordinarily sells about 80,000 units. To test the market, the postal service recently priced a new souvenir sheet at $7.00, and sales increased to 93,600 units.

Required:

1. What total contribution margin did the postal service earn when it sold 80,000 sheets at a price of $8.00 each?

2. By what percentage did the St. Vincent post office decrease its selling price? By what percentage did unit sales increase? (Round your answers to one-tenth of a percent.)

3. What total contribution margin did the postal service earn when it sold 93,600 sheets at a price of $7.00 each?

4. What was the postal service's increase (decrease) in total contribution margin going from the higher price of $8.00 to the lower price of $7.00?

5. How many sheets would the postal service have to sell at the lower price of $7.00 to equal the total contribution margin earned at the higher price of $8.00? (Round your answer up to the nearest whole number.)

6. What percentage increase in the number of sheets sold at $7.00 must be achieved to equal the total contribution margin earned at the higher price of $8.00? (Round your answer up to the nearest one-tenth of a percent.)

7. A financial manager at the postal service has suggested that a more accurate comparison of the two pricing alternatives ($8.00 vs. $7.00) should include an allocation of the postal service's common fixed costs. A portion of the common fixed costs would be allocated to each alternative using total sales dollars as the cost allocation base. He contends that this approach would help ensure that the postal service's common fixed costs are covered by the prices that it charges customers. Do you agree?

PROBLEM 6A–8 Standard Costs; Absorption Costing Approach to Cost-Plus Pricing LO 6–8

Wilderness Products, Inc., has designed a self-inflating sleeping pad for use by backpackers and campers. The following information is available about the new product:

a. An investment of $1,350,000 will be necessary to carry inventories and accounts receivable and to purchase some new equipment needed in the manufacturing process. The company's required rate of return is 24% on all investments.

b. A standard cost card has been prepared for the sleeping pad, as shown below:

	Standard Quantity or Hours	Standard Price or Rate	Standard Cost
Direct materials	4.0 yards	$2.70 per yard	$10.80
Direct labor.	2.4 hours	$8.00 per hour	19.20
Manufacturing overhead (20% variable)	2.4 hours	$12.50 per hour	30.00
Total standard cost per pad.			$60.00

c. The only variable selling and administrative expense will be a sales commission of $9 per pad. The fixed selling and administrative expenses will be $732,000 per year.

d. Because the company manufactures many products, no more than 38,400 direct labor-hours per year can be devoted to production of the new sleeping pads.

e. Manufacturing overhead costs are allocated to products on the basis of direct labor-hours.

Required:

1. Assume the company uses the absorption approach to cost-plus pricing.

   a. Compute the markup percentage that the company needs on the pads to achieve a 24% return on investment (ROI) if it sells all of the pads it can produce.

   b. What selling price per sleeping pad will the company establish if it uses a markup percentage on absorption cost?

   c. Assume the company is able to sell all of the pads that it can produce. Prepare an income statement for the first year of activity. Compute the company's ROI based on the first year of activity.

2. After marketing the sleeping pads for several years, the company is experiencing a falloff in demand due to an economic recession. A large retail outlet will make a bulk purchase of pads if its label is sewn in and if an acceptable price can be worked out. What is the minimum acceptable price for this special order?

PROBLEM 6A–9 Absorption Costing Approach to Cost-Plus Pricing LO 6–8

Aldean Company wants to use absorption cost-plus pricing to set the selling price on a new product. The company plans to invest $200,000 in operating assets to produce and sell 16,000 units. Its required return on investment (ROI) in its operating assets is 18%. The accounting department provided cost estimates for the new product as shown below:

	Per Unit	Total
Direct materials	$7	
Direct labor	$5	
Variable manufacturing overhead	$2	
Fixed manufacturing overhead		$116,000
Variable selling and administrative expenses	$1	
Fixed selling and administrative expenses		$50,000

Required:
1. What is the unit product cost for the new product?
2. What is the markup percentage on absorption cost for the new product?
3. What selling price would the company establish for its new product using a markup percentage on absorption cost? (Round your answer to the nearest penny.)

PROBLEM 6A–10 Absorption Costing Approach to Cost-Plus Pricing LO 6–8

Currington Company wants to use absorption cost-plus pricing to set the selling price on a newly remodeled product. The company plans to invest $150,000 in operating assets to produce and sell 12,000 units. Its required return on investment (ROI) in its operating assets is 16%. The accounting department provided cost estimates for the new product as follows:

	Per Unit	Total
Direct materials	$4	
Direct labor	$3	
Variable manufacturing overhead	$1	
Fixed manufacturing overhead		$66,000
Variable selling and administrative expenses	$1	
Fixed selling and administrative expenses		$45,000

Required:
1. What is the unit product cost for the remodeled product?
2. What is the markup percentage on absorption cost for the remodeled product?
3. What selling price would the company establish for its remodeled product using a markup percentage on absorption cost?
4. Suppose the company actually sold only 10,000 units (instead of its planned sales volume of 12,000 units) at the selling price that you derived in requirement 3. What ROI did the company actually earn at this lower sales volume?
5. Assume the company wants to raise the price of its newly remodeled product with the intention of achieving the product's desired ROI at the lower sales volume of 10,000 units. Using absorption cost-plus pricing, what would be the revised selling price at this lower sales volume? How might customers react to this new price?

PROBLEM 6A–11 Target Costing LO 6–11

National Restaurant Supply, Inc., sells restaurant equipment and supplies throughout most of the United States. Management is considering adding a machine that makes sorbet to its line of ice cream–making machines. Management will negotiate the purchase price of the sorbet machine with its Swedish manufacturer.

Management of National Restaurant Supply believes the sorbet machine can be sold to its customers in the United States for $4,950. At that price, annual sales of the sorbet machine should be 100 units. If the sorbet machine is added to National Restaurant Supply's product lines, the company will have to invest $600,000 in inventories and special warehouse fixtures. The variable cost of selling the sorbet machines would be $650 per machine.

Required:

1. If National Restaurant Supply requires a 15% return on investment (ROI), what is the maximum amount the company would be willing to pay the Swedish manufacturer for the sorbet machines?

2. The manager is flying to Sweden to negotiate the purchase price of the machines and would like to know how the purchase price of the machines would affect National Restaurant Supply's ROI. Construct a chart that shows National Restaurant Supply's ROI as a function of the purchase price of the sorbet machine. Put the purchase price on the X-axis and the resulting ROI on the Y-axis. Plot the ROI for purchase prices between $3,000 and $4,000 per machine.

3. After many hours of negotiations, management has concluded that the Swedish manufacturer is unwilling to sell the sorbet machine at a low enough price so that National Restaurant Supply is able to earn its 15% required ROI. Apart from simply giving up on the idea of adding the sorbet machine to National Restaurant Supply's product lines, what could management do?

PROBLEM 6A–12 Absorption Costing Approach to Cost-Plus Pricing; Customer Latitude and Pricing LO 6–8, LO 6–9

Messina Company wants to use absorption cost-plus pricing to establish the selling price for a new product. The company plans to invest $650,000 in operating assets that provide the capacity to make 30,000 units. Its required return on investment (ROI) in its operating assets is 20%. Messina's Accounting Department set a goal of producing and selling 20,000 units during the new product's first year of availability. It also provided the following cost estimates for the new product:

	Per Unit	Total
Direct materials	$12	
Direct labor	$8	
Variable manufacturing overhead	$3	
Fixed manufacturing overhead		$100,000
Variable selling and administrative expenses	$1	
Fixed selling and administrative expenses		$60,000

Required:

1. If the company plans to produce and sell 20,000 units, what is the absorption unit product cost for its new product?

2. At a planned sales volume of 20,000 units, what is the markup percentage on absorption cost for the new product?

3. Using absorption cost-plus pricing and assuming a planned sales volume of 20,000 units, what selling price would the company establish for its new product?

4. Using an absorption format, calculate Messina's net operating income if it actually produces and sells only 19,000 units (instead of 20,000 units) at the absorption cost-plus price from requirement 3. Calculate the ROI at this lower sales volume.

5. Assume Messina's controller recommends raising the new product's selling price in an effort to achieve the desired ROI at the lower sales volume of 19,000 units.
   a. What would become the new markup percentage? (Round your answer to the nearest one-tenth of a percent.)
   b. What would become the new selling price? (Round your calculations and answer to the nearest penny.)

6. Download the optimal pricing model from www.mhhe.com/noreen_opm. Suppose Messina's Marketing Department surveyed its customers and estimated that an 8% increase in the price of this new product would cause its unit sales to decrease by 22%. The company's marketing managers also believe that Messina's total fixed costs will be unaffected by the pricing decision. Assuming the new product's actual sales volume was 19,000 units and the marketing managers' estimates and assumptions are correct, input all of the pertinent data into the pricing model. Be sure to input the current price (as calculated in requirement 3) in cell B12.

Click on the Data tab in Microsoft Excel and select Solver in the upper right-hand portion of your screen. When the Solver window opens, click "Solve."

a.   What is the optimal selling price?
b.   What profit is earned at the optimal selling price?
c.   Comment on the wisdom of the controller's recommendation to increase the new product's selling price.

PROBLEM 6A–13 Value-Based Pricing LO 6–10

The managers of *Midwest Whitetails* magazine (a magazine dedicated to deer hunters) want to establish a price for customers wishing to place a full-page advertisement in their magazine for one month. To help with the price-setting decision, the managers intend to compute the economic value to the customer (EVC) of a full-page ad in their magazine. They have gathered the following data pertaining to *Midwest Whitetails* magazine, as well as their primary competitor, *Trophy Whitetails* magazine:

	Midwest Whitetails	Trophy Whitetails
Number of readers	130,000	200,000
Percent of readers who buy advertised products each month	0.7%	0.5%
Monthly spending per reader who buys advertised products	$120	$100
Contribution margin ratio of advertisers	40%	40%

Trophy Whitetails magazine charges $4,000 per month for a full-page ad. *Midwest Whitetails'* managers believe they can charge more than $4,000 by quantifying the economic value to its customers of placing an ad in their magazine.

Although *Midwest Whitetails* has fewer readers than *Trophy Whitetails* (130,000 vs. 200,000), *Midwest Whitetails* attracts a segment of hunters who are more likely to buy advertisers' products than the casual hunters who tend to subscribe to *Trophy Whitetails*. Therefore, a higher percentage of *Midwest Whitetails* subscribers buy advertised products (0.7% vs. 0.5%), and they spend more per person on advertised products ($120 vs. $100). The managers of *Midwest Whitetails* assume advertisers in both magazines earn an average contribution margin ratio of 40% on all of their merchandise sales.

Required:

From a value-based pricing standpoint:

1.   What is the reference value that *Midwest Whitetails* should consider when setting the price of a full-page ad in its magazine?
2.   What is the differentiation value offered by a full-page ad placed in *Midwest Whitetails* magazine?
3.   What is the EVC of a full-page ad in *Midwest Whitetails* magazine?
4.   What range of possible prices should *Midwest Whitetails* consider when setting a price for a full-page ad?

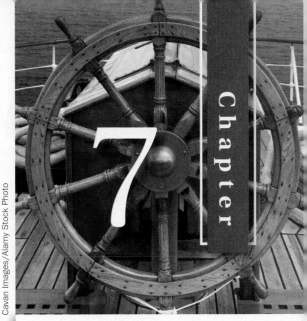
Cavan Images/Alamy Stock Photo

Capital Budgeting Decisions

littlenySTOCK/Shutterstock

ENTREPRENEUR SPOTLIGHT

In 1989, Vera Wang was a bride-to-be who found herself frustrated by the limited selection of available bridal wear. She decided to solve this problem by designing her own wedding gown. A year later, she opened her first bridal boutique on Madison Avenue in New York City. Today Vera Wang is regarded as a fashion design icon whose designs are sold at more than 45 upscale stores worldwide. The Vera Wang Group LLC has also diversified into other product lines, such as eyewear, fragrance, and jewelry.

Managerial Accounting: The Practical Application

When the Vera Wang Group contemplates expanding its brand, such as introducing jewelry or eyewear, it could use capital budgeting techniques to assist in the decision-making process. For example, the company could estimate a new product's future cash inflows and outflows over a 10-year time horizon and then discount those cash flows to their present value. If the net present value is greater than zero, it suggests the investment is worthy of further consideration.

Corporate Social Responsibility: Serving all Stakeholders

Having raised two daughters of her own, Vera Wang was keenly aware of the anxiety that can plague teenagers and young adults. To help respond to this problem, she met with psychiatrist David Shaffer and eventually "one thing led to another and the New York Presbyterian Youth Anxiety Center was established in collaboration with Weill Cornell Medical College and Columbia College of Physicians and Surgeons." Beyond her efforts to address the anxiety challenges of people aged 16 to 28, Wang was chosen by the Breast Cancer Research Foundation as a recipient of the Sandra Taub Humanitarian Award. ■

Sources: www.biography.com/fashion-designer/vera-wang, www.verawang.com/stores, https://variety.com/2016/biz/news/vera-wang-childhood-anxiety-youth-center-1201745494/

LEARNING OBJECTIVES

After studying Chapter 7, you should be able to:

LO 7–1 Determine the payback period for an investment.

LO 7–2 Evaluate the acceptability of an investment project using the net present value method.

LO 7–3 Evaluate the acceptability of an investment project using the internal rate of return method.

LO 7–4 Evaluate an investment project that has uncertain cash flows.

LO 7–5 Rank investment projects in order of preference.

LO 7–6 Compute the simple rate of return for an investment.

LO 7–7 *(Appendix 7A) Understand present value concepts and the use of present value tables.*

LO 7–8 *(Appendix 7C) Include income taxes in a net present value analysis.*

Data Analytics Exercise available in Connect to complement this chapter

Managers often consider decisions that involve an investment today in the hope of realizing future profits. For example, Yum! Brands, Inc., makes an investment when it opens a new Pizza Hut restaurant. L. L. Bean makes an investment when it installs a new computer to handle customer billing. Ford makes an investment when it redesigns a vehicle such as the F-150 pickup truck. Merck & Co. invests in medical research. Amazon.com makes an investment when it redesigns its website. All of these investments require spending money now to realize future net cash inflows.

The term **capital budgeting** is used to describe how managers plan significant investments in projects with long-term implications, such as the purchase of new equipment or the introduction of new products. Most companies have many more potential projects than they can actually fund. Hence, managers must carefully select those projects that promise the greatest future return. How well managers make these capital budgeting decisions is a critical factor in the long-run financial health of the organization. This chapter discusses four methods for making capital budgeting decisions—the *payback method,* the *net present value method,* the *internal rate of return method,* and the *simple rate of return method.*

Capital Budgeting—An Overview

Typical Capital Budgeting Decisions

Any decision involving a cash outlay now to obtain a future return is a capital budgeting decision. Typical capital budgeting decisions include:

1. Cost reduction decisions. Should new equipment be purchased to reduce costs?
2. Expansion decisions. Should a new plant, warehouse, or other facility be acquired to increase capacity and sales?
3. Equipment selection decisions. Which of several available machines should be purchased?
4. Lease or buy decisions. Should new equipment be leased or purchased?
5. Equipment replacement decisions. Should old equipment be replaced now or later?

Capital budgeting decisions fall into two broad categories—*screening decisions* and *preference decisions.* **Screening decisions** relate to whether a proposed project is acceptable—whether it passes a preset hurdle. For example, a company may have a policy of accepting projects only if they provide a return of at least 20 percent on the investment. The required rate of return is the minimum rate of return a project must yield to be acceptable. **Preference decisions,** by contrast, relate to selecting from among several acceptable alternatives. To illustrate, a company may be considering several different machines to replace an existing machine on the assembly line. The choice of which machine to purchase is a preference decision.

Cash Flows versus Net Operating Income

The first three capital budgeting methods discussed in the chapter—the payback method, the net present value method, and internal rate of return method—all focus on analyzing the *cash flows* associated with capital investment projects, whereas the simple rate of return method focuses on *incremental net operating income.* To better prepare you to apply the payback, net present value, and internal rate of return methods, we'd like to define the most common types of cash outflows and cash inflows that accompany capital investment projects.

Typical Cash Outflows Most projects have at least three types of cash outflows. First, they often require an immediate cash outflow in the form of an initial investment in equipment, other assets, and installation costs. Any salvage value realized from the sale of old equipment can be recognized as a reduction in the initial investment or as a cash inflow.

Second, it is important to include the *total cost of ownership* associated with any initial investments in plant and equipment. These costs, also referred to as *life-cycle costs,* may include cash outflows such as annual operating costs, preventive maintenance costs, environmental impact costs, and disposal costs.

Third, some projects require a company to expand its *working capital.* **Working capital** is current assets (e.g., cash, accounts receivable, and inventory) less current liabilities. When a company invests in a new project, the balances in the current asset accounts often increase. For example, opening a new Nordstrom's department store requires additional cash in sales registers and more inventory. These additional working capital needs are treated as part of the initial investment in a project.

Typical Cash Inflows Most projects also have at least three types of cash inflows. First, a project will normally increase revenues or reduce costs. Either way, the amount involved should be treated as a cash inflow for capital budgeting purposes. Notice from a cash flow standpoint, a reduction in costs is equivalent to an increase in revenues. Second, cash inflows are also frequently realized from selling equipment for its salvage value when a project ends, although the company actually may have to pay to dispose of some low-value or hazardous items. Third, any working capital tied up in the project can be released for use elsewhere at the end of the project and should be treated as a cash inflow at that time. Working capital is released, for example, when a company sells off its inventory or collects its accounts receivable.

The Time Value of Money

Beyond defining a capital project's cash outflows and inflows, it is also important to consider when those cash flows occur. For example, if someone offered to give you $1,000 today that you could save toward your eventual retirement or $1,000 a year from now that you could save toward your future retirement, which would you choose? In all likelihood, you would choose to receive $1,000 today because you could invest it and have more than $1,000 a year from now. This simple example illustrates an important capital budgeting concept known as *the time value of money.* The **time value of money** recognizes that a dollar today is worth more than a dollar a year from now if for no other reason than you could put the dollar in a bank today and have more than a dollar a year from now. Because of the time value of money, capital investments that promise earlier cash flows are preferable to those that promise later cash flows.

Although the payback method focuses on cash flows, it does not recognize the time value of money. In other words, it treats a dollar received today as being of equal value to a dollar received at any point in the future. Conversely, the net present value and internal rate of return methods not only focus on cash flows, but they also recognize the time value of those cash flows. These two methods use a technique called *discounting cash flows* to translate the value of future cash flows to their present value. If you are not familiar with the concept of discounting cash flows and the use of present value tables, you should read Appendix 7A: The Concept of Present Value, at the end of the chapter, before studying the net present value and internal rate of return methods.

The Payback Method

The payback method of evaluating capital budgeting projects focuses on the *payback period*. The **payback period** is the length of time that it takes for a project to recover its initial cost from the net cash inflows that it generates. This period is sometimes referred to as "the time that it takes for an investment to pay for itself." The basic premise of the payback method is that the more quickly the cost of an investment can be recovered, the more desirable is the investment.

The payback period is expressed in years. *When the annual net cash inflow is the same every year,* the following formula can be used to compute the payback period:

$$\text{Payback period} = \frac{\text{Investment required}}{\text{Annual net cash inflow}} \qquad (1)$$

To illustrate the payback method, consider the following data:

Example A: York Company needs a new milling machine. The company is considering two machines: machine A and machine B. Machine A costs $15,000, has a useful life of ten years, and will reduce operating costs by $5,000 per year. Machine B costs only $12,000, will also reduce operating costs by $5,000 per year, but has a useful life of only five years.

Required:
Which machine should be purchased according to the payback method?

$$\text{Machine A payback period} = \frac{\$15,000}{\$5,000} = 3.0 \text{ years}$$

$$\text{Machine B payback period} = \frac{\$12,000}{\$5,000} = 2.4 \text{ years}$$

According to the payback calculations, York Company should purchase Machine B because it has a shorter payback period than Machine A.

Evaluation of the Payback Method

The payback method is not a true measure of the profitability of an investment. Rather, it simply tells a manager how many years are required to recover the original investment. Unfortunately, a shorter payback period does not always mean that one investment is more desirable than another.

To illustrate, refer back to Example A. Machine B has a shorter payback period than machine A, but it has a useful life of only 5 years rather than 10 years for machine A. Machine B would have to be purchased twice—once immediately and then again after the fifth year—to provide the same service as just one machine A. Under these circumstances, machine A would probably be a better investment than machine B, even though machine B has a shorter payback period. Unfortunately, the payback method ignores all cash flows that occur after the payback period.

A further criticism of the payback method is that it does not consider the time value of money. A cash inflow to be received several years in the future is weighed the same as a cash inflow received right now. To illustrate, assume for an investment of $8,000 you can purchase either of the two following streams of cash inflows:

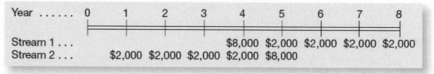

Which stream of cash inflows would you prefer to receive in return for your $8,000 investment? Each stream has a payback period of 4.0 years. Therefore, if payback alone is used to make the decision, the streams would be considered equally desirable. However, from a time value of money perspective, Stream 2 is much more desirable than Stream 1.

On the other hand, under certain conditions the payback method can be very useful. For one thing, it can help identify which investment proposals are in the "ballpark." That is, it can be used as a screening tool to help answer the question, "Should I consider this proposal further?" If a proposal doesn't provide a payback within some specified period, then there may be no need to consider it further. In addition, the payback period is often important to new companies that are "cash poor." When a company is cash poor, a project with a short payback period but a low rate of return might be preferred over another project with a high rate of return but a long payback period. The reason is that the company may simply need a faster return of its cash investment. And finally, the payback method is sometimes used in industries where products become obsolete very rapidly—such as consumer electronics. Because products may last only a year or two, the payback period on investments must be very short.

An Extended Example of Payback

As shown by the payback period formula (formula 1) shown earlier in the chapter, the payback period is computed by dividing the investment in a project by the project's annual net cash inflows. If new equipment is replacing old equipment, then any salvage value to be received when disposing of the old equipment should be deducted from the cost of the new equipment, and only the *incremental* investment should be used in the payback computation. In addition, any depreciation deducted in arriving at the project's net operating income must be added back to obtain the project's expected annual net cash inflow. To illustrate, consider the following data:

Example B: Goodtime Fun Centers, Inc., operates amusement parks. Some of the vending machines in one of its parks provide very little revenue, so the company is considering removing the machines and installing equipment to dispense soft ice cream. The equipment would cost $80,000 and have an eight-year useful life with no salvage value. Incremental annual revenues and costs associated with the sale of ice cream would be as follows:

Sales		$150,000
Variable expenses		90,000
Contribution margin		60,000
Fixed expenses:		
Salaries	$27,000	
Maintenance	3,000	
Depreciation...............................	10,000	40,000
Net operating income.......................		$ 20,000

The vending machines can be sold for a $5,000 scrap value. The company will not purchase the equipment unless it has a payback period of three years or less. Does the ice cream dispenser pass this hurdle?

Exhibit 7–1 computes the payback period for the ice cream dispenser. Several things should be noted. First, depreciation is added back to net operating income to obtain the annual net cash inflow from the new equipment. Depreciation is not a cash outlay; thus, it must be added back to adjust net operating income to a cash basis. Second, the payback computation deducts the salvage value of the old machines from the cost of the new equipment so that only the incremental investment is used in computing the payback period.

Because the proposed equipment has a payback period of less than three years, the company's payback requirement has been met.

Payback and Uneven Cash Flows

When the cash flows associated with an investment project change from year to year, the simple payback formula we outlined earlier cannot be used. Instead, the payback period can be computed as follows (assuming that cash inflows occur evenly throughout the

EXHIBIT 7–1
Computation of the
Payback Period

Step 1:   *Compute the annual net cash inflow.* Because the annual net cash inflow is not given, it must be computed before the payback period can be determined:

Net operating income.	$20,000
Add: Noncash deduction for depreciation	10,000
Annual net cash inflow.	$30,000

Step 2:   *Compute the payback period.* Using the annual net cash inflow from above, the payback period can be determined as follows:

Cost of the new equipment	$80,000
Less salvage value of old equipment	5,000
Investment required	$75,000

$$\text{Payback period} = \frac{\text{Investment required}}{\text{Annual net cash inflow}}$$

$$= \frac{\$75,000}{\$30,000} = 2.5 \text{ years}$$

year): Payback period = Number of years up to the year in which the investment is paid off + (Unrecovered investment at the beginning of the year in which the investment is paid off ÷ Cash inflow in the period in which the investment is paid off). To illustrate how to apply this formula, consider the following data:

Year	Investment	Cash Inflow
1.	$4,000	$1,000
2.		$0
3.		$2,000
4.	$2,000	$1,000
5.		$500
6.		$3,000
7.		$2,000

What is the payback period on this investment? The answer is 5.5 years, computed as follows: 5 + ($1,500 ÷ $3,000) = 5.5 years. In essence, we are tracking the unrecovered investment year by year as shown in Exhibit 7–2. By the middle of the sixth year, sufficient cash inflows will have been realized to recover the entire investment of $6,000 ($4,000 + $2,000).

EXHIBIT 7–2
Payback and Uneven
Cash Flows

Year	Investment	Cash Inflow	Unrecovered Investment*
1	$4,000	$1,000	$3,000
2		$0	$3,000
3		$2,000	$1,000
4	$2,000	$1,000	$2,000
5		$500	$1,500
6		$3,000	$0
7		$2,000	$0

*Year X unrecovered investment = Year (X − 1) unrecovered investment + Year X investment − Year X cash inflow

The Net Present Value Method

As previously mentioned, the *net present value method* and the *internal rate of return method* use discounted cash flows to analyze capital budgeting decisions. The net present value method is discussed in this section, followed by a discussion of the internal rate of return method.

LEARNING OBJECTIVE 7–2
Evaluate the acceptability of an investment project using the net present value method.

The Net Present Value Method Illustrated

The net present value method compares the present value of a project's cash inflows to the present value of its cash outflows. The difference between the present value of these cash flows, called the **net present value,** determines whether or not a project is an acceptable investment.

When performing net present value analysis, managers usually make two important assumptions. First, they assume all cash flows other than the initial investment occur at the end of periods. This assumption is somewhat unrealistic because cash flows typically occur *throughout* a period rather than just at its end; however, it simplifies the computations considerably. Second, managers assume all cash flows generated by an investment project are immediately reinvested at a rate of return equal to the rate used to discount the future cash flows, also known as the *discount rate*. If this condition is not met, the net present value computations will not be accurate.

To illustrate net present analysis, consider the following data:

Example C: Harper Company is contemplating buying a new machine that will cost $50,000 and last five years. The new machine will enable the company to reduce its labor costs by $18,000 per year. At the end of the five-year period, the company will sell the machine for its salvage value of $5,000. Harper Company requires a minimum pretax return of 18% on all investment projects.[1]

Should the machine be purchased? Harper Company must determine whether a cash investment now of $50,000 can be justified if it will result in an $18,000 cost reduction in each of the next five years. The answer may seem obvious given that the total cost savings is $90,000 ($18,000 per year × 5 years); however, the company can earn an 18 percent return by investing its money elsewhere. It is not enough that the annual cost reductions cover just the original cost of the machine; they must also yield a return of at least 18% or the company would be better off investing the money elsewhere.

To determine whether the investment is desirable, the stream of annual $18,000 cost savings and the machine's salvage value of $5,000 should be discounted to their present values and then compared to the cost of the new machine. Exhibits 7–3, 7–4, and 7–5 demonstrate three distinct but equivalent ways of performing these calculations. The approaches in Exhibit 7–3 and 7–4 rely on the discount factors shown in Appendix 7B that have been rounded to three decimal places. The method shown in Exhibit 7–5 derives its answer using unrounded discount factors.

Cell B8 of Exhibit 7–3 calculates the present value of Harper Company's initial cash outlay of $(50,000) by multiplying $(50,000) by 1.000, the present value factor for any cash flow that occurs immediately. Cell C8 calculates the present value of the annual cost savings of $56,286 by multiplying $18,000 by 3.127, the present value factor of a five-year annuity at the discount rate of 18 percent (see Exhibit 7B–2). Cell D8 calculates the present value of the machine's salvage value of $2,185 by multiplying $5,000 by 0.437, the present value factor of a single sum to be received in five years at the discount rate of 18 percent (see Exhibit 7B–1). Finally, cells B8 through D8 are added together to derive the net present value in cell B9 of $8,471.

---

[1] For simplicity, we ignore inflation and taxes. The impact of income taxes on capital budgeting decisions is discussed in Appendix 7C.

EXHIBIT 7–3

Net Present Value Analysis Using Discount Factors from Exhibits 7B–1 and 7B–2 in Appendix 7B

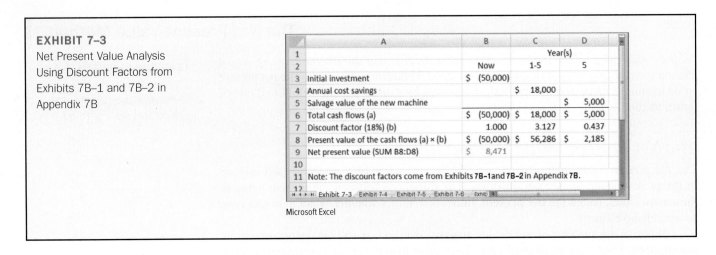

	A	B	C	D
1			Year(s)	
2		Now	1-5	5
3	Initial investment	$ (50,000)		
4	Annual cost savings		$ 18,000	
5	Salvage value of the new machine			$ 5,000
6	Total cash flows (a)	$ (50,000)	$ 18,000	$ 5,000
7	Discount factor (18%) (b)	1.000	3.127	0.437
8	Present value of the cash flows (a) × (b)	$ (50,000)	$ 56,286	$ 2,185
9	Net present value (SUM B8:D8)	$ 8,471		
10				
11	Note: The discount factors come from Exhibits 7B–1 and 7B–2 in Appendix 7B.			
12				

Exhibit 7-3 / Exhibit 7-4 / Exhibit 7-5 / Exhibit 7-6 / Exhibit

Microsoft Excel

Exhibit 7–4 shows another way to calculate the net present value of $8,471. Under this approach, cell B8 calculates the present value of the initial cash outlay of $(50,000) by multiplying $(50,000) by 1.000—just as was done in Exhibit 7–3. However, rather than calculating the present value of the annual cost savings using a discount factor of 3.127 from Exhibit 7B–2, the approach used in Exhibit 7–4 discounts the annual cost savings in Years 1–5 *and* the machine's salvage value in Year 5 to their present values using the discount factors from Exhibit 7B–1. For example, the $18,000 cost savings in Year 3 (cell E6) is multiplied by the discount factor of 0.609 (cell E7) to derive this future cash flow's present value of $10,962 (cell E8). As another example, the $23,000 of total cash flows in Year 5 (cell G6) is multiplied by the discount factor of 0.437 (cell G7) to determine these future cash flows' present value of $10,051 (cell G8). The present values in cells B8 through G8 are then added together to compute the project's net present value of $8,471 (cell B9).

The methods described in Exhibits 7–3 and 7–4 are mathematically equivalent—they both produced a net present value of $8,471. The only difference between these two exhibits relates to the discounting of the annual labor cost savings. In Exhibit 7–3, the labor cost savings are discounted to their present value using the annuity factor of 3.127, whereas in Exhibit 7–4, these cost savings are discounted using five separate factors that sum to 3.127 (0.847 + 0.718 + 0.609 + 0.516 + 0.437 = 3.127).

EXHIBIT 7–4

Net Present Value Analysis Using Discount Factors from Exhibit 7B–1 in Appendix 7B

	A	B	C	D	E	F	G
1					Year		
2		Now	1	2	3	4	5
3	Initial investment	$ (50,000)					
4	Annual labor cost savings		$ 18,000	$ 18,000	$ 18,000	$ 18,000	$ 18,000
5	Salvage value of new machine						$ 5,000
6	Total cash flows (a)	$ (50,000)	$ 18,000	$ 18,000	$ 18,000	$ 18,000	$ 23,000
7	Discount factor (18%) (b)	1.000	0.847	0.718	0.609	0.516	0.437
8	Present value of cash flows (a) × (b)	$ (50,000)	$ 15,246	$ 12,924	$ 10,962	$ 9,288	$ 10,051
9	Net present value (SUM B8:G8)	$ 8,471					
10							
11	Note: The discount factors come from Exhibit 7B–1 in Appendix 7B.						
12							

Exhibit 7-3 / Exhibit 7-4 / Exhibit 7-5 / Exhibit 7-6 / Exhibit

Microsoft Excel

EXHIBIT 7-5
Net Present Value Analysis Using Microsoft Excel's NPV Function

	A	B	C	D	E	F	G
1					Year		
2		Now	1	2	3	4	5
3	Initial investment	$ (50,000)					
4	Annual labor cost savings		$ 18,000	$ 18,000	$ 18,000	$ 18,000	$ 18,000
5	Salvage value of new machine						$ 5,000
6	Total cash flows (a)	$ (50,000)	$ 18,000	$ 18,000	$ 18,000	$ 18,000	$ 23,000
7	Net present value (SUM B8:G8)	$ 8,475					
8							
9	Note: The net present value is computed using the formula =NPV(0.18,C6:G6)+B6						
10							

Exhibit 7-3 Exhibit 7-4 **Exhibit 7-5** Exhibit 7-6 Exl

Microsoft Excel

It bears reemphasizing that the net present values in Exhibits 7–3 and 7–4 are calculated using the *rounded* discount factors from Appendix 7B. However, net present value calculations can also be performed using *unrounded* discount factors. One approach to using unrounded discount factors would be to replace the rounded discount factors shown in row 7 of Exhibits 7–3 and 7–4 with formulas that compute unrounded discount factors. Another approach, as shown in Exhibit 7–5, is to use Microsoft Excel's NPV function to perform the calculations. The NPV function automatically calculates the net present value after specifying three parameters—the discount rate (0.18), the annual cash flows (C6:G6), and the initial cash outlay (+B6). Notice that the net present value in Exhibit 7–5 of $8,475 is $4 higher than the net present value shown in Exhibits 7–3 and 7–4. The trivial $4 difference arises because Microsoft Excel's NPV function uses unrounded discount factors.

During your career, you should feel free to use any of the methods discussed thus far to perform net present value calculations. However, throughout this chapter and its forthcoming exercises and problems, we'll be using the approaches illustrated in Exhibit 7–3 and 7–4 accompanied by the rounded discount factors in Appendix 7B.

Once you have computed a project's net present value, you'll need to interpret your findings. For example, because Harper Company's proposed project has a positive net present value of $8,471, it implies that the company should purchase the new machine. A positive net present value indicates that the project's return exceeds the discount rate. A negative net present value indicates that the project's return is less than the discount rate. Therefore, if the company's minimum required rate of return is used as the discount rate, a project with a positive net present value has a return that exceeds the minimum required rate of return and is acceptable. Conversely, a project with a negative net present value has a return that is less than the minimum required rate of return and is unacceptable. In sum:

If the Net Present Value Is . . .	Then the Project Is . . .
Positive	Acceptable because its return is greater than the required rate of return.
Zero	Acceptable because its return is equal to the required rate of return.
Negative	Not acceptable because its return is less than the required rate of return.

A company's *cost of capital* is usually regarded as its minimum required rate of return. The **cost of capital** is the average rate of return that the company must pay to its long-term creditors and its shareholders for the use of their funds. If a project's rate of return is less than the cost of capital, the company does not earn enough to compensate its creditors and shareholders. Therefore, any project with a rate of return less than the cost of capital should be rejected.

The cost of capital serves as a *screening device*. When the cost of capital is used as the discount rate in net present value analysis, any project with a negative net present value does not cover the company's cost of capital and should be discarded as unacceptable.

Recovery of the Original Investment

The net present value method automatically provides for return of the original investment. Whenever the net present value of a project is positive, the project will recover the original cost of the investment plus sufficient excess cash inflows to compensate the organization for tying up funds in the project. To demonstrate this point, consider the following situation:

Example D: Carver Hospital is considering the purchase of an attachment for its X-ray machine that will cost $3,170. The attachment will be usable for four years, after which time it will have no salvage value. It will increase net cash inflows by $1,000 per year in the X-ray department. The hospital's board of directors requires a rate of return of at least 10% on such investments.

A net present value analysis of the desirability of purchasing the X-ray attachment (using a discount factor of 3.170 from Exhibit 7B–2) is presented in Exhibit 7–6. Notice that the attachment has exactly a 10 percent return on the original investment because the net present value is zero at a 10 percent discount rate.

Each annual $1,000 cash inflow arising from use of the attachment is made up of two parts. One part represents a recovery of a portion *of* the original $3,170 paid for the attachment, and the other part represents a return *on* this investment. The breakdown of each year's $1,000 cash inflow between recovery *of* investment and return *on* investment is shown in Exhibit 7–7.

EXHIBIT 7–6
Carver Hospital—Net Present Value Analysis of X-Ray Attachment

	A	B	C
1			Years
2		Now	1-4
3	Initial investment	$ (3,170)	
4	Annual cost savings		$ 1,000
5	Total cash flows (a)	$ (3,170)	$ 1,000
6	Discount factor (10%) (b)	1.000	3.170
7	Present value of the cash flows (a) × (b)	$ (3,170)	$ 3,170
8	Net present value (SUM B7:C7)	$ 0	
9			
10	Note: The discount factor comes from Exhibit 7B–2 in Appendix 7B.		
11			

⏮ ◀ ▶ ⏭ Exhibit 7-6 / Exhibit 7-7

Microsoft Excel

EXHIBIT 7–7

Carver Hospital—Breakdown of Annual Cash Inflows

	A	B	C	D	E	F
1		(1)	(2)	(3)	(4)	(5)
2	Year	Investment Outstanding during the Year	Cash Inflow	Return on Investment (1) × 10%	Recovery of Investment during the Year (2) – (3)	Unrecovered Investment at the End of the Year (1) – (4)
3	1	$3,170	$1,000	$317	$683	$2,487
4	2	$2,487	$1,000	$249	$751	$1,736
5	3	$1,736	$1,000	$173	$827	$909
6	4	$909	$1,000	$91	$909	$0
7	Total investment recovered				$3,170	

Exhibit 7-6   Exhibit 7-7   Exhibit 7-8   Exhibit 7-9   Exh

Microsoft Excel

The first year's $1,000 cash inflow consists of a return *on* investment of $317 (a 10% return *on* the $3,170 original investment), plus a $683 return *of* that investment. Because the amount of the unrecovered investment decreases each year, the dollar amount of the return on investment also decreases each year. By the end of the fourth year, all $3,170 of the original investment has been recovered.

An Extended Example of the Net Present Value Method

Example E provides an extended example of how the net present value method is used to analyze a proposed project. This example helps tie together and reinforce many of the ideas discussed thus far.

Example E: Under a special licensing arrangement, Swinyard Corporation has an opportunity to market a new product for a five-year period. The product would be purchased from the manufacturer, with Swinyard responsible for promotion and distribution costs. The licensing arrangement could be renewed at the end of the five-year period. After careful study, Swinyard estimated the following costs and revenues for the new product:

Cost of equipment needed	$60,000
Working capital needed	$100,000
Overhaul of the equipment in four years	$5,000
Salvage value of the equipment in five years	$10,000
Annual revenues and costs:	
Sales revenues	$200,000
Cost of goods sold	$125,000
Out-of-pocket operating costs (for salaries, advertising, and other direct costs)	$35,000

At the end of the five-year period, if Swinyard decides not to renew the licensing arrangement, the working capital would be released for investment elsewhere. Swinyard uses a 14 percent discount rate. Would you recommend that the new product be introduced?

EXHIBIT 7–8
The Net Present Value Method—An Extended Example

	A	B	C	D	E	F	G
1					Year		
2		Now	1	2	3	4	5
3	Purchase of equipment	$ (60,000)					
4	Investment in working capital	$ (100,000)					
5	Sales		$ 200,000	$ 200,000	$ 200,000	$ 200,000	$ 200,000
6	Cost of goods sold		$ (125,000)	$ (125,000)	$ (125,000)	$ (125,000)	$ (125,000)
7	Out-of-pocket costs for salaries, advertising, etc.		$ (35,000)	$ (35,000)	$ (35,000)	$ (35,000)	$ (35,000)
8	Overhaul of equipment					$ (5,000)	
9	Salvage value of the equipment						$ 10,000
10	Working capital released						$ 100,000
11	Total cash flows (a)	$ (160,000)	$ 40,000	$ 40,000	$ 40,000	$ 35,000	$ 150,000
12	Discount factor (14%) (b)	1.000	0.877	0.769	0.675	0.592	0.519
13	Present value of cash flows (a) × (b)	$ (160,000)	$ 35,080	$ 30,760	$ 27,000	$ 20,720	$ 77,850
14	Net present value (SUM B13:G13)	$ 31,410					
15							
16	Note: The discount factors come from Exhibit 7B–1 in Appendix 7B.						
17							

Exhibit 7-3 | Exhibit 7-4 | Exhibit 7-5 | Exhibit 7-6 | Exhibit 7-7 | **Exhibit 7-8** | Exhibit

Microsoft Excel

This example involves a variety of cash inflows and cash outflows. The solution (using discount factors from Exhibit 7B–1) is given in Exhibit 7–8.

Notice how the working capital is handled in this exhibit. It is counted as a cash outflow at the beginning of the project (cell B4) and as a cash inflow when it is released at the end of the project (cell G10). Also, notice how the sales revenues, cost of goods sold, and out-of-pocket costs are handled. **Out-of-pocket costs** are actual cash outlays for salaries, advertising, and other operating expenses.

Because the net present value of the proposal is positive, the new product is acceptable.

IN BUSINESS

OAK VIEW GROUP INVESTS IN NEW ARENAS

Oak View Group is a Los Angeles–based company that plans to invest $3.9 billion to build eight new arenas throughout the United States. Rather than relying on professional sports teams to generate revenues at six of these eight venues, the company will rely on concerts from touring musicians such as the Eagles and Harry Styles. Oak View claims that an "arena can generate twice as much net income from hosting a concert than a National Basketball Association or National Hockey League game." While PricewaterhouseCoopers estimates that the live music industry currently generates $28 billion in annual revenues, Oak View expects that figure to grow to $38 billion by 2030.

Source: Anne Steele, "For New Arenas, It's Showtime," *The Wall Street Journal*, November 20, 2019, p. B3.

The Internal Rate of Return Method

LEARNING OBJECTIVE 7–3

Evaluate the acceptability of an investment project using the internal rate of return method.

The **internal rate of return** is the rate of return of an investment project over its useful life. The internal rate of return is computed by finding the discount rate that equates the present value of a project's cash outflows with the present value of its cash inflows. In other words, the internal rate of return is the discount rate that results in a net present value of zero.

The Internal Rate of Return Method Illustrated

To illustrate the internal rate of return method, consider the following data:

Example F: Glendale School District is considering the purchase of a large tractor-pulled lawn mower. At present, the lawn is mowed using a small hand-pushed gas mower. The large, tractor-pulled mower will cost $16,950 and will have a useful life of 10 years. It will have a negligible scrap value, which can be ignored. The tractor-pulled mower would do the job faster than the old mower, resulting in labor savings of $3,000 per year.

  To compute the internal rate of return of the new mower, we must find the discount rate that will result in a zero net present value. How do we do this? The simplest and most direct approach *when the net cash inflow is the same every year* is to divide the investment in the project by the expected annual net cash inflow. This computation yields a factor from which the internal rate of return can be determined. The formula is as follows:

$$\text{Factor of the internal rate of return} = \frac{\text{Investment required}}{\text{Annual net cash inflow}} \qquad (2)$$

  The factor derived from formula (2) is then located in Exhibit 7B–2 in Appendix 7B to see what rate of return it represents. Using formula (2) and the data for the Glendale School District's proposed project, we get:

$$\frac{\text{Investment required}}{\text{Annual net cash inflow}} = \frac{\$16,950}{\$3,000} = 5.650$$

Thus, the discount factor that will equate a series of $3,000 cash inflows with a present investment of $16,950 is 5.650. Now we need to find this factor in Exhibit 7B–2 in Appendix 7B to see what rate of return it represents. We should use the 10-period line in Exhibit 7B–2 because the cash flows for the project continue for 10 years. If we scan along the 10-period line, we find that a factor of 5.650 represents a 12 percent rate of return. Therefore, the internal rate of return of the mower project is 12 percent. We can verify this by computing the project's net present value using a 12 percent discount rate, as shown in Exhibit 7–9.

  Notice from Exhibit 7–9 that using a 12 percent discount rate equates the present value of the annual cost savings with the present value of the initial investment required for the project, leaving a zero net present value. The 12 percent rate therefore represents the internal rate of return of the project.[2]

  Once the Glendale School District computes the project's internal rate of return of 12 percent, it would accept or reject the project by comparing this percentage to the

---

[2] We can also verify the 12% internal rate of return by using the IRR functionality within Microsoft Excel. To do this, you would depict the annual cost savings as 10 single sums rather than a 10-year annuity. In other words, you would create 11 cells of data—one cell would contain the initial investment of $(16,500) and 10 cells would each contain an annual cost savings of $3,000. Then put your cursor in a 12th cell where you would like the internal rate of return to appear. Select the "Formulas" tab in Excel, followed by the "Financial" tab. Scroll down to select IRR. Insert the range of cells that contain your 11 distinct cash flows in the "Values" field that will appear on your screen and then click OK. Microsoft Excel will automatically calculate the IRR and insert it into your chosen cell.

EXHIBIT 7–9
Evaluation of the Mower Using a 12% Discount Rate

	A	B	C
1			Years
2		Now	1-10
3	Initial investment	$ (16,950)	
4	Annual cost savings		$ 3,000
5	Total cash flows (a)	$ (16,950)	$ 3,000
6	Discount factor (12%) (b)	1.000	5.650
7	Present value of the cash flows (a) × (b)	$ (16,950)	$ 16,950
8	Net present value (SUM B7:C7)	$ 0	
9			
10	Note: The discount factor comes from Exhibit 7B–2 in Appendix 7B.		
11			

Exhibit 7-8　Exhibit 7-9　Exhibi

Microsoft Excel

school district's minimum required rate of return. If the internal rate of return is equal to or greater than the required rate of return, then the project is acceptable. If the internal rate of return is less than the required rate of return, then the project is rejected. For example, if we assume Glendale's minimum required rate of return is 15 percent, then the school district would reject this project because the 12 percent internal rate of return does not clear the 15 percent *hurdle rate.*

Comparison of the Net Present Value and Internal Rate of Return Methods

This section compares the net present value and internal rate of return methods in two ways. First, both methods use the cost of capital to screen out undesirable investment projects. When the internal rate of return method is used, the cost of capital is used as the hurdle rate that a project must clear for acceptance. If the internal rate of return of a project is not high enough to clear the cost of capital hurdle, then the project is ordinarily rejected. When the net present value method is used, the cost of capital is the discount rate used to compute the net present value of a proposed project. Any project yielding a negative net present value is rejected unless other factors are significant enough to warrant its acceptance.

Second, the internal rate of return method makes a questionable assumption. Both methods assume that cash flows generated by a project during its useful life are immediately reinvested elsewhere. However, the two methods make different assumptions concerning the rate of return that is earned on those cash flows. The net present value method assumes the rate of return is the discount rate, whereas the internal rate of return method assumes the rate of return earned on cash flows is the internal rate of return on the project. Specifically, if the internal rate of return of the project is high, this assumption may not be realistic. It is generally more realistic to assume that cash inflows can be reinvested at a rate of return equal to the discount rate—particularly if the discount rate is the company's cost of capital or an opportunity rate of return. For example, if the discount rate is the company's cost of capital, this rate of return can be actually realized by paying off the company's creditors and buying back the company's stock with cash flows from the project. In short, when the net present value method and the internal rate of return method do not agree concerning the attractiveness of a project, it is best to go with the net present value method. Of the two methods, it makes the more realistic assumption about the rate of return that can be earned on cash flows from the project.

Expanding the Net Present Value Method

So far, all of our examples have involved an evaluation of a single investment project. In the following section, we use the *total-cost approach* to explain how the net present value method can be used to evaluate two alternative projects.

The total-cost approach is the most flexible method for comparing competing projects. To illustrate the mechanics of the approach, consider the following data:

Example G: Harper Ferry Company operates a high-speed passenger ferry service across the Mississippi River. One of its ferryboats is in poor condition. This ferry can be renovated at an immediate cost of $200,000. Further repairs and an overhaul of the motor will be needed three years from now at a cost of $80,000. In all, the ferry will be usable for 5 years if this work is done. At the end of 5 years, the ferry will have to be scrapped at a salvage value of $60,000. The scrap value of the ferry right now is $70,000. It will cost $300,000 each year to operate the ferry, and revenues will total $400,000 annually.

As an alternative, Harper Ferry Company can purchase a new ferryboat at a cost of $360,000. The new ferry will have a life of 5 years, but it will require some repairs costing $30,000 at the end of 3 years. At the end of 5 years, the ferry will have a scrap value of $60,000. It will cost $210,000 each year to operate the ferry, and revenues will total $400,000 annually.

Harper Ferry Company requires a return of at least 14 percent on all investment projects.

Should the company purchase the new ferry or renovate the old ferry? Exhibit 7–10 shows the solution using the total-cost approach and discount factors from Exhibit 7B–1.

Two points should be noted from the exhibit. First, *all* cash inflows and *all* cash outflows are included in the solution under each alternative. No effort has been made to isolate those cash flows that are relevant to the decision and those that are irrelevant. The inclusion of all cash flows associated with each alternative gives the approach its name— the *total-cost* approach.

Second, notice that a net present value is computed for each alternative. This is a strength of the total-cost approach because an unlimited number of alternatives can be compared side by side to determine the best option. For example, another alternative for Harper Ferry Company would be to get out of the ferry business entirely. If management desired, the net present value of this alternative could be computed to compare with the alternatives shown in Exhibit 7–10. Still other alternatives might be available to the company. In the case at hand, given only two alternatives, the data indicate that the net present value in favor of buying the new ferry is $252,630.[3]

Least-Cost Decisions

Some decisions do not involve any revenues. For example, a company may be trying to decide whether to buy or lease an executive jet. The choice would be made on the basis of which alternative—buying or leasing—would be least costly. In situations such as these, where no revenues are involved, the most desirable alternative is the one with the *least*

---

[3] The alternative with the highest net present value is not always the best choice, although it is the best choice in this case. For further discussion, see the section Preference Decisions—The Ranking of Investment Projects.

EXHIBIT 7–10
The Total-Cost Approach to Project Selection

	A	B	C	D	E	F	G
1	Keep the old ferry:				Year		
2		Now	1	2	3	4	5
3	Renovation	$(200,000)					
4	Annual revenues		$ 400,000	$ 400,000	$ 400,000	$ 400,000	$ 400,000
5	Annual cash operating costs		$(300,000)	$(300,000)	$(300,000)	$(300,000)	$(300,000)
6	Repairs in three years				$ (80,000)		
7	Salvage value of old ferry						$ 60,000
8	Total cash flows (a)	$(200,000)	$ 100,000	$ 100,000	$ 20,000	$ 100,000	$ 160,000
9	Discount factor (14%) (b)	1.000	0.877	0.769	0.675	0.592	0.519
10	Present value of cash flows (a) × (b)	$(200,000)	$ 87,700	$ 76,900	$ 13,500	$ 59,200	$ 83,040
11	Net present value (SUM B10:G10)	$ 120,340					
12							
13	Buy the new ferry:				Year		
14		Now	1	2	3	4	5
15	Initial investment	$(360,000)					
16	Salvage value of the old ferry	$ 70,000					
17	Annual revenues		$ 400,000	$ 400,000	$ 400,000	$ 400,000	$ 400,000
18	Annual cash operating costs		$(210,000)	$(210,000)	$(210,000)	$(210,000)	$(210,000)
19	Repairs in three years				$ (30,000)		
20	Salvage value of new ferry						$ 60,000
21	Total cash flows (a)	$(290,000)	$ 190,000	$ 190,000	$ 160,000	$ 190,000	$ 250,000
22	Discount factor (14%) (b)	1.000	0.877	0.769	0.675	0.592	0.519
23	Present value of cash flows (a) × (b)	$(290,000)	$ 166,630	$ 146,110	$ 108,000	$ 112,480	$ 129,750
24	Net present value (SUM B23:G23)	$ 372,970					
25							
26	Net present value in favor of buying the new ferry (B24-B11)	$ 252,630					
27							
28	Note: The discount factors come from Exhibit 7B–1 in Appendix 7B.						
29							

Exhibit 7-10 / Exhibit 7-11 / Exhibit 7C-1

Microsoft Excel

total cost from a present value perspective. Hence, these are known as least-cost decisions. To illustrate a least-cost decision, consider the following data:

Example H: Val-Tek Company is considering replacing an old threading machine with a new threading machine that would substantially reduce annual operating costs. Selected data relating to the old and new machines are presented below:

	Old Machine	New Machine
Purchase cost when new	$200,000	$250,000
Salvage value now	$30,000	—
Annual cash operating costs	$150,000	$90,000
Overhaul needed immediately	$40,000	—
Salvage value in six years	$0	$50,000
Remaining life	6 years	6 years

Val-Tek Company uses a 10% discount rate.

Exhibit 7–11 analyzes the alternatives using the total-cost approach and discount factors from Exhibits 7B–1 and 7B–2. Because this is a least-cost decision, the present values are negative for both alternatives. However, the present value of the alternative of buying the new machine is $109,500 lower than the other alternative. Therefore, buying the new machine is the less costly alternative.

EXHIBIT 7–11
Least-Cost Decision: A Net Present Value Analysis

	A	B	C	D
			Year(s)	
1	Keep the old machine:			
2		Now	1-6	6
3	Overhaul needed now	$ (40,000)		
4	Annual cash operating costs		$(150,000)	
5	Total cash flows (a)	$ (40,000)	$(150,000)	
6	Discount factor (10%) (b)	1.000	4.355	
7	Present value of the cash flows (a) × (b)	$ (40,000)	$(653,250)	
8	Net present value (SUM B7:C7)	$(693,250)		
9				
10	Buy the new machine:		Year(s)	
11		Now	1-6	6
12	Initial investment	$(250,000)		
13	Salvage value of old machine	$ 30,000		
14	Annual cash operating costs		$ (90,000)	
15	Salvage value of new machine			$50,000
16	Total cash flows (a)	$(220,000)	$ (90,000)	$50,000
17	Discount factor (10%) (b)	1.000	4.355	0.564
18	Present value of the cash flows (a) × (b)	$(220,000)	$(391,950)	$28,200
19	Net present value (SUM B18:D18)	$(583,750)		
20				
21	Net present value in favor of buying the new machine	$ 109,500		
22				
23	Note: The discount factors come from Exhibits 7B–1 and 7B–2 in Appendix 7B.			
24				

|◄ ◄ ► ►| Exhibit 7-10 \ **Exhibit 7-11** \ Exhibit 7C-1

Microsoft Excel

STARBUCKS ADJUSTS CAPITAL INVESTMENT PLAN

Starbucks saw its quarterly revenue decline by more than $3 billion during the coronavirus pandemic. To better position itself in a post–COVID-19 world, the company announced plans to open 40 to 50 pickup-only stores over an 18-month period. Given that to-go orders comprise 80 percent of Starbucks' sales in the United States, the company had already been planning to build more "smaller-footprint" stores over a three- to five-year period. However, when the pandemic unexpectedly arose, the company shortened its capital investment time horizon to 18 months.

Source: Heather Haddon, "Starbucks Speeds Up To-Go Shift," *The Wall Street Journal*, June 11, 2020, pp. B1–B2.

Moomusician/Shutterstock

Uncertain Cash Flows

Thus far, we assumed that all future cash flows are known with certainty. However, future cash flows are often uncertain or difficult to estimate. A number of techniques are available for handling this complication. Some of these techniques are quite technical—involving computer simulations or advanced mathematical skills—and are beyond the scope of this book.

LEARNING OBJECTIVE 7–4
Evaluate an investment project that has uncertain cash flows.

However, we can provide some very useful information to help managers deal with uncertain cash flows without getting too technical.

An Example

As an example of difficult-to-estimate future cash flows, consider the case of investments in automated equipment. The up-front costs of automated equipment and the tangible benefits, such as reductions in operating costs and waste, tend to be relatively easy to estimate. However, the intangible benefits, such as greater reliability, greater speed, and higher quality, are more difficult to quantify in terms of future cash flows. These intangible benefits certainly impact future cash flows—particularly in terms of increased sales and perhaps higher selling prices—but the cash flow effects are difficult to estimate. What can be done?

A fairly simple procedure can be followed when the intangible benefits are likely to be significant. Suppose, for example, that a company with a 12 percent discount rate is considering purchasing automated equipment that would have a 10-year useful life. Also suppose a discounted cash flow analysis of just the tangible costs and benefits shows a negative net present value of $226,000. Clearly, if the intangible benefits are large enough, they could turn this negative net present value into a positive net present value. In this case, the amount of additional cash flow per year from the intangible benefits that would be needed to make the project financially attractive can be computed as follows:

| Net present value excluding the intangible benefits (negative) | $(226,000) |
| Present value factor for an annuity at 12% for 10 periods (from Exhibit 7B–2 in Appendix 7B) | 5.650 |

$$\frac{\text{Negative net present value to be offset, } \$226,000}{\text{Present value factor, 5.650}} = \$40,000$$

Thus, if the intangible benefits of the automated equipment are worth at least $40,000 a year to the company, then the automated equipment should be purchased. If, in the judgment of management, these intangible benefits are not worth $40,000 a year, then the automated equipment should not be purchased.

This technique can be used in other situations in which future cash flows are difficult to estimate. For example, this technique can be used when the salvage value is difficult to estimate. To illustrate, suppose that all of the cash flows from an investment in a supertanker have been estimated—other than its salvage value in 20 years. Using a discount rate of 12 percent, management has determined that the net present value of all of these cash flows is a negative $1.04 million. This negative net present value would be offset by the salvage value of the supertanker. How large would the salvage value have to be to make this investment attractive?

| Net present value excluding salvage value (negative) | $(1,040,000) |
| Present value factor at 12% for 20 periods (from Exhibit 7B–1 in Appendix 7B) | 0.104 |

$$\frac{\text{Negative net present value to be offset, } \$1,040,000}{\text{Present value factor, 0.104}} = \$10,000,000$$

Thus, if the salvage value of the tanker in 20 years is at least $10 million, its net present value would be positive and the investment should be made. However, if management believes the salvage value is unlikely to be as large as $10 million, the investment should not be made.

Preference Decisions—The Ranking of Investment Projects

Recall that when considering investment opportunities, managers must make two types of decisions—screening decisions and preference decisions. Screening decisions, which come first, pertain to whether or not a proposed investment is acceptable. Preference decisions come *after* screening decisions and attempt to answer the following question: "How do the remaining investment proposals, all of which have been screened and provide an acceptable rate of return, rank in terms of preference? That is, which one(s) would be *best* for the company to accept?"

Sometimes preference decisions are called rationing decisions or ranking decisions. Limited investment funds must be rationed among many competing alternatives. Hence, the alternatives must be ranked. Either the internal rate of return method or the net present value method can be used in making preference decisions. However, as discussed earlier, if the two methods are in conflict, it is best to use the net present value method, which is more reliable.

LEARNING OBJECTIVE 7–5
Rank investment projects in order of preference.

Internal Rate of Return Method

When using the internal rate of return method to rank competing investment projects, the preference rule is: *The higher the internal rate of return, the more desirable the project.* An investment project with an internal rate of return of 18 percent usually is considered preferable to another project that has a return of only 15 percent. Internal rate of return is widely used to rank projects.

Net Present Value Method

The net present value of one project cannot be directly compared to the net present value of another project unless the initial investments are equal. For example, assume a company is considering two competing investments, as shown below:

	Investment A	Investment B
Investment required	$(10,000)	$(5,000)
Present value of cash inflows	11,000	6,000
Net present value	$ 1,000	$ 1,000

Although each project has a net present value of $1,000, the projects are not equally desirable if the funds available for investment are limited. The project requiring an investment of only $5,000 is much more desirable than the project requiring an investment of $10,000. This fact can be highlighted by dividing the present value of each project's cash inflows by its investment required. The result, shown below in equation form, is called the **profitability index.**

$$\text{Profitability index} = \frac{\text{Present value of cash inflows}}{\text{Investment required}} \qquad (3)$$

The profitability indexes for the two investments above would be computed as follows:

	Investment A	Investment B
Present value of cash inflows (a)	$11,000	$6,000
Investment required (b)	$10,000	$5,000
Profitability index, (a) ÷ (b)	1.10	1.20

When using the profitability index to rank competing investment projects, the preference rule is: *The higher the profitability index, the more desirable the project.*[4] Applying this rule to the two investments above, Investment B should be chosen over Investment A.

The profitability index is an application of the techniques for utilizing constrained resources discussed in an earlier chapter. In this case, the constrained resource is the limited funds available for investment, and the profitability index is similar to the contribution margin per unit of the constrained resource.

A few details should be clarified with respect to the computation of the profitability index. The "Investment required" refers to any cash outflows that occur at the beginning of the project, reduced by any salvage value recovered from the sale of old equipment. The "Investment required" also includes any investment in working capital that the project may need.

IN BUSINESS

STANLEY BLACK & DECKER MOVES PRODUCTION TO THE UNITED STATES

Stanley Black & Decker is investing $90 million to move production from China to a new manufacturing facility in Fort Worth, Texas. The newly constructed plant will employ 500 people to annually produce 10 million Craftsman wrenches and ratchets as well as 50 million sockets. The Fort Worth facility will rely on robots and fast-forging presses to "boost output about 25% above the older machinery used to make Craftsman wrenches in China." These automation-driven efficiencies coupled with rising tariff costs are also causing other companies, such as Whirlpool and Caterpillar, to bring overseas production back to the United States.

Source: Bob Tita, "Stanley to Make More Craftsman Tools in U.S.," *The Wall Street Journal*, May 16, 2019, p. B2.

The Simple Rate of Return Method

LEARNING OBJECTIVE 7–6
Compute the simple rate of return for an investment.

The **simple rate of return** method is the final capital budgeting technique discussed in the chapter. This method also is often referred to as the accounting rate of return or the unadjusted rate of return. We will begin by explaining how to compute the simple rate of return, followed by a discussion of this method's limitations and its impact on the behavior of investment center managers.

To obtain the simple rate of return, the annual incremental net operating income generated by a project is divided by the initial investment in the project, as shown below.

$$\text{Simple rate of return} = \frac{\text{Annual incremental net operating income}}{\text{Initial investment}} \quad (4)$$

The annual incremental net operating income included in the numerator should be reduced by the depreciation charges that result from making the investment. Furthermore, the initial investment shown in the denominator should be reduced by any salvage value realized from the sale of old equipment.

Example I: Brigham Tea, Inc., is a processor of low-acid tea. The company is contemplating purchasing equipment for an additional processing line that would increase revenues by $90,000 per year. Incremental cash operating expenses would be $40,000 per year. The equipment would cost $180,000 and have a nine-year life with no salvage value.

---

[4] Because of the "lumpiness" of projects, the profitability index ranking may not be perfect. Nevertheless, it is a good starting point.

To apply the formula for the simple rate of return, we must first determine the annual incremental net operating income from the project:

Annual incremental revenues		$90,000
Annual incremental cash operating expenses ...	$40,000	
Annual depreciation ($180,000 − $0) ÷ 9	20,000	
Annual incremental expenses		60,000
Annual incremental net operating income		$30,000

Given that the annual incremental net operating income from the project is $30,000 and the initial investment is $180,000, the simple rate of return is 16.7 percent as shown below:

$$\text{Simple rate of return} = \frac{\text{Annual incremental net operating income}}{\text{Initial investment}}$$

$$= \frac{\$30,000}{\$180,000}$$

$$= 16.7\%$$

Example J: Midwest Farms, Inc., hires people on a part-time basis to sort eggs. The cost of hand sorting is $30,000 per year. The company is investigating an egg-sorting machine that would cost $90,000 and have a 15-year useful life. The machine would have negligible salvage value, and it would cost $10,000 per year to operate and maintain. The egg-sorting equipment currently being used could be sold now for a scrap value of $2,500.

This project is slightly different from the preceding project because it involves cost reductions with no additional revenues. Nevertheless, the annual incremental net operating income can be computed by treating the annual cost savings as if it were incremental revenues as follows:

Annual incremental cost savings		$ 30,000
Annual incremental cash operating expenses	$10,000	
Annual depreciation ($90,000 − $0) ÷ 15	6,000	
Annual incremental expenses		16,000
Annual incremental net operating income		$ 14,000

Thus, even though the new equipment would not generate any additional revenues, it would reduce costs by $14,000 a year. This would have the effect of increasing net operating income by $14,000 a year.

Finally, the salvage value of the old equipment offsets the initial cost of the new equipment as follows:

Cost of the new equipment	$90,000
Less salvage value of the old equipment	2,500
Initial investment	$87,500

Given the annual incremental net operating income of $14,000 and the initial investment of $87,500, the simple rate of return is 16.0 percent computed as follows:

$$\text{Simple rate of return} = \frac{\text{Annual incremental net operating income}}{\text{Initial investment}}$$

$$= \frac{\$14,000}{\$87,500}$$

$$= 16.0\%$$

The simple rate of return suffers from two important limitations. First, it focuses on accounting net operating income rather than cash flows. Thus, if a project does not have constant incremental revenues and expenses over its useful life, the simple rate of return will fluctuate from year to year, thereby possibly causing the same project to appear desirable in some years and undesirable in others. Second, the simple rate of return method does not involve discounting cash flows. It considers a dollar received 10 years from now to be as valuable as a dollar received today.

Given these limitations, it is reasonable to wonder why we bothered discussing this method. First of all, in spite of its limitations, some companies use the simple rate of return to evaluate capital investment proposals. Therefore, you should be familiar with this approach so you can properly critique it in the event that you encounter it in practice. More importantly, you need to understand how the simple rate of return method influences the behavior of investment center managers who are evaluated and rewarded based on their return on investment (ROI).

For example, assume the following three facts. First, assume you are an investment center manager whose pay raises are based solely on ROI. Second, assume last year your division had an ROI of 20 percent. Third, assume your division has the chance to pursue a capital budgeting project that will have a positive net present value and a simple rate of return of 17 percent. Given these three assumptions, would you choose to accept this project or reject it? Although the company would want you to accept it because of its positive net present value, you would probably choose to reject it because the simple rate of return of 17 percent is less than your prior year's ROI of 20 percent. This basic example illustrates how a project's simple rate of return can influence the decisions made by investment center managers. It also highlights an important challenge faced by organizations, namely designing performance measurement systems that align employee actions with organizational goals.

Postaudit of Investment Projects

After an investment project has been approved and implemented, a *postaudit* should be conducted. A **postaudit** involves checking whether or not expected results are actually realized. This is a key part of the capital budgeting process because it helps keep managers honest in their investment proposals. Any tendency to inflate the benefits or downplay the costs in a proposal should become evident after a few postaudits have been conducted. The postaudit also provides an opportunity to reinforce and possibly expand successful projects and to cut losses on floundering projects.

The same capital budgeting method should be used in the postaudit as was used in the original approval process. That is, if a project was approved on the basis of a net present value analysis, then the same procedure should be used in performing the postaudit. However, the data used in the postaudit analysis should be *actual observed data* rather than estimated data. This gives management an opportunity to make a side-by-side comparison to see how well the project has succeeded. It also helps assure that estimated data received on future proposals will be carefully prepared because the people submitting the data know that their estimates will be compared to actual results in the postaudit process. Actual results that are far out of line with original estimates should be carefully reviewed.

VCG/VCG via Getty Images

IN BUSINESS

UNIVERSAL PARKS & RESORTS BETS BIG ON BEIJING

Universal Parks & Resorts is investing $6.5 billion to build a 300-acre theme park in Beijing, China. This investment surpasses Walt Disney Company's $5.5 billion investment to build Shanghai Disney Resort. After Disney's Shanghai theme park attracted 11 million visitors in its first year, Universal decided to double its capital investment in Beijing while increasing its initial projection of 7 million visitors during its first year to 10 million visitors. Mintel, a market research firm, estimates that China's annual theme park revenues will soon exceed $14 billion.

Source: Wayne Ma, "Universal Raises Its Bet on Beijing Park," *The Wall Street Journal,* May 8, 2018, p. B5.

Summary

The payback method of evaluating capital investment projects focuses on the payback period. The payback period is the length of time that it takes for a project to recover its initial cost from the net cash inflows that it generates. The basic premise of the payback method is that the more quickly the cost of an investment can be recovered, the more desirable is the investment.

Investment decisions should take into account the time value of money because a dollar received today is more valuable than a dollar received in the future. The net present value and internal rate of return methods both reflect this fact. In the net present value method, future cash flows are discounted to their present value. The difference between the present value of the cash inflows and the present value of the cash outflows is called a project's net present value. If the net present value of a project is negative, the project is rejected. The discount rate in the net present value method is usually based on a minimum required rate of return, such as a company's cost of capital.

The internal rate of return is the rate of return that equates the present value of the cash inflows and the present value of the cash outflows, resulting in a zero net present value. If the internal rate of return is less than a company's minimum required rate of return, the project is rejected.

After rejecting projects whose net present values are negative or whose internal rates of return are less than the minimum required rate of return, more projects may remain than can be supported with available funds. The remaining projects can be ranked using either the profitability index or internal rate of return. The profitability index is computed by dividing the present value of a project's cash inflows by its required initial investment.

The simple rate of return is determined by dividing a project's annual incremental net operating income by the initial investment in the project. While this method has important limitations, it can influence the decision-making process of investment center managers who are evaluated and rewarded based on their return on investment (ROI).

 Data Analytics Exercise available in Connect to complement this chapter

Review Problem: Comparison of Capital Budgeting Methods

Lamar Company is considering a project that would have a five-year life and require a $2,400,000 investment in equipment. At the end of five years, the project would terminate and the equipment would have no salvage value. The project would provide net operating income each year as follows:

Sales		$3,200,000
Variable expenses		1,800,000
Contribution margin		1,400,000
Fixed expenses:		
Advertising, salaries, and other		
fixed out-of-pocket costs	$700,000	
Depreciation	300,000	
Total fixed expenses		1,000,000
Net operating income		$ 400,000

The company's discount rate is 12%.

Required:

1. Compute the annual net cash inflow from the project.
2. Compute the project's net present value. Is the project acceptable?
3. Find the project's internal rate of return to the nearest whole percent.
4. Compute the project's payback period.
5. Compute the project's simple rate of return.

Solution to Review Problem

1. The annual net cash inflow can be computed by deducting the cash expenses from sales:

Sales	$3,200,000
Variable expenses	1,800,000
Contribution margin	1,400,000
Advertising, salaries, and other	
fixed out-of-pocket costs	700,000
Annual net cash inflow	$ 700,000

Or the annual net cash inflow can be computed by adding depreciation back to net operating income:

Net operating income	$400,000
Add: Noncash deduction for depreciation	300,000
Annual net cash inflow	$700,000

2. The net present value is computed as follows:

	A	B	C	D	E	F	G
1						Year	
2		Now	1	2	3	4	5
3	Initial investment	$ (2,400,000)					
4	Sales		$ 3,200,000	$ 3,200,000	$ 3,200,000	$ 3,200,000	$ 3,200,000
5	Variable expenses		$ (1,800,000)	$ (1,800,000)	$ (1,800,000)	$ (1,800,000)	$ (1,800,000)
6	Fixed out-of-pocket costs		$ (700,000)	$ (700,000)	$ (700,000)	$ (700,000)	$ (700,000)
7	Total cash flows (a)	$ (2,400,000)	$ 700,000	$ 700,000	$ 700,000	$ 700,000	$ 700,000
8	Discount factor (12%) (b)	1.000	0.893	0.797	0.712	0.636	0.567
9	Present value of cash flows (a) × (b)	$ (2,400,000)	$ 625,100	$ 557,900	$ 498,400	$ 445,200	$ 396,900
10	Net present value (SUM B9:G9)	$ 123,500					
11							
12	Note: The discount factors come from Exhibit 7B–1 in Appendix 7B.						

Sheet1 / Sheet2 / Sheet3

Microsoft Excel

Or it can also be computed as follows:

	A	B	C
1			Years
2		Now	1-5
3	Initial investment	$ (2,400,000)	
4	Sales		$ 3,200,000
5	Variable expenses		$ (1,800,000)
6	Fixed out-of-pocket costs		$ (700,000)
7	Total cash flows (a)	$ (2,400,000)	$ 700,000
8	Discount factor (12%) (b)	1.000	3.605
9	Present value of the cash flows (a) × (b)	$ (2,400,000)	$2,523,500
10	Net present value (SUM B9:C9)	$123,500	
11			
12	Note: The discount factor comes from Exhibit 7B–2 in Appendix 7B.		

Sheet1 / Sheet2 / Sheet3

Microsoft Excel

Yes, the project is acceptable because it has a positive net present value.

3. The formula for computing the factor of the internal rate of return is:

$$\text{Factor of the internal rate of return} = \frac{\text{Investment required}}{\text{Annual net cash flow}}$$

$$= \frac{\$2,400,000}{\$700,000} = 3.429$$

Looking in Exhibit 7B–2 in Appendix 7B at the end of the chapter and scanning along the 5-period line, we find that a factor of 3.429 is closest to a factor of 3.433, which corresponds to a rate of return of 14%.

4. The formula for the payback period is:

$$\text{Payback period} = \frac{\text{Investment required}}{\text{Annual net cash flow}}$$

$$= \frac{\$2,400,000}{\$700,000}$$

$$= 3.4 \text{ years (rounded)}$$

5. The formula for the simple rate of return is:

$$\text{Simple rate of return} = \frac{\text{Annual incremental net opeating income}}{\text{Initial investment}}$$

$$= \frac{\$400,000}{\$2,400,000}$$

$$= 16.7\%$$

Glossary

Capital budgeting The process of planning significant investments in projects that have long-term implications, such as the purchase of new equipment or the introduction of a new product. (p. 350)

Cost of capital The average rate of return a company must pay to its long-term creditors and shareholders for the use of their funds. (p. 358)

Internal rate of return The discount rate at which the net present value of an investment project is zero; the rate of return of a project over its useful life. (p. 360)

Net present value The difference between the present value of an investment project's cash inflows and the present value of its cash outflows. (p. 355)

Out-of-pocket costs Actual cash outlays for salaries, advertising, repairs, and similar costs. (p. 360)

Payback period The length of time that it takes for a project to fully recover its initial cost out of the net cash inflows that it generates. (p. 352)

Postaudit The follow-up after a project has been approved and implemented to determine whether expected results were actually realized. (p. 370)

Preference decision A decision in which the acceptable alternatives must be ranked. (p. 350)

Profitability index The present value of a project's cash inflows divided by the investment required. (p. 367)

Screening decision A decision as to whether a proposed investment project is acceptable. (p. 350)

Simple rate of return The rate of return computed by dividing a project's annual incremental net operating income by the initial investment required. (p. 368)

Time value of money The concept that a dollar today is worth more than a dollar a year from now. (p. 351)

Working capital Current assets less current liabilities. (p. 351)

Questions

7–1 What is the difference between capital budgeting screening decisions and capital budgeting preference decisions?

7–2 What is meant by the term *time value of money?*

7–3 What is meant by the term *discounting?*

7–4 Why isn't accounting net income used in the net present value and internal rate of return methods of making capital budgeting decisions?

7–5 Why are discounted cash flow methods of making capital budgeting decisions superior to other methods?

7–6   What is net present value? Can it ever be negative? Explain.

7–7   Identify two simplifying assumptions associated with discounted cash flow methods of making capital budgeting decisions.

7–8   If a company has to pay interest of 14% on long-term debt, then its cost of capital is 14%. Do you agree? Explain.

7–9   What is meant by an investment project's internal rate of return? How is the internal rate of return computed?

7–10   Explain how the cost of capital serves as a screening tool when using (*a*) the net present value method and (*b*) the internal rate of return method.

7–11   As the discount rate increases, the present value of a given future cash flow also increases. Do you agree? Explain.

7–12   Refer to Exhibit 7–8. Is the return on this investment proposal exactly 14%, more than 14%, or less than 14%? Explain.

7–13   How is the profitability index computed, and what does it measure?

7–14   What is meant by the term *payback period?* How is the payback period determined? How can the payback method be useful?

7–15   What is the major criticism of the payback and simple rate of return methods of making capital budgeting decisions?

Applying Excel

LEARNING OBJECTIVES 7–2, 7–3   The Excel worksheet form below is to be used to recreate Example E and Exhibit 7–8. The workbook, and instructions on how to complete the file, can be found in Connect.

	A	B	C	D	E	F	G
1	Chapter 7: Applying Excel						
2							
3	Data						
4	Example E						
5	Cost of equipment needed	$60,000					
6	Working capital needed	$100,000					
7	Overhaul of equipment in four years	$5,000					
8	Salvage value of the equipment in five years	$10,000					
9	Annual revenues and costs:						
10	Sales revenues	$200,000					
11	Cost of goods sold	$125,000					
12	Out-of-pocket operating costs	$35,000					
13	Discount rate	14%					
14							
15	*Enter a formula into each of the cells marked with a ? below*						
16	Exhibit 7-8						
17						Years	
18		Now	1	2	3	4	5
19	Purchase of equipment	?					
20	Investment in working capital	?					
21	Sales		?	?	?	?	?
22	Cost of goods sold		?	?	?	?	?
23	Out-of-pocket operating costs		?	?	?	?	?
24	Overhaul of equipment					?	
25	Salvage value of the equipment						?
26	Working capital released						?
27	Total cash flows (a)	?	?	?	?	?	?
28	Discount factor (14%) (b)	?	?	?	?	?	?
29	Present value of cash flows (a) x (b)	?	?	?	?	?	?
30	Net present value	?					
31							
32	*Use the formulas from Appendix 7B:						
33	Present value of $1 = 1/(1+r)^n						
34	Present value of an annuity of $1 = (1/r)*(1-(1/(1+r)^n))						
35	where n is the number of years and r is the discount rate						
36							

Chapter 7 Form / Filled in Chapter 7 Form / Chapter 7 Formul

Microsoft Excel

You should proceed to the requirements below only after completing your worksheet. Note that you may get a slightly different net present value from that shown in the text due to the precision of the calculations.

Required:

1. Check your worksheet by changing the discount rate to 10%. The net present value should now be between $56,495 and $56,518—depending on the precision of the calculations. If you do not get an answer in this range, find the errors in your worksheet and correct them.

   Explain why the net present value has increased as a result of reducing the discount rate from 14% to 10%.

2. The company is considering another project involving the purchase of new equipment. Change the data area of your worksheet to match the following:

Data	
Example E	
Cost of equipment needed	$120,000
Working capital needed	$80,000
Overhaul of equipment in four years	$40,000
Salvage value of the equipment	
in five years	$20,000
Annual revenues and costs:	
Sales revenues	$255,000
Cost of goods sold	$160,000
Out-of-pocket operating costs	$50,000
Discount rate	14%

   a. What is the net present value of the project?
   b. Experiment with changing the discount rate in one percent increments (e.g., 13%, 12%, 15%, etc.). At what interest rate does the net present value turn from negative to positive?
   c. The internal rate of return is between what two whole discount rates (e.g., between 10% and 11%, between 11% and 12%, between 12% and 13%, between 13% and 14%, etc.)?
   d. Reset the discount rate to 14%. Suppose the salvage value is uncertain. How large would the salvage value have to be to result in a positive net present value?

Mc Graw Hill connect **The Foundational 15**

Cardinal Company is considering a five-year project that would require a $2,975,000 investment in equipment with a useful life of five years and no salvage value. The company's discount rate is 14%. The project would provide net operating income in each of five years as follows:

LEARNING OBJECTIVES 7–1, 7–2, 7–3, 7–5, 7–6

Sales	$2,735,000
Variable expenses	1,000,000
Contribution margin	1,735,000
Fixed expenses:	
Advertising, salaries, and other fixed	
out-of-pocket costs $735,000	
Depreciation 595,000	
Total fixed expenses	1,330,000
Net operating income	$ 405,000

Required:

Answer each question by referring to the original data unless instructed otherwise.

1. Which item(s) in the income statement shown above will not affect cash flows?
2. What are the project's annual net cash inflows?
3. What is the present value of the project's annual net cash inflows?

4. What is the project's net present value?
5. What is the profitability index for this project? (Round your answer to the nearest whole percent.)
6. What is the project's internal rate of return to the nearest whole percent?
7. What is the project's payback period?
8. What is the project's simple rate of return for each of the five years?
9. If the company's discount rate was 16% instead of 14%, would you expect the project's net present value to be higher than, lower than, or the same as your answer to requirement 4? No computations are necessary.
10. If the equipment had a salvage value of $300,000 at the end of five years, would you expect the project's payback period to be higher than, lower than, or the same as your answer to requirement 7? No computations are necessary.
11. If the equipment had a salvage value of $300,000 at the end of five years, would you expect the project's net present value to be higher than, lower than, or the same as your answer to requirement 3? No computations are necessary.
12. If the equipment had a salvage value of $300,000 at the end of five years, would you expect the project's simple rate of return to be higher than, lower than, or the same as your answer to requirement 8? No computations are necessary.
13. Assume a postaudit showed that all estimates (including total sales) were exactly correct except for the variable expense ratio, which actually turned out to be 45%. What was the project's actual net present value?
14. Assume a postaudit showed that all estimates (including total sales) were exactly correct except for the variable expense ratio, which actually turned out to be 45%. What was the project's actual payback period?
15. Assume a postaudit showed that all estimates (including total sales) were exactly correct except for the variable expense ratio, which actually turned out to be 45%. What was the project's actual simple rate of return?

Exercises connect

EXERCISE 7–1 Payback Method LO 7–1
The management of Unter Corporation, an architectural design firm, is considering an investment with the following cash flows:

Year	Investment	Cash Inflow
1	$15,000	$1,000
2	$8,000	$2,000
3		$2,500
4		$4,000
5		$5,000
6		$6,000
7		$5,000
8		$4,000
9		$3,000
10		$2,000

Required:
1. Determine the payback period of the investment.
2. Would the payback period be affected if the cash inflow in the last year were several times as large?

EXERCISE 7–2 Net Present Value Analysis LO 7–2
The management of Kunkel Company is considering the purchase of a $27,000 machine that would reduce operating costs by $7,000 per year. At the end of the machine's five-year useful life, it will have zero salvage value. The company's required rate of return is 12%.

Required:
1. Determine the net present value of the investment in the machine.
2. What is the difference between the total, undiscounted cash inflows and cash outflows over the entire life of the machine?

EXERCISE 7–3 Internal Rate of Return LO 7–3

Wendell's Donut Shoppe is investigating the purchase of a new $18,600 donut-making machine. The new machine would permit the company to reduce the amount of part-time help needed, at a cost savings of $3,800 per year. In addition, the new machine would allow the company to produce one new style of donut, resulting in the sale of 1,000 dozen more donuts each year. The company realizes a contribution margin of $1.20 per dozen donuts sold. The new machine would have a six-year useful life.

Required:
1. What would be the total annual cash inflows associated with the new machine for capital budgeting purposes?
2. What discount factor should be used to compute the new machine's internal rate of return?
3. Using Exhibit 7B–2 in Appendix 7B as a reference, what is the new machine's internal rate of return to the nearest whole percent?
4. In addition to the data given previously, assume the machine will have a $9,125 salvage value at the end of six years. Under these conditions, what is the internal rate of return to the nearest whole percent? (Hint: You may find it helpful to use the net present value approach; find the discount rate that will cause the net present value to be closest to zero.)

EXERCISE 7–4 Uncertain Future Cash Flows LO 7–4

Lukow Products is investigating the purchase of a piece of automated equipment that will save $400,000 each year in direct labor and inventory carrying costs. This equipment costs $2,500,000 and is expected to have a 15-year useful life with no salvage value. The company's required rate of return is 20% on all equipment purchases. Management anticipates this equipment will provide intangible benefits such as greater flexibility and higher-quality output that will result in additional future cash inflows.

Required:
1. What is the net present value of the piece of equipment *before* considering its intangible benefits?
2. What minimum dollar value per year must be provided by the equipment's intangible benefits to justify the $2,500,000 investment?

EXERCISE 7–5 Preference Ranking LO 7–5

Information on four investment proposals is given below:

	Investment Proposal			
	A	B	C	D
Investment required	$(90,000)	$(100,000)	$(70,000)	$(120,000)
Present value of cash inflows	126,000	138,000	105,000	160,000
Net present value	$ 36,000	$ 38,000	$ 35,000	$ 40,000
Life of the project	5 years	7 years	6 years	6 years

Required:
1. Compute the profitability index for each investment proposal.
2. Rank the proposals in terms of preference.

EXERCISE 7–6 Simple Rate of Return Method LO 7–6

The management of Ballard MicroBrew is considering the purchase of an automated bottling machine for $120,000. The machine would replace an old piece of equipment that costs $30,000 per year to operate. The new machine would cost $12,000 per year to operate. The old machine, currently in use, is fully depreciated and could be sold now for a salvage value of $40,000. The new machine would have a useful life of 10 years with no salvage value.

Required:
1. What is the annual depreciation expense associated with the new bottling machine?
2. What is the annual incremental net operating income provided by the new bottling machine?
3. What is the amount of the initial investment associated with this project that should be used for calculating the simple rate of return?
4. What is the simple rate of return on the new bottling machine?

EXERCISE 7–7 Net Present Value Analysis of Two Alternatives LO 7–2

Perit Industries has $100,000 to invest. The company is trying to decide between two alternative uses of the funds. The alternatives are:

	Project A	Project B
Cost of equipment required	$100,000	$0
Working capital investment required	$0	$100,000
Annual cash inflows	$21,000	$16,000
Salvage value of equipment in six years	$8,000	$0
Life of the project	6 years	6 years

The working capital needed for Project B will be released at the end of six years for investment elsewhere. Perit Industries' discount rate is 14%.

Required:
1. Compute the net present value of Project A.
2. Compute the net present value of Project B.
3. Which investment alternative (if either) would you recommend that the company accept?

EXERCISE 7–8 Payback Period and Simple Rate of Return LO 7–1, LO 7–6

Nick's Novelties, Inc., is considering the purchase of new electronic games to place in its amusement houses. The games would cost a total of $300,000, have an eight-year useful life, and have a total salvage value of $20,000. The company estimates annual revenues and expenses associated with the games would be as follows:

Revenues		$200,000
Less operating expenses:		
Commissions to amusement houses	$100,000	
Insurance	7,000	
Depreciation	35,000	
Maintenance	18,000	160,000
Net operating income		$ 40,000

Required:
1. What is the payback period for the new electronic games? Assume Nick's Novelties, Inc., will not purchase new games unless they provide a payback period of five years or less. Would the company purchase the new games?
2. What is the simple rate of return promised by the games? If the company requires a simple rate of return of at least 12%, will the games be purchased?

EXERCISE 7–9 Net Present Value Analysis and Simple Rate of Return LO 7–2, LO 7–6

Derrick Iverson is a divisional manager for Holston Company. His annual pay raises are largely determined by his division's return on investment (ROI), which has been above 20% each of the last three years. Derrick is considering a capital budgeting project that would require a $3,000,000 investment in equipment with a useful life of five years and no salvage value. Holston Company's discount rate is 15%. The project would provide net operating income each year for five years as follows:

Sales		$2,500,000
Variable expenses		1,000,000
Contribution margin		1,500,000
Fixed expenses:		
Advertising, salaries, and other fixed		
out-of-pocket costs	$600,000	
Depreciation	600,000	
Total fixed expenses		1,200,000
Net operating income		$ 300,000

Required:

1. Compute the project's net present value.
2. Compute the project's simple rate of return.
3. Would the company want Derrick to pursue this investment opportunity? Would Derrick be inclined to pursue this investment opportunity? Explain.

EXERCISE 7–10 Net Present Value Analysis LO 7–2

Kathy Myers frequently purchases stocks and bonds, but she is uncertain how to determine the rate of return that she is earning. For example, three years ago she paid $13,000 for 200 shares of Malti Company's common stock. She received a $420 cash dividend on the stock at the end of each year for three years. At the end of three years, she sold the stock for $16,000. Kathy would like to earn a return of at least 14% on all of her investments. She is not sure whether the Malti Company stock provides a 14% return and would like some help with the necessary computations.

Required:

1. Compute the net present value that Kathy earned on her investment in Malti Company stock. Round your answer to the nearest whole dollar.
2. Did the Malti Company stock provide a 14% return?

EXERCISE 7–11 Preference Ranking of Investment Projects LO 7–5

Oxford Company has limited funds available for investment and must ration the funds among four competing projects. Selected information on the four projects follows:

Project	Investment Required	Present Value of Cash Inflows	Life of the Project (years)	Internal Rate of Return
A	$160,000	$204,323	7	18%
B	$135,000	$177,000	12	16%
C	$100,000	$135,035	7	20%
D	$175,000	$213,136	3	22%

The net present values above have been computed using a 10% discount rate. The company wants your assistance in determining which project to accept first, second, and so forth.

Required:

1. Compute the profitability index for each project.
2. In order of preference, rank the four projects in terms of:
   a. Net present value.
   b. Profitability index.
   c. Internal rate of return.
3. Which ranking do you prefer? Why?

EXERCISE 7–12 Uncertain Cash Flows LO 7–4

The Cambro Foundation, a nonprofit organization, is planning to invest $104,950 in a project that will last for three years. The project will produce net cash inflows as follows:

Year 1	$30,000
Year 2	$40,000
Year 3	?

Required:

Assuming the project will yield exactly a 12% rate of return, what is the expected net cash inflow for Year 3?

EXERCISE 7–13 Payback Period and Simple Rate of Return Computations LO 7–1, LO 7–6

A piece of labor-saving equipment has just come onto the market that Mitsui Electronics, Ltd., could use to reduce costs in one of its plants in Japan. Relevant data relating to the equipment follow:

Purchase cost of the equipment	$432,000
Annual cost savings that will be	
provided by the equipment	$90,000
Life of the equipment	12 years

Required:

1. What is the payback period for the equipment? If the company requires a payback period of four years or less, would the equipment be purchased?
2. What is the simple rate of return on the equipment? Use straight-line depreciation based on the equipment's useful life. Would the equipment be purchased if the company's required rate of return is 14%?

EXERCISE 7–14 Comparison of Projects Using Net Present Value LO 7–2

Labeau Products, Ltd., of Perth, Australia, has $35,000 to invest. The company is trying to decide between two alternative uses for the funds as follows:

	Invest in Project X	Invest in Project Y
Investment required	$35,000	$35,000
Annual cash inflows	$12,000	
Single cash inflow at the end of 6 years		$90,000
Life of the project	6 years	6 years

The company's discount rate is 18%.

Required:

1. Compute the net present value of Project X.
2. Compute the net present value of Project Y.
3. Which project would you recommend the company accept?

EXERCISE 7–15 Internal Rate of Return and Net Present Value LO 7–2, LO 7–3

Henrie's Drapery Service is investigating the purchase of a new machine for cleaning and blocking drapes. The machine would cost $137,320, including freight and installation. Henrie's estimated the new machine would increase the company's cash inflows, net of expenses, by $40,000 per year. The machine would have a five-year useful life and no salvage value.

Required:

1. What is the machine's internal rate of return to the nearest whole percent?
2. Using a discount rate of 14%, what is the machine's net present value? Interpret your results.
3. Suppose the new machine would increase the company's annual cash inflows, net of expenses, by only $37,150 per year. Under these conditions, what is the internal rate of return to the nearest whole percent?

Problems

PROBLEM 7–16 Net Present Value Analysis LO 7–2

Windhoek Mines, Ltd., of Namibia, is contemplating the purchase of equipment to exploit a mineral deposit on land to which the company has mineral rights. An engineering and cost analysis has been made, and it is expected that the following cash flows would be associated with opening and operating a mine in the area:

Cost of new equipment and timbers	$275,000
Working capital required	$100,000
Annual net cash receipts	$120,000*
Cost to construct new roads in three years	$40,000
Salvage value of equipment in four years	$65,000

*Receipts from sales of ore, less out-of-pocket costs for salaries, utilities, insurance, and so forth.

The mineral deposit would be exhausted after four years of mining. At that point, the working capital would be released for reinvestment elsewhere. The company's required rate of return is 20%.

Required:

What is the net present value of the proposed mining project? Should the project be accepted? Explain.

PROBLEM 7–17 Net Present Value Analysis; Internal Rate of Return; Simple Rate of Return LO 7–2, LO 7–3, LO 7–6

Casey Nelson is a divisional manager for Pigeon Company. His annual pay raises are largely determined by his division's return on investment (ROI), which has been above 20% each of the last three years. Casey is considering a capital budgeting project that would require a $3,500,000 investment in equipment with a useful life of five years and no salvage value. Pigeon Company's discount rate is 16%. The project would provide net operating income each year for five years as follows:

Sales		$3,400,000
Variable expenses		1,600,000
Contribution margin		1,800,000
Fixed expenses:		
Advertising, salaries, and other fixed out-of-pocket costs	$700,000	
Depreciation	700,000	
Total fixed expenses		1,400,000
Net operating income		$ 400,000

Required:

1. What is the project's net present value?
2. What is the project's internal rate of return to the nearest whole percent?
3. What is the project's simple rate of return?
4. Would the company want Casey to pursue this investment opportunity? Would Casey be inclined to pursue this investment opportunity? Explain.

PROBLEM 7–18 Net Present Value Analysis LO 7–2

Oakmont Company has an opportunity to manufacture and sell a new product for a four-year period. The company's discount rate is 15%. After careful study, Oakmont estimated the following costs and revenues for the new product:

Cost of equipment needed	$130,000
Working capital needed	$60,000
Overhaul of the equipment in two years	$8,000
Salvage value of the equipment in four years	$12,000
Annual revenues and costs:	
Sales revenues	$250,000
Variable expenses	$120,000
Fixed out-of-pocket operating costs	$70,000

When the project concludes in four years, the working capital will be released for investment elsewhere within the company.

Required:

Calculate the net present value of this investment opportunity.

PROBLEM 7–19 Simple Rate of Return; Payback Period LO 7–1, LO 7–6

Paul Swanson has an opportunity to acquire a franchise from The Yogurt Place, Inc., to dispense frozen yogurt products under The Yogurt Place name. Mr. Swanson assembled the following information relating to the franchise:

a. A suitable location in a large shopping mall can be rented for $3,500 per month.
b. Remodeling and necessary equipment would cost $270,000. The equipment would have a 15-year life and an $18,000 salvage value. Straight-line depreciation would be used, and the salvage value would be considered in computing depreciation.
c. Based on similar outlets elsewhere, Mr. Swanson estimates that sales would total $300,000 per year. Ingredients would cost 20% of sales.

d.   Operating costs would include $70,000 per year for salaries, $3,500 per year for insurance, and $27,000 per year for utilities. In addition, Mr. Swanson would have to pay a commission to The Yogurt Place, Inc., of 12.5% of sales.

Required:

1.   Prepare a contribution format income statement that shows the expected net operating income each year from the franchise outlet.
2.   Compute the simple rate of return promised by the outlet. If Mr. Swanson requires a simple rate of return of at least 12%, should he acquire the franchise?
3.   Compute the payback period on the outlet. If Mr. Swanson wants a payback of four years or less, will he acquire the franchise?

PROBLEM 7–20 Net Present Value Analysis; Uncertain Cash Flows LO 7–2, LO 7–4

"I'm not sure we should lay out $250,000 for that automated welding machine," said Jim Alder, president of the Superior Equipment Company. "That's a lot of money, and it would cost us $80,000 for software and installation, and another $36,000 per year just to maintain the thing. In addition, the manufacturer admits it would cost $45,000 more at the end of three years to replace worn-out parts."

"I admit it's a lot of money," said Franci Rogers, the controller. "But you know the turnover problem we've had with the welding crew. This machine would replace six welders at a cost savings of $108,000 per year. And we would save another $6,500 per year in reduced material waste. When you figure that the automated welder would last for six years, I'm sure the return would be greater than our 16% required rate of return."

"I'm still not convinced," countered Mr. Alder. "We can only get $12,000 scrap value out of our old welding equipment if we sell it now, and in six years, the new machine will only be worth $20,000 for parts. But have your people work up the figures, and we'll talk about them at the executive committee meeting tomorrow."

Required:

1.   Compute the annual net cost savings promised by the automated welding machine.
2.   Using the data from (1) above and other data from the problem, compute the automated welding machine's net present value. Would you recommend purchasing the automated welding machine? Explain.
3.   Assume management can identify several intangible benefits associated with the automated welding machine, including greater flexibility in shifting from one type of product to another, improved quality of output, and faster delivery as a result of reduced throughput time. What minimum dollar value per year would management have to attach to these intangible benefits in order to make the new welding machine an acceptable investment?

PROBLEM 7–21 Preference Ranking of Investment Projects LO 7–5

The management of Revco Products is exploring four different investment opportunities. Information on the four projects under study follows:

	Project Number			
	1	2	3	4
Investment required	$(270,000)	$(450,000)	$(360,000)	$(480,000)
Present value of cash inflows	336,140	522,970	433,400	567,270
Net present value	$ 66,140	$ 72,970	$ 73,400	$ 87,270
Life of the project	6 years	3 years	12 years	6 years
Internal rate of return	18%	19%	14%	16%

The net present values above have been computed using a 10% discount rate. Limited funds are available for investment, so the company can't accept all of the available projects.

Required:

1.   Compute the profitability index for each investment project.
2.   Rank the four projects according to preference, in terms of:
    a.   Net present value
    b.   Profitability index
    c.   Internal rate of return
3.   Which ranking do you prefer? Why?

PROBLEM 7–22 Net Present Value Analysis LO 7–2

The Sweetwater Candy Company would like to buy a new machine that would automatically "dip" chocolates. The dipping operation currently is done largely by hand. The machine the company is considering costs $120,000. The manufacturer estimates that the machine would be usable for five years but would require the replacement of several key parts at the end of the third year. These parts would cost $9,000, including installation. After five years, the machine could be sold for $7,500.

The company estimates that the cost to operate the machine will be $7,000 per year. The present method of dipping chocolates costs $30,000 per year. In addition to reducing costs, the new machine will increase production by 6,000 boxes of chocolates per year. The company realizes a contribution margin of $1.50 per box. A 20% rate of return is required on all investments.

Required:
1. What are the annual net cash inflows that will be provided by the new dipping machine?
2. Compute the new machine's net present value. Round all dollar amounts to the nearest whole dollar.

PROBLEM 7–23 Comprehensive Problem LO 7–1, LO 7–2, LO 7–3, LO 7–5, LO 7–6

Lou Barlow, a divisional manager for Sage Company, has an opportunity to manufacture and sell one of two new products for a five-year period. His annual pay raises are determined by his division's return on investment (ROI), which has exceeded 18% each of the last three years. He has computed the cost and revenue estimates for each product as follows:

	Product A	Product B
Initial investment:		
Cost of equipment (zero salvage value)	$170,000	$380,000
Annual revenues and costs:		
Sales revenues	$250,000	$350,000
Variable expenses	$120,000	$170,000
Depreciation expense	$34,000	$76,000
Fixed out-of-pocket operating costs	$70,000	$50,000

The company's discount rate is 16%.

Required:
1. Calculate the payback period for each product.
2. Calculate the net present value for each product.
3. Calculate the internal rate of return for each product.
4. Calculate the profitability index for each product.
5. Calculate the simple rate of return for each product.
6. Which of the two products should Lou's division pursue? Why?

PROBLEM 7–24 Simple Rate of Return; Payback Period; Internal Rate of Return LO 7–1, LO 7–3, LO 7–6

The Elberta Fruit Farm of Ontario has always hired transient workers to pick its annual cherry crop. Janessa Wright, the farm manager, just received information on a cherry-picking machine that is being purchased by many fruit farms. The machine is a motorized device that shakes the cherry tree, causing the cherries to fall onto plastic tarps that funnel the cherries into bins. Ms. Wright has gathered the following information to decide whether a cherry picker would be a profitable investment for the Elberta Fruit Farm:
- *a.* Currently, the farm is paying an average of $40,000 per year to transient workers to pick the cherries.
- *b.* The cherry picker would cost $94,500. It would be depreciated using the straight-line method and would have no salvage value at the end of its 12-year useful life.
- *c.* Annual out-of-pocket costs associated with the cherry picker would include the cost of an operator and an assistant, $14,000; insurance, $200; fuel, $1,800; and a maintenance contract, $3,000.

Required:
1. Determine the annual savings in cash operating costs that would be realized if the cherry picker were purchased.
2. Compute the simple rate of return expected from the cherry picker. Would the cherry picker be purchased if Elberta Fruit Farm's required rate of return is 16%?

3.   Compute the payback period on the cherry picker. The Elberta Fruit Farm will not purchase equipment unless it has a payback period of five years or less. Would the cherry picker be purchased?

4.   Compute (to the nearest whole percent) the internal rate of return promised by the cherry picker. Based on this computation, does it appear that the simple rate of return is an accurate guide in investment decisions?

PROBLEM 7–25 Net Present Value Analysis of a Lease or Buy Decision LO 7–2

The Riteway Ad Agency provides cars for its sales staff. In the past, the company has always purchased its cars from a dealer and then sold the cars after three years of use. The company's present fleet of cars is three years old and will be sold very shortly. To provide a replacement fleet, the company is considering two alternatives:

Purchase alternative: The company can purchase the cars, as in the past, and sell the cars after three years of use. Ten cars will be needed, which can be purchased at a discounted price of $17,000 each. If this alternative is accepted, the following costs will be incurred on the fleet as a whole:

Annual cost of servicing, taxes, and licensing	$3,000
Repairs, first year	$1,500
Repairs, second year	$4,000
Repairs, third year	$6,000

At the end of three years, the fleet could be sold for one-half of the original purchase price.

Lease alternative: The company can lease the cars under a three-year lease contract. The lease cost would be $55,000 per year (the first payment due at the end of Year 1). As part of this lease cost, the owner would provide all servicing and repairs, license the cars, and pay all the taxes. Riteway would be required to make a $10,000 security deposit at the beginning of the lease period, which would be refunded when the cars were returned to the owner at the end of the lease contract.

Riteway Ad Agency's required rate of return is 18%.

Required:

1.   What is the net present value of the cash flows associated with the purchase alternative? Round all dollar amounts to the nearest whole dollar.

2.   What is the net present value of the cash flows associated with the lease alternative? Round all dollar amounts to the nearest whole dollar.

3.   Which alternative should the company accept?

PROBLEM 7–26 Simple Rate of Return; Payback LO 7–1, LO 7–6

Sharkey's Fun Center contains a number of electronic games as well as a miniature golf course and various rides located outside the building. Paul Sharkey, the owner, would like to construct a water slide on one portion of his property. Mr. Sharkey gathered the following information about the slide:

    a.   Water slide equipment could be purchased and installed at a cost of $330,000. According to the manufacturer, the slide would be usable for 12 years, after which it would have no salvage value.

    b.   Mr. Sharkey would use straight-line depreciation on the slide equipment.

    c.   To make room for the water slide, several rides would be dismantled and sold. These rides are fully depreciated, but they could be sold for $60,000 to an amusement park in a nearby city.

    d.   Mr. Sharkey concluded that about 50,000 more people would use the water slide each year than have been using the rides. The admission price would be $3.60 per person (the same price the Fun Center has been charging for the old rides).

    e.   Based on experience at other water slides, Mr. Sharkey estimates that annual incremental operating expenses for the slide would include salaries, $85,000; insurance, $4,200; utilities, $13,000; and maintenance, $9,800.

Required:

1.   Prepare an income statement showing the expected net operating income each year from the water slide.

2.   Compute the simple rate of return expected from the water slide. Based on this computation, would the water slide be constructed if Mr. Sharkey requires a simple rate of return of at least 14% on all investments?

3.   Compute the payback period for the water slide. If Mr. Sharkey accepts any project with a payback period of five years or less, would the water slide be constructed?

PROBLEM 7–27 Net Present Value Analysis LO 7–2

Kent Duncan is exploring the possibility of opening a self-service car wash and operating it for the next five years until he retires. He has gathered the following information:

    a. A building in which a car wash could be installed is available under a five-year lease at a cost of $1,700 per month.

    b. Purchase and installation costs of equipment would total $200,000. In five years, the equipment could be sold for about 10% of its original cost.

    c. An investment of an additional $2,000 would be required to cover working capital needs for cleaning supplies, change funds, and so forth. After five years, this working capital would be released for investment elsewhere.

    d. Both a wash and a vacuum service would be offered. Each customer would pay $2.00 for a wash and $1.00 for access to a vacuum cleaner.

    e. The only variable costs associated with the operation would be 20 cents per wash for water and 10 cents per use of the vacuum for electricity.

    f. In addition to rent, monthly costs of operation would include cleaning, $450; insurance, $75; and maintenance, $500.

    g. Gross receipts from the wash would be about $1,350 per week. According to the experience of other car washes, 60% of the customers using the wash would also use the vacuum.

Mr. Duncan will not open the car wash unless it provides at least a 10% return.

Required:

1. Assuming the car wash will be open 52 weeks a year, compute the expected annual net cash receipts (gross cash receipts less cash disbursements) from its operation. (Do not include the cost of the equipment, the working capital, or the salvage value in these computations.)

2. What is the net present value of the investment in the car wash? Would you advise Mr. Duncan to open the car wash? Round all dollar figures to the nearest whole dollar.

PROBLEM 7–28 Net Present Value Analysis LO 7–2

Bilboa Freightlines, S.A., of Panama, has a small truck that it uses for intracity deliveries. The truck is worn out and must be either overhauled or replaced with a new truck. The company assembled the following information:

	Present Truck	New Truck
Purchase cost (new)	$21,000	$30,000
Remaining book value	$11,500	
Overhaul needed now	$7,000	
Annual cash operating costs	$10,000	$6,500
Salvage value—now	$9,000	
Salvage value—five years from now	$1,000	$4,000

If the company keeps and overhauls its present delivery truck, then the truck will be usable for five more years. If a new truck is purchased, it will be used for five years, after which it will be traded in for another truck. The new truck would be diesel-operated, resulting in a substantial reduction in annual operating costs, as shown above.

    The company computes depreciation on a straight-line basis. All investment projects are evaluated using a 16% discount rate.

Required:

1. What is the net present value of the "keep the old truck" alternative? Round to the nearest whole dollar.

2. What is the net present value of the "purchase the new truck" alternative? Round to the nearest whole dollar.

3. Should Bilboa Freightlines keep the old truck or purchase the new one?

PROBLEM 7–29 Net Present Value Analysis LO 7–2

Linda Clark received $175,000 from her mother's estate. She placed the funds into the hands of a broker, who purchased the following securities on Linda's behalf:

    a. Common stock was purchased at a cost of $95,000. The stock paid no dividends, but it was sold for $160,000 at the end of three years.

    b. Preferred stock was purchased at its par value of $30,000. The stock paid a 6% dividend (based on par value) each year for three years. At the end of three years, the stock was sold for $27,000.

c.   Bonds were purchased at a cost of $50,000. The bonds paid annual interest of $6,000. After three years, the bonds were sold for $52,700.

The securities were all sold at the end of three years so that Linda would have funds available to open a new business venture. The broker stated that the investments had earned more than a 16% return, and he gave Linda the following computations to support his statement:

Common stock:	
Gain on sale ($160,000 − $95,000)	$65,000
Preferred stock:	
Dividends paid (6% × $30,000 × 3 years)	5,400
Loss on sale ($27,000 − $30,000)	(3,000)
Bonds:	
Interest paid ($6,000 × 3 years)	18,000
Gain on sale ($52,700 − $50,000)	2,700
Net gain on all investments	$88,100

$$\frac{\$88,100 \div 3 \text{ years}}{\$175,000} = 16.8\%$$

Required:

1.   Using a 16% discount rate, compute the net present value of each of the three investments. On which investment(s) did Linda earn a 16% rate of return? (Round computations to the nearest whole dollar.)
2.   Considering all three investments together, did Linda earn a 16% rate of return? Explain.
3.   Linda wants to use the $239,700 proceeds ($160,000 + $27,000 + $52,700 = $239,700) from sale of the securities to open a retail store under a 12-year franchise contract. What minimum annual net cash inflow must the store generate for Linda to earn a 14% return over the 12-year period? Round computations to the nearest whole dollar.

PROBLEM 7–30 Net Present Value Analysis; Uncertain Future Cash Flows; Postaudit LO 7–2, LO 7–4
Saxon Products, Inc., is investigating the purchase of a robot for use on the company's assembly line. Selected data relating to the robot are provided below:

Cost of the robot	$1,600,000
Installation and software	$450,000
Annual savings in inventory carrying costs	$210,000
Annual increase in power and maintenance costs	$30,000
Salvage value in 5 years	$70,000
Useful life	5 years

In addition to the data above, engineering studies suggest that use of the robot will result in a savings of 25,000 direct labor-hours each year. The labor rate is $16 per hour. Also, the smoother workflow made possible by the use of automation will allow the company to reduce the amount of inventory on hand by $400,000. This inventory reduction will take place at the end of the first year of operation; the released funds will be available for use elsewhere in the company. Saxon Products has a 20% required rate of return.

Required:

1.   Determine the *annual net* cost savings if the robot is purchased. (Do not include the $400,000 inventory reduction or the salvage value in this computation.)
2.   Compute the net present value of the proposed investment in the robot. Based on these data, would you recommend that the robot be purchased? Explain.
3.   Assume the robot is purchased. However, due to unforeseen problems, software and installation costs were $75,000 more than estimated, and direct labor could only be reduced by 22,500 hours per year, rather than the original estimate of 25,000 hours. Assuming that all other cost data are accurate, what would a postaudit suggest is the actual net present value of this investment? Does it appear that the company made a wise investment?
4.   Upon seeing your analysis in (3) above, Saxon's president stated, "That robot is the worst investment we've ever made. And now we'll be stuck with it for years."

a.   Explain to the president what benefits other than cost savings might accrue from using the new automated equipment.

b.   Compute for the president the minimum dollar amount of annual cash inflow that would be needed from the benefits in (*a*) above for the automated equipment to yield a 20% rate of return.

 Cases

Select cases are available in Connect.

CASE 7–31 Ethics and the Manager

The Fore Corporation is an integrated food processing company that has operations in over two dozen countries. Fore's corporate headquarters are in Chicago, and the company's executives frequently travel to visit Fore's foreign and domestic facilities.

Fore has a fleet of aircraft that consists of two business jets with international range and six smaller turboprop aircraft that are used on shorter flights. Company policy is to assign aircraft to trips on the basis of minimizing cost; however, the practice has been to assign the aircraft based on the organizational rank of the traveler. Fore offers its aircraft for short-term lease or for charter by other organizations whenever Fore itself does not plan to use the aircraft. Fore surveys the market often in order to keep its lease and charter rates competitive.

William Earle, Fore's vice president of finance, has claimed that a third business jet can be justified financially. However, some people in the controller's office have surmised that the real reason for a third business jet was to upgrade the aircraft used by Earle. Presently, the people outranking Earle keep the two business jets busy with the result that Earle usually flies in smaller turboprop aircraft.

The third business jet would cost $11 million. A capital expenditure of this magnitude requires a formal proposal with projected cash flows and net present value computations using Fore's minimum required rate of return. If Fore's president and the finance committee of the board of directors approve the proposal, it will be submitted to the full board of directors. The board has final approval on capital expenditures exceeding $5 million and has established a firm policy of rejecting any discretionary proposal that has a negative net present value.

Earle asked Rachel Arnett, assistant corporate controller, to prepare a proposal on a third business jet. Arnett gathered the following data:

- Acquisition cost of the aircraft, including instrumentation and interior furnishing.
- Operating cost of the aircraft for company use.
- Projected avoidable commercial airfare and other avoidable costs from company use of the plane.
- Projected value of executive time saved by using the third business jet.
- Projected contribution margin from incremental lease and charter activity.
- Estimated resale value of the aircraft.

When Earle reviewed Arnett's completed proposal and saw the large negative net present value figure, he returned the proposal to Arnett. With a glare, Earle commented, "You must have made an error. The proposal should look better than that."

Feeling some pressure, Arnett went back and checked her computations; she found no errors. However, Earle's message was clear. Arnett discarded her projections that she believed were reasonable and replaced them with figures that had a remote chance of actually occurring but were more favorable to the proposal. For example, she used first-class airfares to refigure the avoidable commercial airfare costs, even though company policy was to fly coach. She found revising the proposal to be distressing.

The revised proposal still had a negative net present value. Earle's anger was evident as he told Arnett to revise the proposal again and start with a $100,000 positive net present value and work backwards to compute supporting projections.

Required:

1.   Explain whether Rachel Arnett's revision of the proposal was in violation of the IMA's Statement of Ethical Professional Practice.

2.   Was William Earle in violation of the IMA's Statement of Ethical Professional Practice by telling Arnett specifically how to revise the proposal? Explain your answer.

3.   Identify specific internal controls that Fore Corporation could implement to prevent unethical behavior on the part of the vice president of finance.

(CMA, adapted)

CASE 7–32 Net Present Value Analysis of a New Product LO 7–2

Matheson Electronics has just developed a new electronic device it believes will have broad market appeal. The company has performed marketing and cost studies that revealed the following information:

a. New equipment would have to be acquired to produce the device. The equipment would cost $315,000 and have a six-year useful life. After six years, it would have a salvage value of about $15,000.

b. Sales in units over the next six years are projected to be as follows:

Year	Sales in Units
1	9,000
2	15,000
3	18,000
4–6	22,000

c. Production and sales of the device would require working capital of $60,000 to finance accounts receivable, inventories, and day-to-day cash needs. This working capital would be released at the end of the project's life.

d. The devices would sell for $35 each; variable costs for production, administration, and sales would be $15 per unit.

e. Fixed costs for salaries, maintenance, property taxes, insurance, and straight-line depreciation on the equipment would total $135,000 per year. (Depreciation is based on cost less salvage value.)

f. To gain rapid entry into the market, the company would have to advertise heavily. The advertising costs would be:

Year	Amount of Yearly Advertising
1–2	$180,000
3	$150,000
4–6	$120,000

g. The company's required rate of return is 14%.

Required:

1. Compute the net cash inflow (incremental contribution margin minus incremental fixed expenses) anticipated from sale of the device for each year over the next six years.

2. Using the data computed in (1) above and other data provided in the problem, determine the net present value of the proposed investment. Would you recommend that Matheson accept the device as a new product?

Appendix 7A: The Concept of Present Value

LEARNING OBJECTIVE 7–7

Understand present value concepts and the use of present value tables.

A dollar received today is more valuable than a dollar received a year from now for the simple reason that if you have a dollar today, you can put it in the bank and have more than a dollar a year from now. Because dollars today are worth more than dollars in the future, cash flows that are received at different times must be valued differently.

The Mathematics of Interest

If a bank pays 5 percent interest, then a deposit of $100 today will be worth $105 one year from now. This can be expressed as follows:

$$F_1 = P(1 + r) \tag{1}$$

where F_1 = the balance at the end of one period, P = the amount invested now, and r = the rate of interest per period.

In the case where $100 is deposited in a savings account that earns 5% interest, $P = \$100$ and $r = 0.05$. Under these conditions, $F_1 = \$105$.

The $100 present outlay is called the **present value** of the $105 amount to be received in one year. It is also known as the *discounted value* of the future $105 receipt. The $100 represents the value in present terms of $105 to be received a year from now when the interest rate is 5 percent.

Compound Interest What if the $105 is left in the bank for a second year? In that case, by the end of the second year, the original $100 deposit will have grown to $110.25:

Original deposit	$100.00
Interest for the first year: $100 × 0.05	5.00
Balance at the end of the first year	105.00
Interest for the second year: $105 × 0.05	5.25
Balance at the end of the second year	$110.25

Notice that the interest for the second year is $5.25, as compared to only $5.00 for the first year. This difference arises because interest is being paid on interest during the second year. That is, the $5.00 interest earned during the first year has been left in the account and has been added to the original $100 deposit when computing interest for the second year. This is known as **compound interest.** In this case, the compounding is annual. Interest can be compounded on a semiannual, quarterly, monthly, or even more frequent basis. The more frequently compounding is done, the more rapidly the balance will grow.

We can determine the balance in an account after n periods of compounding using the following equation:

$$F_n = P(1 + r)^n \qquad (2)$$

where $n =$ the number of periods of compounding.

If $n = 2$ years and the interest rate is 5% per year, then the balance in two years will be computed as follows:

$$F_2 = \$100 (1 + 0.05)^2$$
$$F_2 = \$110.25$$

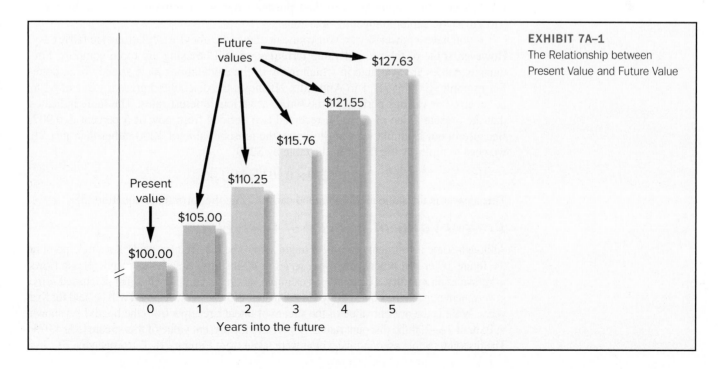

EXHIBIT 7A–1
The Relationship between Present Value and Future Value

Present Value and Future Value   Exhibit 7A–1 shows the relationship between present value and future value. As shown in the exhibit, if $100 is deposited in a bank at 5% interest compounded annually, it will grow to $127.63 by the end of five years.

Computation of Present Value

An investment can be viewed in two ways—either in terms of its future value or in terms of its present value. We have seen from our computations above that if we know the present value of a sum (such as our $100 deposit), the future value in n years can be computed by using equation (2). But what if the situation is reversed and we know the *future* value of some amount, but we do not know its present value?

For example, assume you are to receive $200 two years from now. You know that the future value of this sum is $200 because this is the amount that you will be receiving in two years. But what is the sum's present value—what is it worth *right now?* The present value of any sum to be received in the future can be computed by turning equation (2) around and solving for P:

$$P = \frac{F_n}{(1 + r)^n} \tag{3}$$

In our example, $F_n = \$200$ (the amount to be received in the future), $r = 0.05$ (the annual rate of interest), and $n = 2$ (the number of years in the future that the amount will be received).

$$P = \frac{\$200}{(1 + 0.05)^2}$$

$$P = \frac{\$200}{1.1025}$$

$$P = \$181.40$$

As shown by the computation above, the present value of a $200 amount to be received two years from now is $181.40 if the interest rate is 5 percent. In effect, $181.40 received *right now* is equivalent to $200 received two years from now.

The process of finding the present value of a future cash flow, which we have just completed, is called **discounting.** We have *discounted* the $200 to its present value of $181.40. The 5 percent interest we used to find this present value is called the **discount rate.** Discounting future sums to their present value is a common practice in business, particularly in capital budgeting decisions.

If you have a power key (y^x) on your calculator, the above calculations are fairly easy. However, some of the present value formulas we will be using are more complex. Fortunately, tables are available in which many of the calculations have already been done. For example, Exhibit 7B–1 in Appendix 7B shows the discounted present value of $1 to be received at various periods in the future at various interest rates. The table indicates that the present value of $1 to be received two periods from now at 5 percent is 0.907. Because in our example we want to know the present value of $200 rather than just $1, we need to multiply the factor in the table by $200:

$$\$200 \times 0.907 = \$181.40$$

This answer is the same as we obtained earlier using the formula in equation (3).

Present Value of a Series of Cash Flows

Although some investments involve a single sum to be received (or paid) at a single point in the future, other investments involve a *series* of cash flows. A series of identical cash flows is known as an **annuity.** To provide an example, assume a company has just purchased some government bonds. The bonds will yield interest of $15,000 each year and will be held for five years. What is the present value of the stream of interest receipts from the bonds? As shown in Exhibit 7A–2, if the discount rate is 12 percent, the present value of this stream is $54,075. The discount factors used in this exhibit were taken from Exhibit 7B–1 in Appendix 7B.

Year	Factor at 12% (Exhibit 7B–1)	Interest Received	Present Value
1	0.893	$15,000	$13,395
2	0.797	$15,000	11,955
3	0.712	$15,000	10,680
4	0.636	$15,000	9,540
5	0.567	$15,000	8,505
			$54,075

EXHIBIT 7A–2
Present Value of a Series of Cash Receipts

Exhibit 7A–2 illustrates two important points. First, the present value of the $15,000 interest declines the further it is into the future. The present value of $15,000 received a year from now is $13,395 compared to only $8,505 if received five years from now. This point underscores the time value of money.

The second point is that the computations used in Exhibit 7A–2 involved unnecessary work. The same present value of $54,075 could have been obtained more easily by referring to Exhibit 7B–2 in Appendix 7B. Exhibit 7B–2 contains the present value of $1 to be received each year over a *series* of years at various interest rates. Exhibit 7B–2 has been derived by simply adding together the factors from Exhibit 7B–1, as follows:

Year	Factors at 12% (from Exhibit 7B–1)
1	0.893
2	0.797
3	0.712
4	0.636
5	0.567
	3.605

The sum of these five factors is 3.605. Notice from Exhibit 7B–2 that the factor for $1 to be received each year for five years at 12 percent is also 3.605. If we use this factor and multiply it by the $15,000 annual cash inflow, then we get the same $54,075 present value that we obtained earlier in Exhibit 7A–2.

$$\$15,000 \times 3.605 = \$54,075$$

Therefore, when computing the present value of a series of equal cash flows that begins at the end of period 1, Exhibit 7B–2 should be used.

To summarize, the present value tables in Appendix 7B should be used as follows:

Exhibit 7B–1: This table should be used to find the present value of a single cash flow (such as a single payment or receipt) occurring in the future.

Exhibit 7B–2: This table should be used to find the present value of a series of identical cash flows beginning at the end of the current period and continuing into the future.

The use of both of these tables is illustrated in various exhibits in the main body of the chapter. *When a present value factor appears in an exhibit, you should take the time to trace it back into either Exhibit 7B–1 or Exhibit 7B–2 to get acquainted with the tables and how they work.*

Appendix 7A: Review Problem: Basic Present Value Computations

Each of the following situations is independent. Work out your own solution to each situation, and then check it against the solution provided.

1. John plans to retire in 12 years. Upon retiring, he would like to take an extended vacation, which he expects will cost at least $40,000. What lump-sum amount must he invest now to have $40,000 at the end of 12 years if the rate of return is:
    a.   Eight percent?
    b.   Twelve percent?

2. The Morgans would like to send their daughter to a music camp at the end of each of the next five years. The camp costs $1,000 a year. What lump-sum amount would have to be invested now to have $1,000 at the end of each year if the rate of return is:
    a.   Eight percent?
    b.   Twelve percent?

3. You have just received an inheritance from a relative. You can either receive a $200,000 lump-sum amount at the end of 10 years or receive $14,000 at the end of each year for the next 10 years. If your discount rate is 12%, which alternative would you prefer?

Solution to Review Problem

1. a.   The amount that must be invested now would be the present value of the $40,000, using a discount rate of 8%. From Exhibit 7B–1 in Appendix 7B, the factor for a discount rate of 8% for 12 periods is 0.397. Multiplying this discount factor by the $40,000 needed in 12 years will give the amount of the present investment required: $40,000 × 0.397 = $15,880.
    b.   We will proceed as we did in (a) above, but this time we will use a discount rate of 12%. From Exhibit 7B–1 in Appendix 7B, the factor for a discount rate of 12% for 12 periods is 0.257. Multiplying this discount factor by the $40,000 needed in 12 years will give the amount of the present investment required: $40,000 × 0.257 = $10,280.

    Notice that as the discount rate (desired rate of return) increases, the present value decreases.

2. This part differs from (1) above in that we are now dealing with an annuity rather than with a single future sum. The amount that must be invested now is the present value of the $1,000 needed at the end of each year for five years. Because we are dealing with an annuity, or a series of annual cash flows, we must refer to Exhibit 7B–2 in Appendix 7B for the appropriate discount factor.
    a.   From Exhibit 7B–2 in Appendix 7B, the discount factor for 8% for five periods is 3.993. Therefore, the amount that must be invested now to have $1,000 available at the end of each year for five years is $1,000 × 3.993 = $3,993.
    b.   From Exhibit 7B–2 in Appendix 7B, the discount factor for 12% for five periods is 3.605. Therefore, the amount that must be invested now to have $1,000 available at the end of each year for five years is $1,000 × 3.605 = $3,605.

    Again, notice that as the discount rate increases, the present value decreases. When the rate of return increases, less must be invested today to yield a given amount in the future.

3. For this part, we will need to refer to both Exhibits 7B–1 and 7B–2 in Appendix 7B. From Exhibit 7B–1, we will need to find the discount factor for 12% for 10 periods, then apply it to the $200,000 lump sum to be received in 10 years. From Exhibit 7B–2, we will need to find the discount factor for 12% for 10 periods, then apply it to the series of $14,000 payments to be received over the 10-year period. Whichever alternative has the higher present value is the one that should be selected.

    $$\$200,000 \times 0.322 = \$64,400$$
    $$\$14,000 \times 5.650 = \$79,100$$

    Thus, you should prefer to receive the $14,000 per year for 10 years rather than the $200,000 lump sum. This means that you could invest the $14,000 received at the end of each year at 12% and have *more* than $200,000 at the end of 10 years.

Glossary (Appendix 7A)

Annuity A series of identical cash flows. (p. 390)

Compound interest The process of paying interest on interest in an investment. (p. 389)

Discount rate The rate of return that is used to find the present value of a future cash flow. (p. 390)

Discounting The process of finding the present value of a future cash flow. (p. 390)

Present value The value now of an amount that will be received in some future period. (p. 389)

EXERCISE 7A–1 Basic Present Value Concepts LO 7–7

Annual cash inflows from two competing investment projects are given below:

Year	Investment A	Investment B
1....................	$ 3,000	$12,000
2....................	6,000	9,000
3....................	9,000	6,000
4....................	12,000	3,000
	$30,000	$30,000

The discount rate is 18%.

Required:

Compute the present value of the cash inflows for each investment.

EXERCISE 7A–2 Basic Present Value Concepts LO 7–7

Julie has just retired. Her company's retirement program has two options as to how retirement benefits can be received. Under the first option, Julie would receive a lump sum of $150,000 immediately as her full retirement benefit. Under the second option, she would receive $14,000 each year for 20 years plus a lump-sum payment of $60,000 at the end of the 20-year period.

Required:

If she can invest money at 12%, which option would you recommend that she accept? Use present value analysis.

EXERCISE 7A–3 Basic Present Value Concepts LO 7–7

In three years, when he is discharged from the Air Force, Steve wants to buy an $8,000 power boat.

Required:

What lump-sum amount must Steve invest now to have the $8,000 at the end of three years if he can invest money at:
1. Ten percent?
2. Fourteen percent?

EXERCISE 7A–4 Basic Present Value Concepts LO 7–7

Fraser Company will need a new warehouse in five years. The warehouse will cost $500,000 to build.

Required:

What lump-sum amount should the company invest now to have the $500,000 available at the end of the five-year period? Assume the company can invest money at:
1. Ten percent.
2. Fourteen percent.

EXERCISE 7A–5 Basic Present Value Concepts LO 7–7

The Atlantic Medical Clinic can purchase a new computer system that will save $7,000 annually in billing costs. The computer system will last for eight years and have no salvage value.

Required:

What is the maximum price (i.e., the price that exactly equals the present value of the annual savings in billing costs) that the Atlantic Medical Clinic should be willing to pay for the new computer system if the clinic's required rate of return is:
1. Sixteen percent?
2. Twenty percent?

EXERCISE 7A–6 Basic Present Value Concepts LO 7–7

The *Caldwell Herald* newspaper reported the following story: Frank Ormsby of Caldwell is the state's newest millionaire. By choosing the six winning numbers on last week's state lottery, Mr. Ormsby won the week's grand prize totaling $1.6 million. The State Lottery Commission indicated Mr. Ormsby would receive his prize in 20 annual installments of $80,000 each.

Required:

1. If Mr. Ormsby can invest money at a 12% rate of return, what is the present value of his winnings?
2. Is it correct to say that Mr. Ormsby is the "state's newest millionaire"? Explain your answer.

Appendix 7B: Present Value Tables

EXHIBIT 7B-1
Present Value of $1: $\frac{1}{(1+r)^n}$

Periods	4%	5%	6%	7%	8%	9%	10%	11%	12%	13%	14%	15%	16%	17%	18%	19%	20%	21%	22%	23%	24%	25%
1	0.962	0.952	0.943	0.935	0.926	0.917	0.909	0.901	0.893	0.885	0.877	0.870	0.862	0.855	0.847	0.840	0.833	0.826	0.820	0.813	0.806	0.800
2	0.925	0.907	0.890	0.873	0.857	0.842	0.826	0.812	0.797	0.783	0.769	0.756	0.743	0.731	0.718	0.706	0.694	0.683	0.672	0.661	0.650	0.640
3	0.889	0.864	0.840	0.816	0.794	0.772	0.751	0.731	0.712	0.693	0.675	0.658	0.641	0.624	0.609	0.593	0.579	0.564	0.551	0.537	0.524	0.512
4	0.855	0.823	0.792	0.763	0.735	0.708	0.683	0.659	0.636	0.613	0.592	0.572	0.552	0.534	0.516	0.499	0.482	0.467	0.451	0.437	0.423	0.410
5	0.822	0.784	0.747	0.713	0.681	0.650	0.621	0.593	0.567	0.543	0.519	0.497	0.476	0.456	0.437	0.419	0.402	0.386	0.370	0.355	0.341	0.328
6	0.790	0.746	0.705	0.666	0.630	0.596	0.564	0.535	0.507	0.480	0.456	0.432	0.410	0.390	0.370	0.352	0.335	0.319	0.303	0.289	0.275	0.262
7	0.760	0.711	0.665	0.623	0.583	0.547	0.513	0.482	0.452	0.425	0.400	0.376	0.354	0.333	0.314	0.296	0.279	0.263	0.249	0.235	0.222	0.210
8	0.731	0.677	0.627	0.582	0.540	0.502	0.467	0.434	0.404	0.376	0.351	0.327	0.305	0.285	0.266	0.249	0.233	0.218	0.204	0.191	0.179	0.168
9	0.703	0.645	0.592	0.544	0.500	0.460	0.424	0.391	0.361	0.333	0.308	0.284	0.263	0.243	0.225	0.209	0.194	0.180	0.167	0.155	0.144	0.134
10	0.676	0.614	0.558	0.508	0.463	0.422	0.386	0.352	0.322	0.295	0.270	0.247	0.227	0.208	0.191	0.176	0.162	0.149	0.137	0.126	0.116	0.107
11	0.650	0.585	0.527	0.475	0.429	0.388	0.350	0.317	0.287	0.261	0.237	0.215	0.195	0.178	0.162	0.148	0.135	0.123	0.112	0.103	0.094	0.086
12	0.625	0.557	0.497	0.444	0.397	0.356	0.319	0.286	0.257	0.231	0.208	0.187	0.168	0.152	0.137	0.124	0.112	0.102	0.092	0.083	0.076	0.069
13	0.601	0.530	0.469	0.415	0.368	0.326	0.290	0.258	0.229	0.204	0.182	0.163	0.145	0.130	0.116	0.104	0.093	0.084	0.075	0.068	0.061	0.055
14	0.577	0.505	0.442	0.388	0.340	0.299	0.263	0.232	0.205	0.181	0.160	0.141	0.125	0.111	0.099	0.088	0.078	0.069	0.062	0.055	0.049	0.044
15	0.555	0.481	0.417	0.362	0.315	0.275	0.239	0.209	0.183	0.160	0.140	0.123	0.108	0.095	0.084	0.074	0.065	0.057	0.051	0.045	0.040	0.035
16	0.534	0.458	0.394	0.339	0.292	0.252	0.218	0.188	0.163	0.141	0.123	0.107	0.093	0.081	0.071	0.062	0.054	0.047	0.042	0.036	0.032	0.028
17	0.513	0.436	0.371	0.317	0.270	0.231	0.198	0.170	0.146	0.125	0.108	0.093	0.080	0.069	0.060	0.052	0.045	0.039	0.034	0.030	0.026	0.023
18	0.494	0.416	0.350	0.296	0.250	0.212	0.180	0.153	0.130	0.111	0.095	0.081	0.069	0.059	0.051	0.044	0.038	0.032	0.028	0.024	0.021	0.018
19	0.475	0.396	0.331	0.277	0.232	0.194	0.164	0.138	0.116	0.098	0.083	0.070	0.060	0.051	0.043	0.037	0.031	0.027	0.023	0.020	0.017	0.014
20	0.456	0.377	0.312	0.258	0.215	0.178	0.149	0.124	0.104	0.087	0.073	0.061	0.051	0.043	0.037	0.031	0.026	0.022	0.019	0.016	0.014	0.012
21	0.439	0.359	0.294	0.242	0.199	0.164	0.135	0.112	0.093	0.077	0.064	0.053	0.044	0.037	0.031	0.026	0.022	0.018	0.015	0.013	0.011	0.009
22	0.422	0.342	0.278	0.226	0.184	0.150	0.123	0.101	0.083	0.068	0.056	0.046	0.038	0.032	0.026	0.022	0.018	0.015	0.013	0.011	0.009	0.007
23	0.406	0.326	0.262	0.211	0.170	0.138	0.112	0.091	0.074	0.060	0.049	0.040	0.033	0.027	0.022	0.018	0.015	0.012	0.010	0.009	0.007	0.006
24	0.390	0.310	0.247	0.197	0.158	0.126	0.102	0.082	0.066	0.053	0.043	0.035	0.028	0.023	0.019	0.015	0.013	0.010	0.008	0.007	0.006	0.005
25	0.375	0.295	0.233	0.184	0.146	0.116	0.092	0.074	0.059	0.047	0.038	0.030	0.024	0.020	0.016	0.013	0.010	0.009	0.007	0.006	0.005	0.004
26	0.361	0.281	0.220	0.172	0.135	0.106	0.084	0.066	0.053	0.042	0.033	0.026	0.021	0.017	0.014	0.011	0.009	0.007	0.006	0.005	0.004	0.003
27	0.347	0.268	0.207	0.161	0.125	0.098	0.076	0.060	0.047	0.037	0.029	0.023	0.018	0.014	0.011	0.009	0.007	0.006	0.005	0.004	0.003	0.002
28	0.333	0.255	0.196	0.150	0.116	0.090	0.069	0.054	0.042	0.033	0.026	0.020	0.016	0.012	0.010	0.008	0.006	0.005	0.004	0.003	0.002	0.002
29	0.321	0.243	0.185	0.141	0.107	0.082	0.063	0.048	0.037	0.029	0.022	0.017	0.014	0.011	0.008	0.006	0.005	0.004	0.003	0.002	0.002	0.002
30	0.308	0.231	0.174	0.131	0.099	0.075	0.057	0.044	0.033	0.026	0.020	0.015	0.012	0.009	0.007	0.005	0.004	0.003	0.003	0.002	0.002	0.001
40	0.208	0.142	0.097	0.067	0.046	0.032	0.022	0.015	0.011	0.008	0.005	0.004	0.003	0.002	0.001	0.001	0.001	0.000	0.000	0.000	0.000	0.000

EXHIBIT 7B-2

Present Value of an Annuity of $1 in Arrears; $\dfrac{1}{r}\left[1 - \dfrac{1}{(1+r)^n}\right]$

Periods	4%	5%	6%	7%	8%	9%	10%	11%	12%	13%	14%	15%	16%	17%	18%	19%	20%	21%	22%	23%	24%	25%
1	0.962	0.952	0.943	0.935	0.926	0.917	0.909	0.901	0.893	0.885	0.877	0.870	0.862	0.855	0.847	0.840	0.833	0.826	0.820	0.813	0.806	0.800
2	1.886	1.859	1.833	1.808	1.783	1.759	1.736	1.713	1.690	1.668	1.647	1.626	1.605	1.585	1.566	1.547	1.528	1.509	1.492	1.474	1.457	1.440
3	2.775	2.723	2.673	2.624	2.577	2.531	2.487	2.444	2.402	2.361	2.322	2.283	2.246	2.210	2.174	2.140	2.106	2.074	2.042	2.011	1.981	1.952
4	3.630	3.546	3.465	3.387	3.312	3.240	3.170	3.102	3.037	2.974	2.914	2.855	2.798	2.743	2.690	2.639	2.589	2.540	2.494	2.448	2.404	2.362
5	4.452	4.329	4.212	4.100	3.993	3.890	3.791	3.696	3.605	3.517	3.433	3.352	3.274	3.199	3.127	3.058	2.991	2.926	2.864	2.803	2.745	2.689
6	5.242	5.076	4.917	4.767	4.623	4.486	4.355	4.231	4.111	3.998	3.889	3.784	3.685	3.589	3.498	3.410	3.326	3.245	3.167	3.092	3.020	2.951
7	6.002	5.786	5.582	5.389	5.206	5.033	4.868	4.712	4.564	4.423	4.288	4.160	4.039	3.922	3.812	3.706	3.605	3.508	3.416	3.327	3.242	3.161
8	6.733	6.463	6.210	5.971	5.747	5.535	5.335	5.146	4.968	4.799	4.639	4.487	4.344	4.207	4.078	3.954	3.837	3.726	3.619	3.518	3.421	3.329
9	7.435	7.108	6.802	6.515	6.247	5.995	5.759	5.537	5.328	5.132	4.946	4.772	4.607	4.451	4.303	4.163	4.031	3.905	3.786	3.673	3.566	3.463
10	8.111	7.722	7.360	7.024	6.710	6.418	6.145	5.889	5.650	5.426	5.216	5.019	4.833	4.659	4.494	4.339	4.192	4.054	3.923	3.799	3.682	3.571
11	8.760	8.306	7.887	7.499	7.139	6.805	6.495	6.207	5.938	5.687	5.453	5.234	5.029	4.836	4.656	4.486	4.327	4.177	4.035	3.902	3.776	3.656
12	9.385	8.863	8.384	7.943	7.536	7.161	6.814	6.492	6.194	5.918	5.660	5.421	5.197	4.988	4.793	4.611	4.439	4.278	4.127	3.985	3.851	3.725
13	9.986	9.394	8.853	8.358	7.904	7.487	7.103	6.750	6.424	6.122	5.842	5.583	5.342	5.118	4.910	4.715	4.533	4.362	4.203	4.053	3.912	3.780
14	10.563	9.899	9.295	8.745	8.244	7.786	7.367	6.982	6.628	6.302	6.002	5.724	5.468	5.229	5.008	4.802	4.611	4.432	4.265	4.108	3.962	3.824
15	11.118	10.380	9.712	9.108	8.559	8.061	7.606	7.191	6.811	6.462	6.142	5.847	5.575	5.324	5.092	4.876	4.675	4.489	4.315	4.153	4.001	3.859
16	11.652	10.838	10.106	9.447	8.851	8.313	7.824	7.379	6.974	6.604	6.265	5.954	5.668	5.405	5.162	4.938	4.730	4.536	4.357	4.189	4.033	3.887
17	12.166	11.274	10.477	9.763	9.122	8.544	8.022	7.549	7.120	6.729	6.373	6.047	5.749	5.475	5.222	4.990	4.775	4.576	4.391	4.219	4.059	3.910
18	12.659	11.690	10.828	10.059	9.372	8.756	8.201	7.702	7.250	6.840	6.467	6.128	5.818	5.534	5.273	5.033	4.812	4.608	4.419	4.243	4.080	3.928
19	13.134	12.085	11.158	10.336	9.604	8.950	8.365	7.839	7.366	6.938	6.550	6.198	5.877	5.584	5.316	5.070	4.843	4.635	4.442	4.263	4.097	3.942
20	13.590	12.462	11.470	10.594	9.818	9.129	8.514	7.963	7.469	7.025	6.623	6.259	5.929	5.628	5.353	5.101	4.870	4.657	4.460	4.279	4.110	3.954
21	14.029	12.821	11.764	10.836	10.017	9.292	8.649	8.075	7.562	7.102	6.687	6.312	5.973	5.665	5.384	5.127	4.891	4.675	4.476	4.292	4.121	3.963
22	14.451	13.163	12.042	11.061	10.201	9.442	8.772	8.176	7.645	7.170	6.743	6.359	6.011	5.696	5.410	5.149	4.909	4.690	4.488	4.302	4.130	3.970
23	14.857	13.489	12.303	11.272	10.371	9.580	8.883	8.266	7.718	7.230	6.792	6.399	6.044	5.723	5.432	5.167	4.925	4.703	4.499	4.311	4.137	3.976
24	15.247	13.799	12.550	11.469	10.529	9.707	8.985	8.348	7.784	7.283	6.835	6.434	6.073	5.746	5.451	5.182	4.937	4.713	4.507	4.318	4.143	3.981
25	15.622	14.094	12.783	11.654	10.675	9.823	9.077	8.422	7.843	7.330	6.873	6.464	6.097	5.766	5.467	5.195	4.948	4.721	4.514	4.323	4.147	3.985
26	15.983	14.375	13.003	11.826	10.810	9.929	9.161	8.488	7.896	7.372	6.906	6.491	6.118	5.783	5.480	5.206	4.956	4.728	4.520	4.328	4.151	3.988
27	16.330	14.643	13.211	11.987	10.935	10.027	9.237	8.548	7.943	7.409	6.935	6.514	6.136	5.798	5.492	5.215	4.964	4.734	4.524	4.332	4.154	3.990
28	16.663	14.898	13.406	12.137	11.051	10.116	9.307	8.602	7.984	7.441	6.961	6.534	6.152	5.810	5.502	5.223	4.970	4.739	4.528	4.335	4.157	3.992
29	16.984	15.141	13.591	12.278	11.158	10.198	9.370	8.650	8.022	7.470	6.983	6.551	6.166	5.820	5.510	5.229	4.975	4.743	4.531	4.337	4.159	3.994
30	17.292	15.372	13.765	12.409	11.258	10.274	9.427	8.694	8.055	7.496	7.003	6.566	6.177	5.829	5.517	5.235	4.979	4.746	4.534	4.339	4.160	3.995
40	19.793	17.159	15.046	13.332	11.925	10.757	9.779	8.951	8.244	7.634	7.105	6.642	6.233	5.871	5.548	5.258	4.997	4.760	4.544	4.347	4.166	3.999

Appendix 7C: Income Taxes and the Net Present Value Method

This appendix discusses the impact of income taxes on the net present value method of making capital budgeting decisions. We ignored income taxes throughout the chapter for two reasons. First, many organizations do not pay income taxes. Nonprofit organizations, such as hospitals and charitable foundations, and government agencies are exempt from income taxes. Second, capital budgeting is complex and best absorbed in small doses. Now that we have a solid foundation in the concept of discounting cash flows, we can explore the impact of income taxes on the net present value method.

To keep this discussion within reasonable bounds, we make three simplifying assumptions. First, although the tax law allows companies to expense the entire cost of some fixed assets in the year the assets are placed into service, we will assume a company's taxable income equals its net income for financial reporting purposes and that the company always uses straight-line depreciation with zero salvage value. Second, we assume a flat tax rate of 30% (a 21% federal income tax rate plus 9% for state and local income taxes). Third, we assume there are no gains or losses on the sale of noncurrent assets.

Key Concepts

This appendix takes everything you have already learned about the net present value method and simply adds one more type of cash flow to the computations—it adds income tax expense as a *cash outflow*. To calculate the amount of income tax expense associated with a capital budgeting project, we'll be using a two-step process. The first step is to calculate the incremental net income earned during each year of the project. The second step is to multiply each year's incremental net income by the tax rate to determine the income tax expense. Each year's income tax expense is then discounted to its present value along with all other cash flows realized over the life of the project.

A capital budgeting project's incremental net income computation *includes* annual revenues minus annual cash operating expenses (including variable expenses and fixed out-of-pocket costs), annual depreciation expense, and any one-time expenses. Notice that *depreciation expense is included in the computation of incremental net income.* Although depreciation expense is a noncash expense, it does impact the computation of taxable income, which in turn affects the cash outflows pertaining to income tax expense. A capital budgeting project's incremental net income computation *does not include* immediate cash outflows in the form of initial investments in equipment, other assets, and installation costs. It also *does not include* investments in working capital, the release of working capital at the end of a project, and the proceeds from selling a noncurrent asset when no gain or loss is realized on the sale.

To summarize, the items that should be included and excluded from a capital budgeting project's incremental net income computations are as follows:

Include in the computation of incremental net income:
Annual revenues
Annual cash operating expenses
Annual depreciation expense
One-time expenses

Exclude from the computation of incremental net income:
Initial investments in equipment, other assets, and installation costs
Investment in working capital
Release of working capital at the end of a project
Proceeds from selling noncurrent assets when no gain or loss is realized

Income Taxes and Net Present Value Analysis: An Example

Holland Company owns the mineral rights to land that has a deposit of ore. The company is uncertain if it should purchase equipment and open a mine on the property. After careful study, the company gathered the following data:

Initial investment in equipment..............................	$275,000
Initial investment in working capital.........................	$50,000
Estimated annual sales of ore...............................	$250,000
Estimated annual cash operating expenses..................	$150,000
Cost of road repairs needed in 3 years......................	$30,000

The ore in the mine would be exhausted after five years, at which time the mine would be closed, and the working capital would be released and redeployed by the company. The equipment has a useful life of five years and a salvage value of zero. The company uses straight-line depreciation for financial reporting and tax purposes. Its after-tax cost of capital is 12 percent, and its tax rate is 30 percent. To be consistent, when we take the net present value of after-tax cash flows, we use the *after-tax* cost of capital as the discount rate.

Should Holland Company purchase the equipment and open a mine on the property? Exhibit 7C–1 shows a net present value analysis that incorporates the impact of income taxes on this decision. The top portion of the exhibit computes the project's incremental net income for Years 1–5 and the income tax expense for each of those years. The incremental net income computations include the annual sales ($250,000), the annual cash operating expenses ($150,000), the road repairs in Year 3 ($30,000), and the annual depreciation expense of $55,000 ($275,000 ÷ 5 years = $55,000 per year). Each year's incremental net income is multiplied by the tax rate of 30 percent to determine the income tax expense.

The bottom portion of Exhibit 7C–1 calculates the net present value of the mining project. The cash flows summarized in this portion of the exhibit include the initial outlays for

EXHIBIT 7C–1
Holland Company: Income Taxes and Net Present Value Analysis

the purchase of equipment ($275,000) and the investment in working capital ($50,000), the annual sales ($250,000), the annual cash operating expenses ($150,000), the road repairs in Year 3 ($30,000), the release of working capital in Year 5 ($50,000), and the annual income tax expense. Notice that the amounts of income tax expense shown in cells C19 through G19 come directly from the calculations previously performed in cells C10 through G10. Each year's total cash flows in cells B20 through G20 are multiplied by the appropriate discount factor for 12 percent to compute their present value. The present values in cells B22 through G22 are combined to determine the project's net present value of $231. Because the net present value is positive, it indicates that Holland Company should proceed with the mining project.

Summary (Appendix 7C)

Unless the organization is tax-exempt, such as a nonprofit school or a governmental body, income taxes should be considered when using net present value analysis to make capital budgeting decisions. Calculating the amount of income tax expense associated with a capital budgeting project is a two-step process. The first step is to calculate the incremental net income earned during each year of the project. The second step is to multiply each year's incremental net income by the tax rate to determine the income tax expense. Each year's income tax expense is then discounted to its present value along with all other cash flows realized over the life of the project.

A capital budgeting project's incremental net income computation includes annual revenues minus annual cash operating expenses, annual depreciation expense, and any one-time expenses. It does not include immediate cash outflows in the form of initial investments in equipment, other assets, and installation costs, as well as investments in working capital, the release of working capital at the end of a project, and the proceeds from selling a noncurrent asset where no gain or loss is realized on the sale.

Appendix 7C: Exercises and Problems

EXERCISE 7C–1 Income Taxes and Net Present Value Analysis LO 7–8
Gaston Company is considering a capital budgeting project that would require a $2,000,000 investment in equipment with a useful life of five years and no salvage value. The company's tax rate is 30%, and its after-tax cost of capital is 13%. It uses the straight-line depreciation method for financial reporting and tax purposes. The project would provide net operating income each year for five years as follows:

Sales		$2,800,000
Variable expenses		1,600,000
Contribution margin		1,200,000
Fixed expenses:		
Advertising, salaries, and other fixed		
out-of-pocket costs	$500,000	
Depreciation	400,000	
Total fixed expenses		900,000
Net operating income		$ 300,000

Required:
Compute the project's net present value.

EXERCISE 7C–2 Income Taxes and Net Present Value Analysis LO 7–8
Winthrop Company has an opportunity to manufacture and sell a new product for a five-year period. To pursue this opportunity, the company would need to purchase a piece of equipment for $130,000. The equipment would have a useful life of five years and zero salvage value. It would be

depreciated for financial reporting and tax purposes using the straight-line method. After careful study, Winthrop estimated the following annual costs and revenues for the new product:

Annual revenues and costs:	
Sales revenues	$250,000
Variable expenses	$120,000
Fixed out-of-pocket operating costs	$70,000

The company's tax rate is 30% and its after-tax cost of capital is 15%.

Required:
1. Calculate the annual income tax expense that will arise as a result of this investment.
2. Calculate the net present value of this investment opportunity.

PROBLEM 7C–3 Income Taxes and Net Present Value Analysis LO 7–8
Lander Company has an opportunity to pursue a capital budgeting project with a five-year time horizon. After careful study, Lander estimated the following costs and revenues for the project:

Cost of equipment needed	$250,000
Working capital needed	$60,000
Repair the equipment in two years	$18,000
Annual revenues and costs:	
Sales revenues	$350,000
Variable expenses	$180,000
Fixed out-of-pocket operating costs	$80,000

The piece of equipment mentioned above has a useful life of five years and zero salvage value. Lander uses straight-line depreciation for financial reporting and tax purposes. The company's tax rate is 30%, and its after-tax cost of capital is 12%. When the project concludes in five years, the working capital will be released for investment elsewhere within the company.

Required:
1. Calculate the annual income tax expense for each of years 1 through 5 that will arise as a result of this investment opportunity.
2. Calculate the net present value of this investment opportunity.

PROBLEM 7C–4 Income Taxes and Net Present Value Analysis LO 7–8
Rosman Company has an opportunity to pursue a capital budgeting project with a five-year time horizon. After careful study, Rosman estimated the following costs and revenues for the project:

Cost of new equipment needed	$420,000
Sale of old equipment no longer needed	$80,000
Working capital needed	$65,000
Equipment maintenance in each of Years 3 and 4	$20,000
Annual revenues and costs:	
Sales revenues	$410,000
Variable expenses	$175,000
Fixed out-of-pocket operating costs	$100,000

The new piece of equipment mentioned above has a useful life of five years and zero salvage value. The old piece of equipment mentioned above would be sold at the beginning of the project, and there would be no gain or loss realized on its sale. Rosman uses the straight-line depreciation method for financial reporting and tax purposes. The company's tax rate is 30%, and its after-tax cost of capital is 12%. When the project concludes in five years, the working capital will be released for investment elsewhere within the company.

Required:
1. Calculate the annual income tax expense for each of years 1 through 5 that will arise as a result of this investment opportunity.
2. Calculate the net present value of this investment opportunity.

PROBLEM 7C–5 Income Taxes and Net Present Value Analysis LO 7–5, LO 7–8

Shimano Company has an opportunity to manufacture and sell one of two new products for a five-year period. The company's tax rate is 30% and its after-tax cost of capital is 14%. The cost and revenue estimates for each product are as follows:

	Product A	Product B
Initial investment in equipment	$400,000	$550,000
Initial investment in working capital	$85,000	$60,000
Annual sales	$370,000	$390,000
Annual cash operating expenses	$200,000	$170,000
Cost of repairs needed in three years	$45,000	$70,000

The equipment pertaining to both products has a useful life of five years and no salvage value. The company uses the straight-line depreciation method for financial reporting and tax purposes. At the end of five years, each product's working capital will be released for investment elsewhere within the company.

Required:

1. Calculate the annual income tax expense for each of years 1 through 5 that will arise if Product A is introduced.
2. Calculate the net present value of the investment opportunity pertaining to Product A.
3. Calculate the annual income tax expense for each of years 1 through 5 that will arise if Product B is introduced.
4. Calculate the net present value of the investment opportunity pertaining to Product B.
5. Calculate the profitability index for Product A and Product B. Which of the two products should the company pursue? Why?

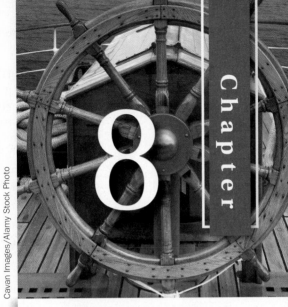

Cavan Images/Alamy Stock Photo

Chapter 8

Master Budgeting

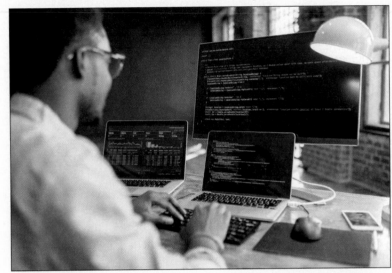

rh2010/123RF

ENTREPRENEUR SPOTLIGHT

Trinity Heavenz came from an impoverished neighborhood of Uganda to found era92—a tech company that provides a range of services for its clients including web and mobile design, landing page design, brand identity design, magazine and brochure design, and print, packaging, and merchandise design. To date, the company has developed more than 300 websites. Its client list includes Stanbic Bank, Impact Nations, The Remnant Generation, The Institute for Social Transformation, and Fields of Life.

Managerial Accounting: The Practical Application

To aid in its annual planning process, era92 could create a master budget. The budget could be broken down into various business segments. For example, Merline Ulysse, who is in charge of Business Development in the United Kingdom, could have her own budget. Similarly, Brenda Nassali (Digital Projects Manager) and Shamir Kwizera (Photography & Film) could also rely on their own budgets to execute their responsibilities. All of these individual budgets would roll up into the companywide budget Trinity would use to coordinate and allocate resources across the organization.

Corporate Social Responsibility: Serving all Stakeholders

Heavenz believes that "talent is equally distributed but the opportunity is not." To address this problem, he started era92's Elevate program, which provides "a new pathway for youth in education, employment, and empowerment, proving that by learning and improving digital skills, one can increase their chances of becoming employed or starting their own business or freelance career in Uganda." He also started a nonprofit organization called 92hands.org that serves its communities through five programs—One Child Education, US4 Women, Feeding Kosovo, The Wise Builders, and Kids Back to School. ∎

Sources: https://era92.com/our-story, https://era92elevate.org/elevate/, https://92hands.org/about-us

LEARNING OBJECTIVES

After studying Chapter 8, you should be able to:

LO 8–1 Understand why organizations budget and the processes they use to create budgets.

LO 8–2 Prepare a sales budget, including a schedule of expected cash collections.

LO 8–3 Prepare a production budget.

LO 8–4 Prepare a direct materials budget, including a schedule of expected cash disbursements for purchases of materials.

LO 8–5 Prepare a direct labor budget.

LO 8–6 Prepare a manufacturing overhead budget.

LO 8–7 Prepare a selling and administrative expense budget.

LO 8–8 Prepare a cash budget.

LO 8–9 Prepare a budgeted income statement.

LO 8–10 Prepare a budgeted balance sheet.

Data Analytics Exercise available in Connect to complement this chapter

In this chapter, we describe how organizations strive to achieve their financial goals by preparing *budgets*. A **budget** is a detailed plan for the future that is usually expressed in formal quantitative terms. A company's budget ordinarily covers a one-year period corresponding to its fiscal year, and it is often broken down into quarterly and monthly budgets. Some companies also use a *perpetual budget,* which is a 12-month budget that continuously rolls forward one month (or quarter) at a time as the current month (or quarter) is completed. This approach keeps managers continually focused one year ahead.

Why and How Do Organizations Create Budgets?

LEARNING OBJECTIVE 8–1
Understand why organizations budget and the processes they use to create budgets.

Budgets are used for two distinct purposes—*planning* and *control*. **Planning** involves developing goals and preparing various budgets to achieve those goals. **Control** involves gathering feedback to ensure that the plan is being properly executed or modified as circumstances change. To be effective, a good budgeting system must provide for both planning and control.

Why Do Organizations Create Budgets?

From a planning standpoint, organizations use budgets to:

1. Encourage managers to *think about* and *plan* for the future.
2. *Communicate* financial goals throughout the organization.
3. *Allocate resources* within the organization where they can be used most effectively.
4. *Coordinate* the plans and activities of departmental managers.
5. Uncover potential *bottlenecks* before they occur.

From a control standpoint, organizations compare their budgets to actual results to:

1. *Improve* the efficiency and effectiveness of operations.
2. *Evaluate* and *reward* employees.

skodonnell/Shutterstock

AMAZON EXPANDS ITS TRAINING BUDGET

Amazon.com is spending $700 million over six years to retrain its workforce. Beth Galetti, the company's senior vice president of worldwide HR, says, "The most consistent thing we see that's changing is the need for some level of technical skills in any job." For example, the company's fulfillment center employees need to learn how to work with a variety of automated tools, whereas its software engineers need to acquire more advanced skills, such as machine learning. Amazon has also seen a 500 percent growth rate in job openings for data scientists as well as networking and security engineers, all of whom need continuous training to update their technical skills.

Source: Chip Cutter, "Amazon Retrains More of Its Staff for Digital Future," *The Wall Street Journal,* December 11, 2019, p. B4.

How Do Organizations Create Budgets?

Companies usually create budgets by relying on some combination of top-down budgeting and *self-imposed budgeting*. A **self-imposed budget** or **participative budget** is a budget prepared with the full cooperation and participation of managers at all levels.

With a top-down approach, top-level managers initiate the budgeting process by issuing profit targets. Lower-level managers are directed to prepare budgets that meet those targets. This approach often demoralizes lower-level managers because it ignores their knowledge and opinions. Furthermore, the targets imposed by top-level managers, who may possess strategic vision while lacking operational knowledge, may be unrealistically high or unknowingly too low. If the targets are too high and top-level managers penalize lower-level managers for not meeting them, it will generate resentment rather than cooperation and commitment.

Given these complications, many companies choose to involve lower-level managers in the budgeting process because:

1. It shows respect for their opinions.
2. It leverages their knowledge to provide more accurate estimates than those imposed by top-level managers who have less intimate knowledge of day-to-day operations.
3. It increases their motivation to achieve their own self-imposed goals.
4. It empowers them to take ownership of the budget and be accountable for deviations from it.

While it may be tempting to conclude that companies should rely entirely on self-imposed budgets, this approach has two important limitations. First, lower-level managers may make suboptimal budgeting estimates if they lack the broad strategic perspective possessed by top managers. Second, if the budget is used to reward employees, then lower-level managers may create too much *budgetary slack* in an effort to ensure that their actual results exceed the plan. For these reasons, most companies use a combination of inputs from top-level managers and lower-level managers when creating their budgets. The budget estimates prepared by lower-level managers are usually scrutinized by higher levels of management. Without such a review, self-imposed budgets may fail to support the organization's strategy or may be too slack, resulting in suboptimal performance.

When managers throughout the organization work collaboratively to prepare a budget, they often strive to establish challenging but "highly achievable" targets. Highly achievable goals are likely to build a lower-level manager's confidence and commitment to the budget while also reducing the likelihood that they will engage in undesirable behavior to secure their desired compensation. Finally, top-level managers should not pressure lower-level managers to take extreme measures to "meet the budget." Creating this type of budgeting environment breeds hostility, tension, and mistrust rather than a cooperative pursuit of continuous process improvement.

The Master Budget: An Overview

For the remainder of the chapter, we will illustrate a type of integrated business plan known as a *master budget*. The **master budget** consists of a number of separate but interdependent budgets that formally lay out the company's sales, production, and financial goals. The master budget culminates in a cash budget, a budgeted income statement, and a budgeted balance sheet. Exhibit 8–1 provides an overview of the various parts of the master budget and how they are related.

The first step in the budgeting process is preparing a **sales budget,** which is a detailed schedule showing the expected sales for the budget period. An accurate sales budget is the key to the entire budgeting process. As illustrated in Exhibit 8–1, all other parts of the master budget depend on the sales budget. If the sales budget is inaccurate, the rest of the budget will be inaccurate. The sales budget is based on the company's sales forecast, which may require the use of sophisticated mathematical models and statistical tools that are beyond the scope of this course.

The sales budget influences the variable portion of the selling and administrative expense budget, and it feeds into the production budget, which defines how many units need to be produced during the budget period. The production budget, in turn, is used to determine the direct materials, direct labor, and manufacturing overhead budgets. Once a company has prepared these three manufacturing cost budgets, it can prepare the ending finished goods inventory budget.

The master budget concludes with the preparation of a cash budget, income statement, and balance sheet. Information from the sales budget, selling and administrative expense budget, and the manufacturing cost budgets all influence the preparation of

EXHIBIT 8–1
The Master Budget
Interrelationships

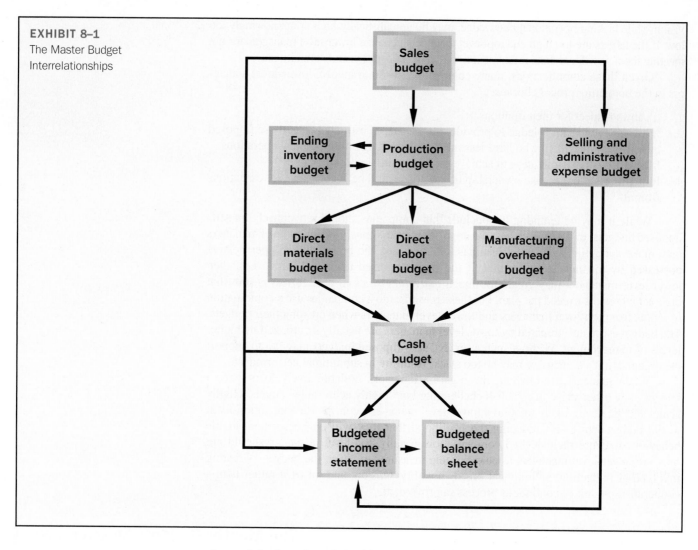

the *cash budget*. A **cash budget** is a detailed plan showing how cash resources will be acquired and used. The budgeted income statement provides an estimate of net income for the budget period, and it relies on information from the sales budget, ending finished goods inventory budget, selling and administrative expense budget, and cash budget. The final schedule of the master budget is the balance sheet, which estimates a company's assets, liabilities, and stockholders' equity at the end of a budget period.

Seeing the Big Picture

The 10 schedules contained in a master budget can be overwhelming; therefore, it is important to see the big picture in two respects. First, a master budget for a manufacturing company is designed to answer 10 key questions as follows:

1. How much sales will we earn?
2. How much cash will we collect from customers?
3. How many units of finished goods do we need to produce?
4. How much raw material will we need to purchase?
5. How much conversion cost (direct labor and manufacturing overhead) will we incur?
6. How much cash will we pay to our suppliers and our direct laborers, and how much will we pay for manufacturing overhead resources?
7. How much selling and administrative expense will we incur, and how much cash will we pay related to those expenses?
8. How will our cash balance and financing needs change?
9. How much net income will we earn?
10. What will our balance sheet look like at the end of the budget period?

EXHIBIT 8–2
Estimates and Assumptions for a Master Budget

Sales budget:
1. What are the budgeted unit sales?
2. What is the budgeted selling price per unit?
3. What percentage of accounts receivable will be collected in the current and subsequent periods?

Production budget:
1. What percentage of next period's unit sales needs to be maintained in ending finished goods inventory?

Direct materials budget:
1. How many units of raw materials are needed to make one unit of finished goods?
2. What is the budgeted cost for one unit of raw materials?
3. What percentage of next period's production needs should be maintained in ending raw materials inventory?
4. What percentage of raw materials purchases will be paid in the current and subsequent periods?

Direct labor budget:
1. How many direct labor-hours are required per unit of finished goods?
2. What is the budgeted direct labor wage rate per hour?

Manufacturing overhead budget:
1. What is the budgeted variable overhead cost per unit of the allocation base?
2. What is the total budgeted fixed overhead cost per period?
3. What is the budgeted depreciation expense on factory assets per period?

Selling and administrative expense budget:
1. What is the budgeted variable selling and administrative expense per unit sold?
2. What is the total budgeted fixed selling and administrative expense per period?
3. What is the budgeted depreciation expense on nonfactory assets per period?

Cash budget:
1. What is the budgeted minimum cash balance?
2. What are our estimated expenditures for noncurrent asset purchases and dividends?
3. What is the estimated interest rate on borrowed funds?

Second, it is important to understand that many of the schedules in a master budget hinge on a variety of estimates and assumptions managers must make when preparing those schedules. Exhibit 8–2 summarizes the questions that underlie these estimates and assumptions for seven of the schedules included in a master budget. As you study the forthcoming budget schedules, keep these two "big picture" insights in mind—the budget is designed to answer 10 key questions, and it is based on various estimates and assumptions—because they will help you understand *why* and *how* a master budget is created.

Preparing the Master Budget

Tom Wills is the majority stockholder and chief executive officer of Hampton Freeze, Inc., a company he started two years ago. The company makes premium popsicles using only natural ingredients and featuring exotic flavors such as tangy tangerine and minty mango. The company's business is highly seasonal, with most of the sales occurring in spring and summer.

In the company's second year of operations, a major cash crunch in the first and second quarters almost forced it into bankruptcy. In spite of this cash crunch, the year turned out to be a very successful year in terms of both cash flow and net income. Partly as a result of that harrowing experience, Tom decided it was time to hire a professional financial manager. He interviewed several promising candidates for the job and settled on Larry Giano, who had considerable experience in the packaged foods industry.

MANAGERIAL ACCOUNTING IN ACTION

The Issue

In the job interview, Tom questioned Larry about the steps he would take to prevent a recurrence of this year's cash crunch:

Tom: As I mentioned earlier, we are going to end this year with a very nice profit. What you may not know is that we had some very big financial problems this year.

Larry: Let me guess. You ran out of cash sometime in the first or second quarter.

Tom: How did you know?

Larry: Most of your sales are in the second and third quarter, right?

Tom: Sure, everyone wants to buy popsicles in the spring and summer, but nobody wants them when the weather turns cold.

Larry: So you don't have many sales in the first quarter?

Tom: Right.

Larry: And in the second quarter, which is the spring, you are producing like crazy to fill orders?

Tom: Sure.

Larry: Do your customers, the grocery stores, pay you the day you make your deliveries?

Tom: Are you kidding? Of course not.

Larry: So in the first quarter, you don't have many sales. In the second quarter, you are producing like crazy, which eats up cash, but you aren't paid by your customers until long after you have paid your employees and suppliers. No wonder you had a cash problem. I see this pattern all the time in food processing because of the seasonality of the business.

Tom: So what can we do about it?

Larry: The first step is to predict the magnitude of the problem before it occurs. If we can predict early in the year what the cash shortfall is going to be, we can go to the bank and arrange for credit before we really need it. Bankers tend to be leery of panicky people who show up begging for emergency loans. They are much more likely to make the loan if you look like you are in control of the situation.

Tom: How can we predict the cash shortfall?

Larry: You can put together a cash budget. In fact, while you're at it, you might as well do a master budget. You'll find it well worth the effort because we can use a master budget to estimate the financial statement implications of numerous "what-if" questions. For example, with the click of a mouse, we can answer questions such as: If unit sales are 10 percent less than our original forecast, what will be the impact on profits? Or what if we increase our selling price by 15 percent and unit sales drop by 5 percent? What will be the impact on profits?

Tom: That sounds great, Larry! Not only do we need a cash budget, but I would love to have a master budget that could quickly answer the types of "what-if" questions that you just described. As far as I'm concerned, the sooner you get started, the better.

With the full backing of Tom Wills, Larry Giano set out to create the company's master budget for next year. In his planning for the budgeting process, Larry drew up the following list of documents that would be a part of the master budget:

1. A sales budget, including a schedule of expected cash collections.
2. A production budget (a merchandise purchases budget would be used in a merchandising company).
3. A direct materials budget, including a schedule of expected cash disbursements for purchases of materials.
4. A direct labor budget.
5. A manufacturing overhead budget.
6. An ending finished goods inventory budget.
7. A selling and administrative expense budget.
8. A cash budget.
9. A budgeted income statement.
10. A budgeted balance sheet.

Larry felt it was important to have everyone's cooperation in the budgeting process, so he asked Tom to call a companywide meeting to explain the budgeting process. At the meeting, there was initially some grumbling, but Tom was able to convince nearly everyone of the necessity for planning and getting better control over spending. It helped that the cash crisis earlier in the year was still fresh in everyone's minds. As much as some people disliked the idea of budgets, they liked their jobs more.

In the months that followed, Larry worked closely with all of the managers involved in the master budget, gathering data from them and making sure that they understood and fully supported the parts of the master budget that would affect them.

The interdependent documents that Larry Giano prepared for Hampton Freeze are Schedules 1 through 10 of the company's master budget. In this section, we will study these schedules as well as the beginning balance sheet and the budgeting assumptions that Larry included in his master budget to help answer the types of "what-if" questions that he discussed with Tom Wills.

The Beginning Balance Sheet

Exhibit 8–3 shows the first tab included in Larry's Microsoft Excel master budget file. It contains Hampton Freeze's beginning balance sheet for next year. Larry included this balance sheet in his master budget file so he could link some of these data to subsequent schedules. For example, as you'll eventually see, he used cell references within Excel to link the beginning accounts receivable balance of $90,000 to the schedule of expected cash collections. He also used cell references to link the beginning cash balance of $42,500 to the cash budget.

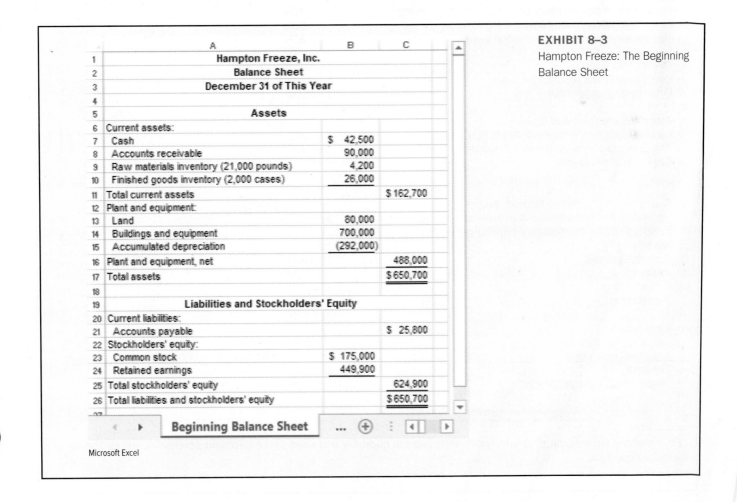

	A	B	C
1	Hampton Freeze, Inc.		
2	Balance Sheet		
3	December 31 of This Year		
4			
5	Assets		
6	Current assets:		
7	Cash	$ 42,500	
8	Accounts receivable	90,000	
9	Raw materials inventory (21,000 pounds)	4,200	
10	Finished goods inventory (2,000 cases)	26,000	
11	Total current assets		$ 162,700
12	Plant and equipment:		
13	Land	80,000	
14	Buildings and equipment	700,000	
15	Accumulated depreciation	(292,000)	
16	Plant and equipment, net		488,000
17	Total assets		$650,700
18			
19	Liabilities and Stockholders' Equity		
20	Current liabilities:		
21	Accounts payable		$ 25,800
22	Stockholders' equity:		
23	Common stock	$ 175,000	
24	Retained earnings	449,900	
25	Total stockholders' equity		624,900
26	Total liabilities and stockholders' equity		$650,700

Beginning Balance Sheet

Microsoft Excel

EXHIBIT 8–3

Hampton Freeze: The Beginning Balance Sheet

The Budgeting Assumptions

Exhibit 8–4 shows the second tab included in Larry's master budget file. It is labeled Budgeting Assumptions and contains all of Hampton Freeze's answers to the questions summarized in Exhibit 8–2. The data included in Exhibit 8–4 summarize the estimates and assumptions that provide the foundation for Hampton Freeze's entire master budget,

EXHIBIT 8–4
Hampton Freeze: Budgeting Assumptions

	A	B	C	D	E	F
1		Hampton Freeze, Inc.				
2		Budgeting Assumptions				
3		For the Year Ended December 31 of Next Year				
4						
5		All 4 Quarters		Quarter		
6	Sales Budget		1	2	3	4
7	Budgeted sales in cases		10,000	30,000	40,000	20,000
8	Selling price per case	$ 20.00				
9	Percentage of sales collected in the quarter of sale	70%				
10	Percentage of sales collected in the quarter after sale	30%				
11						
12	Production Budget					
13	Percentage of next quarter's sales in ending finished goods inventory	20%				
14						
15	Direct Materials Budget					
16	Pounds of sugar per case	15				
17	Cost per pound of sugar	$ 0.20				
18	Percentage of next quarter's production needs in ending inventory	10%				
19	Percentage of purchases paid in the quarter purchased	50%				
20	Percentage of purchases paid in the quarter after purchase	50%				
21						
22	Direct Labor Budget					
23	Direct labor-hours required per case	0.40				
24	Direct labor cost per hour	$ 15.00				
25						
26	Manufacturing Overhead Budget					
27	Variable manufacturing overhead per direct labor-hour	$ 4.00				
28	Fixed manufacturing overhead per quarter	$ 60,600				
29	Depreciation per quarter	$ 15,000				
30						
31						
32	Selling and Administrative Expense Budget					
33	Variable selling and administrative expense per case	$ 1.80				
34	Fixed selling and administrative expense per quarter:					
35	Advertising	$ 20,000				
36	Executive salaries	$ 55,000				
37	Insurance	$ 10,000				
38	Property tax	$ 4,000				
39	Depreciation	$ 10,000				
40						
41	Cash Budget					
42	Minimum cash balance	$ 30,000				
43	Equipment purchases		$ 50,000	$ 40,000	$ 20,000	$ 20,000
44	Dividends	$ 8,000				
45	Simple interest rate per quarter	3%				
46						

Budgeting Assumptions	Schedule

* For simplicity, we assume all quarterly estimates, except quarterly unit sales and equipment purchases, will be the same for all four quarters.

Microsoft Excel

so it is important to familiarize yourself with this information now. Beginning with the estimates underlying the sales budget, Exhibit 8–4 shows that Hampton Freeze's budgeted quarterly unit sales are 10,000, 30,000, 40,000, and 20,000 cases. Its budgeted selling price is $20 per case. The company expects to collect 70 percent of its credit sales in the quarter of sale, and the remaining 30 percent of credit sales will be collected in the quarter after sale. The company's bad debts are negligible.

Exhibit 8–4 also shows that the production budget is based on the assumption that Hampton Freeze will maintain ending finished goods inventory equal to 20 percent of the next quarter's unit sales. In terms of the company's only direct material, high fructose sugar, it budgets 15 pounds of sugar per case of popsicles at a cost of $0.20 per pound.[1] It expects to maintain ending raw materials inventory equal to 10 percent of the raw materials needed to satisfy the following quarter's production. In addition, the company plans to pay for 50 percent of its materials purchases within the quarter of purchase and the remaining 50 percent in the following quarter.

Continuing with a summary of Exhibit 8–4, the two key assumptions underlying the direct labor budget are that 0.40 direct labor-hours are required per case of popsicles, and the direct labor cost per hour is $15. The manufacturing overhead budget is based on three underlying assumptions—the variable overhead cost per direct labor-hour is $4.00, the total fixed overhead per quarter is $60,600, and the quarterly depreciation on factory assets is $15,000. Exhibit 8–4 also shows that the budgeted variable selling and administrative expense per case of popsicles is $1.80, and the fixed selling and administrative expenses per quarter include advertising ($20,000), executive salaries ($55,000), insurance ($10,000), property tax ($4,000), and depreciation expense ($10,000). The remaining budget assumptions depicted in Exhibit 8–4 pertain to the cash budget. The company expects to maintain a minimum cash balance each quarter of $30,000; it plans to make quarterly equipment purchases of $50,000, $40,000, $20,000, and $20,000;[2] it plans to pay quarterly dividends of $8,000; and it expects to pay simple interest on borrowed money of 3 percent per quarter.

Before reading further, it is important to understand why Larry created the Budgeting Assumptions tab shown in Exhibit 8–4. He did it because it simplifies the process of using a master budget to answer "what-if" questions. For example, assume Larry wanted to answer the question: What if we increase the selling price per unit by $2 and expect sales to drop by 1,000 units per quarter; what would be the impact on profits? With a properly constructed Budgeting Assumptions tab, Larry would only need to make a few adjustments to the data within this tab, and the formulas embedded in each of the budget schedules would automatically update the projected financial results. This is much simpler than attempting to adjust data inputs within each of the master budget schedules.

The Sales Budget

LEARNING OBJECTIVE 8–2
Prepare a sales budget, including a schedule of expected cash collections.

Schedule 1 contains Hampton Freeze's sales budget for next year. As you study this schedule, keep in mind that all of its numbers are derived from cell references to the Budgeting Assumptions tab and formulas—none of the numbers appearing in the schedule were actually keyed into their respective cells. Furthermore, it bears emphasizing that all remaining schedules in the master budget are prepared in the same fashion—they rely almost exclusively on cell references and formulas.

For the year, Hampton Freeze expects to sell 100,000 cases of popsicles at a price of $20 per case for total budgeted sales of $2,000,000. The budgeted unit sales for each quarter (10,000, 30,000, 40,000, and 20,000) come from cells C7 through F7 in the Budgeting Assumptions tab shown in Exhibit 8–4, and the selling price per case ($20.00) comes from cell B8 in the Budgeting Assumptions tab. Schedule 1 also shows that the company's expected cash collections for next year are $1,970,000. The accounts receivable balance of $90,000 that is collected in the first quarter comes from cell B8 of the

---

[1] While popsicle manufacturing is likely to involve other raw materials, such as popsicle sticks and packaging materials, for simplicity, we have limited our scope to high fructose sugar.

[2] For simplicity, we assume depreciation on these newly acquired assets is included in the quarterly depreciation estimates included in the Budgeting Assumptions tab.

SCHEDULE 1

	A	B	C	D	E	F
1		Hampton Freeze, Inc.				
2		Sales Budget				
3		For the Year Ended December 31 of Next Year				
4						
5		Quarter				
6		1	2	3	4	Year
7	Budgeted unit sales (in cases)	10,000	30,000	40,000	20,000	100,000
8	Selling price per unit	$ 20.00	$ 20.00	$ 20.00	$ 20.00	$ 20.00
9	Total sales	$200,000	$600,000	$800,000	$400,000	$2,000,000
10						
11		70%	30%			
12		Schedule of Expected Cash Collections				
13	Beginning accounts receivable[1]	$ 90,000				$ 90,000
14	First-quarter sales[2]	140,000	$ 60,000			200,000
15	Second-quarter sales[3]		420,000	$180,000		600,000
16	Third-quarter sales[4]			560,000	$240,000	800,000
17	Fourth-quarter sales[5]				280,000	280,000
18	Total cash collections[6]	$230,000	$480,000	$740,000	$520,000	$1,970,000
19						
20						
21						
22						

◄ ► ... **Schedule 1** Schedule ... ⊕ ┊ ◄

[1] Cash collections from last year's fourth-quarter sales. See the beginning balance sheet in Exhibit 8–3.
[2] $200,000 × 70%; $200,000 × 30%.
[3] $600,000 × 70%; $600,000 × 30%.
[4] $800,000 × 70%; $800,000 × 30%.
[5] $400,000 × 70%.
[6] Uncollected fourth-quarter sales ($120,000) appear as accounts receivable on the company's end-of-year budgeted balance sheet (see Schedule 10).

Microsoft Excel

beginning balance sheet shown in Exhibit 8–3. All other cash collections rely on the estimated cash collection percentages from cells B9 and B10 of the Budgeting Assumptions tab. For example, Schedule 1 shows that the budgeted sales for the first quarter equal $200,000. In the first quarter, Hampton Freeze expects to collect 70 percent of this amount, or $140,000. In the second quarter, the company expects to collect the remaining 30 percent of this amount, or $60,000.

IN BUSINESS

BUDGETING FOR HOLIDAY RETURNS

In addition to preparing sales budgets, companies need to budget for the expense of managing sales returns. B-Stock Solutions, which runs online liquidation sites for major retailers, estimates that customers return more than $90 billion worth of merchandise purchased during the holiday season. The National Retail Federation estimates that 80 percent of shoppers prefer in-store returns rather than returning items through carriers, such as UPS and FedEx. Given this reality, many e-commerce merchants are providing ways for customers to return digital purchases to physical locations. For example, Amazon offers free returns at more than 18,000 drop-off locations.

Source: Jennifer Smith, "Retailers Brace for Holiday Returns," *The Wall Street Journal*, December 20, 2019, p. B2.

The Production Budget

The production budget is prepared after the sales budget. The **production budget** lists the number of units that must be produced to satisfy sales needs and to provide for the desired ending finished goods inventory. Production needs can be determined as follows:

LEARNING OBJECTIVE 8–3
Prepare a production budget.

Budgeted unit sales	XXX
Add desired units of ending finished goods inventory	XXX
Total needs	XXX
Less units of beginning finished goods inventory	XXX
Required production in units	XXX

Note the production requirements are influenced by the desired level of the ending finished goods inventory. Inventories should be carefully planned. Excessive inventories tie up funds and create storage problems. Insufficient inventories can lead to lost sales or last-minute, high-cost production efforts.

Schedule 2 contains the production budget for Hampton Freeze. The budgeted sales data come from cells B7 through E7 of the sales budget. The desired ending finished goods inventory for the first quarter of 6,000 cases is computed by multiplying budgeted sales from the second quarter (30,000 cases) by the desired ending finished goods inventory percentage (20%) shown in cell B13 of the Budgeting Assumptions tab. The total needs for the first quarter (16,000 cases) are determined by adding together the budgeted sales of 10,000 cases for the quarter and the desired ending inventory of 6,000 cases. As discussed above, the ending inventory is intended to provide some cushion in the event that problems develop in production or sales increase unexpectedly. Because the company

---

SCHEDULE 2

	A	B	C	D	E	F
3	Hampton Freeze, Inc.					
4	Production Budget					
5	For the Year Ended December 31 of Next Year					
6	(in cases)					
7						Assumed
8			Quarter			
9		1	2	3	4	Year
10	Budgeted unit sales (Schedule 1)	10,000	30,000	40,000	20,000	100,000
11	Add desired units of ending finished goods inventory*	6,000	8,000	4,000	3,000	3,000
12	Total needs	16,000	38,000	44,000	23,000	103,000
13	Less units of beginning finished goods inventory†	2,000	6,000	8,000	4,000	2,000
14	Required production in units	14,000	32,000	36,000	19,000	101,000
15						

(Row 10 to 11 shows 20% arrows between quarters)

Tabs: Beginning Balance Sheet | Budgeting Assumptions | Schedule 1 | **Schedule 2** | ... ⊕

* Twenty percent of next quarter's sales. For example, the second-quarter sales are 30,000 cases. Therefore, the desired ending inventory of finished goods for the first quarter would be 20% × 30,000 cases = 6,000 cases.

† The beginning inventory in each quarter is the same as the prior quarter's ending inventory.

Microsoft Excel

already has 2,000 cases in beginning finished goods inventory (as shown in the beginning balance sheet in Exhibit 8–3), only 14,000 cases need to be produced in the first quarter.

Pay particular attention to the Year column to the right of the production budget in Schedule 2. In some instances (e.g., budgeted unit sales and required production in units), the amount listed for the year is the sum of the quarterly amounts for the item. In other cells (e.g., desired units of ending finished goods inventory and units of beginning finished goods inventory), the amount listed for the year is not the sum of the quarterly amounts. From the standpoint of the entire year, the ending finished goods inventory, which Larry Giano assumed to be 3,000 units, is the same as the ending finished goods inventory for the fourth quarter—it is *not* the sum of the ending finished goods inventories for all four quarters. Similarly, from the standpoint of the entire year, the beginning finished goods inventory (2,000 units) is the same as the beginning finished goods inventory for the first quarter—it is *not* the sum of the beginning finished goods inventories for all four quarters. It is important to pay attention to such distinctions in all schedules that follow.

Inventory Purchases—Merchandising Company

Hampton Freeze prepares a production budget because it is a *manufacturing* company. If it were a *merchandising* company, instead it would prepare a **merchandise purchases budget** showing the amount of goods to be purchased from suppliers during the period.

The format of the merchandise purchases budget is shown below:

Budgeted cost of goods sold	XXX
Add desired ending merchandise inventory	XXX
Total needs	XXX
Less beginning merchandise inventory	XXX
Required purchases	XXX

A merchandising company would prepare a merchandise purchases budget, such as the one above, for each item carried in stock. The merchandise purchases budget can be expressed in dollars (using the headings shown above) or units. The top line of a merchandise purchases budget based on units would say Budgeted unit sales instead of Budgeted cost of goods sold.

A merchandise purchases budget is usually accompanied by a schedule of expected cash disbursements for merchandise purchases. The format of this schedule mirrors the approach used for the schedule of expected cash disbursements for purchases of materials that is illustrated at the bottom of Schedule 3.

The Direct Materials Budget

LEARNING OBJECTIVE 8–4
Prepare a direct materials budget, including a schedule of expected cash disbursements for purchases of materials.

A *direct materials budget* is prepared after the production requirements have been computed. The **direct materials budget** details the raw materials that must be purchased to fulfill the production budget and to provide for adequate inventories. The required purchases of raw materials are computed as follows:

Required production in units of finished goods	XXX
Units of raw materials needed per unit of finished goods	XXX
Units of raw materials needed to meet production	XXX
Add desired units of ending raw materials inventory	XXX
Total units of raw materials needed	XXX
Less units of beginning raw materials inventory	XXX
Units of raw materials to be purchased	XXX
Unit cost of raw materials	XXX
Cost of raw materials to be purchased	XXX

Schedule 3 contains the direct materials budget for Hampton Freeze. The first line of this budget contains the required production for each quarter, which is taken directly from cells B14 through E14 of the production budget (Schedule 2). The second line of the direct materials budget recognizes that 15 pounds of sugar (see cell B16 from the Budgeting Assumptions tab) are required to make one case of popsicles. The third line of the budget presents the raw materials needed to meet production. For example, in the first quarter, the required production of 14,000 cases is multiplied by 15 pounds to equal 210,000 pounds of sugar needed to meet production. The fourth line shows the desired units of ending raw materials inventory. For the first quarter, this amount is computed by multiplying the raw materials needed to meet production in the second quarter of 480,000 pounds by the desired ending inventory percentage of 10 percent as shown in cell B18 of the Budgeting Assumptions tab. The desired units of ending raw materials inventory of

SCHEDULE 3

	A	B	C	D	E	F
3		Hampton Freeze, Inc.				
4		Direct Materials Budget				
5		For the Year Ended December 31 of Next Year				
6						Assumed
7			Quarter			
8		1	2	3	4	Year
9	Required production in cases (Schedule 2)	14,000	32,000	36,000	19,000	101,000
10	Units of raw materials needed per case	15	15	15	15	15
11	Units of raw materials needed to meet production	210,000	480,000	540,000	285,000	1,515,000
12	Add desired units of ending raw materials inventory[1]	48,000 10%	54,000 10%	28,500 10%	22,500	22,500
13	Total units of raw materials needed	258,000	534,000	568,500	307,500	1,537,500
14	Less units of beginning raw materials inventory	21,000	48,000	54,000	28,500	21,000
15	Units of raw materials to be purchased	237,000	486,000	514,500	279,000	1,516,500
16	Cost of raw materials per pound	$ 0.20	$ 0.20	$ 0.20	$ 0.20	$ 0.20
17	Cost of raw materials to be purchased	$ 47,400	$ 97,200	$ 102,900	$ 55,800	$ 303,300
18						
19			50%	50%		
20	Schedule of Expected Cash Disbursements for Purchases of Materials					
21						
22	Beginning accounts payable[2]	$ 25,800				$ 25,800
23	First-quarter purchases[3]	23,700	$ 23,700			47,400
24	Second-quarter purchases[4]		48,600	$ 48,600		97,200
25	Third-quarter purchases[5]			51,450	$ 51,450	102,900
26	Fourth-quarter purchases[6]	-	-	-	27,900	27,900
27	Total cash disbursements for materials	$ 49,500	$ 72,300	$ 100,050	$ 79,350	$ 301,200
28						

Schedule 1 | Schedule 2 | **Schedule 3** | Schedule 4 | Sch ... ⊕

[1] Ten percent of the next quarter's production needs. For example, the second-quarter production needs are 480,000 pounds. Therefore, the desired ending inventory for the first quarter would be 10% × 480,000 pounds = 48,000 pounds. The desired ending inventory for quarter 4 (22,500 pounds) assumes the first quarter production needs in the following year are 225,000 pounds (225,000 pounds × 10% = 22,500 pounds).

[2] Cash payments for last year's fourth-quarter purchases. See the beginning-of-year balance sheet in Exhibit 8–3.

[3] $47,400 × 50%; $47,400 × 50%.

[4] $97,200 × 50%; $97,200 × 50%.

[5] $102,900 × 50%; $102,900 × 50%.

[6] $55,800 × 50%. Unpaid fourth-quarter purchases ($27,900) appear as accounts payable on the company's end-of-year budgeted balance sheet (see Schedule 10).

Microsoft Excel

48,000 pounds are added to 210,000 pounds to provide the total units of raw materials needed of 258,000 pounds. However, because the company already has 21,000 pounds of sugar in beginning inventory (as shown in cell A9 in the beginning balance sheet in Exhibit 8–3), only 237,000 pounds of sugar need to be purchased in the first quarter. Because the budgeted cost of raw materials per pound is $0.20 (see cell B17 from the Budgeting Assumptions tab), the cost of raw materials to be purchased in the first quarter is $47,400. For the entire year, the company plans to purchase $303,300 of raw materials.

Schedule 3 also shows that the company's expected cash disbursements for materials purchases for next year are $301,200. The accounts payable balance of $25,800 paid in the first quarter comes from cell C21 of the beginning balance sheet shown in Exhibit 8–3. All other cash disbursement computations rely on the estimated cash payment percentages (both of which are 50%) from cells B19 and B20 of the Budgeting Assumptions tab. For example, Schedule 3 shows that the budgeted raw materials purchases for the first quarter equal $47,400. In the first quarter, Hampton Freeze expects to pay 50 percent of this amount, or $23,700. In the second quarter, the company expects to pay the remaining 50 percent of this amount, or $23,700.

The Direct Labor Budget

LEARNING OBJECTIVE 8–5

Prepare a direct labor budget.

The **direct labor budget** shows the direct labor-hours required to satisfy the production budget. By knowing in advance how much labor time will be needed throughout the budget year, the company can develop plans to adjust the labor force as the situation requires. Companies that neglect the budgeting process run the risk of facing labor shortages or having to hire and lay off workers at awkward times. Erratic labor policies lead to insecurity, low morale, and inefficiency.

The direct labor budget for Hampton Freeze is shown in Schedule 4. The first line in the direct labor budget consists of the required production for each quarter, which is taken directly from cells B14 through E14 of the production budget (Schedule 2). The direct labor requirement for each quarter is computed by multiplying the number of units to be produced in each quarter by the 0.40 direct labor-hours required to make one unit (see cell B23 from the Budgeting Assumptions tab). For example, 14,000 cases are to be produced in the first quarter, and each case requires 0.40 direct labor-hours, so a total of 5,600 direct labor-hours (14,000 cases × 0.40 direct labor-hours per case) will be required

SCHEDULE 4

	A	B	C	D	E	F
1		Hampton Freeze, Inc.				
2		Direct Labor Budget				
3		For the Year Ended December 31 of Next Year				
4						
5				Quarter		
6		1	2	3	4	Year
7	Required production in cases (Schedule 2)	14,000	32,000	36,000	19,000	101,000
8	Direct labor-hours per case	0.40	0.40	0.40	0.40	0.40
9	Total direct labor-hours needed	5,600	12,800	14,400	7,600	40,400
10	Direct labor cost per hour	$ 15.00	$ 15.00	$ 15.00	$ 15.00	$ 15.00
11	Total direct labor cost	$ 84,000	$ 192,000	$ 216,000	$ 114,000	$ 606,000
12						

Schedule 1 | Schedule 2 | Schedule 3 | **Schedule 4** | Sch ... ⊕

* This schedule assumes that the direct labor workforce will be fully adjusted to the total direct labor-hours needed each quarter.

Microsoft Excel

in the first quarter. The direct labor requirements are then translated into budgeted direct labor costs by simply multiplying the direct labor-hour requirements by the direct labor rate of $15 per hour (see cell B24 from the Budgeting Assumptions tab). For example, the direct labor cost in the first quarter is $84,000 (5,600 direct labor-hours × $15 per direct labor-hour).[3]

WILL CHECKOUT COUNTERS BECOME OBSOLETE?

Most retailers continue to rely heavily on cashiers to tally a customer's amount due and to process the corresponding payment. However, Amazon.com's new Amazon Go store in Seattle, Washington, uses computer technology to replace cashiers and to eliminate the need for any type of barcode-scanning checkout process. The company's innovative new store relies on "computer vision and machine-learning algorithms to track shoppers and charge them for what they select, thereby eliminating checkout counters. . . . A customer entering the store scans his or her phone and then becomes represented as a 3-D object to the system." While the Amazon Go model holds much promise for future development, the company currently has no plans to use this technology within its Whole Foods Market grocery stores.

Source: Laura Stevens, "Amazon's Cashierless 'Go' Convenience Store Set to Open," *The Wall Street Journal,* January 20, 2018.

MariaX/Shutterstock

The Manufacturing Overhead Budget

The **manufacturing overhead budget** lists all costs of production other than direct materials and direct labor. Schedule 5 shows the manufacturing overhead budget for Hampton Freeze. At Hampton Freeze, manufacturing overhead is separated into variable and fixed components. As shown in the Budgeting Assumptions tab (Exhibit 8–4), the variable component is $4 per direct labor-hour, and the fixed component is $60,600 per quarter. Because the variable component of manufacturing overhead depends on direct labor, the first line in the manufacturing overhead budget consists of the budgeted direct labor-hours from cells B9 through E9 of the direct labor budget (Schedule 4). The budgeted direct labor-hours in each quarter are multiplied by the variable overhead rate to determine the variable component of manufacturing overhead. For example, the variable manufacturing overhead for the first quarter is $22,400 (5,600 direct labor-hours × $4.00 per direct labor-hour). This is added to the fixed manufacturing overhead for the quarter to determine the total manufacturing overhead for the quarter of $83,000 ($22,400 + $60,600).

The last line of Schedule 5 for Hampton Freeze shows the budgeted cash disbursements for manufacturing overhead. Because some of the overhead costs are not cash outflows, the total budgeted manufacturing overhead costs must be adjusted to determine the cash disbursements for manufacturing overhead. At Hampton Freeze, the only significant noncash manufacturing overhead cost is depreciation, which is $15,000 per quarter (see cell B29 in the Budgeting Assumptions tab). These noncash depreciation charges are deducted from the total budgeted manufacturing overhead to determine each quarter's expected cash disbursements. Hampton Freeze pays all overhead costs involving cash disbursements in the quarter incurred. Note that the company's predetermined overhead

LEARNING OBJECTIVE 8–6
Prepare a manufacturing overhead budget.

---

[3] Many companies have employment policies or contracts that require them to pay overtime premiums and that prevent them from laying off and rehiring workers as needed. The costs associated with the idle time and overtime that can result from these policies are usually treated as part of manufacturing overhead. In this chapter, for simplicity, we bypass these considerations by always assuming that the direct labor workforce is adjusted as needed to match the budgeted production needs.

SCHEDULE 5

	A	B	C	D	E	F
1		Hampton Freeze, Inc.				
2		Manufacturing Overhead Budget				
3		For the Year Ended December 31 of Next Year				
4						
5		Quarter				
6		1	2	3	4	Year
7	Budgeted direct labor-hours (Schedule 4)	5,600	12,800	14,400	7,600	40,400
8	Variable manufacturing overhead rate	$ 4.00	$ 4.00	$ 4.00	$ 4.00	$ 4.00
9	Variable manufacturing overhead	$ 22,400	$ 51,200	$ 57,600	$ 30,400	$ 161,600
10	Fixed manufacturing overhead	60,600	60,600	60,600	60,600	242,400
11	Total manufacturing overhead	83,000	111,800	118,200	91,000	404,000
12	Less depreciation	15,000	15,000	15,000	15,000	60,000
13	Cash disbursements for manufacturing overhead	$ 68,000	$ 96,800	$ 103,200	$ 76,000	$ 344,000
14						
15	Total manufacturing overhead (a)					$ 404,000
16	Budgeted direct labor-hours (b)					40,400
17	Predetermined overhead rate for the year (a)÷(b)					$10.00

Schedule 3 | Schedule 4 | **Schedule 5** | Schedule 6 | ... ⊕

Microsoft Excel

rate for the year is $10 per direct labor-hour, which is determined by dividing the total budgeted manufacturing overhead for the year ($404,000) by the total budgeted direct labor-hours for the year (40,400).

The Ending Finished Goods Inventory Budget

After completing Schedules 1–5, Larry Giano had all of the data he needed to compute the absorption unit product cost for the units produced during the budget year. This computation was needed for two reasons: first, to help determine cost of goods sold on the budgeted income statement; and, second, to value ending inventories on the budgeted balance sheet. The cost of unsold units is computed on the **ending finished goods inventory budget.**[4]

Schedule 6 shows that Hampton Freeze's absorption unit product cost is $13 per case of popsicles—consisting of $3 of direct materials, $6 of direct labor, and $4 of manufacturing overhead. Notice that manufacturing overhead has been applied to units of product using the rate of $10 per direct labor-hour from cell F17 of the Manufacturing Overhead budget. The budgeted carrying cost of the ending inventory is $39,000.

The Selling and Administrative Expense Budget

LEARNING OBJECTIVE 8–7
Prepare a selling and administrative expense budget.

The **selling and administrative expense budget** lists the budgeted expenses for areas other than manufacturing. In large organizations, this budget would be a compilation of many smaller, individual budgets submitted by department heads and other

_____

[4] For simplicity, the beginning balance sheet and the ending finished goods inventory budget both report a unit product cost of $13. For purposes of answering "what-if" questions, this schedule would assume a FIFO inventory flow. In other words, the ending inventory would consist solely of units that are produced during the budget year.

SCHEDULE 6

	A	B	C	D	E	F	G	H
1			Hampton Freeze, Inc.					
2			Ending Finished Goods Inventory Budget					
3			(absorption costing basis)					
4			For the Year Ended December 31 of Next Year					
5								
6	Item	Quantity			Cost			Total
7	Production cost per case:							
8	Direct materials	15.00	pounds		$ 0.20	per pound		$ 3.00
9	Direct labor	0.40	hours		$15.00	per hour		6.00
10	Manufacturing overhead	0.40	hours		$10.00	per hour		4.00
11	Unit product cost							$ 13.00
12								
13	Budgeted finished goods inventory:							
14	Ending finished goods inventory in cases (Schedule 2)							3,000
15	Unit product cost (see above)							$ 13.00
16	Ending finished goods inventory in dollars							$ 39,000

... | Schedule 5 | **Schedule 6** | Sch ... | (+) | ◄

Microsoft Excel

persons responsible for selling and administrative expenses. For example, the marketing manager would submit a budget detailing the advertising expenses for each budget period.

Schedule 7 contains the selling and administrative expense budget for Hampton Freeze. Like the manufacturing overhead budget, the selling and administrative expense budget is divided into variable and fixed cost components. Consequently, budgeted sales in cases for each quarter are entered at the top of the schedule. These data are taken from cells B7 through E7 of the sales budget (Schedule 1). The budgeted variable selling and administrative expenses are determined by multiplying the budgeted cases sold by the variable selling and administrative expense of $1.80 per case (see cell B33 from the Budgeting Assumptions tab). For example, the budgeted variable selling and administrative expense for the first quarter is $18,000 (10,000 cases × $1.80 per case). The fixed selling and administrative expenses of $99,000 per quarter (see cells B35 through B39 from the Budgeting Assumptions tab) are then added to the variable selling and administrative expenses to arrive at the total budgeted selling and administrative expenses. Finally, to determine the cash disbursements for selling and administrative items, the total budgeted selling and administrative expense is adjusted by subtracting any noncash selling and administrative expenses (in this case, just depreciation).[5]

---

[5] Other adjustments might need to be made for differences between cash flows on the one hand and revenues and expenses on the other hand. For example, if property taxes are paid twice a year in installments of $8,000 each, the expense for property tax would have to be "backed out" of the total budgeted selling and administrative expenses and the cash installment payments added to the appropriate quarters to determine the cash disbursements. Similar adjustments might also need to be made in the manufacturing overhead budget. We generally ignore these complications in this chapter.

SCHEDULE 7

	1	2	3	4	Year
Hampton Freeze, Inc.					
Selling and Administrative Expense Budget					
For the Year Ended December 31 of Next Year					
			Quarter		
	1	2	3	4	Year
Budgeted units sales (Schedule 1)	10,000	30,000	40,000	20,000	100,000
Variable selling and administrative expense per case	$ 1.80	$ 1.80	$ 1.80	$ 1.80	$ 1.80
Variable selling and administrative expense	$ 18,000	$ 54,000	$ 72,000	$ 36,000	$180,000
Fixed selling and administrative expenses:					
Advertising	20,000	20,000	20,000	20,000	80,000
Executive salaries	55,000	55,000	55,000	55,000	220,000
Insurance	10,000	10,000	10,000	10,000	40,000
Property taxes	4,000	4,000	4,000	4,000	16,000
Depreciation	10,000	10,000	10,000	10,000	40,000
Total fixed selling and administrative expenses	99,000	99,000	99,000	99,000	396,000
Total selling and administrative expenses	117,000	153,000	171,000	135,000	576,000
Less depreciation	10,000	10,000	10,000	10,000	40,000
Cash disbursements for selling and administrative expenses	$107,000	$143,000	$161,000	$125,000	$536,000

◄ ► ...   Schedule 5   Schedule 6   **Schedule 7**   ... ⊕

Microsoft Excel

JLMcAnally/Shutterstock

P&G MANAGES THE RISK ASSOCIATED WITH TIDE PODS

Procter & Gamble (P&G) would prefer to spend its marketing budget on advertising campaigns that motivate customers to use its products rather than compensating a spokesman to admonish them not to abuse its products. However, when teens starting taking the "Tide pods challenge" by eating and vaping the company's laundry detergent and then posting their experiences online, it needed to shift into damage control mode. P&G hired retired professional football player Rob Gronkowski to record a video saying, "No. No. No. What the heck is going on, people. Use Tide pods for washing, not eating." The company then posted the video on Twitter, Facebook, and YouTube. In a two-year span, more than 130 teenagers were poisoned by intentionally ingesting laundry detergent pods.

Source: Imani Moise and Sharon Terlep, "P&G Wrestles with Tide Pods Challenge," *The Wall Street Journal*, January 22, 2018, pp. B1–B2.

The Cash Budget

LEARNING OBJECTIVE 8–8

Prepare a cash budget.

The cash budget is composed of four main sections:

1. The cash receipts section.
2. The cash disbursements section.
3. The cash excess or deficiency section.
4. The financing section.

The receipts section lists all of the cash inflows, except from financing, expected during the budget period. Generally, the major source of receipts is from sales. The disbursements section summarizes all cash payments that are planned for the budget period.

These payments include raw materials purchases, direct labor payments, manufacturing overhead costs, and so on, as contained in their respective budgets. In addition, other cash disbursements such as equipment purchases and dividends are listed.

The cash excess or deficiency section is computed as follows:

Beginning cash balance	XXX
Add cash receipts	XXX
Total cash available	XXX
Less cash disbursements	XXX
Excess (deficiency) of cash available over disbursements	XXX

If a cash deficiency exists during any budget period or if there is a cash excess during any budget period that is less than the minimum required cash balance, the company will need to borrow money. Conversely, if there is a cash excess during any budget period that is greater than the minimum required cash balance, the company can invest the excess funds or repay principal and interest to lenders.

IN BUSINESS

MISMATCHED CASH FLOWS—CLIMBING THE HILLS AND VALLEYS

The Washington Trails Association (WTA) is a private, nonprofit organization primarily concerned with protecting and maintaining hiking trails in the state of Washington. Some 2,000 WTA volunteer workers donate more than 80,000 hours per year maintaining trails in rugged landscapes on federal, state, and private lands. The organization is supported by membership dues, voluntary contributions, grants, and some contract work for the government.

The organization's income and expenses are erratic—although somewhat predictable—over the course of the year as shown in the following chart. Expenses tend to be highest in the spring and summer when most of the trail maintenance work is done. However, income spikes in December well after the expenses have been incurred. With cash outflows running ahead of cash inflows for much of the year, it is very important for the WTA to carefully plan its cash budget and to maintain adequate cash reserves to be able to pay its bills.

Eric W. Noreen

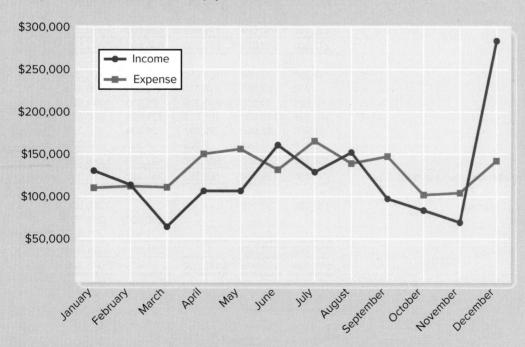

Note: Total income and total expense are approximately equal over the course of the year.

Sources: Conversation with Elizabeth Lunney, President of the Washington Trails Association; WTA documents; and the WTA website www.wta.org.

The financing section of the cash budget details the borrowings and principal and interest repayments projected to take place during the budget period. *In this chapter, unless explicitly stated otherwise, we'll always assume all borrowings take place on the first day of the borrowing period and all repayments take place on the last day of the final period included in the cash budget.* To calculate borrowings and interest payments, you'll need to pay attention to the company's desired minimum cash balance and the terms of the company's loan agreement with the bank. For example, Hampton Freeze's desired minimum cash balance is $30,000 (see cell B42 in the Budgeting Assumptions tab). Furthermore, *we are going to assume Hampton Freeze's loan agreement stipulates it must borrow money in increments of $10,000* and it must pay simple interest of 3 percent per quarter (as shown in cell B45 in Exhibit 8–4).[6]

The cash balances at both the beginning and end of the year may be adequate even though a serious cash deficit occurs at some point during the year. Consequently, the cash budget should be broken down into time periods that are short enough to capture major fluctuations in cash balances. While a monthly cash budget is most common, some organizations budget cash on a weekly or even daily basis. At Hampton Freeze, Larry Giano prepared a quarterly cash budget that can be further refined as necessary. This budget appears in Schedule 8.

The beginning cash balance in the first quarter of $42,500 agrees with cell B7 of the beginning balance sheet in Exhibit 8–3. Each quarter's collections from customers come

SCHEDULE 8

Hampton Freeze, Inc.
Cash Budget
For the Year Ended December 31 of Next Year

	Schedule	Quarter 1	Quarter 2	Quarter 3	Quarter 4	Year
Beginning cash balance		$42,500	$36,000	$33,900	$165,650	$42,500
Add cash receipts:						
Collections from customers	1	230,000	480,000	740,000	520,000	1,970,000
Total cash available		272,500	516,000	773,900	685,650	2,012,500
Less cash disbursements:						
Direct materials	3	49,500	72,300	100,050	79,350	301,200
Direct labor	4	84,000	192,000	216,000	114,000	606,000
Manufacturing overhead	5	68,000	96,800	103,200	76,000	344,000
Selling and administrative	7	107,000	143,000	161,000	125,000	536,000
Equipment purchases		50,000	40,000	20,000	20,000	130,000
Dividends		8,000	8,000	8,000	8,000	32,000
Total cash disbursements		366,500	552,100	608,250	422,350	1,949,200
Excess (deficiency) of cash available over disbursements		(94,000)	(36,100)	165,650	263,300	63,300
Financing:						
Borrowings (at the beginnings of quarters)		130,000	70,000	-	-	200,000
Repayments (at end of the year)		-	-	-	(200,000)	(200,000)
Interest		-	-	-	(21,900)	(21,900)
Total financing		130,000	70,000	-	(221,900)	(21,900)
Ending cash balance		$36,000	$33,900	$165,650	$41,400	$41,400

◄ ► ... | Schedule 5 | Schedule 6 | Schedule 7 | **Schedule 8** | S(... ⊕ ⋮ ◄ [   ] ►

Microsoft Excel

---

[6] We use simple interest rather than compound interest throughout the chapter for simplicity.

from cells B18 through E18 of the schedule of expected cash collections in Schedule 1. Each quarter's beginning cash balance plus the collections from customers equals the total cash available. For example, in the first quarter, the beginning cash balance of $42,500 plus the collections from customers of $230,000 equals the total cash available of $272,500.

The disbursements section of the cash budget includes six types of cash disbursements. Each quarter's cash disbursements for direct materials come from cells B27 through E27 of the schedule of expected cash disbursements for materials (see Schedule 3). The quarterly cash payments for direct labor were calculated in cells B11 through E11 of the direct labor budget (see Schedule 4), whereas the quarterly cash payments related to manufacturing overhead were calculated in cells B13 through E13 of the manufacturing overhead budget (see Schedule 5). The quarterly cash payments for selling and administrative expenses come from cells B19 through E19 of the selling and administrative expense budget (see Schedule 7). So putting it all together, in the first quarter, the cash disbursements for direct materials ($49,500), direct labor ($84,000), manufacturing overhead ($68,000), selling and administrative expenses ($107,000), equipment purchases ($50,000), and the dividend ($8,000) (see cells C43 and B44 in Exhibit 8–4) equal the total cash disbursements of $366,500.

Each quarter's total cash available minus its total disbursements equals the excess (deficiency) of cash available over disbursements. For example, in the first quarter, the total cash available of $272,500 minus the total disbursements of $366,500 results in a cash deficiency of $94,000. The excess or deficiency of cash directly influences whether Hampton Freeze will need to borrow money, as shown in the Financing section of the cash budget.

The first row in the Financing section of the cash budget relates to projected borrowings. In any period where a company's excess of cash available over disbursements is greater than its desired minimum cash balance, the company will not need to borrow money during that period. In the case of Hampton Freeze, the company wants to maintain a minimum cash balance of $30,000; therefore, it will not need to borrow money in any quarter where its excess of cash available over disbursements is greater than $30,000. However, in the first quarter of next year Hampton Freeze estimates it will have a cash deficiency of $94,000; consequently, the company's minimum required borrowings at the beginning of the first quarter would be computed as follows:

Required Borrowings at the Beginning of the First Quarter:	
Desired ending cash balance	$ 30,000
Plus deficiency of cash available over disbursements	94,000
Minimum required borrowings	$124,000

Recall that the bank requires loans be made in increments of $10,000. Because Hampton Freeze needs to borrow at least $124,000, it will have to borrow $130,000.

In next year's second quarter, Hampton Freeze estimates it will have another cash deficiency of $36,100; therefore, the company's minimum required borrowings at the beginning of the second quarter would be computed as follows:

Required Borrowings at the Beginning of the Second Quarter:	
Desired ending cash balance	$30,000
Plus deficiency of cash available over disbursements	36,100
Minimum required borrowings	$66,100

Again, recall that the bank requires loans be made in increments of $10,000. Because Hampton Freeze needs to borrow at least $66,100 at the beginning of the second quarter, the company will have to borrow $70,000 from the bank.

In the third and fourth quarters, Hampton Freeze has an excess of cash available over disbursements greater than $30,000, so it will not need to borrow money in these two quarters. Notice that in the third quarter Hampton Freeze has excess cash of $165,650, yet the cash budget does not include any principal or interest repayments during this quarter. This occurs because, unless stated otherwise, we always assume the company will, as far as it is able, repay the loan plus accumulated interest on the *last day of the final period* included in the cash budget. Because Hampton Freeze has excess cash of $263,300 in the fourth quarter, on the last day of the fourth quarter, it would be able to repay the $200,000 that it borrowed from the lender plus $21,900 of interest computed as follows:

Interest on the $130,000 borrowed at the beginning of the first quarter:	
$130,000 × 0.03 per quarter × 4 quarters*	$15,600
Interest on the $70,000 borrowed at the beginning of the second quarter:	
$70,000 × 0.03 per quarter × 3 quarters*	6,300
Total interest accrued to the end of the fourth quarter	$21,900

* Simple, rather than compounded, interest is assumed for simplicity

The ending cash balance for each period is computed by taking the excess (deficiency) of cash available over disbursements plus the total financing. For example, in the first quarter, Hampton Freeze's cash deficiency of $(94,000) plus its total financing of $130,000 equals its ending cash balance of $36,000. The ending cash balance for each quarter then becomes the beginning cash balance for the next quarter. Also, the amounts under the Year column in the cash budget are not always the sum of the amounts for the four quarters. In particular, the beginning cash balance for the year is the same as the beginning cash balance for the first quarter, and the ending cash balance for the year is the same as the ending cash balance for the fourth quarter.

The Budgeted Income Statement

Schedule 9 contains the budgeted income statement for Hampton Freeze. All of the sales and expenses shown on the budgeted income statement come from the data in the beginning balance sheet and the data developed in Schedules 1–8. The sales of $2,000,000 come from cell F9 of the sales budget (Schedule 1). Given that the unit product cost of the year's beginning inventory and the year's production both equal $13 per unit, the cost of goods sold of $1,300,000 can be computed by multiplying 100,000 units sold (see cell F7 from Schedule 1) by the unit product cost of $13 per unit (see cell H11 in Schedule 6).[7] The selling and administrative expenses of $576,000 come from cell F17 of the selling and administrative expenses budget (Schedule 7). Finally, the interest expense of $21,900 comes from cell G23 of the cash budget (Schedule 8).

The budgeted income statement is one of the key schedules in the budget process. It shows the company's planned profit and serves as a benchmark against which subsequent company performance can be measured. Because Larry Giano created a Budgeting Assumptions tab in his Excel file (see Exhibit 8–4) and linked all of his budget schedules together using properly constructed Excel formulas, he can make changes to his underlying budgeting assumptions and instantly see the impact of the change on all of the schedules and on net income. For example, if Larry wanted to estimate the profit impact if fourth-quarter sales are 18,000 cases instead of 20,000 cases, he would simply

---

[7] Cost of goods sold can also be computed using equations introduced in earlier chapters. Manufacturing companies can use the equation: Cost of goods sold = Beginning finished goods inventory + Cost of goods manufactured − Ending finished goods inventory. Merchandising companies can use the equation: Cost of goods sold = Beginning merchandise inventory + Purchases − Ending merchandise inventory.

	A	B	C
1	**Hampton Freeze, Inc.**		
2	**Budgeted Income Statement**		
3	**For the Year Ended December 31 of Next Year**		
4			
5		*Schedules*	
6	Sales	1	$ 2,000,000
7	Cost of goods sold	1, 6	1,300,000
8	Gross margin		700,000
9	Selling and administrative expenses	7	576,000
10	Net operating Income		124,000
11	Interest expense	8	21,900
12	Net Income		$ 102,100

Schedule 9   Schedule 10   (+)

Microsoft Excel

change the 20,000 cases shown in cell F7 of his Budgeting Assumptions worksheet to 18,000 cases. The revised net income of $87,045 would instantly appear in cell C12 of the budgeted income statement.

The Budgeted Balance Sheet

The budgeted balance sheet is developed using data from the balance sheet from the beginning of the budget period (see Exhibit 8–3) and data contained in the various schedules. Hampton Freeze's budgeted balance sheet accompanied by explanations of how the numbers were derived is presented in Schedule 10.

LEARNING OBJECTIVE 8–10
Prepare a budgeted balance sheet.

After completing the master budget, Larry Giano took the documents to Tom Wills, chief executive officer of Hampton Freeze, for his review.

MANAGERIAL ACCOUNTING IN ACTION
The Wrap-Up

Larry: Here's the budget. Overall, the income is excellent, and the net cash flow for the entire year is positive.
Tom: Yes, but I see on this cash budget that we have the same problem with negative cash flows in the first and second quarters that we had this year.
Larry: That's true. I don't see any way around that problem. However, there is no doubt in my mind that if you take this budget to the bank today, they'll approve an open line of credit that will allow you to borrow enough money to make it through the first two quarters without any problem.
Tom: Are you sure? They didn't seem very happy to see me this year when I came in for an emergency loan.
Larry: Did you repay the loan on time?
Tom: Sure.
Larry: I don't see any problem. You won't be asking for an emergency loan this time. The bank will have plenty of warning. And with this budget, you have a solid plan that shows when and how you are going to pay off the loan. Trust me, they'll go for it. Also, keep in mind that the master budget contains all the embedded formulas you'll need to answer the types of "what-if" questions that we discussed earlier. If you want to calculate the financial impact of changing any of your master budget's underlying estimates or assumptions, you can do it with the click of a mouse!
Tom: This sounds fabulous, Larry. Thanks for all of your work on this project.

SCHEDULE 10

	A	B	C	D	E
1	Hampton Freeze, Inc.				
2	Budgeted Balance Sheet				
3	December 31 of Next Year				
4					
5	Assets				
6	Current assets:				
7	Cash	$ 41,400	(a)		
8	Accounts receivable	120,000	(b)		
9	Raw materials inventory	4,500	(c)		
10	Finished goods inventory	39,000	(d)		
11	Total current assets			$ 204,900	
12	Plant and equipment:				
13	Land	80,000	(e)		
14	Buildings and equipment	830,000	(f)		
15	Accumulated depreciation	(392,000)	(g)		
16	Plant and equipment, net			518,000	
17	Total assets			$ 722,900	
18					
19	Liabilities and Stockholders' Equity				
20	Current liabilities:				
21	Accounts payable (raw materials)			$ 27,900	(h)
22	Stockholders' equity:				
23	Common stock, no par	$ 175,000	(i)		
24	Retained earnings	520,000	(j)		
25	Total stockholders' equity			695,000	
26	Total liabilities and stockholders' equity			$ 722,900	
27					

◀　▶　... e 9　**Schedule 10**　⊕　⋮　◀ [　　] ▶

Microsoft Excel

Explanations of December 31 budgeted balance sheet figures:
(a) From cell G25 of the cash budget (Schedule 8).
(b) Thirty percent of fourth-quarter sales, from Schedule 1 ($400,000 × 30% = $120,000).
(c) From the direct materials budget (Schedule 3). Cell E12 multiplied by cell E16. In other words, 22,500 pounds × $0.20 per pound = $4,500.
(d) From cell H16 of the ending finished goods inventory budget (Schedule 6).
(e) From cell B13 of the beginning balance sheet (Exhibit 8–3).
(f) Cell B14 of the beginning balance sheet (Exhibit 8–3) plus cell G16 from the cash budget (Schedule 8). In other words, $700,000 + $130,000 = $830,000.
(g) The beginning balance of $292,000 (from cell B15 of the beginning balance sheet in Exhibit 8–3) plus the depreciation of $60,000 included in cell F12 of the manufacturing overhead budget (Schedule 5) plus depreciation expense of $40,000 included in cell F18 in the selling and administrative expense budget (Schedule 7). In other words, $292,000 + $60,000 + $40,000 = $392,000.
(h) One-half of fourth-quarter raw materials purchases, from Schedule 3 ($55,800 × 50% = $27,900).
(i) From cell B23 of the beginning balance sheet (Exhibit 8–3).
(j)

Beginning balance, from cell B24 of Exhibit 8–3	$ 449,900
Add net income, from cell C12 of Schedule 9	102,100
	552,000
Deduct dividends paid, from cell G17 of Schedule 8	32,000
Ending balance	$ 520,000

PLANNING FOR A CRISIS—CIVIL WAR TRUST

The Civil War Trust (CWT) is a private, nonprofit organization with 70,000 members that works to preserve the nation's remaining Civil War battlefields—many of which are threatened by commercial development, such as shopping centers, houses, industrial parks, and casinos. To forestall development, the CWT typically purchases the land or development rights to the land. The CWT has saved over 25,000 acres from development, including, for example, 698 acres of battlefield at Gettysburg.

The CWT is wholly supported by contributions from its members. When the economy stagnates, it complicates the CWT's ability to predict the amount of future donations. The CWT responds to this uncertainty by creating an annual budget that contains three variations based on progressively pessimistic economic assumptions. The more pessimistic budgets were called contingent budgets. If member contributions decline somewhat due to economic woes, the CWT can switch to its first contingent budget. In the past, rolling to the contingent budget required a number of actions to reduce costs, including a hiring freeze and a salary freeze while maintaining an aggressive program of protecting battlefield acreage through purchases of land and development rights. In more dire circumstances, the CWT can switch to its most pessimistic budget—which would involve layoffs and other extraordinary cost-saving measures.

Instead of reacting in a panic mode to unfavorable developments, CWT uses the budgeting process to carefully plan in advance for a number of possible contingencies.

Sources: Communications with James Lighthizer, president, and David Duncan, director of membership and development, Civil War Trust; and the CWT website, www.civilwar.org.

Sandee Noreen

Summary

This chapter describes the budgeting process and shows how the various operating budgets relate to each other. The sales budget is the foundation for a master budget. Once the sales budget has been set, the production budget and the selling and administrative expense budget can be prepared because they depend on how many units are to be sold. The production budget determines how many units are to be produced, so after it is prepared, the various manufacturing cost budgets can be prepared. All of these budgets feed into the cash budget, and the budgeted income statement and balance sheet. The parts of the master budget are connected in many ways. For example, the schedule of expected cash collections, which is completed in connection with the sales budget, provides data for both the cash budget and the budgeted balance sheet.

The material in this chapter is just an introduction to master budgeting. In later chapters, we will see how budgets are used to control day-to-day operations and how they are used in performance evaluation.

Data Analytics Exercise available in Connect to complement this chapter

Review Problem: Budget Schedules

Mynor Corporation manufactures and sells a seasonal product that has peak sales in the third quarter. The following information concerns operations for Year 2—the coming year—and for the first two quarters of Year 3:

a. The company's single product sells for $8 per unit. Budgeted unit sales for the next six quarters are as follows (all sales are on credit):

	Year 2 Quarter				Year 3 Quarter	
	1	2	3	4	1	2
Budgeted sales in units	40,000	60,000	100,000	50,000	70,000	80,000

b. Sales are collected in the following pattern: 75 percent in the quarter the sales are made, and the remaining 25 percent in the following quarter. On January 1, Year 2, the company's balance sheet showed $65,000 in accounts receivable, all of which will be collected in the first quarter of the year. Bad debts are negligible and can be ignored.

c. The company desires an ending finished goods inventory at the end of each quarter equal to 30 percent of the budgeted unit sales for the next quarter. On December 31, Year 1, the company had 12,000 units on hand.

d. Five pounds of raw materials are required to complete one unit of product. The company requires ending raw materials inventory at the end of each quarter equal to 10 percent of the following quarter's production needs. On December 31, Year 1, the company had 23,000 pounds of raw materials on hand.

e. The raw material costs $0.80 per pound. Raw materials purchases are paid for in the following pattern: 60 percent paid in the quarter the purchases are made, and the remaining 40 percent paid in the following quarter. On January 1, Year 2, the company's balance sheet showed $81,500 in accounts payable for raw materials purchases, all of which will be paid for in the first quarter of the year.

Required:

Prepare the following budgets and schedules for the year, showing both quarterly and total figures:

1. A sales budget and a schedule of expected cash collections.
2. A production budget.
3. A direct materials budget and a schedule of expected cash payments for purchases of materials.

Solution to Review Problem

1. The sales budget is prepared as follows:

	Year 2 Quarter				Year 2
	1	2	3	4	
Budgeted unit sales	40,000	60,000	100,000	50,000	250,000
Selling price per unit . . .	× $8	× $8	× $8	× $8	× $8
Total sales	$ 320,000	$ 480,000	$ 800,000	$ 400,000	$ 2,000,000

Based on the budgeted sales above, the schedule of expected cash collections is prepared as follows:

	Year 2 Quarter				Year 2
	1	2	3	4	
Beginning accounts receivable	$ 65,000				$ 65,000
First-quarter sales ($320,000 × 75%, 25%)	240,000	$ 80,000			320,000
Second-quarter sales ($480,000 × 75%, 25%)		360,000	$ 120,000		480,000
Third-quarter sales ($800,000 × 75%, 25%)			600,000	$ 200,000	800,000
Fourth-quarter sales ($400,000 × 75%)				300,000	300,000
Total cash collections	$ 305,000	$ 440,000	$ 720,000	$ 500,000	$ 1,965,000

2. Based on the sales budget in units, the production budget is prepared as follows:

| | Year 2 Quarter | | | | | Year 3 Quarter | |
	1	2	3	4	Year 2	1	2
Budgeted unit sales	40,000	60,000	100,000	50,000	250,000	70,000	80,000
Add desired ending finished goods inventory*	18,000	30,000	15,000	21,000[†]	21,000	24,000	
Total needs	58,000	90,000	115,000	71,000	271,000	94,000	
Less beginning finished goods inventory	12,000	18,000	30,000	15,000	12,000	21,000	
Required production	46,000	72,000	85,000	56,000	259,000	73,000	

* 30% of the following quarter's budgeted unit sales.
† 30% of the budgeted Year 3 first-quarter sales.

3. Based on the production budget, raw materials will need to be purchased during the year as follows:

| | Year 2 Quarter | | | | | Year 3 Quarter |
	1	2	3	4	Year 2	1
Required production in units of finished goods	46,000	72,000	85,000	56,000	259,000	73,000
Units of raw materials needed per unit of finished goods	× 5	× 5	× 5	× 5	× 5	× 5
Units of raw materials needed to meet production	230,000	360,000	425,000	280,000	1,295,000	365,000
Add desired units of ending raw materials inventory*	36,000	42,500	28,000	36,500[†]	36,500	
Total units of raw materials needed	266,000	402,500	453,000	316,500	1,331,500	
Less units of beginning raw materials inventory	23,000	36,000	42,500	28,000	23,000	
Units of raw materials to be purchased	243,000	366,500	410,500	288,500	1,308,500	
Unit cost of raw materials	× $0.80	× $0.80	× $0.80	× $0.80	× $0.80	
Cost of raw materials to be purchased	$194,400	$293,200	$328,400	$230,800	$1,046,800	

* 10% of the following quarter's production needs in pounds.
† 10% of the Year 3 first-quarter production needs in pounds.

Based on the raw materials purchases above, expected cash payments are computed as follows:

| | Year 2 Quarter | | | | |
	1	2	3	4	Year 2
Beginning accounts payable	$ 81,500				$ 81,500
First-quarter purchases ($194,400 × 60%, 40%)	116,640	$ 77,760			194,400
Second-quarter purchases ($293,200 × 60%, 40%)		175,920	$117,280		293,200
Third-quarter purchases ($328,400 × 60%, 40%)			197,040	$131,360	328,400
Fourth-quarter purchases ($230,800 × 60%)				138,480	138,480
Total cash disbursements	$198,140	$253,680	$314,320	$269,840	$1,035,980

Glossary

Budget A detailed plan for the future that is usually expressed in formal quantitative terms. (p. 402)

Cash budget A detailed plan showing how cash resources will be acquired and used over a specific time period. (p. 404)

Control The process of gathering feedback to ensure that a plan is being properly executed or modified as circumstances change. (p. 402)

Direct labor budget A detailed plan that shows the direct labor-hours required to fulfill the production budget. (p. 414)

Direct materials budget A detailed plan showing the amount of raw materials that must be purchased to fulfill the production budget and to provide for adequate inventories. (p. 412)

Ending finished goods inventory budget A budget showing the dollar amount of unsold finished goods inventory that will appear on the ending balance sheet. (p. 416)

Manufacturing overhead budget A detailed plan showing the production costs, other than direct materials and direct labor, that will be incurred over a specified time period. (p. 415)

Master budget A number of separate but interdependent budgets that formally lay out the company's sales, production, and financial goals and culminate in a cash budget, budgeted income statement, and budgeted balance sheet. (p. 403)

Merchandise purchases budget A detailed plan used by a merchandising company that shows the amount of goods that must be purchased from suppliers during the period. (p. 412)

Participative budget See *Self-imposed budget.* (p. 402)

Planning The process of establishing goals and specifying how to achieve them. (p. 402)

Production budget A detailed plan showing the number of units that must be produced during a period in order to satisfy both sales and inventory needs. (p. 411)

Sales budget A detailed schedule showing expected sales expressed in both dollars and units. (p. 403)

Self-imposed budget A method of preparing budgets in which managers prepare their own budgets. These budgets are then reviewed by higher-level managers, and any issues are resolved by mutual agreement. (p. 402)

Selling and administrative expense budget A detailed schedule of planned expenses that will be incurred in areas other than manufacturing during a budget period. (p. 416)

Questions

8–1 What is a budget? What is budgetary control?

8–2 Discuss some of the major reasons why companies prepare budgets.

8–3 What is a perpetual budget?

8–4 What is a master budget? Briefly describe its contents.

8–5 Why is the sales forecast the starting point in budgeting?

8–6 "As a practical matter, planning and control mean exactly the same thing." Do you agree? Explain.

8–7 Why is it a good idea to create a "Budgeting Assumptions" tab when creating a master budget in Microsoft Excel?

8–8 What is a self-imposed budget? What are the major advantages of self-imposed budgets? What caution must be exercised in their use?

8–9 How can budgeting assist a company in planning its workforce staffing levels?

8–10 "The principal purpose of the cash budget is to see how much cash the company will have in the bank at the end of the year." Do you agree? Explain.

Applying Excel   Mc Graw Hill connect

LEARNING OBJECTIVES 8–2, 8–3, 8–4   The Excel worksheet form below is to be used to recreate the Review Problem related to Mynor Corporation. The workbook, and instructions on how to complete the file, can be found in Connect.

	A	B	C	D	E	F	G	H	I
1	Chapter 8: Applying Excel								
2									
3	Data			Year 2 Quarter			Year 3 Quarter		
4			1	2	3	4	1	2	
5	Budgeted unit sales		40,000	60,000	100,000	50,000	70,000	80,000	
6									
7	• Selling price per unit	$8							
8	• Accounts receivable, beginning balance	$65,000							
9	• Sales collected in the quarter sales are made	75%							
10	• Sales collected in the quarter after sales are made	25%							
11	• Desired ending finished goods inventory is	30%	of the budgeted unit sales of the next quarter						
12	• Finished goods inventory, beginning	12,000	units						
13	• Raw materials required to produce one unit	5	pounds						
14	• Desired ending inventory of raw materials is	10%	of the next quarter's production needs						
15	• Raw materials inventory, beginning	23,000	pounds						
16	• Raw materials costs	$0.80	per pound						
17	• Raw materials purchases are paid	60%	in the quarter the purchases are made						
18	and	40%	in the quarter following purchase						
19	• Accounts payable for raw materials, beginning balance	$81,500							
20									
21	*Enter a formula into each of the cells marked with a ? below*								
22	Review Problem: Budget Schedules								
23									
24	*Construct the sales budget*			Year 2 Quarter			Year 3 Quarter		
25			1	2	3	4	1	2	
26	Budgeted unit sales		?	?	?	?	?	?	
27	Selling price per unit		?	?	?	?	?	?	
28	Total sales		?	?	?	?	?	?	
29									
30	*Construct the schedule of expected cash collections*			Year 2 Quarter					
31			1	2	3	4	Year		
32	Beginning balance accounts receivable		?				?		
33	First-quarter sales		?	?			?		
34	Second-quarter sales			?	?		?		
35	Third-quarter sales				?	?	?		
36	Fourth-quarter sales					?	?		
37	Total cash collections		?	?	?	?	?		
38									
39	*Construct the production budget*			Year 2 Quarter				Year 3 Quarter	
40			1	2	3	4	Year	1	2
41	Budgeted unit sales		?	?	?	?	?	?	?
42	Add desired ending finished goods inventory		?	?	?	?	?	?	
43	Total needs		?	?	?	?	?	?	
44	Less beginning finished goods inventory		?	?	?	?	?	?	
45	Required production in units		?	?	?	?	?	?	
46									
47	*Construct the raw materials purchases budget*			Year 2 Quarter				Year 3 Quarter	
48			1	2	3	4	Year	1	
49	Required production (units)		?	?	?	?	?	?	
50	Raw materials required to produce one unit (pounds)		?	?	?	?	?	?	
51	Production needs (pounds)		?	?	?	?	?	?	
52	Add desired ending inventory of raw materials (pounds)		?	?	?	?	?		
53	Total needs (pounds)		?	?	?	?	?		
54	Less beginning inventory of raw materials (pounds)		?	?	?	?	?		
55	Raw materials to be purchased (pounds)		?	?	?	?	?		
56	Cost of raw materials per pound		?	?	?	?	?		
57	Cost of raw materials to be purchased		?	?	?	?	?		
58									
59	*Construct the schedule of expected cash payments*			Year 2 Quarter					
60			1	2	3	4	Year		
61	Beginning balance accounts payable		?				?		
62	First-quarter purchases		?	?			?		
63	Second-quarter purchases			?	?		?		
64	Third-quarter purchases				?	?	?		
65	Fourth-quarter purchases					?	?		
66	Total cash disbursements		?	?	?	?	?		
67									

H ◀ ▶ H   **Chapter 8 Form** / Filled in Chapter 8 Form / Chapter 8 Formulas / Chapter 8 Requiremen

Microsoft Excel

You should proceed to the requirements below only after completing your worksheet.

Required:

1. Check your worksheet by changing the budgeted unit sales in Quarter 2 of Year 2 in cell C5 to 75,000 units. The total expected cash collections for the year should now be $2,085,000. The required production for the year should be 274,000 units. The cost of raw materials to be purchased for the year should be $1,106,800, whereas the total cash disbursements for the year should be $1,095,980. If you do not get these answers, find the errors in your worksheet and correct them. Why have the total cash disbursements for raw materials increased?

2. The company just hired a new marketing manager who insists that unit sales can be dramatically increased by dropping the selling price from $8 to $7. The marketing manager would like to use the following projections in the budget:

	Year 2 Quarter				Year 3 Quarter	
	1	2	3	4	1	2
Budgeted unit sales	50,000	70,000	120,000	80,000	90,000	100,000
Selling price per unit	$7					

    a. What are the total expected cash collections for the year under this revised budget?
    b. What is the total required production for the year under this revised budget?
    c. What is the total cost of raw materials to be purchased for the year under this revised budget?
    d. What are the total expected cash disbursements for raw materials for the year under this revised budget?
    e. After seeing this revised budget, the production manager cautioned that due to the limited availability of a complex milling machine, the plant can produce no more than 90,000 units in any one quarter. Is this a potential problem? If so, what can be done about it?

The Foundational 15   Mc Graw Hill **connect**

LEARNING OBJECTIVES 8–2, 8–3, 8–4, 8–5, 8–7, 8–9, 8–10

Morganton Company makes one product, and it provided the following information to help prepare the master budget:

    a. The budgeted selling price per unit is $70. Budgeted unit sales for June, July, August, and September are 8,400, 10,000, 12,000, and 13,000 units, respectively. All sales are on credit.
    b. Forty percent of credit sales are collected in the month of the sale and 60% in the following month.
    c. The ending finished goods inventory equals 20% of the following month's unit sales.
    d. The ending raw materials inventory equals 10% of the following month's raw materials production needs. Each unit of finished goods requires 5 pounds of raw materials. The raw materials cost $2.00 per pound.
    e. Thirty percent of raw materials purchases are paid for in the month of purchase and 70% in the following month.
    f. The direct labor wage rate is $15 per hour. Each unit of finished goods requires two direct labor-hours.
    g. The variable selling and administrative expense per unit sold is $1.80. The fixed selling and administrative expense per month is $60,000.

Required:

1. What are the budgeted sales for July?
2. What are the expected cash collections for July?
3. What is the accounts receivable balance at the end of July?
4. According to the production budget, how many units should be produced in July?
5. If 61,000 pounds of raw materials are needed to meet production in August, how many pounds of raw materials should be purchased in July?
6. What is the estimated cost of raw materials purchases for July?
7. In July, what are the total estimated cash disbursements for raw materials purchases? Assume the cost of raw material purchases in June is $88,880.
8. What is the estimated accounts payable balance at the end of July?
9. What is the estimated raw materials inventory balance at the end of July?
10. What is the total estimated direct labor cost for July?

11. If we assume there is no fixed manufacturing overhead and the variable manufacturing overhead is $10 per direct labor-hour, what is the estimated unit product cost?
12. What is the estimated finished goods inventory balance at the end of July?
13. What are the estimated cost of goods sold and gross margin for July?
14. What is the estimated total selling and administrative expense for July?
15. What is the estimated net operating income for July?

Exercises

EXERCISE 8–1 Schedule of Expected Cash Collections LO 8–2

Silver Company makes a product that is very popular as a Mother's Day gift. Thus, peak sales occur in May of each year, as shown in the company's sales budget for the second quarter given below:

	April	May	June	Total
Budgeted sales (all on account).........	$300,000	$500,000	$200,000	$1,000,000

From past experience, the company learned that 20% of a month's sales are collected in the month of sale, another 70% are collected in the month following sale, and the remaining 10% are collected in the second month following sale. Bad debts are negligible and can be ignored. February sales totaled $230,000, and March sales totaled $260,000.

Required:
1. Using Schedule 1 as your guide, prepare a schedule of expected cash collections from sales, by month and in total, for the second quarter.
2. What is the accounts receivable balance on June 30th?

EXERCISE 8–2 Production Budget LO 8–3

Down Under Products, Ltd., of Australia has budgeted sales of its popular boomerang for the next four months as follows:

	Unit Sales
April..................	50,000
May	75,000
June	90,000
July	80,000

The company is now in the process of preparing a production budget for the second quarter. Past experience has shown that end-of-month inventory levels must equal 10% of the following month's unit sales. The inventory at the end of March was 5,000 units.

Required:
Using Schedule 2 as your guide, prepare a production budget, by month and in total, for the second quarter.

EXERCISE 8–3 Direct Materials Budget LO 8–4

Three grams of musk oil are required for each bottle of Mink Caress, a very popular perfume made by a small company in western Siberia. The cost of the musk oil is $1.50 per gram. Budgeted production of Mink Caress is given below by quarters for Year 2 and for the first quarter of Year 3:

	Year 2				Year 3
	First	Second	Third	Fourth	First
Budgeted production, in bottles	60,000	90,000	150,000	100,000	70,000

The inventory of musk oil at the end of a quarter must be equal to 20% of the following quarter's production needs. Some 36,000 grams of musk oil will be on hand to start the first quarter of Year 2.

Required:

Using Schedule 3 as your guide, prepare a direct materials budget for musk oil, by quarter and in total, for Year 2.

EXERCISE 8–4 Direct Labor Budget LO 8–5

The production manager of Rordan Corporation submitted the following quarterly production forecast for the upcoming fiscal year:

	1st Quarter	2nd Quarter	3rd Quarter	4th Quarter
Units to be produced	8,000	6,500	7,000	7,500

Each unit requires 0.35 direct labor-hours, and direct laborers are paid $15.00 per hour.

Required:

Using Schedule 4 as your guide, prepare the company's direct labor budget for the upcoming fiscal year.

EXERCISE 8–5 Manufacturing Overhead Budget LO 8–6

The direct labor budget of Yuvwell Corporation for the upcoming fiscal year contains the following details concerning budgeted direct labor-hours:

	1st Quarter	2nd Quarter	3rd Quarter	4th Quarter
Budgeted direct labor-hours	8,000	8,200	8,500	7,800

The company uses direct labor-hours as its overhead allocation base. The variable portion of its predetermined manufacturing overhead rate is $3.25 per direct labor-hour and its total fixed manufacturing overhead is $48,000 per quarter. The only noncash item included in fixed manufacturing overhead is depreciation, which is $16,000 per quarter.

Required:

1. Using Schedule 5 as your guide, prepare the company's manufacturing overhead budget for the upcoming fiscal year.
2. Compute the company's predetermined overhead rate (including both variable and fixed manufacturing overhead) for the upcoming fiscal year. Round off to the nearest whole cent.

EXERCISE 8–6 Selling and Administrative Expense Budget LO 8–7

Weller Company's budgeted unit sales for the upcoming fiscal year are provided below:

	1st Quarter	2nd Quarter	3rd Quarter	4th Quarter
Budgeted unit sales	15,000	16,000	14,000	13,000

The company's variable selling and administrative expense per unit is $2.50. Fixed selling and administrative expenses include advertising expenses of $8,000 per quarter, executive salaries of $35,000 per quarter, and depreciation of $20,000 per quarter. In addition, the company will make insurance payments of $5,000 in the first quarter and $5,000 in the third quarter. Finally, property taxes of $8,000 will be paid in the second quarter.

Required:

Using Schedule 7 as your guide, prepare the company's selling and administrative expense budget for the upcoming fiscal year.

EXERCISE 8–7 Cash Budget LO 8–8

Garden Depot is a retailer that is preparing its budget for the upcoming fiscal year. Management prepared the following summary of its budgeted cash flows:

	1st Quarter	2nd Quarter	3rd Quarter	4th Quarter
Total cash receipts	$180,000	$330,000	$210,000	$230,000
Total cash disbursements	$260,000	$230,000	$220,000	$240,000

The company's beginning cash balance for the upcoming fiscal year will be $20,000. The company requires a minimum cash balance of $10,000 and may borrow any amount needed from a local bank at a quarterly interest rate of 3%. The company may borrow any amount at the beginning of any quarter and may repay its loans, or any part of its loans, at the end of any quarter. Interest payments are due on any principal at the time it is repaid. For simplicity, assume interest is not compounded.

Required:
Using Schedule 8 as your guide, prepare the company's cash budget for the upcoming fiscal year.

EXERCISE 8–8 Budgeted Income Statement LO 8–9

Gig Harbor Boating is the wholesale distributor of a small recreational catamaran sailboat. Management prepared the following summary data to use in its annual budgeting process:

Budgeted unit sales	460
Selling price per unit	$1,950
Cost per unit	$1,575
Variable selling and administrative expense (per unit)	$75
Fixed selling and administrative expense (per year)	$105,000
Interest expense for the year	$14,000

Required:
Using Schedule 9 as your guide, prepare the company's budgeted income statement for the year.

EXERCISE 8–9 Budgeted Balance Sheet LO 8–10

The management of Mecca Copy, a photocopying center located on University Avenue, compiled the following data to use in preparing its budgeted balance sheet for next year:

	Ending Balances
Cash	?
Accounts receivable	$8,100
Supplies inventory	$3,200
Equipment	$34,000
Accumulated depreciation	$16,000
Accounts payable	$1,800
Common stock	$5,000
Retained earnings	?

The beginning balance of retained earnings was $28,000, net income is budgeted to be $11,500, and dividends are budgeted to be $4,800.

Required:
Prepare the company's budgeted balance sheet.

EXERCISE 8–10 Production and Direct Materials Budgets LO 8–3, LO 8–4

Pearl Products Limited of Shenzhen, China, manufactures and distributes toys throughout Southeast Asia. Three cubic centimeters (cc) of solvent H300 are required to manufacture each unit of Supermix, one of the company's products. The company is planning its raw materials needs for the third quarter, the quarter in which peak sales of Supermix occur. To keep production and sales moving smoothly, the company has the following inventory requirements:

a. The finished goods inventory on hand at the end of each month must equal 3,000 units of Supermix plus 20% of the next month's sales. The finished goods inventory on June 30 is budgeted to be 10,000 units.

b. The raw materials inventory on hand at the end of each month must equal one-half of the following month's production needs for raw materials. The raw materials inventory on June 30 is budgeted to be 54,000 cc of solvent H300.

c.   The company maintains no work in process inventories.

A monthly sales budget for Supermix for the third and fourth quarters of the year follows.

	Budgeted Unit Sales
July	35,000
August	40,000
September	50,000
October	30,000
November	20,000
December	10,000

Required:

1.   Prepare a production budget for Supermix for the months July, August, September, and October.

2.   Examine the production budget that you prepared in (1) above. Why will the company produce more units than it sells in July and August, and fewer units than it sells in September and October?

3.   Prepare a direct materials budget showing the quantity of solvent H300 to be purchased for July, August, and September, and for the quarter in total.

EXERCISE 8–11 Cash Budget Analysis LO 8–8

A cash budget, by quarters, is given below for a retail company (000 omitted). The company requires a minimum cash balance of at least $5,000 to start each quarter.

	Quarter				
	1	2	3	4	Year
Cash balance, beginning	$ 6	$?	$?	$?	$?
Add collections from customers	?	?	96	?	323
Total cash available	71	?	?	?	?
Less disbursements:					
Purchase of inventory	35	45	?	35	?
Selling and administrative expenses	?	30	30	?	113
Equipment purchases	8	8	10	?	36
Dividends.....................................	2	2	2	2	?
Total disbursements	?	85	?	?	?
Excess (deficiency) of cash available over disbursements	(2)	?	11	?	?
Financing:					
Borrowings	?	15	—	—	?
Repayments (including interest)*	—	—	(?)	(17)	(?)
Total financing	?	?	?	?	?
Cash balance, ending	$?	$?	$?	$?	$?

* Interest will total $1,000 for the year.

Required:

Fill in the missing amounts in the above table.

EXERCISE 8–12 Schedules of Expected Cash Collections and Disbursements; Income Statement; Balance Sheet LO 8–2, LO 8–4, LO 8–9, LO 8–10

Beech Corporation is a merchandising company that is preparing a master budget for the third quarter of the calendar year. The company's balance sheet as of June 30th is shown below:

Beech Corporation Balance Sheet June 30	
Assets	
Cash	$ 90,000
Accounts receivable	136,000
Inventory	62,000
Plant and equipment, net of depreciation	210,000
Total assets	$498,000
Liabilities and Stockholders' Equity	
Accounts payable	$ 71,100
Common stock	327,000
Retained earnings	99,900
Total liabilities and stockholders' equity	$498,000

Beech's managers have made the following additional assumptions and estimates:

1. Estimated sales for July, August, September, and October will be $210,000, $230,000, $220,000, and $240,000, respectively.

2. All sales are on credit, and all credit sales are collected. Each month's credit sales are collected 35% in the month of sale and 65% in the month following the sale. All of the accounts receivable at June 30 will be collected in July.

3. Each month's ending inventory must equal 30% of the cost of next month's sales. The cost of goods sold is 60% of sales. The company pays for 40% of its merchandise purchases in the month of the purchase and the remaining 60% in the month following the purchase. All of the accounts payable at June 30 will be paid in July.

4. Monthly selling and administrative expenses are always $60,000. Each month $5,000 of this total amount is depreciation expense, and the remaining $55,000 relates to expenses that are paid in the month they are incurred.

5. The company does not plan to borrow money or pay or declare dividends during the quarter ended September 30. The company does not plan to issue any common stock or repurchase its own stock during the quarter ended September 30.

Required:

1. Prepare a schedule of expected cash collections for July, August, and September. Also, compute total cash collections for the quarter ended September 30.

2. *a.* Prepare a merchandise purchases budget for July, August, and September. Also, compute total merchandise purchases for the quarter ended September 30.

   b. Prepare a schedule of expected cash disbursements for merchandise purchases for July, August, and September. Also compute total cash disbursements for merchandise purchases for the quarter ended September 30.

3. Using Schedule 9 as your guide, prepare an income statement that computes net operating income for the quarter ended September 30.

4. Prepare a balance sheet as of September 30.

EXERCISE 8–13 Schedules of Expected Cash Collections and Disbursements; Income Statement; Balance Sheet LO 8–2, LO 8–4, LO 8–9, LO 8–10

Refer to the data for Beech Corporation in Exercise 8–12. The company is considering making the following changes to the assumptions underlying its master budget:

1. Each month's credit sales are collected 45% in the month of sale and 55% in the month following the sale.

2. Each month's ending inventory must equal 20% of the cost of next month's sales.
3. The company pays for 30% of its merchandise purchases in the month of the purchase and the remaining 70% in the month following the purchase.

All other information from Exercise 8–12 that is not mentioned above remains the same.

Required:

Using the new assumptions described above, complete the following requirements:

1. Prepare a schedule of expected cash collections for July, August, and September. Also compute total cash collections for the quarter ended September 30.
2.   *a.* Prepare a merchandise purchases budget for July, August, and September. Also compute total merchandise purchases for the quarter ended September 30.
    b. Prepare a schedule of expected cash disbursements for merchandise purchases for July, August, and September. Also, compute total cash disbursements for merchandise purchases for the quarter ended September 30.
3. Using Schedule 9 as your guide, prepare an income statement for the quarter ended September 30.
4. Prepare a balance sheet as of September 30.

EXERCISE 8–14 Sales and Production Budgets LO 8–2, LO 8–3

The marketing department of Jessi Corporation submitted the following sales forecast for the upcoming fiscal year (all sales are on account):

	1st Quarter	2nd Quarter	3rd Quarter	4th Quarter
Budgeted unit sales	11,000	12,000	14,000	13,000

The selling price of the company's product is $18.00 per unit. Management expects to collect 65% of sales in the quarter in which the sales are made, 30% in the following quarter, and 5% of sales are expected to be uncollectible. The beginning balance of accounts receivable, all of which is expected to be collected in the first quarter, is $70,200.

    The company expects to start the first quarter with 1,650 units in finished goods inventory. Management desires an ending finished goods inventory in each quarter equal to 15% of the next quarter's budgeted sales. The desired ending finished goods inventory for the fourth quarter is 1,850 units.

Required:

1. Calculate the estimated sales for each quarter of the fiscal year and for the year as a whole. (Hint: Refer to Schedule 1 for guidance.)
2. Calculate the expected cash collections for each quarter of the fiscal year and for the year as a whole. (Hint: Refer to Schedule 1 for guidance.)
3. Calculate the required production in units of finished goods for each quarter of the fiscal year and for the year as a whole. (Hint: Refer to Schedule 2 for guidance.)

EXERCISE 8–15 Direct Labor and Manufacturing Overhead Budgets LO 8–5, LO 8–6

The Production Department of Hruska Corporation submitted the following forecast of units to be produced by quarter for the upcoming fiscal year:

	1st Quarter	2nd Quarter	3rd Quarter	4th Quarter
Units to be produced	12,000	10,000	13,000	14,000

Each unit requires 0.2 direct labor-hours and direct laborers are paid $16.00 per hour.

    In addition, the variable manufacturing overhead rate is $1.75 per direct labor-hour. The fixed manufacturing overhead is $86,000 per quarter. The only noncash element of manufacturing overhead is depreciation, which is $23,000 per quarter.

Required:

1. Calculate the company's total estimated direct labor cost for each quarter of the upcoming fiscal year and for the year as a whole. (Hint: Refer to Schedule 4 for guidance.)
2. Calculate the company's total estimated manufacturing overhead cost for each quarter of the upcoming fiscal year and for the year as a whole. (Hint: Refer to Schedule 5 for guidance.)
3. Calculate the company's cash disbursements for manufacturing overhead for each quarter of the the upcoming fiscal year and for the year as a whole. (Hint: Refer to Schedule 5 for guidance.)

EXERCISE 8–16 Direct Materials and Direct Labor Budgets LO 8–4, LO 8–5

The production department of Zan Corporation submitted the following forecast of units to be produced by quarter for the upcoming fiscal year:

	1st Quarter	2nd Quarter	3rd Quarter	4th Quarter
Units to be produced	5,000	8,000	7,000	6,000

In addition, 6,000 grams of raw materials inventory is on hand at the start of the 1st Quarter and the beginning accounts payable for the 1st Quarter is $2,880.

Each unit requires 8 grams of raw materials that cost $1.20 per gram. Management desires to end each quarter with an inventory of raw materials equal to 25% of the following quarter's production needs. The desired ending inventory for the 4th Quarter is 8,000 grams. Management plans to pay for 60% of raw materials purchases in the quarter acquired and 40% in the following quarter. Each unit requires 0.20 direct labor-hours and direct laborers are paid $15 per hour.

Required:
1. Calculate the estimated grams of raw materials that need to be purchased each quarter and for the year as a whole. (Hint: Refer to Schedule 3 for guidance.)
2. Calculate the cost of raw materials purchases for each quarter and for the year as a whole. (Hint: Refer to Schedule 3 for guidance.)
3. Calculate the expected cash disbursements for purchases of materials for each quarter and for the year as a whole. (Hint: Refer to Schedule 3 for guidance.)
4. Calculate the estimated direct labor cost for each quarter and for the year as a whole. (Hint: Refer to Schedule 4 for guidance.)

EXERCISE 8–17 Cash Flows; Budgeted Income Statement and Balance Sheet LO 8–2, LO 8–3, LO 8–4, LO 8–9, LO 8–10

Wheeling Company is a merchandiser that provided a balance sheet as of September 30 as shown below:

Wheeling Company Balance Sheet September 30	
Assets	
Cash	$ 59,000
Accounts receivable	90,000
Inventory	32,400
Buildings and equipment, net of depreciation	214,000
Total assets	$395,400
Liabilities and Stockholders' Equity	
Accounts payable	$ 73,000
Common stock	216,000
Retained earnings	106,400
Total liabilities and stockholders' equity	$395,400

The company is in the process of preparing a budget for October and assembled the following data:
1. Sales are budgeted at $240,000 for October and $250,000 for November. Of these sales, 35% will be for cash; the remainder will be credit sales. Forty percent of a month's credit sales are collected in the month the sales are made, and the remaining 60% are collected in the following month. All of the September 30 accounts receivable will be collected in October.
2. The budgeted cost of goods sold is always 45% of sales, and the ending merchandise inventory is always 30% of the following month's cost of goods sold.
3. All merchandise purchases are on account. Thirty percent of all purchases are paid for in the month of purchase, and 70% are paid for in the following month. All of the September 30 accounts payable to suppliers will be paid during October.
4. Selling and administrative expenses for October are budgeted at $78,000, exclusive of depreciation. These expenses will be paid in cash. Depreciation is budgeted at $2,000 for the month.

Required:

1. Using the information provided, calculate or prepare the following:
    a. The budgeted cash collections for October.
    b. The budgeted merchandise purchases for October.
    c. The budgeted cash disbursements for merchandise purchases for October.
    d. The budgeted net operating income for October.
    e. A budgeted balance sheet at October 31.

2. Assume the following changes to the underlying budgeting assumptions: (1) 50% of a month's credit sales are collected in the month the sales are made, and the remaining 50% are collected in the following month; (2) the ending merchandise inventory is always 10% of the following month's cost of goods sold; and (3) 20% of all purchases are paid for in the month of purchase, and 80% are paid for in the following month. Using these new assumptions, calculate or prepare the following:
    a. The budgeted cash collections for October.
    b. The budgeted merchandise purchases for October.
    c. The budgeted cash disbursements for merchandise purchases for October.
    d. Net operating income for the month of October.
    e. A budgeted balance sheet at October 31.

3. Compare your answers in requirement 1 to those that you obtained in requirement 2. If Wheeling Company is able to achieve the budgeted projections described in requirement 2, will it improve the company's financial performance relative to the projections that you derived in requirement 1?

EXERCISE 8–18 Cash Flows; Budgeted Income Statement and Balance Sheet LO 8–2, LO 8–3, LO 8–9, LO 8–10

Wolfpack Company is a merchandising company that is preparing a budget for the month of July. It provided the following information:

Wolfpack Company Balance Sheet June 30	
Assets	
Cash	$ 75,000
Accounts receivable	50,000
Inventory	30,000
Buildings and equipment, net of depreciation	150,000
Total assets	$305,000
Liabilities and Stockholders' Equity	
Accounts payable	$ 35,300
Common stock	100,000
Retained earnings	169,700
Total liabilities and stockholders' equity	$305,000

Budgeting Assumptions:

1. All sales are on account. Thirty percent of the credit sales are collected in the month of sale, and the remaining 70% are collected in the month subsequent to the sale. The accounts receivable at June 30 will be collected in July.
2. All merchandise purchases are on account. Twenty percent of merchandise inventory purchases are paid in the month of the purchase, and the remaining 80% are paid in the month after the purchase.
3. The budgeted inventory balance at July 31 is $22,000.
4. Depreciation expense is $3,000 per month. All other selling and administrative expenses are paid in full in the month the expense is incurred.
5. The company's cash budget for July shows expected cash collections of $77,000, expected cash disbursements for merchandise purchases of $44,500, and cash paid for selling and administrative expenses of $15,000.

Required:

1. For the month of July, calculate the following:
   a. Budgeted sales
   b. Budgeted merchandise purchases
   c. Budgeted cost of goods sold
   d. Budgeted net operating income
2. Prepare a budgeted balance sheet as of July 31.

 Problems

PROBLEM 8–19 Cash Budget; Income Statement; Balance Sheet LO 8–2, LO 8–4, LO 8–8, LO 8–9, LO 8–10

Minden Company is a wholesale distributor of premium European chocolates. The company's balance sheet as of April 30 is given below:

Minden Company Balance Sheet April 30	
Assets	
Cash	$ 9,000
Accounts receivable	54,000
Inventory	30,000
Buildings and equipment, net of depreciation	207,000
Total assets	$300,000
Liabilities and Stockholders' Equity	
Accounts payable	$ 63,000
Note payable	14,500
Common stock	180,000
Retained earnings	42,500
Total liabilities and stockholders' equity	$300,000

The company is in the process of preparing a budget for May and assembled the following data:

a. Sales are budgeted at $200,000 for May. Of these sales, $60,000 will be for cash; the remainder will be credit sales. One-half of a month's credit sales are collected in the month the sales are made, and the remainder is collected in the following month. All of the April 30 accounts receivable will be collected in May.

b. Purchases of inventory are expected to total $120,000 during May. These purchases will all be on account. Forty percent of all purchases are paid for in the month of purchase; the remainder are paid in the following month. All of the April 30 accounts payable to suppliers will be paid during May.

c. The May 31 inventory balance is budgeted at $40,000.

d. Selling and administrative expenses for May are budgeted at $72,000, exclusive of depreciation. These expenses will be paid in cash. Depreciation is budgeted at $2,000 for the month.

e. The note payable on the April 30 balance sheet will be paid during May, with $100 in interest. (All of the interest relates to May.)

f. New refrigerating equipment costing $6,500 will be purchased for cash during May.

g. During May, the company will borrow $20,000 from its bank by giving a new note payable to the bank for that amount. The new note will be due in one year.

Required:

1. Calculate the expected cash collections from customers for May.
2. Calculate the expected cash disbursements for merchandise purchases for May.
3. Prepare a cash budget for May.
4. Using Schedule 9 as your guide, prepare a budgeted income statement for May.
5. Prepare a budgeted balance sheet as of May 31.

PROBLEM 8–20 Cash Budget; Income Statement; Balance Sheet; Changing Assumptions LO 8–2, LO 8–4, LO 8–8, LO 8–9, LO 8–10

Refer to the data for Minden Company in Problem 8–19. The company is considering making the following changes to the assumptions underlying its master budget:

1. Sales are budgeted for $220,000 for May.
2. Each month's credit sales are collected 60% in the month of sale and 40% in the month following the sale.
3. The company pays for 50% of its merchandise purchases in the month of the purchase and the remaining 50% in the month following the purchase.

All other information from Problem 8–19 that is not mentioned above remains the same.

Required:

Using the new assumptions described above, complete the following requirements:
1. Calculate the expected cash collections for May.
2. Calculate the expected cash disbursements for merchandise purchases for May.
3. Prepare a cash budget for May.
4. Using Schedule 9 as your guide, prepare a budgeted income statement for May.
5. Prepare a budgeted balance sheet as of May 31.

PROBLEM 8–21 Schedules of Expected Cash Collections and Disbursements LO 8–2, LO 8–4, LO 8–8

You have been asked to prepare a December cash budget for Ashton Company, a distributor of exercise equipment. The following information is available about the company's operations:
a. The cash balance on December 1 is $40,000.
b. Actual sales for October and November and expected sales for December are as follows:

	October	November	December
Cash sales	$65,000	$70,000	$83,000
Sales on account	$400,000	$525,000	$600,000

Sales on account are collected over a three-month period as follows: 20% collected in the month of sale, 60% collected in the month following sale, and 18% collected in the second month following sale. The remaining 2% are uncollectible.
c. Purchases of inventory will total $280,000 for December. Thirty percent of a month's inventory purchases are paid during the month of purchase. The accounts payable remaining from November's inventory purchases total $161,000, all of which will be paid in December.
d. Selling and administrative expenses are budgeted at $430,000 for December. Of this amount, $50,000 is for depreciation.
e. A new web server for the Marketing Department costing $76,000 will be purchased for cash during December, and dividends totaling $9,000 will be paid during the month.
f. The company maintains a minimum cash balance of $20,000. An open line of credit is available from the company's bank to increase its cash balance as needed.

Required:
1. Calculate the expected cash collections for December.
2. Calculate the expected cash disbursements for merchandise purchases for December.
3. Prepare a cash budget for December. Indicate in the financing section any borrowing that will be needed during the month. Assume any interest will not be paid until the following month.

PROBLEM 8–22 Evaluating a Company's Budget Procedures LO 8–1

Springfield Corporation operates on a calendar-year basis. It begins the annual budgeting process in late August, when the president establishes targets for total sales dollars and net operating income before taxes for the next year.

The sales target is given to the Marketing Department, where the marketing manager formulates a sales budget by product line in both units and dollars. From this budget, sales quotas by product line in units and dollars are established for each of the corporation's sales districts.

The marketing manager also estimates the cost of the marketing activities required to support the target sales volume and prepares a tentative marketing expense budget.

The executive vice president uses the sales and profit targets, the sales budget by product line, and the tentative marketing expense budget to determine the dollar amounts that can be devoted to manufacturing and corporate office expense. The executive vice president prepares the budget for corporate expenses, and then forwards to the Production Department the product-line sales budget in units and the total dollar amount that can be devoted to manufacturing.

The production manager meets with the factory managers to develop a manufacturing plan that will produce the required units when needed within the cost constraints set by the executive vice president. The budgeting process usually comes to a halt at this point because the Production Department does not consider its allocated financial resources to be adequate.

When this standstill occurs, the vice president of finance, the executive vice president, the marketing manager, and the production manager meet to determine the final budgets for each of the areas. This normally results in a modest increase in the total amount available for manufacturing costs, while the marketing expense and corporate office expense budgets are cut. The total sales and net operating income figures proposed by the president are seldom changed. Although the participants are seldom pleased with the compromise, these budgets are final. Each executive then develops a new detailed budget for the operations in his or her area.

None of the areas achieved its budget in recent years. Sales often run below the target. When budgeted sales are not achieved, each area is expected to cut costs so that the president's profit target can still be met. However, the profit target is seldom met because costs are not cut enough. In fact, costs often run above the original budget in all functional areas. The president is disturbed that Springfield has not been able to meet the sales and profit targets. He hired a consultant with considerable relevant industry experience. The consultant reviewed the budgets for the past four years. He concluded that the product-line sales budgets were reasonable and that the cost and expense budgets were adequate for the budgeted sales and production levels.

Required:
1. Discuss how Springfield Corporation's budgeting process contributes to its failure to achieve the president's sales and profit targets.
2. Suggest how Springfield Corporation's budgeting process could be revised to correct the problem.
3. Should the functional areas be expected to cut their costs when sales volume falls below budget? Explain your answer.

(CMA, adapted)

PROBLEM 8–23 Schedule of Expected Cash Collections; Cash Budget LO 8–2, LO 8–8

The president of the retailer Prime Products just approached the company's bank with a request for a $30,000, 90-day loan. The purpose of the loan is to assist the company in acquiring inventories. Because the company has had some difficulty in paying off its loans in the past, the loan officer asked for a cash budget to help determine whether the loan should be made. The following data are available for the months April through June, during which the loan will be used:

a. On April 1, the start of the loan period, the cash balance will be $24,000. Accounts receivable on April 1 will total $140,000, of which $120,000 will be collected during April and $16,000 will be collected during May. The remainder will be uncollectible.

b. Past experience shows that 30% of a month's sales are collected in the month of sale, 60% in the month following sale, and 8% in the second month following sale. The other 2% are bad debts that are never collected. Budgeted sales and expenses for the three-month period follow:

	April	May	June
Sales (all on account)	$300,000	$400,000	$250,000
Merchandise purchases	$210,000	$160,000	$130,000
Payroll	$20,000	$20,000	$18,000
Lease payments	$22,000	$22,000	$22,000
Advertising	$60,000	$60,000	$50,000
Equipment purchases	—	—	$65,000
Depreciation	$15,000	$15,000	$15,000

c. Merchandise purchases are paid in full during the month following purchase. Accounts payable for merchandise purchases during March, which will be paid in April, total $140,000.

d. In preparing the cash budget, assume the $30,000 loan will be made in April and repaid in June. Interest on the loan will total $1,200.

Required:

1. Calculate the expected cash collections for April, May, and June, and for the three months in total.
2. Prepare a cash budget, by month and in total, for the three-month period.
3. If the company needs a minimum cash balance of $20,000 to start each month, can the loan be repaid as planned? Explain.

PROBLEM 8–24 Cash Budget with Supporting Schedules LO 8–2, LO 8–4, LO 8–8

Garden Sales, Inc., sells garden supplies. Management is planning its cash needs for the second quarter. The company usually has to borrow money during this quarter to support peak sales of lawn care equipment, which occur during May. The following information has been assembled to assist in preparing a cash budget for the quarter:

a. Budgeted monthly absorption costing income statements for April–July are:

	April	May	June	July
Sales	$600,000	$900,000	$500,000	$400,000
Cost of goods sold	420,000	630,000	350,000	280,000
Gross margin	180,000	270,000	150,000	120,000
Selling and administrative expenses:				
Selling expense	79,000	120,000	62,000	51,000
Administrative expense*	45,000	52,000	41,000	38,000
Total selling and administrative expenses . . .	124,000	172,000	103,000	89,000
Net operating income	$ 56,000	$ 98,000	$ 47,000	$ 31,000

* Includes $20,000 of depreciation each month.

b. Sales are 20% for cash and 80% on account.

c. Sales on account are collected over a three-month period, with 10% collected in the month of sale, 70% collected in the first month following the month of sale, and the remaining 20% collected in the second month following the month of sale. February's sales totaled $200,000, and March's sales totaled $300,000.

d. Inventory purchases are paid for within 15 days. Therefore, 50% of a month's inventory purchases are paid for in the month of purchase. The remaining 50% are paid in the following month. Accounts payable at March 31 for inventory purchases during March total $126,000.

e. Each month's ending inventory must equal 20% of the cost of the merchandise to be sold in the following month. The merchandise inventory at March 31 is $84,000.

f. Dividends of $49,000 will be declared and paid in April.

g. Land costing $16,000 will be purchased for cash in May.

h. The cash balance at March 31 is $52,000; the company must maintain a cash balance of at least $40,000 at the end of each month.

i. The company has an agreement with a local bank that allows the company to borrow in increments of $1,000 at the beginning of each month, up to a total loan balance of $200,000. The interest rate on these loans is 1% per month, and for simplicity we will assume interest is not compounded. The company would, as far as it is able, repay the loan plus accumulated interest at the end of the quarter.

Required:

1. Prepare a schedule of expected cash collections for April, May, and June, and for the quarter in total.
2. Prepare the following for merchandise inventory:
   a. A merchandise purchases budget for April, May, and June.
   b. A schedule of expected cash disbursements for merchandise purchases for April, May, and June, and for the quarter in total.
3. Prepare a cash budget for April, May, and June, as well as in total for the quarter.

PROBLEM 8–25 Cash Budget with Supporting Schedules; Changing Assumptions LO 8–2,
LO 8–4, LO 8–8

Refer to the data for Garden Sales, Inc., in Problem 8–24. The company's president is interested in knowing how reducing inventory levels and collecting accounts receivable sooner will impact the cash budget. He revises the cash collection and ending inventory assumptions as follows:

1. Sales continue to be 20% for cash and 80% on credit. However, credit sales from April, May, and June are collected over a three-month period with 25% collected in the month of sale, 65% collected in the month following sale, and 10% in the second month following sale. Credit sales from February and March are collected during the second quarter using the collection percentages specified in Problem 8–24.

2. The company maintains its ending inventory levels for April, May, and June at 15% of the cost of merchandise to be sold in the following month. The merchandise inventory at March 31 remains $84,000, and accounts payable for inventory purchases at March 31 remains $126,000.

All other information from Problem 8–24 that is not referred to above remains the same.

Required:

1. Using the president's new assumptions in (1) above, prepare a schedule of expected cash collections for April, May, and June and for the quarter in total.

2. Using the president's new assumptions in (2) above, prepare the following for merchandise inventory:
    a. A merchandise purchases budget for April, May, and June.
    b. A schedule of expected cash disbursements for merchandise purchases for April, May, and June and for the quarter in total.

3. Using the president's new assumptions, prepare a cash budget for April, May, and June, and for the quarter in total.

4. Prepare a brief memorandum for the president explaining how his revised assumptions affect the cash budget.

PROBLEM 8–26 Behavioral Aspects of Budgeting; Ethics and the Manager LO 8–1

Norton Company, a manufacturer of infant furniture and carriages, is in the initial stages of preparing the annual budget for next year. Scott Ford has recently joined Norton's accounting staff and wants to learn as much as possible about the company's budgeting process. During a recent lunch with Marge Atkins, sales manager, and Pete Granger, production manager, Ford initiated the following conversation.

Ford: Because I'm new around here and am going to be involved with the preparation of the annual budget, I'd be interested to learn how the two of you estimate sales and production numbers.

Atkins: We start out very methodically by looking at recent history, discussing what we know about current accounts, potential customers, and the general state of consumer spending. Then, we add that usual dose of intuition to come up with the best forecast we can.

Granger: I usually take the sales projections as the basis for my projections. Of course, we have to make an estimate of what this year's ending inventories will be, which is sometimes difficult.

Ford: Why does that present a problem? There must have been an estimate of ending inventories in the budget for the current year.

Granger: Those numbers aren't always reliable because Marge makes some adjustments to the sales numbers before passing them on to me.

Ford: What kind of adjustments?

Atkins: Well, we don't want to fall short of the sales projections, so we generally give ourselves a little breathing room by lowering the initial sales projection anywhere from 5% to 10%.

Granger: So, you can see why this year's budget is not a very reliable starting point. We always have to adjust the projected production rates as the year progresses, and, of course, this changes the ending inventory estimates. By the way, we make similar adjustments to expenses by adding at least 10% to the estimates; I think everyone around here does the same thing.

Required:

1. Marge Atkins and Pete Granger have described the use of what is sometimes called *budgetary slack.*
    a. Explain why Atkins and Granger behave in this manner and describe the benefits they expect to realize from the use of budgetary slack.
    b. Explain how the use of budgetary slack can adversely affect Atkins and Granger.
2. As a management accountant, Scott Ford believes that the behavior described by Marge Atkins and Pete Granger may be unethical. By referring to the IMA's Statement of Ethical Professional Practice in the Prologue, explain why the use of budgetary slack may be unethical.

(CMA, adapted)

PROBLEM 8–27 Cash Collections; Cash Disbursements; Budgeted Balance Sheet LO 8–2, LO 8–3, LO 8–4, LO 8–10

Deacon Company is a merchandising company that is preparing a budget for the three-month period ended June 30. The following information is available:

Deacon Company Balance Sheet March 31	
Assets	
Cash	$ 55,000
Accounts receivable	36,000
Inventory	40,000
Buildings and equipment, net of depreciation	100,000
Total assets	$231,000
Liabilities and Stockholders' Equity	
Accounts payable	$ 51,300
Common Stock	70,000
Retained earnings	109,700
Total liabilities and stockholders' equity	$231,000

Budgeted Income Statements	April	May	June
Sales	$100,000	$110,000	$130,000
Cost of goods sold	60,000	66,000	78,000
Gross margin	40,000	44,000	52,000
Selling and administrative expenses	15,000	16,500	19,500
Net operating income	$ 25,000	$ 27,500	$ 32,500

Budgeting Assumptions:

1. Sixty percent of sales are cash sales and 40% of sales are credit sales. Twenty percent of all credit sales are collected in the month of sale, and the remaining 80% are collected in the month subsequent to the sale.
2. Budgeted sales for July are $140,000.
3. Ten percent of merchandise inventory purchases are paid in cash at the time of the purchase. The remaining 90% of purchases are credit purchases. All purchases on credit are paid in the month subsequent to the purchase.
4. Each month's ending merchandise inventory should equal $10,000 plus 50% of the next month's cost of goods sold.
5. Depreciation expense is $1,000 per month. All other selling and administrative expenses are paid in full in the month the expense is incurred.

Required:

1. Calculate the expected cash collections for April, May, and June.
2. Calculate the budgeted merchandise purchases for April, May, and June.
3. Calculate the expected cash disbursements for merchandise purchases for April, May, and June.
4. Prepare a budgeted balance sheet at June 30. (Hint: You need to calculate the cash paid for selling and administrative expenses during April, May, and June to determine the cash balance in your June 30 balance sheet.)

PROBLEM 8–28 Cash Budget with Supporting Schedules LO 8–2, LO 8–4, LO 8–7, LO 8–8

Westex Products is a wholesale distributor of industrial cleaning products. When the treasurer of Westex Products approached the company's bank late in the current year seeking short-term financing, he was told that money was very tight and that any borrowing over the next year would have to be supported by a detailed statement of cash collections and disbursements. The treasurer also was told it would be very helpful to the bank if borrowers would indicate the quarters in which they need funds, as well as the amounts needed, and the quarters in which repayments could be made.

Because the treasurer is unsure as to the particular quarters in which bank financing will be needed, he assembled the following information to assist in preparing a detailed cash budget:

a. Budgeted sales and merchandise purchases for next year, as well as actual sales and purchases for the last quarter of the current year, are:

	Sales	Merchandise Purchases
Current Year:		
Fourth quarter actual	$200,000	$126,000
Next Year:		
First quarter estimated	$300,000	$186,000
Second quarter estimated	$400,000	$246,000
Third quarter estimated	$500,000	$305,000
Fourth quarter estimated	$200,000	$126,000

b. All sales are on account. The company normally collects 65% of a quarter's sales before the quarter ends and another 33% in the following quarter. The remainder is uncollectible. This pattern of collections is now being experienced in the current year's fourth-quarter actual data.

c. Eighty percent of a quarter's merchandise purchases are paid for within the quarter. The remainder is paid for in the following quarter.

d. Selling and administrative expenses for next year are budgeted at $50,000 per quarter plus 15% of sales. Of the fixed amount, $20,000 each quarter is depreciation.

e. The company will pay $10,000 in dividends each quarter.

f. Land purchases of $75,000 will be made in the second quarter, and purchases of $48,000 will be made in the third quarter. These purchases will be for cash.

g. The Cash account contained $10,000 at the end of the current year. The treasurer feels that this represents a minimum balance that must be maintained.

h. The company's bank allows borrowing in increments of $1,000 at the beginning of each quarter, up to a total loan balance of $100,000. The interest rate on these loans is 2.5% per quarter, and, for simplicity, we will assume interest is not compounded. The company would, as far as it is able, repay the loan plus accumulated interest at the end of the year.

i. At present, the company has no loans outstanding.

Required:

1. Calculate the expected cash collections by quarter and in total for next year.
2. Calculate the expected cash disbursements for merchandise purchases by quarter and in total for next year.
3. Calculate the expected cash disbursements for selling and administrative expenses, by quarter and in total for next year.
4. Prepare a cash budget by quarter and in total for next year.

PROBLEM 8–29 Completing a Master Budget LO 8–2, LO 8–4, LO 8–7, LO 8–8, LO 8–9, LO 8–10

The following data relate to the operations of Shilow Company, a wholesale distributor of consumer goods:

Current assets as of March 31:	
Cash	$8,000
Accounts receivable	$20,000
Inventory	$36,000
Building and equipment, net	$120,000
Accounts payable	$21,750
Common stock	$150,000
Retained earnings	$12,250

a. The gross margin is 25% of sales.
b. Actual and budgeted sales data:

March (actual)	$50,000
April	$60,000
May	$72,000
June	$90,000
July	$48,000

c. Sales are 60% for cash and 40% on credit. Credit sales are collected in the month following sale. The accounts receivable at March 31 are a result of March credit sales.
d. Each month's ending inventory should equal 80% of the following month's budgeted cost of goods sold.
e. One-half of a month's inventory purchases is paid for in the month of purchase; the other half is paid for in the following month. The accounts payable at March 31 are the result of March purchases of inventory.
f. Monthly expenses are as follows: commissions, 12% of sales; rent, $2,500 per month; other expenses (excluding depreciation), 6% of sales. Assume these expenses are paid monthly. Depreciation is $900 per month (includes depreciation on new assets).
g. Equipment costing $1,500 will be purchased for cash in April.
h. Management would like to maintain a minimum cash balance of at least $4,000 at the end of each month. The company has an agreement with a local bank that allows the company to borrow in increments of $1,000 at the beginning of each month, up to a total loan balance of $20,000. The interest rate on these loans is 1% per month, and for simplicity, we will assume interest is not compounded. The company would, as far as it is able, repay the loan plus accumulated interest at the end of the quarter.

Required:

Using the preceding data:

1. Complete the following schedule:

Schedule of Expected Cash Collections

	April	May	June	Quarter
Cash sales	$36,000			
Credit sales	20,000			
Total collections	$56,000			

2. Complete the following:

Merchandise Purchases Budget

	April	May	June	Quarter
Budgeted cost of goods sold	$45,000*	$54,000		
Add desired ending inventory	43,200†			
Total needs	88,200			
Less beginning inventory	36,000			
Required purchases	$52,200			

* For April sales: $60,000 sales × 75% cost ratio = $45,000.
† $54,000 × 80% = $43,200

Schedule of Expected Cash Disbursements—Merchandise Purchases

	April	May	June	Quarter
March purchases	$21,750			$21,750
April purchases	26,100	$26,100		52,200
May purchases				
June purchases				
Total disbursements	$47,850			

3. Complete the following cash budget:

Cash Budget

	April	May	June	Quarter
Beginning cash balance	$ 8,000			
Add cash collections	56,000			
Total cash available	64,000			
Less cash disbursements:				
For inventory	47,850			
For expenses	13,300			
For equipment	1,500			
Total cash disbursements	62,650			
Excess (deficiency) of cash	1,350			
Financing:				
Etc.				

4. Using Schedule 9 as your guide, prepare an absorption costing income statement for the quarter ended June 30.

5. Prepare a balance sheet as of June 30.

PROBLEM 8–30 Integration of the Sales, Production, and Direct Materials Budgets LO 8–2, LO 8–3, LO 8–4

Milo Company manufactures beach umbrellas. The company is preparing detailed budgets for the third quarter and assembled the following information to assist in the budget preparation:

a. The Marketing Department estimated sales as follows for the remainder of the year (in units):

July	30,000	October	20,000
August	70,000	November	10,000
September	50,000	December	10,000

The selling price of the beach umbrellas is $12 per unit.

b.   All sales are on account. Based on past experience, sales are collected in the following pattern:

> 30% in the month of sale
> 65% in the month following sale
> 5% uncollectible

Sales for June totaled $300,000.

c.   The company maintains finished goods inventories equal to 15% of the following month's sales. This requirement will be met at the end of June.

d.   Each beach umbrella requires 4 feet of Gilden, a material that is sometimes hard to acquire. Therefore, the company requires that the ending inventory of Gilden be equal to 50% of the following month's production needs. The inventory of Gilden on hand at the beginning and end of the quarter will be:

> June 30 .... 72,000 feet
> September 30 .... ?   feet

e.   Gilden costs $0.80 per foot. One-half of a month's purchases of Gilden is paid for in the month of purchase; the remainder is paid for in the following month. The accounts payable on July 1 for purchases of Gilden during June will be $76,000.

Required:

1.   Calculate the estimated sales, by month and in total, for the third quarter. (Hint: Refer to Schedule 1 for guidance.)

2.   Calculate the expected cash collections, by month and in total, for the third quarter. (Hint: Refer to Schedule 1 for guidance.)

3.   Calculate the estimated quantity of beach umbrellas that need to be produced in July, August, September, and October. (Hint: Refer to Schedule 2 for guidance.)

4.   Calculate the quantity of Gilden (in feet) that needs to be purchased by month and in total for the third quarter. (Hint: Refer to Schedule 3 for guidance.)

5.   Calculate the cost of the raw material (Gilden) purchases by month and in total for the third quarter. (Hint: Refer to Schedule 3 for guidance.)

6.   Calculate the expected cash disbursements for raw material (Gilden) purchases, by month and in total, for the third quarter. (Hint: Refer to Schedule 3 for guidance.)

PROBLEM 8–31 Completing a Master Budget LO 8–2, LO 8–4, LO 8–7, LO 8–8, LO 8–9, LO 8–10

Hillyard Company, an office supplies specialty store, prepares its master budget on a quarterly basis. The following data have been assembled to assist in preparing the master budget for the first quarter:

a.   As of December 31 (the end of the prior quarter), the company's general ledger showed the following account balances:

	Debits	Credits
Cash	$ 48,000	
Accounts receivable	224,000	
Inventory	60,000	
Buildings and equipment (net)	370,000	
Accounts payable		$ 93,000
Common stock		500,000
Retained earnings		109,000
	$702,000	$702,000

b.   Actual sales for December and budgeted sales for the next four months are as follows:

> December (actual) $280,000
> January....................... $400,000
> February...................... $600,000
> March $300,000
> April......................... $200,000

c. Sales are 20% for cash and 80% on credit. All payments on credit sales are collected in the month following sale. The accounts receivable at December 31 are a result of December credit sales.

d. The company's gross margin is 40% of sales. (In other words, cost of goods sold is 60% of sales.)

e. Monthly expenses are budgeted as follows: salaries and wages, $27,000 per month; advertising, $70,000 per month; shipping, 5% of sales; other expenses, 3% of sales. Depreciation, including depreciation on new assets acquired during the quarter, will be $42,000 for the quarter.

f. Each month's ending inventory should equal 25% of the following month's cost of goods sold.

g. One-half of a month's inventory purchases is paid for in the month of purchase; the other half is paid in the following month.

h. During February, the company will purchase a new copy machine for $1,700 cash. During March, other equipment will be purchased for cash at a cost of $84,500.

i. During January, the company will declare and pay $45,000 in cash dividends.

j. Management wants to maintain a minimum cash balance of $30,000. The company has an agreement with a local bank that allows the company to borrow in increments of $1,000 at the beginning of each month. The interest rate on these loans is 1% per month, and for simplicity, we will assume interest is not compounded. The company would, as far as it is able, repay the loan plus accumulated interest at the end of the quarter.

Required:

Using the data above, complete the following statements and schedules for the first quarter:

1. Schedule of expected cash collections:

	January	February	March	Quarter
Cash sales	$ 80,000			
Credit sales	224,000			
Total cash collections	$304,000			

2. a. Merchandise purchases budget:

	January	February	March	Quarter
Budgeted cost of goods sold	$ 240,000*	$360,000		
Add desired ending inventory	90,000†			
Total needs	330,000			
Less beginning inventory	60,000			
Required purchases	$ 270,000			

* $400,000 sales × 60% cost ratio = $240,000.
† $360,000 × 25% = $90,000.

b. Schedule of expected cash disbursements for merchandise purchases:

	January	February	March	Quarter
December purchases	$ 93,000			$ 93,000
January purchases	135,000	135,000		270,000
February purchases	—			
March purchases	—			
Total cash disbursements for purchases	$228,000			

3. Cash budget:

	January	February	March	Quarter
Beginning cash balance	$ 48,000			
Add cash collections	304,000			
Total cash available	352,000			
Less cash disbursements:				
Inventory purchases	228,000			
Selling and administrative expenses	129,000			
Equipment purchases	—			
Cash dividends	45,000			
Total cash disbursements	402,000			
Excess (deficiency) of cash	(50,000)			
Financing:				
Etc.				

4. Using Schedule 9 as your guide, prepare an absorption costing income statement for the quarter ending March 31.
5. Prepare a balance sheet as of March 31.

Cases   connect

Select cases are available in Connect.

CASE 8–32   Evaluating a Company's Budget Procedures   LO 8–1

Tom Emory and Jim Morris strolled back to their plant from the administrative offices of Ferguson & Son Manufacturing Company. Tom is manager of the machine shop in the company's factory; Jim is manager of the equipment maintenance department.

The men had just attended the monthly performance evaluation meeting for plant department heads. These meetings had been held on the third Tuesday of each month since Robert Ferguson Jr., the president's son, had become plant manager a year earlier.

As they were walking, Tom Emory spoke: "Boy, I hate those meetings! I never know whether my department's accounting reports will show good or bad performance. I'm beginning to expect the worst. If the accountants say I saved the company a dollar, I'm called 'Sir,' but if I spend even a little too much—boy, do I get in trouble. I don't know if I can hold on until I retire."

Tom had just been given the worst evaluation he had ever received in his long career with Ferguson & Son. He was the most respected of the experienced machinists in the company. He had been with Ferguson & Son for many years and was promoted to supervisor of the machine shop when the company expanded and moved to its present location. The president (Robert Ferguson Sr.) often stated that the company's success was due to the high-quality work of machinists like Tom. As supervisor, Tom stressed the importance of craftsmanship and told his workers he wanted no sloppy work coming from his department.

When Robert Ferguson Jr. became the plant manager, he directed that monthly performance comparisons be made between actual and budgeted costs for each department. The departmental budgets were intended to encourage the supervisors to reduce inefficiencies and to seek cost reduction opportunities. The company controller was instructed to have his staff "tighten" the budget slightly whenever a department attained its budget in a given month; this was done to reinforce the plant manager's desire to reduce costs. The young plant manager often stressed the importance of continued progress toward attaining the budget; he also made it known that he kept a file of these performance reports for future reference when he succeeded his father.

Tom Emory's conversation with Jim Morris continued as follows:

Emory: I really don't understand. We've worked so hard to meet the budget, and the minute we do so, they tighten it on us. We can't work any faster and still maintain quality. I think my men are ready to quit trying. Besides, those reports don't tell the whole story. We always seem to be interrupting the big jobs for all those small rush orders. All that setup and machine adjustment time is killing us. And quite frankly, Jim, you were no help. When our hydraulic press broke down last month, your people were nowhere to be found. We had to take it apart ourselves and got stuck with all that idle time.

Morris: I'm sorry about that, Tom, but you know my department has had trouble making budget, too. We were running well behind at the time of that problem, and if we'd spent a day on that old machine, we would never have made it up. Instead, we made the scheduled inspections of the forklift trucks because we knew we could do those in less than the budgeted time.

Emory: Well, Jim, at least you have some options. I'm locked into what the scheduling department assigns to me, and you know they're being harassed by sales for those special orders. Incidentally, why didn't your report show all the supplies you guys wasted last month when you were working in Bill's department?

Morris: We're not out of the woods on that deal yet. We charged the maximum we could to other work and haven't even reported some of it yet.

Emory: Well, I'm glad you have a way of getting out of the pressure. The accountants seem to know everything that's happening in my department, sometimes even before I do. I thought all that budget and accounting stuff was supposed to help, but it just gets me into trouble. It's all a big pain. I'm trying to put out quality work; they're trying to save pennies.

Required:

1. Identify the problems that appear to exist in Ferguson & Son Manufacturing Company's budgetary control system and explain how the problems are likely to reduce the effectiveness of the system.

2. Explain how Ferguson & Son Manufacturing Company's budgetary control system could be revised to improve its effectiveness.

(CMA, adapted)

CASE 8–33 Master Budget with Supporting Schedules LO 8–2, LO 8–4, LO 8–8, LO 8–9, LO 8–10

You have just been hired as a new management trainee by Earrings Unlimited, a distributor of earrings to various retail outlets located in shopping malls across the country. In the past, the company has done very little in the way of budgeting and, at certain times of the year, has experienced a shortage of cash. Because you are well trained in budgeting, you have decided to prepare a master budget for the upcoming second quarter. To this end, you have worked with accounting and other areas to gather the information assembled below.

The company sells many styles of earrings, but all are sold for the same price—$10 per pair. Actual sales of earrings for the last three months and budgeted sales for the next six months follow (in pairs of earrings):

January (actual)	20,000	June (budget)	50,000
February (actual)	26,000	July (budget)	30,000
March (actual)	40,000	August (budget)	28,000
April (budget)	65,000	September (budget)	25,000
May (budget)	100,000		

The concentration of sales before and during May is due to Mother's Day. Sufficient inventory should be on hand at the end of each month to supply 40% of the earrings sold in the following month.

Suppliers are paid $4 for a pair of earrings. One-half of a month's purchases is paid for in the month of purchase; the other half is paid for in the following month. All sales are on credit. Only 20% of a month's sales are collected in the month of sale. An additional 70% are collected in the following month, and the remaining 10% are collected in the second month following sale. Bad debts have been negligible.

Monthly operating expenses for the company are given below:

Variable:	
Sales commissions	4% of sales
Fixed:	
Advertising	$200,000
Rent	$18,000
Salaries	$106,000
Utilities	$7,000
Insurance	$3,000
Depreciation	$14,000

Insurance is paid on an annual basis, in November of each year.

The company plans to purchase $16,000 in new equipment during May and $40,000 in new equipment during June; both purchases will be for cash. The company declares dividends of $15,000 each quarter, payable in the first month of the following quarter.

The company's balance sheet as of March 31 is given below:

Assets	
Cash	$ 74,000
Accounts receivable ($26,000 February sales;	
$320,000 March sales)	346,000
Inventory	104,000
Prepaid insurance	21,000
Property and equipment (net)	950,000
Total assets	$1,495,000
Liabilities and Stockholders' Equity	
Accounts payable	$ 100,000
Dividends payable	15,000
Common stock	800,000
Retained earnings	580,000
Total liabilities and stockholders' equity	$1,495,000

The company maintains a minimum cash balance of $50,000. All borrowing is done at the beginning of a month; any repayments are made at the end of a month.

The company has an agreement with a bank that allows the company to borrow in increments of $1,000 at the beginning of each month. The interest rate on these loans is 1% per month, and for simplicity, we will assume interest is not compounded. At the end of the quarter, the company would pay the bank all of the accumulated interest on the loan and as much of the loan as possible (in increments of $1,000), while still retaining at least $50,000 in cash.

Required:
Prepare a master budget for the three-month period ending June 30. Include the following detailed schedules:

1. *a.* A sales budget, by month and in total.
   b. A schedule of expected cash collections, by month and in total.
   c. A merchandise purchases budget in units and in dollars. Show the budget by month and in total.
   d. A schedule of expected cash disbursements for merchandise purchases, by month and in total.
2. A cash budget. Show the budget by month and in total. Determine any borrowing that would be needed to maintain the minimum cash balance of $50,000.
3. A budgeted income statement for the three-month period ending June 30. Use the contribution approach.
4. A budgeted balance sheet as of June 30.

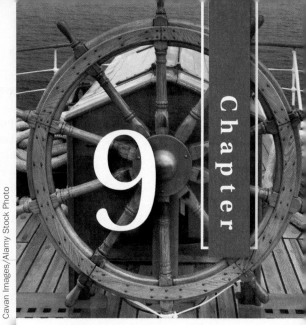

Flexible Budgets and Performance Analysis

Chapter 9

Craig Barritt/Getty Images

ENTREPRENEUR SPOTLIGHT

Taraji Henson has had an interest in hair care her entire life. Eventually, she turned that passion into a new business called TPH by Taraji. Her company's scalp-first approach to hair care "creates the optimal environment for healthy hair no matter the style." Its product categories include scalp care, cleanse, intense moisture, and repair for coily, curly, wavy, and straight hair. Taraji's products are sold at Amazon.com and Target, as well as through her own website at www.tphbytaraji.com. Her business venture caught the attention of *Entrepreneur's Handbook*, which named her one of seven "entrepreneurs to watch in 2021."

Managerial Accounting: The Practical Application
TPH by Taraji launched in January 2020—a couple months before the COVID-19 pandemic began crippling the economy. Any budgeted expectations the company may have had in January 2020 needed to be flexed throughout the year to adjust for the pandemic's impact on sales. For example, as millions of Americans lost their jobs or were furloughed, it lowered their disposable incomes, which quite possibly reduced the amount of money they could spend on hair care products.

Corporate Social Responsibility: Serving all Stakeholders
Taraji Henson founded the Boris Henson Foundation to change "the perception of mental illness in the African-American community by encouraging those who suffer with this debilitating illness to get the help they need." Taraji named the organization in honor of her father, who suffered from mental health issues following his service in the Vietnam War. The Boris Henson Foundation supports numerous initiatives, such as increasing mental health resources in urban schools, reducing prison recidivism rates, and increasing the number of African American therapists. ■

Sources: https://entrepreneurshandbook.co/7-entrepreneurs-to-watch-in-2021-6a3ca4da3d0, https://tphbytaraji.com/pages/about-us, https://borislhensonfoundation.org/

LEARNING OBJECTIVES

After studying Chapter 9, you should be able to:

LO 9–1 Prepare a planning budget and a flexible budget with one cost driver.

LO 9–2 Calculate and interpret activity variances.

LO 9–3 Calculate and interpret revenue and spending variances.

LO 9–4 Prepare a performance report with one cost driver that combines activity variances and revenue and spending variances.

LO 9–5 Prepare a planning budget and a flexible budget with more than one cost driver.

LO 9–6 Prepare a performance report with more than one cost driver that combines activity variances and revenue and spending variances.

Data Analytics Exercise available in Connect to complement this chapter

453

In the last chapter, we explored how budgets are developed before a period begins. In this chapter, we explain how budgets can be adjusted to help guide actual operations and influence the performance evaluation process. For example, an organization's actual expenses will rarely equal its budgeted expenses as estimated at the beginning of the period. The reason is that the actual level of activity (such as unit sales) will rarely be the same as the budgeted activity; therefore, many actual expenses and revenues will naturally differ from what was budgeted. Should a manager be penalized for spending 10 percent more than budgeted for a variable expense like direct materials if unit sales are 10 percent higher than budgeted? Of course not. After studying this chapter, you'll know how to adjust a budget to enable meaningful comparisons to actual results.

The Variance Analysis Cycle

Companies use the *variance analysis cycle,* as illustrated in Exhibit 9–1, to evaluate and improve performance. The cycle begins with the preparation of performance reports in the accounting department. These reports highlight variances, which are the differences between the actual results and what should have occurred according to the budget. The variances raise questions. Why did this variance occur? Why is this variance larger than it was last period? The significant variances are investigated so that their root causes can be either replicated or eliminated. Then, next period's operations are carried out, and the cycle begins again with the preparation of a new performance report for the latest period. The emphasis should be on highlighting superior and unsatisfactory results, finding the root causes of these outcomes, and then replicating the sources of superior achievement and eliminating the sources of unsatisfactory performance. The variance analysis cycle should not be used to assign blame for poor performance.

Managers frequently use the concept of *management by exception* in conjunction with the variance analysis cycle. **Management by exception** is a management system that compares actual results to a budget so that significant deviations can be flagged as exceptions and investigated further. This approach enables managers to focus on the most important variances while bypassing trivial discrepancies between the budget and actual results. For example, a variance of $5 is probably not big enough to warrant attention, whereas a variance of $5,000 might be worth tracking down. Another clue is the size of the variance relative to the amount of spending. A variance that is only 0.1 percent of

EXHIBIT 9–1
The Variance Analysis Cycle

Variance Analysis Cycle

spending on an item is probably caused by random factors. On the other hand, a variance of 10 percent of spending is much more likely to be a signal that something is wrong. In addition to watching for unusually large variances, the pattern of the variances should be monitored. For example, a run of steadily mounting variances should trigger an investigation even though none of the variances is large enough by itself to warrant investigation.

Next, we explain how organizations use flexible budgets to compare actual results to what should have occurred according to the budget.

Preparing Planning Budgets and Flexible Budgets with One Cost Driver

Characteristics of a Flexible Budget

The budgets that we explored in the last chapter were *planning budgets*. A **planning budget** is prepared before the period begins and is valid for only the planned level of activity. A static planning budget is suitable for planning but is inappropriate for evaluating how well costs are controlled. If the actual level of activity differs from what was planned, it would be misleading to compare actual costs to the static, unchanged planning budget. If activity is higher than expected, variable costs should be higher than expected; and if activity is lower than expected, variable costs should be lower than expected.

Flexible budgets take into account how changes in activity affect costs. A **flexible budget** is an estimate of what revenues and costs should have been, given the actual level of activity for the period. When a flexible budget is used in performance evaluation, actual costs are compared to what the costs *should have been for the actual level of activity during the period* rather than to the static planning budget. This is a very important distinction. If adjustments for the level of activity are not made, it is very difficult to interpret discrepancies between budgeted and actual costs.

LEARNING OBJECTIVE 9–1
Prepare a planning budget and a flexible budget with one cost driver.

IN BUSINESS

WHY DO COMPANIES NEED FLEXIBLE BUDGETS?

The difficulty of accurately predicting future financial performance can be readily understood by reading the annual report of any publicly traded company. For example, Nucor Corporation, a steel manufacturer headquartered in Charlotte, North Carolina, cites numerous reasons why its actual results may differ from expectations, including the following: (1) changes in the supply and cost of raw materials; (2) changes in the availability and cost of electricity and natural gas; (3) changes in the market demand for steel products; (4) fluctuations in currency conversion rates; (5) significant changes in laws or government regulations; and (6) the cyclical nature of the steel industry.

Source: Nucor Corporation 2020 Annual Report.

Michael Sears/MCT/Newscom

Deficiencies of the Static Planning Budget

To illustrate the difference between a static planning budget and a flexible budget, consider Rick's Hairstyling, an upscale hairstyling salon located in Beverly Hills owned and managed by Rick Manzi. Recently Rick has been attempting to get better control of his revenues and costs. At the urging of his accounting and business adviser, Victoria Kho, he has begun to prepare monthly budgets.

At the end of February, Rick prepared the March budget in Exhibit 9–2. Rick believes the number of customers served in a month (also known as the number of client-visits) is the best way to measure the overall level of activity in his salon. A customer who comes into the salon and has his or her hair styled is counted as one client-visit.

EXHIBIT 9–2
Planning Budget

Rick's Hairstyling
Planning Budget
For the Month Ended March 31

Budgeted client-visits (q)	1,000
Revenue ($180.00q)	$180,000
Expenses:	
Wages and salaries ($65,000 + $37.00q)	102,000
Hairstyling supplies ($1.50q)	1,500
Client gratuities ($4.10q)	4,100
Electricity ($1,500 + $0.10q)	1,600
Rent ($28,500)	28,500
Liability insurance ($2,800)	2,800
Employee health insurance ($21,300)	21,300
Miscellaneous ($1,200 + $0.20q)	1,400
Total expense	163,200
Net operating income	$ 16,800

Note that the term *revenue* is used in the planning budget rather than *sales*. We use the term *revenue* throughout the chapter because some organizations have sources of revenue other than sales. For example, donations, as well as sales, are counted as revenue in nonprofit organizations.

Rick identified eight major categories of costs—wages and salaries, hairstyling supplies, client gratuities, electricity, rent, liability insurance, employee health insurance, and miscellaneous. Client gratuities consist of flowers, candies, and glasses of champagne that Rick gives to his customers while they are in the salon.

Working with Victoria, Rick estimated a cost formula for each cost. For example, the cost formula for electricity is $1,500 + $0.10q$, where q equals the number of client-visits. In other words, electricity is a mixed cost with a $1,500 fixed element and a $0.10 per client-visit variable element. Once the budgeted level of activity was set at 1,000 client-visits, Rick computed the budgeted amount for each line item in the budget. For example, using the cost formula, he set the budgeted cost for electricity at $1,600 (= $1,500 + $0.10 × 1,000$). To finalize his budget, Rick computed his expected net operating income for March of $16,800.

At the end of March, Rick prepared the income statement in Exhibit 9–3, which shows that 1,100 clients actually visited his salon in March and his actual net operating income for the month was $21,230. It is important to realize that the actual results are *not* determined by plugging the actual number of client-visits into the revenue and cost formulas. The formulas are simply estimates of what the revenues and costs should be for a given level of activity. What actually happens usually differs from what is supposed to happen.

The first thing Rick noticed when comparing Exhibits 9–2 and 9–3 is the actual profit of $21,230 (from Exhibit 9–3) was substantially higher than the budgeted profit of $16,800 (from Exhibit 9–2). This was, of course, good news, but Rick wanted to know more. Business was up by 10 percent—the salon had 1,100 client-visits instead of the budgeted 1,000 client-visits. Could this alone explain the higher net operating income? The answer is no. An increase in net operating income of 10 percent would have resulted in net operating income of only $18,480 (= 1.1 × $16,800$), not the $21,230 actually earned during the month. What is responsible for this better outcome? Higher prices? Lower costs? Something else? Whatever the cause, Rick would like to know the answer and then hopefully repeat the same performance next month.

In an attempt to analyze what happened in March, Rick prepared the report comparing actual to budgeted costs in Exhibit 9–4. Note that most of the variances in this report

EXHIBIT 9–3

Actual Results—Income Statement

Rick's Hairstyling
Income Statement
For the Month Ended March 31

Actual client-visits	1,100
Revenue	$194,200
Expenses:	
Wages and salaries	106,900
Hairstyling supplies	1,620
Client gratuities	6,870
Electricity	1,550
Rent	28,500
Liability insurance	2,800
Employee health insurance	22,600
Miscellaneous	2,130
Total expense	172,970
Net operating income	$ 21,230

EXHIBIT 9–4

Comparison of Actual Results to the Static Planning Budget

Rick's Hairstyling
Comparison of Actual Results to the Planning Budget
For the Month Ended March 31

	Actual Results	Planning Budget	Variances*
Client-visits	1,100	1,000	
Revenue	$194,200	$180,000	$14,200 F
Expenses:			
Wages and salaries	106,900	102,000	4,900 U
Hairstyling supplies	1,620	1,500	120 U
Client gratuities	6,870	4,100	2,770 U
Electricity	1,550	1,600	50 F
Rent	28,500	28,500	0
Liability insurance	2,800	2,800	0
Employee health insurance	22,600	21,300	1,300 U
Miscellaneous	2,130	1,400	730 U
Total expense	172,970	163,200	9,770 U
Net operating income	$ 21,230	$ 16,800	$ 4,430 F

*The revenue variance is labeled favorable (unfavorable) when the actual revenue is greater than (less than) the planning budget. The expense variances are labeled favorable (unfavorable) when the actual expense is less than (greater than) the planning budget.

are labeled unfavorable (U) rather than favorable (F) even though net operating income was actually higher than expected. For example, wages and salaries show an unfavorable variance of $4,900 because the actual wages and salaries expense was $106,900, whereas the budget called for wages and salaries of $102,000. The problem with the report, as Rick immediately realized, is that it compares revenues and costs at one level of activity (1,000 client-visits) to revenues and costs at a different level of activity (1,100 client-visits). This is like comparing apples to oranges. Because Rick had 100 more client-visits than expected, some of his costs should be higher than budgeted. From Rick's standpoint, the increase in activity was good; however, it appears to be having a negative impact on most of the costs in the report. Rick knew that something would have to be done to make the report more meaningful, but he was unsure what to do. So he made an appointment to meet with Victoria Kho to discuss the next step.

Victoria: How is the budgeting going?

Rick: Pretty well. I didn't have any trouble putting together the budget for March. I also prepared a report comparing the actual results for March to the budget, but that report isn't giving me what I really want to know.

Victoria: Because your actual level of activity didn't match your budgeted activity?

Rick: Right. I know the level of activity shouldn't affect my fixed costs, but we had more client-visits than I had expected, and that had to affect my other costs.

Victoria: So you want to know whether the higher actual costs are justified by the higher level of activity?

Rick: Precisely.

Victoria: If you leave your reports and data with me, I can work on it later today, and by tomorrow I'll have a report to show you.

How a Flexible Budget Works

A flexible budget adjusts to show what costs *should be* for the actual level of activity. To illustrate how flexible budgets work, Victoria prepared the report in Exhibit 9–5 that shows what the *revenues and costs should have been given the actual level of activity* in March. Preparing the report is straightforward. The cost formula for each cost is used to estimate what the cost should have been for 1,100 client-visits—the actual level of activity for March. For example, using the cost formula $1,500 + $0.10q, the cost of electricity in March *should have been* $1,610 (= $1,500 + $0.10 × 1,100). Also, notice that the amounts of rent ($28,500), liability insurance ($2,800), and employee health insurance ($21,300) in the flexible budget equal the corresponding amounts in the planning budget (see Exhibit 9–2). This occurs because fixed costs are not affected by the activity level.

We can see from the flexible budget that the net operating income in March *should have been* $30,510, but recall from Exhibit 9–3 that the net operating income was actually

EXHIBIT 9–5
Flexible Budget Based on Actual Activity

Rick's Hairstyling
Flexible Budget
For the Month Ended March 31

Actual client-visits (q)	1,100
Revenue ($180.00q)	$198,000
Expenses:	
Wages and salaries ($65,000 + $37.00q)	105,700
Hairstyling supplies ($1.50q)	1,650
Client gratuities ($4.10q)	4,510
Electricity ($1,500 + $0.10q)	1,610
Rent ($28,500)	28,500
Liability insurance ($2,800)	2,800
Employee health insurance ($21,300)	21,300
Miscellaneous ($1,200 + $0.20q)	1,420
Total expense	167,490
Net operating income	$ 30,510

only $21,230. The results are not as good as we thought. Why? We will answer that question shortly.

To summarize to this point, Rick had budgeted for a profit of $16,800. The actual profit was quite a bit higher—$21,230. However, Victoria's analysis shows that given the actual number of client-visits in March, the profit should have been even higher—$30,510. What are the causes of these discrepancies? Rick would like to build on the positive factors, while working to reduce the negative factors. But what are they?

Flexible Budget Variances

To answer Rick's questions concerning the discrepancies between budgeted and actual costs, Victoria broke down the variances shown in Exhibit 9–4 into two types of variances—activity variances and revenue and spending variances. We explain how she did it in the next two sections.

Activity Variances

Part of the discrepancy between the budgeted profit and the actual profit is due to the fact that the actual level of activity in March was higher than expected. How much of this discrepancy was due to this single factor? Victoria prepared the report in Exhibit 9–6 to answer this question. In that report, the flexible budget based on the actual level of activity for the period is compared to the planning budget from the beginning of the period. The flexible budget shows what should have happened at the actual level of activity, whereas the planning budget shows what should have happened at the budgeted level of activity. Therefore, the differences between the flexible budget and the planning budget show what should have happened solely because the actual level of activity differed from what had been expected.

LEARNING OBJECTIVE 9–2
Calculate and interpret activity variances.

Rick's Hairstyling Activity Variances For the Month Ended March 31			
	Flexible Budget	Planning Budget	Activity Variances*
Client-visits	1,100	1,000	
Revenue ($180.00q)	$198,000	$180,000	$18,000 F
Expenses:			
Wages and salaries ($65,000 + $37.00q)	105,700	102,000	3,700 U
Hairstyling supplies ($1.50q)	1,650	1,500	150 U
Client gratuities ($4.10q)	4,510	4,100	410 U
Electricity ($1,500 + $0.10q)	1,610	1,600	10 U
Rent ($28,500)	28,500	28,500	0
Liability insurance ($2,800)	2,800	2,800	0
Employee health insurance ($21,300)	21,300	21,300	0
Miscellaneous ($1,200 + $0.20q)	1,420	1,400	20 U
Total expense	167,490	163,200	4,290 U
Net operating income	$ 30,510	$ 16,800	$ 13,710 F

*The revenue variance is labeled favorable (unfavorable) when the revenue in the flexible budget is greater than (less than) the planning budget. The expense variances are labeled favorable (unfavorable) when the expense in the flexible budget is less than (greater than) the planning budget.

EXHIBIT 9–6
Activity Variances from Comparing the Flexible Budget Based on Actual Activity to the Planning Budget

For example, the flexible budget based on 1,100 client-visits shows revenue of $198,000 (= $180 per client-visit × 1,100 client-visits). The planning budget based on 1,000 client-visits shows revenue of $180,000 (= $180 per client-visit × 1,000 client-visits). Because the salon had 100 more client-visits than anticipated in the planning budget, actual revenue should have been higher than planned revenue by $18,000 (= $198,000 − $180,000). This activity variance is shown on the report as $18,000 F (favorable). Similarly, the flexible budget based on 1,100 client-visits shows electricity cost of $1,610 (= $1,500 + $0.10 per client-visit × 1,100 client-visits). The planning budget based on 1,000 client-visits shows electricity cost of $1,600 (= $1,500 + $0.10 per client-visit × 1,000 client-visits). Because the salon had 100 more client-visits than anticipated in the planning budget, the actual electricity cost should have been higher than the planned cost by $10 (= $1,610 − $1,600). The activity variance for electricity is shown on the report as $10 U (unfavorable). Note that in this case, the label "unfavorable" may be a little misleading. The electricity cost *should* be $10 higher because business was up by 100 client-visits; therefore, it would be misleading to describe this variance in negative terms given that it was a necessary cost of serving more customers. For reasons such as this, we would like to caution you against assuming that unfavorable variances always indicate bad performance and favorable variances always indicate good performance.

Because all of the variances on this report are solely due to the difference between the actual level of activity and the level of activity in the planning budget from the beginning of the period, they are called **activity variances.** For example, the activity variance for revenue is $18,000 F, the activity variance for electricity is $10 U, and so on. The most important activity variance appears at the very bottom of the report; namely, the $13,710 F (favorable) variance for net operating income. This variance says that because activity was higher than expected in the planning budget, the net operating income should have been $13,710 higher. We caution against placing too much emphasis on any other single variance in this report. As we have said above, one would expect some costs to be higher as a consequence of more business. It is misleading to think of these unfavorable variances as indicative of poor performance.

On the other hand, the favorable activity variance for net operating income is important. Let's explore this variance a bit more thoroughly. First, as we have already noted, activity was up by 10 percent, but the flexible budget indicates that net operating income should have increased much more than 10 percent. A 10 percent increase in net operating income from the $16,800 in the planning budget would result in net operating income of $18,480 (= 1.1 × $16,800); however, the flexible budget shows much higher net operating income of $30,510. Why? The short answer is: Because of the presence of fixed costs. When we apply the 10 percent increase to the budgeted net operating income to estimate the profit at the higher level of activity, we implicitly assume that the revenues and *all* of the costs increase by 10 percent. But they do not. Note that when the activity level increases by 10 percent, three of the costs—rent, liability insurance, and employee health insurance—do not increase at all. These are all entirely fixed costs. So while sales do increase by 10 percent, these costs do not increase. This results in net operating income increasing by more than 10 percent. A similar effect occurs with the mixed costs, which contain fixed cost elements—wages and salaries, electricity, and miscellaneous. While sales increase by 10 percent, these mixed costs increase by less than 10 percent, resulting in an overall increase in net operating income of more than 10 percent. Because of the existence of fixed costs, net operating income does not change in proportion to changes in the level of activity. There is a leverage effect. The percentage changes in net operating income are ordinarily larger than the percentage increases in activity.

Revenue and Spending Variances

LEARNING OBJECTIVE 9–3
Calculate and interpret revenue and spending variances.

In the last section, we answered the question, "What impact did the change in activity have on our revenues, costs, and profit?" In this section, we answer the question, "How well did we control our revenues, our costs, and our profit?"

EXHIBIT 9–7
Revenue and Spending Variances from Comparing Actual Results to the Flexible Budget

Rick's Hairstyling
Revenue and Spending Variances
For the Month Ended March 31

	Actual Results	Flexible Budget	Revenue and Spending Variances*
Client-visits	1,100	1,100	
Revenue ($180.00q)	$194,200	$198,000	$3,800 U
Expenses:			
Wages and salaries ($65,000 + $37.00q)	106,900	105,700	1,200 U
Hairstyling supplies ($1.50q)	1,620	1,650	30 F
Client gratuities ($4.10q)	6,870	4,510	2,360 U
Electricity ($1,500 + $0.10q)	1,550	1,610	60 F
Rent ($28,500)	28,500	28,500	0
Liability insurance ($2,800)	2,800	2,800	0
Employee health insurance ($21,300)	22,600	21,300	1,300 U
Miscellaneous ($1,200 + $0.20q)	2,130	1,420	710 U
Total expense	172,970	167,490	5,480 U
Net operating income	$ 21,230	$ 30,510	$9,280 U

*The revenue variance is labeled favorable (unfavorable) when the actual revenue is greater than (less than) the flexible budget. The expense variances are labeled favorable (unfavorable) when the actual expense is less than (greater than) the flexible budget.

Recall that the flexible budget based on the actual level of activity in Exhibit 9–5 shows what *should have happened given the actual level of activity*. Therefore, Victoria's next step was to compare actual results to the flexible budget—in essence comparing what actually happened to what should have happened. Her work is shown in Exhibit 9–7.

Focusing first on revenue, the actual revenue totaled $194,200. However, the flexible budget indicates that, given the actual level of activity, revenue should have been $198,000. Consequently, revenue was $3,800 less than it should have been, given the actual number of client-visits for the month. This discrepancy is labeled as a $3,800 U (unfavorable) variance and is called a *revenue variance*. A **revenue variance** is the

PANDEMIC CAUSES SHIFT IN BEER SALES

A company's actual results can differ from its plans for many unanticipated reasons. For example, the coronavirus lockdown "reversed the trajectory of long-declining beers such as Bud Light, Miller Lite, and Coors Light" by shifting consumer purchases "from tap rooms to grocery store aisles." As many people lost their jobs and bars, tap rooms, and restaurants closed, beer drinkers dropped their usual higher-priced craft beers in favor of cheaper national brands bought at grocery stores and big box stores. They also bought beer in 24- and 30-packs to reduce the number of trips to those stores. At the same time, retailers and distributors decided to simplify their supply chains by reducing the number craft brands that they carried. Collectively, these market dynamics increased pandemic-period sales of mainstream beers like Coors Light and Miller Lite by 10.7 percent compared to the same period from the prior year, which stands in stark contrast to the 3.1 percent decline in sales these same brands experienced throughout 2019.

Ingram Publishing/Alamy Stock Photo

Source: Jennifer Maloney, "Pandemic Boosts Big Beer Brands," *The Wall Street Journal*, May 19, 2020, p. B3.

difference between the actual total revenue and what the total revenue should have been, given the actual level of activity for the period. If actual revenue exceeds what the revenue should have been, the variance is labeled favorable. If actual revenue is less than what the revenue should have been, the variance is labeled unfavorable. Why would actual revenue be less than or more than it should have been, given the actual level of activity? Basically, the revenue variance is favorable if the average selling price is greater than expected; it is unfavorable if the average selling price is less than expected. This could happen for a variety of reasons, including a change in selling price, a different mix of products sold, a change in the amount of discounts given, poor accounting controls, and so on.

Focusing next on costs, the actual electricity cost was $1,550; however, the flexible budget indicates that electricity costs should have been $1,610 for the 1,100 client-visits in March. Because the cost was $60 less than we would have expected for the actual level of activity during the period, it is labeled as a favorable variance, $60 F. This is an example of a *spending variance*. A **spending variance** is the difference between the actual amount of the cost and how much a cost should have been, given the actual level of activity. If the actual cost is greater than what the cost should have been, the variance is labeled as unfavorable. If the actual cost is less than what the cost should have been, the variance is labeled as favorable. Why would a cost have a favorable or unfavorable variance? There are many possible explanations including paying a higher price for inputs than should have been paid, using too many inputs for the actual level of activity, a change in technology, and so on. In the next chapter, we will explore these types of explanations in greater detail.

Note from Exhibit 9–7 that the overall net operating income variance is $9,280 U (unfavorable). This means that given the actual level of activity for the period, the net operating income was $9,280 lower than it should have been. There are a number of reasons for this. The most prominent is the unfavorable revenue variance of $3,800. Next in line is the $2,360 unfavorable variance for client gratuities. Looking at this in another way, client gratuities were more than 50 percent larger than they should have been according to the flexible budget. This is a variance that Rick would almost certainly want to investigate further. He may find that this unfavorable variance is not necessarily a bad thing. It is possible, for example, that more lavish use of gratuities led to the 10 percent increase in client-visits.

Exhibit 9–7 also includes a $1,300 unfavorable variance related to employee health insurance, thereby highlighting how a fixed cost can have a spending variance. While fixed costs do not depend on the level of activity, the actual amount of a fixed cost can differ from the estimated amount included in a flexible budget. For example, perhaps Rick's employee health insurance premiums unexpectedly increased by $1,300 during March.

In conclusion, the revenue and spending variances in Exhibit 9–7 will help Rick better understand why his actual net operating income differs from what should have happened given the actual level of activity.

A Performance Report Combining Activity and Revenue and Spending Variances

LEARNING OBJECTIVE 9–4
Prepare a performance report with one cost driver that combines activity variances and revenue and spending variances.

Exhibit 9–8 displays Victoria's performance report that combines the activity variances (from Exhibit 9–6) with the revenue and spending variances (from Exhibit 9–7). The report brings together information from those two earlier exhibits in a way that makes it easier to interpret what happened during the period. The format of this report is a bit different from the format of the previous reports in that the variances appear between the amounts being compared rather than after them. For example, the activity variances appear between the flexible budget amounts and the planning budget amounts. In Exhibit 9–6, the activity variances appeared after the flexible budget and the planning budget.

Note two numbers in particular in the performance report—the activity variance for net operating income of $13,710 F (favorable) and the overall revenue and spending variance for net operating income of $9,280 U (unfavorable). It is worth repeating what those two numbers mean. The $13,710 favorable activity variance occurred because

EXHIBIT 9–8
Performance Report Combining Activity Variances with Revenue and Spending Variances

Rick's Hairstyling
Flexible Budget Performance Report
For the Month Ended March 31

	(1) Actual Results	Revenue and Spending Variances (1) – (2)	(2) Flexible Budget	Activity Variances (2) – (3)	(3) Planning Budget
Client-visits	1,100		1,100		1,000
Revenue ($180.00q)	$194,200	$3,800 U	$198,000	$18,000 F	$180,000
Expenses:					
Wages and salaries ($65,000 + $37.00q)	106,900	1,200 U	105,700	3,700 U	102,000
Hairstyling supplies ($1.50q)	1,620	30 F	1,650	150 U	1,500
Client gratuities ($4.10q)	6,870	2,360 U	4,510	410 U	4,100
Electricity ($1,500 + $0.10q)	1,550	60 F	1,610	10 U	1,600
Rent ($28,500)	28,500	0	28,500	0	28,500
Liability insurance ($2,800)	2,800	0	2,800	0	2,800
Employee health insurance ($21,300)	22,600	1,300 U	21,300	0	21,300
Miscellaneous ($1,200 + $0.20q)	2,130	710 U	1,420	20 U	1,400
Total expense	172,970	5,480 U	167,490	4,290 U	163,200
Net operating income	$ 21,230	$9,280 U	$ 30,510	$13,710 F	$ 16,800

actual activity (1,100 client-visits) was greater than the budgeted level of activity (1,000 client-visits). The $9,280 unfavorable overall revenue and spending variance occurred because the profit was not as large as it should have been for the actual level of activity for the period. These two different variances mean very different things and call for different types of actions. To generate a favorable activity variance for net operating income, managers must take actions to increase client-visits. To generate a favorable overall revenue and spending variance, managers must take actions to protect selling prices, increase operating efficiency, and reduce the prices of inputs.

The performance report in Exhibit 9–8 provides much more useful information to managers than a simple comparison of the planning budget with actual results as shown in Exhibit 9–4. In Exhibit 9–4, the effects of changes in activity were jumbled together with the effects of how well prices were controlled and operations were managed. The performance report in Exhibit 9–8 clearly separates these effects, allowing managers to take a much more focused approach in evaluating operations.

To get a better idea of how the performance report accomplishes this task, look at hairstyling supplies in the performance report. The actual cost of hairstyling supplies was $1,620 for the period, whereas in the planning budget, this cost was $1,500. In the comparison of the actual results to the planning budget in Exhibit 9–4, this difference is shown as an unfavorable variance of $120. Exhibit 9–4 uses a static planning budget approach that compares actual costs at one level of activity to budgeted costs at a different level of activity. As we said before, this is like comparing apples to oranges. This variance is actually a mixture of two different effects. This becomes clear in the performance report in Exhibit 9–8. The $120 difference between the actual results and the budgeted amount is composed of two different variances—a favorable spending variance of $30 and an unfavorable activity variance of $150. The favorable spending variance occurred because less was spent on hairstyling supplies than one would have expected, given the actual level of activity for the month. The activity variance occurs because activity was greater than anticipated in the planning budget, which naturally resulted in a higher total cost for this variable cost.

The flexible budget performance report in Exhibit 9–8 provides a more valid assessment of performance than simply comparing actual costs to static planning budget costs because actual costs are compared to what costs should have been at the actual level of activity. In other words, apples are compared to apples. When this is done, we see that the spending variance for hairstyling supplies is $30 F (favorable) rather than $120 U (unfavorable) as it was in the original static planning budget performance report (see Exhibit 9–4). In some cases, as with hairstyling supplies in Rick's report, an unfavorable static planning budget variance may be transformed into a favorable revenue or spending variance when an increase in activity is properly taken into account. The following discussion took place the next day at Rick's salon.

RICK'S
Hairstyling Salon

Victoria: Let me show you what I've got. [Victoria shows Rick the flexible budget performance report in Exhibit 9–8.] I simply used the cost formulas to update the budget to reflect the increase in client-visits you experienced in March. That allowed me to come up with a better benchmark for what the costs should have been.

Rick: That's what you labeled the "flexible budget based on 1,100 client-visits"?

Victoria: That's right. Your original budget was based on 1,000 client-visits, so it understated what some of the costs should have been when you actually served 1,100 customers.

Rick: That's clear enough. These spending variances aren't quite as shocking as the variances on my first report.

Victoria: Yes, but you still have an unfavorable variance of $2,360 for client gratuities.

Rick: I know how that happened. In March, there was a big political fundraising dinner that I forgot about when I prepared the March budget. To fit all of our regular clients in, we had to push them through here pretty fast. Everyone still got top-rate service, but I felt bad about not being able to spend as much time with each customer. I wanted to give my customers a little extra something to compensate them for the less personal service, so I ordered a lot of flowers, which I gave away by the bunch.

Victoria: With the prices you charge, Rick, I am sure the gesture was appreciated.

Rick: One thing bothers me about the report. When we discussed my costs before, you called rent, liability insurance, and employee health insurance fixed costs. How can I have a variance for a fixed cost? Doesn't fixed mean that it doesn't change?

Victoria: We call these costs *fixed* because they shouldn't be affected by *changes in the level of activity.* However, that doesn't mean that they can't change for other reasons. Also, the use of the term *fixed* suggests to people that the cost can't be controlled, but that isn't true. It is often easier to control fixed costs than variable costs. For example, it would be fairly easy for you to change your insurance bill by adjusting the amount of insurance you carry. It would be much more difficult for you to significantly reduce your spending on hairstyling supplies—a variable cost that is a necessary part of serving customers.

Rick: I think I understand, but it *is* confusing.

Victoria: Just remember that a cost is called variable if it is proportional to activity; it is called fixed if it does not depend on the level of activity. However, fixed costs can change for reasons unrelated to changes in the level of activity. And controllability has little to do with whether a cost is variable or fixed. Fixed costs are often more controllable than variable costs.

URBAN OUTFITTERS' SALES GROWTH RATE DECLINES

Urban Outfitters sells record players, vinyl albums, and vintage film cameras to "hipster millenials and teens" longing to connect with the culture of the 1980s and 1990s. When the company's sales growth rate during the holiday season dropped from 3.6 percent to 1 percent, the company's chief financial officer, Frank Conforti, conceded that the drop-off was "worse than what we had anticipated."

In 2015, the company's sales of vinyl records were growing at a rate of 38 percent, but more recently, they had slowed to 2 percent, thus highlighting the challenges of forecasting sales in the fickle and fashion-conscious teenage market. The company claims to be the world's top seller of vinyl records "with a vast offering of classics like Beatles albums to the latest from Kendrick Lamar."

Source: Chelsey Dulaney, "Record Players and Polaroids Are So Over," *The Wall Street Journal,* January 10, 2018.

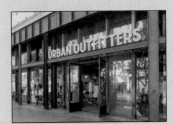

Ken Wolter/Shutterstock

Performance Reports in Nonprofit Organizations

The performance reports in nonprofit organizations are basically the same as the performance reports we have considered so far—with one prominent difference. Nonprofit organizations usually receive a significant amount of funding from sources other than sales. For example, universities receive their funding from sales (i.e., tuition charged to students), from endowment income and donations, and—in the case of public universities—from state appropriations. This means that, like costs, the revenue in governmental and nonprofit organizations may consist of both fixed and variable elements. For example, the Seattle Opera Company's revenue in a recent year consisted of grants and donations of $12,719,000 and ticket sales of $8,125,000 (or about $75.35 per ticket sold). Consequently, the revenue formula for the opera company can be written as:

$$\text{Revenue} = \$12,719,000 + \$75.35q$$

where q is the number of tickets sold. In other respects, the performance report for the Seattle Opera Company and other nonprofit organizations would be similar to the performance report in Exhibit 9–8.

Performance Reports in Cost Centers

Performance reports are often prepared for organizations that do not have any source of outside revenue. In particular, in a large organization, a performance report may be prepared for each department—including departments that do not sell anything to outsiders. For example, a performance report is very commonly prepared for production departments in manufacturing companies. Such reports should be prepared using the same principles we have discussed and should look very much like the performance report in Exhibit 9–8—with the exception that revenue, and consequently net operating income, will not appear on the report. Because the managers in these departments are responsible for costs but not revenues, they are often called *cost centers.*

Preparing Planning Budgets and Flexible Budgets with Multiple Cost Drivers

At Rick's Hairstyling, we have assumed there is only one cost driver—the number of client-visits. However, in the activity-based costing chapter, we found more than one cost driver might be needed to adequately explain all of the costs in an organization. For example, some of the costs at Rick's Hairstyling probably depend more on the number of hours

LEARNING OBJECTIVE 9–5
Prepare a planning budget and a flexible budget with more than one cost driver.

the salon is open for business than the number of client-visits. Specifically, most of Rick's employees are paid salaries, but some are paid on an hourly basis. None of the employees is paid on the basis of the number of customers actually served. Consequently, the cost formula for wages and salaries would be more accurate if it were stated in terms of the hours of operation rather than the number of client-visits. The cost of electricity is even more complex. Some of the cost is fixed—the heat must be kept at some minimum level even at night when the salon is closed. Some of the cost depends on the number of client-visits—the power consumed by hair dryers depends on the number of customers served. Some of the cost depends on the number of hours the salon is open—the costs of lighting the salon and heating it to a comfortable temperature. Consequently, the cost formula for electricity would be more accurate if it were stated in terms of both the number of client-visits and the hours of operation rather than just in terms of the number of client-visits.

Exhibit 9–9 shows a planning budget in which these changes have been made. It includes two cost drivers—client-visits and hours of operation—where q_1 refers to client-visits and q_2 refers to hours of operation. The budgeted number of client visits is 1,000, and the budgeted hours of operation is 190.

As expected, the planning budget based on two cost drivers differs from the planning budget based on one cost driver shown in Exhibit 9–2. For example, the revised cost formula for wages and salaries, which is $65,000 + $220q_2$, now depends on the hours of operation rather than the number of client-visits. Because the salon is expected to operate for 190 hours, the planning budget includes wages and salaries of $106,800 (= $65,000 + $220 × 190). The electricity cost depends on both client-visits and the hours of operation, and its cost formula is $390 + $0.10q_1 + $6.00q_2$. Because the planned number of client-visits was 1,000 and the salon was expected to operate for 190 hours, the planning budget includes electricity expense of $1,630 (= $390 + $0.10 × 1,000 + $6.00 × 190). Notice that the net operating income in the planning budget based on two cost drivers is $11,970, whereas the net operating income in the planning budget based on one cost driver (see Exhibit 9–2) is $16,800. These two amounts differ because the planning budget based on two cost drivers is more accurate than the planning budget based on one driver.

If we assume Rick's salon actually had 1,100 client-visits during the month and it actually operated for the budgeted amount of 190 hours, the cost formulas shown in Exhibit 9–9 can also be used to create the flexible budget shown in Exhibit 9–10. The flexible budget based on two cost drivers differs from the flexible budget based on one cost driver shown in Exhibit 9–5. For example, the wages and salaries shown in Exhibit 9–10 are $106,800, whereas the wages and salaries shown in Exhibit 9–5 are $105,700.

EXHIBIT 9–9

Planning Budget Based on More Than One Cost Driver

Rick's Hairstyling
Planning Budget
For the Month Ended March 31

Budgeted client-visits (q_1)	1,000
Budgeted hours of operation (q_2)	190
Revenue ($180.00q_1$)	$180,000
Expenses:	
Wages and salaries ($65,000 + $220q_2$)	106,800
Hairstyling supplies ($1.50q_1$)	1,500
Client gratuities ($4.10q_1$)	4,100
Electricity ($390 + $0.10q_1 + $6.00q_2$)	1,630
Rent ($28,500)	28,500
Liability insurance ($2,800)	2,800
Employee health insurance ($21,300)	21,300
Miscellaneous ($1,200 + $0.20q_1$)	1,400
Total expense	168,030
Net operating income	$ 11,970

EXHIBIT 9–10
Flexible Budget Based on More than One Cost Driver

Rick's Hairstyling
Flexible Budget
For the Month Ended March 31

Actual client-visits (q_1)	1,100
Actual hours of operation (q_2)	190
Revenue ($\$180.00q_1$)	$\underline{\$198,000}$
Expenses:	
Wages and salaries ($\$65,000 + \$220q_2$)	106,800
Hairstyling supplies ($\$1.50q_1$)	1,650
Client gratuities ($\$4.10q_1$)	4,510
Electricity ($\$390 + \$0.10q_1 + \$6.00q_2$)	1,640
Rent ($\$28,500$)	28,500
Liability insurance ($\$2,800$)	2,800
Employee health insurance ($\$21,300$)	21,300
Miscellaneous ($\$1,200 + \$0.20q_1$)	$\underline{1,420}$
Total expense	168,620
Net operating income	$\underline{\underline{\$\ 29,380}}$

The difference arises because the variable portion of this expense is driven by the hours of operation in Exhibit 9–10; however, it is assumed to be a function of client-visits in Exhibit 9–5. The flexible budgets in these two exhibits also report different net operating incomes. The flexible budget in Exhibit 9–5, which is based on one cost driver, shows a net operating income of $30,510. The flexible budget in Exhibit 9–10, which is based on two cost drivers, shows a net operating income of $29,380.

The revised flexible budget based on both client-visits and hours of operation can be used to create the performance report shown in Exhibit 9–11. The difference

LEARNING OBJECTIVE 9–6
Prepare a performance report with more than one cost driver that combines activity variances and revenue and spending variances.

EXHIBIT 9–11
Performance Report with More Than One Cost Driver That Combines Activity Variances with Revenue and Spending Variances

Rick's Hairstyling
Flexible Budget Performance Report
For the Month Ended March 31

	Actual Results	Revenue and Spending Variances	Flexible Budget	Activity Variances	Planning Budget
Client-visits (q_1)	1,100		1,100		1,000
Hours of operation (q_2)	190		190		190
Revenue ($\$180.00q_1$)	$194,200	$ 3,800 U	$198,000	$ 18,000 F	$180,000
Expenses:					
Wages and salaries ($\$65,000 + \$220.00q_2$)	106,900	100 U	106,800	0	106,800
Hairstyling supplies ($\$1.50q_1$)	1,620	30 F	1,650	150 U	1,500
Client gratuities ($\$4.10q_1$)	6,870	2,360 U	4,510	410 U	4,100
Electricity ($\$390 + \$0.10q_1 + \$6.00q_2$)	1,550	90 F	1,640	10 U	1,630
Rent ($\$28,500$)	28,500	0	28,500	0	28,500
Liability insurance ($\$2,800$)	2,800	0	2,800	0	2,800
Employee health insurance ($\$21,300$)	22,600	1,300 U	21,300	0	21,300
Miscellaneous ($\$1,200 + \$0.20q_1$)	2,130	710 U	1,420	20 U	1,400
Total expense	172,970	4,350 U	168,620	590 U	168,030
Net operating income	$ 21,230	$ 8,150 U	$ 29,380	$ 17,410 F	$ 11,970

between this performance report and the one shown in Exhibit 9–8 is that the cost formulas based on more than one cost driver are more accurate than the cost formulas based on just one cost driver; hence, the variances will also be more accurate. For example, the spending variance for electricity is $60 F when the flexible budget is based on one cost driver (see Exhibit 9–8), but it is $90 F when computed using two cost drivers (see Exhibit 9–11).

Summary

Directly comparing actual revenues and costs to static planning budget revenues and costs can easily lead to erroneous conclusions. Actual revenues and costs differ from budgeted revenues and costs for a variety of reasons, but one of the biggest is a change in the level of activity. One would expect actual revenues and costs to increase or decrease as the activity level increases or decreases. Flexible budgets enable managers to isolate the various causes of the differences between budgeted and actual revenues and costs.

A flexible budget is a budget that is adjusted to the actual level of activity. It is the best estimate of what revenues and costs should have been, given the actual level of activity during the period. The flexible budget can be compared to the budget from the beginning of the period or to the actual results.

When the flexible budget is compared to the planning budget, activity variances are the result. An activity variance shows how a revenue or cost should have changed in response to the difference between actual and planned activity.

When actual results are compared to the flexible budget, revenue and spending variances are the result. A favorable revenue variance indicates that revenue was larger than should have been expected, given the actual level of activity. An unfavorable revenue variance indicates that revenue was less than it should have been, given the actual level of activity. A favorable spending variance indicates that the cost was less than expected, given the actual level of activity. An unfavorable spending variance indicates that the cost was greater than it should have been, given the actual level of activity. A flexible budget performance report combines activity variances and revenue and spending variances on one report.

Planning budgets, flexible budgets, and flexible budget performance reports can be prepared using more than one cost driver. When a company uses multiple cost drivers to compare its actual results to the budget, it should result in more accurate and insightful variances than those computed using only one cost driver.

 Data Analytics Exercise available in Connect to complement this chapter

Review Problem: Variance Analysis Using a Flexible Budget

Harrald's Fish House is a family-owned restaurant specializing in Scandinavian-style seafood. Data concerning the restaurant's monthly revenues and costs appear below (*q* refers to the number of meals served):

	Formula
Revenue	$16.50*q*
Cost of ingredients	$6.25*q*
Wages and salaries	$10,400
Utilities	$800 + $0.20*q*
Rent	$2,200
Miscellaneous	$600 + $0.80*q*

Required:
1. Prepare the restaurant's planning budget for April assuming 1,800 meals are served.
2. Assume 1,700 meals were actually served in April. Prepare a flexible budget for this level of activity.
3. The actual results for April appear below. Prepare a flexible budget performance report for the restaurant for April.

Revenue	$27,920
Cost of ingredients	$11,110
Wages and salaries	$10,130
Utilities	$1,080
Rent	$2,200
Miscellaneous	$2,240

Solution to Review Problem

1. The planning budget for April appears below:

Harrald's Fish House Planning Budget For the Month Ended April 30	
Budgeted meals served (*q*)	1,800
Revenue ($16.50*q*)	$29,700
Expenses:	
Cost of ingredients ($6.25*q*)	11,250
Wages and salaries ($10,400)	10,400
Utilities ($800 + $0.20*q*)	1,160
Rent ($2,200)	2,200
Miscellaneous ($600 + $0.80*q*)	2,040
Total expense	27,050
Net operating income	$ 2,650

2.   The flexible budget for April appears below:

Harrald's Fish House Flexible Budget For the Month Ended April 30	
Actual meals served (q)	1,700
Revenue ($16.50q)	$28,050
Expenses:	
Cost of ingredients ($6.25q)	10,625
Wages and salaries ($10,400)	10,400
Utilities ($800 + $0.20q)	1,140
Rent ($2,200)	2,200
Miscellaneous ($600 + $0.80q)....................	1,960
Total expense	26,325
Net operating income	$ 1,725

3.   The flexible budget performance report for April appears below:

Harrald's Fish House Flexible Budget Performance Report For the Month Ended April 30					
	(1) Actual Results	Revenue and Spending Variances (1) – (2)	(2) Flexible Budget	Activity Variances (2) – (3)	(3) Planning Budget
Meals served	1,700		1,700		1,800
Revenue ($16.50q)	$27,920	$ 130 U	$28,050	$1,650 U	$29,700
Expenses:					
Cost of ingredients ($6.25q)	11,110	485 U	10,625	625 F	11,250
Wages and salaries ($10,400)	10,130	270 F	10,400	0	10,400
Utilities ($800 + $0.20q)	1,080	60 F	1,140	20 F	1,160
Rent ($2,200)	2,200	0	2,200	0	2,200
Miscellaneous ($600 + $0.80q)	2,240	280 U	1,960	80 F	2,040
Total expense	26,760	435 U	26,325	725 F	27,050
Net operating income	$ 1,160	$ 565 U	$ 1,725	$ 925 U	$ 2,650

Glossary

Activity variance The difference between a revenue or cost item in the flexible budget and the same item in the static planning budget. An activity variance is due solely to the difference between the actual level of activity used in the flexible budget and the level of activity assumed in the planning budget. (p. 460)

Flexible budget A report showing estimates of what revenues and costs should have been, given the actual level of activity for the period. (p. 455)

Management by exception A management system in which actual results are compared to a budget. Significant deviations from the budget are flagged as exceptions and investigated further. (p. 454)

Planning budget A budget created at the beginning of the budgeting period that is valid only for the planned level of activity. (p. 455)

Revenue variance The difference between the actual revenue for the period and how much the revenue should have been, given the actual level of activity. A favorable (unfavorable) revenue variance occurs because the revenue is higher (lower) than expected, given the actual level of activity for the period. (p. 461)

Spending variance The difference between the actual amount of the cost and how much the cost should have been, given the actual level of activity. A favorable (unfavorable) spending variance occurs because the cost is lower (higher) than expected, given the actual level of activity for the period. (p. 462)

Questions

9–1   What is a static planning budget?

9–2   What is a flexible budget and how does it differ from a static planning budget?

9–3   What are some of the possible reasons that actual results may differ from what had been budgeted at the beginning of a period?

9–4   Why is it difficult to interpret a difference between how much expense was budgeted and how much was actually spent?

9–5   What is an activity variance, and what does it mean?

9–6   If the actual level of activity is greater than the planned level of activity, would you expect the activity variances for variable expenses to be favorable, unfavorable, or a combination of the two?

9–7   What is a revenue variance, and what does it mean?

9–8   What is a spending variance, and what does it mean?

9–9   What does a flexible budget performance report do that a simple comparison of budgeted to actual results does not do?

9–10   How does a flexible budget based on two cost drivers differ from a flexible budget based on one cost driver?

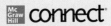 Applying Excel

The Excel worksheet form on the next page is to be used to recreate the Review Problem relating to Harrald's Fish House. The workbook, and instructions on how to complete the file, can be found in Connect.

    You should proceed to the requirements below only after completing your worksheet.

LEARNING OBJECTIVES 9–1, 9–2, 9–3, 9–4

Required:

1. Check your worksheet by changing the revenue in cell D4 to $16.00; the cost of ingredients in cell D5 to $6.50; and the wages and salaries in cell B6 to $10,000. The activity variance for net operating income should now be $850 U, and the spending variance for total expenses should be $410 U. If you do not get these answers, find the errors in your worksheet and correct them.

   a.   What is the activity variance for revenue? Explain this variance.

   b.   What is the spending variance for the cost of ingredients? Explain this variance.

	A	B	C	D	E	F	G	H
1	Chapter 9: Applying Excel							
2								
3	**Data**							
4	Revenue			$16.50 q				
5	Cost of ingredients			$6.25 q				
6	Wages and salaries	$10,400						
7	Utilities	$800	+	$0.20 q				
8	Rent	$2,200						
9	Miscellaneous	$600	+	$0.80 q				
10								
11	Actual results:							
12	Revenue	$27,920						
13	Cost of ingredients	$11,110						
14	Wages and salaries	$10,130						
15	Utilities	$1,080						
16	Rent	$2,200						
17	Miscellaneous	$2,240						
18								
19	Planning budget activity	1,800	meals served					
20	Actual activity	1,700	meals served					
21								
22	*Enter a formula into each of the cells marked with a ? below*							
23	**Review Problem: Variance Analysis Using a Flexible Budget**							
24								
25	*Construct a flexible budget performance report*							
26			Revenue					
27			and					
28		Actual	Spending		Flexible	Activity		Planning
29		Results	Variances		Budget	Variances		Budget
30	Meals served	?			?			?
31	Revenue	?	?		?	?		?
32	Expenses:							
33	Cost of ingredients	?	?		?	?		?
34	Wages and salaries	?	?		?	?		?
35	Utilities	?	?		?	?		?
36	Rent	?	?		?	?		?
37	Miscellaneous	?	?		?	?		?
38	Total expenses	?	?		?	?		?
39	Net operating income	?	?		?	?		?
40								

Chapter 9 Form　Filled in Chapter 9 Form　Chapter 9 Form

Microsoft Excel

2. Revise the data in your worksheet to reflect the results for the following year:

Data

Revenue	$16.50q
Cost of ingredients	$6.25q
Wages and salaries	$10,400
Utilities	$800 + $0.20q
Rent	$2,200
Miscellaneous	$600 + $0.80q
Actual results:	
Revenue	$28,900
Cost of ingredients	$11,300
Wages and salaries	$10,300
Utilities	$1,120
Rent	$2,300
Miscellaneous	$2,020
Planning budget activity	1,700 meals served
Actual activity	1,800 meals served

Using the flexible budget performance report, briefly evaluate the company's performance for the year and indicate where attention should be focused.

The Foundational 15

Adger Corporation is a service company that measures its output based on the number of customers served. The company provided the following fixed and variable cost estimates that it uses for budgeting purposes and the actual results for May as shown below:

LEARNING OBJECTIVES 9–1, 9–2, 9–3

	Fixed Element per Month	Variable Element per Customer Served	Actual Total for May
Revenue		$5,000	$160,000
Employee salaries and wages	$50,000	$1,100	$88,000
Travel expenses		$600	$19,000
Other expenses	$36,000		$34,500

When preparing its planning budget, the company estimated it would serve 30 customers per month; however, during May, the company actually served 35 customers.

Required (all computations pertain to the month of May):

1. What amount of revenue would be included in Adger's flexible budget?
2. What amount of employee salaries and wages would be included in Adger's flexible budget?
3. What amount of travel expenses would be included in Adger's flexible budget?
4. What amount of other expenses would be included in Adger's flexible budget?
5. What net operating income would appear in Adger's flexible budget?
6. What is Adger's revenue variance?
7. What is Adger's employee salaries and wages spending variance?
8. What is Adger's travel expenses spending variance?
9. What is Adger's other expenses spending variance?
10. What amount of revenue would be included in Adger's planning budget?
11. What amount of employee salaries and wages would be included in Adger's planning budget?
12. What amount of travel expenses would be included in Adger's planning budget?
13. What amount of other expenses would be included in Adger's planning budget?
14. What activity variance would Adger report with respect to its revenue?
15. What activity variances would Adger report with respect to each of its expenses?

Exercises

EXERCISE 9–1 Prepare a Flexible Budget LO 9–1

Puget Sound Divers is a company that provides diving services such as underwater ship repairs to clients in the Puget Sound area. The company's planning budget for May appears below:

Puget Sound Divers Planning Budget For the Month Ended May 31	
Budgeted diving-hours (q)	100
Revenue (365.00q$)	$36,500
Expenses:	
Wages and salaries ($8,000 + 125.00q$)	20,500
Supplies (3.00q$)	300
Equipment rental ($1,800 + 32.00q$)	5,000
Insurance ($3,400)	3,400
Miscellaneous ($630 + 1.80q$)	810
Total expense	30,010
Net operating income	$ 6,490

During May, the company's actual activity was 105 diving-hours.

Required:

Using Exhibit 9–5 as your guide, prepare a flexible budget for May.

EXERCISE 9–2 Activity Variances LO 9–2

Flight Café prepares in-flight meals for airlines in its kitchen located next to a local airport. The company's planning budget for July appears below:

Flight Café Planning Budget For the Month Ended July 31	
Budgeted meals (q)	18,000
Revenue ($4.50q)	$81,000
Expenses:	
Raw materials ($2.40q)	43,200
Wages and salaries ($5,200 + $0.30q)	10,600
Utilities ($2,400 + $0.05q)	3,300
Facility rent ($4,300)	4,300
Insurance ($2,300)	2,300
Miscellaneous ($680 + $0.10q)	2,480
Total expense	66,180
Net operating income	$14,820

In July, 17,800 meals were actually served. The company's flexible budget for this level of activity appears below:

Flight Café Flexible Budget For the Month Ended July 31	
Budgeted meals (q)	17,800
Revenue ($4.50q)	$80,100
Expenses:	
Raw materials ($2.40q)	42,720
Wages and salaries ($5,200 + $0.30q)	10,540
Utilities ($2,400 + $0.05q)	3,290
Facility rent ($4,300)	4,300
Insurance ($2,300)	2,300
Miscellaneous ($680 + $0.10q)	2,460
Total expense	65,610
Net operating income	$14,490

Required:

1. Calculate the company's activity variances for July. (Hint: Refer to Exhibit 9–6.)
2. Which of the activity variances should be of concern to management? Explain.

EXERCISE 9–3 Revenue and Spending Variances LO 9–3

Quilcene Oysteria farms and sells oysters in the Pacific Northwest. The company harvested and sold 8,000 pounds of oysters in August. The company's flexible budget for August appears below:

Quilcene Oysteria Flexible Budget For the Month Ended August 31	
Actual pounds (q)	8,000
Revenue ($4.00q)	$ 32,000
Expenses:	
Packing supplies ($0.50q)	4,000
Oyster bed maintenance ($3,200)	3,200
Wages and salaries ($2,900 + $0.30q)	5,300
Shipping ($0.80q)	6,400
Utilities ($830)	830
Other ($450 + $0.05q)	850
Total expense	20,580
Net operating income	$ 11,420

The actual results for August were as follows:

Quilcene Oysteria Income Statement For the Month Ended August 31	
Actual pounds	8,000
Revenue	$35,200
Expenses:	
Packing supplies	4,200
Oyster bed maintenance	3,100
Wages and salaries	5,640
Shipping	6,950
Utilities	810
Other	980
Total expense	21,680
Net operating income	$13,520

Required:

Calculate the company's revenue and spending variances for August. (Hint: Refer to Exhibit 9–7.)

EXERCISE 9–4 Prepare a Flexible Budget Performance Report LO 9–4

Vulcan Flyovers offers scenic overflights of Mount St. Helens, the volcano in Washington State that explosively erupted in 1982. Data concerning the company's operations in July appear below:

Vulcan Flyovers Operating Data For the Month Ended July 31	Actual Results	Flexible Budget	Planning Budget
Flights (q)	48	48	50
Revenue ($320.00q)	$13,650	$15,360	$16,000
Expenses:			
Wages and salaries ($4,000 + $82.00q)	8,430	7,936	8,100
Fuel ($23.00q)	1,260	1,104	1,150
Airport fees ($650 + $38.00q)	2,350	2,474	2,550
Aircraft depreciation ($7.00q)	336	336	350
Office expenses ($190 + $2.00q)	460	286	290
Total expense	12,836	12,136	12,440
Net operating income	$ 814	$ 3,224	$ 3,560

The company measures its activity in terms of flights. Customers can buy individual tickets for overflights or hire an entire plane at a discount.

Required:

1. Using Exhibit 9–8 as your guide, prepare a flexible budget performance report for July that includes revenue and spending variances and activity variances.
2. Which of the variances should be of concern to management? Explain.

EXERCISE 9–5 Prepare a Flexible Budget with More Than One Cost Driver LO 9–5

Alyeski Tours operates day tours of coastal glaciers in Alaska on its tour boat, the Blue Glacier. Management identified two cost drivers—the number of cruises and the number of passengers—it uses in its budgeting and performance reports. The company publishes a schedule of day cruises that it may supplement with special sailings if there is sufficient demand. Up to 80 passengers can be accommodated on the tour boat. Data concerning the company's cost formulas appear below:

	Fixed Cost per Month	Cost per Cruise	Cost per Passenger
Vessel operating costs	$5,200	$480.00	$2.00
Advertising	$1,700		
Administrative costs	$4,300	$24.00	$1.00
Insurance	$2,900		

For example, vessel operating costs should be $5,200 per month plus $480 per cruise plus $2 per passenger. The company's sales should average $25 per passenger. In July, the company provided 24 cruises for a total of 1,400 passengers.

Required:

Using Exhibit 9–10 as your guide, prepare the company's flexible budget for July.

EXERCISE 9–6 Working with More Than One Cost Driver LO 9–2, LO 9–3, LO 9–5, LO 9–6

The Gourmand Cooking School runs short cooking courses at its small campus. Management has identified two cost drivers it uses in its budgeting and performance reports—the number of courses and the total number of students. For example, the school might run two courses in a month and have a total of 50 students enrolled in those two courses. Data concerning the company's cost formulas appear below:

	Fixed Cost per Month	Cost per Course	Cost per Student
Instructor wages		$3,080	
Classroom supplies			$260
Utilities	$870	$130	
Campus rent	$4,200		
Insurance	$1,890		
Administrative expenses	$3,270	$15	$4

For example, administrative expenses should be $3,270 per month plus $15 per course plus $4 per student. The company's sales should average $800 per student.

The company planned to run three courses with a total of 45 students; however, it actually ran three courses with a total of only 42 students. The actual operating results for September were as follows:

	Actual
Revenue	$32,400
Instructor wages	$9,080
Classroom supplies	$8,540
Utilities	$1,530
Campus rent	$4,200
Insurance	$1,890
Administrative expenses	$3,790

Required:

Using Exhibit 9–11 as your guide, prepare a flexible budget performance report that shows both revenue and spending variances and activity variances for September.

EXERCISE 9–7 Flexible Budgets and Activity Variances LO 9–1, LO 9–2

Jake's Roof Repair provided the following data concerning its costs:

	Fixed Cost per Month	Cost per Repair-Hour
Wages and salaries	$23,200	$16.30
Parts and supplies		$8.60
Equipment depreciation	$1,600	$0.40
Truck operating expenses	$6,400	$1.70
Rent	$3,480	
Administrative expenses	$4,500	$0.80

For example, wages and salaries should be $23,200 plus $16.30 per repair-hour. The company expected to work 2,800 repair-hours in May, but actually worked 2,900 repair-hours. The company expects its sales to be $44.50 per repair-hour.

Required:

Compute the company's activity variances for May. (Hint: Refer to Exhibit 9–6.)

EXERCISE 9–8 Planning Budget LO 9–1

Wyckam Manufacturing Inc. provided the following estimates concerning its manufacturing costs:

	Fixed Cost per Month	Cost per Machine-Hour
Direct materials		$4.25
Direct labor	$36,800	
Supplies		$0.30
Utilities	$1,400	$0.05
Depreciation	$16,700	
Insurance	$12,700	

For example, utilities should be $1,400 per month plus $0.05 per machine-hour. The company expects to work 5,000 machine-hours in June. Note that the company's direct labor is a fixed cost.

Required:

Using Exhibit 9–2 as your guide, prepare the company's planning budget for June.

EXERCISE 9–9 Planning Budget LO 9–1

Lavage Rapide is a Canadian company that owns and operates a large automatic car wash facility near Montreal. The following table provides estimates concerning the company's costs:

	Fixed Cost per Month	Cost per Car Washed
Cleaning supplies		$0.80
Electricity	$1,200	$0.15
Maintenance		$0.20
Wages and salaries	$5,000	$0.30
Depreciation	$6,000	
Rent	$8,000	
Administrative expenses	$4,000	$0.10

For example, electricity costs should be $1,200 per month plus $0.15 per car washed. The company expects to wash 9,000 cars in August and to collect an average of $4.90 per car washed.

Required:

Using Exhibit 9–2 as your guide, prepare the company's planning budget for August.

EXERCISE 9–10 Flexible Budget LO 9–1

Refer to the data for Lavage Rapide in Exercise 9–9. The company actually washed 8,800 cars in August.

Required:

Using Exhibit 9–5 as your guide, prepare the company's flexible budget for August.

EXERCISE 9–11 Activity Variances LO 9–2

Refer to the data for Lavage Rapide in Exercise 9–9. The company actually washed 8,800 cars in August.

Required:

Calculate the company's activity variances for August. (Hint: Refer to Exhibit 9–6.)

EXERCISE 9–12 Revenue and Spending Variances LO 9–3

Refer to the data for Lavage Rapide in Exercise 9–9. Also assume the company's actual operating results for August are as follows:

Lavage Rapide Income Statement For the Month Ended August 31	
Actual cars washed	8,800
Revenue	$43,080
Expenses:	
Cleaning supplies	7,560
Electricity	2,670
Maintenance	2,260
Wages and salaries	8,500
Depreciation	6,000
Rent	8,000
Administrative expenses	4,950
Total expense	39,940
Net operating income	$ 3,140

Required:

Calculate the company's revenue and spending variances for August. (Hint: Refer to Exhibit 9–7.)

EXERCISE 9–13 Prepare a Flexible Budget Performance Report LO 9–4

Refer to the data for Lavage Rapide in Exercises 9–9 and 9–12.

Required:

Using Exhibit 9–8 as your guide, prepare a flexible budget performance report that shows the company's revenue and spending variances and activity variances for August.

EXERCISE 9–14 Flexible Budget Performance Report in a Cost Center LO 9–1, LO 9–2, LO 9–3, LO 9–4

Packaging Solutions Corporation manufactures and sells a wide variety of packaging products. Performance reports are prepared monthly for each department. The planning budget and flexible budget for the Production Department are based on the following formulas, where q is the number of labor-hours worked in a month:

	Cost Formulas
Direct labor	$15.80q$
Indirect labor	$8,200 + $1.60q$
Utilities	$6,400 + $0.80q$
Supplies	$1,100 + $0.40q$
Equipment depreciation	$23,000 + $3.70q$
Factory rent	$8,400
Property taxes	$2,100
Factory administration	$11,700 + $1.90q$

The Production Department planned to work 8,000 labor-hours in March; however, it actually worked 8,400 labor-hours during the month. Its actual costs incurred in March are listed below:

	Actual Cost Incurred in March
Direct labor	$134,730
Indirect labor	$19,860
Utilities	$14,570
Supplies	$4,980
Equipment depreciation	$54,080
Factory rent	$8,700
Property taxes	$2,100
Factory administration	$26,470

Required:

1. Using Exhibit 9–2 as your guide, prepare the Production Department's planning budget for the month.
2. Using Exhibit 9–5 as your guide, prepare the Production Department's flexible budget for the month.
3. Using Exhibit 9–8 as your guide, prepare the Production Department's flexible budget performance report for March, including both the spending and activity variances.
4. What aspects of the flexible budget performance report should be brought to management's attention? Explain.

EXERCISE 9–15 Flexible Budgets and Revenue and Spending Variances LO 9–1, LO 9–3

Via Gelato is a popular neighborhood gelato shop. The company provided the following cost formulas and actual results for the month of June:

	Fixed Element per Month	Variable Element per Liter	Actual Total for June
Revenue		$12.00	$71,540
Raw materials		$4.65	$29,230
Wages	$5,600	$1.40	$13,860
Utilities	$1,630	$0.20	$3,270
Rent	$2,600		$2,600
Insurance	$1,350		$1,350
Miscellaneous	$650	$0.35	$2,590

While gelato is sold by the cone or cup, the shop measures its activity in terms of the total number of liters of gelato sold. For example, wages should be $5,600 plus $1.40 per liter of gelato sold, and the actual wages for June were $13,860. Via Gelato expected to sell 6,000 liters in June, but actually sold 6,200 liters.

Required:

Calculate Via Gelato revenue and spending variances for June. (Hint: Refer to Exhibit 9–7.)

EXERCISE 9–16 Flexible Budget Performance Report LO 9–1, LO 9–2, LO 9–3, LO 9–4

AirQual Test Corporation provides on-site air quality testing services. The company provided the following cost formulas and actual results for the month of February:

	Fixed Component per Month	Variable Component per Job	Actual Total for February
Revenue		$360	$18,950
Technician wages	$6,400		$6,450
Mobile lab operating expenses	$2,900	$35	$4,530
Office expenses	$2,600	$2	$3,050
Advertising expenses	$970		$995
Insurance	$1,680		$1,680
Miscellaneous expenses	$500	$3	$465

The company uses the number of jobs as its measure of activity. For example, mobile lab operating expenses should be $2,900 plus $35 per job, and the actual mobile lab operating expenses for February were $4,530. The company expected to work 50 jobs in February, but actually worked 52 jobs.

Required:

Using Exhibit 9–8 as your guide, prepare a flexible budget performance report showing AirQual Test Corporation's revenue and spending variances and activity variances for February.

Problems   connect

PROBLEM 9–17 Flexible Budget Performance Reports; Working Backwards LO 9–1, LO 9–2, 9–3, 9–4

Ray Company provided the following excerpts from its Production Department's flexible budget performance report:

	Actual Results	Spending Variances	Flexible Budget	Activity Variances	Planning Budget
Ray Company Production Department Flexible Budget Performance Report For the Month Ended August 31					
Labor-hours (q)	9,480		?		9,000
Direct labor ($?q)	$134,730	$?	$132,720	$?	$?
Indirect labor ($? + $1.50q)	?	1,780 F	21,640	?	?
Utilities ($6,500 + $?q)	?	1,450 U	?	336 U	12,800
Supplies ($? + $?q)	4,940	?	4,444	?	4,300
Equipment depreciation ($78,400)	?	0	?	?	?
Factory administration ($18,700 + $1.90q)	?	?	?	?	?
Total expense	$288,088	$?	$?	$?	$?

Required:

Complete the Production Department's Flexible Budget Performance Report by filling in all the question marks.

PROBLEM 9–18 Activity and Spending Variances LO 9–1, LO 9–2, LO 9–3

You have just been hired by FAB Corporation, the manufacturer of a revolutionary new garage door opening device. The president asked you to review the company's costing system and "do what you can to help us get better control of our manufacturing overhead costs." You find that the company has never used a flexible budget, and you suggest that preparing such a budget would be an excellent first step in overhead planning and control.

After much effort and analysis, you determined the following cost formulas and gathered the following actual cost data for March:

	Cost Formula	Actual Cost in March
Utilities	$20,600 + $0.10 per machine-hour	$24,200
Maintenance	$40,000 + $1.60 per machine-hour	$78,100
Supplies	$0.30 per machine-hour	$8,400
Indirect labor	$130,000 + $0.70 per machine-hour	$149,600
Depreciation	$70,000	$71,500

During March, the company worked 26,000 machine-hours and produced 15,000 units. The company had originally planned to work 30,000 machine-hours during March.

Required:

1. Calculate the activity variances for March. (Hint: Refer to Exhibit 9–6.) Explain what these variances mean.
2. Calculate the spending variances for March. (Hint: Refer to Exhibit 9–7.) Explain what these variances mean.

PROBLEM 9–19 More Than One Cost Driver LO 9–2, LO 9–3, LO 9–5, LO 9–6

Milano Pizza is a small neighborhood pizzeria with a small area for in-store dining as well as offering take-out and free home delivery services. The pizzeria's owner has determined that the shop has two major cost drivers—the number of pizzas sold and the number of deliveries made.

The pizzeria's cost formulas appear below:

	Fixed Cost per Month	Cost per Pizza	Cost per Delivery
Pizza ingredients		$3.80	
Kitchen staff	$5,220		
Utilities	$630	$0.05	
Delivery person			$3.50
Delivery vehicle	$540		$1.50
Equipment depreciation	$275		
Rent	$1,830		
Miscellaneous	$820	$0.15	

In November, the pizzeria budgeted for 1,200 pizzas at an average selling price of $13.50 per pizza and for 180 deliveries.

Data concerning the pizzeria's actual results in November were as follows:

	Actual Results
Pizzas	1,240
Deliveries	174
Revenue	$17,420
Pizza ingredients	$4,985
Kitchen staff	$5,281
Utilities	$984
Delivery person	$609
Delivery vehicle	$655
Equipment depreciation	$275
Rent	$1,830
Miscellaneous	$954

Required:

1. Using Exhibit 9–11 as your guide, prepare a flexible budget performance report that shows both revenue and spending variances and activity variances for the pizzeria for November.
2. Explain the activity variances.

PROBLEM 9–20 Critique a Report; Prepare a Performance Report LO 9–1, LO 9–2, LO 9–3, LO 9–4

TipTop Flight School offers flying lessons at a small municipal airport. The school's owner and manager have been attempting to evaluate performance and control costs using a variance report that compares the planning budget to actual results. A recent variance report appears below:

TipTop Flight School Variance Report For the Month Ended July 31	Actual Results	Planning Budget	Variances	
Lessons	155	150		
Revenue	$33,900	$33,000	$900	F
Expenses:				
Instructor wages	9,870	9,750	120	U
Aircraft depreciation	5,890	5,700	190	U
Fuel	2,750	2,250	500	U
Maintenance	2,450	2,330	120	U
Ground facility expenses	1,540	1,550	10	F
Administration	3,320	3,390	70	F
Total expense	25,820	24,970	850	U
Net operating income	$ 8,080	$ 8,030	$ 50	F

After several months of using these reports, the owner has become frustrated. For example, she is quite confident that instructor wages were very tightly controlled in July, but the report shows an unfavorable variance.

The planning budget was developed using the following formulas, where q is the number of lessons sold:

	Cost Formulas
Revenue	$220q
Instructor wages	$65q
Aircraft depreciation	$38q
Fuel	$15q
Maintenance	$530 + $12q
Ground facility expenses	$1,250 + $2q
Administration	$3,240 + $1q

Required:

1. Should the owner feel frustrated with the variance reports? Explain.
2. Using Exhibit 9–8 as your guide, prepare a flexible budget performance report for the school for July.
3. Evaluate the school's performance for July.

PROBLEM 9–21 Performance Report for a Nonprofit Organization LO 9–1, LO 9–2, LO 9–3, LO 9–4
The St. Lucia Blood Bank, a private charity partly supported by government grants, is located on the Caribbean island of St. Lucia. The blood bank has just finished its operations for September, which was a very busy month due to a powerful hurricane that hit neighboring islands causing many injuries. The hurricane largely bypassed St. Lucia, but residents of St. Lucia willingly donated their blood to help people on other islands. As a consequence, the blood bank collected and processed over 20% more blood than had been originally planned for the month.

A report prepared by a government official comparing actual costs to budgeted costs for the blood bank appears below. Continued support from the government depends on the blood bank's ability to demonstrate control over its costs.

St. Lucia Blood Bank Cost Control Report For the Month Ended September 30	Actual Results	Planning Budget	Variances
Liters of blood collected	620	500	
Medical supplies	$ 9,250	$ 7,500	$1,750 U
Lab tests	6,180	6,000	180 U
Equipment depreciation	2,800	2,500	300 U
Rent	1,000	1,000	0
Utilities	570	500	70 U
Administration	11,740	11,250	490 U
Total expense	$31,540	$28,750	$2,790 U

The managing director of the blood bank was very unhappy with this report, claiming his costs were higher than expected due to the emergency on the neighboring islands. He also pointed out that the additional costs had been fully covered by payments from grateful recipients on the other islands. The government official who prepared the report countered that all of the figures had been submitted by the blood bank to the government; he was just pointing out that actual costs were a lot higher than promised in the budget.

The following cost formulas were used to construct the planning budget:

Cost Formulas	
Medical supplies	$15.00q
Lab tests	$12.00q
Equipment depreciation	$2,500
Rent	$1,000
Utilities	$500
Administration	$10,000 + $2.50q

Required:

1. Using Exhibit 9–8 as your guide, prepare a flexible budget performance report for September.
2. Do you think any of the variances in the report you prepared should be investigated? Why?

PROBLEM 9–22 Critiquing a Variance Report; Preparing a Performance Report LO 9–1, LO 9–2, LO 9–3, LO 9–4

Several years ago, Westmont Corporation developed a comprehensive budgeting system for planning and control purposes. While departmental supervisors have been happy with the system, the factory manager expressed considerable dissatisfaction with the information being generated by the system.

A report for the company's Assembly Department for the month of March follows:

Assembly Department Cost Report For the Month Ended March 31	Actual Results	Planning Budget	Variances
Machine-hours	35,000	40,000	
Variable costs:			
Supplies	$ 29,700	$ 32,000	$2,300 F
Scrap	19,500	20,000	500 F
Indirect materials	51,800	56,000	4,200 F
Fixed costs:			
Wages and salaries	79,200	80,000	800 F
Equipment depreciation	60,000	60,000	—
Total cost	$240,200	$248,000	$7,800 F

After receiving a copy of this cost report, the supervisor of the Assembly Department stated, "These reports are super. It makes me feel really good to see how well things are going in my department. I can't understand why those people upstairs complain so much about the reports."

For the last several years, the company's marketing department chronically failed to meet the sales goals expressed in the company's monthly budgets.

Required:

1. The company's president is uneasy about the cost reports and would like you to evaluate their usefulness to the company.
2. What changes, if any, should be made in the reports to give better insight into how well departmental supervisors are controlling costs?
3. Using Exhibit 9–8 as your guide, prepare a new performance report for the quarter, incorporating any changes you suggested in question (2) above.
4. How well were costs controlled in the Assembly Department in March?

PROBLEM 9–23 Critiquing a Cost Report; Preparing a Performance Report LO 9–1, LO 9–2, LO 9–3, LO 9–4

Frank Weston, supervisor of the Freemont Corporation's Machining Department, was visibly upset after being reprimanded for his department's poor performance over the prior month. The department's cost control report is given below:

Freemont Corporation—Machining Department Cost Control Report For the Month Ended June 30	Actual Results	Planning Budget	Variances
Machine-hours	38,000	35,000	
Direct labor wages	$ 86,100	$ 80,500	$ 5,600 U
Supplies	23,100	21,000	2,100 U
Maintenance	137,300	134,000	3,300 U
Utilities	15,700	15,200	500 U
Supervision	38,000	38,000	0
Depreciation	80,000	80,000	0
Total	$380,200	$368,700	$11,500 U

"I just can't understand all of these unfavorable variances," Weston complained to the supervisor of another department. "When the boss called me in, I thought he was going to give me a pat on the back because I know for a fact that my department worked more efficiently last month than it has ever worked before. Instead, he tore me apart. I thought for a minute it might be over the supplies that were stolen out of our warehouse last month. But they only amounted to a couple of hundred dollars, and just look at this report. Everything is unfavorable."

Direct labor wages and supplies are variable costs; supervision and depreciation are fixed costs; and maintenance and utilities are mixed costs. The fixed component of the budgeted maintenance cost is $92,000; the fixed component of the budgeted utilities cost is $11,700.

Required:

1. Evaluate the company's cost control report and explain why the variances were all unfavorable.
2. Using Exhibit 9–8 as your guide, prepare a performance report that will help Mr. Weston's superiors assess how well costs were controlled in the Machining Department.

Cases | McGraw Hill **connect**

Select cases are available in Connect.

CASE 9–24 Ethics and the Manager LO 9–3

Tom Kemper is the controller of the Wichita manufacturing facility of Prudhom Enterprises, Inc.

The annual cost control report is one of the many reports that must be filed with corporate headquarters and is due at corporate headquarters shortly after the beginning of the New Year. Kemper does not like putting work off to the last minute, so just before Christmas, he prepared a preliminary draft of the cost control report. Some adjustments would later be required for transactions that occur between Christmas and New Year's Day. A copy of the preliminary draft report, which Kemper completed on December 21, follows:

Wichita Manufacturing Facility Cost Control Report December 21 Preliminary Draft			
	Actual Results	Flexible Budget	Spending Variances
Labor-hours	18,000	18,000	
Direct labor	$ 326,000	$ 324,000	$ 2,000 U
Power	19,750	18,000	1,750 U
Supplies	105,000	99,000	6,000 U
Equipment depreciation	343,000	332,000	11,000 U
Supervisory salaries	273,000	275,000	2,000 F
Insurance	37,000	37,000	0
Industrial engineering	189,000	210,000	21,000 F
Factory building lease	60,000	60,000	0
Total expense	$1,352,750	$1,355,000	$ 2,250 F

Melissa Ilianovitch, the general manager at the Wichita facility, asked to see a copy of the preliminary draft report. Kemper carried a copy of the report to her office, where the following discussion took place:

Ilianovitch: Wow! Almost all of the variances on the report are unfavorable. The only favorable variances are for supervisory salaries and industrial engineering. How did we have an unfavorable variance for depreciation?

Kemper: Do you remember that milling machine that broke down because the wrong lubricant was used by the machine operator?

Ilianovitch: Yes.

Kemper: We couldn't fix it. We had to scrap the machine and buy a new one.

Ilianovitch: This report doesn't look good. I was raked over the coals last year when we had just a few unfavorable variances.

Kemper: I'm afraid the final report is going to look even worse.

Ilianovitch: Oh?

Kemper: The line item for industrial engineering on the report is for work we hired Ferguson Engineering to do for us. The original contract was for $210,000, but we asked them to do some additional work that was not in the contract. We have to reimburse Ferguson Engineering for the costs of that additional work. The $189,000 in actual costs that appears on the preliminary draft report reflects only their billings up through December 21. The last bill they had sent us was on November 28, and they completed the project just last week. Yesterday I got a call from Laura Sunder over at Ferguson, and she said they would be sending us a final bill for the project before the end of the year. The total bill, including the reimbursements for the additional work, is going to be . . .

Ilianovitch: I am not sure I want to hear this.

Kemper: $225,000

Ilianovitch: Ouch!

Kemper: The additional work added $15,000 to the cost of the project.

Ilianovitch: I can't turn in a report with an overall unfavorable variance! They'll kill me at corporate headquarters. Call up Laura at Ferguson and ask her not to send the bill until after the first of the year. We have to have that $21,000 favorable variance for industrial engineering on the report.

Required:

What should Tom Kemper do? Explain.

CASE 9–25 Critiquing a Report; Calculating Spending Variances LO 9–3, LO 9–5

Boyne University offers an extensive continuing education program in many cities throughout the state. For the convenience of its faculty and administrative staff and to save costs, the university operates a motor pool. The motor pool's monthly planning budget is based on operating 20 vehicles; however, for the month of March, the university purchased one additional vehicle. The motor pool furnishes gasoline, oil, and other supplies for its automobiles. A mechanic does routine maintenance and minor repairs. Major repairs are performed at a nearby commercial garage.

The following cost control report shows actual operating costs for March of the current year compared to the planning budget for March.

Boyne University Motor Pool Cost Control Report For the Month Ended March 31	March Actual	Planning Budget	(Over) Under Budget
Miles	63,000	50,000	
Autos	21	20	
Gasoline	$ 9,350	$ 7,500	$(1,850)
Oil, minor repairs, parts	2,360	2,000	(360)
Outside repairs	1,420	1,500	80
Insurance	2,120	2,000	(120)
Salaries and benefits	7,540	7,540	0
Vehicle depreciation	5,250	5,000	(250)
Total	$28,040	$25,540	$(2,500)

The planning budget was based on the following assumptions:
a. $0.15 per mile for gasoline.
b. $0.04 per mile for oil, minor repairs, and parts.
c. $75 per automobile per month for outside repairs.
d. $100 per automobile per month for insurance.
e. $7,540 per month for salaries and benefits.
f. $250 per automobile per month for depreciation.

The supervisor of the motor pool is unhappy with the report, claiming it paints an unfair picture of the motor pool's performance.

Required:
1. Calculate the spending variances for March. (Hint: Refer to Exhibit 9–7.)
2. What are the deficiencies in the original cost control report? How do your calculations in part (1) above overcome these deficiencies?

(CMA, adapted)

CASE 9–26 Performance Report with More Than One Cost Driver LO 9–2, LO 9–3, LO 9–5, LO 9–6

The Little Theatre is a nonprofit organization devoted to staging plays for children. The theater has a very small full-time professional administrative staff. Through a special arrangement with the actors' union, actors and directors rehearse without pay and are paid only for actual performances.

The Little Theatre had tentatively planned to put on six different productions with a total of 108 performances. For example, one of the productions was *Peter Rabbit,* which had a six-week run with three performances on each weekend. The costs from the current year's planning budget appear below.

The Little Theatre Costs from the Planning Budget For the Year Ended December 31	
Budgeted number of productions	6
Budgeted number of performances	108
Actors and directors wages	$216,000
Stagehands wages	32,400
Ticket booth personnel and ushers wages	16,200
Scenery, costumes, and props	108,000
Theater hall rent	54,000
Printed programs	27,000
Publicity	12,000
Administrative expenses	43,200
Total	$508,800

Some of the costs vary with the number of productions, some with the number of perfor-mances, and some are fixed and depend on neither the number of productions nor the number of performances. The costs of scenery, costumes, props, and publicity vary with the number of pro-ductions. It doesn't make any difference how many times *Peter Rabbit* is performed, the cost of the scenery is the same. Likewise, the cost of publicizing a play with posters and radio commercials is the same whether there are 10, 20, or 30 performances of the play. On the other hand, the wages of the actors, directors, stagehands, ticket booth personnel, and ushers vary with the number of per-formances. The greater the number of performances, the higher the wage costs will be. Similarly, the costs of renting the hall and printing the programs will vary with the number of performances. Administrative expenses are more difficult to analyze, but the best estimate is approximately 75% of the budgeted costs are fixed, 15% depend on the number of productions staged, and the remain-ing 10% depend on the number of performances.

After the beginning of the year, the board of directors of the theater authorized expanding the theater's program to seven productions and a total of 168 performances. Not surprisingly, actual costs were considerably higher than the costs from the planning budget. (Grants from donors and ticket sales were also correspondingly higher but are not shown here.) Data concerning the actual costs were as follows:

The Little Theatre	
Actual Costs	
For the Year Ended December 31	
Actual number of productions	7
Actual number of performances	168
Actors and directors wages	$341,800
Stagehands wages	49,700
Ticket booth personnel and ushers wages	25,900
Scenery, costumes, and props	130,600
Theater hall rent	78,000
Printed programs	38,300
Publicity	15,100
Administrative expenses	47,500
Total	$726,900

Required:
1. Using Exhibit 9–11 as your guide, prepare a flexible budget performance report for the year that shows both spending variances and activity variances.
2. If you were on the board of directors of the theater, would you be pleased with how well costs were controlled during the year? Why, or why not?
3. The cost formulas provide figures for the average cost per production and average cost per performance. How accurate do you think these figures would be for predicting the cost of a new production or of an additional performance of a particular production?

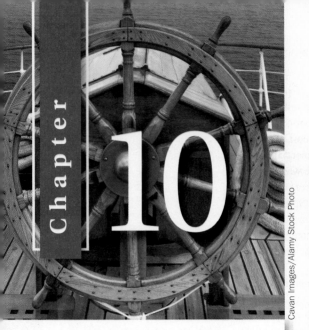
Standard Costs and Variances

Johnny Nunez/WireImage/Getty Images

LEARNING OBJECTIVES

After studying Chapter 10, you should be able to:

LO 10–1 Compute the direct materials price and quantity variances and explain their significance.

LO 10–2 Compute the direct labor rate and efficiency variances and explain their significance.

LO 10–3 Compute the variable manufacturing overhead rate and efficiency variances and explain their significance.

LO 10–4 *(Appendix 10A) Compute and interpret the fixed overhead budget and volume variances.*

Data Analytics Exercise available in Connect to complement this chapter

ENTREPRENEUR SPOTLIGHT

After completing a 12-year career as a professional basketball player, Ulysses "Junior" Bridgeman and two colleagues started Bridgeman Foods by purchasing five underperforming Wendy's restaurants. Eventually, the Bridgeman Hospitality Group grew to more than 300 restaurants including various brands, such as Wendy's, Chili's, Perkins, and Fazoli's. In 2017, Bridgeman divested his ownership stake in the Bridgeman Hospitality Group and became the president and CEO of Coca-Cola Heartland, which owns a production facility in Lenexa, Kansas, and 18 regional distribution centers.

Managerial Accounting: The Practical Application
Restaurant owners pay very close attention to ingredient (materials) quantity standards. For example, if Wendy's beef patties are too large, it will cause cost overruns that lower profits, whereas if the patties are too small, it will lead to dissatisfied customers, which in turn lowers sales and profits. Managing the purchase price of ingredients also requires managerial attention. While it may be tempting to conclude that lower purchase prices always lead to higher profits, that is not true. An excessive focus on driving down the price of ingredients may lower product quality, increase storage costs, and increase spoilage, all of which adversely affect profits.

Corporate Social Responsibility: Serving all Stakeholders
Coca-Cola Heartland's website says, "our culture is built around putting people first, and that starts with continuing to embrace and serve our local community." The company focuses its philanthropic efforts in four areas: education, health and well-being, diversity, and the environment. It supports numerous organizations such as Boys & Girls Clubs of America, Susan G. Komen, Special Olympics Illinois, the Negro League's Baseball Museum, and the Veterans Community Project. ■

Sources: Jack Dougherty, "Junior Bridgeman Used Fast Food to Become One of the 5 Richest Former Athletes in the World," *Sportscasting,* April 21, 2020 (https://www.sportscasting.com/junior-bridgeman-used-fast-food-to-become-one-of-the-5-richest-former-athletes-in-the-world/); https://www.celebritynetworth.com/richest-athletes/nba/junior-bridgeman-net-worth/; https://bfcompanies.com/bridgemanhospitality/#!company; https://www.heartlandcocacola.com/community

I n the last chapter, we investigated flexible budget variances. These variances provide feedback concerning how well an organization performed in relation to its budget. The impact on profit of a change in the level of activity is captured in the overall net operating income activity variance. The revenue and spending variances indicate how well revenues and costs were controlled given the actual level of activity. However, with regard to spending variances, we can often get even more detail about how well costs were controlled. For example, at Rick's Hairstyling, an unfavorable spending variance for hairstyling supplies could be due to paying too much for the supplies or using too many supplies, or some combination of the two. In this chapter, we learn how to use standard costs to decompose spending variances into two parts—a part that measures how well the acquisition prices of resources were controlled and a part that measures how efficiently those resources were used.

Standard Costs—Setting the Stage

A *standard* is a benchmark for measuring performance. Standards are found everywhere. Auto service centers like Firestone and Sears, for example, often set specific labor time standards for the completion of certain tasks, such as installing a carburetor or doing a valve job, and then measure actual performance against these standards. Fast-food outlets such as McDonald's and Subway have exacting standards for the quantity of meat going into a sandwich, as well as standards for the cost of the meat. Your doctor evaluates your weight using standards for individuals of your age, height, and gender. The buildings we live in conform to standards set in building codes.

Standards also are widely used in managerial accounting where they relate to the *quantity* and acquisition *price* of inputs used in manufacturing goods or providing services. *Quantity standards* specify how much of an input should be used to make a product or provide a service. *Price standards* specify how much should be paid for each unit of the input. If either the quantity or acquisition price of an input departs significantly from the standard, managers investigate the discrepancy to find the cause of the problem and eliminate it.

Next, we'll demonstrate how a company can establish quantity and price standards for direct materials, direct labor, and variable manufacturing overhead, and then we'll discuss how those standards can be used to calculate variances and manage operations.

The Colonial Pewter Company makes only one product—an elaborate reproduction of an 18th-century pewter statue. The statue is made largely by hand, using traditional metalworking tools. Consequently, the manufacturing process is labor-intensive and requires a high level of skill.

Colonial Pewter has recently expanded its workforce to take advantage of unexpected demand for the statue as a gift. The company started with a small cadre of experienced pewter workers but has had to hire less-experienced workers as a result of the expansion. The president of the company, J. D. Wriston, has called a meeting to discuss production problems. Attending the meeting are Tom Kuchel, the production manager; Janet Warner, the purchasing manager; and Terry Sherman, the corporate controller.

MANAGERIAL ACCOUNTING IN ACTION

The Issue

Colonial
Pewter
Company

J. D.:   I've got a feeling that we aren't getting the production we should out of our new people.

Tom: Give us a chance. Some of the new people have been with the company for less than a month.

Janet: Let me add that production seems to be wasting an awful lot of material—particularly pewter. That stuff is very expensive.

Tom: What about the shipment of defective pewter that you bought—the one with the iron contamination? That caused us major problems.

Janet: How was I to know it was off-grade? Besides, it was a great deal.

J. D.:   Calm down everybody. Let's get the facts before we start attacking each other.

Tom: I agree. The more facts the better.

J. D.:   Okay, Terry, it's your turn. Facts are the controller's department.

Terry: I'm afraid I can't provide the answers off the top of my head, but if you give me about a week I can set up a system that can routinely answer questions relating to worker productivity, material waste, and input prices.

J. D.:   Let's mark it on our calendars.

Setting Direct Materials Standards

Terry Sherman's first task was to prepare quantity and price standards for the company's only significant raw material, pewter ingots. The **standard quantity per unit** defines the amount of direct materials that should be used for each unit of finished product, including an allowance for normal inefficiencies, such as scrap and spoilage.[1] After consulting with the production manager, Tom Kuchel, Terry set the quantity standard for pewter at 3.0 pounds per statue.

The **standard price per unit** defines the price that should be paid for each unit of direct materials, and it should reflect the final, delivered cost of those materials. After consulting with purchasing manager Janet Warner, Terry set the standard price of pewter at $4.00 per pound.

Once Terry established the quantity and price standards, he computed the standard direct materials cost per statue as follows:

$$3.0 \text{ pounds per statue} \times \$4.00 \text{ per pound} = \$12.00 \text{ per statue}$$

IN BUSINESS

Fabrice Dimier/Bloomberg/Getty Images

MANAGING MATERIALS AND LABOR

Schneider Electric's Oxford, Ohio, plant manufactures *busways* that transport electricity from its point of entry into a building to remote locations throughout the building. The plant's managers pay close attention to direct materials costs because they are more than half of the plant's total manufacturing costs. To help control scrap rates for direct materials such as copper, steel, and aluminum, the accounting department prepares direct materials quantity variances. These variances compare the amount of direct materials that were actually used to the standard quantity of direct materials that should have been used to make a product (according to computations by the plant's engineers). Keeping a close eye on these differences helps to identify and deal with the causes of excessive scrap, such as an inadequately trained machine operator, poor-quality raw materials inputs, or a malfunctioning machine.

Because direct labor is also a significant component of the plant's total manufacturing costs, the management team daily monitors the direct labor efficiency variance. This variance compares the actual amount of labor time used to the standard amount of labor time allowed to make a product. When idle workers cause an unfavorable labor efficiency variance, managers temporarily move workers from departments with slack to departments with a backlog of work to be done.

Source: Author's conversation with Doug Taylor, plant controller, Schneider Electric's Oxford, Ohio, plant.

Setting Direct Labor Standards

Direct labor quantity and price standards are usually expressed in terms of labor-hours or a labor rate. The **standard hours per unit** defines the amount of direct labor-hours that should be used to produce one unit of finished goods. One approach used to determine

---

[1] Although companies often create "practical" rather than "ideal" materials quantity standards that include allowances for normal inefficiencies such as scrap, spoilage, and rejects, this practice is often criticized because it contradicts the zero defects goal that underlies many process improvement programs. If these types of allowances are built into materials quantity standards, they should be periodically reviewed and reduced over time to reflect improved processes, better training, and better equipment.

this standard is for an industrial engineer to do a time and motion study, actually clocking the time required for each task. Throughout the chapter, we'll assume that "tight but attainable" labor standards are used rather than "ideal" standards that can only be attained by the most skilled and efficient employees working at peak effort 100% of the time. Therefore, after consulting with the production manager and considering reasonable allowances for breaks, personal needs of employees, cleanup, and machine downtime, Terry set the standard hours per unit at 0.50 direct labor-hours per statue.

The **standard rate per hour** defines the company's expected direct labor wage rate per hour, including employment taxes and fringe benefits. Using wage records and in consultation with the production manager, Terry Sherman established a standard rate per hour of $22.00. This standard rate reflects the expected "mix" of workers, even though the actual hourly wage rates may vary somewhat from individual to individual due to differing skills or seniority.

Once Terry established the time and rate standards, he computed the standard direct labor cost per statue as follows:

0.50 direct labor-hours per statue × $22.00 per direct labor-hour = $11.00 per statue

Setting Variable Manufacturing Overhead Standards

As with direct labor, the quantity and price standards for variable manufacturing overhead are usually expressed in terms of hours and a rate. The *standard hours per unit* for variable overhead measures the amount of the allocation base from a company's predetermined overhead rate that is required to produce one unit of finished goods. In the case of Colonial Pewter, we will assume that the company uses direct labor-hours as the allocation base in its predetermined overhead rate. Therefore, the standard hours per unit for variable overhead is exactly the same as the standard hours per unit for direct labor—0.50 direct labor-hours per statue.

The *standard rate per unit* that a company expects to pay for variable overhead equals *the variable portion of the predetermined overhead rate*. At Colonial Pewter, the variable portion of the predetermined overhead rate is $6.00 per direct labor-hour. Therefore, Terry computed the standard variable manufacturing overhead cost per statue as follows:

0.50 direct labor-hours per statue × $6.00 per direct-labor hour = $3.00 per statue

This $3.00-per-unit cost for variable manufacturing overhead appears along with direct materials ($12 per unit) and direct labor ($11 per unit) on the *standard cost card* in Exhibit 10–1. A **standard cost card** shows the standard quantity (or hours) and standard price (or rate) of the inputs required to produce a unit of a specific product. The **standard cost per unit** for all three variable manufacturing costs is computed the same way. The standard quantity (or hours) per unit is multiplied by the standard price (or rate) per unit to obtain the standard cost per unit.

Inputs	(1) Standard Quantity or Hours	(2) Standard Price or Rate	Standard Cost (1) × (2)
Direct materials	3.0 pounds	$4.00 per pound	$12.00
Direct labor	0.50 hours	$22.00 per hour	11.00
Variable manufacturing overhead	0.50 hours	$6.00 per hour	3.00
Total standard cost per unit			$26.00

EXHIBIT 10–1
Standard Cost Card—
Variable Manufacturing Costs

Using Standards in Flexible Budgets

Once Terry Sherman created the standard cost card shown in Exhibit 10–1, he was ready to use this information to calculate direct materials, direct labor, and variable manufacturing overhead variances. Therefore, he gathered the following data for the month of June:

Planned output in June	2,100 statues
Actual output in June	2,000 statues
Actual direct materials cost in June*	$24,700
Actual direct labor cost in June	$22,680
Actual variable manufacturing overhead cost in June	$7,140

*There were no beginning or ending inventories of raw materials in June; all materials purchased were used.

Using the above data and the standard cost data from Exhibit 10–1, Terry computed the spending and activity variances shown in Exhibit 10–2. Notice that the actual results and flexible budget columns are each based on the actual output of 2,000 statues. The planning budget column is based on the planned output of 2,100 statues. The standard costs of $12.00 per unit for materials, $11.00 per unit for direct labor, and $3.00 per unit for variable manufacturing overhead are each multiplied by the actual output of 2,000 statues to compute the amounts in the flexible budget column. For example, the standard direct labor cost per unit of $11.00 multiplied by 2,000 statues equals the direct labor flexible budget of $22,000. Similarly, the three standard variable cost figures are multiplied by 2,100 statues to compute the amounts in the planning budget column. For example, the direct labor cost for the planning budget is $23,100 (= $11.00 per unit × 2,100 units).

The spending variances shown in Exhibit 10–2 are computed by taking the amounts in the actual results column and subtracting the amounts in the flexible budget column. For all three variable manufacturing costs, this computation results in a positive number because the actual amount of the cost incurred to produce 2,000 statues exceeds the standard cost allowed for 2,000 statues. Because, in all three instances, the actual cost incurred exceeds the standard cost allowed for the actual level of output, the variance is labeled unfavorable (U). Had any of the actual costs incurred been less than the standard cost allowed for the actual level of output, the corresponding variances would have been labeled favorable (F).

The activity variances shown in the exhibit are computed by taking the amounts in the flexible budget column and subtracting the amounts in the planning budget column. For all three variable manufacturing costs, these computations result in negative

EXHIBIT 10–2

Flexible Budget Performance Report for Variable Manufacturing Costs

Colonial Pewter
Flexible Budget Performance Report—Variable Manufacturing Costs
For the Month Ended June 30

	Actual Results	Spending Variances	Flexible Budget	Activity Variances	Planning Budget
Statues produced (q)	2,000		2,000		2,100
Direct materials ($12.00q)	$24,700	$700 U	$24,000	$1,200 F	$25,200
Direct labor ($11.00q)	$22,680	$680 U	$22,000	$1,100 F	$23,100
Variable manufacturing overhead ($3.00q)	$7,140	$1,140 U	$6,000	$300 F	$6,300

numbers and what are labeled as favorable (F) variances. The label favorable is used in these instances because the standard cost allowed for the actual output is less than the standard cost allowed for the planned output. Had the actual level of activity been greater than the planned level of activity, all of the computations would have resulted in positive numbers and unfavorable (U) activity variances.

While the performance report in Exhibit 10–2 is useful, it would be even more useful if the spending variances could be broken down into their price-related and quantity-related components. For example, the direct materials spending variance in the report is $700 unfavorable. This means that, given the actual level of production for the period, direct materials costs were too high by $700—at least according to the standard costs. Was this due to higher-than-expected prices for materials? Or was it due to too much material being used? The standard cost variances we will be discussing in the rest of the chapter are designed to answer these questions.

A General Model for Standard Cost Variance Analysis

Standard cost variance analysis decomposes spending variances from the flexible budget into two elements—one due to the price paid for the input and the other due to the amount of the input that is used. A **price variance** is the difference between the actual amount paid for an input and the standard amount that should have been paid, multiplied by the actual amount of the input purchased. A **quantity variance** is the difference between how much of an input was actually used and how much should have been used for the actual level of output and is stated in dollar terms using the standard price of the input.

Why are standards separated into two categories—price and quantity? Price variances and quantity variances usually have different causes. In addition, different managers are usually responsible for buying and using inputs. For example, in the case of a raw material, the purchasing manager is responsible for its price and the production manager is responsible for the amount of the raw material actually used to make products. Therefore, it is important to clearly distinguish between deviations from price standards (the responsibility of the purchasing manager) and deviations from quantity standards (the responsibility of the production manager).

Exhibit 10–3 presents a general model that can be used to decompose the spending variance for a variable cost into a *price variance* and a *quantity variance*.[2] Column (1) corresponds with the Actual Results column in Exhibit 10–2. Column (3) corresponds with the Flexible Budget column in Exhibit 10–2. Column (2) has been inserted into Exhibit 10–3 to enable separating the spending variance into a price variance and a quantity variance.

Three things should be noted from Exhibit 10–3. First, it can be used to compute a price variance and a quantity variance for each of the three variable cost elements—direct materials, direct labor, and variable manufacturing overhead—even though the variances have different names. A price variance is called a *materials price variance* in the case of direct materials, a *labor rate variance* in the case of direct labor, and a *variable overhead rate variance* in the case of variable manufacturing overhead. A quantity variance is called a *materials quantity variance* in the case of direct materials, a *labor efficiency variance* in the case of direct labor, and a *variable overhead efficiency variance* in the case of variable manufacturing overhead.

Second, all three columns in the exhibit are based on the *actual amount of output* produced during the period. Even the flexible budget column (column 3) depicts

---

[2] This general model can always be used to compute direct labor and variable manufacturing overhead variances. However, it can be used to compute direct materials variances only when the actual quantity of materials purchased equals the actual quantity of materials used in production. Later in the chapter, we will explain how to compute direct materials variances when these quantities differ.

EXHIBIT 10–3
A General Model for Standard Cost Variance Analysis—Variable Manufacturing Costs

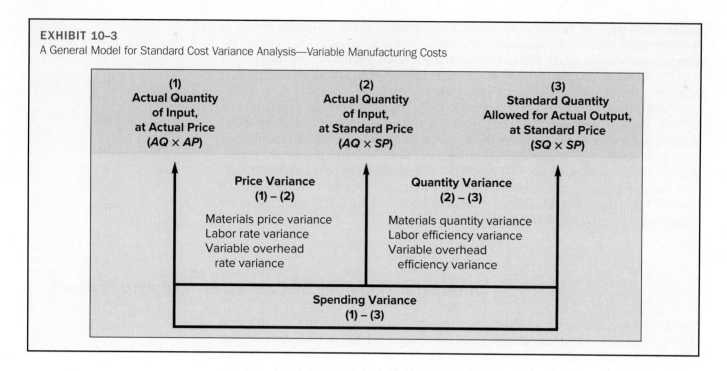

the standard cost allowed for the *actual amount of output* produced during the period. The key to understanding the flexible budget column in Exhibit 10–3 is to grasp the meaning of the term *standard quantity allowed (SQ)*. The **standard quantity allowed** (when computing direct materials variances) or **standard hours allowed** (when computing direct labor and variable manufacturing overhead variances) refers to the amount of an input *that should have been used* to manufacture the actual output of finished goods produced during the period. It is computed by multiplying the actual output by the standard quantity (or hours) per unit. The standard quantity (or hours) allowed is then multiplied by the standard price (or rate) per unit of the input to obtain the total cost according to the flexible budget. For example, if a company actually produced 100 units of finished goods during the period and its standard quantity per unit of finished goods for direct materials is 5 pounds, then its *standard quantity allowed (SQ)* would be 500 pounds (= 100 units × 5 pounds per unit). If the company's standard cost per pound of direct materials is \$2.00, then the total direct materials cost in its flexible budget would be \$1,000 (= 500 pounds × \$2.00 per pound).

Third, the spending, price, and quantity variances—regardless of what they are called—are computed exactly the same way regardless of whether one is dealing with direct materials, direct labor, or variable manufacturing overhead. The spending variance is computed by taking the total cost in column (1) and subtracting the total cost in column (3). The price variance is computed by taking the total cost in column (1) and subtracting the total cost in column (2). The quantity variance is computed by taking the total cost in column (2) and subtracting the total cost in column (3). In all of these variance calculations, a positive number should be labeled as an unfavorable (U) variance and a negative number should be labeled as a favorable (F) variance. An unfavorable price variance indicates that the actual price (AP) per unit of the input was greater than the standard price (SP) per unit. A favorable price variance indicates that the actual price (AP) of the input was less than the standard price per unit (SP). An unfavorable quantity variance indicates that the actual quantity (AQ) of the input used was greater than the standard quantity allowed (SQ). Conversely, a favorable quantity variance indicates that the actual quantity (AQ) of the input used was less than the standard quantity allowed (SQ).

With this general model as the foundation, we will now calculate Colonial Pewter's price and quantity variances.

Using Standard Costs—Direct Materials Variances

After determining Colonial Pewter Company's standard costs for direct materials, direct labor, and variable manufacturing overhead, Terry Sherman's next step was to compute the company's variances for June. As discussed in the preceding section, variances are computed by comparing actual costs to standard costs. Terry referred to the standard cost card in Exhibit 10–1 that shows the standard direct materials cost per statue was computed as follows:

LEARNING OBJECTIVE 10–1

Compute the direct materials price and quantity variances and explain their significance.

$$3.0 \text{ pounds per statue} \times \$4.00 \text{ per pound} = \$12.00 \text{ per statue}$$

Colonial Pewter's records for June showed that the actual quantity (AQ) of pewter purchased was 6,500 pounds at an actual price (AP) of $3.80 per pound, for a total cost of $24,700. All of the material purchased was used during June to manufacture 2,000 statues.[3] Using these data and the standard costs from Exhibit 10–1, Terry computed the price and quantity variances shown in Exhibit 10–4.

Notice that the variances in this exhibit are based on three different total costs— $24,700, $26,000, and $24,000. The first, $24,700, is the actual amount paid for the actual amount of pewter purchased. The third total cost figure, $24,000, refers to how much should have been spent on pewter to produce the actual output of 2,000 statues. The standards call for 3 pounds of pewter per statue. Because 2,000 statues were produced, 6,000 pounds of pewter should have been used. As mentioned earlier in the chapter, this is referred to as the *standard quantity allowed* (SQ), and its computation can be stated in formula form as follows:

$$\text{Standard quantity allowed} = \text{Actual output} \times \text{Standard quantity per unit}$$

If 6,000 pounds of pewter had been purchased at the standard price of $4.00 per pound, the company would have spent $24,000. This is the amount that appears in the company's

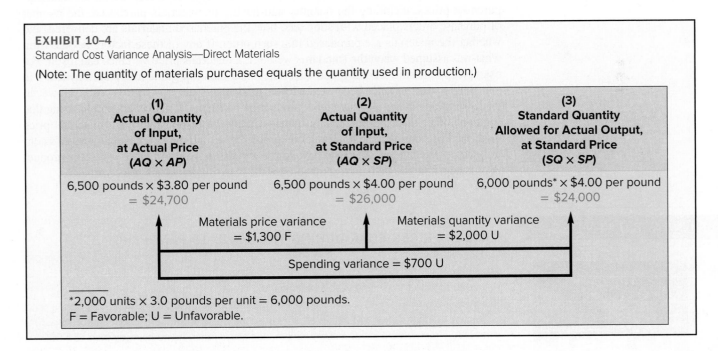

EXHIBIT 10–4
Standard Cost Variance Analysis—Direct Materials

(Note: The quantity of materials purchased equals the quantity used in production.)

(1) Actual Quantity of Input, at Actual Price ($AQ \times AP$)	(2) Actual Quantity of Input, at Standard Price ($AQ \times SP$)	(3) Standard Quantity Allowed for Actual Output, at Standard Price ($SQ \times SP$)
6,500 pounds × $3.80 per pound = $24,700	6,500 pounds × $4.00 per pound = $26,000	6,000 pounds* × $4.00 per pound = $24,000

Materials price variance = $1,300 F   Materials quantity variance = $2,000 U

Spending variance = $700 U

*2,000 units × 3.0 pounds per unit = 6,000 pounds.
F = Favorable; U = Unfavorable.

---

[3] Throughout this section, we assume zero beginning and ending inventories of materials and that all materials purchased during the period are used during that period. The more general case in which there are beginning and ending inventories of materials and materials are not necessarily used during the period in which they are purchased is considered later in the chapter.

flexible budget for the month. The difference between the $24,700 actually spent and the $24,000 that should have been spent is the spending variance for the month of $700 U. This variance is unfavorable (denoted by U) because the amount that was actually spent exceeds the amount that should have been spent. Also, note that this spending variance agrees with the direct materials spending variance in Exhibit 10–2.

The second total cost figure in Exhibit 10–4, $26,000, is the key that allows us to decompose the spending variance into two distinct elements—one due to price and one due to quantity. It represents how much the company should have spent if it had purchased the actual amount of input, 6,500 pounds, at the standard price of $4.00 a pound rather than the actual price of $3.80 a pound.

The Materials Price Variance

Using the $26,000 total cost figure in column (2) of Exhibit 10–4, we can make two comparisons—one with the total cost of $24,700 in column (1) and one with the total cost of $24,000 in column (3). The difference between the $24,700 in column (1) and the $26,000 in column (2) is the *materials price variance* of $1,300, which is labeled as favorable (denoted by F). A **materials price variance** measures the difference between a direct material's actual price per unit and its standard price per unit, multiplied by the actual quantity purchased.

To understand the materials price variance, note that the actual price of $3.80 per pound of pewter is $0.20 less than the standard price of $4.00 per pound. Because 6,500 pounds were purchased, the total amount of the variance is $1,300 (= $0.20 per pound × 6,500 pounds). This variance is labeled favorable (F) because the actual purchase price per pound is less than the standard purchase price per pound. Conversely, the materials price variance would have been labeled unfavorable (U) if the actual purchase price per pound had exceeded the standard purchase price per pound.

Generally speaking, the purchasing manager controls the price paid for materials and is therefore responsible for the materials price variance. Many factors influence materials purchase prices, including the quantity and quality of materials purchased, the number of purchase orders placed with suppliers, how the purchased materials are delivered, and whether the materials are purchased in a rush order. If any of these factors deviate from what was assumed when the standards were set, a materials price variance can result. For example, purchasing second-grade materials rather than top-grade materials may result in a favorable price variance because the lower-grade materials may be less costly. However, the lower-grade materials may create production problems. It also bears emphasizing that someone other than the purchasing manager could be responsible for a materials price variance. For example, due to production problems beyond the purchasing manager's control, the purchasing manager may have to use express delivery. In these cases, the production manager should be held responsible for the resulting materials price variances.

The Materials Quantity Variance

Referring again to Exhibit 10–4, the difference between the $26,000 in column (2) and the $24,000 in column (3) is the *materials quantity variance* of $2,000, which is labeled as unfavorable (denoted by U). The **materials quantity variance** measures the difference between the actual quantity of materials used in production and the standard quantity of materials allowed for the actual output, multiplied by the standard price per unit of materials. It is labeled as unfavorable (favorable) when the actual quantity of material used in production is greater than (less than) the quantity of material that should have been used according to the standard.

To understand the materials quantity variance, note that the actual amount of pewter used in production was 6,500 pounds. However, the standard amount of pewter allowed for the 2,000 statues that were actually produced is only 6,000 pounds. Therefore, too much pewter was used to produce the actual output—by a total of 500 pounds. To express this in dollar terms, the 500 pounds is multiplied by the standard price of $4.00 per pound to yield the quantity variance of $2,000 U. Why is the standard price of pewter, rather than the actual price, used in this calculation? The production manager is ordinarily responsible for the materials quantity variance. If the actual price were used in the calculation of the materials quantity variance, the production manager's performance evaluation would be unfairly influenced by the efficiency or inefficiency of the purchasing manager.

Excessive materials usage can result from many factors, including faulty machines, inferior materials quality, untrained workers, and poor supervision. Generally speaking, it is the responsibility of the production manager to see that material usage is kept in line with standards. There may be times, however, when the *purchasing* manager is responsible for an unfavorable materials quantity variance. For example, if the purchasing manager buys inferior materials at a lower price, the materials may be unsuitable for use and may result in excessive waste. Thus, the purchasing manager rather than the production manager would be responsible for the materials quantity variance.

Thus far, we have shown how to compute direct materials variances using the general model depicted in Exhibit 10–4; however, these variances can also be calculated using basic mathematical equations. Exhibit 10–5 shows how Colonial Pewter can compute its direct materials variances using the equations-based approach.

EXHIBIT 10–5
Direct Materials Variances: The Equations-Based Approach

Materials Price Variance:

Materials price variance = $(AQ \times AP) - (AQ \times SP)$
Materials price variance = $AQ(AP - SP)$
Materials price variance = 6,500 pounds ($3.80 per pound − $4.00 per pound)
Materials price variance = $1,300 F

Materials Quantity Variance:

Materials quantity variance = $(AQ \times SP) - (SQ \times SP)$
Materials quantity variance = $SP(AQ - SQ)$
Materials quantity variance = $4.00 per pound (6,500 pounds − 6,000 pounds)
Materials quantity variance = $2,000 U

where:
AQ = Actual quantity of inputs purchased and used in production
SQ = Standard quantity of inputs allowed for the actual output
AP = Actual price per unit of the input
SP = Standard price per unit of the input

STANDARD COSTS APPLY TO SERVICE COMPANIES TOO

Many manufacturers use standard cost systems; however, service companies can also use price and quantity standards for management control purposes. For example, the average cost of a burger sold at American restaurants is $1.86, consisting of $1.05 for the beef patty, $0.52 for the bun, $0.12 for lettuce, $0.07 for the tomato, and $0.10 for onion, mayonnaise, ketchup, and mustard.

At restaurants such as McDonald's, Burger King, Five Guys, and Steak 'n Shake, managers can use price and quantity standards to control their ingredient costs. If the average amount of beef being used in each burger exceeds the quantity standard, thereby shrinking the profit margin per burger sold, managers can solve the problem by reducing the amount of beef in a patty. Conversely, if the average portion of meat being used in each burger is less than the standard quantity, thereby leading to dissatisfied customers and lost sales, managers can resolve the issue by "beefing-up" the size of their burgers.

Source: Julie Jargon, "Diners Lose Taste for Pricey Burgers," *The Wall Street Journal*, June 1, 2017, pp. B1–B2.

Foodcollection/StockFood

Using Standard Costs—Direct Labor Variances

LEARNING OBJECTIVE 10–2
Compute the direct labor rate and efficiency variances and explain their significance.

Terry Sherman's next step in determining Colonial Pewter's variances for June was to compute the direct labor variances for the month. Recall from Exhibit 10–1 that the standard direct labor cost per statue is $11, computed as follows:

$$0.50 \text{ hours per statue} \times \$22.00 \text{ per hour} = \$11.00 \text{ per statue}$$

In addition, Colonial Pewter's records for June showed that 1,050 direct labor-hours were actually worked. Given that the company paid its direct labor workers a total of $22,680 (including payroll taxes and fringe benefits), the average actual wage rate was $21.60 per hour (= $22,680 ÷ 1,050 hours). Using these data and the standard costs from Exhibit 10–1, Terry computed the direct labor rate and efficiency variances that appear in Exhibit 10–6.

Notice that the column headings in Exhibit 10–6 are the same as those used in Exhibits 10–3 and 10–4, except that in Exhibit 10–6, the terms *rate* and *hours* are used in place of the terms *price* and *quantity*.

EXHIBIT 10–6
Standard Cost Variance Analysis—Direct Labor

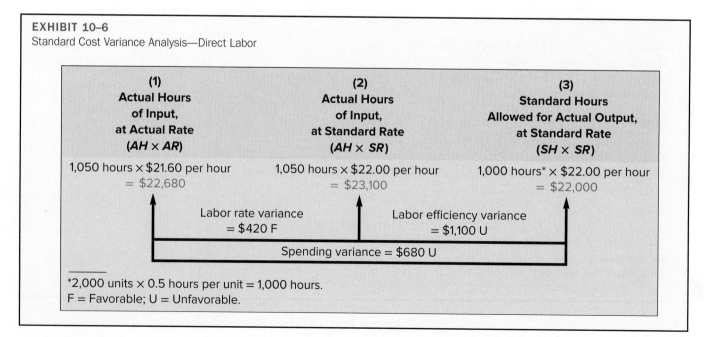

(1) Actual Hours of Input, at Actual Rate (AH × AR)	(2) Actual Hours of Input, at Standard Rate (AH × SR)	(3) Standard Hours Allowed for Actual Output, at Standard Rate (SH × SR)
1,050 hours × $21.60 per hour = $22,680	1,050 hours × $22.00 per hour = $23,100	1,000 hours* × $22.00 per hour = $22,000

Labor rate variance = $420 F

Labor efficiency variance = $1,100 U

Spending variance = $680 U

*2,000 units × 0.5 hours per unit = 1,000 hours.
F = Favorable; U = Unfavorable.

The Labor Rate Variance

Using the $23,100 total cost figure in column (2) of Exhibit 10–6, we can make two comparisons—one with the total cost of $22,680 in column (1) and one with the total cost of $22,000 in column (3). The difference between the $22,680 in column (1) and the $23,100 in column (2) is the *labor rate variance* of $420 F. The **labor rate variance** measures the difference between the actual hourly rate and the standard hourly rate, multiplied by the actual number of hours worked during the period.

To understand the labor rate variance, note that the actual hourly rate of $21.60 is $0.40 less than the standard rate of $22.00 per hour. Because 1,050 hours were actually worked, the total amount of the variance is $420 (= $0.40 per hour × 1,050 hours). The variance is labeled favorable (F) because the actual hourly rate is less than the standard hourly rate. If the actual hourly rate had been greater than the standard hourly rate, the variance would have been labeled unfavorable (U).

In most companies, the wage rates paid to workers are quite predictable. Nevertheless, rate variances can arise based on how production supervisors use their direct labor workers. Skilled workers with high hourly rates of pay may be given duties that require little skill and call for lower hourly rates of pay. This will result in an unfavorable labor rate variance because the actual hourly rate of pay will exceed the standard rate specified for the particular task. In contrast, a favorable rate variance would result when workers who are paid at a rate lower than specified in the standard are assigned to the task. However, the lower-paid workers may not be as efficient. Finally, overtime work at premium rates will result in an unfavorable labor rate variance if the overtime premium is charged to the direct labor account.

The Labor Efficiency Variance

Referring back to Exhibit 10–6, the difference between the $23,100 in column (2) and the $22,000 in column (3) is the *labor efficiency variance* of $1,100 unfavorable (U). The **labor efficiency variance** measures the difference between the actual labor-hours used and the standard hours allowed for the actual output, multiplied by the standard hourly rate.

To understand Colonial Pewter's labor efficiency variance, note that the actual labor-hours used in production was 1,050 hours. However, the standard amount of hours allowed for the 2,000 statues actually produced is 1,000 hours. Therefore, the company used 50 more hours for the actual output than the standards allow. To express this in dollar terms, the 50 hours are multiplied by the standard rate of $22.00 per labor-hour to yield the efficiency variance of $1,100 U.

Possible causes of an unfavorable labor efficiency variance include poorly trained or motivated workers; poor-quality materials, requiring more labor time; faulty equipment causing breakdowns and work interruptions; and poor supervision of workers. The managers in charge of production would usually be responsible for control of the labor efficiency variance. However, the purchasing manager could be held responsible if the purchase of poor-quality materials resulted in excessive labor processing time.

IN BUSINESS

CHINA'S LABOR COST ADVANTAGE IS SHRINKING

For many years, manufacturers such as TAL Group, Coach, Inc., and Samsung Electronics moved their operations to China in an effort to lower their labor cost per unit. However, as China's average labor cost of $3.60 per hour continues to rise, many of those manufacturers are relocating to cheaper-labor countries such as Sri Lanka, where factory wages are $0.50 per hour. China's Pearl River Delta region, once known as a thriving manufacturing hub, now has for-lease signs appearing at abandoned factories and worker dormitories inside one of its industrial parks.

Sources: Sophia Yan, "'Made in China' Isn't So Cheap Anymore, and That Could Spell Headache for Beijing," CNBC, February 27, 2017, https://www.cnbc.com/2017/02/27/chinese-wages-rise-made-in-china-isnt-so-cheap-anymore; and Kathy Chu, "China Loses Edge on Labor Costs," *The Wall Street Journal*, December 3, 2015, pp. B1, B4.

Another important cause of an unfavorable labor efficiency variance may be insufficient demand for the company's products. Managers in some companies argue that it is difficult, and perhaps unwise, to constantly adjust the workforce in response to changes in the amount of work that needs to be done. In such companies, the direct labor workforce is essentially fixed in the short run. If demand is insufficient to keep everyone busy, workers are not laid off, which in turn creates an unfavorable labor efficiency variance.

If customer orders are insufficient to keep the workers busy, the work center manager has two options—either accept an unfavorable labor efficiency variance or build inventory. A central lesson of Lean Production is that building inventory with no immediate prospect of sale is a bad idea. Excessive inventory—particularly work in process inventory—leads to high defect rates, obsolete goods, and inefficient operations. As a consequence, when the workforce is fixed in the short term, managers must be cautious about how labor efficiency variances are used. Some experts advocate eliminating labor efficiency variances in such situations—at least for the purposes of motivating and controlling workers on the shop floor.

Direct labor variances can also be computed using equations instead of the general model depicted in Exhibit 10–6. Exhibit 10–7 shows how Colonial Pewter can compute its direct labor variances using the equations-based approach.

EXHIBIT 10–7
Direct Labor Variances: The Equations-Based Approach

Labor Rate Variance:

Labor rate variance = $(AH \times AR) - (AH \times SR)$
Labor rate variance = $AH(AR - SR)$
Labor rate variance = 1,050 hours ($21.60 per hour − $22.00 per hour)
Labor rate variance = $420 F

Labor Efficiency Variance:

Labor efficiency variance = $(AH \times SR) - (SH \times SR)$
Labor efficiency variance = $SR(AH - SH)$
Labor efficiency variance = $22.00 per hour (1,050 hours − 1,000 hours)
Labor efficiency variance = $1,100 U

where:
AH = Actual quantity of labor-hours used in production
SH = Standard quantity of labor-hours allowed for the actual output
AR = Actual rate per direct labor-hour
SR = Standard rate per direct labor-hour

Using Standard Costs—Variable Manufacturing Overhead Variances

LEARNING OBJECTIVE 10–3
Compute the variable manufacturing overhead rate and efficiency variances and explain their significance.

The final step in Terry Sherman's analysis of Colonial Pewter's variances for June was to compute the variable manufacturing overhead variances. The variable portion of manufacturing overhead can be analyzed using the same basic formulas that we used to analyze direct materials and direct labor. Recall from Exhibit 10–1 that the standard variable manufacturing overhead is $3.00 per statue, computed as follows:

0.50 hours per statue × $6.00 per hour = $3.00 per statue

Also recall that Colonial Pewter's cost records showed that the total actual variable manufacturing overhead cost for June was $7,140 and that 1,050 direct labor-hours were worked in June to produce 2,000 statues. Terry's analysis of this overhead data appears in Exhibit 10–8.

Notice the similarities between Exhibits 10–6 and 10–8. These similarities arise from the fact that direct labor-hours are being used as the base for allocating overhead

EXHIBIT 10–8
Standard Cost Variance Analysis—Variable Manufacturing Overhead

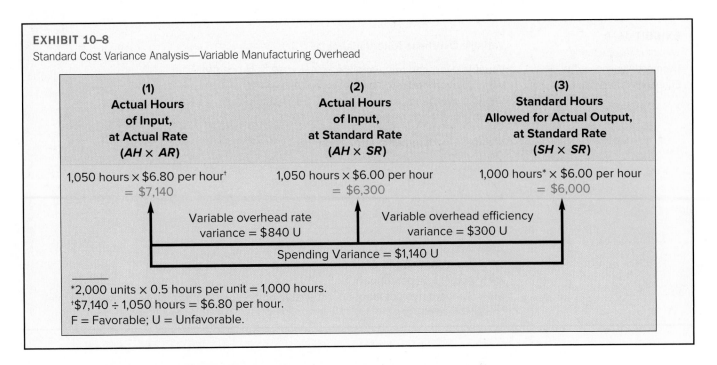

(1) **Actual Hours** **of Input,** **at Actual Rate** **(AH × AR)**	(2) **Actual Hours** **of Input,** **at Standard Rate** **(AH × SR)**	(3) **Standard Hours** **Allowed for Actual Output,** **at Standard Rate** **(SH × SR)**
1,050 hours × $6.80 per hour† = $7,140	1,050 hours × $6.00 per hour = $6,300	1,000 hours* × $6.00 per hour = $6,000

Variable overhead rate
variance = $840 U

Variable overhead efficiency
variance = $300 U

Spending Variance = $1,140 U

*2,000 units × 0.5 hours per unit = 1,000 hours.
†$7,140 ÷ 1,050 hours = $6.80 per hour.
F = Favorable; U = Unfavorable.

cost to units of product; thus, the same hourly figures appear in Exhibit 10–8 for variable manufacturing overhead as in Exhibit 10–6 for direct labor. The main difference between the two exhibits is in the standard hourly rate being used, which in this company is much lower for variable manufacturing overhead than for direct labor.

The Variable Manufacturing Overhead Rate and Efficiency Variances

Using the $6,300 total cost figure in column (2) of Exhibit 10–8, we can make two comparisons—one with the total cost of $7,140 in column (1) and one with the total cost of $6,000 in column (3). The difference between the $7,140 in column (1) and the $6,300 in column (2) is the *variable overhead rate variance* of $840 U. The **variable overhead rate variance** measures the difference between the actual variable overhead cost incurred during the period and the standard cost that should have been incurred based on the actual activity of the period. The difference between the $6,300 in column (2) and the $6,000 in column (3) is the *variable overhead efficiency variance* of $300 U. The **variable overhead efficiency variance** measures the difference between the actual level of activity and the standard activity allowed for the actual output, multiplied by the variable part of the predetermined overhead rate.

To understand Colonial Pewter's variable overhead efficiency variance, note that the actual amount of labor-hours used in production was 1,050 hours. However, the standard amount of labor-hours allowed for the actual output is 1,000 hours. Therefore, the company used 50 more hours for the actual output than the standards allow. To express this in dollar terms, the 50 hours are multiplied by the variable part of the predetermined overhead rate of $6.00 per labor-hour to yield the variable overhead efficiency variance of $300 U.

The interpretation of the variable overhead variances is not as clear as the direct materials and direct labor variances. In particular, the variable overhead efficiency variance is exactly the same as the direct labor efficiency variance except for one detail—the rate that is used to translate the variance into dollars. In both cases, the variance is the difference between the actual hours worked and the standard hours allowed for the actual output. In the case of the direct labor efficiency variance, this difference is multiplied by the standard direct labor rate. In the case of the variable overhead efficiency variance, this difference is multiplied by the variable portion of the predetermined overhead rate. So when direct labor is used as the overhead allocation base, whenever the direct labor

EXHIBIT 10–9
Variable Manufacturing
Overhead Variances: The
Equations-Based Approach

Variable Overhead Rate Variance:

Variable overhead rate variance = $(AH \times AR) - (AH \times SR)$
Variable overhead rate variance = $AH(AR - SR)$
Variable overhead rate variance = 1,050 hours ($6.80 − $6.00)
Variable overhead rate variance = $840 U

Variable Overhead Efficiency Variance:

Variable overhead efficiency variance = $(AH \times SR) - (SH \times SR)$
Variable overhead efficiency variance = $SR(AH - SH)$
Variable overhead efficiency variance = $6.00 per hour (1,050 hours − 1,000 hours)
Variable overhead efficiency variance = $300 U

where:
AH = Actual quantity of labor-hours used in production
SH = Standard quantity of labor-hours allowed for the actual output
AR = Actual rate per labor-hour
SR = Standard rate per labor-hour (Variable portion of the predetermined overhead rate)

efficiency variance is favorable, the variable overhead efficiency variance will also be favorable. And whenever the direct labor efficiency variance is unfavorable, the variable overhead efficiency variance will be unfavorable. Indeed, the variable overhead efficiency variance really doesn't tell us anything about how efficiently overhead resources were used. It depends solely on how efficiently direct labor was used.

Variable manufacturing overhead variances can also be computed using equations instead of the general model depicted in Exhibit 10–8. Exhibit 10–9 shows how Colonial Pewter can compute its variable overhead variances using the equations-based approach.

In preparation for the scheduled meeting to discuss his analysis of Colonial Pewter's standard costs and variances, Terry summarized his manufacturing cost variances as follows:

Materials price variance	$1,300 F
Materials quantity variance	2,000 U
Labor rate variance	420 F
Labor efficiency variance	1,100 U
Variable overhead rate variance	840 U
Variable overhead efficiency variance	300 U
Total of the variances	$2,520 U

MANAGERIAL ACCOUNTING IN ACTION

The Wrap-Up

Colonial Pewter Company

He distributed these results to the management group of Colonial Pewter, which included J. D. Wriston, the president of the company; Tom Kuchel, the production manager; and Janet Warner, the purchasing manager. J. D. Wriston opened the meeting with the following question:

J. D.: Terry, I think I understand what you have done, but just to make sure, would you mind summarizing the highlights of what you found?

Terry: As you can see, the biggest problems are the unfavorable materials quantity variance of $2,000 and the unfavorable labor efficiency variance of $1,100.

J. D.: Tom, you're the production boss. What do you think is causing the unfavorable labor efficiency variance?

Tom: It has to be the new production workers. Our experienced workers shouldn't have much problem meeting the standard of half an hour per unit. We all knew that there would be some inefficiency for a while as we brought new people on board. My plan for overcoming the problem is to pair up each of the new guys with one of our old-timers and have them work together for a while. It would slow down our older guys a bit, but I'll bet the unfavorable variance disappears, and our new workers would learn a lot.

J. D.:   Sounds good. Now, what about that $2,000 unfavorable materials quantity variance?

Terry: Tom, are the new workers generating a lot of scrap?

Tom: Yeah, I guess so.

J. D.:   I think that could be part of the problem. Can you do anything about it?

Tom: I can watch the scrap closely for a few days to see where it's being generated. If it is the new workers, I can have the old-timers work with them on the problem when I team them up.

J. D.:   Janet, the favorable materials price variance of $1,300 isn't helping us if it is contributing to the unfavorable materials quantity and labor efficiency variances. Let's make sure that our raw materials purchases conform to our quality standards.

Janet: Will do.

J. D.:   Good. Let's reconvene in a few weeks to see what has happened. Hopefully, we can get those unfavorable variances under control.

An Important Subtlety in the Materials Variances

Most companies use the *quantity of materials purchased* to compute the materials price variance and the *quantity of materials used* in production to compute the materials quantity variance. There are two reasons for this practice. First, delaying the computation of the price variance until the materials are used would result in less timely variance reports. Second, computing the price variance when the materials are purchased allows materials to be carried in the inventory accounts at their standard cost. This greatly simplifies bookkeeping.

When we computed materials price and quantity variances for Colonial Pewter in Exhibit 10–4, we assumed 6,500 pounds of materials were purchased and used in production. However, it is very common for a company's quantity of materials purchased to differ from its quantity used in production. When this happens, the materials price variance is computed using the *quantity of materials purchased,* whereas the materials quantity variance is computed using the *quantity of materials used* in production.

To illustrate, assume during June, Colonial Pewter purchased 7,000 pounds of materials at $3.80 per pound instead of 6,500 pounds as assumed earlier in the chapter. Also assume the company continued to use 6,500 pounds of materials in production and that the standard price remained at $4.00 per pound.

Given these assumptions, Exhibit 10–10 shows how to compute the materials price variance of $1,400 F and the materials quantity variance of $2,000 U. Note that the price variance is based on the pounds purchased, whereas the quantity variance is based on the pounds used in production. Column (2) of Exhibit 10–10 contains two different total costs for this reason. When the price variance is computed, the total cost used from column (2) is $28,000—which is the cost of the pounds *purchased,* evaluated at the standard price. When the quantity variance is computed, the total cost used from column (2) is $26,000—which is the cost of the actual pounds *used,* evaluated at the standard price.

Exhibit 10–10 shows that the price variance is computed on the entire amount of material purchased (7,000 pounds), whereas the quantity variance is computed only on the amount of materials used in production during the month (6,500 pounds). What about the other 500 pounds of material that were purchased during the period but have not yet been used? When those materials are used in future periods, a quantity variance will be computed. However, a price variance will not be computed when the materials are finally used because the price variance was computed when the materials were purchased.

Because the price variance is based on the amount purchased and the quantity variance is based on the amount used, the two variances do not generally sum to the spending variance from the flexible budget, which is wholly based on the amount used. We would

EXHIBIT 10–10

Standard Cost Variance Analysis—Direct Materials

(Note: The quantity of materials purchased does not equal the quantity used in production.)

(1) Actual Quantity of Input, at Actual Price (AQ × AP)	(2) Actual Quantity of Input, at Standard Price (AQ × SP)	(3) Standard Quantity Allowed for Actual Output, at Standard Price (SQ × SP)
7,000 pounds × \$3.80 per pound = \$26,600	7,000 pounds × \$4.00 per pound = \$28,000	6,000 pounds* × \$4.00 per pound = \$24,000

Price variance = \$1,400 F

6,500 Pounds × \$4.00 per pound
= \$26,000

Quantity variance = \$2,000 U

In this case, the price variance and the quantity variance do not sum to the spending variance because the price variance is based on the quantity purchased, whereas the quantity variance is based on the quantity used in production, and the two numbers differ.

―――――
*2,000 units × 3.0 pounds per unit = 6,000 pounds.
F = Favorable; U = Unfavorable.

also like to emphasize that the variances depicted in Exhibit 10–10 also can be computed using the equations shown in Exhibit 10–11. The approaches shown in *Exhibits 10–10 and 10–11 can always be used to compute direct materials variances. However, Exhibits 10–4 and 10–5 only can be used in the special case when the quantity of materials purchased equals the quantity of materials used.*

EXHIBIT 10–11

Direct Materials Variances: The Equations-Based Approach (when the quantity of materials purchased does not equal the quantity used in production)

Materials Price Variance:

Materials price variance = $(AQ \times AP) - (AQ \times SP)$
Materials price variance = $AQ(AP - SP)$
Materials price variance = 7,000 pounds (\$3.80 per pound − \$4.00 per pound)
Materials price variance = \$1,400 F

where:
AQ = Actual quantity of inputs *purchased*
AP = Actual price per unit of the input
SP = Standard price per unit of the input

Materials Quantity Variance:

Materials quantity variance = $(AQ \times SP) - (SQ \times SP)$
Materials quantity variance = $SP(AQ - SQ)$
Materials quantity variance = \$4.00 per pound (6,500 pounds − 6,000 pounds)
Materials quantity variance = \$2,000 U

where:
AQ = Actual quantity of inputs *used in production*
SQ = Standard quantity of inputs allowed for the actual output
SP = Standard price per unit of the input

Standard Costs—Managerial Implications

Advantages of Standard Costs

Standard cost systems have a number of advantages.

1. Standard costs are a key element in a management by exception approach as defined in the previous chapter. If costs conform to the standards, managers can focus on other issues. When costs are significantly outside the standards, managers are alerted that problems may exist that require attention. This approach helps managers focus on important issues.
2. Standards that are viewed as reasonable by employees can promote economy and efficiency. They provide benchmarks that individuals can use to judge their own performance.
3. Standard costs can greatly simplify bookkeeping. Instead of recording actual costs for each job, the standard costs for direct materials, direct labor, and overhead can be charged to jobs.
4. Standard costs fit naturally in an integrated system of "responsibility accounting." The standards establish what costs should be, who should be responsible for them, and whether actual costs are under control.

Potential Problems with Standard Costs

The improper use of standard costs can present a number of potential problems.

1. Standard cost variance reports are usually prepared on a monthly basis and often are released days or even weeks after the end of the month. As a consequence, the information in the reports may be so outdated that it is almost useless. Timely, frequent reports that are approximately correct are better than infrequent reports that are very precise but out of date by the time they are released. Some companies are now reporting variances and other key operating data daily or even more frequently.
2. If managers use variances only to assign blame and punish subordinates, morale may suffer. Furthermore, subordinates may be tempted to cover up unfavorable variances or take actions that are not in the best interests of the company to make sure the variances are favorable.
3. Labor-hour standards and efficiency variances make two important assumptions. First, they assume that the production process is labor-paced; if labor works faster, output will go up. However, output in many companies is not determined by how fast labor works; rather, it is determined by the processing speed of machines. Second, the computations assume that labor is a variable cost. However, direct labor can often be a fixed cost. If labor is fixed, then an undue emphasis on labor efficiency variances creates pressure to build excess inventories.
4. In some cases, a "favorable" variance can be worse than an "unfavorable" variance. For example, Hardee's has a standard for the amount of hamburger meat that should be in a beef patty. A "favorable" variance would mean that less meat was used than the standard specifies. The result is substandard hamburgers and possibly numerous dissatisfied customers.
5. Too much emphasis on meeting the standards may overshadow other important objectives such as maintaining and improving quality, on-time delivery, and customer satisfaction. This tendency can be reduced by using supplemental performance measures that focus on these other objectives.
6. Just meeting standards is not sufficient because companies need to continually improve to remain competitive. For this reason, some companies focus on the trends in their standard cost variances—aiming for continual improvement rather than just meeting the standards. In other companies, engineered standards are replaced either by a rolling average of actual costs, which is expected to decline, or by very challenging target costs.

In sum, managers should exercise considerable care when using a standard cost system. It is particularly important that managers go out of their way to focus on the positive, rather than just on the negative, and be aware of possible unintended consequences.

Summary

A standard is a benchmark for measuring performance. Standards are set for both the quantity and the cost of inputs needed to manufacture goods or to provide services. Quantity standards indicate how much of an input, such as labor time or raw materials, should be used to make a product or provide a service. Cost standards indicate what the cost per unit of the input should be.

When standards are compared to actual performance, the difference is referred to as a *variance*. Variances are computed and reported to management on a regular basis for both the quantity and the price elements of direct materials, direct labor, and variable overhead. Price variances are computed by taking the difference between actual and standard prices and multiplying the result by the amount of input purchased. Quantity variances are computed by taking the difference between the actual amount of the input used and the amount of input that is allowed for the actual output, and then multiplying the result by the standard price per unit of the input.

Standard cost systems provide companies with a number of advantages, such as supporting the management by exception approach, simplifying bookkeeping, and providing a benchmark that employees can use to judge their own performance. However, critics of standard cost systems argue that they provide information that is outdated, they can motivate employees to make poor decisions in an effort to generate favorable variances, and they fail to adequately embrace the mindset of continuous process improvement.

Traditional standard cost variance reports are often supplemented with other performance measures to ensure that overemphasis on standard cost variances does not lead to problems in other critical areas such as product quality, inventory levels, and on-time delivery.

 Data Analytics Exercise available in Connect to complement this chapter

Review Problem: Standard Costs

Xavier Company produces a single product. Variable manufacturing overhead is applied to products on the basis of direct labor-hours. The standard cost card for one unit of product is as follows:

Inputs	(1) Standard Quantity or Hours	(2) Standard Price or Rate	Standard Cost (1) × (2)
Direct materials	6 ounces	$0.50 per ounce	$ 3.00
Direct labor.	0.6 hours	$30.00 per hour	18.00
Variable manufacturing overhead	0.6 hours	$10.00 per hour	6.00
Total standard cost per unit.			$27.00

During June, 2,000 units were produced. The costs associated with June's operations were as follows:

Material purchased: 18,000 ounces at $0.60 per ounce	$10,800
Material used in production: 14,000 ounces	—
Direct labor: 1,100 hours at $30.50 per hour	$33,550
Variable manufacturing overhead costs incurred	$12,980

Required:

Compute the direct materials, direct labor, and variable manufacturing overhead variances.

Solution to Review Problem

Direct Materials Variances

Actual Quantity of Input, at Actual Price (AQ × AP)	Actual Quantity of Input at Standard Price (AQ × SP)	Standard Quantity Allowed for Actual Output, at Standard Price (SQ × SP)
18,000 ounces × $0.60 per ounce = $10,800	18,000 ounces × $0.50 per ounce = $9,000	12,000 ounces* × $0.50 per ounce = $6,000

Price variance = $1,800 U

14,000 ounces × $0.50 per ounce = $7,000

Quantity variance = $1,000 U

_____

*2,000 units × 6 ounces per unit = 12,000 ounces.
F = Favorable; U = Unfavorable.

Using formulas, the same variances would be computed as follows:

$$\text{Materials price variance} = (AQ \times AP) - (AQ \times SP)$$
$$= AQ(AP - SP)$$
$$= 18,000 \text{ ounces } (\$0.60 \text{ per ounce} - \$0.50 \text{ per ounce})$$
$$= \$1,800 \text{ U}$$

$$\text{Materials quantity vaiance} = (AQ \times SP) - (SQ \times SP)$$
$$= SP(AQ - SQ)$$
$$= \$0.50 \text{ per ounce } (14,000 \text{ ounces} - 12,000 \text{ ounces})$$
$$= \$1,000 \text{ U}$$

Direct Labor Variances

Actual Hours of Input, at Actual Rate (AH × AR)	Actual Hours of Input, at Standard Rate (AH × SR)	Standard Hours Allowed for Actual Output, at Standard Rate (SH × SR)
1,100 hours × $30.50 per hour = $33,550	1,100 hours × $30.00 per hour = $33,000	1,200 hours* × $30.00 per hour = $36,000

Labor rate variance = $550 U

Labor efficiency variance = $3,000 F

Spending variance = $2,450 F

_____

*2,000 units × 0.6 hours per unit = 1,200 hours.
F = Favorable; U = Unfavorable.

Using formulas, the same variances can be computed as follows:

$$\text{Labor rate variance} = (AH \times AR) - (AH \times SR)$$
$$= AH(AR - SR)$$
$$= 1{,}100 \text{ hours } (\$30.50 \text{ per hour} - \$30.00 \text{ per hour})$$
$$= \$550 \text{ U}$$

$$\text{Labor efficiency variance} = (AH \times SR) - (SH \times SR)$$
$$= SR(AH - SH)$$
$$= \$30.00 \text{ per hour } (1{,}100 \text{ hours} - 1{,}200 \text{ hours})$$
$$= \$3{,}000 \text{ F}$$

Variable Manufacturing Overhead Variances

Actual Hours of Input, at Actual Rate (AH × AR)	Actual Hours of Input, at Standard Rate (AH × SR)	Standard Hours Allowed for Actual Output, at Standard Rate (SH × SR)
1,100 hours × $11.80 per hour† = $12,980	1,100 hours × $10.00 per hour = $11,000	1,200 hours* × $10.00 per hour = $12,000

Variable overhead rate variance = $1,980 U   Variable overhead efficiency variance = $1,000 F

Spending variance = $980 U

*2,000 units × 0.6 hours per unit = 1,200 hours.
†$12,980 ÷ 1,100 hours = $11.80 per hour.
F = Favorable; U = Unfavorable.

Using formulas, the same variances can be computed as follows:

$$\text{Variable overhead rate variance} = (AH \times AR) - (AH \times SR)$$
$$= AH(AR - SR)$$
$$= 1{,}100 \text{ hours } (\$11.80 \text{ per hour} - \$10.00 \text{ per hour})$$
$$= \$1{,}980 \text{ U}$$

$$\text{Variable overhead efficiency variance} = (AH \times SR) - (SH \times SR)$$
$$= SR(AH - SH)$$
$$= \$10.00 \text{ per hour } (1{,}100 \text{ hours} - 1{,}200 \text{ hours})$$
$$= \$1{,}000 \text{ F}$$

Glossary

Labor efficiency variance The difference between the actual labor-hours taken to complete a task and the standard hours allowed for the actual output, multiplied by the standard hourly labor rate. (p. 499)

Labor rate variance The difference between the actual hourly labor rate and the standard rate, multiplied by the number of hours worked during the period. (p. 499)

Materials price variance The difference between a direct material's actual price per unit and its standard price per unit, multiplied by the quantity purchased. (p. 496)

Materials quantity variance The difference between the actual quantity of materials used in production and the standard quantity allowed for the actual output, multiplied by the standard price per unit of materials. (p. 497)

Price variance A variance computed by taking the difference between the actual price and the standard price and multiplying the result by the actual quantity of the input. (p. 493)

Quantity variance A variance computed by taking the difference between the actual quantity of the input used and the amount of the input that should have been used for the actual level of output and multiplying the result by the standard price of the input. (p. 493)

Standard cost card A detailed listing of the standard amounts of inputs and their costs that are required to produce one unit of a specific product. (p. 491)

Standard cost per unit The standard quantity allowed of an input per unit of a specific product, multiplied by the standard price of the input. (p. 491)

Standard hours allowed The time that should have been taken to complete the period's output. It is computed by multiplying the actual number of units produced by the standard hours per unit. (p. 494)

Standard hours per unit The amount of direct labor time that should be required to complete a single unit of product, including allowances for breaks, machine downtime, cleanup, rejects, and other normal inefficiencies. (p. 490)

Standard price per unit The price that should be paid for each unit of direct materials. It should reflect the final, delivered cost of those materials. (p. 490)

Standard quantity allowed The amount of direct materials that should have been used to complete the period's actual output. It is computed by multiplying the actual number of units produced by the standard quantity per unit. (p. 494)

Standard quantity per unit The amount of direct materials that should be used for each unit of finished product, including an allowance for normal inefficiencies, such as scrap and spoilage. (p. 490)

Standard rate per hour The labor rate that should be incurred per hour of labor time, including employment taxes and fringe benefits. (p. 491)

Variable overhead efficiency variance The difference between the actual level of activity (direct labor-hours, machine-hours, or some other base) and the standard activity allowed, multiplied by the variable part of the predetermined overhead rate. (p. 501)

Variable overhead rate variance The difference between the actual variable overhead cost incurred during a period and the standard cost that should have been incurred based on the actual activity of the period. (p. 501)

Questions

10–1 What is a quantity standard? What is a price standard?

10–2 Why are separate price and quantity variances computed?

10–3 Who is generally responsible for the materials price variance? The materials quantity variance? The labor efficiency variance?

10–4 The materials price variance can be computed at what two different points in time? Which point is better? Why?

10–5 If the materials price variance is favorable, but the materials quantity variance is unfavorable, what might this indicate?

10–6 Should standards be used to identify who to blame for problems?

10–7 "Our workers are all under labor contracts; therefore, our labor rate variance is bound to be zero." Discuss.

10–8 What effect, if any, would you expect poor-quality materials to have on direct labor variances?

10–9 If variable manufacturing overhead is applied to production on the basis of direct labor-hours and the direct labor efficiency variance is unfavorable, will the variable overhead efficiency variance be favorable or unfavorable, or could it be either? Explain.

10–10 Why can undue emphasis on labor efficiency variances lead to excess work in process inventories?

 Applying Excel

LEARNING OBJECTIVES 10–1, 10–2, 10–3

The Excel worksheet form on the next page is to be used to recreate the main example in the text pertaining to Colonial Pewter Company. The workbook, and instructions on how to complete the file, can be found in Connect.

You should proceed to the requirements below only after completing your worksheet.

Required:

1. Check your worksheet by changing the direct materials standard quantity in cell B6 to 2.9 pounds, the direct labor standard quantity in cell B7 to 0.6 hours, and the variable manufacturing overhead in cell B8 to 0.6 hours. The materials spending variance should now be

$1,500 U, the labor spending variance should now be $3,720 F, and the variable overhead spending variance should now be $60 F. If you do not get these answers, find the errors in your worksheet and correct them.

   a.   What is the materials quantity variance? Explain this variance.

   b.   What is the labor rate variance? Explain this variance.

	A	B	C	D	E	F	G
1	Chapter 10: Applying Excel						
2							
3	**Data**						
4	***Exhibit 10-1: Standard Cost Card***						
5	*Inputs*	*Standard Quantity*		*Standard Price*			
6	Direct materials	3.0 pounds		$4.00 per pound			
7	Direct labor	0.50 hours		$22.00 per hour			
8	Variable manufacturing overhead	0.50 hours		$6.00 per hour			
9							
10	Actual results:						
11	Actual output	2,000 units					
12	Actual variable manufacturing overhead cost	$7,140					
13		*Actual Quantity*		*Actual price*			
14	Actual direct materials cost	6,500 pounds		$3.80 per pound			
15	Actual direct labor cost	1,050 hours		$21.60 per hour			
16							
17	*Enter a formula into each of the cells marked with a ? below*						
18	**Main Example: Chapter 10**						
19							
20	***Exhibit 10-4: Standard Cost Variance Analysis–Direct Materials***						
21	Actual Quantity of Input, at Actual Price		? pounds ×		? per pound =	?	
22	Actual Quantity of Input, at Standard Price		? pounds ×		? per pound =	?	
23	Standard Quantity Allowed for the Actual Output, at Standard Price		? pounds ×		? per pound =	?	
24	Direct materials variances:						
25	Materials price variance		?				
26	Materials quantity variance		?				
27	Materials spending variance		?				
28							
29	***Exhibit 10-6: Standard Cost Variance Analysis–Direct Labor***						
30	Actual Hours of Input, at Actual Rate		? hours ×		? per hour =	?	
31	Actual Hours of Input, at Standard Rate		? hours ×		? per hour =	?	
32	Standard Hours Allowed for the Actual Output, at Standard Rate		? hours ×		? per hour =	?	
33	Direct labor variances:						
34	Labor rate variance		?				
35	Labor efficiency variance		?				
36	Labor spending variance		?				
37							
38	***Exhibit 10-8: Standard Cost Variance Analysis–Variable Manufacturing Overhead***						
39	Actual Hours of Input, at Actual Rate		? hours ×		? per hour =	?	
40	Actual Hours of Input, at Standard Rate		? hours ×		? per hour =	?	
41	Standard Hours Allowed for the Actual Output, at Standard Rate		? hours ×		? per hour =	?	
42	Variable overhead variances:						
43	Variable overhead rate variance		?				
44	Variable overhead efficiency variance		?				
45	Variable overhead spending variance		?				
46							

⊮ ◂ ▸ ⊯   Chapter 10 Form   Filled in Chapter 10 Form   Chapter 10 Formulas

Microsoft Excel

2.   Revise the data in your worksheet to reflect the results for the subsequent period:

Data

Exhibit 10–1: Standard Cost Card

Inputs	Standard Quantity	Standard Price
Direct materials	3.0 pounds	$4.00 per pound
Direct labor.	0.50 hours	$22.00 per hour
Variable manufacturing overhead	0.50 hours	$6.00 per hour
Actual results:		
Actual output	2,100 units	
Actual variable manufacturing overhead cost	$5,100	
	Actual Quantity	Actual price
Actual direct materials cost	6,350 pounds	$4.10 per pound
Actual direct labor cost.	1,020 hours	$22.10 per hour

a. What is the materials quantity variance? What is the materials price variance?
b. What is the labor efficiency variance? What is the labor rate variance?
c. What is the variable overhead efficiency variance? What is the variable overhead rate variance?

McGraw Hill **connect** **The Foundational 15**

Preble Company manufactures one product. Its variable manufacturing overhead is applied to production based on direct labor-hours and its standard cost card per unit is as follows:

LEARNING OBJECTIVES 10–1, 10–2, 10–3

Inputs	(1) Standard Quantity or Hours	(2) Standard Price or Rate	Standard Cost (1) × (2)
Direct materials	5 pounds	$8.00 per pound	$40.00
Direct labor.	2 hours	$14 per hour	28.00
Variable overhead.	2 hours	$5 per hour	10.00
Total standard cost per unit.			$78.00

The planning budget for March was based on producing and selling 25,000 units. However, during March the company actually produced and sold 30,000 units and incurred the following costs:
a. Purchased 160,000 pounds of raw materials at a cost of $7.50 per pound. All of this material was used in production.
b. Direct laborers worked 55,000 hours at a rate of $15.00 per hour.
c. Total variable manufacturing overhead for the month was $280,500.

Required:
1. What raw materials cost would be included in the company's planning budget for March?
2. What raw materials cost would be included in the company's flexible budget for March?
3. What is the materials price variance for March?
4. What is the materials quantity variance for March?
5. If Preble had purchased 170,000 pounds of materials at $7.50 per pound and used 160,000 pounds in production, what would be the materials price variance for March?
6. If Preble had purchased 170,000 pounds of materials at $7.50 per pound and used 160,000 pounds in production, what would be the materials quantity variance for March?
7. What direct labor cost would be included in the company's planning budget for March?
8. What direct labor cost would be included in the company's flexible budget for March?
9. What is the labor rate variance for March?
10. What is the labor efficiency variance for March?
11. What is the labor spending variance for March?
12. What variable manufacturing overhead cost would be included in the company's planning budget for March?
13. What variable manufacturing overhead cost would be included in the company's flexible budget for March?
14. What is the variable overhead rate variance for March?
15. What is the variable overhead efficiency variance for March?

McGraw Hill **connect** **Exercises**

EXERCISE 10–1 Direct Materials Variances LO 10–1
Bandar Industries manufactures sporting equipment. One of the company's products is a football helmet that requires special plastic. During the quarter ending June 30, the company manufactured 35,000 helmets, using 22,500 kilograms of plastic. The plastic cost the company $171,000.

According to the standard cost card, each helmet should require 0.6 kilograms of plastic, at a cost of $8 per kilogram.

Required:

1. What is the standard quantity of kilograms of plastic (*SQ*) that is allowed to make 35,000 helmets?
2. What is the standard materials cost allowed (*SQ* × *SP*) to make 35,000 helmets?
3. What is the materials spending variance?
4. What are the materials price variance and the materials quantity variance?

EXERCISE 10–2 Direct Labor Variances LO 10–2

SkyChefs, Inc., prepares in-flight meals for a number of major airlines. One of the company's products is grilled salmon with new potatoes and mixed vegetables. During the most recent week, the company prepared 4,000 of these meals using 960 direct labor-hours. The company paid its direct labor workers a total of $19,200 for this work, or $20.00 per hour.

According to the standard cost card for this meal, it should require 0.25 direct labor-hours at a cost of $19.75 per hour.

Required:

1. What is the standard labor-hours allowed (*SH*) to prepare 4,000 meals?
2. What is the standard labor cost allowed (*SH* × *SR*) to prepare 4,000 meals?
3. What is the labor spending variance?
4. What are the labor rate variance and the labor efficiency variance?

EXERCISE 10–3 Variable Overhead Variances LO 10–3

Logistics Solutions provides order fulfillment services for dot.com merchants. The company maintains warehouses that stock items carried by its dot.com clients. When a client receives an order from a customer, the order is forwarded to Logistics Solutions, which pulls the item from storage, packs it, and ships it to the customer. The company uses a predetermined variable overhead rate based on direct labor-hours.

In the most recent month, 120,000 items were shipped to customers using 2,300 direct labor-hours. The company incurred a total of $7,360 in variable overhead costs.

According to the company's standards, 0.02 direct labor-hours are required to fulfill an order for one item, and the variable overhead rate is $3.25 per direct labor-hour.

Required:

1. What is the standard labor-hours allowed (*SH*) to ship 120,000 items to customers?
2. What is the standard variable overhead cost allowed (*SH* × *SR*) to ship 120,000 items to customers?
3. What is the variable overhead spending variance?
4. What are the variable overhead rate variance and the variable overhead efficiency variance?

EXERCISE 10–4 Direct Labor and Variable Manufacturing Overhead Variances LO 10–2, LO 10–3

Erie Company manufactures a mobile fitness device called the Jogging Mate. The company uses standards to control its costs. The labor standards for one Jogging Mate are as follows:

Standard Hours	Standard Rate per Hour	Standard Cost
18 minutes	$17.00	$5.10

During August, 5,750 hours of direct labor time were needed to make 20,000 units of the Jogging Mate. The direct labor cost totaled $102,350 for the month.

Required:

1. What is the standard labor-hours allowed (*SH*) to makes 20,000 Jogging Mates?
2. What is the standard labor cost allowed (*SH* × *SR*) to make 20,000 Jogging Mates?
3. What is the labor spending variance?
4. What are the labor rate variance and the labor efficiency variance?
5. The budgeted variable manufacturing overhead rate is $4 per direct labor-hour. During August, the company incurred $21,850 in variable manufacturing overhead cost. Compute the variable overhead rate and efficiency variances for the month.

EXERCISE 10–5 Working Backwards from Labor Variances LO 10–2

Quality Motor Company is an auto repair shop that uses standards to control its labor time and labor cost. The standard labor cost for a motor tune-up is:

	Standard Hours	Standard Rate	Standard Cost
Motor tune-up	2.5	$25.00	$62.50

The record showing the time spent in the shop last week on motor tune-ups has been misplaced. However, the shop supervisor recalls that 50 tune-ups were completed during the week, and the controller recalls the following variance data relating to tune-ups:

Labor rate variance.....................	$150 F
Labor spending variance...............	$200 U

Required:
1. Determine the number of actual labor-hours spent on tune-ups during the week.
2. Determine the actual hourly pay rate for tune-ups last week. (Round your answer to the nearest cent.)

(*Hint:* A useful way to proceed would be to work from known to unknown data either by using the variance formulas in Exhibit 10–7 or by using the columnar format shown in Exhibit 10–6.)

EXERCISE 10–6 Direct Materials and Direct Labor Variances LO 10–1, LO 10–2

Huron Company produces a commercial cleaning compound known as Zoom. The direct materials and direct labor standards for one unit of Zoom are given below:

	Standard Quantity or Hours	Standard Price or Rate	Standard Cost
Direct materials	4.6 pounds	$2.50 per pound	$11.50
Direct labor............	0.2 hours	$18.00 per hour	$3.60

During the most recent month, the following activity was recorded:
a. Twenty thousand pounds of material were purchased at a cost of $2.35 per pound.
b. All of the material purchased was used to produce 4,000 units of Zoom.
c. 750 hours of direct labor time were recorded at a total labor cost of $14,925.

Required:
1. Compute the materials price and quantity variances for the month.
2. Compute the labor rate and efficiency variances for the month.

EXERCISE 10–7 Direct Materials Variances LO 10–1

Refer to the data in Exercise 10–6. Assume that instead of producing 4,000 units during the month, the company produced only 3,000 units, using 14,750 pounds of material. (The rest of the material purchased remained in raw materials inventory.)

Required:
Compute the materials price and quantity variances for the month.

EXERCISE 10–8 Direct Materials and Direct Labor Variances LO 10–1, LO 10–2

Dawson Toys, Ltd., produces a toy called the Maze. The company has recently created a standard cost system to help control costs and established the following standards for the Maze toy:

Direct materials: 6 microns per toy at $1.50 per micron	
Direct labor: 1.3 hours per toy at $21 per hour	

During July, the company produced 3,000 Maze toys. The toy's production data for the month are as follows:

Direct materials: 25,000 microns were purchased at a cost of $1.48 per micron. 5,000 of these microns were still in inventory at the end of the month.

Direct labor: 4,000 direct labor-hours were worked at a cost of $88,000.

Required:
1. Compute the following variances for July:
   a. The materials price and quantity variances.
   b. The labor rate and efficiency variances.
2. Prepare a brief explanation of the possible causes of each variance.

Problems Mc Graw Hill connect

PROBLEM 10–9 Comprehensive Variance Analysis LO 10–1, LO 10–2, LO 10–3

Marvel Parts, Inc., manufactures auto accessories. One of the company's products is a set of seat covers that can be adjusted to fit nearly any small car. The company uses a standard cost system for all of its products. According to the standards set for the seat covers, the factory should work 2,850 hours each month to produce 1,900 sets of covers. The standard costs associated with this level of production are:

	Total	Per Set of Covers
Direct materials	$42,560	$22.40
Direct labor	$51,300	27.00
Variable manufacturing overhead (based on direct labor-hours)	$ 6,840	3.60
		$53.00

During August, the factory worked only 2,800 direct labor-hours and produced 2,000 sets of covers. The following actual costs were recorded during the month:

	Total	Per Set of Covers
Direct materials (12,000 yards)	$45,600	$22.80
Direct labor	$49,000	24.50
Variable manufacturing overhead	$ 7,000	3.50
		$50.80

At standard, each set of covers should require 5.6 yards of material. All of the materials purchased during the month were used in production.

Required:
Compute the following variances for August:
1. The materials price and quantity variances.
2. The labor rate and efficiency variances.
3. The variable overhead rate and efficiency variances.

PROBLEM 10–10 Multiple Products, Materials, and Processes LO 10–1, LO 10–2

Mickley Corporation produces two products, Alpha6s and Zeta7s, which pass through two operations, Sintering and Finishing. Each of the products uses two raw materials—X442 and Y661. The company uses a standard cost system, with the following standards for each product (on a per-unit basis):

	Raw Material		Standard Labor Time	
Product	X442	Y661	Sintering	Finishing
Alpha6	1.8 kilos	2.0 liters	0.20 hours	0.80 hours
Zeta7	3.0 kilos	4.5 liters	0.35 hours	0.90 hours

Information relating to materials purchased and materials used in production during May follows:

Material	Purchases	Purchase Cost	Standard Price	Used in Production
X442	14,500 kilos	$52,200	$3.50 per kilo	8,500 kilos
Y661	15,500 liters	$20,925	$1.40 per liter	13,000 liters

The following additional information is available:
a. The company recognizes price variances when materials are purchased.
b. The standard labor rate is $19.80 per hour in Sintering and $19.20 per hour in Finishing.
c. During May, 1,200 direct labor-hours were worked in Sintering at a total labor cost of $27,000, and 2,850 direct labor-hours were worked in Finishing at a total labor cost of $59,850.
d. Production during May was 1,500 Alpha6s and 2,000 Zeta7s.

Required:
1. Prepare a standard cost card for each product, showing the standard cost of direct materials and direct labor.
2. Compute the materials price and quantity variances for each material.
3. Compute the labor rate and efficiency variances for each operation.

PROBLEM 10–11 Direct Materials and Direct Labor Variances; Computations from Incomplete Data LO 10–1, LO 10–2

Sharp Company manufactures a product for which the following standards have been set:

	Standard Quantity or Hours	Standard Price or Rate	Standard Cost
Direct materials	3 feet	$11 per foot	$33
Direct labor.	? hours	? per hour	?

During March, the company purchased direct materials at a cost of $111,300, all of which were used in the production of 3,200 units of product. In addition, 4,900 direct labor-hours were worked on the product during the month. The cost of this labor time was $95,550. The following variances have been computed for the month:

Materials quantity variance	$4,400 U
Labor spending variance.	$450 F
Labor efficiency variance.	$2,000 U

Required:
1. For direct materials:
   a. Compute the actual cost per foot of materials for March.
   b. Compute the price variance and the spending variance.
2. For direct labor:
   a. Compute the standard direct labor rate per hour.
   b. Compute the standard hours allowed for the month's production.
   c. Compute the standard hours allowed per unit of product.

(*Hint:* In completing the problem, it may be helpful to move from known to unknown data either by using the columnar format shown in Exhibits 10–4 and 10–6 or by using the variance formulas in Exhibits 10–5 and 10–7.)

PROBLEM 10–12 Variance Analysis in a Hospital LO 10–1, LO 10–2, LO 10–3

John Fleming, chief administrator for Valley View Hospital, is concerned about the costs for tests in the hospital's lab. Charges for lab tests are consistently higher at Valley View than at other hospitals and have resulted in many complaints. Also, because of strict regulations on amounts reimbursed for lab tests, payments received from insurance companies and governmental units have not been high enough to cover lab costs.

Mr. Fleming asked you to evaluate costs in the hospital's lab for the past month. The following information is available:

a. Two types of tests are performed in the lab—blood tests and smears. During the past month, 1,800 blood tests and 2,400 smears were performed in the lab.

b. Small glass plates are used in both types of tests. During the past month, the hospital purchased 12,000 plates at a cost of $56,400. 1,500 of these plates were unused at the end of the month; no plates were on hand at the beginning of the month.

c. During the past month, 1,150 hours of labor time were recorded in the lab at a cost of $21,850.

d. The lab's variable overhead cost last month totaled $7,820.

Valley View Hospital never used standard costs. By searching industry literature, however, you determined the following nationwide averages for hospital labs:

Plates: Two plates are required per lab test. These plates cost $5.00 each and are disposed of after the test is completed.

Labor: Each blood test should require 0.3 hours to complete, and each smear should require 0.15 hours to complete. The average cost of this lab time is $20 per hour.

Overhead: Overhead cost is based on direct labor-hours. The average rate for variable overhead is $6 per hour.

Required:

1. Compute a materials price variance for the plates purchased last month and a materials quantity variance for the plates used last month.

2. For labor cost in the lab:
   a. Compute a labor rate variance and a labor efficiency variance.
   b. In most hospitals, one-half of the workers in the lab are senior technicians and one-half are assistants. In an effort to reduce costs, Valley View Hospital employs only one-fourth senior technicians and three-fourths assistants. Would you recommend this policy be continued? Explain.

3. Compute the variable overhead rate and efficiency variances. Is there any relation between the variable overhead efficiency variance and the labor efficiency variance? Explain.

PROBLEM 10–13 Basic Variance Analysis; the Impact of Variances on Unit Costs LO 10–1, LO 10–2, LO 10–3

Koontz Company manufactures a number of products. The standards relating to one of these products are shown, along with actual cost data for May.

	Standard Cost per Unit	Actual Cost per Unit
Direct materials:		
Standard: 1.80 feet at $3.00 per foot	$ 5.40	
Actual: 1.80 feet at $3.30 per foot.		$ 5.94
Direct labor:		
Standard: 0.90 hours at $18.00 per hour.	16.20	
Actual: 0.92 hours at $17.50 per hour		16.10
Variable overhead:		
Standard: 0.90 hours at $5.00 per hour.	4.50	
Actual: 0.92 hours at $4.50 per hour		4.14
Total cost per unit	$26.10	$26.18
Excess of actual cost over standard cost per unit.		$0.08

The production superintendent was pleased when he saw this report and commented: "This $0.08 excess cost is well within the 2% limit management has set for acceptable variances. It's obvious there's not much to worry about with this product."

Actual production for the month was 12,000 units. Variable overhead cost is assigned to products on the basis of direct labor-hours. There were no beginning or ending inventories of materials.

Required:

1. Compute the following variances for May:
   a. Materials price and quantity variances.
   b. Labor rate and efficiency variances.
   c. Variable overhead rate and efficiency variances.
2. How much of the $0.08 excess unit cost is traceable to each of the variances computed in (1) above.
3. How much of the $0.08 excess unit cost is traceable to apparent inefficient use of labor time?
4. Do you agree that the excess unit cost is not of concern?

PROBLEM 10–14 Basic Variance Analysis LO 10–1, LO 10–2, LO 10–3

Becton Labs, Inc., produces various chemical compounds for industrial use. One compound, called Fludex, is prepared using an elaborate distilling process. The company developed standard costs for one unit of Fludex, as follows:

	Standard Quantity or Hours	Standard Price or Rate	Standard Cost
Direct materials	2.5 ounces	$20.00 per ounce	$50.00
Direct labor.	1.4 hours	$22.50 per hour	31.50
Variable manufacturing overhead	1.4 hours	$3.50 per hour	4.90
Total standard cost per unit.			$86.40

During November, the following activity was recorded related to the production of Fludex:
a. Materials purchased, 12,000 ounces at a cost of $225,000.
b. There was no beginning inventory of materials; however, at the end of the month, 2,500 ounces of material remained in ending inventory.
c. The company employs 35 lab technicians to work on the production of Fludex. During November, they each worked an average of 160 hours at an average pay rate of $22 per hour.
d. Variable manufacturing overhead is assigned to Fludex on the basis of direct labor-hours. Variable manufacturing overhead costs during November totaled $18,200.
e. During November, the company produced 3,750 units of Fludex.

Required:

1. For direct materials:
   a. Compute the price and quantity variances.
   b. The materials were purchased from a new supplier who is anxious to enter into a long-term purchase contract. Would you recommend the company sign the contract? Explain.
2. For direct labor:
   a. Compute the rate and efficiency variances.
   b. In the past, the 35 technicians employed in the production of Fludex consisted of 20 senior technicians and 15 assistants. During November, the company experimented with fewer senior technicians and more assistants in order to reduce labor costs. Would you recommend the new labor mix be continued? Explain.
3. Compute the variable overhead rate and efficiency variances. What relation can you see between this efficiency variance and the labor efficiency variance?

PROBLEM 10–15 Comprehensive Variance Analysis LO 10–1, LO 10–2, LO 10–3

Miller Toy Company manufactures a plastic swimming pool at its Westwood Plant. The plant has been experiencing problems as shown by its June contribution format income statement below:

	Flexible Budget	Actual
Sales (15,000 pools)...	$675,000	$675,000
Variable expenses:		
Variable cost of goods sold*.................................	435,000	461,890
Variable selling expenses	20,000	20,000
Total variable expenses..	455,000	481,890
Contribution margin	220,000	193,110
Fixed expenses:		
Manufacturing overhead......................................	130,000	130,000
Selling and administrative....................................	84,000	84,000
Total fixed expenses..	214,000	214,000
Net operating income (loss)	$ 6,000	$ (20,890)

*Contains direct materials, direct labor, and variable manufacturing overhead.

Janet Dunn, who has just been appointed general manager of the Westwood Plant, has been given instructions to "get things under control." Upon reviewing the plant's income statement, Ms. Dunn concluded that the major problem lies in the variable cost of goods sold. She has been provided with the following standard cost per swimming pool:

	Standard Quantity or Hours	Standard Price or Rate	Standard Cost
Direct materials	3.0 pounds	$5.00 per pound	$15.00
Direct labor................................	0.8 hours	$16.00 per hour	12.80
Variable manufacturing overhead	0.4 hours*	$3.00 per hour	1.20
Total standard cost per unit..................			$29.00

*Based on machine-hours.

During June the plant produced 15,000 pools and incurred the following costs:
a. Purchased 60,000 pounds of materials at a cost of $4.95 per pound.
b. Used 49,200 pounds of materials in production. (Finished goods and work in process inventories are insignificant and can be ignored.)
c. Worked 11,800 direct labor-hours at a cost of $17.00 per hour.
d. Incurred variable manufacturing overhead cost totaling $18,290 for the month. A total of 5,900 machine-hours was recorded.
It is the company's policy to close all variances to cost of goods sold on a monthly basis.

Required:
1. Compute the following variances for June:
    a. Materials price and quantity variances.
    b. Labor rate and efficiency variances.
    c. Variable overhead rate and efficiency variances.
2. Summarize the variances you computed in (1) above by showing the net overall favorable or unfavorable variance for the month. What impact did this figure have on the company's income statement? Show computations.
3. Pick out the two most significant variances you computed in (1) above. Explain to Ms. Dunn possible causes of these variances.

PROBLEM 10–16 Comprehensive Variance Analysis LO 10–1, LO 10–2, LO 10–3
Highland Company produces a lightweight backpack popular with college students. Standard variable costs relating to a single backpack are given below:

	Standard Quantity or Hours	Standard Price or Rate	Standard Cost
Direct materials	?	$6 per yard	$?
Direct labor.	?	?	?
Variable manufacturing overhead . . .	?	$3 per direct labor-hour	?
Total standard cost per unit.			$?

Overhead is applied to production on the basis of direct labor-hours. During March, 1,000 backpacks were manufactured and sold. Selected information relating to the month's production is given below:

	Materials Used	Direct Labor	Variable Manufacturing Overhead
Total standard cost allowed*	$16,800	$21,000	$4,200
Actual costs incurred	$15,000	?	$3,600
Materials price variance.	?		
Materials quantity variance	$ 1,200 U		
Labor rate variance.		?	
Labor efficiency variance.		?	
Variable overhead rate variance			?
Variable overhead efficiency variance			?

*For the month's production.

The following additional information is available for March's production:

Actual direct labor-hours	1,500
Difference between standard and actual cost per backpack produced during March	$0.15 F

Required: (Hint: It may be helpful to complete a general model diagram for direct materials, direct labor, and variable manufacturing overhead before attempting to answer any of the requirements.)
1. What is the standard cost of a single backpack?
2. What was the actual cost per backpack produced during March?
3. How many yards of material are required at standard per backpack?
4. What was the materials price variance for March if there were no beginning or ending inventories of materials?
5. What is the standard direct labor rate per hour?
6. What was the labor rate variance for March? The labor efficiency variance?
7. What was the variable overhead rate variance for March? The variable overhead efficiency variance?
8. Prepare a standard cost card for one backpack.

Mc Graw Hill **connect** **Case**

Select cases are available in Connect.

CASE 10–17 Working Backwards from Variance Data LO 10–1, LO 10–2, LO 10–3
Vitex, Inc. manufactures a popular consumer product and provided the following data excerpts from its standard cost system:

Inputs	(1) Standard Quantity or Hours	(2) Standard Price or Rate	Standard Cost (1) × (2)
Direct materials............................	6 pounds	$3 per pound	$18.00
Direct labor................................	0.8 hours	$15 per hour	12.00
Variable manufacturing overhead............	0.8 hours	$3 per hour	2.40
Total standard cost per unit.................			$32.40

	Total Standard Cost*	Variances Reported Price or Rate	Quantity or Efficiency
Direct materials............................	$405,000	$6,900 F	$9,000 U
Direct labor................................	$270,000	$14,550 U	$21,000 U
Variable manufacturing overhead............	$54,000	$1,300 F	$? U

*Applied to Work in Process during the period.

The company's manufacturing overhead cost is applied to production on the basis of direct labor-hours. All of the materials purchased during the period were used in production. Work in process inventories are insignificant and can be ignored.

Required:
1. How many units were produced last period?
2. How many pounds of direct material were purchased and used in production?
3. What was the actual cost per pound of material?
4. How many actual direct labor-hours were worked during the period?
5. What was the actual rate paid per direct labor-hour?
6. How much actual variable manufacturing overhead cost was incurred during the period?

Appendix 10A: Predetermined Overhead Rates and Overhead Analysis in a Standard Costing System

LEARNING OBJECTIVE 10–4
Compute and interpret the fixed overhead budget and volume variances.

In this appendix, we explain how the predetermined overhead rates that were discussed in the job-order costing chapters can be used in a standard costing system. Throughout this appendix, we assume an absorption costing system is used in which *all* manufacturing costs—both variable and fixed—are included in product costs.

MicroDrive Corporation: An Example

Exhibit 10A–1 pertains to MicroDrive Corporation, a company that produces miniature electric motors. The data within this exhibit are divided into three sections. The first section summarizes the budgeted overhead costs and budgeted machine-hours included in the company's planning budget. Note that the company's planning budget is based on producing 25,000 motors. Given that two machine-hours are allowed per motor, the planning budget allows for 50,000 machine-hours. At this level of activity, the budgeted variable manufacturing overhead is $75,000, and the budgeted fixed manufacturing overhead is $300,000.

EXHIBIT 10A–1
MicroDrive Corporation Data

Budgeted (Planned) Overhead:	
Budgeted variable manufacturing overhead	$ 75,000
Budgeted fixed manufacturing overhead.......	300,000
Total budgeted manufacturing overhead	$375,000
Budgeted production (a)	25,000 motors
Standard machine-hours per motor (b)	2 machine-hours per motor
Budgeted machine-hours (a) × (b)	50,000 machine-hours

Applying Overhead:	
Actual production (a)........................	20,000 motors
Standard machine-hours per motor (b)	2 machine-hours per motor
Standard machine-hours allowed for the	
actual production (a) × (b)	40,000 machine-hours

Actual Overhead and Machine-Hours:	
Actual variable manufacturing overhead	$ 71,400
Actual fixed manufacturing overhead	308,000
Total actual manufacturing overhead	$379,400
Actual machine-hours........................	42,000 machine-hours

The second section includes information that MicroDrive will use to apply overhead costs to production. Notice that the company actually produced 20,000 motors instead of the 25,000 motors included in the planning budget. Given that two machine-hours are allowed per motor, the standard machine-hours allowed for the actual production is 40,000 machine-hours. This is the quantity of machine-hours that the company will use to apply variable and fixed overhead costs to production.

The third section summarizes the company's actual variable and fixed manufacturing overhead costs for the period as well as its actual machine-hours used during the period. As we will describe in greater detail shortly, *it is very important to understand that in a standard cost system, the actual hours (42,000 machine-hours) are not used to apply overhead costs to production. Variable and fixed overhead costs are applied to production using the standard hours allowed for the actual production (40,000 machine-hours).*

Predetermined Overhead Rates

Recall from earlier chapters that the following formula is used to establish the predetermined overhead rate at the beginning of the period:

$$\frac{\text{Predetermined}}{\text{overhead rate}} = \frac{\text{Estimated total manufacturing overhead cost}}{\text{Estimated total amount of the allocation base}}$$

The estimated total amount of the allocation base in the formula for the predetermined overhead rate is called the **denominator activity.**

Once the predetermined overhead rate has been established, it remains unchanged throughout the period, even if the actual level of activity differs from what was estimated. Consequently, the amount of overhead applied to each unit of product is the same regardless of when it is produced during the period.

As alluded to in Exhibit 10A–1, MicroDrive Corporation uses 50,000 budgeted machine-hours as its denominator activity in the predetermined overhead rate. Consequently, the company's predetermined overhead rate would be computed as follows:

$$\text{Predetermined overhead rate} = \frac{\$375,000}{50,000 \text{ MHs}} = \$7.50 \text{ per MH}$$

This predetermined overhead rate can be broken down into its variable and fixed components as follows:

$$\text{Variable component of the predetermined overhead rate} = \frac{\$75,000}{50,000 \text{ MHs}} = \$1.50 \text{ per MH}$$

$$\text{Fixed component of the predetermined overhead rate} = \frac{\$300,000}{50,000 \text{ MHs}} = \$6.00 \text{ per MH}$$

For every standard machine-hour recorded, work in process is charged with $7.50 of manufacturing overhead, of which $1.50 represents variable manufacturing overhead and $6.00 represents fixed manufacturing overhead. In total, MicroDrive Corporation would apply $300,000 of overhead to work in process as shown:

$$\text{Overhead applied} = \text{Predetermined overhead rate} \times \text{Standard hours allowed for the actual output}$$
$$= \$7.50 \text{ per machine-hour} \times 40,000 \text{ machine-hours}$$
$$= \$300,000$$

Overhead Application in a Standard Cost System

To understand fixed overhead variances, we first have to realize how overhead is applied to work in process in a standard cost system. Recall that in the job-order costing chapters, we applied overhead to work in process on the basis of the actual level of activity (e.g., the actual direct labor-hours worked or the actual machine-hours used). This procedure was correct because, at the time, we were dealing with a normal cost system.[4] However, we are now dealing with a standard cost system. In such a system, overhead is applied to work in process on the basis of the *standard hours allowed for the actual output of the period* rather than on the basis of the actual number of hours worked. Exhibit 10A–2 illustrates this point. In a standard cost system, every unit of output is charged with the same amount of overhead cost, regardless of how much time the unit actually requires for processing.

EXHIBIT 10A–2
Applied Overhead Costs: Normal Cost System versus Standard Cost System

Normal Cost System		Standard Cost System	
Manufacturing Overhead		Manufacturing Overhead	
Actual overhead costs incurred.	Applied overhead costs: Actual hours × Predetermined overhead rate.	Actual overhead costs incurred.	Applied overhead costs: Standard hours allowed for actual output × Predetermined overhead rate.
Underapplied or overapplied overhead		Underapplied or overapplied overhead	

---

[4] Normal cost systems are defined in the Chapter 3 glossary.

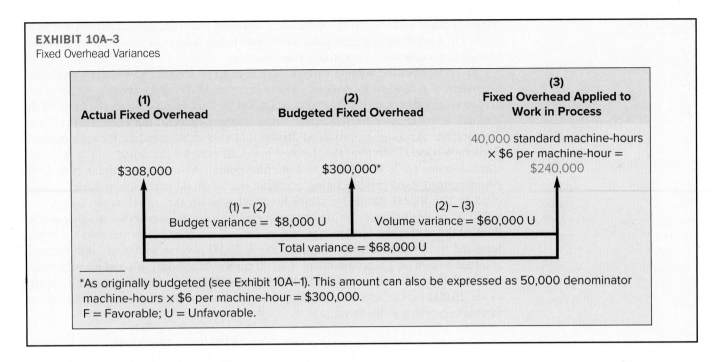

EXHIBIT 10A–3
Fixed Overhead Variances

		(3)
(1)	**(2)**	**Fixed Overhead Applied to**
Actual Fixed Overhead	**Budgeted Fixed Overhead**	**Work in Process**

40,000 standard machine-hours
× $6 per machine-hour =
$240,000

$308,000 $300,000*

(1) – (2)   (2) – (3)
Budget variance = $8,000 U   Volume variance = $60,000 U

Total variance = $68,000 U

*As originally budgeted (see Exhibit 10A–1). This amount can also be expressed as 50,000 denominator machine-hours × $6 per machine-hour = $300,000.
F = Favorable; U = Unfavorable.

Budget Variance

Two fixed manufacturing overhead variances are computed in a standard costing system—a *budget variance* and a *volume variance*. These variances are computed in Exhibit 10A–3. The **budget variance** is simply the difference between the actual fixed manufacturing overhead and the budgeted fixed manufacturing overhead for the period. The formula is:

$$\text{Budget variance} = \text{Actual fixed overhead} - \text{Budgeted fixed overhead}$$

If the actual fixed overhead cost exceeds the budgeted fixed overhead cost, the budget variance is labeled unfavorable. If the actual fixed overhead cost is less than the budgeted fixed overhead cost, the budget variance is labeled favorable.

Applying the formula to the MicroDrive Corporation data, the budget variance is computed as follows:

$$\text{Budget variance} = \$308,000 - \$300,000 = \$8,000 \text{ U}$$

According to the budget, the fixed manufacturing overhead should have been $300,000, but it was actually $308,000. Because the actual cost exceeds the budget by $8,000, the variance is labeled as unfavorable; however, this label does not automatically signal ineffective managerial performance. For example, this variance may be the result of waste and inefficiency, or it may be due to an unforeseen yet prudent investment in fixed overhead resources that improves product quality or manufacturing cycle efficiency.

Volume Variance

The **volume variance** is defined by the following formula:

$$\text{Volume variance} = \frac{\text{Budgeted fixed}}{\text{overhead}} - \frac{\text{Fixed overhead applied}}{\text{to work in process}}$$

When the budgeted fixed manufacturing overhead exceeds the fixed manufacturing overhead applied to work in process, the volume variance is labeled as unfavorable. When the budgeted fixed manufacturing overhead is less than the fixed manufacturing overhead applied to work in process, the volume variance is labeled as favorable. As we shall see, caution is advised when interpreting this variance.

To understand the volume variance, we need to understand how fixed manufacturing overhead is applied to work in process in a standard costing system. As discussed earlier, fixed manufacturing overhead is applied to work in process on the basis of the standard hours allowed for the actual output of the period. In the case of MicroDrive Corporation, the company produced 20,000 motors and the standard for each motor is 2 machine-hours. Therefore, the standard hours allowed for the actual output is 40,000 machine-hours (= 20,000 motors × 2 machine-hours). As shown in Exhibit 10A–3, the predetermined fixed manufacturing overhead rate of $6.00 per machine-hour is multiplied by the 40,000 standard machine-hours allowed for the actual output to arrive at $240,000 of fixed manufacturing overhead applied to work in process. Another way to think of this is that the standard for each motor is 2 machine-hours. Because the predetermined fixed manufacturing overhead rate is $6.00 per machine-hour, each motor is assigned $12.00 (= 2 machine-hours × $6.00 per machine-hour) of fixed manufacturing overhead. Consequently, a total of $240,000 of fixed manufacturing overhead is applied to the 20,000 motors that are actually produced. Under either explanation, the volume variance according to the formula is:

$$\text{Volume variance} = \$300,000 - \$240,000 = \$60,000 \text{ U}$$

The key to interpreting the volume variance is to understand that it depends on the difference between the hours used in the denominator to compute the predetermined overhead rate and the standard hours allowed for the actual output of the period. In other words, the volume variance can also be computed using the following formula:

$$\frac{\text{Volume}}{\text{variance}} = \frac{\text{Fixed component of the}}{\text{predetermined overhead rate}} \times \left(\frac{\text{Denominator}}{\text{hours}} - \frac{\text{Standard hours allowed}}{\text{for the actual output}} \right)$$

In the case of MicroDrive Corporation, the volume variance can be computed using this formula as follows:

$$\text{Volume variance} = \frac{\$6.00 \text{ per}}{\text{machine-hour}} \times \left(\frac{50,000}{\text{machine-hours}} - \frac{40,000}{\text{machine-hours}} \right)$$
$$= \$6.00 \text{ per machine-hour} \times 10,000 \text{ machine-hours}$$
$$= \$60,000 \text{ U}$$

Note that this agrees with the volume variance computed using the earlier formula.

Focusing on this new formula, if the denominator hours exceed the standard hours allowed for the actual output, the volume variance is unfavorable. If the denominator hours are less than the standard hours allowed for the actual output, the volume variance is favorable. Stated differently, the volume variance is unfavorable if the actual level of activity is less than expected. The volume variance is favorable if the actual level of activity is greater than expected. It is important to note that the volume variance does not measure overspending or underspending. A company should incur the same dollar amount of fixed overhead cost regardless of whether the period's activity was above or below the planned (denominator) level.

The volume variance is often viewed as a measure of the utilization of facilities. If the standard hours allowed for the actual output are greater than (less than) the denominator hours, it signals efficient (inefficient) usage of facilities. However, other measures of utilization—such as the percentage of capacity utilized—are easier to compute and understand. Perhaps a better interpretation of the volume variance is that it is the error that occurs when the level of activity is incorrectly estimated, and the costing system assumes fixed costs behave as if they are variable. This interpretation may be clearer in the next section that graphically analyzes the fixed manufacturing overhead variances.

Graphic Analysis of Fixed Overhead Variances

Exhibit 10A–4 shows a graphic analysis that offers insights into the fixed overhead budget and volume variances. As shown in the graph, fixed overhead cost is applied to work in process at the predetermined rate of $6.00 for each standard hour of activity. (The applied-cost line is the upward-sloping line on the graph.) Because a denominator level of 50,000 machine-hours was used in computing the $6.00 rate, the applied-cost line crosses the budget-cost line at exactly 50,000 machine-hours. If the denominator hours and the standard hours allowed for the actual output are the same, there is no volume variance. It is only when the standard hours differ from the denominator hours that a volume variance arises.

In MicroDrive's case, the standard hours allowed for the actual output (40,000 hours) are less than the denominator hours (50,000 hours). The result is an unfavorable volume variance because less cost was applied to production than was originally budgeted. If the situation had been reversed and the standard hours allowed for the actual output had exceeded the denominator hours, then the volume variance on the graph would have been favorable.

Cautions in Fixed Overhead Analysis

A volume variance for fixed overhead arises because when applying the costs to work in process, we act *as if* the fixed costs are variable. The graph in Exhibit 10A–4 illustrates this point. Notice from the graph that fixed overhead costs are applied to work in process at a rate of $6 per hour *as if* they are variable. Treating these costs as if they are variable is necessary for product costing purposes, but some real dangers lurk here. Managers can easily be misled into thinking that fixed costs are, *in fact,* variable.

Keep clearly in mind that fixed overhead costs come in large chunks. Expressing fixed costs on a unit or per-hour basis, though necessary for product costing for external reports,

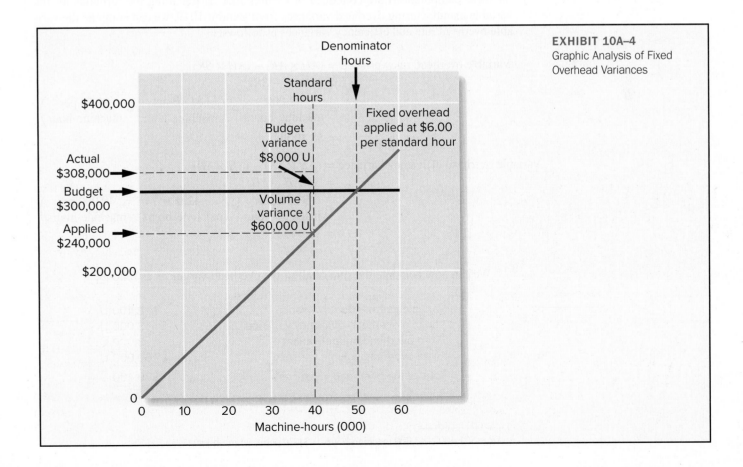

EXHIBIT 10A–4
Graphic Analysis of Fixed Overhead Variances

is artificial. Increases or decreases in activity, in fact, have no effect on total fixed costs within the relevant range of activity. Even though fixed costs are expressed on a unit or per-hour basis, they are *not* proportional to activity. In a sense, the volume variance is the error that occurs as a result of treating fixed costs as variable costs in the costing system.

Reconciling Overhead Variances and Underapplied or Overapplied Overhead

In a standard cost system, the underapplied or overapplied overhead for a period equals the sum of the overhead variances. To see this, we will return to the MicroDrive Corporation example.

As discussed earlier, in a standard cost system, overhead is applied to work in process on the basis of the standard hours allowed for the actual output of the period. The following table shows how the underapplied or overapplied overhead for MicroDrive is computed.

Predetermined overhead rate (a)	$7.50 per machine-hour
Standard machine-hours allowed for the actual production [Exhibit 10A–1] (b)	40,000 machine-hours
Manufacturing overhead applied (a) × (b)	$300,000
Total actual manufacturing overhead [Exhibit 10A–1]	$379,400
Manufacturing overhead underapplied or overapplied	$79,400 underapplied

We previously computed the budget variance and the volume variance for this company. We also need to compute the variable manufacturing overhead variances. The data for these computations are contained in Exhibit 10A–1. Recalling the formulas for the variable manufacturing overhead variances from Exhibit 10–9, we can compute the variable overhead rate and efficiency variances as follows:

$$
\begin{aligned}
\text{Variable overhead rate variance} &= (AH \times AR) - (AH \times SR) \\
&= AH(AR - SR) \\
&= \frac{42{,}000}{\text{machine-hours}} - \left(\frac{\$1.70 \text{ per}}{\text{machine-hour}^5} - \frac{\$1.50 \text{ per}}{\text{machine-hour}} \right) \\
&= \$8{,}400 \text{ U}
\end{aligned}
$$

$$
\begin{aligned}
\text{Variable overhead efficiency variance} &= (AH \times SR) - (SH \times SR) \\
&= SR(AH - SH) \\
&= \frac{\$1.50 \text{ per}}{\text{machine-hour}} - \left(\frac{42{,}000}{\text{machine-hours}} - \frac{40{,}000 \text{ per}}{\text{machine-hours}} \right) \\
&= \$3{,}000 \text{ U}
\end{aligned}
$$

We can now compute the sum of all of the overhead variances as follows:

Variable overhead rate variance	$ 8,400 U
Variable overhead efficiency variance	3,000 U
Fixed overhead budget variance	8,000 U
Fixed overhead volume variance	60,000 U
Total of the overhead variances	$79,400 U

---

[5] $AR = \$71{,}400 \div 42{,}000 \text{ machine-hours} = \$1.70 \text{ per machine-hour.}$

Note that the total of the overhead variances is $79,400, which equals the underapplied overhead of $79,400. In general, if the overhead is underapplied, the total of the standard cost overhead variances is unfavorable. If the overhead is overapplied, the total of the standard cost overhead variances is favorable.

Glossary (Appendix 10A)

Budget variance The difference between the actual fixed overhead costs and the budgeted fixed overhead costs for the period. (p. 523)

Denominator activity The level of activity used to compute the predetermined overhead rate. (p. 521)

Volume variance The variance that arises whenever the standard hours allowed for the actual output of a period are different from the denominator activity level that was used to compute the predetermined overhead rate. It is computed by multiplying the fixed component of the predetermined overhead rate by the difference between the denominator hours and the standard hours allowed for the actual output. (p. 523)

connect Appendix 10A: Exercises and Problems

EXERCISE 10A–1 Fixed Overhead Variances LO 10–4

Primara Corporation has a standard cost system in which it applies overhead to products based on the standard direct labor-hours allowed for the actual output of the period. Data concerning the most recent year appear below:

Total budgeted fixed overhead cost for the year.	$250,000
Actual fixed overhead cost for the year	$254,000
Budgeted direct labor-hours (denominator level of activity)	25,000
Actual direct labor-hours	27,000
Standard direct labor-hours allowed for the actual output	26,000

Required:

1. Compute the fixed portion of the predetermined overhead rate for the year.
2. Compute the fixed overhead budget variance and volume variance.

EXERCISE 10A–2 Predetermined Overhead Rate; Overhead Variances LO 10–3, LO 10–4

Norwall Company's budgeted variable manufacturing overhead cost is $3.00 per machine-hour and its budgeted fixed manufacturing overhead is $300,000 per month.

The following information is available for a recent month:

a. The denominator activity of 60,000 machine-hours is used to compute the predetermined overhead rate.

b. At a denominator activity of 60,000 machine-hours, the company should produce 40,000 units of product.

c. The company's actual operating results were:

Number of units produced.	42,000
Actual machine-hours.	64,000
Actual variable manufacturing overhead cost	$185,600
Actual fixed manufacturing overhead cost.	$302,400

Required:

1. Compute the predetermined overhead rate and break it down into variable and fixed cost elements.
2. Compute the standard hours allowed for the actual production.
3. Compute the variable overhead rate and efficiency variances and the fixed overhead budget and volume variances.

EXERCISE 10A–3 Applying Overhead in a Standard Costing System LO 10–4

Privack Corporation has a standard cost system in which it applies overhead to products based on the standard direct labor-hours allowed for the actual output of the period. Data concerning the most recent year appear below:

Budgeted variable overhead cost per direct labor-hour	$2
Total budgeted fixed overhead cost per year	$250,000
Budgeted direct labor-hours (denominator level of activity)	40,000
Actual direct labor-hours	39,000
Standard direct labor-hours allowed for the actual output	38,000

Required:

1. Compute the predetermined overhead rate for the year. Be sure to include the total budgeted fixed overhead and the total budgeted variable overhead in the numerator of your rate.
2. Compute the amount of overhead that would be applied to the output of the period.

EXERCISE 10A–4 Fixed Overhead Variances LO 10–4

Selected operating information on three different companies for a recent year is given below:

	Company		
	A	B	C
Full-capacity machine-hours	10,000	18,000	20,000
Budgeted machine-hours*	9,000	17,000	20,000
Actual machine-hours	9,000	17,800	19,000
Standard machine-hours allowed for actual production	9,500	16,000	20,000

*Denominator activity for computing the predetermined overhead rate.

Required:

For each company, state whether the company would have a favorable or unfavorable volume variance and why.

EXERCISE 10A–5 Using Fixed Overhead Variances LO 10–4

The standard cost card for the single product manufactured by Cutter, Inc., is given below:

Inputs	(1) Standard Quantity or Hours	(2) Standard Price or Rate	Standard Cost (1) × (2)
Direct materials	3 yards	$6.00 per yard	$ 18
Direct labor	4 hours	$15.50 per hour	62
Variable overhead	4 hours	$1.50 per hour	6
Fixed overhead	4 hours	$5.00 per hour	20
Total standard cost per unit			$106

Manufacturing overhead is applied to production on the basis of standard direct labor-hours. During the year, the company worked 37,000 hours and manufactured 9,500 units of product. Selected data relating to the company's fixed manufacturing overhead cost for the year are shown:

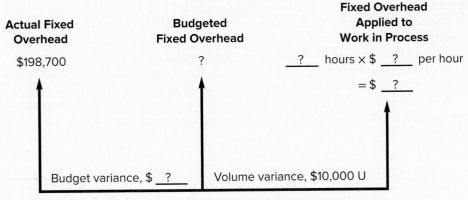

Actual Fixed Overhead	Budgeted Fixed Overhead	Fixed Overhead Applied to Work in Process
$198,700	?	__?__ hours × $ __?__ per hour = $ __?__

Budget variance, $ __?__ | Volume variance, $10,000 U

Required:

1. What were the standard hours allowed for the year's production?
2. What was the amount of budgeted fixed overhead cost for the year?
3. What was the fixed overhead budget variance for the year?
4. What denominator activity level did the company use in setting the predetermined overhead rate for the year?

EXERCISE 10A–6 Predetermined Overhead Rate LO 10–4

Lasser Company plans to produce 10,000 units next period at a denominator activity of 30,000 direct labor-hours. The direct labor wage rate is $12 per hour. The company's standards allow 2.5 yards of direct materials for each unit of product; the standard materials cost is $8.60 per yard. The company's budget includes variable manufacturing overhead cost of $1.90 per direct labor-hour and fixed manufacturing overhead of $168,000 per period.

Required:

1. Using 30,000 direct labor-hours as the denominator activity, compute the predetermined overhead rate and break it down into variable and fixed elements.
2. Complete the standard cost card below for one unit of product:

Inputs	(1) Standard Quantity or Hours	(2) Standard Price or Rate	Standard Cost (1) × (2)
Direct materials	2.5 yards	$8.60 per yard	$21.50
Direct labor.	?	?	?
Variable manufacturing overhead	?	?	?
Fixed manufacturing overhead.	?	?	?
Total standard cost per unit.			$?

EXERCISE 10A–7 Relations Among Fixed Overhead Variances LO 10–4

Selected information relating to Yost Company's operations for the most recent year is given below:

Activity:	
Denominator activity (machine-hours).	45,000
Standard hours allowed per unit	3
Actual number of units produced.	14,000
Costs:	
Actual fixed overhead costs incurred	$267,000
Fixed overhead budget variance	$3,000 F

The company applies overhead cost to products on the basis of standard machine-hours.

Required:

1. What were the standard machine-hours allowed for the actual number of units produced?
2. What was the total budgeted fixed overhead cost for the period?
3. What was the fixed portion of the predetermined overhead rate?
4. What was the fixed overhead volume variance?

PROBLEM 10A–8 Applying Overhead; Overhead Variances LO 10–3, LO 10–4

Lane Company manufactures a single product that requires a great deal of hand labor. Overhead cost is applied on the basis of standard direct labor-hours. The budgeted variable manufacturing overhead is $2 per direct labor-hour, and the budgeted fixed manufacturing overhead is $480,000 per year.

The standard quantity of materials is 3 pounds per unit, and the standard cost is $7 per pound. The standard direct labor-hours per unit is 1.5 hours, and the standard labor rate is $12 per hour.

The company planned to operate at a denominator activity level of 60,000 direct labor-hours and to produce 40,000 units of product during the most recent year. Actual activity and costs for the year were as follows:

Actual number of units produced.	42,000
Actual direct labor-hours worked.	65,000
Actual variable manufacturing overhead cost incurred	$123,500
Actual fixed manufacturing overhead cost incurred	$483,000

Required:

1. Compute the predetermined overhead rate for the year. Break the rate down into variable and fixed elements.
2. Prepare a standard cost card for the company's product; show the details for all manufacturing costs on your standard cost card.
3. Do the following:
   a. Compute the standard direct labor-hours allowed for the year's production.
   b. Complete the following Manufacturing Overhead T-account for the year:

Manufacturing Overhead

?	?
?	?

4. Determine the reason for any underapplied or overapplied overhead for the year by computing the variable overhead rate and efficiency variances and the fixed overhead budget and volume variances.
5. Suppose the company had chosen 65,000 direct labor-hours as the denominator activity rather than 60,000 hours. State which, if any, of the variances computed in (4) above would have changed, and explain how the variance(s) would have changed. No computations are necessary.

PROBLEM 10A–9 Applying Overhead; Overhead Variances LO 10–3, LO 10–4

Baird Company makes classic Polish sausage. The company uses a standard cost system to help control costs. Manufacturing overhead is applied to production on the basis of standard direct labor-hours. According to the company's planning budget, the following manufacturing overhead costs should be incurred at an activity level of 35,000 labor-hours (the denominator activity level):

Variable manufacturing overhead cost	$ 87,500
Fixed manufacturing overhead cost	210,000
Total manufacturing overhead cost	$297,500

During the most recent year, the following operating results were recorded:

Activity:	
Actual labor-hours worked	30,000
Standard labor-hours allowed for the actual output	32,000
Cost:	
Actual variable manufacturing overhead cost incurred	$78,000
Actual fixed manufacturing overhead cost incurred	$209,400

At the end of the year, the company's Manufacturing Overhead account contained the following data:

Manufacturing Overhead

Actual	287,400	Applied	272,000
	15,400		

Management would like to determine the cause of the $15,400 underapplied overhead.

Required:
1. Compute the predetermined overhead rate. Break the rate down into variable and fixed cost elements.
2. Show how the $272,000 Applied figure in the Manufacturing Overhead account was computed.
3. Break down the $15,400 underapplied overhead into four components: (1) variable overhead rate variance, (2) variable overhead efficiency variance, (3) fixed overhead budget variance, and (4) fixed overhead volume variance.
4. Explain the meaning of each variance you computed in (3) above.

PROBLEM 10A–10 Comprehensive Standard Cost Variances LO 10–1, LO 10–2, LO 10–3, LO 10–4

"Wonderful! Not only did our salespeople do a good job in meeting the sales budget this year, but our production people did a good job in controlling costs as well," said Kim Clark, president of Martell Company. "Our $18,300 overall manufacturing cost variance is only 1.2% of the $1,536,000 standard cost of products made during the year. That's well within the 3% parameter set by management for acceptable variances. It looks like everyone will be in line for a bonus this year."

The company produces and sells a single product. The standard cost card for the product follows:

Inputs	(1) Standard Quantity or Hours	(2) Standard Price or Rate	Standard Cost (1) × (2)
Direct materials	2 feet	$8.45 per foot	$16.90
Direct labor.	1.4 hours	$16 per hour	22.40
Variable overhead.	1.4 hours	$2.50 per hour	3.50
Fixed overhead	1.4 hours	$6 per hour	8.40
Total standard cost per unit.			$51.20

The following additional information is available for the year just completed:

a. The company manufactured 30,000 units of product during the year.

b. A total of 64,000 feet of material was purchased during the year at a cost of $8.55 per foot. All of this material was used to manufacture the 30,000 units produced. There were no beginning or ending inventories for the year.

c. The company worked 43,500 direct labor-hours during the year at a direct labor cost of $15.80 per hour.

d. Overhead is applied to products on the basis of standard direct labor-hours. Data relating to manufacturing overhead costs follow:

Denominator activity level (direct labor-hours)	35,000
Budgeted fixed overhead costs	$210,000
Actual variable overhead costs incurred.	$108,000
Actual fixed overhead costs incurred	$211,800

Required:
1. Compute the materials price and quantity variances for the year.
2. Compute the labor rate and efficiency variances for the year.

3. For manufacturing overhead compute:
   a. The variable overhead rate and efficiency variances for the year.
   b. The fixed overhead budget and volume variances for the year.
4. Total the variances you have computed, and compare the net amount with the $18,300 mentioned by the president. Do you agree that bonuses should be given to everyone for good cost control during the year? Explain.

PROBLEM 10A–11 Comprehensive Standard Cost Variances LO 10–1, LO 10–2, LO 10–3, LO 10–4

Flandro Company uses a standard cost system and sets its predetermined overhead rate on the basis of direct labor-hours. The following data are taken from the company's planning budget for the current year:

Denominator activity (direct labor-hours)	5,000
Variable manufacturing overhead cost	$25,000
Fixed manufacturing overhead cost	$59,000

The standard cost card for the company's only product is given below:

Inputs	(1) Standard Quantity or Hours	(2) Standard Price or Rate	Standard Cost (1) × (2)
Direct materials	3 yards	$4.40 per yard	$13.20
Direct labor.	1 hour	$12 per hour	12.00
Manufacturing overhead	1 hour	$16.80 per hour	16.80
Total standard cost per unit.			$42.00

During the year, the company produced 6,000 units of product and incurred the following actual results:

Materials purchased, 24,000 yards at $4.80 per yard	$115,200
Materials used in production (in yards)	18,500
Direct labor cost incurred, 5,800 hours at $13 per hour	$75,400
Variable manufacturing overhead cost incurred	$29,580
Fixed manufacturing overhead cost incurred.	$60,400

Required:
1. Create a new standard cost card that separates the variable manufacturing overhead per unit and the fixed manufacturing overhead per unit.
2. Compute the materials price and quantity variances. Also, compute the labor rate and efficiency variances.
3. Compute the variable overhead rate and efficiency variances. Also, compute the fixed overhead budget and volume variances.
4. What effect, if any, does the choice of a denominator activity level have on unit standard costs? Is the volume variance a controllable variance from a spending point of view? Explain.

PROBLEM 10A–12 Selection of a Denominator; Overhead Analysis; Standard Cost Card LO 10–3, LO 10–4

Morton Company's budgeted variable manufacturing overhead is $4.50 per direct labor-hour, and its budgeted fixed manufacturing overhead is $270,000 per year.

The company manufactures a single product whose standard direct labor-hours per unit is 2 hours. The standard direct labor wage rate is $15 per hour. The standards also allow 4 feet of raw material per unit at a standard cost of $8.75 per foot.

Although normal activity is 30,000 direct labor-hours each year, the company expects to operate at a 40,000-hour level of activity this year.

Required:

1. Assume the company chooses 30,000 direct labor-hours as the denominator level of activity. Compute the predetermined overhead rate, breaking it down into variable and fixed cost elements.
2. Assume the company chooses 40,000 direct labor-hours as the denominator level of activity. Compute the predetermined overhead rate, breaking it down into variable and fixed cost elements.
3. Complete two standard cost cards as outlined below.

Inputs	(1) Standard Quantity or Hours	(2) Standard Price or Rate	Standard Cost (1) × (2)
Denominator Activity: 30,000 Direct Labor-Hours			
Direct materials	4 feet	$8.75 per foot	$35.00
Direct labor.	?	?	?
Variable manufacturing overhead	?	?	?
Fixed manufacturing overhead.	?	?	?
Total standard cost per unit.			$?
Denominator Activity: 40,000 Direct Labor-Hours			
Direct materials	4 feet	$8.75 per foot	$35.00
Direct labor.	?	?	?
Variable manufacturing overhead	?	?	?
Fixed manufacturing overhead.	?	?	?
Total standard cost per unit.			$?

4. Assume the company actually produces 18,000 units and works 38,000 direct labor-hours during the year. Actual manufacturing overhead costs for the year are:

Variable manufacturing overhead cost	$174,800
Fixed manufacturing overhead cost	271,600
Total manufacturing overhead cost	$446,400

Do the following:

a. Compute the standard direct labor-hours allowed for this year's production.
b. Complete the Manufacturing Overhead T-account below. Assume the company uses 30,000 direct labor-hours (normal activity) as the denominator activity in computing predetermined overhead rates, as you have done in (1) above.

Manufacturing Overhead

Actual costs	446,400	Applied costs	?
	?		?

c. Determine the cause of the underapplied or overapplied overhead for the year by computing the variable overhead rate and efficiency variances and the fixed overhead budget and volume variances.

5. Looking at the variances you computed, what appears to be the major disadvantage of using normal activity rather than expected actual activity as a denominator in computing the predetermined overhead rate? What advantages can you see to offset this disadvantage?

Responsibility Accounting Systems

JHVEPhoto/Shutterstock

LEARNING OBJECTIVES

After studying Chapter 11, you should be able to:

LO 11–1 Compute return on investment (ROI) and show how changes in sales, expenses, and assets affect ROI.

LO 11–2 Compute residual income and understand its strengths and weaknesses.

LO 11–3 Determine the range, if any, within which a negotiated transfer price should fall.

LO 11–4 Charge operating departments for services provided by service departments.

ENTREPRENEUR SPOTLIGHT

Sara Blakely was selling fax machines, had only $5,000 in savings, and had just moved out of her mom's house when she came up with a life-changing idea. While getting dressed for a party, she cut the feet out of some control top pantyhose and wore them beneath her pants. Blakely noted, "I looked fabulous. I felt great. I had no panty lines, I looked thinner and smoother, but they rolled up my legs all night." Eventually, she worked out the kinks and created shapewear by Spanx. Today, Spanx sells shapewear, leggings, clothing, bras, panties, hosiery, activewear, and men's wear in over 50 countries.

Managerial Accounting: The Practical Application

Spanx can use responsibility accounting for management control purposes. For example, the company might define its responsibility centers by product line, such as leggings, shapewear, and hosiery. Or it might define responsibility centers by sales channel, such as Spanx retail stores, Spanx partner stores, and e-commerce. It might further divide Spanx partner stores by geographic region. If the managers in charge of the company's responsibility centers had control over costs and revenue, then they would be managing profit centers. If they also had the authority to make investments in operating assets, then they would be managing investment centers.

Corporate Social Responsibility: Serving all Stakeholders

Sara Blakely supports women because she believes it "offers one of the greatest returns on investment." In 2006, she founded the Spanx by Sara Blakely Foundation, which supports numerous initiatives, such as the Red Backpack Fund that has donated $5,000 to each of 1,000 female-owned businesses. Sara also created The Belly Art Project, which donates 100% of its proceeds to Every Mother Counts, which works to make pregnancy and childbirth safe for all women. In 2013 she "became the first self-made female billionaire to sign the Melinda and Bill Gates' and Warren Buffett's Giving Pledge, promising to give at least half her wealth to charity." ■

Sources: https://www.inc.com/sara-blakely/how-sara-blakley-started-spanx.html, https://www.spanx.com, https://www.forbes.com/profile/sara-blakely/?sh=4b61b8d276bb, http://www.spanxfoundation.com/about/, http://www.bellyartproject.org/about.

Data Analytics Exercise available in Connect to complement this chapter

Except in very small organizations, a company's owners and its top managers must delegate decision-making authority to others. When a company's owners (e.g., stockholders) delegate decision-making authority to top managers, they employ *corporate governance systems* to direct and control the actions of those managers. When properly implemented, corporate governance systems provide incentives and feedback mechanisms to help ensure that a company's board of directors and top managers pursue goals that align with the owners' interests.[1] Similarly, when a company's top managers delegate decision-making authority to subordinates, they employ *management control systems* to direct and control the actions of those subordinates. When properly implemented, management control systems provide incentives and feedback mechanisms to help ensure that all of a company's employees pursue goals that align with its interests.

This chapter explains a variety of performance measures and management controls that a company can use to align its employees' incentives and actions with its overall interests. First, it discusses the advantages and disadvantages of decentralization. Next, it provides a brief overview of responsibility accounting systems followed by a discussion of two performance measures commonly used within those systems—return on investment (ROI) and residual income. The chapter concludes with an overview of transfer pricing and service department charges.

Decentralization in Organizations

In a **decentralized organization,** decision-making authority is spread throughout the organization rather than being confined to a few top executives. As noted above, out of necessity, all large organizations are decentralized to some extent. Organizations do differ, however, in the extent to which they are decentralized. In strongly centralized organizations, decision-making authority is reluctantly delegated to lower-level managers who have little freedom to make decisions. In strongly decentralized organizations, even the lowest-level managers are empowered to make as many decisions as possible. Most organizations fall somewhere between these two extremes.

Advantages and Disadvantages of Decentralization

The major advantages of decentralization include:

1. By delegating day-to-day problem solving to lower-level managers, top-level managers can concentrate on bigger issues, such as overall strategy.
2. Empowering lower-level managers to make decisions puts the decision-making authority in the hands of those who tend to have the most detailed and up-to-date information about day-to-day operations.
3. By eliminating layers of decision making and approvals, organizations can respond more quickly to customers and changes in the operating environment.
4. Granting decision-making authority helps train lower-level managers for higher-level positions.
5. Empowering lower-level managers to make decisions can increase their motivation and job satisfaction.

The major disadvantages of decentralization include:

1. Lower-level managers may make decisions without fully understanding the company's overall strategy.
2. If lower-level managers make their own decisions independently of each other, coordination may be lacking.

---

[1] These comments on corporate governance were adapted from the 2004 report titled *OECD Principles of Corporate Governance,* published by the Organization for Economic Co-operation and Development.

3. Lower-level managers may have objectives that clash with the objectives of the entire organization.[2] For example, a manager may be more interested in increasing the size of his or her department, leading to more power and prestige, than in increasing the department's effectiveness.

4. Spreading innovative ideas may be difficult in a decentralized organization. Someone in one part of the organization may have a terrific idea that would benefit other parts of the organization, but without strong central direction, the idea may not be shared with, and adopted by, other parts of the organization.

Responsibility Accounting

Many decentralized organizations use *responsibility accounting* systems to link lower-level managers' decision-making authority with accountability for the outcomes of those decisions. The basic idea underlying **responsibility accounting** is that a manager should be held responsible for those items—and *only* those items—that the manager can actually control to a significant extent. Each line item (i.e., revenue or cost) in the budget is the responsibility of a manager who is held responsible for explaining and productively responding to large deviations between the budgeted and actual amounts. In effect, responsibility accounting *personalizes* accounting information by holding individuals responsible for revenues and costs.

The term **responsibility center** is used for any part of an organization whose manager has control over and is accountable for cost, profit, or investments. The three primary types of responsibility centers are *cost centers, profit centers,* and *investment centers.*

Cost, Profit, and Investment Centers

Cost Center   The manager of a **cost center** has control over costs but not over revenue or the use of investment funds. Service departments such as accounting, finance, general administration, legal, and personnel are usually classified as cost centers. In addition, manufacturing facilities are often treated as cost centers. The managers of cost centers are expected to minimize costs while providing the level of products and services needed by other parts of the organization. For example, the manager of a manufacturing facility would be evaluated at least in part by comparing actual costs to how much costs should have been for the actual level of output during the period. Flexible budget variances and standard cost variances, such as those discussed in earlier chapters, are often used to evaluate cost center performance.

Profit Center   The manager of a **profit center** has control over both costs and revenue, but not over the use of investment funds. For example, the manager in charge of a Six Flags amusement park would be responsible for both the revenues and costs, and hence the profits, of the amusement park but may not have control over major investments in the park. Profit center managers are often evaluated by comparing actual profit to budgeted profit.

Investment Center   The manager of an **investment center** has control over cost, revenue, and investments in operating assets. For example, General Motors' vice president

---

[2] Similar problems exist with top-level managers as well. The shareholders of the company delegate their decision-making authority to the top managers. Unfortunately, top managers may abuse that trust by rewarding themselves and their friends too generously, spending too much company money on palatial offices, and so on. The issue of how to ensure that top managers act in the best interests of the company's owners continues to challenge experts. To a large extent, the owners rely on performance evaluation using return on investment and residual income measures, as discussed later in the chapter, and on bonuses and stock options. The stock market is also an important disciplining mechanism. If top managers squander the company's resources, the price of the company's stock will almost surely fall—possibly resulting in a loss of prestige, bonuses, and a job. And, of course, particularly outrageous self-dealing may land a CEO in court.

of manufacturing in North America would have a great deal of discretion over investments in manufacturing—such as investing in equipment to produce more fuel-efficient engines. Once General Motors' top-level managers and board of directors approve the vice president's investment proposals, he is held responsible for making them pay off. As discussed in the next section, investment center managers are often evaluated using return on investment (ROI) or residual income measures.

Evaluating Investment Center Performance—Return on Investment

R*eturn on investment* (ROI) is a financial measure that is commonly used to evaluate investment center performance. **Return on investment (ROI)** is defined as net operating income divided by average operating assets:

LEARNING OBJECTIVE 11–1
Compute return on investment (ROI) and show how changes in sales, expenses, and assets affect ROI.

$$\text{ROI} = \frac{\text{Net operating income}}{\text{Average operating assests}}$$

The goal is to increase ROI because it indicates that more profit is being earned per dollar invested in operating assets.

Net Operating Income and Operating Assets Defined

Note that *net operating income,* rather than net income, is used in the ROI formula. **Net operating income** is income before interest and taxes and is sometimes referred to as EBIT (earnings before interest and taxes). Net operating income is used in the formula because the base (i.e., denominator) consists of *operating assets.* To be consistent, we use net operating income in the numerator.

Operating assets include cash, accounts receivable, inventory, plant and equipment, and all other assets held for operating purposes. Examples of assets that are not included in operating assets (i.e., examples of nonoperating assets) include land held for future use, an investment in another company, or a building rented to someone else. These assets are not held for operating purposes and therefore are excluded from operating assets. The operating assets base used in the formula is typically computed as the average of the operating assets between the beginning and the end of the year.

Most companies use the net book value (i.e., acquisition cost less accumulated depreciation) of depreciable assets to calculate average operating assets. This approach has drawbacks. An asset's net book value decreases over time as the accumulated depreciation increases. This decreases the denominator in the ROI calculation, thus increasing ROI. Consequently, ROI mechanically increases over time. Moreover, replacing old depreciated equipment with new equipment increases the book value of depreciable assets and decreases ROI. Hence, using net book value in the calculation of average operating assets results in a predictable pattern of increasing ROI over time as accumulated depreciation grows and discourages replacing old equipment with new, updated equipment. An alternative to using net book value is the gross cost of the asset, which ignores accumulated depreciation. Gross cost stays constant over time because depreciation is ignored; therefore, ROI does not grow automatically over time, and replacing a fully depreciated asset with a comparably priced new asset will not adversely affect ROI.

Nevertheless, most companies use the net book value approach to computing average operating assets because it is consistent with their financial reporting practices of recording the net book value of assets on the balance sheet and including depreciation as an operating expense on the income statement. Therefore, we will always use the net book value approach.

Understanding ROI

The equation for ROI, net operating income divided by average operating assets, can also be expressed in terms of **margin** and **turnover** as follows:

$$\text{ROI} = \text{Margin} \times \text{Turnover}$$

where

$$\text{Margin} = \frac{\text{Net operating income}}{\text{Sales}}$$

and

$$\text{Turnover} = \frac{\text{Sales}}{\text{Average operating assests}}$$

Note that the sales terms in the margin and turnover formulas cancel out when they are multiplied together, yielding the original formula for ROI stated in terms of net operating income and average operating assets. So, either formula for ROI will give the same answer.

However, the margin and turnover formulas provide some additional insights that help managers better understand how to increase ROI. All other things the same, margin is ordinarily improved by increasing selling prices, reducing operating expenses, or increasing unit sales. Increasing selling prices and reducing operating expenses both increase net operating income and, therefore, margin. Increasing unit sales also ordinarily increases the margin because of operating leverage. As discussed in a previous chapter, because of operating leverage, a given percentage increase in unit sales usually leads to an even larger percentage increase in net operating income. Therefore, an increase in unit sales ordinarily has the effect of increasing margin.

Some managers tend to focus too much on margin and ignore turnover. However, turnover incorporates a crucial area of a manager's responsibility—the investment in operating assets. Excessive funds tied up in operating assets (e.g., cash, accounts receivable, inventories, plant and equipment, and other assets) depress turnover and lower ROI. In fact, excessive operating assets can be just as much of a drag on ROI as excessive operating expenses, which depress margin.

HARLEY-DAVIDSON TAKES STEPS TO INCREASE ITS ROI

When the COVID-19 pandemic caused Harley-Davidson's quarterly sales to drop by 27%, the company responded by reducing the number of models that it manufactures by one-third. Jochen Zeitz, the company's CEO, said that through "years of expansion . . . it was evident to me that we had lost our focus." Reducing the number of models will enable the company to increase its return on investment (ROI) in two ways. First, by discontinuing low-margin models, the company can now pay greater attention to producing and promoting its higher-margin touring-bike models. Second, with less manufacturing complexity, the company hopes to cut expenses by $250 million per year.

Source: Bob Tita, "Harley Sales Decline as It Shifts Strategy," *The Wall Street Journal*, July 29, 2020, p. B8.

Andrey Armyagov/Shutterstock

Managers can seek to increase ROI by taking a variety of actions that change sales, expenses, and operating assets. For example, a manager may make an investment in (i.e., increase) operating assets to reduce operating expenses or increase sales. Whether the net effect is favorable or not is judged in terms of its overall impact on ROI.

For example, suppose the Montvale Burger Grill expects the following operating results next month:

Sales	$100,000
Operating expenses	$90,000
Net operating income	$10,000
Average operating assets	$50,000

The expected return on investment (ROI) for the month is computed as follows:

$$\text{ROI} = \text{Margin} \times \text{Turnover}$$

$$\text{ROI} = \frac{\text{Net operating income}}{\text{Sales}} \times \frac{\text{Sales}}{\text{Average operating assests}}$$

$$= \frac{\$10,000}{\$100,000} \times \frac{\$100,000}{\$50,000}$$

$$= 10\% \times 2 = 20\%$$

Now let's suppose the manager of the Montvale Burger Grill is considering investing $2,000 in a state-of-the-art soft-serve ice cream machine that can dispense a number of different flavors. This new machine would boost sales by $4,000 but would require additional operating expenses of $1,000. Thus, net operating income would increase by $3,000, to $13,000. The new ROI would be:

$$\text{ROI} = \text{Margin} \times \text{Turnover}$$

$$\text{ROI} = \frac{\text{Net operating income}}{\text{Sales}} \times \frac{\text{Sales}}{\text{Average operating assests}}$$

$$= \frac{\$13,000}{\$104,000} \times \frac{\$104,000}{\$52,000}$$

$$= 12.5\% \times 2 = 25\% \text{ (as compared to 20\% originally)}$$

In this particular example, the investment increases ROI, but that will not always happen.

E.I. du Pont de Nemours and Company (better known as DuPont) pioneered the use of ROI and recognized the importance of looking at both margin and turnover in assessing a manager's performance. ROI reflects in a single figure many aspects of the manager's responsibilities. It can be compared to the returns of other investment centers in the organization, the returns of other companies in the industry, and the past returns of the investment center itself. DuPont also developed the diagram that appears in Exhibit 11–1 to help managers better understand how they can increase ROI.

IN BUSINESS

STARBUCKS GROWS MARGINS WHILE CUSTOMER TRAFFIC DECLINES

Moomusician/Shutterstock

In a recent quarter, Starbucks' stock price rose 9 percent on the news of 4 percent same-store sales growth—which exceeded analysts' expectations of 2–3 percent growth. The favorable results were driven by an increase in margins as the company saw its average ticket price rise by 5 percent. On the contrary, the company's number of transactions declined by 1 percent. Chief Operating Officer Rosalind Brewer views transaction growth as the company's largest opportunity. However, increasing the company's turnover presents some challenges given that Starbucks faces stiff competition from lower-priced competitors, such as Dunkin' Brands, as well growing competition from higher-priced specialty coffee shops.

Source: Julie Jargon, "Starbucks Gets Jolt from Higher Prices," *The Wall Street Journal,* November 2, 2018, p. B1.

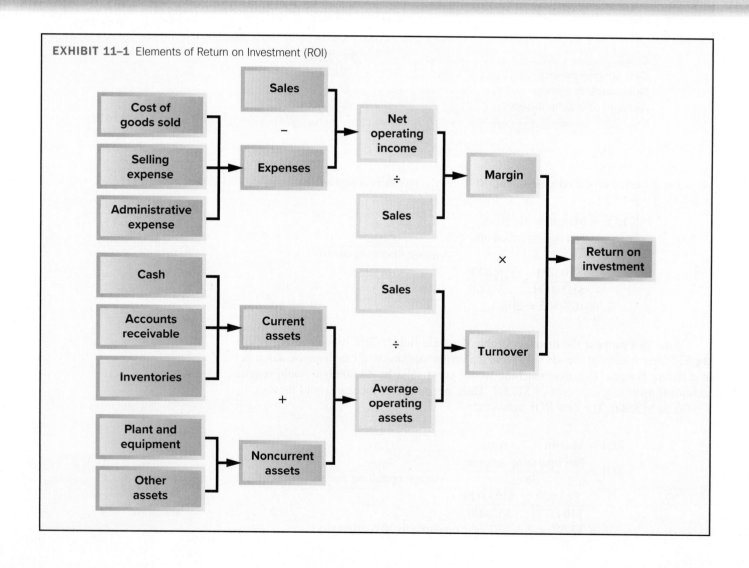

EXHIBIT 11–1 Elements of Return on Investment (ROI)

Criticisms of ROI

Although ROI is widely used in evaluating investment center performance, it has three important limitations:

1. Just telling managers to increase ROI may not be enough. Managers may not know how to increase ROI; they may increase ROI in a way that is inconsistent with the company's strategy; or they may take actions that increase ROI in the short run but harm the company in the long run (such as cutting back on research and development). This is why ROI is best used as part of a balanced scorecard performance measurement system, as discussed in the next chapter.
2. When managers take over an investment center, they typically inherit many committed costs that are beyond their control. While these committed costs are pertinent when calculating the investment center's ROI, they make it difficult to fairly assess the managers' performance based solely on controllable results.
3. As discussed in the next section, managers who are evaluated based on ROI may reject investment opportunities that lower their investment center's ROI even though those investments are desirable from the company's perspective.

Residual Income

Residual income is another approach to measuring an investment center's performance. **Residual income** is the net operating income that an investment center earns above the minimum required return on its operating assets. In equation form, residual income is calculated as follows:[3]

LEARNING OBJECTIVE 11–2
Compute residual income and understand its strengths and weaknesses.

$$\frac{\text{Residual}}{\text{income}} = \frac{\text{Net operating}}{\text{income}} - \left(\frac{\text{Average operating}}{\text{assets}} \times \frac{\text{Minimum required}}{\text{rate of return}} \right)$$

When residual income is used to measure performance, the objective is to maximize the total amount of residual income, not to maximize ROI. This is an important distinction. If the objective were to maximize ROI, then every company should divest all of its products except the single product with the highest ROI.

For purposes of illustration, consider the following data for an investment center—the Ketchikan Division of Alaskan Marine Services Corporation.

Alaskan Marine Services Corporation Ketchikan Division Basic Data for Performance Evaluation	
Average operating assets	$100,000
Net operating income	$20,000
Minimum required rate of return	15%

Alaskan Marine Services Corporation has long had a policy of using ROI to evaluate its investment center managers, but it is considering switching to residual income. The controller of the company, who is in favor of the change to residual income, has provided the

---

[3] Economic Value Added (EVA™) is an adaptation of residual income that has been trademarked by Stern Stewart & Company. Under EVA, companies often modify their accounting principles in various ways. For example, funds used for research and development are often treated as investments rather than as expenses. In this text, we will not draw any distinction between residual income and EVA.

following table that shows how the performance of the division would be evaluated under each of the two methods:

Alaskan Marine Services Corporation
Ketchikan Division

	Alternative Performance Measures	
	ROI	Residual Income
Average operating assets (a)	$100,000	$100,000
Net operating income (b)	$ 20,000	$ 20,000
ROI, (b) ÷ (a)	20%	
Minimum required return (15% × $100,000) ...		15,000
Residual income		$ 5,000

The reasoning underlying the residual income calculation is straightforward. The company is able to earn a rate of return of at least 15 percent on its investments. Because the company has invested $100,000 in the Ketchikan Division in the form of operating assets, the company should be able to earn at least $15,000 (15% × $100,000) on this investment. Because the Ketchikan Division's net operating income is $20,000, the residual income above and beyond the minimum required return is $5,000. If residual income is adopted as the performance measure to replace ROI, the manager of the Ketchikan Division would be evaluated based on the growth in residual income from year to year.

Motivation and Residual Income

One of the primary reasons why the controller of Alaskan Marine Services Corporation would like to switch from ROI to residual income relates to how managers view new investments under the two performance measurement methods. The residual income approach encourages managers to make investments that are profitable for the entire company but that would be rejected by managers who are evaluated using the ROI formula.

To illustrate this limitation of ROI, suppose that the manager of the Ketchikan Division is considering purchasing a computerized diagnostic machine to aid in servicing marine diesel engines. The machine would cost $25,000 and is expected to generate additional operating income of $4,500 a year. From the standpoint of the company, this would be a good investment because it promises a rate of return of 18 percent ($4,500 ÷ $25,000), which exceeds the company's minimum required rate of return of 15 percent.

If the manager of the Ketchikan Division is evaluated based on residual income, she would be in favor of the investment in the diagnostic machine as shown below:

Alaskan Marine Services Corporation
Ketchikan Division
Performance Evaluated Using Residual Income

	Present	New Project	Overall
Average operating assets	$100,000	$25,000	$125,000
Net operating income	$ 20,000	$ 4,500	$ 24,500
Minimum required return	15,000	3,750*	18,750
Residual income	$ 5,000	$ 750	$ 5,750

*$25,000 × 15% = $3,750

Because the project would increase the residual income of the Ketchikan Division by $750, the manager would choose to invest in the new diagnostic machine.

Now suppose the manager of the Ketchikan Division is evaluated based on ROI. The effect of the diagnostic machine on the division's ROI is computed below:

Alaskan Marine Services Corporation
Ketchikan Division
Performance Evaluated Using ROI

	Present	New Project	Overall
Average operating assets (a)	$100,000	$25,000	$125,000
Net operating income (b)	$20,000	$4,500	$24,500
ROI, (b) ÷ (a)	20%	18%	19.6%

The new project reduces the division's ROI from 20 percent to 19.6 percent. This happens because the 18 percent rate of return on the new diagnostic machine, while above the company's 15 percent minimum required rate of return, is below the division's current ROI of 20 percent. Therefore, the new diagnostic machine would decrease the division's ROI even though it would be a good investment from the standpoint of the company as a whole. If the manager of the division is evaluated based on ROI, she will be reluctant to even propose such an investment.

Generally, a manager who is evaluated based on ROI will reject any project whose rate of return is below the division's current ROI even if the rate of return on the project is above the company's minimum required rate of return. In contrast, managers who are evaluated using residual income will pursue any project whose rate of return is above the minimum required rate of return because it will increase their residual income. Because it is in the best interests of the company as a whole to accept any project whose rate of return is above the minimum required rate of return, managers who are evaluated based on residual income will tend to make better decisions concerning investment projects than managers who are evaluated based on ROI.[4]

APPAREL RETAILERS LOOK TO GROW SALES THROUGH PLUS-SIZE OFFERINGS

Amanda Gilliam, a college-admissions consultant in New Jersey, offered a stinging critique of clothing retailers by saying, "Plus-size clothes are often at the back of the store, the departments aren't well-stocked, and the experience is so uninviting. . . . It's very short-sighted of brands not to make plus sizes. They are missing out on so many people who are prepared to spend money." The likes of Amanda's concerns, coupled with data indicating that 70 percent of adults in the United States are overweight or obese, is starting to capture the attention of numerous retailers.

Nordstrom is adding plus sizes from 100 brands, Target plans to expand its plus-size departments in 300 stores, and REI has increased its plus-size offerings by 50 percent. Moreover, these clothing sellers are starting to merge plus-size clothing together with regular sizes instead of isolating plus sizes in separate departments. Target will sell plus-size swimsuits, athletic gear, and lingerie next to their corresponding regular-size items. While many retailers are initially focusing on women's clothing, they are quick to point out that the same concerns and opportunities exist in men's apparel.

Source: Suzanne Kapner, "Once Shunned, Plus Sizes Embraced by Stores," *The Wall Street Journal*, May 8, 2018.

Transfer Pricing

A company's profit centers and investment centers often supply goods and services to other responsibility centers within the same company. For example, the truck division of Toyota (an investment center) supplies trucks to other Toyota divisions to use in their operations. When these responsibility centers are evaluated based on their profit, ROI,

---

[4] The residual income approach has one major disadvantage. Larger divisions often have more residual income than smaller divisions, not necessarily because they are better managed, but simply because they are bigger. Therefore, residual income can't be used to compare the performance of divisions of different sizes.

or residual income, a price must be established for such a transfer—otherwise, the truck division will not be allowed to recognize any financial benefit related to the transfer and the other divisions will not be required to incur any cost associated with the transfer. The price in such a situation is called a *transfer price*. A **transfer price** is the price charged when one responsibility center within a company provides goods or services to another responsibility center in the same company.

For example, most companies in the oil industry, such as Royal Dutch Shell, have petroleum refining and retail sales divisions that are evaluated based on ROI or residual income. The petroleum refining division processes crude oil into gasoline, kerosene, lubricants, and other end products. The retail sales division takes these end products from the refining division and sells them through the company's chain of service stations.

Creating a transfer price for each product enables the petroleum refining division to recognize revenue on its transfers while also requiring the retail sales division to recognize a corresponding expense. For example, if we assume that the transfer price for gasoline is $0.80 a gallon, then the refining division would recognize revenue of $0.80 a gallon on its segment income statement, whereas the retail sales division would record an expense of $0.80 a gallon on its income statement. Clearly, the refining division would like the transfer price to be as high as possible to maximize its profits, whereas the retailing division would like the transfer price to be as low as possible for the same reason. However, the transaction has no direct effect on the entire company's reported profit. It is like taking money out of one pocket and putting it into the other.

Profit center and investment center managers are intensely interested in how transfer prices are set because their financial compensation is directly influenced by their responsibility center's profits. Similarly, a company's senior leaders, such as its chief executive officer (CEO) and chief financial officer (CFO), also have a strong interest in how transfer prices are established because they have a strong desire to maximize companywide profits. Unfortunately, the goals of a company's senior leaders and its responsibility center managers do not always align. In fact, situations can arise where a responsibility center manager's transfer pricing decisions actually decrease profits for the company as a whole. We refer to this counterproductive scenario as *suboptimization*. **Suboptimization** occurs when responsibility center managers forgo additional company-wide profits by making decisions that are not in the best interests of the overall company or even in the best interests of their own responsibility center.

The fundamental objective in setting transfer prices is to avoid suboptimization by motivating managers to act in the best interests of the overall company.[5] Three common approaches (each discussed in turn) are used to set transfer prices:

1. Allow the managers involved in the transfer to negotiate the transfer price.
2. Set transfer prices at cost using either variable cost or full (absorption) cost.
3. Set transfer prices at the market price.

While each of these approaches has its strengths and weaknesses, none of them completely eliminates the risk of suboptimization.

Negotiated Transfer Prices

LEARNING OBJECTIVE 11–3
Determine the range, if any, within which a negotiated transfer price should fall.

As the name implies, a *negotiated transfer price* involves a negotiation between two responsibility center managers—a prospective buyer and a seller. If the negotiation is successful, it results in a **negotiated transfer price** that has been agreed to by the buyer and the seller. If the negotiation is unsuccessful, the two parties will not exchange products or services because they failed to agree on a mutually acceptable transfer price.

---

[5] The dynamics of transfer pricing decisions become more complex with multinational corporations. In this context, the objectives of international transfer pricing expand to include minimizing taxes, duties, and foreign exchange risks, along with enhancing a company's competitive position and improving its relations with foreign governments.

When a company allows its responsibility center managers to negotiate their own transfer prices, it provides two important benefits. First, it preserves the autonomy of the negotiating parties, which is consistent with the spirit of decentralization. Second, it acknowledges that the managers involved in the negotiation are likely to have much better information about the potential costs and benefits of the transfer than others in the company.

However, negotiated transfer prices also have two important disadvantages—not all managers understand their own businesses, and not all managers are cooperative negotiators. As a result, negotiations often break down even when it would be in the managers' own best interests (and the company's best interests) to come to an agreement. Sometimes failed negotiations arise from the way that managers are evaluated and rewarded. If managers are pitted against each other rather than against their own past performance or reasonable benchmarks, a noncooperative negotiating atmosphere is almost guaranteed.

Generally speaking, two responsibility center managers will agree to a transfer of products or services only if the transfer price falls within a **range of acceptable transfer prices** that increases both the buyer's and seller's profits. The lower limit for this range of acceptable transfer prices is determined by the situation of the seller, whereas the upper limit of this range is determined by the situation of the buyer. Next, we'll introduce an example that explains how the range of acceptable transfer prices is calculated.

Negotiated Transfer Prices: An Example

Harris & Louder, Ltd., owns fast-food restaurants and snack food and beverage manufacturers in the United Kingdom. One of its restaurants, Pizza Maven, serves pizza and a variety of beverages, including ginger beer, which it serves on tap. Harris & Louder has just purchased a new company, Imperial Beverages, that produces ginger beer. The managing director of Imperial Beverages has approached the managing director of Pizza Maven about purchasing Imperial Beverages' ginger beer to sell at Pizza Maven restaurants rather than its usual brand of ginger beer. Because managers at Pizza Maven agree that the quality of Imperial Beverages' ginger beer is comparable to the quality of their regular brand, their decision hinges largely on the transfer price that they'd have to pay to Imperial Beverages.

As mentioned above, the managers of these two responsibility centers (hereafter referred to as divisions) are likely to agree on a transfer price only if it increases both of their profits. The formulas for computing the range of acceptable transfer prices that will increase both parties' profits will be derived using the following information:

Imperial Beverages:	
Ginger beer production capacity per month	10,000 barrels
Variable cost per barrel of ginger beer	$8 per barrel
Fixed costs per month	$70,000
Selling price of Imperial Beverages ginger beer on the outside market	$20 per barrel
Pizza Maven:	
Purchase price of regular brand of ginger beer	$18 per barrel
Monthly consumption of ginger beer	2,000 barrels

The Selling Division's Lowest Acceptable Transfer Price The selling division, Imperial Beverages, will agree to a transfer price only if it increases divisional profits. Thus, the transfer price must exceed Imperial Beverages' variable cost per barrel of $8 plus an amount that covers any contribution margin that could have been earned serving regular customers that gets sacrificed by serving Pizza Maven. In sum, if the transfer has no effect on fixed costs, then from the selling division's standpoint, the transfer price must be greater than or equal to its variable cost per unit plus the opportunity cost, if any, from lost sales to regular customers. This can be expressed in equation form as follows.

Seller's perspective:

$$\frac{\text{Transfer}}{\text{price}} \geq \frac{\text{Variable cost}}{\text{per unit}} + \frac{\text{Total contribution margin on lost sales}}{\text{Number of units transferred}}$$

The Buying Division's Highest Acceptable Transfer Price

The buying division, Pizza Maven, will agree to a transfer price only if it increases divisional profits. In cases like this where the buying division (Pizza Maven) has an outside supplier, the buying division's decision is simple—buy from the inside supplier if the price is less than or equal to the price offered by the outside supplier.

Buyer's perspective:

$$\text{Transfer price} \leq \text{Cost of buying from outside supplier}$$

Or if an outside supplier does not exist:

$$\text{Transfer price} \leq \text{Profit to be earned per unit sold (not including the transfer price)}$$

Next, we use these formulas to compute the range of acceptable transfer prices for three scenarios (1) the selling division has idle capacity, (2) the selling division has no idle capacity, and (3) the selling division has some idle capacity.

Selling Division Has Idle Capacity

Suppose Imperial Beverages has sufficient idle capacity to satisfy Pizza Maven's demand for ginger beer without sacrificing any sales of ginger beer to its regular customers. To be specific, let's suppose Imperial Beverages is selling only 7,000 barrels of ginger beer a month on the outside market. That leaves unused capacity of 3,000 barrels a month—more than enough to satisfy Pizza Maven's requirement of 2,000 barrels a month. What range of transfer prices, if any, would make both divisions better off with the transfer of 2,000 barrels a month?

1. The selling division, Imperial Beverages, will be interested in the transfer only if:

$$\frac{\text{Transfer}}{\text{price}} \geq \frac{\text{Variable cost}}{\text{per unit}} + \frac{\text{Total contribution margin on lost sales}}{\text{Number of units transferred}}$$

Because Imperial Beverages has more than enough idle capacity, it will not have to sacrifice any sales to regular customers. Therefore, the variable cost per unit of $8 becomes the lowest acceptable transfer price:

$$\text{Transfer price} \geq \$8 + \frac{\$0}{2,000} = \$8$$

2. The buying division, Pizza Maven, can buy similar ginger beer from an outside supplier for $18. Therefore, this purchase price becomes the highest acceptable transfer price:

$$\text{Transfer price} \leq \text{Cost of buying from outside supplier} = \$18$$

3. Combining the requirements of both the selling division and the buying division, the range of acceptable transfer prices in this situation is:

$$\$8 \leq \text{Transfer price} \leq \$18$$

Assuming the managers understand their own businesses and are cooperative, they should be able to agree on a transfer price within this range.

Selling Division Has No Idle Capacity

Suppose Imperial Beverages is selling 10,000 barrels of ginger beer a month on the outside market at $20 per barrel. In this situation, Imperial Beverages has no idle capacity so it would have to divert 2,000 barrels of ginger beer from its regular customers to fill the order from Pizza Maven. What range of transfer prices, if any, would make both divisions better off transferring the 2,000 barrels within the company?

1. The selling division, Imperial Beverages, will be interested in the transfer only if:

$$\frac{\text{Transfer}}{\text{price}} \geq \frac{\text{Variable cost}}{\text{per unit}} + \frac{\text{Total contribution margin on lost sales}}{\text{Number of units transferred}}$$

Because Imperial Beverages has no idle capacity, there *are* lost outside sales. Given that the contribution margin per barrel on these outside sales is $12 ($20 − $8), the lowest acceptable transfer price of $20 is computed as follows:

$$\text{Transfer price} \geq \$8 + \frac{(\$20 - \$8) \times 2{,}000}{2{,}000} = \$8 + (\$20 - \$8) = \$20$$

As the formula shows, from the selling division's standpoint, the transfer price must at least cover the revenue on the lost sales, which is $20 per barrel. This makes sense because the cost of producing the 2,000 barrels is the same whether they are sold to Pizza Maven or to regular customers. The only difference is that Imperial Beverages loses the revenue of $20 per barrel if it transfers the barrels to Pizza Maven.

2. As before, the buying division, Pizza Maven, can buy similar ginger beer from an outside supplier for $18. Therefore, this purchase price becomes the highest acceptable transfer price:

$$\text{Transfer price} \leq \text{Cost of buying from outside supplier} = \$18$$

3. Therefore, the selling division would insist on a transfer price of at least $20. But the buying division would refuse any transfer price above $18. Because there is no range of acceptable transfer prices, the negotiation process will fail and no transfer will take place. Is this good? The answer is yes. From the standpoint of the entire company, the transfer doesn't make sense. Why give up sales of $20 to save costs of $18?

Basically, the transfer price is a mechanism for dividing between the two divisions any profit the entire company earns as a result of the transfer. If the company as a whole loses money on the transfer, there will be no profit to divide up, and it will be impossible for the two divisions to come to an agreement. On the other hand, if the company as a whole makes money on the transfer, there will be a profit to share, and it will always be possible for the two divisions to find a mutually agreeable transfer price that increases the profits of both divisions.

Selling Division Has Some Idle Capacity Suppose Imperial Beverages is selling 9,000 barrels of ginger beer a month on the outside market. Pizza Maven can only sell one kind of ginger beer on tap. It cannot buy 1,000 barrels from Imperial Beverages and 1,000 barrels from its regular supplier; it must buy all of its 2,000 barrels of ginger beer from one source.

To fill the entire 2,000-barrel-a-month order from Pizza Maven, Imperial Beverages would have to divert 1,000 barrels from its regular customers who are paying $20 per barrel. The other 1,000 barrels can be made using idle capacity. What range of transfer prices, if any, would make both divisions better off transferring the 2,000 barrels within the company?

1. As before, the selling division, Imperial Beverages, will insist on a transfer price that at least covers its variable cost and opportunity cost:

$$\frac{\text{Transfer}}{\text{price}} \geq \frac{\text{Variable cost}}{\text{per unit}} + \frac{\text{Total contribution margin on lost sales}}{\text{Number of units transferred}}$$

Because Imperial Beverages does not have enough idle capacity to fill the entire order for 2,000 barrels, there *are* lost outside sales. Given that the contribution margin per barrel on these outside sales is $12 ($20 − $8), the lowest acceptable transfer price of $14 is computed as follows:

$$\text{Transfer price} \geq \$8 + \frac{(\$20 - \$8) \times 1,000}{2,000} = \$8 + \$6 = \$14$$

Thus, as far as the selling division is concerned, the transfer price must cover the variable cost of $8 plus the average opportunity cost of lost sales of $6.

2. As before, the buying division, Pizza Maven, can buy similar ginger beer from an outside supplier for $18. Therefore, this purchase price becomes the highest acceptable transfer price:

$$\text{Transfer price} \leq \text{Cost of buying from outside supplier} = \$18$$

3. Combining the requirements for both the selling and buying divisions, the range of acceptable transfer prices is:

$$\$14 \leq \text{Transfer price} \leq \$18$$

Again, assuming the managers understand their own businesses and are cooperative, they should be able to agree on a transfer price within this range.

No Outside Supplier   If Pizza Maven has no outside supplier for the ginger beer, the highest price the buying division would be willing to pay depends on how much the buying division expects to make on the transferred units—excluding the transfer price. If, for example, Pizza Maven expects to earn $30 per barrel of ginger beer after paying its own expenses, then it should be willing to pay up to $30 per barrel to Imperial Beverages. Remember, however, that this assumes Pizza Maven cannot buy ginger beer from other sources.

Evaluation of Negotiated Transfer Prices   As discussed earlier, if an internal transfer results in higher companywide profits, there is always a range of transfer prices that enables the selling and buying divisions to each earn higher profits. Therefore, if the managers understand their own businesses and are cooperative, then they should always be able to agree on a transfer price if it is in the best interests of the company that they do so. However, given the disputes that often accompany the negotiation process, many companies rely on some other means of setting transfer prices, such as cost-based and market-based transfer prices.

Transfers at the Cost to the Selling Division

Many companies set transfer prices at either the variable cost or full (absorption) cost incurred by the selling division. Although the cost approach to setting transfer prices is relatively simple to apply, it has some major defects.

First, the use of cost—particularly full cost—as a transfer price can lead to suboptimization. Return to the example involving the ginger beer. The full cost of ginger beer can never be less than $15 per barrel ($8 per barrel variable cost + $7 per barrel fixed cost at capacity). What if the cost of buying the ginger beer from an outside supplier is less than $15—for example, $14 per barrel? If the transfer price were set at full cost, then Pizza Maven would never want to buy ginger beer from Imperial Beverages because it could buy its ginger beer from an outside supplier at a lower price. However, from the standpoint of the company as a whole, ginger beer should be transferred from Imperial Beverages to Pizza Maven whenever Imperial Beverages has idle capacity. Why? Because when Imperial Beverages has idle capacity, it only costs the company $8 in variable cost to produce a barrel of ginger beer, but it costs $14 per barrel to buy from an outside supplier.

Second, if cost is used as the transfer price, the selling division will never show a profit on any internal transfer. The only division that shows a profit is the division that makes the final sale to an outside party.

Third, cost-based prices do not provide incentives to control costs. If the actual costs of one division are simply passed on to the next, there is little incentive for anyone to strive to reduce costs. This problem can be overcome by using budgeted costs or standard costs rather than actual costs for transfer prices.

Despite these shortcomings, cost-based transfer prices are often used in practice. Advocates argue that they are easily understood and convenient to use.

Transfers at Market Price

Using a product or service's **market price** (i.e., the price charged for an item on the open market) as a transfer price is possible in situations where there is an *outside market of customers* that routinely purchase the transferred product or service.

When a selling division has no idle capacity, the market price is the optimal transfer price. This is because, from the company's perspective, the real cost of the transfer is the opportunity cost of the lost revenue on the outside sale. Whether the item is transferred internally or sold on the outside market, the production costs are exactly the same. If the market price is used as the transfer price, the selling division manager will not lose anything by making the transfer, and the buying division manager will get the correct signal about how much it really costs the company for the transfer to take place.

While market-based transfer prices work well when the selling division has no idle capacity, they do not work well when the selling division has idle capacity. Recalling once again the ginger beer example, the outside market price for the ginger beer produced by Imperial Beverages is $20 per barrel. However, Pizza Maven can purchase all of the ginger beer it wants from its own outside supplier for $18 per barrel. Thus, Pizza Maven would never willingly accept a transfer price of $20 from Imperial Beverages when it can buy ginger beer from its own supplier at a price of $18 per barrel. Thus, a market-based transfer price of $20 per barrel would lead to suboptimization. It would motivate Pizza Maven to pay an outside supplier $18 per barrel instead of making the optimal choice from a companywide standpoint, which is choosing to obtain additional barrels of ginger beer from Imperial Beverages at a variable manufacturing cost of $8 per barrel (assuming that Imperial Beverages has idle capacity).

In some market-based transfer pricing schemes, the transfer price would be lowered to $18, the outside supplier's market price. Pizza Maven would be directed to pay Imperial Beverages a transfer price of $18 per barrel as long as Imperial Beverages is willing to sell. This scheme can work reasonably well, but a drawback is that managers at Pizza Maven will regard the cost of ginger beer as $18 rather than the $8, which is the real cost to the company when the selling division has idle capacity. Consequently, the managers of Pizza Maven will make pricing and other decisions based on an incorrect cost.

Unfortunately, none of the possible solutions to the transfer pricing problem are perfect—not even market-based transfer prices. Next, we discuss service department charges, which can be viewed as transfer prices that are charged for services provided by service departments to operating departments.

Service Department Charges

Most large organizations have both *operating departments* and *service departments*. The central purposes of the organization are carried out in the **operating departments.** In contrast, **service departments** do not directly engage in operating activities. Instead, they provide services or assistance to the operating departments. Examples of service departments include Cafeteria, Internal Auditing, Human Resources, Cost Accounting, and Purchasing.

LEARNING OBJECTIVE 11–4
Charge operating departments for services provided by service departments.

Service department costs are charged to operating departments for a variety of reasons, including:

- To encourage operating departments to make wise use of service department resources. If the services were provided for free, operating managers would be inclined to waste these resources.
- To provide operating departments with more complete cost data for making decisions. Actions taken by operating departments have impacts on service department costs. For example, hiring another employee will increase costs in the human resources department. Such service department costs should be charged to the operating departments; otherwise, the operating departments will not take them into account when making decisions.
- To help measure the profitability of operating departments. Charging service department costs to operating departments provides a more complete accounting of the costs incurred as a consequence of activities in the operating departments.
- To create an incentive for service departments to operate efficiently. Charging service department costs to operating departments provides a system of checks and balances in the sense that cost-conscious operating departments will take an active interest in keeping service department costs low.

Service Department Charges: Key Concepts

There are two key concepts for calculating service department charges. First, variable and fixed service department costs should be charged to operating departments separately because it provides more useful data for planning and control purposes. Second, a service department's *budgeted costs,* rather than its actual costs, should be charged to operating departments. This prohibits a service department from passing on cost overruns to operating departments. We expand on these concepts below.

Variable Costs

A service department's variable costs should be charged to operating departments according to whatever activity causes the incurrence of the cost. For example, variable costs of a maintenance department that are caused by the number of machine-hours worked in the operating departments should be charged to the operating departments on the basis of machine-hours. The equation for charging a service department's variable costs to operating departments is as follows:

$$\text{Variable costs charged to operating departments} = \text{Budgeted variable rate} \times \text{Actual level of activity}$$

Notice the service department's *budgeted* variable rate per unit is used in this equation rather than its actual variable rate. This ensures that service departments remain solely responsible for explaining any differences between their actual and budgeted variable rate. If service departments could base their charges on the actual variable rate, then operating departments would be unfairly charged for and held accountable for cost inefficiencies in the service departments.

Also, note that the operating department's actual level of activity (rather than its budgeted level of activity) is used in the above equation. This ensures that the total amount charged to operating departments varies in direct proportion to their actual usage of service department resources. Conversely, if the operating department's budgeted level of activity were used in the above equation, it would unfairly allow operating departments to exceed their budgeted usage of service department resources free-of-charge.

Fixed Costs

The fixed costs of service departments are charged to operating departments in a three-step process. First, the operating and service department managers agree on the operating department's estimated future usage of the service department's fixed cost resources. In this chapter, this estimated future usage will always be quantified in terms of the operating department's peak-period service needs or its long-run average needs. Second, the service department managers make the fixed cost commitments required to deliver the estimated peak-period or long-run average needs as specified by the operating departments. Third, service departments use the equation below to charge *predetermined lump-sum amounts* of fixed costs to operating departments as follows:

$$\begin{array}{l}\text{Fixed costs}\\\text{charged to operating} = \text{Budgeted total fixed costs} \times \text{Peak-period capacity required}\\\text{departments}\end{array}$$

Notice that the service department's *budgeted* total fixed costs are used in this equation rather than its actual total fixed costs. This ensures that service departments remain solely responsible for explaining any differences between their actual and budgeted fixed costs.

Also, note that the service department's budgeted fixed costs are charged to operating departments based on peak-period capacity required rather than a variable allocation base. This ensures that the service department's fixed costs are borne by operating departments in proportion to the amount of capacity each operating department requires. The fact that an operating department does not need the peak level of service every period is immaterial; the capacity to deliver this level of service must be available, and the budgeted cost of providing that capacity should be charged to the operating department accordingly.

Service Department Charges: An Example

Seaboard Airlines has a Maintenance Department that provides services to two operating departments—the Freight Division and the Passenger Division. The Maintenance Department's variable servicing costs are budgeted at $10 per flight-hour, and its total fixed costs are budgeted at $750,000 for the year. The fixed costs are allocated to the operating departments based on their peak-period service needs. Approximately 40 percent of the Maintenance Department's peak-period capacity is used by the Freight Division, and 60 percent is used by the Passenger Division.

At the end of the year, the Freight and Passenger Divisions actually logged 8,000 and 17,000 flight-hours, respectively. The Maintenance Department also actually incurred total variable and fixed costs of $260,000 and $780,000, respectively. Given this information, the amount of Maintenance Department cost charged to each division for the year would be computed as follows:

		Actual activity	Division	
			Freight	Passenger
	Variable cost charges:			
Budgeted variable rate →	$10 per flight-hour ×	8,000 flight-hours	$ 80,000	
	$10 per flight-hour ×	17,000 flight-hours		$170,000
	Fixed cost charges:			
Peak-period capacity required →	40% × $750,000	....	300,000	
	60% × $750,000	....		450,000
	Total charges	....	$380,000	$620,000
		Budgeted fixed cost		

Notice that variable servicing costs are charged to the operating divisions based on the budgeted rate ($10 per hour) and the *actual activity* for the year. In contrast, the charges for fixed costs are based entirely on budgeted data. Also note that the two operating divisions are *not* charged for the actual costs of the service department, which are influenced by how well the service department is managed. Instead, the service department is held responsible for the actual costs not charged to other departments as shown below:

	Variable	Fixed
Total actual costs incurred	$260,000	$780,000
Total charges to operating departments	250,000*	750,000**
Spending variance—responsibility of the Maintenance Department	$ 10,000	$ 30,000

*$80,000 + $170,000 = $250,000
**$300,000 + $450,000 = $750,000

Some Cautions in Allocating Service Department Costs

Pitfalls in Allocating Fixed Costs

Rather than charge fixed costs to operating departments in predetermined lump-sum amounts, some companies allocate them using a *variable* allocation base that fluctuates from period to period. This practice can distort decisions and create serious inequities between departments. The inequities arise from the fact that the fixed costs allocated to one department are heavily influenced by what happens in *other* departments.

Sales dollars is an example of a variable allocation base that is often used to allocate fixed costs from service departments to operating departments. Using sales dollars as a base is simple, straightforward, and easy to use. Furthermore, people tend to view sales dollars as a measure of ability to pay, and, hence, as a measure of how readily costs can be absorbed from other parts of the organization.

Unfortunately, sales dollars is often a very poor base for allocating or charging costs because sales dollars vary from period to period, whereas the costs are often largely *fixed.* Therefore, if one department's sales decline, it will shift allocated costs from that department to other departments whose sales have grown or at least held constant. In effect, the departments with growing sales tend to be penalized in the form of higher cost allocations. The result is often bitterness and resentment on the part of the managers of the better departments.

For example, let's assume a large men's clothing store has one service department and three sales departments—Suits, Shoes, and Accessories. The service department's costs total $60,000 per period and are allocated to the three sales departments according to sales dollars. A recent period showed the following allocation:

	Departments			
	Suits	**Shoes**	**Accessories**	**Total**
Sales by department	$260,000	$40,000	$100,000	$400,000
Percentage of total sales	65%	10%	25%	100%
Allocation of service department costs, based on percentage of total sales	$39,000	$6,000	$15,000	$60,000

In the following period, let's assume the manager of the Suits Department launched a successful program to expand sales in his department by $100,000. Furthermore, let's assume that sales in the other two departments remained unchanged, total service department costs remained unchanged, and the sales departments' expected usage of service department resources remained unchanged. Given these assumptions, the service department cost allocations to the sales departments would change as shown below:

	Departments			
	Suits	**Shoes**	**Accessories**	**Total**
Sales by department	$360,000	$40,000	$100,000	$500,000
Percentage of total sales	72%	8%	20%	100%
Allocation of service department costs, based on percentage of total sales	$43,200	$4,800	$12,000	$60,000
Increase (or decrease) from prior allocation.	$4,200	$(1,200)	$(3,000)	$0

After seeing these allocations, the manager of the Suits Department is likely to complain because by growing sales in his department, he is being forced to carry a larger share of the service department costs. In essence, this manager is being punished for his outstanding performance by being saddled with a greater proportion of service department costs. On the other hand, the managers of the departments that showed no sales growth are being relieved of a portion of the costs they had been carrying. Yet, there was no change in the amount of services provided for any department across the two periods.

This example shows why a variable allocation base such as sales dollars should only be used as a base for allocating costs in those cases where service department costs actually vary with the chosen allocation base. When service department costs are fixed, they should be charged to operating departments according to the guidelines mentioned earlier.

Summary

Many companies use responsibility accounting systems that classify their business units as cost centers, profit centers, and investment centers. Responsibility accounting systems personalize accounting information by holding the managers of these responsibility centers accountable for their revenues and costs.

Return on investment (ROI) and residual income are widely used to evaluate the performance of investment centers. ROI, which can also be expressed as a function of margin and turnover, suffers from the underinvestment problem—managers are reluctant to invest in projects that would exceed the company's required rate of return but decrease their investment center's ROI. The residual income approach solves this problem by giving managers full credit for any returns that a project earns in excess of the company's required rate of return.

A transfer price is the price charged when one responsibility center within a company provides goods or services to another responsibility center in the same company. Using a transfer price enables the provider of these goods and services to recognize a financial benefit associated with the transaction while also requiring the recipient to pay for the goods and services received.

Service department charges can be viewed as transfer prices that are charged for services provided by service departments to operating departments. Variable and fixed service department costs should be charged to operating departments separately. A service department's budgeted costs, rather than its actual costs, should be charged to operating departments. The operating departments should be charged for variable costs based on their actual level of activity rather than their budgeted usage. They should also be charged for fixed costs based on their peak-period requirements.

 Data Analytics Exercise available in Connect to complement this chapter

Review Problem 1: Return on Investment (ROI) and Residual Income

The Magnetic Imaging Division of Medical Diagnostics, Inc., has reported the following results for last year's operations:

Sales	$25 million
Net operating income	$3 million
Average operating assets	$10 million

Required:
1. Compute the Magnetic Imaging Division's margin, turnover, and ROI.
2. If Medical Diagnostics, Inc., has a minimum required rate of return on average operating assets of 25%, then what is the Magnetic Imaging Division's residual income for the year?

Solution to Review Problem

1. The required calculations follow:

$$\text{Margin} = \frac{\text{Net operating income}}{\text{Sales}}$$
$$= \frac{\$3,000,000}{\$25,000,000}$$
$$= 12\%$$

$$\text{Turnover} = \frac{\text{Sales}}{\text{Average operating assets}}$$
$$= \frac{\$25,000,000}{\$10,000,000}$$
$$= 2.5$$

$$\text{ROI} = \text{Margin} \times \text{Turnover}$$
$$= 12\% \times 2.5$$
$$= 30\%$$

2. The Magnetic Imaging Division's residual income is computed as follows:

Average operating assets	$10,000,000
Net operating income	$ 3,000,000
Minimum required return (25% × $10,000,000)	2,500,000
Residual income	$ 500,000

Review Problem 2: Transfer Pricing

Situation A

Collyer Products, Inc., has a Valve Division that manufactures and sells a standard valve:

Capacity in units	100,000
Selling price to outside customers.	$30
Variable costs per unit	$16
Fixed costs per unit (based on capacity).	$9

The company has a Pump Division that could use this valve in one of its pumps. The Pump Division is currently purchasing 10,000 valves per year from an overseas supplier at a cost of $29 per valve.

Required:
1. Assume the Valve Division has enough idle capacity to handle all of the Pump Division's needs. What is the range of acceptable transfer prices, if any, for the transfer between the two divisions?
2. Assume the Valve Division is selling all of the valves it can produce to outside customers. What is the range of acceptable transfer prices, if any, for the transfer between the two divisions?
3. Assume again the Valve Division is selling all of the valves it can produce to outside customers. Also assume that $3 in variable expenses can be avoided on transfers within the company, due to reduced selling costs. What is the range of acceptable transfer prices, if any, for the transfer between the two divisions?

Solution to Situation A

1. Because the Valve Division has idle capacity, it does not have to give up any outside sales to take on the Pump Division's business. Applying the formula for the lowest acceptable transfer price from the viewpoint of the selling division, we get:

$$\text{Transfer price} \geq \frac{\text{Variable cost}}{\text{per unit}} + \frac{\text{Total contribution margin on lost sales}}{\text{Number of units transferred}}$$

$$\text{Transfer price} \geq \$16 + \frac{\$0}{10{,}000} = \$16$$

The Pump Division would be unwilling to pay more than $29, the price it is currently paying an outside supplier for its valves. Therefore, the transfer price must fall within the range:

$$\$16 \leq \text{Transfer price} \leq \$29$$

2. Because the Valve Division has no idle capacity, there *are* lost outside sales. Given the contribution margin per unit on these outside sales is $14 ($30 − $16), the lowest acceptable transfer price of $30 is computed as follows:

$$\text{Transfer price} \geq \frac{\text{Variable cost}}{\text{per unit}} + \frac{\text{Total contribution margin on lost sales}}{\text{Number of units transferred}}$$

$$\text{Transfer price} \geq \$16 + \frac{(\$30 - \$16) \times 10{,}000}{10{,}000} = \$16 + \$14 = \$30$$

Because the Pump Division can purchase valves from an outside supplier at only $29 per unit, no transfers will be made between the two divisions.

3. Applying the formula for the lowest acceptable transfer price from the viewpoint of the selling division, we get:

$$\text{Transfer price} \geq \frac{\text{Variable cost}}{\text{per unit}} + \frac{\text{Total contribution margin on lost sales}}{\text{Number of units transferred}}$$

$$\text{Transfer price} \geq (\$16 - \$3) + \frac{(\$30 - \$16) \times 10,000}{10,000} = \$13 + \$14 = \$27$$

In this case, the transfer price must fall within the range:

$$\$27 \leq \text{Transfer price} \leq \$29$$

Situation B

Refer to the original data in situation A above. Assume the Pump Division needs 20,000 special high-pressure valves per year. The Valve Division's variable costs to manufacture and ship the special valve would be $20 per unit. To produce these special valves, the Valve Division would have to reduce its production and sales of regular valves from 100,000 units per year to 70,000 units per year.

Required:

From the Valve Division's perspective, what is the lowest acceptable transfer price?

Solution to Situation B

To produce the 20,000 special valves, the Valve Division will have to give up sales of 30,000 regular valves to outside customers. Applying the formula for the lowest acceptable transfer price from the viewpoint of the selling division, we get:

$$\text{Transfer price} \geq \text{Variable cost per unit} + \frac{\text{Total contribution margin on lost sales}}{\text{Number of units transferred}}$$

$$\text{Transfer price} \geq \$20 + \frac{(\$30 - \$16) \times 30,000}{20,000} = \$20 + \$21 = \$41$$

Glossary

Cost center A business segment whose manager has control over cost but has no control over revenue or investments in operating assets. (p. 536)

Decentralized organization An organization in which decision-making authority is not confined to a few top executives but rather is spread throughout the organization. (p. 535)

Investment center A business segment whose manager has control over cost, revenue, and investments in operating assets. (p. 536)

Margin Net operating income divided by sales. (p. 538)

Market price The price charged for an item on the open market. (p. 549)

Negotiated transfer price A transfer price agreed on between buying and selling divisions. (p. 544)

Net operating income Income before interest and income taxes have been deducted. (p. 537)

Operating assets Cash, accounts receivable, inventory, plant and equipment, and all other assets held for operating purposes. (p. 537)

Operating department A department in which the central purposes of the organization are carried out. (p. 549)

Profit center A business segment whose manager has control over cost and revenue but has no control over investments in operating assets. (p. 536)

Range of acceptable transfer prices The range of transfer prices within which the profits of both the selling division and the buying division would increase as a result of a transfer. (p. 545)

Residual income The net operating income that an investment center earns above the minimum required return on its operating assets. (p. 541)

Responsibility accounting A manager should be held responsible for those items—and *only* those items—that the manager can actually control to a significant extent. (p. 536)

Responsibility center Any business segment whose manager has control over costs, revenues, or investments in operating assets. (p. 536)

Return on investment (ROI) Net operating income divided by average operating assets. It also equals margin multiplied by turnover. (p. 537)

Service department A department that does not directly engage in operating activities; rather, it provides services or assistance to the operating departments. (p. 549)

Suboptimization An overall level of profits that is less than a segment or a company is capable of earning. (p. 544)

Transfer price The price charged when one responsibility center within a company provides goods or services to another responsibility center in the same company. (p. 544)

Turnover Sales divided by average operating assets. (p. 538)

Questions

11–1   What is meant by the term *decentralization?*
11–2   What benefits result from decentralization?
11–3   Distinguish between a cost center, a profit center, and an investment center.
11–4   What is meant by the terms *margin* and *turnover* in ROI calculations?
11–5   What is meant by residual income?
11–6   In what way can the use of ROI as a performance measure for investment centers lead to bad decisions? How does the residual income approach overcome this problem?
11–7   What is a transfer price?
11–8   What does suboptimization mean?
11–9   Why should a service department's budgeted costs, rather than its actual costs, be charged to operating departments?
11–10   Why is using sales dollars as an allocation base usually a poor choice for allocating fixed costs to operating departments?

 Applying Excel

The Excel worksheet form below is to be used to recreate the Review Problem pertaining to the Magnetic Imaging Division of Medical Diagnostics, Inc. The workbook, and instructions on how to complete the file, can be found in Connect.

LEARNING OBJECTIVES 11–1, 11–2

	A	B	C	D	E
1	Chapter 11: Applying Excel				
2					
3	**Data**				
4	Sales	$25,000,000			
5	Net operating income	$3,000,000			
6	Average operating assets	$10,000,000			
7	Minimum required rate of return	25%			
8					
9	*Enter a formula into each of the cells marked with a ? below*				
10	**Review Problem: Return on Investment (ROI) and Residual Income**				
11					
12	*Compute the ROI*				
13	Margin	?			
14	Turnover	?			
15	ROI	?			
16					
17	*Compute the residual income*				
18	Average operating assets	?			
19	Net operating income	?			
20	Minimum required return	?			
21	Residual income	?			
22					

Chapter 11 Form   Filled in Chapter 11 Form

Microsoft Excel

You should proceed to the requirements below only after completing your worksheet.

Required:

1. Check your worksheet by changing the average operating assets in cell B6 to $8,000,000. The ROI should now be 38% and the residual income should now be $1,000,000. If you do not get these answers, find the errors in your worksheet and correct them.

    Explain why the ROI and the residual income both increase when the average operating assets decrease.

2. Revise the data in your worksheet as follows:

Data	
Sales	$1,200
Net operating income.	$72
Average operating assets	$500
Minimum required rate of return.	15%

    a. What is the ROI?
    b. What is the residual income?
    c. Explain the relationship between the ROI and the residual income.

The Foundational 15   connect

LEARNING OBJECTIVES 11–1, 11–2

Westerville Company reported the following results from last year's operations:

Sales	$1,000,000
Variable expenses	300,000
Contribution margin	700,000
Fixed expenses	500,000
Net operating income	$ 200,000
Average operating assets	$ 625,000

At the beginning of this year, the company has a $120,000 investment opportunity with the following cost and revenue characteristics:

Sales	$200,000
Contribution margin ratio	60% of sales
Fixed expenses	$90,000

The company's minimum required rate of return is 15%.

Required:

1. What is last year's margin?
2. What is last year's turnover?
3. What is last year's return on investment (ROI)?
4. What is the margin related to this year's investment opportunity?
5. What is the turnover related to this year's investment opportunity?
6. What is the ROI related to this year's investment opportunity?
7. If the company pursues the investment opportunity and otherwise performs the same as last year, what margin will it earn this year?
8. If the company pursues the investment opportunity and otherwise performs the same as last year, what turnover will it earn this year?
9. If the company pursues the investment opportunity and otherwise performs the same as last year, what ROI will it earn this year?
10. If Westerville's chief executive officer will earn a bonus only if her ROI from this year exceeds her ROI from last year, would she pursue the investment opportunity? Would the owners of the company want her to pursue the investment opportunity?

11. What is last year's residual income?
12. What is the residual income of this year's investment opportunity?
13. If the company pursues the investment opportunity and otherwise performs the same as last year, what residual income will it earn this year?
14. If Westerville's chief executive officer will earn a bonus only if her residual income from this year exceeds her residual income from last year, would she pursue the investment opportunity?
15. Assume that the contribution margin ratio of the investment opportunity was 50% instead of 60%. If Westerville's chief executive officer will earn a bonus only if her residual income from this year exceeds her residual income from last year, would she pursue the investment opportunity? Would the owners of the company want her to pursue the investment opportunity?

Mc Graw Hill connect   **Exercises**

EXERCISE 11–1 Compute the Return on Investment (ROI) LO 11–1

Alyeska Services Company, a division of a major oil company, provides various services to the operators of the North Slope oil field in Alaska. Data concerning the most recent year follow:

Sales	$7,500,000
Net operating income	$600,000
Average operating assets	$5,000,000

Required:
1. Compute the margin.
2. Compute the turnover.
3. Compute the return on investment (ROI).

EXERCISE 11–2 Residual Income LO 11–2

Juniper Design Ltd. of Manchester, England, provides design services to residential developers. Last year, the company had net operating income of $600,000 on sales of $3,000,000. The company's average operating assets for the year were $2,800,000, and its minimum required rate of return was 18%.

Required:
Compute the company's residual income for the year.

EXERCISE 11–3 Transfer Pricing Basics LO 11–3

Sako Company's Audio Division produces a speaker that is used by manufacturers of various audio products. Sales and cost data on the speaker follow:

Selling price per unit on the intermediate market	$60
Variable costs per unit	$42
Fixed costs per unit (based on capacity)	$8
Capacity in units	25,000

Sako Company has a Hi-Fi Division that could use this speaker in one of its products. The Hi-Fi Division will need 5,000 speakers per year. It has received a quote of $57 per speaker from another manufacturer. Sako Company evaluates division managers on the basis of divisional profits.

Required:
1. Assume the Audio Division sells only 20,000 speakers per year to outside customers.
   a. From the standpoint of the Audio Division, what is the lowest acceptable transfer price for speakers sold to the Hi-Fi Division?
   b. From the standpoint of the Hi-Fi Division, what is the highest acceptable transfer price for speakers acquired from the Audio Division?
   c. What is the range of acceptable transfer prices (if any) between the two divisions? If left free to negotiate without interference, would you expect the division managers to

voluntarily agree to the transfer of 5,000 speakers from the Audio Division to the Hi-Fi Division? Why or why not?

     d. From the standpoint of the entire company, should the transfer take place? Why or why not?

2. Assume the Audio Division is selling 22,500 speakers per year to outside customers.

     a. From the standpoint of the Audio Division, what is the lowest acceptable transfer price for speakers sold to the Hi-Fi Division?

     b. From the standpoint of the Hi-Fi Division, what is the highest acceptable transfer price for speakers acquired from the Audio Division?

     c. What is the range of acceptable transfer prices (if any) between the two divisions? If left free to negotiate without interference, would you expect the division managers to voluntarily agree to the transfer of 5,000 speakers from the Audio Division to the Hi-Fi Division? Why or why not?

     d. From the standpoint of the entire company, should the transfer take place? Why or why not?

3. Assume the Audio Division is selling 25,000 speakers per year to outside customers.

     a. From the standpoint of the Audio Division, what is the lowest acceptable transfer price for speakers sold to the Hi-Fi Division?

     b. From the standpoint of the Hi-Fi Division, what is the highest acceptable transfer price for speakers acquired from the Audio Division?

     c. What is the range of acceptable transfer prices (if any) between the two divisions? If left free to negotiate without interference, would you expect the division managers to voluntarily agree to the transfer of 5,000 speakers from the Audio Division to the Hi-Fi Division? Why or why not?

     d. From the standpoint of the entire company, should the transfer take place? Why or why not?

EXERCISE 11–4 Service Department Charges LO 11–4

Hannibal Steel Company has a Transport Services Department that provides trucks to haul ore from the company's mine to its two steel mills—the Northern Plant and the Southern Plant. Budgeted costs for the Transport Services Department total $350,000 per year, consisting of $0.25 per ton variable cost and $300,000 fixed cost. The level of fixed cost is determined by peak-period requirements. During the peak period, the Northern Plant requires 70% of the Transport Services Department's capacity, and the Southern Plant requires 30%.

During the year, the Transport Services Department actually hauled 130,000 tons of ore to the Northern Plant and 50,000 tons to the Southern Plant. The Transport Services Department incurred $364,000 in cost during the year, of which $54,000 was variable cost and $310,000 was fixed cost.

Required:

1. How much of the Transport Services Department's variable costs should be charged to each plant?

2. How much of the Transport Services Department's fixed costs should be charged to each plant?

3. Should any of the Transport Services Department's actual total cost of $364,000 be treated as a spending variance and not charged to the plants? Explain.

EXERCISE 11–5 Return on Investment (ROI) LO 11–1

Provide the missing data in the following table for a distributor of martial arts products:

	Division		
	Alpha	Bravo	Charlie
Sales	$?	$11,500,000	$?
Net operating income	$?	$ 920,000	$210,000
Average operating assets	$800,000	$?	$?
Margin	4%	?	7%
Turnover	5	?	?
Return on investment (ROI)	?	20%	14%

EXERCISE 11–6 Contrasting Return on Investment (ROI) and Residual Income LO 11–1, LO 11–2

Tan Corporation of Japan has two regional divisions with headquarters in Osaka and Yokohama. Selected data on the two divisions follow:

	Division	
	Osaka	Yokohama
Sales	$3,000,000	$9,000,000
Net operating income	$210,000	$720,000
Average operating assets	$1,000,000	$4,000,000

Required:

1. For each division, compute the margin, turnover, and return on investment (ROI). Where necessary, carry computations to two decimal places.
2. Assume the company evaluates performance using residual income and the minimum required rate of return for any division is 15%. Compute the residual income for each division.

EXERCISE 11–7 Transfer Pricing from the Viewpoint of the Entire Company LO 11–3

Division A manufactures electronic circuit boards. The boards can be sold either to Division B of the same company or to outside customers. Last year, the following activity occurred in Division A:

Selling price per circuit board	$125
Variable cost per circuit board	$90
Number of circuit boards:	
Produced during the year	20,000
Sold to outside customers	16,000
Sold to Division B	4,000

Sales to Division B were at the same price as sales to outside customers. The circuit boards purchased by Division B were used in an electronic instrument manufactured by that division (one board per instrument). Division B incurred $100 in additional variable cost per instrument and then sold the instruments for $300 each.

Required:

1. Calculate the net operating incomes earned by Division A, Division B, and the company as a whole.
2. Assume Division A's manufacturing capacity is 20,000 circuit boards. Next year, Division B wants to purchase 5,000 circuit boards from Division A rather than 4,000. (Circuit boards of this type are not available from outside sources.) From the standpoint of the company as a whole, should Division A sell the 1,000 additional circuit boards to Division B or continue to sell them to outside customers? Explain.

EXERCISE 11–8 Computing and Interpreting Return on Investment (ROI) LO 11–1

Selected operating data for two divisions of Outback Brewing, Ltd., of Australia are given below:

	Division	
	Queensland	New South Wales
Sales	$4,000,000	$7,000,000
Average operating assets	$2,000,000	$2,000,000
Net operating income	$360,000	$420,000
Property, plant, and equipment (net)	$950,000	$800,000

Required:

1. Compute each division's margin, turnover, and return on investment (ROI).
2. Which divisional manager seems to be doing the better job? Why?

EXERCISE 11–9 Return on Investment (ROI) and Residual Income Relations LO 11–1, LO 11–2

A family friend has asked your help in analyzing the operations of three anonymous companies operating in the same service sector industry. Supply the missing data in the table below:

	Company		
	A	B	C
Sales	$9,000,000	$7,000,000	$4,500,000
Net operating income	$?	$ 280,000	$?
Average operating assets	$3,000,000	$?	$1,800,000
Return on investment (ROI)	18%	14%	?
Minimum required rate of return:			
Percentage	16%	?	15%
Dollar amount	$?	$ 320,000	$?
Residual income	$?	$?	$ 90,000

EXERCISE 11–10 Sales Dollars as an Allocation Base for Fixed Costs LO 11–4

Konig Enterprises, Ltd., owns and operates three restaurants in Vancouver, B.C. The company allocates its fixed administrative expenses to the three restaurants on the basis of sales dollars. Last year, the fixed administrative expenses totaled $2,000,000 and were allocated as follows:

	Restaurants			
	Rick's Harborside	Imperial Garden	Ginger Wok	Total
Total sales—last year	$16,000,000	$15,000,000	$9,000,000	$40,000,000
Percentage of total sales ...	40%	37.5%	22.5%	100%
Allocation (based on the above percentages)	$800,000	$750,000	$450,000	$2,000,000

This year the Imperial Garden restaurant increased its sales by $10 million. The sales levels in the other two restaurants remained unchanged. The company's sales data for this year were as follows:

	Restaurants			
	Rick's Harborside	Imperial Garden	Ginger Wok	Total
Total sales—this year	$16,000,000	$25,000,000	$9,000,000	$50,000,000
Percentage of total sales	32%	50%	18%	100%

Fixed administrative expenses for this year remained unchanged at $2,000,000.

Required:

1. Using sales dollars as an allocation base, show the allocation of the fixed administrative expenses among the three restaurants for this year.
2. Calculate the change in each restaurant's allocated cost from last year to this year. As the manager of the Imperial Garden, how would you feel about the amount charged to you for this year?
3. Comment on the usefulness of sales dollars as an allocation base.

EXERCISE 11–11 Cost-Volume-Profit Analysis and Return on Investment (ROI) LO 11–1

Posters.com is a small Internet retailer of high-quality posters. The company has $1,000,000 in operating assets and fixed expenses of $150,000 per year. With this level of operating assets and fixed expenses, the company can support sales of up to $3,000,000 per year. The company's contribution margin ratio is 25%, which means that an additional dollar of sales results in additional contribution margin, and net operating income, of 25 cents.

Required:
1. Complete the following table showing the relation between sales and return on investment (ROI).

Sales	Net Operating Income	Average Operating Assets	ROI
$2,500,000	$475,000	$1,000,000	?
$2,600,000	$?	$1,000,000	?
$2,700,000	$?	$1,000,000	?
$2,800,000	$?	$1,000,000	?
$2,900,000	$?	$1,000,000	?
$3,000,000	$?	$1,000,000	?

2. What happens to the company's return on investment (ROI) as sales increase? Explain.

EXERCISE 11–12 Effects of Changes in Profits and Assets on Return on Investment (ROI) LO 11–1

Fitness Fanatics is a regional chain of health clubs. The managers of the clubs, who have authority to make investments as needed, are evaluated based largely on return on investment (ROI). The company's Springfield Club reported the following results for the past year:

Sales	$1,400,000
Net operating income	$70,000
Average operating assets	$350,000

Required:
The following questions are to be considered independently. Carry out all computations to two decimal places.
1. Compute the Springfield club's return on investment (ROI).
2. Assume the manager of the club is able to increase sales by $70,000 and, as a result, net operating income increases by $18,200. Further assume, this is possible without any increase in average operating assets. What would be the club's return on investment (ROI)?
3. Assume the manager of the club is able to reduce expenses by $14,000 without any change in sales or average operating assets. What would be the club's return on investment (ROI)?
4. Assume the manager of the club is able to reduce average operating assets by $70,000 without any change in sales or net operating income. What would be the club's return on investment (ROI)?

EXERCISE 11–13 Transfer Pricing Situations LO 11–3

In each of the cases below, assume Division X has a product that can be sold either to outside customers or to Division Y of the same company for use in its production process. The managers of the divisions are evaluated based on their divisional profits.

	Case	
	A	B
Division X:		
Capacity in units	200,000	200,000
Number of units being sold to outside customers	200,000	160,000
Selling price per unit to outside customers	$90	$75
Variable costs per unit	$70	$60
Fixed costs per unit (based on capacity)	$13	$8
Division Y:		
Number of units needed for production	40,000	40,000
Purchase price per unit now being paid		
to an outside supplierr	$86	$74

Required:

1. Refer to the data in case A above. Assume in this case that $3 per unit in variable selling costs can be avoided on intracompany sales.
    a. What is the lowest acceptable transfer price from the perspective of the selling division?
    b. What is the highest acceptable transfer price from the perspective of the buying division?
    c. What is the range of acceptable transfer prices (if any) between the two divisions? If the managers are free to negotiate and make decisions on their own, will a transfer probably take place? Explain.
2. Refer to the data in case B above. In this case, there will be no savings in variable selling costs on intracompany sales.
    a. What is the lowest acceptable transfer price from the perspective of the selling division?
    b. What is the highest acceptable transfer price from the perspective of the buying division?
    c. What is the range of acceptable transfer prices (if any) between the two divisions? If the managers are free to negotiate and make decisions on their own, will a transfer probably take place? Explain.

EXERCISE 11–14 Evaluating New Investments Using Return on Investment (ROI) and Residual Income LO 11–1, LO 11–2

Selected sales and operating data for three divisions of different structural engineering firms are given as follows:

	Division A	Division B	Division C
Sales	$12,000,000	$14,000,000	$25,000,000
Average operating assets	$3,000,000	$7,000,000	$5,000,000
Net operating income	$600,000	$560,000	$800,000
Minimum required rate of return	14%	10%	16%

Required:

1. Compute the margin, turnover, and return on investment (ROI) for each division.
2. Compute the residual income for each division.
3. Assume each division is presented with an investment opportunity that would yield a 15% rate of return.
    a. If performance is being measured by ROI, which division or divisions will probably accept the opportunity? Reject? Why?
    b. If performance is being measured by residual income, which division or divisions will probably accept the opportunity? Reject? Why?

EXERCISE 11–15 Service Department Charges LO 11–4

Korvanis Corporation operates a Medical Services Department for its employees. Charges to the company's operating departments for the variable costs of the Medical Services Department are based on the actual number of employees in each department. Charges for the fixed costs of the Medical Services Department are based on the long-run average number of employees in each operating department.

Variable Medical Services Department costs are budgeted at $80 per employee. Fixed Medical Services Department costs are budgeted at $400,000 per year. Actual Medical Services Department costs for the most recent year were $41,000 for variable costs and $408,000 for fixed costs. Data concerning employees in the three operating departments follow:

	Cutting	Milling	Assembly
Budgeted number of employees	170	100	280
Actual number of employees for the most recent year	150	80	270
Long-run average number of employees	180	120	300

Required:

1. Determine the Medical Services Department charges for the year to each of the operating departments—Cutting, Milling, and Assembly.
2. How much, if any, of the actual Medical Services Department costs for the year should be treated as a spending variance and not charged to the operating departments?

EXERCISE 11–16 Effects of Changes in Sales, Expenses, and Assets on ROI LO 11–1

CommercialServices.com Corporation provides business-to-business services on the Internet. Data concerning the most recent year appear below:

Sales	$3,000,000
Net operating income	$150,000
Average operating assets	$750,000

Required:

Consider each question below independently. Carry out all computations to two decimal places.

1. Compute the company's return on investment (ROI).
2. The entrepreneur who founded the company is convinced sales will increase next year by 50% and net operating income will increase by 200%, with no increase in average operating assets. What would be the company's ROI?
3. The chief financial officer of the company believes a more realistic scenario would be a $1,000,000 increase in sales, requiring a $250,000 increase in average operating assets, with a resulting $200,000 increase in net operating income. What would be the company's ROI in this scenario?

McGraw Hill connect   **Problems**

PROBLEM 11–17 Return on Investment (ROI) and Residual Income LO 11–1, LO 11–2

Financial data for Joel de Paris, Inc., for last year follow:

Joel de Paris, Inc. Balance Sheet	Beginning Balance	Ending Balance
Assets		
Cash	$ 140,000	$ 120,000
Accounts receivable	450,000	530,000
Inventory	320,000	380,000
Plant and equipment, net	680,000	620,000
Investment in Buisson, S.A.	250,000	280,000
Land (undeveloped)	180,000	170,000
Total assets	$2,020,000	$2,100,000
Liabilities and Stockholders' Equity		
Accounts payable	$ 360,000	$ 310,000
Long-term debt	1,500,000	1,500,000
Stockholders' equity	160,000	290,000
Total liabilities and stockholders' equity	$2,020,000	$2,100,000

Joel de Paris, Inc. Income Statement		
Sales		$4,050,000
Operating expenses		3,645,000
Net operating income		405,000
Interest and taxes:		
Interest expense	$150,000	
Tax expense...................................	110,000	260,000
Net income....................................		$ 145,000

The company paid dividends of $15,000 last year. The "Investment in Buisson, S.A." on the balance sheet represents an investment in the stock of another company. The company's minimum required rate of return of 15%.

Required:
1. Compute the company's average operating assets for last year.
2. Compute the company's margin, turnover, and return on investment (ROI) for last year. (Hint: Should you use net income or net operating income in your calculations?)
3. What was the company's residual income last year?

PROBLEM 11–18 Service Department Charges LO 11–4

Tasman Products, Ltd., of Australia has a Maintenance Department that services the equipment in the company's Forming Department and Assembly Department. The cost of this servicing is charged to the operating departments on the basis of machine-hours. Cost and other data relating to the Maintenance Department and to the other two departments for the most recent year are presented below.

Data for the Maintenance Department follow:

	Budget	Actual
Variable costs for lubricants	$96,000*	$110,000
Fixed costs for salaries and other	$150,000	$153,000

*Budgeted at $0.40 per machine-hour.

Data for the Forming and Assembly Departments follow:

	Percentage of Peak-Period Capacity Required	Machine-Hours	
		Budget	Actual
Forming Department	70%	160,000	190,000
Assembly Department	30%	80,000	70,000
Total	100%	240,000	260,000

The level of fixed costs in the Maintenance Department is determined by peak-period requirements.

Required:
1. How much Maintenance Department cost should be charged to the Forming Department and to the Assembly Department?
2. How much, if any, of the actual Maintenance Department costs for the year should be treated as a spending variance and not charged to the Forming and Assembly departments? Explain the rationale for your answer.

PROBLEM 11–19 Comparison of Performance Using Return on Investment (ROI) LO 11–1

Comparative data on three companies in the same service industry are given below:

	Company		
	A	B	C
Sales	$600,000	$500,000	$?
Net operating income	$ 84,000	$ 70,000	$?
Average operating assets	$300,000	$?	$1,000,000
Margin	?	?	3.5%
Turnover	?	?	2
ROI	?	7%	?

Required:
1. What advantages are there to breaking down the ROI computation into two separate elements, margin and turnover?
2. Fill in the missing information above, and comment on the relative performance of the three companies in as much detail as the data permit. Make *specific recommendations* about how to improve the ROI.

(Adapted from National Association of Accountants,
Research Report No. 35, p. 34)

PROBLEM 11–20 Transfer Price with an Outside Market LO 11–3

Hrubec Products, Inc., operates a Pulp Division that manufactures wood pulp for use in the production of various paper goods. Revenue and costs associated with a ton of pulp follow:

Selling price		$70
Expenses:		
Variable	$42	
Fixed (based on a capacity of		
50,000 tons per year)	18	60
Net operating income		$10

Hrubec Products just acquired a small company that manufactures paper cartons. Hrubec plans to treat its newly acquired Carton Division as a profit center. The manager of the Carton Division is currently purchasing 5,000 tons of pulp per year from a supplier at a cost of $63 per ton. Hrubec's president is anxious for the Carton Division to begin purchasing its pulp from the Pulp Division if the managers of the two divisions can negotiate an acceptable transfer price.

Required:

For (1) and (2) below, assume the Pulp Division can sell all of its pulp to outside customers for $70 per ton.

1. What is the Pulp Division's lowest acceptable transfer price? What is the Carton Division's highest acceptable transfer price? What is the range of acceptable transfer prices (if any) between the two divisions? Are the managers of the Carton and Pulp Divisions likely to voluntarily agree to a transfer price for 5,000 tons of pulp next year? Why or why not?

2. If the Pulp Division meets the price that the Carton Division is currently paying to its supplier and sells 5,000 tons of pulp to the Carton Division each year, what will be the effect on the profits of the Pulp Division, the Carton Division, and the company as a whole?

For (3)–(6) below, assume that the Pulp Division is currently selling only 30,000 tons of pulp each year to outside customers at the stated $70 price.

3. What is the Pulp Division's lowest acceptable transfer price? What is the Carton Division's highest acceptable transfer price? What is the range of acceptable transfer prices (if any) between the two divisions? Are the managers of the Carton and Pulp Divisions likely to voluntarily agree to a transfer price for 5,000 tons of pulp next year? Why or why not?

4. Suppose the Carton Division's outside supplier drops its price to only $59 per ton. Should the Pulp Division meet this price? Explain. If the Pulp Division does *not* meet the $59 price, what will be the effect on the profits of the company as a whole?

5. Refer to (4) above. If the Pulp Division refuses to meet the $59 price, should the Carton Division be required to purchase from the Pulp Division at a higher price for the good of the company as a whole?

6. Refer to (4) above. Assume that due to inflexible management policies, the Carton Division is required to purchase 5,000 tons of pulp each year from the Pulp Division at $70 per ton. What will be the effect on the profits of the company as a whole?

PROBLEM 11–21 Return on Investment (ROI) and Residual Income LO 11–1, LO 11–2

"I know headquarters wants us to add that new product line," said Dell Havasi, manager of Billings Company's Office Products Division. "But I want to see the numbers before I make any move. Our division's return on investment (ROI) has led the company for three years, and I don't want any letdown."

Billings Company is a decentralized wholesaler with five autonomous divisions. The divisions are evaluated on the basis of ROI, with year-end bonuses given to the divisional managers who have the highest ROIs. Operating results for the company's Office Products Division for this year are given below:

Sales	$10,000,000
Variable expenses	6,000,000
Contribution margin	4,000,000
Fixed expenses	3,200,000
Net operating income	$ 800,000
Divisional average operating assets	$ 4,000,000

The company had an overall return on investment (ROI) of 15% this year (considering all divisions). Next year the Office Products Division has an opportunity to add a new product line that would require an additional investment that would increase average operating assets by $1,000,000. The cost and revenue characteristics of the new product line per year would be:

Sales	$2,000,000
Variable expenses	60% of sales
Fixed expenses	$640,000

Required:
1. Compute the Office Products Division's margin, turnover, and ROI for this year.
2. Compute the Office Products Division's margin, turnover, and ROI for the new product line by itself.
3. Compute the Office Products Division's margin, turnover, and ROI for next year assuming that it performs the same as this year and adds the new product line.
4. If you were in Dell Havasi's position, would you accept or reject the new product line? Explain.
5. Why do you suppose headquarters is anxious for the Office Products Division to add the new product line?
6. Suppose that the company's minimum required rate of return on operating assets is 12% and that performance is evaluated using residual income.
    a.   Compute the Office Products Division's residual income for this year.
    b.   Compute the Office Products Division's residual income for the new product line by itself.
    c.   Compute the Office Products Division's residual income for next year assuming that it performs the same as this year and adds the new product line.
    d.   Using the residual income approach, if you were in Dell Havasi's position, would you accept or reject the new product line? Explain.

PROBLEM 11–22 Service Department Charges LO 11–4

Sharp Motor Company has two operating divisions—an Auto Division and a Truck Division. The company has a cafeteria that serves the employees of both divisions. The costs of operating the cafeteria are budgeted at $40,000 per month plus $3 per meal served. The company pays all the cost of the meals.

The fixed costs of the cafeteria are determined by peak-period requirements. The Auto Division is responsible for 65% of the peak-period requirements, and the Truck Division is responsible for the other 35%.

For June, the Auto Division estimated it would need 35,000 meals served, and the Truck Division estimated it would need 20,000 meals served. However, due to unexpected layoffs of employees during the month, only 20,000 meals were served to the Auto Division. Another 20,000 meals were served to the Truck Division as planned.

The cafeteria's actual fixed costs for June totaled $42,000, and its actual meal costs totaled $128,000.

Required:
1. How much cafeteria cost should be charged to each division for June?
2. Assume the company follows the practice of allocating *all* cafeteria costs incurred each month to the divisions in proportion to the number of meals served to each division during the month. On this basis, how much cost would be allocated to each division for June?
3. What criticisms can you make of the allocation method used in part (2) above?
4. If managers of operating departments know that fixed service costs are going to be allocated on the basis of peak-period requirements, what will be their probable strategy as they report their estimate of peak-period requirements to the company's budget committee? As a member of top management, what would you do to neutralize such strategies?

PROBLEM 11–23 Market-Based Transfer Price LO 11–3

Stavos Company's Screen Division manufactures a standard screen for high-definition televisions (HDTVs). The cost per screen is:

Variable cost per screen	$ 70
Fixed cost per screen	30*
Total cost per screen	$100

*Based on a capacity of 10,000 screens per year.

Part of the Screen Division's output is sold to outside manufacturers of HDTVs and part is sold to Stavos Company's Quark Division, which produces an HDTV under its own name. The Screen Division charges $140 per screen for all sales.

The net operating income associated with the Quark Division's HDTV is computed as follows:

Selling price per unit		$480
Variable cost per unit:		
Cost of the screen	$140	
Variable cost of electronic parts	210	
Total variable cost		350
Contribution margin		130
Fixed costs per unit		80*
Net operating income per unit		$ 50

*Based on a capacity of 3,000 units per year.

The Quark Division has an order from an overseas source for 1,000 HDTVs. The overseas source wants to pay only $340 per unit.

Required:

1. Assume the Quark Division has enough idle capacity to fill the 1,000-unit order. Is the division likely to accept the $340 price or to reject it? Explain.
2. Assume both the Screen Division and the Quark Division have idle capacity. Under these conditions, what is the financial advantage (disadvantage) for the company as a whole (on a per-unit basis) if the Quark Division *rejects* the $340 price?
3. Assume the Quark Division has idle capacity, but the Screen Division is operating at capacity and could sell all of its screens to outside manufacturers. Under these conditions, what is the financial advantage (disadvantage) for the company as a whole (on a per-unit basis) if the Quark Division *accepts* the $340 unit price?
4. What conclusions do you draw concerning the use of market price as a transfer price in intracompany transactions?

PROBLEM 11–24 Return on Investment (ROI) Analysis LO 11–1

The contribution format income statement for Huerra Company for last year is given below:

	Total	Unit
Sales	$4,000,000	$80.00
Variable expenses	2,800,000	56.00
Contribution margin	1,200,000	24.00
Fixed expenses...................	840,000	16.80
Net operating income	360,000	7.20
Income taxes @ 30%	108,000	2.16
Net income	$ 252,000	$ 5.04

The company had average operating assets of $2,000,000 during the year.

Required:

1. Compute the company's margin, turnover, and return on investment (ROI) for the period.

For each of the following questions, indicate whether the margin and turnover will increase, decrease, or remain unchanged as a result of the events described, and then compute the new ROI figure. Consider each question separately, starting in each case from the data used to compute the original ROI in (1) above.

2. Using Lean Production, the company is able to reduce the average level of inventory by $400,000.
3. The company achieves a cost savings of $32,000 per year by using less costly materials.
4. The company purchases machinery and equipment that increases average operating assets by $500,000. Sales remain unchanged. The new, more efficient equipment reduces production costs by $20,000 per year.

5. As a result of a more intense effort by salespeople, sales are increased by 20%; operating assets remain unchanged.

6. At the beginning of the year, obsolete inventory carried on the books at a cost of $40,000 is scrapped and written off as a loss, thereby lowering net operating income.

7. At the beginning of the year, the company uses $200,000 of cash (received on accounts receivable) to repurchase some of its common stock.

PROBLEM 11–25 Basic Transfer Pricing LO 11–3

Alpha and Beta are divisions within the same company. The managers of both divisions are evaluated based on their own division's return on investment (ROI). Assume the following information relative to the two divisions:

		Case		
	1	2	3	4
Alpha Division:				
Capacity in units	80,000	400,000	150,000	300,000
Number of units now being sold to outside				
customers	80,000	400,000	100,000	300,000
Selling price per unit to outside customers	$30	$90	$75	$50
Variable costs per unit	$18	$65	$40	$26
Fixed costs per unit (based on capacity)	$6	$15	$20	$9
Beta Division:				
Number of units needed annually	5,000	30,000	20,000	120,000
Purchase price now being paid to an				
outside supplier	$27	$89	$75*	—

*Before any purchase discount.

Required:

1. Refer to case 1 shown above. Alpha Division can avoid $2 per unit in commissions on any sales to Beta Division.
    a. What is Alpha Divisions's lowest acceptable transfer price?
    b. What is Beta Division's highest acceptable transfer price?
    c. What is the range of acceptable transfer prices (if any) between the two divisions? Will the managers probably agree to a transfer? Explain.

2. Refer to case 2 shown above. A study indicates Alpha Division can avoid $5 per unit in shipping costs on any sales to Beta Division.
    a. What is Alpha Divisions's lowest acceptable transfer price?
    b. What is Beta Division's highest acceptable transfer price?
    c. What is the range of acceptable transfer prices (if any) between the two divisions? Would you expect any disagreement between the two divisional managers over what the exact transfer price should be? Explain.
    d. Assume Alpha Division offers to sell 30,000 units to Beta Division for $88 per unit and that Beta Division refuses this price. What will be the loss in potential profits for the company as a whole?

3. Refer to case 3 shown above. Assume Beta Division is now receiving an 8% price discount from the outside supplier.
    a. What is Alpha Divisions's lowest acceptable transfer price?
    b. What is Beta Division's highest acceptable transfer price?
    c. What is the range of acceptable transfer prices (if any) between the two divisions? Will the managers probably agree to a transfer? Explain.
    d. Assume Beta Division offers to purchase 20,000 units from Alpha Division at $60 per unit. If Alpha Division accepts this price, would you expect its ROI to increase, decrease, or remain unchanged? Why?

4. Refer to case 4 shown above. Assume Beta Division wants Alpha Division to provide it with 120,000 units of a *different* product from the one Alpha Division is producing now. The new product would require $21 per unit in variable costs and would require that Alpha Division cut back production of its present product by 45,000 units annually. What is Alpha Division's lowest acceptable transfer price?

Select cases are available in Connect.

CASE 11–26 Transfer Pricing; Divisional Performance LO 11–3

Weller Industries is a decentralized organization with six divisions. The company's Electrical Division produces a variety of electrical items, including an X52 electrical fitting. The Electrical Division (which is operating at capacity) sells this fitting to its regular customers for $7.50 each; the fitting has a variable manufacturing cost of $4.25.

The company's Brake Division has asked the Electrical Division to supply it with a large quantity of X52 fittings for only $5 each. The Brake Division, which is operating at 50% of capacity, will put the fitting into a brake unit that it will produce and sell to a large commercial airplane manufacturer. The cost of the brake unit being built by the Brake Division follows:

Purchased parts (from outside vendors)	$22.50
Electrical fitting X52.	5.00
Other variable costs.	14.00
Fixed overhead and administration.	8.00
Total cost per brake unit	$49.50

Although the $5 price for the X52 fitting represents a substantial discount from the regular $7.50 price, the manager of the Brake Division believes the price concession is necessary if his division is to get the contract for the airplane brake units. He has heard "through the grapevine" that the airplane manufacturer plans to reject his bid if it is more than $50 per brake unit. Thus, if the Brake Division is forced to pay the regular $7.50 price for the X52 fitting, either it will not get the contract, or it will suffer a substantial loss at a time when it is already operating at only 50% of capacity. The manager of the Brake Division argues that the price concession is imperative to the well-being of both his division and the company as a whole.

Weller Industries uses return on investment (ROI) to measure divisional performance.

Required:

1. What is the Electrical Division's lowest acceptable transfer price? If you were the manager of the Electrical Division, would you supply the X52 fitting to the Brake Division for $5 each as requested? Why or why not?

2. Assuming the airplane brakes can be sold for $50, what is the financial advantage (disadvantage) for the company as a whole (on a per-unit basis) if the Electrical Division supplies fittings to the Brake Division? Explain your answer.

3. What is the Brake Division's highest acceptable transfer price? In principle, should it be possible for the two divisional managers to agree to a transfer price in this particular situation?

4. Discuss the organizational behavior problems, if any, inherent in this situation. What would you advise the company's president to do in this situation?

(CMA, adapted)

Strategic Performance Measurement

Hillary Kladke/Moment/Getty Images

LEARNING OBJECTIVES

After studying Chapter 12, you should be able to:

LO 12–1 Identify examples of performance measures that are appropriate for each of the four balanced scorecard categories.

LO 12–2 Identify the four types of quality costs and use them to create a quality cost report.

LO 12–3 Understand how to calculate throughput (manufacturing cycle) time, delivery cycle time, manufacturing cycle efficiency (MCE), and overall equipment effectiveness (OEE).

LO 12–4 Understand how to construct and use a balanced scorecard.

Data Analytics available in Connect to complement this chapter

ENTREPRENEUR SPOTLIGHT

Collette DiVitto developed a passion for baking while attending high school. After experimenting with numerous recipes, she created a cinnamon chocolate chip cookie her friends and family described as amazing! After completing Clemson University's LIFE program, she founded ColletLey's Cookies (www.colletteys.com), which sells "The Amazing Cookie" as well as other tempting treats, such as oatmeal raisin cookies, peanut butter cookies, and gluten-free cinnamon chocolate chip cookies. In addition to internet sales, Collette's products are sold in nine stores across three states.

Managerial Accounting: The Practical Application

Collettey's Cookies maintains a strategic performance measurement dashboard on its website that separates its goals into three phases (https://www.colletteys.com /company-growth/). Some of its goals across these phases include "move to a commercial kitchen" (100% achieved), "build corporate accounts" (27% achieved), "create PR strategy" (82% achieved), and "design and launch merchandise" (62% achieved).

Corporate Social Responsibility: Serving all Stakeholders

Collettey's Cookies' mission includes creating jobs for people with special needs, changing the public's perception of this population's capabilities, and advocating for tax incentives for employers that hire workers with special needs. Her website notes, "82% of people with a disability are unemployed. Many of them want to work, have valuable skills to contribute, and ache for the chance to prove themselves and earn a living." Her dashboard includes numerous measures that support the company's mission, such as "open the world's eye to see abilities" (65% achieved), "develop workshops for others struggling with employment" (85% achieved), and "visit and speak at schools" (78% achieved). ■

Source: www.colletteys.com

A **company uses performance measures** for a variety of reasons such as providing information that enables its employees to execute strategies and then influencing their rewards for doing so. The centerpiece of this chapter is a particular type of performance measurement system called a *balanced scorecard*. A **balanced scorecard** consists of an integrated set of performance measures that are derived from and support a company's strategy.

The Balanced Scorecard: An Overview

Exhibit 12–1 highlights four key concepts related to the balanced scorecard. First, as shown on the left side of the exhibit, a company's balanced scorecard must emanate from its vision and *strategy* for succeeding in the marketplace. A **strategy** is a "game plan" that enables a company to attract customers by distinguishing itself from competitors. These distinguishing characteristics, or what are more formally called *customer value propositions,* are the essence of strategy.

As discussed in the Prologue, customer value propositions tend to fall into three broad categories—*customer intimacy, operational excellence,* and *product leadership.* Companies that adopt a *customer intimacy* strategy are in essence saying to their customers, "You should choose us because we can customize our products and services to meet your individual needs better than our competitors." Companies that pursue the second customer value proposition, called *operational excellence,* are saying to their target customers, "You should choose us because we deliver products and services faster, more conveniently, and at a lower price than our competitors." Companies pursuing the third

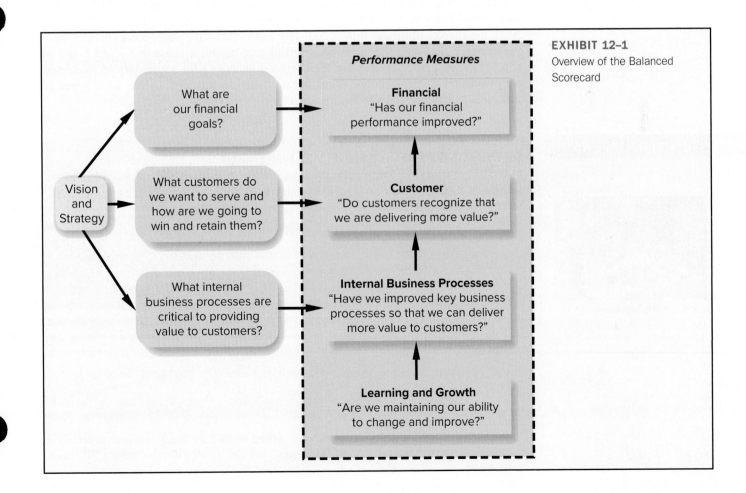

EXHIBIT 12–1
Overview of the Balanced Scorecard

customer value proposition, called *product leadership*, are saying to their target customers, "You should choose us because we offer more innovative and higher quality products than our competitors."[1]

The second key point from Exhibit 12–1 is that the measures included in a balanced scorecard usually fall into four categories: learning and growth, internal business processes, customer, and financial. Internal business processes are what the company does in an attempt to satisfy customers. For example, in a manufacturing company, assembling a product is an internal business process. In an airline, handling baggage is an internal business process. Some of the measures included in these categories may be financial, while others may be nonfinancial in nature.

The third insight from Exhibit 12–1 is that a company's strategy has an important influence on the measures it will include in the four categories of its balanced scorecard. For example, a company focused on product leadership might create learning and growth measures related to its engineering training program, internal business process measures related to its research and development process, customer measures related to their perceptions of product innovation, and financial measures related to sales growth from new products. All of these measures have a shared emphasis on new product development, which would be very important to a company pursuing a product leadership customer value proposition.

The fourth key idea related to the balanced scorecard (as indicated by the vertical arrows in Exhibit 12–1) is that the four categories of measures are linked to one another in a cause-and-effect fashion as follows: a company's employees need to continuously learn in order to improve internal business processes; improving business processes is necessary to improve customer satisfaction; and improving customer satisfaction is necessary to improve financial results.

The remainder of the chapter is organized in three main sections. The first section describes a variety of performance measures for each of the four balanced scorecard categories—learning and growth, internal business processes, customer, and financial. Next, the chapter illustrates how a company can build a complete scorecard, including performance measures that have been linked together on a cause-and-effect basis, to support its strategic goals. Finally, the chapter concludes with a summary of social and environmental performance measures because many companies include these types of measures within their balanced scorecards.

IN BUSINESS

SAUL LOEB/AFP/Getty Images

RETHINKING PERFORMANCE MEASUREMENT

As restaurants started reopening during the COVID-19 (coronavirus) pandemic, "service with safety" became an imperative. Restaurant staff were retrained in numerous ways, such as ripping up "disposable menus in front of customers after taking their orders to assure them that they aren't being reused" and limiting contact with diners by "uncorking a bottle of wine and setting it on the table instead of filling their glasses."

In this chapter, you'll learn how companies use the balanced scorecard to organize their performance measures into four categories—financial, customer, internal business process, and learning and growth. The intuitive appeal of these four categories can be readily understood through the eyes of post-COVID-19 restaurant owners as they confronted the new reality that their financial success was going to be heavily influenced by their customers' intensified attention to cleanliness, which in turn had important implications for redesigning their business processes and training their employees.

Source: Te-Ping Chen and Heather Haddon, "Rules Press Restaurant Staff," *The Wall Street Journal*, June 15, 2020, pp. B1–B2.

---

[1] These three customer value propositions were defined by Michael Treacy and Fred Wiersema in "Customer Intimacy and Other Value Disciplines," *Harvard Business Review,* Volume 71 Issue 1, pp. 84–93.

EXHIBIT 12–2
Examples of Learning and Growth Performance Measures

Recruiting:

- Percent of "outstanding" interview candidates that accepted our job offer (+)
- Recruiting expenditures per hired employee (−)

Skills development:

- Percent of employees that strongly agree with the statement "I am consistently given the resources that I need to do my job." (+)
- Average mentorship hours per employee (+)
- Average training hours per employee (+)

Compensation and advancement:

- Percent of leadership positions filled with internal candidates (+)
- Percent of workforce promoted within the last three years (+)
- Average pay raise percentage per employee (+)

Wellness/safety:

- Absenteeism rate (−)
- Average number of workplace accidents per employee (−)

Job satisfaction:

- Percent of employees that strongly agree with the statement "This is a great place to work." (+)
- Percent of employees that strongly agree with the statement "My contribution to the company is recognized and respected by my co-workers." (+)
- Number of process improvement suggestions per employee (+)

Retention:

- Employee turnover percentage (−)
- Average years of tenure per employee (+)

Learning and Growth Measures

It is often said by business leaders and consultants that a company's employees are its most important asset. This axiom is grounded in the belief that if a company with a viable strategy enables its employees to continuously learn and expand their capabilities, it should ultimately improve financial performance.

Exhibit 12–2 contains 15 examples of learning and growth measures that organizations might include in their balanced scorecards. The measures are organized under six headings that influence employee learning and growth—recruiting, skills development, compensation and advancement, wellness/safety, job satisfaction, and retention. Each measure contains a parenthetical + or − to indicate if the goal is to increase or decrease the measure. For example, the measure *percent of "outstanding" interview candidates that accepted our job offer* has a parenthetical + sign because it would be expected to increase over time.

Each measure included in the learning and growth section of a balanced scorecard should influence other measures within the scorecard. For example, a company may hypothesize that increasing its *average training hours per employee* will lead to process improvements such as fewer errors. Or it may hypothesize that lowering its employee turnover percentage will lead to greater loyalty from customers who appreciate working with a "familiar face."

LEARNING OBJECTIVE 12–1
Identify examples of performance measures that are appropriate for each of the four balanced scorecard categories.

IN BUSINESS

TOUGHER INTERVIEWS INCREASE JOB ACCEPTANCE RATES

Research from Glassdoor suggests that job acceptance rates from candidates between the ages of 25 and 34 rise by 3.1 percent when they perceive job interviews to be increasingly difficult. Glassdoor's senior economist Daniel Zhao said, "job seekers, especially younger ones, want the chance to perform and be assessed for the unique skills they bring to the table. . . [; therefore,] having candidates complete skills tests as part of the vetting process raises acceptance rates by 2.5 percentage points." On the contrary, when these same job applicants are asked to take a personality test, it decreases their job acceptance rate by 2.3 percent.

From a balanced scorecard perspective, a company's job offer acceptance rate is an important learning and growth measure that can eventually drive improvements in other measures related to internal business process performance, customer satisfaction, and profits.

Source: Kathryn Dill, "Tough Interview Process is Linked to a Higher Job-Acceptance Rate," *The Wall Street Journal,* February 27, 2020, p. B4.

EXHIBIT 12–3

Examples of Internal Business Process Measures

Innovation:

- Number of new products designed (+)
- Number of patents approved (+)
- Percentage of previously designed parts used in new products (+)

Product and service quality:

- Number of warranty claims (–)
- Defect-free units as a percentage of completed units (+)
- Percent of customer complaints settled on first contact (+)

Agility:

- Number of modular product designs (+)
- Percent of suppliers with long-term contracts (+)
- Average batch size (–)

Cost:

- Cost of quality (–)
- Non-value-added activity costs (–)
- Lost sales due to out-of-stock merchandise (–)

Time:

- Delivery cycle time (–)
- Throughput (Manufacturing cycle) time (–)
- Manufacturing cycle efficiency (MCE) (+)

Lean resource management:

- Overall equipment effectiveness (OEE) (+)
- WIP Inventory as a percent of sales (+)
- Workstation cleanliness score (+)

Internal Business Process Measures

Effective managers understand that *business processes,* rather than functional departments, serve the needs of a company's most important stakeholders—its customers. A **business process** is a series of steps that are followed in order to carry out some task in a business. These steps often span departmental boundaries, thereby requiring managers to cooperate to improve internal business process performance measures.

Exhibit 12–3 contains 18 examples of internal business process measures that organizations might include in their balanced scorecards. The measures are organized under six dimensions of business process performance—innovation, product and service quality, agility (which refers to a company's ability to adapt or change quickly), cost, time, and lean resource management (as described in the Prologue). Each measure contains a parenthetical + or – to indicate if the goal is to increase or decrease the measure.

As mentioned earlier, each company's internal business process measures will vary depending on its strategy. A company focused on product leadership may choose business process measures related to innovation and product quality. A company that differentiates itself from competitors based on operational excellence may select process measures related to cost and time. Finally, a company with a customer intimacy strategy may focus on service quality and agility measures.

Customer Measures

Exhibit 12–4 contains 18 examples of customer measures that organizations might include in their balanced scorecards. The measures are organized under six headings—customer satisfaction, customer acquisition/retention, customer lifetime value, customer loyalty, customer service, and customer value proposition.

If a company improves its learning and growth and internal business process measures, these improvements must ultimately have a positive influence on its customer measures. If this cause-and-effect relationship does not materialize, it suggests the company does not have a complete understanding of the performance attributes shaping its customers' perceptions and behaviors.

EXHIBIT 12–4

Example of Customer Measures

Customer satisfaction:

- Percent of customers that strongly agree with the statement "I would readily recommend your company to someone else." (+)
- Number of customer referrals (+)

Customer acquisition/retention:

- Market share percentage (+)
- Customer defection rate (−)
- Average customer acquisition cost (−)
- Percent of customer leads that generate a sale (+)

Customer lifetime value:

- Average revenue per order (+)
- Average gross margin per order (+)
- Average time between purchases (−)

Customer loyalty:

- Percent of a customer's overall spending committed to our company (also called "share of wallet") (+)
- Number of collaborative customer-driven product innovations (+)

Customer service:

- Percent of customers that strongly agree with the statement "My order was delivered on time." (+)
- Percent of customers that strongly agree with the statement "My problem was resolved quickly." (+)
- Percent of customers that strongly agree with the statement "Your website was easy to use." (+)
- Percent of customers that strongly agree with the statement "Your employees treated me courteously." (+)

Customer value proposition:

- Customer perception of our product leadership (+)
- Customer perception of our operational excellence (+)
- Customer perception of our customer intimacy (+)

IN BUSINESS

AMAZON'S CUSTOMER SATISFACTION DROPS, BUT ITS SALES GROW

Usually, companies expect to see a correlation between customer satisfaction and sales—as customer satisfaction grows, so do sales. However, during the COVID-19 pandemic, this was not the case at Amazon.com. Research conducted by RBC Capital Markets showed a "sharp rise in the number of Amazon customers who made at least two to three purchases a month, as well as the number of those who claim to have spent $200 or more on Amazon over past 90 days." Conversely, the number of customers who were "very satisfied or extremely satisfied" with Amazon dipped from 73% the prior year to 64%. Given that investors expect Amazon's sales to grow 18% per year, the company will be working hard to reverse its decline in customer satisfaction.

Source: Dan Gallagher, "Amazon Doesn't Need No Satisfaction," *The Wall Street Journal*, June 9, 2020, p. B12.

Ross D Franklin/AP/Shutterstock

Financial Measures

Exhibit 12–5 includes 20 examples of financial measures that are organized under six headings—sales, profits, profitability ratios, trend performance, cash flows, and market performance. The balanced scorecard framework rejects the notion that improving process-oriented measures automatically leads to financial success. On the contrary, the scorecard includes a financial perspective for the express purpose of holding organizations accountable for translating improvements in nonfinancial performance to "bottom-line" results. If favorable trends in a company's learning and growth, internal business processes, and customer measures do not translate to financial results, the balanced scorecard is designed to force the organization to reexamine its strategy for differentiating itself from competitors.

EXHIBIT 12–5

Examples of Financial Measures

Sales:

- Sales from new customers (+)
- Sales from products less than three years old (+)
- Patent-protected sales (+)

Profitability ratios:

- Gross margin percentage (+)
- Net profit margin percentage (+)
- Return on assets (ROA) (+)
- Return on equity (ROE) (+)

Cash flows:

- Net cash flow from operating activities (+)
- Net cash flow from operating activities ÷ average operating assets (+)
- Net cash flow from operating activities ÷ sales (+)

Profits:

- Contribution margin (+)
- Net operating income (+)
- Residual income (+)

Trend performance:

- Sales growth rate (+)
- Contribution margin growth rate (+)
- Net operating income growth rate (+)
- Net cash flow from operating activities growth rate (+)

Market performance:

- Stock price (+)
- Earnings-per-share (EPS) (+)
- Price-earnings ratio (+)

Cost of Quality: A Closer Look

This section takes a closer look at one of the internal business process measures included in Exhibit 12–3—the cost of quality. It defines four types of quality costs and explains how to compute the cost of quality.

Cost of Quality

LEARNING OBJECTIVE 12–2

Identify the four types of quality costs and use them to create a quality cost report.

A product that meets or exceeds its design specifications and is free of defects that degrade its appearance or diminish its performance is said to have high **quality of conformance.** Preventing, detecting, and dealing with defects that lower the quality of conformance causes the incurrence of four types of quality costs—*prevention costs, appraisal costs, internal failure costs,* and *external failure costs.* **Prevention costs** support activities whose purpose is to prevent defects from occurring. **Appraisal costs,** which are sometimes called *inspection costs,* are incurred to identify production defects *before* they are shipped to customers. **Internal failure costs** result from identifying defects before they are shipped to customers. **External failure costs** result when a defective product is delivered to customers. Exhibit 12–6 contains examples of costs within each of these four categories.

The sum of these four types of costs is called the **cost of quality.** A company's goal is to lower its cost of quality over time. The key to accomplishing this goal is recognizing the following distinction—prevention costs and appraisal costs are incurred in an effort to keep production defects from falling into the hands of customers, whereas internal failure costs and external failure costs are incurred because defects occur despite efforts to prevent them. Thus, the objective of an effective quality management program is to make additional investments in prevention and appraisal that are more than offset by reductions in internal and external failure costs. Preventing defects from occurring is preferable to detecting them after they have occurred.

A company can prepare a *quality cost report* to help monitor its progress in terms of lowering its overall cost of quality. A **quality cost report** details the prevention costs, appraisal costs, and the costs of internal and external failures that arise from the

EXHIBIT 12–6
Examples of Quality Costs

Prevention Costs:

Systems development
Quality engineering
Quality training
Quality circles
Statistical process control activities
Supervision of prevention activities
Quality data gathering, analysis, and reporting
Quality improvement projects
Technical support provided to suppliers
Audits of the effectiveness of the quality system

Appraisal Costs:

Test and inspection of incoming materials
Test and inspection of in-process goods
Final product testing and inspection
Supplies used in testing and inspection
Supervision of testing and inspection activities
Depreciation of test equipment
Maintenance of test equipment
Plant utilities in the inspection area
Field testing and appraisal at customer site

Internal Failure Costs:

Net cost of scrap
Net cost of spoilage
Rework labor and overhead
Reinspection of reworked products
Retesting of reworked products
Downtime caused by quality problems
Disposal of production defects
Analysis of the cause of defects in production
Reentering data because of keying errors
Debugging software errors

External Failure Costs:

Cost of field servicing and handling complaints
Warranty repairs and replacements
Repairs and replacements beyond the warranty period
Product recalls
Liability arising from production defects
Returns and allowances arising from quality problems
Lost sales arising from a reputation for poor quality

company's current quality management efforts. Exhibit 12–7 contains an example of a quality cost report for Ventura Company.

Several things should be noted from the data in the exhibit. First, Ventura Company's quality costs are poorly distributed in both years, with most of the costs due to either internal failure or external failure. The external failure costs are particularly high in Year 1 in comparison to other costs.

Second, note that the company increased its spending on prevention and appraisal activities in Year 2. As a result, internal failure costs went up in that year (from $2 million in Year 1 to $3 million in Year 2), but external failure costs dropped sharply (from $5.15 million in Year 1 to only $2 million in Year 2). Because of the increase in appraisal activity in Year 2, more defects were caught inside the company before they were shipped to customers. This resulted in more cost for scrap, rework, and so forth, but saved huge amounts in warranty repairs, warranty replacements, and other external failure costs.

Third, note that as a result of greater emphasis on prevention and appraisal, *total* quality cost decreased in Year 2. As continued emphasis is placed on prevention and appraisal in future years, total quality cost should continue to decrease. That is, future increases in prevention and appraisal costs should be more than offset by decreases in failure costs. Moreover, appraisal costs should also decrease over time as more effort is placed into prevention.

Quality Cost Reports: Strengths and Limitations

A quality cost report has several uses. First, quality cost information helps managers see the financial significance of defects. Managers usually are not aware of the magnitude of their quality costs because these costs cut across departmental lines and are not normally tracked and accumulated by the cost system. Thus, when first presented with a quality cost report, managers often are surprised by the amount of cost attributable to poor quality.

EXHIBIT 12–7
Quality Cost Report

Ventura Company
Quality Cost Report
For Years 1 and 2

	Year 1		Year 2	
	Amount	Percent*	Amount	Percent*
Prevention costs:				
Systems development	$ 270,000	0.54%	$ 400,000	0.80%
Quality training	130,000	0.26%	210,000	0.42%
Supervision of prevention activities	40,000	0.08%	70,000	0.14%
Quality improvement projects	210,000	0.42%	320,000	0.64%
Total prevention cost	650,000	1.30%	1,000,000	2.00%
Appraisal costs:				
Inspection	560,000	1.12%	600,000	1.20%
Reliability testing	420,000	0.84%	580,000	1.16%
Supervision of testing and inspection	80,000	0.16%	120,000	0.24%
Depreciation of test equipment	140,000	0.28%	200,000	0.40%
Total appraisal cost	1,200,000	2.40%	1,500,000	3.00%
Internal failure costs:				
Net cost of scrap	750,000	1.50%	900,000	1.80%
Rework labor and overhead	810,000	1.62%	1,430,000	2.86%
Downtime due to defects in quality	100,000	0.20%	170,000	0.34%
Disposal of production defects	340,000	0.68%	500,000	1.00%
Total internal failure cost	2,000,000	4.00%	3,000,000	6.00%
External failure costs:				
Warranty repairs	900,000	1.80%	400,000	0.80%
Warranty replacements	2,300,000	4.60%	870,000	1.74%
Allowances	630,000	1.26%	130,000	0.26%
Cost of field servicing	1,320,000	2.64%	600,000	1.20%
Total external failure cost	5,150,000	10.30%	2,000,000	4.00%
Total quality cost	$9,000,000	18.00%	$7,500,000	15.00%

*As a percentage of total sales. In each year, sales totaled $50,000,000.

Second, quality cost information helps managers identify the relative importance of the quality problems faced by their companies. For example, the quality cost report may show that scrap is a major quality problem or that the company is incurring huge warranty costs. With this information, managers have a better idea of where to focus their efforts.

Third, quality cost information helps managers see whether their quality costs are poorly distributed. In general, quality costs should be distributed more toward prevention and appraisal activities and less toward failures.

Counterbalancing these uses, quality cost information has three limitations. First, simply measuring and reporting quality costs does not solve quality problems. Problems can be solved only by taking action. Second, results usually lag behind quality improvement programs. Initially, total quality cost may even increase as quality control systems are designed and installed. Decreases in quality costs may not begin to occur until the quality program has been in effect for some time. And third, the most important quality cost, lost sales arising from customer ill will, is usually omitted from the quality cost report because it is difficult to estimate.

Operating Performance Measures: A Closer Look

This section takes a closer look at four of the internal business process measures included in Exhibit 12–3—throughput (manufacturing cycle) time, delivery cycle time, manufacturing cycle efficiency (MCE), and overall equipment effectiveness (OEE).

LEARNING OBJECTIVE 12–3
Understand how to calculate throughput (manufacturing cycle) time, delivery cycle time, manufacturing cycle efficiency (MCE), and overall equipment effectiveness (OEE).

Throughput (Manufacturing Cycle) Time

The elapsed time from when production is started until finished goods are shipped to customers is called **throughput time,** or *manufacturing cycle time.* The goal is to continuously reduce this measure; the formula for computing it is as follows:

$$\text{Throughput (manufacturing cycle) time} =$$
$$\text{Process time} + \text{Inspection time} + \text{Move time} + \text{Queue time}$$

Process time is the amount of time work is actually done on the product. *Inspection time* is the amount of time spent ensuring that the product is not defective. *Move time* is the time required to move materials or partially completed products from workstation to workstation. *Queue time* is the amount of time a product spends waiting to be worked on, to be moved, to be inspected, or to be shipped. Only one of these four activities adds value to the product—process time. The other three activities—inspecting, moving, and queuing—add no value and should be eliminated as much as possible.

Delivery Cycle Time

The elapsed time from when a customer order is received until the finished goods are shipped is called **delivery cycle time.** The goal is to reduce this measure; the formula for computing it is as follows:

$$\text{Delivery cycle time} = \text{Wait time} + \text{Throughput time}$$

Wait time is the elapsed time from when a customer order is received until production of the order is started. This is a non-value-added activity that should be reduced or eliminated. When companies succeed in drastically reducing or eliminating wait time plus the non-value-added components of throughput time, it often enables them to increase customer satisfaction and profits. The relation between throughput (manufacturing cycle) time and delivery cycle time is illustrated in Exhibit 12–8.

IN BUSINESS

PANERA SLICES ITS WAIT TIME

Panera's customers used to wait in line for eight minutes to place an order, and then they had to stand in what the company's CEO called a "mosh pit" to receive their order—which was fulfilled incorrectly 10 percent of the time. Over the course of six years, the company reduced its wait time to one minute and eliminated the "mosh pit" by implementing self-ordering kiosks, food delivery to the customers' table, digital ordering, and off-site food delivery. Digital orders now comprise 26 percent of total sales at Panera's 900 company-owned locations. The company also plans to add 10,000 delivery drivers to the 4,000 that it currently employs.

Source: Julie Jargon, "Panera Slices Lines with Mobile," *The Wall Street Journal,* June 3–4, 2017, pp. B1–B2.

Ken Wolter/Shutterstock

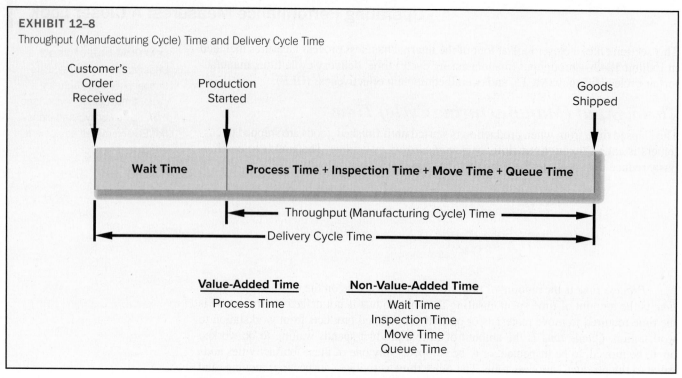

EXHIBIT 12–8
Throughput (Manufacturing Cycle) Time and Delivery Cycle Time

Manufacturing Cycle Efficiency (MCE)

Through concerted efforts to eliminate the *non-value-added* activities of inspecting, moving, and queuing, some companies have reduced their throughput time to only a fraction of previous levels. In turn, this has helped to reduce the delivery cycle time from months to only weeks or hours. Throughput time, which is a key measure in delivery performance, can be put into better perspective by computing the **manufacturing cycle efficiency (MCE).** The MCE is computed by relating the value-added time to the throughput time. The goal is to increase this measure; the formula for computing it is as follows:

$$MCE = \frac{\text{Value-added time (Process time)}}{\text{Throughput (manufacturing cycle) time}}$$

Any non-value-added time results in an MCE of less than 1. An MCE of 0.5, for example, would mean that half of the total production time consists of inspection, moving, and similar non-value-added activities. In many manufacturing companies, the MCE is less than 0.1 (10%), which means that 90 percent of the time a unit is in process is spent on activities that do not add value to the product. Monitoring the MCE helps companies to reduce non-value-added activities and thus get products into the hands of customers more quickly and at a lower cost.

Example To provide an example of these measures, consider the following data for Novex Company:

Novex Company keeps careful track of the time to complete customer orders. During the most recent quarter, it recorded the following average times per order:

	Days
Wait time	17.0
Inspection time	0.4
Process time	2.0
Move time	0.6
Queue time	5.0

Goods are shipped as soon as production is completed.

Required:

1. Compute the throughput (manufacturing cycle) time.
2. Compute the manufacturing cycle efficiency (MCE).
3. What percentage of the production time is spent in non-value-added activities?
4. Compute the delivery cycle time.

Solution

1. Throughput time = Process time + Inspection time + Move time + Queue time

   = 2.0 days + 0.4 days + 0.6 days + 5.0 days

   = 8.0 days

2. Only process time represents value-added time; therefore, MCE would be computed as follows:

$$\text{MCE} = \frac{\text{Value-added time}}{\text{Throughput time}} = \frac{2.0 \text{ days}}{8.0 \text{ days}}$$

$$= 0.25$$

   Thus, once put into production, a typical order is actually being worked on only 25 percent of the time.

3. Because the MCE is 25 percent, 75 percent (100% − 25%) of total production time is spent in non-value-added activities.

4. Delivery cycle time = Wait time + Throughput time

   = 17.0 days + 8.0 days

   = 25.0 days

Overall Equipment Effectiveness (OEE)

Overall equipment effectiveness (OEE) is a performance measure used by many lean manufacturers. **Overall equipment effectiveness** measures the productivity of a piece of equipment in terms of three dimensions—utilization, efficiency, and quality. The equation for calculating OEE is as follows:

OEE = Utilization rate × Efficiency rate × Quality rate

where:

Utilization rate = Actual run time ÷ Machine time available
Efficiency rate = Actual run rate ÷ Ideal run rate
Quality rate = Defect-free output ÷ Total output

The keys to increasing the utilization rate include avoiding machine breakdowns and minimizing average setup times. The efficiency rate is maximized by avoiding minor work stoppages and by retaining and properly training operators to run and regularly maintain the machine. The quality rate is improved by reducing the number of defective units produced as a percent of the total output.

Example Jayson Company has demand for its only product that exceeds its manufacturing capacity. The company provided the following information for a machine whose limited capacity is prohibiting the company from producing and selling additional units.

Actual run time this week	4,550 minutes
Machine time available per week.	6,500 minutes
Actual run rate this week.	3.8 units per minute
Ideal run rate	4.0 units per minute
Defect-free output this week.	16,000 units
Total output this week (including defects).	17,290 units

Calculate the machine's OEE:

$$
\begin{aligned}
\text{Utilization rate} &= \text{Actual run time} \div \text{Machine time available} \\
&= 4{,}550 \text{ minutes} \div 6{,}500 \text{ minutes} \\
&= 0.70 \\
\text{Efficiency rate} &= \text{Actual run rate} \div \text{Ideal run rate} \\
&= 3.8 \text{ units per minute} \div 4.0 \text{ units per miute} \\
&= 0.95 \\
\text{Quality rate} &= \text{Defect-free output} \div \text{Total output} \\
&= 16{,}000 \text{ units} \div 17{,}290 \text{ units} \\
&= 0.925 \\
\text{OEE} &= \text{Utilization rate} \times \text{Efficiency rate} \times \text{Quality rate} \\
&= 0.70 \times 0.95 \times 0.925 \\
&= 0.615
\end{aligned}
$$

The overall equipment effectiveness can also be analyzed in terms of units produced as follows:

Maximum possible output (6,500 × 4.0) (a)		26,000
Utilization loss [(6,500 − 4,550) × 4.0]	7,800	
Efficiency loss [(4.0 − 3.8) × 4,550].	910	
Quality loss (17,290 − 16,000)	1,290	10,000
Defect-free output (b).		16,000
OEE (b) ÷ (a)		0.615

This analysis reveals that Jayson Company sacrificed 10,000 units of production (due to utilization, efficiency, and quality losses) that probably could have been sold to customers.

Constructing a Balanced Scorecard

LEARNING OBJECTIVE 12–4
Understand how to construct and use a balanced scorecard.

Earlier in the chapter, we introduced more than 70 examples of measures that companies might include in their balanced scorecards. Now we are shifting our focus to assembling these measures into a complete balanced scorecard. Our discussion will proceed in two steps. First, we'll demonstrate how companies can select strategy-driven measures and then link them together in a series of testable if-then hypothesis statements. Second, we'll discuss some important issues related to using balanced scorecard measures to evaluate and reward employees.

Selecting Balanced Scorecard Measures

At the beginning of the chapter, we mentioned that the four categories of a balanced scorecard are interrelated to one another. Those interrelationships were depicted by the vertical arrows in Exhibit 12–1—a company's employees need to continuously learn and grow in order to improve internal business processes; improving business processes is necessary to improve customer satisfaction; and improving customer satisfaction is necessary to improve financial results.

To illustrate these interrelationships, let's suppose that Jaguar's strategy is to offer distinctive, richly finished luxury automobiles to wealthy individuals who prize hand-crafted, individualized products. To deliver this customer intimacy value proposition to its wealthy target customers, Jaguar might create such a large number of options for details, such as leather seats, interior and exterior color combinations, and wooden dash-boards, that each car becomes virtually one of a kind. Instead of just offering tan or blue leather seats in standard cowhide, the company may offer customers the choice of an almost infinite palette of colors in any of a number of different exotic leathers. For such a system to work effectively, Jaguar would have to be able to deliver a completely custom-ized car within a reasonable amount of time—and without incurring more cost for this customization than the customer is willing to pay.

Exhibit 12–9 suggests how Jaguar might reflect this strategy in its balanced score-card. Each measure contains a parenthetical + or − to indicate if the goal is to increase or decrease the measure. The exhibit also contains arrows that link the measures together on a cause-and-effect basis. Each link can be read as a hypothesis in the form "If we improve this measure, then this other performance measure should also improve." Starting from the bottom of Exhibit 12–9, we can read the links between performance measures as follows.

If we increase our employee retention rate and our average training hours per employee, then it will increase the number of options available while decreasing the aver-age number of errors per vehicle and the average time to install an option. If we increase the number of options available, decrease the average number of errors per vehicle, and decrease the average time to install an option, then it will increase our customers' satis-faction with the number of options available, which in turn will increase our market share percentage in the luxury car market.

Continuing up Exhibit 12–9, if we increase our customers' satisfaction with the number of options available and decrease the average time to install an option, it will

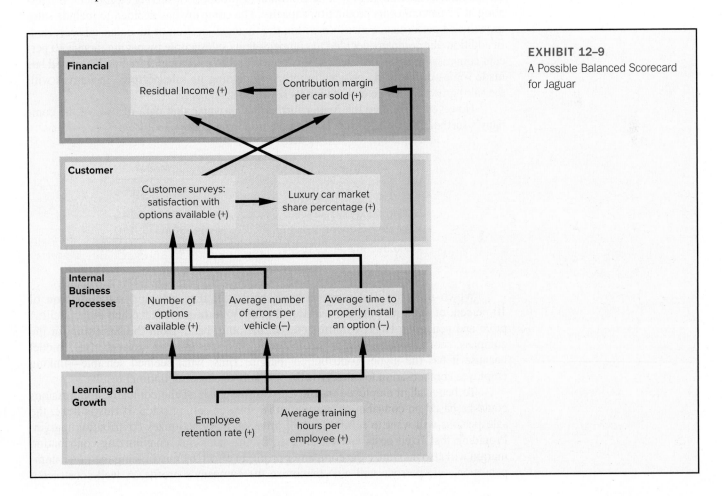

EXHIBIT 12–9
A Possible Balanced Scorecard for Jaguar

increase our contribution margin per car sold. Finally, if we increase our market share percentage in the luxury car market and our contribution margin per car sold, it will increase our residual income.

In essence, the balanced scorecard lays out a theory of how the company can take concrete actions to attain its desired outcomes (financial, in this case). The strategy laid out in Exhibit 12–9 seems plausible, but it should be regarded as only a theory. For example, if the company succeeds in increasing the number of options available and in decreasing its average number of errors per vehicle and its average time to install an option and yet there is no increase in customer satisfaction, the market share percentage, the contribution margin per car, or residual income, the strategy would have to be reconsidered. One of the advantages of the balanced scorecard is that it continually tests the theories underlying management's strategy. If a strategy is not working, it should become evident when some of the predicted effects (i.e., higher residual income) don't occur. Without this feedback, an organization may drift on indefinitely with an ineffective strategy based on faulty assumptions.

Tying Compensation to the Balanced Scorecard

Incentive compensation for employees, such as bonuses, can, and probably should, be tied to balanced scorecard performance measures. However, this should be done only after the organization has been successfully managed with the scorecard for some time—perhaps a year or more. Managers must be confident that the performance measures are reliable, sensible, understood by those who are being evaluated, and not easily manipulated.

While selecting measures for a balanced scorecard and then using those measures to reward employees may seem pretty straightforward, too often organizations use performance measures to reward employees in ways that cause suboptimal results. To illustrate this point, let's assume that Pipeline Unlimited, a producer of surfing equipment, is operating at 75 percent of its production capacity. The company has decided to include sales growth as a performance measure within the financial portion of its balanced scorecard. In addition, the company decided to compensate its salespeople by paying them a 10 percent commission based on sales. At this point, it seems as though Pipeline Unlimited has made some very sensible choices in terms of aligning its salespersons' incentives with the sales growth measure included in its balanced scorecard.

However, to explore the matter further, let's assume that data for two of the company's surfboards, the XR7 and Turbo models, appear below:

	Model	
	XR7	Turbo
Selling price	$695	$749
Variable expenses	344	410
Contribution margin	$351	$339

Which model will salespeople push hardest if they are paid a commission of 10 percent of sales revenue? The answer is the Turbo because it has the higher selling price and hence the larger commission. On the other hand, from the standpoint of the company, profits will be greater if salespeople steer customers toward the XR7 model because it has the higher contribution margin. Thus, what seemed sensible—linking employee compensation to sales growth—is likely to cause suboptimal results.

To better align employee incentives with the goals of the company, commissions could be based on contribution margin rather than on selling price. If this is done, the salespersons will want to sell the mix of products that maximizes contribution margin. Providing that fixed costs are not affected by the sales mix, maximizing contribution margin will also maximize the company's profit. In effect, by maximizing their own compensation, salespersons will also maximize the company's profits. A well-constructed balanced scorecard should achieve similar alignment. It should motivate employees to choose actions that align with the company's overall strategic goals, and it should properly reward them for doing so.

STARBUCKS ATTENDS TO ITS SOCIAL RESPONSIBILITIES

Starbucks is setting ambitious goals for reducing its impact on the environment. The company is looking at numerous opportunities such as reducing food and packaging waste, expanding the use of reusable coffee cups, adding plant-based options to its menu, improving the energy efficiency of newly constructed stores, and improving its suppliers' environmental practices. Kevin Johnson, the company's CEO, said, "the journey we undertake is not only the right one for Starbuck's responsibility as a corporate citizen of the world but is also fundamental to our brand relevance." In terms of measurable goals, by 2030, the company plans to reduce its carbon emissions and the waste it sends to landfills by 50%.

Source: Heather Haddon, "Starbucks Pledges to Slash Water Use, Waste, Emissions," *The Wall Street Journal*, January 22, 2020, p. B7.

Andrew Balcombe/Shutterstock

Corporate Social Responsibility Performance Measures

As stated in the Prologue, companies are responsible for creating strategies that produce financial results that satisfy stockholders. However, they also have a *corporate social responsibility* to serve other stakeholders—such as customers, employees, suppliers, communities, and environmental and human rights advocates—whose interests are tied to the company's performance. **Corporate social responsibility** (CSR) is a concept whereby organizations consider the needs of all stakeholders when making decisions. CSR extends beyond legal compliance to include voluntary actions that satisfy stakeholder expectations.

Many of the world's largest companies prepare corporate social responsibility performance reports (also called sustainability reports) that are shared with their external stakeholders. In addition, a growing percentage of these companies are hiring public accounting firms to provide assurance services that lend additional credibility to the disclosures contained in those reports. While many of these companies undoubtedly feel a moral obligation to serve diverse stakeholders, these same companies also understand that social and environmental issues provide them with immense *opportunities* and *risks*.

From an opportunity management standpoint, some companies have responded to social and environmental challenges by making strategic investments in product, service, and process innovations that increase stakeholder satisfaction and profits. For example, Toyota developed the hybrid-engine Prius to respond to societal concerns about auto emissions and to grow stockholder wealth. Timberland uses recycled plastic from millions of water bottles in the manufacture of its Earthkeepers® footwear product line. In turn, the Earthkeepers® collection has become one of Timberland's fastest growing and most profitable product lines. Procter & Gamble decided to consolidate its distribution centers, thereby lowering its transportation costs while simultaneously reducing its fuel consumption and the associated emissions.

From a risk management standpoint, most companies understand that if they overlook their social and environmental responsibilities, it will damage their reputations. For example, if a company discharges lethal pollutants into the environment, purchases products from an overseas supplier that employs child labor, or systematically discriminates against a group of its employees, the adverse consequences of those actions will cause negative publicity. This, in turn, will trigger undesirable after-effects such as customer boycotts or defections, a decline in job applications from top-notch candidates, an increase in employee turnover, disenchanted investors, and possibly even lawsuits and government-imposed fines.

Whether a company's interest in CSR is grounded in morality, opportunism, risk management, or a combination of all three, it needs to accompany this interest with measures and reports that can be tracked by managers and shared with external stakeholders.

Global Reporting Initiative

The Global Reporting Initiative (GRI) is a leading organization in the field of social and environmental performance measurement.[2] It has created a widely adopted sustainability reporting framework that includes three universal standards and three sets of topic-specific standards related to economic, environmental, and social performance.

The universal standards require companies to provide disclosures related to topics such as strategy and analysis, stakeholder engagement, and governance. More specifically, they require a company's most senior decision maker (such as its CEO) to describe the company's strategic priorities, plans, and achievements with respect to corporate social performance. They also mandate that a company identify its stakeholders and summarize the means and frequency of its communications with them. Finally, the universal standards ask a company to describe the role of its highest governing body (such as its board of directors) in managing risks; evaluating social, environmental, and economic performance; and reporting results to external stakeholders.

The three topic-specific standards parallel the phrases "triple bottom-line" and "people, planet, and profit" that are commonly used to summarize a company's expanded set of corporate social responsibilities. The economic standards pertain to topics such as funding employee retirement benefits, procuring supplies and hiring senior managers from the local community, analyzing entry-level wages by gender, and assessing the financial implications of climate change. The environmental standards relate to issues such as water usage, waste management, energy consumption, biodiversity preservation, and emissions control. Finally, the social standards focus on a range of topics, including occupational health and safety, human rights, training and education, diversity and equal opportunity, customer health and safety, as well as marketing and labeling.

Corporate Social Responsibility and the Balanced Scorecard

The balanced scorecard provides a useful framework for organizing and managing the types of social and environmental performance measures that companies often include in their sustainability reports. Exhibit 12–10 provides examples of social and environmental performance measures for each of the four balanced scorecard categories.

While some companies incorporate social and environmental performance measures into their existing balanced scorecards, others implement a variety of adaptations. For example, some companies add a fifth category to their scorecards that purposely focuses on an expanded set of stakeholders. Other companies establish separate scorecards dedicated to their own and/or their suppliers' social and environmental performance. Regardless of these diverse formatting choices, a company should always connect its scorecard measures using if-then hypothesis statements. Individual measures are of limited value unless they ultimately drive the attainment of larger strategic goals. Furthermore, a company's scorecard measures need to be linked to how its senior leaders and managers are evaluated and rewarded. Otherwise, a company's proclaimed commitment to fulfilling its social and environmental responsibilities may not lead to corresponding actions and results.

---

[2] You can learn more about the Global Reporting Initiative by visiting www.globalreporting.org.

EXHIBIT 12–10
Examplesl of Corporate Social Responsibility Measures for the Balanced Scorecard

Learning and Growth:

- Number of occupational injuries/accidents (–)
- Average compensation for female employees ÷ average compensation for male employees (+)
- Number of job applicants from underrepresented groups (+)
- Average community service hours per employee (+)

Customer:

- Percent of customers that strongly agree with the statement "Your company cares about the communities where it operates." (+)
- Percent of customers that strongly agree with the statement "Your company has a superior commitment to product safety." (+)
- Percent of customers that strongly agree with the statement "Your company is committed to environmental stewardship." (+)
- Percent of customers that strongly agree with the statement "Your company provides me with the information that I need to assess its social and environmental performance." (+)

Internal Business Processes:

- Average water consumed per unit produced (–)
- Percent of raw material inputs that have been recycled (+)
- Average carbon emissions per unit produced (–)
- Pounds of waste produced (–)

Financial:

- Percent of revenue from eco-conscious products (+)
- Average fuel cost per sales dollar (–)
- Total workers' compensation costs
- Capital expenditures on "green" products and processes

IN BUSINESS

GOLDMAN SACHS WORKS TO CLOSE ITS GENDER PAY GAP

Goldman Sachs' female employees in the United Kingdom make 36 percent less than its male employees—this is based on data from 5,000 employees, or 13 percent of Goldman's global workforce. Only 15 percent of Goldman's partners are women, whereas women comprise a much higher percentage of back-office jobs such as human resources, compliance, and legal. "Of the four women with a seat on Goldman's management committee, only one runs a business that makes money for the firm. There are 27 men on the panel." Eighty-three percent of the company's highest quartile of earners are men.

Goldman is aware of these gender-based disparities and is taking steps to remedy them. The company hopes that in the near future, women will comprise 50 percent of its incoming analyst classes. The company also began tracking its summer interns, "who account for about 75% of its incoming analyst class, with the goal of retaining nontraditional candidates who might fall behind."

Source: Liz Hoffman and Margot Patrick, "Goldman's Gender Pay Gap Reflects Wider Issue," *The Wall Street Journal*, March 17–18, 2018, p. B10.

Summary

The centerpiece of this chapter is the balanced scorecard, which is an integrated set of performance measures that are derived from and support a company's strategy. Performance measures used in balanced scorecards tend to fall into four categories—learning and growth, internal business processes, customer, and financial.

A company's internal business process measures can include the cost of quality, which quantifies the sum of prevention costs, appraisal costs, internal failure costs, and external failure costs. Generally speaking, management should focus its attention on preventing defects because small investments in prevention can lead to dramatic reductions in appraisal costs as well as internal and external failure costs. The costs of quality are often summarized in a quality cost report that helps managers understand the importance of quality costs, spot problem areas, and assess the way in which the quality costs are distributed.

Internal business process measures can also include time-based measures such as throughput time, delivery cycle time, and manufacturing cycle efficiency, as well as overall equipment effectiveness—which considers machine utilization, efficiency, and quality. The goals are to decrease throughput time and delivery cycle time while increasing manufacturing cycle efficiency (MCE) and overall equipment effectiveness (OEE).

The process of constructing a balanced scorecard begins with an organization defining its strategy. Then, the organization translates this strategy into accompanying performance measures that track its progress in executing the strategy. These performance measures should be linked together in a cause-and-effect manner. One of the advantages of the balanced score-card is that it continually tests the theories underlying management's strategy. If a strategy is not working, it should become evident when some of the predicted if-then relationships don't occur. The measures contained in a balanced scorecard should also be linked to how employees are evaluated and rewarded; otherwise, the measures are likely to be ignored.

Many organizations prepare corporate social responsibility performance reports that are shared with their external stakeholders. The Global Reporting Initiative (GRI) has created a widely adopted sustainability reporting framework that includes three universal standards as well as standards related to economic, environmental, and social performance. The balanced scorecard provides a useful framework for organizing and managing the types of social and environmental performance measures that companies often include in their sustainability reports.

 Data Analytics available in Connect to complement this chapter

---

Review Problem: Operating Performance Measures

Codington Corporation records the time required to fill customer orders. It recorded the following data for a particular order:

	Hours
Wait time..................................	20.8
Process time.............................	2.2
Inspection time	0.2
Move time................................	4.8
Queue time...............................	18.6

Required:
1. Determine the throughput (manufacturing cycle) time.
2. Determine the manufacturing cycle efficiency (MCE).
3. Determine the delivery cycle time.

Solution to Review Problem

1. The throughput time is computed as follows:

    Throughput time = Process time + Inspection time + Move time + Queue time

    Throughput time = 2.2 hours + 0.2 hours + 4.8 hours + 18.6 hours

    Throughput time = 25.8 hours

2. The manufacturing cycle efficiency (MCE) is computed as follows:

    MCE = Value-added time (Process time)/Throughput time

    MCE = 2.2 hours/25.8 hours

    MCE = 0.09 (rounded)

3. The delivery cycle time is computed as follows:

    Delivery cycle time = Wait time + Throughput time

    Delivery cycle time = 20.8 hours + 25.8 hours

    Delivery cycle time = 46.6 hours

Glossary

Appraisal costs Costs that are incurred to identify production defects before the products are shipped to customers. (p. 578)

Balanced scorecard An integrated set of performance measures that are derived from and support the organization's strategy. (p. 573)

Business process A series of steps that are followed in order to carry out some task in a business. (p. 576)

Corporate social responsibility A concept whereby organizations consider the needs of all stakeholders when making decisions. (p. 587)

Cost of quality The sum of prevention costs, appraisal costs, internal failure costs, and external failure costs. (p. 578)

Delivery cycle time The elapsed time from when a customer order is received until the finished goods are shipped. (p. 581)

External failure costs Costs that are incurred when a product or service that is defective is delivered to a customer. (p. 578)

Internal failure costs Costs that are incurred as a result of identifying production defects before they are shipped to customers. (p. 578)

Manufacturing cycle efficiency (MCE) Process (value-added) time as a percentage of throughput time. (p. 582)

Overall equipment effectiveness A ratio that measures the productivity of a piece of equipment. (p. 583)

Prevention costs Costs that are incurred to keep defects from occurring. (p. 578)

Quality cost report A report that details prevention costs, appraisal costs, and the costs of internal and external failures. (p. 578)

Quality of conformance The degree to which a product or service meets or exceeds its design specifications and is free of defects or other problems that mar its appearance or degrade its performance. (p. 578)

Strategy A company's "game plan" for attracting customers by distinguishing itself from competitors. (p. 573)

Throughput time The elapsed time from when production is started until finished goods are shipped. (p. 581)

Questions

12–1 What are the four categories of measures in a balanced scorecard?

12–2 What are the four types of costs summarized in a quality cost report? How do companies generally seek to lower their cost of quality?

12–3 What is the difference between delivery cycle time and throughput time? What four elements make up throughput time? What elements of throughput time are value-added and what elements are non-value-added?

12–4 What does a manufacturing cycle efficiency (MCE) of less than 1 mean? How would you interpret an MCE of 0.40?

12–5 Why do the measures used in a balanced scorecard differ from company to company?

12–6 Why should the measures included in a balanced scorecard be linked together in the form of if-then hypothesis statements?

12–7 Why does the balanced scorecard include financial performance measures as well as measures of how well internal business processes are doing?

12–8 Why should companies link their balanced scorecard measures to their employee reward systems?

12–9 Why do companies measure their corporate social responsibility performance?

12–10 What is the Global Reporting Initiative?

Applying Excel   **Mc Graw Hill connect**

LEARNING OBJECTIVE 12–3

The Excel worksheet form below is to be used to recreate the Review Problem pertaining to Codington Corporation. The workbook, and instructions on how to complete the file, can be found in Connect.

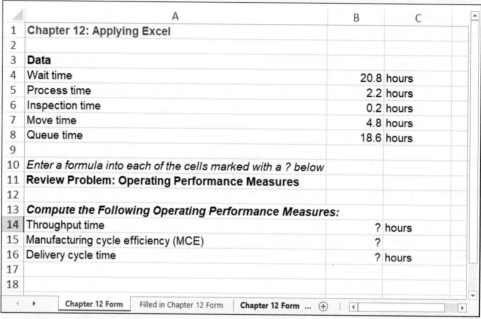

	A	B	C
1	Chapter 12: Applying Excel		
2			
3	**Data**		
4	Wait time	20.8	hours
5	Process time	2.2	hours
6	Inspection time	0.2	hours
7	Move time	4.8	hours
8	Queue time	18.6	hours
9			
10	*Enter a formula into each of the cells marked with a ? below*		
11	**Review Problem: Operating Performance Measures**		
12			
13	***Compute the Following Operating Performance Measures:***		
14	Throughput time	?	hours
15	Manufacturing cycle efficiency (MCE)	?	
16	Delivery cycle time	?	hours
17			
18			

Chapter 12 Form   Filled in Chapter 12 Form   Chapter 12 Form ...

Microsoft Excel

You should proceed to the requirements below only after completing your worksheet.

Required:

1. Check your worksheet by changing the wait time in cell B4 to 5.8 hours and the queue time in cell B8 to 8.6 hours. The throughput time should now be 15.8 hours. The manufacturing cycle efficiency (MCE) should now be 0.14, and the delivery cycle time should now be 21.6 hours. If you do not get these answers, find the errors in your worksheet and correct them.

    Explain why the throughput time and delivery cycle time both decreased. Why did the manufacturing cycle efficiency (MCE) increase?

2. Revise the data in your worksheet as follows:

Data	
Wait time	1.0 hours
Process time	2.2 hours
Inspection time	0.2 hours
Move time	0.8 hours
Queue time	0.6 hours

a. What is the throughput time?

b. What is the manufacturing cycle efficiency (MCE)?

c. What is the delivery cycle time?

Exercises

EXERCISE 12–1 Examples of Balanced Scorecard Performance Measures LO 12–1

Reid Company would like to implement a balanced scorecard performance measurement system. Its senior management team has assembled the measures shown below for possible inclusion in its scorecard.

Required:

For each measure, indicate by placing an X in the appropriate column whether it would most likely be classified in the learning and growth, internal business process, customer, or financial category of the company's balanced scorecard.

Item	Learning & Growth	Internal Business Process	Customer	Financial
Ex. Employee absenteeism rate	X			
1. Sales from new customers...				
2. Customer defection rate..				
3. Average fuel cost per sales dollar				
4. Average number of workplace accidents per employee				
5. Delivery cycle time				
6. Average training hours per employee.....................................				
7. Number of job applicants from underrepresented groups...................				
8. Percent of customers that strongly agree with the statement "Your employees treated me courteously."				
9. Return on assets				
10. Percent of customers that strongly agree with the statement "Your company has a superior commitment to product safety."				
11. Number of modular product designs.....................................				
12. Lost sales due to out-of-stock merchandise..............................				
13. Pounds of waste produced				
14. Number of customer referrals...				
15. Residual income...				
16. Average mentorship hours per employee				

EXERCISE 12–2 Classification of Quality Costs LO 12–2

A number of activities that are part of a company's quality control system are listed below:

a. Product testing.
b. Product recalls.
c. Rework labor and overhead.
d. Quality circles.
e. Downtime caused by defects.
f. Cost of field servicing.
g. Inspection of goods.
h. Quality engineering.
i. Warranty repairs.
j. Statistical process control.
k. Net cost of scrap.
l. Depreciation of test equipment.
m. Returns and allowances arising from poor quality.
n. Disposal of production defects.
o. Technical support to suppliers.
p. Systems development.
q. Warranty replacements.
r. Field testing at customer site.
s. Quality training.

Required:

1. Classify the costs associated with each of these activities into one of the following categories: prevention cost, appraisal cost, internal failure cost, or external failure cost.
2. Which of the four types of costs in (1) above are incurred in an effort to keep poor quality of conformance from occurring? Which of the four types of costs in (1) above are incurred because poor quality of conformance has occurred?

EXERCISE 12–3 Measures of Internal Business Process Performance LO 12–3

Management of Mittel Company would like to reduce the amount of time between when a customer places an order and when the order is shipped. For the first quarter of operations during the current year, the following data were reported:

Inspection time	0.3 days
Wait time (from order to start of production)	14.0 days
Process time	2.7 days
Move time	1.0 days
Queue time	5.0 days

Required:

1. Compute the throughput time.
2. Compute the manufacturing cycle efficiency (MCE) for the quarter.
3. What percentage of the throughput time was spent in non-value-added activities?
4. Compute the delivery cycle time.
5. If by using Lean Production all queue time during production is eliminated, what will be the new MCE?

EXERCISE 12–4 Building a Balanced Scorecard LO 12–4

Lost Peak ski resort was for many years a small, family-owned resort serving day skiers from nearby towns. Lost Peak was recently acquired by Western Resorts, a major ski resort operator. The new owners have plans to upgrade the resort into a destination resort for vacationers. As part of this plan, the new owners would like to make major improvements in the Powder 8 Lodge, the resort's on-the-hill cafeteria. The menu at the lodge is very limited—hamburgers, hot dogs, chili, tuna fish sandwiches, pizzas, french fries, and packaged snacks. With little competition, the previous owners of the resort felt no urgency to upgrade the food service at the lodge. If skiers want lunch on the mountain, the only alternatives are the Powder 8 Lodge or a brown bag lunch brought from home.

As part of the deal when acquiring Lost Peak, Western Resorts agreed to retain all of the current resort employees. The manager of the lodge, while hardworking and enthusiastic, has very little experience in the restaurant business. The manager is responsible for selecting the menu, finding and training employees, and overseeing daily operations. The kitchen staff prepare food and wash dishes. The dining room staff take orders, serve as cashiers, and clean the dining room area.

Shortly after taking over Lost Peak, management of Western Resorts held a day-long meeting with all of the employees of the Powder 8 Lodge to discuss the future of the ski resort and the new management's plans for the lodge. At the end of this meeting, management and lodge employees selected the following performance measures to be used in creating a balanced scorecard:

a. Weekly Powder 8 Lodge sales
b. Weekly Powder 8 Lodge profit
c. Number of menu items
d. Dining area cleanliness as rated by a representative from Western Resorts management
e. Customer satisfaction with menu choices as measured by customer surveys
f. Customer satisfaction with service as measured by customer surveys
g. Average time to take an order
h. Average time to prepare an order
i. Percentage of kitchen staff completing a reimbursed cooking course at the local community college
j. Percentage of dining room staff completing a reimbursed hospitality course at the local community college

Required:

1.   Using the above performance measures, construct a balanced scorecard for the Powder 8 Lodge. Use Exhibit 12–9 as a guide. Use arrows to show causal links and indicate with a + or – whether the performance measure should increase or decrease.
2.   What hypotheses are built into the balanced scorecard for the Powder 8 Lodge? Which of these hypotheses do you believe are most questionable? Why?
3.   How will management know if one of the hypotheses underlying the balanced scorecard is false?

EXERCISE 12–5 Overall Equipment Effectiveness LO 12–3

Jefferson Company's demand for its only product exceeds its manufacturing capacity. The company provided the following information for the machine whose limited capacity is prohibiting the company from producing and selling additional units.

Actual run time this week	4,900 minutes
Machine time available per week.	7,000 minutes
Actual run rate this week.	3.8 units per minute
Ideal run rate	4.0 units per minute
Defect-free output this week.	15,827 units
Total output this week (including defects).	18,620 units

Required:

1.   Compute the utilization rate.
2.   Compute the efficiency rate
3.   Compute the quality rate
4.   Compute the overall equipment effectiveness (OEE).

EXERCISE 12–6 Defining Balanced Scorecard Measures LO 12–1, LO 12–4

Askew Company is interested in adopting the balanced scorecard. As a first step, the company just completed a brainstorming activity to define areas where it needs to improve with respect to learning and growth, internal business process performance, customer satisfaction, and financial results. The results of its brainstorming session are summarized below:

Learning and Growth	Internal Business Process
"Too many customer service employees leave our company to work for other employers." "We are not providing enough training to our employees." "Our employees are not generating enough ideas to help improve what we do."	"Customers are returning too many defective products." "It is taking too long to make products and ship them to customers." "Customers have to call us repeatedly to get problems solved."
Customer	**Financial**
"The number of customers we are serving seems to be shrinking." "Customers are complaining about excessive delays with respect to receiving what they ordered." "We are acquiring fewer new customers from our current customers' word-of-mouth."	"Wall Street is becoming very concerned about our future." "Sales are decreasing instead of increasing." "It takes too long to convert customer orders into cash."

The company asked you to guide its balanced scorecard implementation process from this point forward.

Required:

1.   As a first step, you decide to explain that the insights from the company's brainstorming session need to be translated into performance measures that can be tracked and managed. To illustrate this point, provide one example of a plausible performance measure for each comment raised during the company's brainstorming session.

2. As a second step, you decide to highlight the importance of defining a strategy and then linking performance measures together using if-then hypothesis statements in a manner that reflects the chosen strategy. To illustrate this point, choose a strategy for the company based on its brainstorming goals (either product leadership, operational excellence, or customer intimacy) and define three plausible if-then hypothesis statements using some of your measures from requirement 1. Use a + or − to indicate whether each performance measure should increase or decrease.

EXERCISE 12–7 If-Then Hypothesis Statements LO 12–4

The table below contains five measures under the column heading If and five measures under the column heading Then.

If	Then
Employee turnover percentage	⟶ Number of warranty claims
Customer defection rate	⟶ Sales growth rate
Number of new products designed	⟶ Percent of a customer's overall spending committed to our company
Non-value-added activity costs	⟶ Net operating income
Number of process improvement suggestions per employee	⟶ Non-value-added activity costs

Required:
1. For each row in the table, write an if-then hypothesis statement that connects the two measures. Be sure to indicate whether each measure is expected to increase or decrease.
2. For each row in the table, provide one possible reason why a company that is able to improve each of the five "if" measures may not see the expected improvement in its associated "then" measure.

EXERCISE 12–8 Cost of Quality LO 12–2

Walton Company measured its quality costs for the past two years and summarized those costs using the four categories shown below:

	Last Year	This Year
Prevention costs	$357,000	$650,000
Appraisal costs	$445,000	$545,000
Internal failure costs	$790,000	$500,000
External failure costs	$1,100,000	$680,000

Required:
1. Calculate the total cost of quality last year and this year.
2. For last year, calculate the cost in each of the four categories as a percent of the total cost of quality.
3. For this year, calculate the cost in each of the four categories as a percent of the total cost of quality.
4. Discuss the company's efforts to manage its costs of quality over the two-year period. Is performance trending in a favorable or unfavorable direction? Why?

EXERCISE 12–9 Balanced Scorecard Performance Measures LO 12–1, LO 12–4

The table below contains four performance measures for four different companies. Each set of performance measures contains one measure for each of the four perspectives of the balanced scorecard.

Company A:

Average years of tenure per employee
Sales from products less than three years old
Market share percentage
Number of new products designed

Company B:

Customer perception of our product
   leadership
Percent of "outstanding" interview candidates
   that accepted our job offer
Number of patents approved
Patent-protected sales

Company C:

Pounds of waste produced
Percent of revenue from eco-conscious
   products
Number of process improvement suggestions
   per employee
Percent of customers that strongly agree with
   the statement "Your company is committed
   to environmental stewardship."

Company D:

Net operating income growth rate
Manufacturing cycle efficiency
Percent of customers that strongly agree
   with the statement "My order was delivered
   on time."
Average training hours per employee

Required:

1. For each of companies A, B, C, and D:
    a. Label each of the four measures as relating to the Learning & Growth, Internal Business
        Process, Customer, or Financial perspective. Indicate whether each measure is expected
        to increase or decrease.
    b. Create three if-then hypothesis statements that link (1) the Learning & Growth measure
        with the Internal Business Process measure, (2) the Internal Business Process measure to
        the Customer measure, and (3) the Customer measure to the Financial measure.
2. For each of companies A, B, C, and D, describe whether its set of four measures reflect an opera-
    tional excellence, customer intimacy, or product leadership customer value proposition. Why?

EXERCISE 12–10 Internal Business Process Measures and Customer Value Propositions LO 12–1
The table shown contains a variety of performance measures that companies might use as internal
business process measures in their balanced scorecards. Each measure is accompanied by a + or −
to indicate whether the performance measure should increase or decrease over time.

Required:

For each measure, place an *X* in one of the first three columns to indicate whether the measure would
most likely be adopted by a company pursuing a strategy focused on operational excellence, product
leadership, or customer intimacy. In the fourth column, provide an explanation for your answer.

Item	Operational Excellence	Product Leadership	Customer Intimacy	Explanation
Ex. Number of patents approved		X		Patents often provide the foundation for delivering new and innovative products to customers.
1. Delivery cycle time (−)				
2. Number of new products designed (+)				
3. Average contact hours per customer (+)				
4. Non-value-added activity costs (−)				
5. Percent of suppliers with long-term contracts (+)				
6. Number of modular product designs (+)				
7. Number of customized products co-designed with customers (+)				
8. Defect-free units as a percentage of completed units (+)				
9. Number of options available for customers to choose from (+)				

EXERCISE 12–11 Using If-Then Hypothesis Statements to Connect Balanced Scorecard Performance Measures LO 12–4

The table shown below contains three performance measures for each of the four perspectives of the balanced scorecard.

Learning and Growth:	*Internal Business Process:*
Percent of employees that strongly agree with the statement "I am consistently given the resources that I need to do my job."	Throughput time
	Percent of customer complaints settled on first contact
Absenteeism rate	Cost of quality
Percent of employees that strongly agree with the statement "I would say that this is a great place to work."	
Customer:	*Financial:*
Average gross margin per order	Net cash flow from operating activities
Customer perception of operational excellence	Gross margin percentage
Percent of customers that strongly agree with the statement "My problem was resolved quickly."	Net profit margin percentage

Required:

1. Choose one of the three learning and growth measures and write an if-then hypothesis statement that connects it to one of the three internal business process measures. Then create an if-then hypothesis statement that connects your chosen internal business process measure to one of the three customer measures. Finally, write an if-then hypothesis statement that connects your chosen customer measure to one of the three financial measures. Be sure to indicate whether each measure is expected to increase or decrease.

2. Choose one of the two remaining learning and growth measures and write an if-then hypothesis statement that connects it to one of the two remaining internal business process measures. Then create an if-then hypothesis statement that connects your chosen internal business process measure to one of the two remaining customer measures. Finally, write an if-then hypothesis statement that connects your chosen customer measure to one of the two remaining financial measures. Be sure to indicate whether each measure is expected to increase or decrease.

3. Write an if-then hypothesis statement that connects your remaining learning and growth measure to your remaining internal business process measure. Then create an if-then hypothesis statement that connects your remaining internal business process measure to your remaining customer measure. Finally, write an if-then hypothesis statement that connects your remaining customer measure to your remaining financial measure. Be sure to indicate whether each measure is expected to increase or decrease.

Problems connect

PROBLEM 12–12 Overall Equipment Effectiveness LO 12–3

Kilmer Company has demand for its only product that exceeds its manufacturing capacity. The company provided the following information for the machine whose limited capacity is prohibiting the company from producing and selling additional units.

Actual run time this week	6,600 minutes
Machine time available per week	11,000 minutes
Actual run rate this week	5.1 units per minute
Ideal run rate	6.0 units per minute
Defect-free output this week	23,562 units
Total output this week (including defects)	33,660 units

Required:

1. With respect to the company's overall equipment effectiveness, calculate the following:
   a. The utilization rate.
   b. The efficiency rate.
   c. The quality rate
   d. The overall equipment effectiveness (OEE).
2. With respect to the company's overall equipment effectiveness, calculate the following:
   a. The utilization loss in units during the week.
   b. The efficiency loss in units during the week.
   c. The quality loss in units during the week.

PROBLEM 12–13 Creating Balanced Scorecards That Support Different Strategies LO 12–4

The Midwest Consulting Group (MCG) helps companies build balanced scorecards. As part of its marketing efforts, MCG conducts an annual balanced scorecard workshop for prospective clients. As MCG's newest employee, your boss has asked you to participate in this year's workshop by explaining to attendees how a company's strategy determines the measures that are appropriate for its balanced scorecard. Your boss has provided you with the excerpts below from the annual reports of two current MCG clients. She has asked you to use these excerpts in your portion of the workshop.

Excerpt from Applied Pharmaceuticals' annual report:

> The keys to our business are consistent and timely new product introductions and manufacturing process integrity. The new product introduction side of the equation is a function of research and development (R&D) yield (e.g., the number of marketable drug compounds created relative to the total number of potential compounds pursued). We seek to optimize our R&D yield and first-to-market capability by investing in state-of-the-art technology, hiring the highest possible percentage of the "best and the brightest" engineers that we pursue, and providing world-class training to those engineers. Manufacturing process integrity is all about establishing world-class quality specifications and then relentlessly engaging in prevention and appraisal activities to minimize defect rates. Our customers must have an awareness of and respect for our brand image of being "first to market and first in quality." If we deliver on this pledge to our customers, then our financial goal of increasing our return on stockholders' equity should take care of itself.

Excerpt from Destination Resorts International's annual report:

> Our business succeeds or fails based on the quality of the service that our front-line employees provide to customers. Therefore, it is imperative that we strive to maintain high employee morale and minimize employee turnover. In addition, it is critical that we train our employees to use technology to create one seamless worldwide experience for our repeat customers. Once an employee enters a customer preference (e.g., provide two extra pillows in the room, deliver fresh brewed coffee to the room at 8:00 A.M., etc.) into our database, our worldwide workforce strives to ensure that a customer will never need to repeat it at any of our destination resorts. If we properly train and retain a motivated workforce, we should see continuous improvement in our percentage of error-free repeat customer check-ins, the time taken to resolve customer complaints, and our independently assessed room cleanliness. This in turn should drive improvement in our customer retention, which is the key to meeting our revenue growth goals.

Required:

1. Based on the excerpts above, compare and contrast the strategies of Applied Pharmaceuticals and Destination Resorts International.
2. Select balanced scorecard measures for each company and link the scorecard measures using the framework from Exhibit 12–9. Use arrows to show the causal links between the performance measures and show whether the performance measure should increase or decrease over time. Feel free to create measures that may not be specifically mentioned in the chapter but nonetheless make sense given the strategic goals of each company.
3. What hypotheses are built into each balanced scorecard? Why do the hypotheses differ between the two companies?

PROBLEM 12–14 Dysfunctional Effects of Some Performance Measures LO 12–1

There is often more than one way to improve a performance measure. Unfortunately, some of the actions taken by managers to make their performance look better may actually harm the organization. For example, suppose the marketing department is held responsible only for increasing the performance measure "total revenues." Increases in total revenues may be achieved by working harder and smarter, but they can also usually be achieved by simply cutting prices. The increase in volume from cutting prices almost always results in greater total revenues; however, it does not always lead to greater total profits. Those who design performance measurement systems need to keep in mind that managers who are under pressure to perform may take actions to improve performance measures that have negative consequences elsewhere.

Required:

For each of the following situations, describe actions managers might take to show improvement in the performance measure but which do not actually lead to improvement in the organization's overall performance.

1. Concerned with the slow rate at which new products are brought to market, top management of a consumer electronics company introduces a new performance measure—speed-to-market. The research and development department is given responsibility for this performance measure, which measures the average amount of time a product is in development before it is released to the market for sale.

2. The CEO of an airline company is dissatisfied with the amount of time her ground crews are taking to unload luggage from airplanes. To solve the problem, she decides to measure the average elapsed time from when an airplane parks at the gate to when all pieces of luggage are unloaded from the airplane. For each month that an airport's ground crew can lower its "average elapsed time" relative to the prior month, the CEO pays a lump-sum bonus to be split equally among members of the crew.

3. A manufacturing company has been plagued by the chronic failure to ship orders to customers by the promised date. To solve this problem, the production manager has been given the responsibility of increasing the percentage of orders shipped on time. When a customer calls in an order, the production manager and the customer agree to a delivery date. If the order is not completed by that date, it is counted as a late shipment.

4. Concerned with the productivity of employees, the board of directors of a large multinational corporation has dictated that the manager of each subsidiary will be held responsible for increasing the revenue per employee of his or her subsidiary.

PROBLEM 12–15 Internal Business Process Performance Measures LO 12–3

Tombro Industries is in the process of automating one of its plants and developing a flexible manufacturing system. The company is finding it necessary to make many changes in operating procedures. Progress has been slow, particularly in trying to develop new performance measures for the factory.

In an effort to evaluate performance and determine where improvements can be made, management has gathered the following data relating to activities over the last four months:

	Month			
	1	2	3	4
Quality control measures:				
Number of defects	185	163	124	91
Number of warranty claims	46	39	30	27
Number of customer complaints	102	96	79	58
Material control measures:				
Purchase order lead time	8 days	7 days	5 days	4 days
Scrap as a percent of total cost	1%	1%	2%	3%
Machine performance measures:				
Machine downtime as a percentage of availability	3%	4%	4%	6%
Use as a percentage of availability	95%	92%	89%	85%
Setup time (hours)	8	10	11	12
Delivery performance measures:				
Throughput time	?	?	?	?
Manufacturing cycle efficiency (MCE)	?	?	?	?
Delivery cycle time	?	?	?	?
Percentage of on-time deliveries	96%	95%	92%	89%

The president has read in industry journals that throughput time, MCE, and delivery cycle time are important measures of performance, but no one is sure how they are computed. You have been asked to assist the company, and you have gathered the following data relating to these measures:

	Average per Month (in days)			
	1	2	3	4
Wait time per order before start of production	9.0	11.5	12.0	14.0
Inspection time per unit	0.8	0.7	0.7	0.7
Process time per unit	2.1	2.0	1.9	1.8
Queue time per unit	2.8	4.4	6.0	7.0
Move time per unit	0.3	0.4	0.4	0.5

Required:

1. For each month, compute the following performance measures:
   a. Throughput time.
   b. MCE.
   c. Delivery cycle time.
2. Using the performance measures given in the main body of the problem and the performance measures computed in (1) above, do the following:
   a. Identify areas where the company seems to be improving.
   b. Identify areas where the company seems to be deteriorating.
3. Refer to the inspection time, process time, and so forth, given for month 4.
   a. Assume in month 5, the inspection time, process time, and so forth are the same as for month 4, except that the company is able to completely eliminate the queue time during production using Lean Production. Compute the new throughput time and MCE.
   b. Assume in month 6, the inspection time, process time, and so forth are the same as in month 4, except that the company is able to eliminate both the queue time during production and the inspection time using Lean Production. Compute the new throughput time and MCE.

PROBLEM 12–16 Creating a Balanced Scorecard LO 12–4

Mason Paper Company (MPC) manufactures commodity grade papers for use in computer printers and photocopiers. MPC has reported net operating losses for the last two years due to intense price pressure from much larger competitors. The MPC management team—including Kristen Townsend (CEO), Mike Martinez (VP of Manufacturing), Tom Andrews (VP of Marketing), and Wendy Chen (CFO)—is contemplating a change in strategy to save the company from impending bankruptcy. Excerpts from a recent management team meeting are shown below:

Townsend: As we all know, the commodity paper manufacturing business is all about economies of scale. The largest competitors with the lowest cost per unit win. The limited capacity of our older machines prohibits us from competing in the high-volume commodity paper grades. Furthermore, expanding our capacity by acquiring a new paper-making machine is out of the question given the extraordinarily high price tag. Therefore, I propose that we abandon cost reduction as a strategic goal and instead pursue manufacturing flexibility as the key to our future success.

Chen: Manufacturing flexibility? What does that mean?

Martinez: It means we have to abandon our "crank out as many tons of paper as possible" mentality. Instead, we need to pursue the low-volume business opportunities that exist in the nonstandard, specialized paper grades. To succeed in this regard, we'll need to improve our flexibility in three ways. First, we must improve our ability to switch between paper grades. Right now, we require an average of four hours to change over to another paper grade. Timely customer deliveries are a function of changeover performance. Second, we need to expand the range of paper grades that we can manufacture. Currently, we can only manufacture three paper grades. Our customers must perceive that we are a "one-stop shop" that can meet all of their paper grade needs. Third, we will need to improve our yields (e.g., tons of acceptable output relative to total tons processed) in the nonstandard paper grades. Our percentage of waste within these grades will be unacceptably high unless we do something to improve our processes. Our variable costs will go through the roof if we cannot increase our yields!

Chen: Wait just a minute! These changes are going to destroy our equipment utilization numbers!

Andrews: You're right, Wendy; however, equipment utilization is not the name of the game when it comes to competing in terms of flexibility. Our customers don't care about our equipment utilization. Instead, as Mike just alluded to, they want just-in-time delivery of smaller quantities of a full range of paper grades. If we can shrink the elapsed time from order placement to order delivery and expand our product offerings, it will increase sales from current customers and bring in new customers. Furthermore, we will be able to charge a premium price because of the limited competition within this niche from our cost-focused larger competitors. Our contribution margin per ton should drastically improve!

Martinez: Of course, executing the change in strategy will not be easy. We'll need to make a substantial investment in training because ultimately it is our people who create our flexible manufacturing capabilities.

Chen: If we adopt this new strategy, it is definitely going to impact how we measure performance. We'll need to create measures that motivate our employees to make decisions that support our flexibility goals.

Townsend: Wendy, you hit the nail right on the head. For our next meeting, could you pull together some potential measures that support our new strategy?

Required:

1. Contrast MPC's previous manufacturing strategy with its new manufacturing strategy.
2. Generally speaking, why would a company that changes its strategic goals need to change its performance measurement system as well? What are some examples of measures that would have been appropriate for MPC prior to its change in strategy? Why would those measures fail to support MPC's new strategy?
3. Construct a balanced scorecard that would support MPC's new manufacturing strategy. Use arrows to show the causal links between the performance measures and show whether the performance measure should increase or decrease over time. Feel free to create measures that may not be specifically mentioned in the chapter, but nonetheless make sense given the strategic goals of the company.
4. What hypotheses are built into MPC's balanced scorecard? Which of these hypotheses do you believe are most questionable and why?

PROBLEM 12–17 Analyzing a Quality Cost Report LO 12–2

Mercury, Inc., produces cell phones at its plant in Texas. In recent years, the company's market share has been eroded by stiff competition from overseas. Price and product quality are the two key areas in which companies compete in this market.

A year ago, the company's cell phones had been ranked low in product quality in a consumer survey. Shocked by this result, Jorge Gomez, Mercury's president, initiated an intense effort to improve product quality. Gomez set up a task force to implement a formal quality improvement program. Included on this task force were representatives from the Engineering, Marketing, Customer Service, Production, and Accounting departments. The broad representation was needed because Gomez believed that this was a companywide program and that all employees should share the responsibility for its success.

After the first meeting of the task force, Holly Elsoe, manager of the Marketing Department, asked John Tran, production manager, what he thought of the proposed program. Tran replied, "I have reservations. Quality is too abstract to be attaching costs to it and then to be holding you and me responsible for cost improvements. I like to work with goals that I can see and count! I'm nervous about having my annual bonus based on a decrease in quality costs; there are too many variables that we have no control over."

Mercury's quality improvement program has now been in operation for one year. The company's most recent quality cost report is shown below:

Mercury, Inc. Quality Cost Report (in thousands)		
	Last Year	This Year
Prevention costs:		
Machine maintenance	$ 70	$ 120
Training suppliers	0	10
Quality circles	0	20
Total prevention cost	70	150
Appraisal costs:		
Incoming inspection	20	40
Final testing	80	90
Total appraisal cost.	100	130
Internal failure costs:		
Rework	50	130
Scrap.	40	70
Total internal failure cost	90	200
External failure costs:		
Warranty repairs	90	30
Customer returns	320	80
Total external failure cost	410	110
Total quality cost	$ 670	$ 590
Total production cost	$4,200	$4,800

As they were reviewing the report, Elsoe asked Tran what he now thought of the quality improvement program. Tran replied, "I'm relieved that the new quality improvement program hasn't hurt our bonuses, but the program has increased the workload in the Production Department. It is true that customer returns are way down, but the cell phones that were returned by customers to retail outlets were rarely sent back to us for rework."

Required:

1. Expand the company's quality cost report by showing the costs in both years as percentages of both total production cost and total quality cost. Carry all computations to one decimal place. By analyzing the report, determine if Mercury, Inc.'s quality improvement program has been successful. List specific evidence to support your answer.

2. Do you expect the improvement program as it progresses to continue to increase the workload in the Production Department?

3. Jorge Gomez believed the quality improvement program was essential and that Mercury, Inc., could no longer afford to ignore the importance of product quality. Discuss how Mercury, Inc., could measure the cost of *not* implementing the quality improvement program.

(CMA, adapted)

PROBLEM 12–18 Creating a Balanced Scorecard LO 12–4

Ariel Tax Services prepares tax returns for individual and corporate clients. As the company has gradually expanded to 10 offices, the founder, Max Jacobs, has begun to feel as though he is losing control of operations. In response to this concern, he has decided to implement a performance measurement system that will help control current operations and facilitate his plans of expanding to 20 offices.

Jacobs describes the keys to the success of his business as follows:

"Our only real asset is our people. We must keep our employees highly motivated, and we must hire the 'cream of the crop.' Interestingly, employee morale and recruiting success are both driven by the same two factors—compensation and career advancement. In other words, providing superior compensation relative to the industry average coupled with fast-track career advancement opportunities keeps morale high and makes us a very attractive place to work. It drives a high rate of job offer acceptances relative to job offers tendered."

"Hiring highly qualified people and keeping them energized ensures operational success, which in our business is a function of productivity, efficiency, and effectiveness. Productivity boils down to employees being billable rather than idle. Efficiency relates to the time required to complete a tax return. Finally, effectiveness is critical to our business in the sense that we cannot tolerate errors. Completing a tax return quickly is meaningless if the return contains errors."

"Our growth depends on acquiring new customers through word of mouth from satisfied repeat customers. We believe that our customers come back year after year because they value error-free, timely, and courteous tax return preparation. Common courtesy is an important aspect of our business! We call it service quality, and it all ties back to employee morale in the sense that happy employees treat their clients with care and concern."

"While sales growth is obviously important to our future plans, growth without a corresponding increase in profitability is useless. Therefore, we understand that increasing our profit margin is a function of cost-efficiency as well as sales growth. Given that payroll is our biggest expense, we must maintain an optimal balance between staffing levels and the revenue being generated. As I alluded to earlier, the key to maintaining this balance is employee productivity. If we can achieve cost-efficient sales growth, we should eventually have 20 profitable offices!"

Required:
1. Create a balanced scorecard for Ariel Tax Services. Link your scorecard measures using the framework from Exhibit 12–9. Indicate whether each measure is expected to increase or decrease. Feel free to create measures that may not be specifically mentioned in the chapter but make sense given the strategic goals of the company.
2. What hypotheses are built into the balanced scorecard for Ariel Tax Services? Which of these hypotheses do you believe are most questionable and why?
3. Discuss the potential advantages and disadvantages of implementing an internal business process measure called *total dollar amount of tax refunds generated.* Would you recommend using this measure in Ariel's balanced scorecard?
4. Would it be beneficial to attempt to measure each office's individual performance with respect to the scorecard measures you created? Why or why not?

PROBLEM 12–19 Quality Cost Report LO 12–2
In response to intensive foreign competition, the management of Florex Company has attempted over the past year to improve the quality of its products. A statistical process control system has been installed, and other steps have been taken to decrease the amount of warranty and other field costs, which have been trending upward over the past several years. Costs relating to quality and quality control over the last two years (in thousands) are given below:

	Costs (in thousands)	
	Last Year	This Year
Inspection	$750	$900
Quality engineering	$420	$570
Depreciation of test equipment	$210	$240
Rework labor	$1,050	$1,500
Statistical process control	$0	$180
Cost of field servicing	$1,200	$900
Supplies used in testing	$30	$60
Systems development	$480	$750
Warranty repairs	$3,600	$1,050
Net cost of scrap	$630	$1,125
Product testing	$810	$1,200
Product recalls	$2,100	$750
Disposal of production defects	$720	$975

Sales have been flat over the past few years, at $75,000,000 per year. A great deal of money has been spent in the effort to upgrade quality, and management is anxious to see whether or not the effort has been effective.

Required:

1. Prepare a quality cost report that contains data for both this year and last year. Carry percentage computations to two decimal places.
2. Prepare a written evaluation to accompany the reports you have prepared in requirement 1. This evaluation should discuss the distribution of quality costs in the company, changes in this distribution that you see taking place, the reasons for changes in costs in the various categories, and any other information that would be of value to management.

PROBLEM 12–20 Measures of Internal Business Process Performance LO 12–3

DataSpan, Inc., automated its plant at the start of the current year and installed a flexible manufacturing system. The company is also evaluating its suppliers and moving toward Lean Production. Many adjustment problems have been encountered, including problems relating to performance measurement. After much study, the company has decided to use the performance measures below, and it has gathered data relating to these measures for the first four months of operations.

	Month			
	1	2	3	4
Throughput time (days)	?	?	?	?
Delivery cycle time (days)	?	?	?	?
Manufacturing cycle efficiency (MCE)	?	?	?	?
Percentage of on-time deliveries	91%	86%	83%	79%
Total sales (units)	3,210	3,072	2,915	2,806

Management has asked for your help in computing throughput time, delivery cycle time, and MCE. The following average times have been logged over the last four months:

	Average per Month (in days)			
	1	2	3	4
Move time per unit	0.4	0.3	0.4	0.4
Process time per unit	2.1	2.0	1.9	1.8
Wait time per order before start of production	16.0	17.5	19.0	20.5
Queue time per unit	4.3	5.0	5.8	6.7
Inspection time per unit	0.6	0.7	0.7	0.6

Required:

1. For each month, compute the following:
   a. The throughput time.
   b. The delivery cycle time.
   c. The manufacturing cycle efficiency (MCE).
2. Evaluate the company's performance over the last four months.
3. Refer to the move time, process time, and so forth, given above for month 4.
   a. Assume in month 5, the move time, process time, and so forth, are the same as in month 4, except that through the use of Lean Production the company is able to completely eliminate the queue time during production. Compute the new throughput time and MCE.

> b. Assume in month 6, the move time, process time, and so forth, are again the same as in month 4, except that the company is able to completely eliminate both the queue time during production and the inspection time. Compute the new throughput time and MCE.

Case   connect

Select cases are available in Connect.

CASE 12–21 Balanced Scorecard LO 12–4

Haglund Department Store is located in the downtown area of a small city. While the store had been profitable for many years, it is facing increasing competition from large national chains that have set up stores on the outskirts of the city. Recently the downtown area has been undergoing revitalization, and the owners of Haglund Department Store are somewhat optimistic that profitability can be restored.

In an attempt to accelerate the return to profitability, management of Haglund Department Store is in the process of designing a balanced scorecard for the company. Management believes the company should focus on two key problems. First, customers are taking longer and longer to pay the bills they incur using the department store's charge card, and the company has far more bad debts than are normal for the industry. If this problem were solved, the company would have more cash to make much-needed renovations. Investigation has revealed that much of the problem with late payments and unpaid bills results from customers disputing incorrect charges on their bills. These incorrect charges usually occur because salesclerks incorrectly enter data on the charge account slip. Second, the company has been incurring large losses on unsold seasonal apparel. Such items are ordinarily resold at a loss to discount stores that specialize in such distress items.

The meeting in which the balanced scorecard approach was discussed was disorganized and ineffectively led—possibly because no one other than one of the vice presidents had read anything about how to build a balanced scorecard. Nevertheless, a number of potential performance measures were suggested by various managers. These potential performance measures are:

a. Percentage of charge account bills containing errors.
b. Percentage of salesclerks trained to correctly enter data on charge account slips.
c. Average age of accounts receivable.
d. Profit per employee.
e. Customer satisfaction with accuracy of charge account bills from monthly customer survey.
f. Total sales revenue.
g. Sales per employee.
h. Travel expenses for buyers for trips to fashion shows.
i. Unsold inventory at the end of the season as a percentage of total cost of sales.
j. Courtesy shown by junior staff members to senior staff members based on surveys of senior staff.
k. Percentage of suppliers making just-in-time deliveries.
l. Sales per square foot of floor space.
m. Written-off accounts receivable (bad debts) as a percentage of sales.
n. Quality of food in the staff cafeteria based on staff surveys.
o. Percentage of employees who have attended the city's cultural diversity workshop.
p. Total profit.

Required:

1. As someone with more knowledge of the balanced scorecard than almost anyone else in the company, you have been asked to build an integrated balanced scorecard. In your scorecard, use only performance measures listed previously. You do not have to use all of the performance measures suggested by the managers, but you should build a balanced scorecard that

reveals a strategy for dealing with the problems with accounts receivable and with unsold merchandise. Construct the balanced scorecard following the format used in Exhibit 12–9. Do not be concerned with whether a specific performance measure falls within the learning and growth, internal business process, customer, or financial perspective. However, use arrows to show the causal links between performance measures within your balanced scorecard and explain whether the performance measures should show increases or decreases.

2. Assume the company adopts your balanced scorecard. After operating for a year, some performance measures show improvements, but not others. What should management do next?

3. *a.* Suppose customers express greater satisfaction with the accuracy of their charge account bills, but the performance measures for the average age of accounts receivable and for bad debts do not improve. Explain why this might happen.

   b. Suppose the performance measures for the average age of accounts receivable, bad debts, and unsold inventory improve, but total profits do not. Explain why this might happen. Assume in your answer that the explanation lies within the company.

Integration Exercises: An Overview

Successful managers rely on an integrated set of managerial accounting competencies to solve complex real-world problems. Therefore, we have created 12 integration exercises to help you develop these critically important managerial skills. This collective group of exercises will enable you to see how the learning objectives throughout the book interrelate with one another. As you begin to understand "how it all fits together," you will start the exciting evolution from "number cruncher" to a manager-in-training.

Integration Exercises

INTEGRATION EXERCISE 1 Activity Variance, Spending Variance, Materials Price Variance, Materials Quantity Variance LO 9–1, LO 9–2, LO 9–3, LO 10–1

Southside Pizzeria wants to improve its ability to manage the ingredient costs associated with making and selling its pizzas. For the month of June, the company plans to make 1,000 pizzas. It created a planning budget that includes a cost formula for mozzarella cheese of $2.40 per pizza. At the end of June, Southside actually sold 1,100 pizzas, and the actual cost of the cheese it used during the month was $2,632.

Required:

1. What is the mozzarella cheese activity variance for June?
2. What is the mozzarella cheese spending variance for June?
3. Assume the company establishes a price standard of $0.30 per ounce for mozzarella cheese and a quantity standard of eight ounces of cheese per pizza. Also, assume Southside actually used 9,400 ounces of cheese during the month to make 1,100 pizzas.
    a. What is the materials price variance for mozzarella cheese for June?
    b. What is the materials quantity variance for mozzarella cheese for June?
    c. What is the materials spending variance for mozzarella cheese for June?

INTEGRATION EXERCISE 2 Different Costs for Different Purposes, Cost-Volume-Profit-Relationships LO 1–1, LO 1–2, LO 1–3, LO 1–4, LO 1–5, LO 1–6, LO 2–1, LO 2–3, LO 2–5, LO 2–7, LO 2–8

Hixson Company manufactures and sells one product for $34 per unit. The company maintains no beginning or ending inventories and its relevant range of production is 20,000 units to 30,000 units. When Hixson produces and sells 25,000 units, its unit costs are as follows:

	Amount Per Unit
Direct materials	$8.00
Direct labor.	$5.00
Variable manufacturing overhead	$1.00
Fixed manufacturing overhead.	$6.00
Fixed selling expense.	$3.50
Fixed administrative expense	$2.50
Sales commissions	$4.00
Variable administrative expense.	$1.00

Required:

1. For financial accounting purposes, what is the total amount of product costs incurred to make 25,000 units? What is the total amount of period costs incurred to sell 25,000 units?

2. If 24,000 units are produced, what is the variable manufacturing cost per unit produced? What is the average fixed manufacturing cost per unit produced?

3. If 26,000 units are produced, what is the variable manufacturing cost per unit produced? What is the average fixed manufacturing cost per unit produced?

4. If 27,000 units are produced, what are the total amounts of direct and indirect manufacturing costs incurred to support this level of production?

5. What total incremental manufacturing cost will Hixson incur if it increases production from 25,000 to 25,001 units?

6. What is Hixson's contribution margin per unit? What is its contribution margin ratio?

7. What is Hixson's break-even point in unit sales? What is its break-even point in dollar sales?

8. How much will Hixson's net operating income increase if it can grow production and sales from 25,000 units to 26,500 units?

9. What is Hixson's margin of safety at a sales volume of 25,000 units?

10. What is Hixson's degree of operating leverage at a sales volume of 25,000 units?

INTEGRATION EXERCISE 3 Absorption Costing, Variable Costing, Cost-Volume-Profit-Relationships

LO 2–4, LO 2–5, LO 2–7, LO 4–1, LO 4–2

Newton Company manufactures and sells one product. The company assembled the following projections for its first year of operations:

Variable costs per unit:	
Manufacturing:	
Direct materials	$20
Direct labor.	$16
Variable manufacturing overhead	$4
Variable selling and administrative	$2
Fixed costs per year:	
Fixed manufacturing overhead.	$450,000
Fixed selling and administrative expenses.	$70,000

During its first year of operations, Newton expects to produce 25,000 units and sell 20,000 units. The budgeted selling price of the company's only product is $66 per unit.

Required *(answer each question independently by referring to the original data):*

1. Assuming Newton's projections are accurate, what will be its absorption costing net operating income in its first year of operations?

2. Newton is considering investing in a higher quality raw material that will increase its direct materials cost by $1 per unit. It estimates the higher quality raw material will increase sales by 1,000 units. What will be the company's revised absorption costing net operating income if it invests in the higher quality raw material and continues to *produce* 25,000 units?

3. Newton is considering raising its selling price by $1.00 per unit with an expectation that it will lower unit sales by 1,500 units. What will be the company's revised absorption costing net operating income if it raises its price by $1.00 and continues to *produce* 25,000 units?

4. Assuming Newton's projections are accurate, what will be its variable costing net operating income in its first year of operations?

5. Newton is considering investing in a higher quality raw material that will increase its direct materials cost by $1 per unit. It estimates the higher quality raw material will increase sales by 1,000 units. What will be the company's revised variable costing net operating income if it invests in the higher quality raw material and continues to *produce* 25,000 units?

6. Newton is considering raising its selling price by $1.00 per unit with an expectation it will lower unit sales by 1,500 units. What will be the company's revised variable costing net operating income if it raises its price by $1.00 and continues to *produce* 25,000 units?

7. What is Newton's break-even point in unit sales? What is its break-even point in dollar sales?

8. What is the company's projected margin of safety in its first year of operations?

INTEGRATION EXERCISE 4 Plantwide and Departmental Overhead Allocation; Activity-Based Costing; Segmented Income Statements LO 3–1, LO 3–2, LO 3–3, LO 3–4, LO 4–4, LO 4–5, LO 5–1, LO 5–3, LO 5–4

Koontz Company manufactures two models of industrial components—a Basic model and an Advanced Model. The company considers all of its manufacturing overhead costs to be fixed, and it uses plantwide manufacturing overhead cost allocation based on direct labor-hours. Koontz's controller prepared the segmented income statement that is shown below for the most recent year (he allocated selling and administrative expenses to products based on sales dollars):

	Basic	Advanced	Total
Number of units produced and sold	20,000	10,000	30,000
Sales	$3,000,000	$2,000,000	$5,000,000
Cost of goods sold	2,300,000	1,350,000	3,650,000
Gross margin	700,000	650,000	1,350,000
Selling and administrative expenses	720,000	480,000	1,200,000
Net operating income (loss)	$ (20,000)	$ 170,000	$ 150,000

Direct laborers are paid $20 per hour. Direct materials cost $40 per unit for the Basic model and $60 per unit for the Advanced model. Koontz is considering a change from plantwide overhead allocation to a departmental approach. The overhead costs in the company's Molding Department would be allocated based on machine-hours, and the overhead costs in its Assemble and Pack Department would be allocated based on direct labor-hours. To enable further analysis, the controller gathered the following information:

	Molding	Assemble and Pack	Total
Manufacturing overhead costs	$787,500	$562,500	$1,350,000
Direct labor-hours:			
Basic	10,000	20,000	30,000
Advanced	5,000	10,000	15,000
Machine-hours:			
Basic	12,000	—	12,000
Advanced	10,000	—	10,000

Required:
1. Using the plantwide approach:
    a. Calculate the plantwide overhead rate.
    b. Calculate the amount of overhead that would be assigned to each product.

2. Using a departmental approach:
   a. Calculate the departmental overhead rates.
   b. Calculate the total amount of overhead that would be assigned to each product.
   c. Using your departmental overhead cost allocations, redo the controller's segmented income statement (continue to allocate selling and administrative expenses based on sales dollars).

3. Koontz's production manager has suggested using activity-based costing instead of either the plantwide or departmental approaches. To facilitate the necessary calculations, she assigned the company's total manufacturing overhead cost to five activity cost pools as follows:

Activity Cost Pool	Activity Measure	Manufacturing Overhead
Machining...............	Machine-hours in Molding	$ 417,500
Assemble and pack	Direct labor-hours in Assemble and Pack	282,500
Order processing	Number of customer orders	230,000
Setups..................	Setup hours	340,000
Other (unused capacity)....		80,000
		$1,350,000

She also determined that the average order sizes for the Basic and Advanced models are 400 units and 50 units, respectively. The molding machines require a setup for each order. One setup hour is required for each customer order of the Basic model, and three hours are required to set up for an order of the Advanced model.

The company pays a sales commission of 5% for the Basic model and 10% for the Advanced model. Its traceable fixed advertising costs include $150,000 for the Basic model and $200,000 for the Advanced model. The remainder of the company's selling and administrative costs are organization-sustaining in nature.

Using the additional information provided by the production manager, calculate:
   a. An activity rate for each activity cost pool.
   b. The total manufacturing overhead cost allocated to the Basic model and the Advanced model using the activity-based approach.
   c. The total selling and administrative cost traced to the Basic model and the Advanced model using the activity-based approach.

4. Using your activity-based cost assignments from requirement 3, prepare a contribution format segmented income statement adapted from Exhibit 4–8. (Hint: Organize all of the company's costs into three categories: variable expenses, traceable fixed expenses, and common fixed expenses.)

5. Using your contribution format segmented income statement from requirement 4, calculate the break-even point in dollar sales for the Advanced model.

6. Explain how Koontz's activity-based costing approach differs from its plantwide and departmental approaches.

INTEGRATION EXERCISE 5 Capital Budgeting, Return on Investment, Residual Income LO 7–2, LO 11–1, LO 11–2

Simmons Company is a merchandiser with multiple store locations. One of its store managers is considering a shift in her store's product mix in anticipation of a strengthening economy. Her store would invest $800,000 in more expensive merchandise (an increase in its working capital) with the expectation that it would increase annual sales and variable expenses by $400,000 and $250,000, respectively, for three years. At the end of the three-year period, the store manager believes that the economic surge will subside; therefore, she will release the additional investment in working capital. The store manager's pay raises are largely determined by her store's return on investment (ROI), which has exceeded 22% each of the last three years.

Required:
1. Assuming the company's discount rate is 16%, calculate the net present value of the store manager's investment opportunity.

2. Calculate the annual margin, turnover, and return on investment (ROI) provided by the store manager's investment opportunity.

3. Assuming the company's minimum required rate of return is 16%, calculate the residual income earned by the store manager's investment opportunity for each of years 1 through 3.

4. Do you think the store manager would choose to pursue this investment opportunity? Do you think the company would want the store manager to pursue it? Why?

5. Using a discount rate of 16%, calculate the present value of your residual incomes for years 1 through 3. Is your answer greater than, less than, or equal to the net present value that you computed in (1) above? Why? Support your explanation with computations.

INTEGRATION EXERCISE 6 Variance Analysis and Internal Business Process Performance Measures LO 10–1, LO 10–2, LO 10–3, LO 12–3

"I thought Lean Production was supposed to make us more efficient," commented Ben Carrick, manufacturing vice president of Vorelli Industries. "But just look at June's manufacturing variances for Zets. The labor efficiency variance was $240,000 unfavorable—four times higher than it's ever been before. If you add on the $102,000 unfavorable materials price variance, that's $342,000 down the drain in a single month on just one product."

"Now take it easy, Ben," replied Sandi Shipp, the company's purchasing manager. "We knew the switch to Lean Production was going to increase our materials costs. But now, we're partnering with top-notch suppliers who deliver raw materials to our plant three times a day. In a few months, we'll be able to offset most of our higher purchasing costs by vacating three rented warehouses."

"And I know our labor efficiency variance looks bad," responded Raul Duvall, the company's production manager, "but it doesn't tell the whole story. The just-in-time flow in our production lines has made our plant more efficient than ever before. Plus, our investment in automation is reducing our materials waste each month."

"How can you say you're more efficient when you took 90,000 direct labor-hours to produce just 30,000 Zets last month?" asked Ben Carrick. "That's an average of 3 hours per unit, whereas the Zets' standard cost card only allows 2.5 hours per unit."

Raul explained that "part of our lean transformation requires cutting back production to reduce excess finished goods inventories. In a few months, our finished goods inventories will be depleted, and we'll be able to match production with demand. In the meantime, don't forget that our line people aren't just standing around when their machines are idle. Under the lean approach, they're doing their own inspections and equipment maintenance."

Ben replied, "We can't let this go on a few more months . . . at least not if you want to earn a bonus this year. I've been looking at these reports for 30 years, and I know inefficiency when I see it. Let's get things back under control."

After leaving Ben's office, Raul asked for your help in developing some performance measures that will highlight the benefits of the company's lean transformation. Working with Raul, you gathered the following information:

a. A standard cost card for Zets (one of the company's many products) is given below:

	Standard Quantity or Hours	Standard Price or Rate	Standard Cost
Direct materials	18 feet	$3.00 per foot	$ 54.00
Direct labor.	2.5 hours	$16.00 per hour	40.00
Variable manufacturing overhead	2.5 hours	$2.80 per hour	7.00
Total standard cost			$101.00

b. During June, the company purchased 510,000 feet of material for production of Zets at a cost of $3.20 per foot. All of this material was used to make 30,000 units during the month.

c. The company maintains a stable workforce to produce Zets. Employees who previously performed inspections and maintenance have been reassigned as direct labor workers. During June, direct laborers worked 90,000 hours on the Zets production lines at an average pay rate of $15.85 per hour.

d. Variable manufacturing overhead cost is allocated to products based on direct labor-hours. During June, the company incurred $207,000 in variable manufacturing overhead costs associated with the manufacture of Zets.

e. As workers have become more familiar with Lean Production methods, the following trends (per unit) have emerged over the last three months:

	April	May	June
Processing time..............	2.6 hours	2.5 hours	2.4 hours
Inspection time	1.3 hours	0.9 hours	0.1 hours
Move time.................	1.9 hours	1.4 hours	0.6 hours
Queue time................	8.2 hours	5.2 hours	1.9 hours

Required:

1. For direct materials:
    a. Compute the price and quantity variances.
    b. Is the decrease in waste that was mentioned by Raul apparent from your variance calculations? Explain.
    c. What standard price per foot should the company use going forward to compute the materials price variance? Why?

2. For direct labor:
    a. Compute the rate and efficiency variances.
    b. Is the company's labor efficiency variance a useful performance measure in its lean environment? Why?

3. For variable manufacturing overhead:
    a. Compute the rate and efficiency variances.
    b. Is direct labor-hours an appropriate cost driver for variable manufacturing overhead in the company's lean environment? Explain.

4. Compute the following for April, May, and June:
    a. The throughput time per unit.
    b. The manufacturing cycle efficiency (MCE).

5. Which performance measures do you think are more appropriate in the company's lean environment—the labor efficiency variance or throughput time per unit and manufacturing cycle efficiency?

INTEGRATION EXERCISE 7 Segmented Income Statements; Activity Rates and Activity-Based Cost Allocation LO 4–4, LO 5–3, LO 5–4

Morley Products is a wholesale distributor that competes in three markets—Commercial, Home, and School. It prepared the following segmented income statement:

	Total Company		Commercial Market	Home Market	School Market
Sales	$20,000,000	100.0%	$ 8,000,000	$5,000,000	$7,000,000
Less expenses:					
Cost of goods sold...............	9,500,000	47.5%	3,900,000	2,400,000	3,200,000
Sales support	3,600,000	18.0%	1,440,000	900,000	1,260,000
Order processing.................	1,720,000	8.6%	688,000	430,000	602,000
Warehousing.....................	940,000	4.7%	376,000	235,000	329,000
Packing and shipping	520,000	2.6%	208,000	130,000	182,000
Advertising	1,690,000	8.5%	676,000	422,500	591,500
General management	1,310,000	6.5%	524,000	327,500	458,500
Total expenses	19,280,000	96.4%	7,812,000	4,845,000	6,623,000
Net operating income	$ 720,000	3.6%	$ 188,000	$ 155,000	$ 377,000

Although the Commercial Market has the highest sales, it reports much lower profit than the School Market. Therefore, management is considering shifting attention and resources away from the Commercial Market and towards the School Market. They have asked for your recommendation on how to proceed. You have decided to create a properly formatted segmented income statement. To assist in this endeavor, you have gathered the following information:

a.   The cost of goods sold figures shown in the income statement above are traceable to their respective markets.

b.   Sales support, order processing, and packing and shipping are variable costs. Warehousing, general management, and advertising are fixed costs. In the income statement above, all of these costs have been allocated to the three markets on the basis of sales dollars.

c.   Using your knowledge of activity-based costing, you have compiled the following data:

Cost Pool and (Allocation Base)	Total Cost	Amount of Activity			
		Commercial Market	Home Market	School Market	Total
Sales support (number of calls)	$3,600,000	8,000	5,000	11,000	24,000
Order processing (number of orders)............	$1,720,000	1,750	5,200	1,650	8,600
Warehousing (square feet of space).............	$940,000	35,000	65,000	17,500	117,500
Packing and shipping (pounds shipped)	$520,000	24,000	16,000	64,000	104,000

d.   You have also determined the following breakdown of the company's advertising expense and general management expense:

	Total	Commercial Market	Home Market	School Market
Advertising:				
Traceable......................	$1,460,000	$700,000	$180,000	$580,000
Common	$230,000			
General management:				
Traceable salaries	$410,000	$150,000	$120,000	$140,000
Common	$900,000			

Required:

1.   Refer to the data in part (c) above. Calculate an activity rate for each cost pool. Then, using those rates, allocate each cost pool to the company's three markets.

2.   Prepare a revised contribution format segmented income statement for the company. Include an "Amount" column and a "Percent" column for the company as a whole and for each market segment.

3.   What insights from your segmented income statement should be brought to management's attention? Explain.

INTEGRATION EXERCISE 8 Transfer Pricing and Differential Analysis LO 6–1, LO 11–3

Bend Corporation consists of three decentralized divisions—Grant Division, Able Division, and Facet Division. The division managers are evaluated and rewarded based on their division's profit. They each can choose to sell their products to outside customers or to sell their products to other divisions within the company. They also have the authority to set their own selling prices to outside customers and to negotiate transfer prices with other divisions.

The manager of the Able Division is considering two alternative orders.

Alternative 1:

The Able Division could sell 2,000 motors to the Facet Division for a transfer price of $1,600 per motor. To manufacture each motor, Able would buy one component part from Grant Division at a transfer price of $400 per unit. Able would then further process each part it receives from Grant at a variable cost of $450 per unit. In addition, Able would use five machine-hours to complete each motor. Its fixed manufacturing overhead rate is $23 per machine-hour.

Grant incurs a variable cost of $200 per unit before selling each part to Able for $400. It also uses 2.5 machine-hours to manufacture each part it sells to Able. Grant has a fixed manufacturing overhead rate of $38 per machine-hour.

If Able declines this opportunity (and pursues alternative 2 as described in the next paragraph), the Facet Division will buy 2,000 motors from Waverly Corporation for a price of $1,600 per motor. To produce each motor, Waverly would buy a component part from Grant Division for $350 per unit. Grant would use 2.5 machine-hours to make each part; however, because the part differs from the one it would produce for Able, the variable cost per unit is only $175 per unit.

Alternative 2:

The Able Division could sell 2,500 motors to Tech Corporation for a price of $1,200 per motor. To manufacture each unit of this particular motor, Able would buy one component part from Grant Division at a transfer price of $200 per unit. From Grant's perspective, this part would have a variable cost per unit of $100, and it would require two machine-hours to produce. Able would further process each part it receives from Grant at a variable cost of $470 per unit. Able would also use four machine-hours to complete each motor.

Able Division's plant capacity is limited; therefore, it can only choose one of the two alternatives. The company's total general fixed overhead would not be affected by this decision.

Required:

1. If the manager of the Able Division wants to maximize the division's profits, which alternative should be accepted—the order from the Facet Division or the order from Tech Corporation? Support your answer with computations.

2. Which of the two alternatives will maximize profits for the company as a whole? Support your answer with computations.

INTEGRATION EXERCISE 9 Segmented Income Statements; Contribution Margin Ratio; Activity-Based Cost Allocation LO2–3, LO4–4, LO5–4

Diversified Products, Inc., recently acquired a small publishing company that offers three books for sale—a cookbook, a travel guide, and a handy speller. Each book sells for $10. The publishing company's most recent monthly income statement is shown below.

	Total Company	Product Line		
		Cookbook	Travel Guide	Handy Speller
Sales................................	$300,000	$ 90,000	$150,000	$60,000
Expenses:				
Printing costs	102,000	27,000	63,000	12,000
Advertising	36,000	13,500	19,500	3,000
General sales	18,000	5,400	9,000	3,600
Salaries	33,000	18,000	9,000	6,000
Equipment depreciation	9,000	3,000	3,000	3,000
Sales commissions................	30,000	9,000	15,000	6,000
General administration	42,000	14,000	14,000	14,000
Warehouse rent	12,000	3,600	6,000	2,400
Depreciation—office facilities.......	3,000	1,000	1,000	1,000
Total expenses	285,000	94,500	139,500	51,000
Net operating income (loss)..........	$ 15,000	$ (4,500)	$ 10,500	$ 9,000

The following additional information is available:

a.   Only printing costs and sales commissions are variable; all other costs are fixed. The printing costs (which include materials, labor, and variable overhead) are traceable to the three product lines shown in the income statement above. Sales commissions are 10% of sales.

b.   The same equipment is used to produce all three books, so the equipment depreciation expense has been allocated equally among the three product lines. An analysis of the company's activities indicates that the equipment is used 30% of the time to produce cookbooks, 50% of the time to produce travel guides, and 20% of the time to produce handy spellers.

c.   The warehouse is used to store finished units of product, so the rental cost has been allocated to the product lines on the basis of sales dollars. The warehouse rental cost is $3 per square foot per year. The warehouse contains 48,000 square feet of space, of which 7,200 square feet are used by the cookbook line, 24,000 square feet by the travel guide line, and 16,800 square feet by the handy speller line.

d.   The general sales cost above includes the salary of the sales manager and other sales costs not traceable to any specific product line. This cost has been allocated to the product lines on the basis of sales dollars.

e.   The general administration cost and depreciation of office facilities both relate to administration of the company as a whole. These costs have been allocated equally to the three product lines.

f.   All other costs are traceable to the three product lines in the amounts shown on the income statement above.

The management of Diversified Products, Inc., is anxious to improve the publishing company's 5% return on sales.

Required:

1.   Prepare a new contribution format segmented income statement for the month. Adjust allocations of equipment depreciation and warehouse rent as indicated by the additional information provided.

2.   Based on the segmented income statements given in the problem, management plans to eliminate the cookbook because it is not returning a profit and to focus all available resources on promoting the travel guide. However, based on the new contribution format segmented income statement that you prepared:

a.   Do you agree with management's plan to eliminate the cookbook? Explain.

b.   Do you agree with the decision to focus all available resources on promoting the travel guide? Assume that an ample market is available for all three product lines. (*Hint:* Compute the contribution margin ratio for each product.)

INTEGRATION EXERCISE 10 Master Budgeting LO 8–2, LO 8–3, LO 8–4, LO 8–5, LO 8–6, LO 8–7, LO 8–8, LO 8–9, LO 8–10

Endless Mountain Company manufactures a single product popular with outdoor recreation enthusiasts. The company sells its product to retailers throughout the northeastern quadrant of the United States. It is in the process of creating a master budget for 2023 and reports a balance sheet at December 31, 2022, as follows:

	A	B	C	
1	**Endless Mountain Company**			
2	**Balance Sheet**			
3	**December 31, 2022**			
4				
5	**Assets**			
6	Current assets:			
7	Cash	$ 46,200		
8	Accounts receivable	260,000		
9	Raw materials inventory (4,500 yards)	11,250		
10	Finished goods inventory (1,500 units)	32,250		
11	Total current assets		$349,700	
12	Plant and equipment:			
13	Buildings and equipment	900,000		
14	Accumulated depreciation	(292,000)		
15	Plant and equipment, net		608,000	
16	Total assets		$957,700	
17				
18	**Liabilities and Stockholders' Equity**			
19	Current liabilities:			
20	Accounts payable		$158,000	
21	Stockholders' equity:			
22	Common stock	$ 419,800		
23	Retained earnings	379,900		
24	Total stockholders' equity		799,700	
25	Total liabilities and stockholders' equity		$957,700	
26				

Beginning Balance Sheet   ... ⊕ ⁞ ◀ ▶

Microsoft Excel

The company's chief financial officer (CFO), in consultation with various managers across the organization, has developed the following set of assumptions to help create the 2023 budget:

1. The budgeted unit sales are 12,000 units, 37,000 units, 15,000 units, and 25,000 units for quarters 1–4, respectively. Notice that the company experiences peak sales in the second and fourth quarters. The budgeted selling price for the year is $32 per unit. The budgeted unit sales for the first quarter of 2024 is 13,000 units.

2. All sales are on credit. Uncollectible accounts are negligible and can be ignored. Seventy-five percent of all credit sales are collected in the quarter of the sale, and 25% are collected in the subsequent quarter.

3. Each quarter's ending finished goods inventory should equal 15% of the next quarter's unit sales.

4. Each unit of finished goods requires 3.5 yards of raw material that costs $3.00 per yard. Each quarter's ending raw materials inventory should equal 10% of the next quarter's production needs. The estimated ending raw materials inventory on December 31, 2023, is 5,000 yards.

5. Seventy percent of each quarter's purchases are paid for in the quarter of purchase. The remaining 30% of each quarter's purchases are paid in the following quarter.

6. Direct laborers are paid $18 an hour, and each unit of finished goods requires 0.25 direct labor-hours to complete. All direct labor costs are paid in the quarter incurred.

7. The budgeted variable manufacturing overhead per direct labor-hour is $3.00. The quarterly fixed manufacturing overhead is $150,000, including $20,000 of depreciation on equipment. The number of direct labor-hours is used as the allocation base for the budgeted plantwide overhead rate. All overhead costs (excluding depreciation) are paid in the quarter incurred.

8. The budgeted variable selling and administrative expense is $1.25 per unit sold. The fixed selling and administrative expenses per quarter include advertising ($25,000), executive salaries ($64,000), insurance ($12,000), property tax ($8,000), and depreciation expense ($8,000). All selling and administrative expenses (excluding depreciation) are paid in the quarter incurred.

9. The company plans to maintain a minimum cash balance at the end of each quarter of $30,000. Assume that any borrowings take place on the first day of the quarter. To the extent possible, the company will repay principal and interest on any borrowings on the last day of the fourth quarter. The company's lender imposes a simple interest rate of 3% per quarter on any borrowings.

10. Dividends of $15,000 will be declared and paid in each quarter.

11. The company uses a last-in, first-out (LIFO) inventory flow assumption. This means that the most recently purchased raw materials are the "first-out" to production and the most recently completed finished goods are the "first-out" to customers.

Required:

The company's CFO has asked you to use Microsoft Excel to prepare the 2023 master budget. Your Excel file should include a tab that contains the December 31, 2022, balance sheet; a tab that summarizes the budgeting assumptions; and tabs corresponding to the following budget schedules and financial statements:

1. Quarterly sales budget, including a schedule of expected cash collections.
2. Quarterly production budget.
3. Quarterly direct materials budget, including a schedule of expected cash disbursements for purchases of materials.
4. Quarterly direct labor budget.
5. Quarterly manufacturing overhead budget.
6. Ending finished goods inventory budget at December 31, 2023.
7. Quarterly selling and administrative expense budget.
8. Quarterly cash budget.
9. Income statement for the year ended December 31, 2023.
10. Balance sheet at December 31, 2023.

INTEGRATION EXERCISE 11 Cost-Volume-Profit Relationships, Variable Costing LO 1–4, LO 2–1, LO 2–5, LO 2–7, LO 2–8, LO 4–1, LO 4–2, LO 4–3

Refer to the information pertaining to Endless Mountain Company that is provided in Integration Exercise 10. In addition to the budget schedules you prepared in Integration Exercise 10, insert two new tabs in your Microsoft Excel worksheet titled "CVP Analysis" and "Variable Costing."

Required (For all questions, be sure to use formulas that link to the other tabs in your Microsoft Excel worksheet when performing your calculations):

1. Calculate the following budgeted figures for 2023:
   a. The total fixed cost.
   b. The variable cost per unit sold.
   c. The contribution margin per unit sold.
   d. The break-even point in unit sales and dollar sales.
   e. The margin of safety.
   f. The degree of operating leverage
2. Calculate the following budgeted figures for 2023:
   a. A variable costing income statement. Stop your computations at net operating income.
   b. A reconciliation that explains the difference in the absorption costing and variable costing net operating incomes.

INTEGRATION EXERCISE 12 Master Budgeting, Cost-Volume-Profit Relationships, Variable Costing LO 2–5, LO 4–2, LO 8–5, LO 8–6, LO 8–8, LO 8–9, LO 8–10

Refer to the information pertaining to Endless Mountain Company provided in Integration Exercise 10 as well as the schedules you prepared in answering Integration Exercises 10 and 11.

Required:

1. Assume the company expects to collect all of its credit sales in the quarter of sale rather than the original assumption it will collect 75% of credit sales in the quarter of sale and the remaining 25% in the subsequent quarter. *Without changing any of the underlying assumptions in*

your budgeting assumptions tab, calculate the revised net income (absorption basis) for the 2023 budget.

2. Go to the Budgeting Assumptions tab in your Microsoft Excel worksheet. Change the percentage of sales collected in the quarter of sale to 100% and the percentage of sales collected in the quarter after sale to 0%. Does your answer to requirement 1 match the net income that appears in your Excel worksheet? If not, why?

3. Refer to the original budgeting assumptions from Integration Exercise 10. Assume the company expects to pay its direct laborers $19 per hour instead of the original estimate of $18 per hour. *Without changing any of the underlying assumptions in your budgeting assumptions tab,* calculate the following revised figures related to the 2023 budget:
   a. Ending finished goods inventory at December 31, 2023.
   b. The break-even point in unit sales.
   c. Variable costing net operating income

4. Go to the Budgeting Assumptions tab in your Microsoft Excel worksheet. Change the direct labor cost per hour from $18 to $19. Do your answers to 3a through 3c match the numbers that appear in your Excel worksheet? If not, why?

Index